THE COMPLETE TRANSCRIPTS OF THE

Clarence Thomas—Anita Hill Hearings

OCTOBER 11, 12, 13, 1991

THE COMPLETE TRANSCRIPTS OF THE

CLARENCE THOMAS—ANITA HILL HEARINGS

OCTOBER 11, 12, 13, 1991

PREFACE BY NINA TOTENBERG

EDITED BY ANITA MILLER

Academy Chicago Publishers

Published by
Academy Chicago Publishers
363 West Erie Street
Chicago, Illinois 60610

First Printing, 1994

Printed and bound in the U.S.A.

ISBN 0-89733-408-6

Library of Congress Cataloging-in-Publication Data

United States. Congress. Senate. Committee on the Judiciary.
The Clarence Thomas—Anita Hill hearings.
p. cm.
ISBN 0-89733-408-6: $22.95
1. Thomas, Clarence, 1948— . 2. Hill, Anita. 3. United States. Supreme Court. 4. Judges—Selection and appointment—United States. 5. Sexual harassment of women—United States. I. Title.
KF8745.T48U55 1994
347.73'2634—dc20 94-15891
[347.3073534] CIP

This book is gratefully dedicated to Mark Crispin Miller,
who conceived the idea of this project.

CONTENTS

COMMITTEE ON THE JUDICIARY

JOSEPH R. BIDEN, Jr., Delaware, *Chairman*

EDWARD M.KENNEDY, Massachusetts
HOWARD M. METZENBAUM, Ohio
DENNIS DECONCINI, Arizona
PATRICK J. LEAHY, Vermont
HOWELL HEFLIN, Alabama
PAUL SIMON, Illinois
HERBERT KOHL, Wisconsin

STROM THURMOND, South Carolina
ORRIN G. HATCH, Utah
ALAN K. SIMPSON, Wyoming
CHARLES E. GRASSLEY, Iowa
ARLEN SPECTER, Pennsylvania
HANK BROWN, Colorado

RONALD A. KLAIN, *Chief Counsel*
JEFFERY J. PECK, *Staff Director*
TERRY L. WOOTEN, *Minority Chief Counsel and Staff Director*

HEARINGS HELD

FRIDAY, OCTOBER 11, 1991

OPENING STATEMENTS OF COMMITTEE MEMBERS

WITNESSES

Saturday, October 12, 1991

WITNESS

Sunday, October 13, 1991

CHRONOLOGICAL LIST OF WITNESSES

INTRODUCTION
BY NINA TOTENBERG

Today we think of the Clarence Thomas/Anita Hill hearings as a watershed in American political and social life. But as I walked into the Russell Senate Office Building in the early hours of October 11,1991 and headed for the NPR/PBS broadcast stand overlooking the Rotunda, I had no notion of what those hearings would come to mean.

The story at that moment was nothing more to me than Clarence Thomas, Round II of the confirmation process. To my astonishment, though, the building was not its usual quiet self. Workers were everywhere. Cables, lights, cameras were everywhere. Network anchors were munching catered food, going over scripts, talking on telephones. Crews were frantically taping down wires, hauling in more and more equipment. Everywhere I looked I half expected someone to yell, "Lights, cameras, action!"

And suddenly I realized the Clarence Thomas/Anita Hill hearings would be broadcast live, not just by NPR and PBS (as the first round had been), but by every network that could buy, rent, or steal the equipment necessary to do it. The *world* was going to carry this hearing, in living color and lurid detail. My mouth literally fell open as I recognized, for the first time I think, that the story I had broken just a few days earlier had turned into a mega-story.

It was a story I had been working on for some time—indeed, ever since I had learned that Anita Hill had informed the Judiciary Committee of her charges in early September, before the first round of Thomas hearings began. I eventually determined that the chairman of the committee, Joseph Biden, had not pursued the charges at all initially—had not even talked to Anita Hill, on the grounds that if she was not willing to go public, he would not investigate. Only at the eleventh hour, with the first round of hearings over, did Biden finally succumb to pressure from some Democrats. But the investigative step he took was minimal: he asked the White House to have Hill and Thomas each interviewed by the FBI. There was no follow-up, no further investigation. Nothing. And on the day the committee was to vote on the Thomas nomination, committee members were given a copy of the affidavit Hill sent Biden outlining her charges. I saw Senators reading a document as they prepared to vote, and I began to smell a rat.

As I began to dig for facts, it seemed to me that the story was not just Anita Hill and Clarence Thomas, but the story of the Judiciary Committee and how it did its job. And even after my October 6th broadcast, the Senate seemed little interested in pursuing the Hill allegations. It was only after the phone lines jammed and the FAX machines nearly vaporized, that the body politic began to realize that these were charges that, true or not, could not be ignored.

Less than a week earlier, after many difficult conversations, I had finally told Professor Hill that I had a copy of her affidavit charging Supreme Court nominee Clarence Thomas with sexual harassment. It was only then that she resolved her ambivalence and agreed to an interview. I listened to that interview in full not long ago. It lasted about a half hour. And what is remarkable about it is how little has changed about her charges, and how little evidence the beleaguered Senate Judiciary Committee managed to collect as it stumbled and smashed its way through three days of tumultuous testimony.

Why would a woman of hard-earned and high professional and personal repute make up such a story? Was she credible? Was he credible? Who do you believe? Those questions crackled through the air as the hearings opened.

Who can forget Anita Hill, trembling almost imperceptibly, as she walked into the ornate Senate Caucus Room, and seeming to gain strength as she testified. Political operatives at the White House initially were so impressed with her steady performance as a witness that they privately concluded on Day One that Clarence Thomas could not be confirmed. Only a few die-hards in the White House counsel's office continued to insist that Thomas could prevail, and they eventually won the chance to try. Thomas, who has told friends he felt hung out to dry by the White House, came into the hearing with a fiery rage that impressed the audience and shrank the Democrats into sniveling submission.

The spectacle laid out for the public played like a three-act play that lasted three very long days. The protagonists, of course, were Thomas and Hill. But the supporting characters were just as important in this drama. First, the Judiciary Committee. The attack dogs on the Republican side—Orrin Hatch, Alan Simpson, and Arlen Specter. And the befuddled Democrats—Joseph Biden, Patrick Leahy, and Howell Heflin—looking pained and inept. Then there were the spear carriers—Sen. John Danforth for Thomas, and Harvard Law Professor Charles Ogletree for Hill. Then too, there were the small character parts. John Doggett, the guy who thought he was God's gift to women, and to Anita Hill; Ellen Wells, who testified that Hill had told her about Thomas's alleged abuse at the time it happened. Her emotional testimony, and her GOP credentials, silenced Republican efforts to discredit her. And there were the panel of witnesses—the many women who had worked with Thomas and Hill and said it was inconceivable Thomas would do such a thing, or conversely, the panelists who testified that Hill told each of them about Thomas's alleged abuse at the time it occurred.

Despite the fact that Hill took and passed a lie detector test, the two sides were no match for each other. The Thomas forces, frantic but unified, marched together to a strategic tune composed by Thomas and Danforth and orchestrated by the White House. Hill's forces, inexperienced, in disarray, and with little or no support from Senate Democrats, were left to flounder.

When it was over, public opinion polls showed that people believed Clarence Thomas by a margin of two to one, a ratio that would reverse itself in less than two years.

The Senate had held hearings with no thought, planning, rules, or investigation, and the Senate had resolved nothing. Clarence Thomas was confirmed by a two-vote margin, but women voters rebelled—first ousting Illinois Democrat Alan Dixon, one of the only eleven Democrats to vote for Thomas. Dixon was beaten in a primary by Carol Moseley-Braun, a little known Cook County official with almost no campaign money, who decided to get into the race because of her outrage at the Hill/Thomas hearings. With her primary win, she would become the first of four new women to win Senate victories in 1992.

Outside the body politic, social volcanoes were erupting elsewhere. The hearings ripped open the subject of sexual harassment like some sort of long-festering sore. It oozed over every workplace, creating everything from heated discussions to an avalanche of lawsuits. In 1992, the number of sexual harassment charges filed through the Equal Employment Opportunities Commission and Fair Employment Practices Agencies had increased by nearly seventy-two percent from the number of charges brought in 1990.

In the publishing world, books about the hearing continue to proliferate. Both *Newsday* reporter Tim Phelps and Sen. Paul Simon wrote interesting volumes. Conservative polemicist David Brock caused quite a stir with his book, *The Real Anita Hill*, a work that, although well-reviewed in some places, is widely viewed by journalists who covered the hearings as riddled with factual errors. Eagerly awaited is an investigative book in the works by two first-rate *Wall Street Journal* reporters, Jill Abramson and Jane Mayer.

In short, the Clarence Thomas/Anita Hill controversy has become the Alger Hiss case of our times. Hill and Thomas partisans in the thousands can and do debate the minutiae of every witness's testimony, pro and con. Some Republicans have grilled and held up Clinton Administration nominees because of their role in helping Hill during those fateful days. But true believers on both sides would probably argue that for good or ill, the hearings spurred political and cultural revolution across the country.

For me, much of these hearings were a blur. Trying to be a reporter for those three days and to be fair was like trying to keep your feet on the ground during a tornado; you just do your best and try to get through it. As time has gone by, though, I have frequently longed to sit down with a copy of the hearings and read them without the cacophony of sound that accompanied them at the time.

Now I can, and so can you. While the Senate, incredibly, published only 500 copies of the record in these hearings, they are now available affordably and in full in this volume. Here are the transcripts of the hearings, and the important exhibits that were submitted—affidavits aimed at discrediting Hill, and the sworn testimony of the so-called "other woman," Angela Wright, who had worked for Thomas and, like Hill, claimed he had made lewd and inappropriate remarks to her. The Judiciary Committee staff took Wright's testimony under oath. The Democrats, in what they now admit was a tactical error, yielded to Republican pressure and decided not to call Wright for fear she would be discredited.

You can read her closed door testimony here. You can read the hearings, the affidavits about character and lack of it. And finally, you can decide for yourself what it all means.

Editor's Note

It should be pointed out that the Government Printing Office publication of these hearings contains much "submitted material": newspaper and magazine articles, and letters from individuals and organizations, all arguing for or against the confirmation of the nominee. When this material was read into the record, it is of course included here.

However, submitted material which was not transcribed during the course of the hearings, we have chosen not to reprint—with one exception—since our focus is on the actual hearings themselves. On occasion, enough of the material was read into the record to carry its point. For instance, Senator Simpson read aloud relevant sentences from a letter written by Andrew Fishel contesting some of Anita Hill's testimony. We have not included the letter, but Senator Simpson's reading of a portion of it suffices to make Mr Fishel's point. At another moment, Senator Heflin submitted several newspaper stories. We have not included these, but Senator Heflin read enough information into the transcript so that anyone can find these articles without too much difficulty.

A complete list of the submitted material is included in Appendix B, separated into categories of general interest, of support and of opposition. Appendix A contains the only exception to our rule: a letter from Sukari Hardnett included because this submission illuminates an otherwise obscure reference in the text.

We have included also the telephone logs submitted by Senator Hatch, since this is clearly something readers should see for themselves.

There are three indices. The first is an alphabetical list of witnesses with the page numbers of their testimony. The second, called "Colloquy", identifies page numbers of each senator's questioning of each witness. The third locates names mentioned in the text apart from testimony. In this index, under the senators' names, we have isolated comments, discussion and submissions apart from the questioning of witnesses.

Obvious typos in the Government transcripts have been silently corrected; spelling and capitalization have been made consistent throughout. When a question exists about the intention of a speaker, we have put brackets around what seemed to us to be the logical correction.

Fairly often statements or questions by some senators—especially Biden and Specter—are couched in language so involuted as to be virtually incomprehensible. On occasion we have used [*sic*] to indicate that these are not the result of printers' errors—at least on our part; most of the time we have simply let these sentences stand without comment. The reader should be aware that these statements and questions have been carefully proofread and that these men frequently talk this way.

NOMINATION OF JUDGE CLARENCE THOMAS TO BE ASSOCIATE JUSTICE OF THE SUPREME COURT OF THE UNITED STATES

FRIDAY, OCTOBER 11, 1991

U.S. SENATE,
COMMITTEE ON THE JUDICIARY
Washington, DC

The committee met, pursuant to notice, at 10:01 a.m., in room SD-325, Russell Senate Office Building, Hon. Joseph R. Biden, Jr. (chairman of the committee) presiding.

Present: Senators Biden, Kennedy, Metzenbaum, DeConcini, Leahy, Heflin, Simon, Kohl, Thurmond, Hatch, Simpson, Grassley, Specter, and Brown.

OPENING STATEMENT OF CHAIRMAN JOSEPH R. BIDEN, JR., A U.S. SENATOR FROM THE STATE OF DELAWARE

THE CHAIRMAN: The hearing will come to order.

Let me inform the Capitol Hill Police that, if there is not absolute order and decorum in here, we will recess the hearing and those who engage in any outburst at all will be asked to leave the committee room.

Good morning, Judge.

Today, the Senate Judiciary Committee is meeting to hear evidence on sexual harassment charges that have been made against Judge Clarence Thomas, who has been nominated to be an Associate Justice of the Supreme Court.

I want to speak very briefly about the circumstances that have caused us to convene these hearings. We are here today to hold open hearings on Professor Anita Hill's allegations concerning Judge Thomas. This committee's handling of her charges has been criticized. Professor Hill made two requests to this committee: First, she asked us to investigate her charges against Judge Thomas, and, second, she asked that these charges remain confidential, that they not be made public and not shared with anyone beyond this committee. I believe that we have honored both of her requests.

Some have asked how we could have the U.S. Senate vote on Judge Thomas's nomination and leave Senators in the dark about Professor Hill's charges. To this, I answer, how could we have forced Professor Hill against her will into the blinding light where you see her today.

But I am deeply sorry that our actions in this respect have been seen by many across this country as a sign that this committee does not take the charge of sexual harassment seriously. We emphatically do.

I hope we all learn from the events of the past week. As one person who has spent the past two years attempting to combat violence of all kinds against women through legislative efforts, I can assure you that I take the charge of sexual harassment seriously.

The committee's ability to investigate and hold hearings on Professor Hill's charges has now been dramatically changed by the events which forced Professor Hill, against her wishes, to publicly discuss these charges. The landscape has changed. We are, thus, here today free from the restrictions which had previously limited our work.

Sexual harassment is a serious matter and, in my view, any person guilty of this offense is unsuited to serve, not only the nation's highest court, but any position of responsibility, of high responsibility in or out of government. Sexual harassment of working women is an issue of national concern.

With that said, let me make clear that this is not, I emphasize, this is not a hearing about the extent and nature of sexual harassment in America. That question is for a different sort of meeting of this or any other committee.

This is a hearing convened for a specific purpose, to air specific allegations against one specific individual, allegations which may be true or may not be true.

Whichever may be the case, this hearing has not been convened to investigate the widespread problem, and it is indisputably widespread, the widespread problem of sexual harassment in this country.

Those watching these proceedings will see witnesses being sworn and testifying pursuant to a subpoena. But I want to emphasize that this is not a trial, this is not a courtroom. At the end of our proceedings, there will be no formal verdict of guilt or innocence, nor any finding of civil liability.

Because this is not a trial, the proceedings will not be conducted the way in which a sexual harassment trial would be handled in a court of law. For example, on the advice of the nonpartisan Senate legal counsel, the rules of evidence that apply in courtrooms will not apply here today. Thus, evidence and questions that would not be permitted in the court of law must, under Senate rules, be allowed here.

This is a fact-finding hearing, and our purpose is to help our colleagues in the U.S. Senate determine whether Judge Thomas should be confirmed to the Supreme Court. We are not here, or at least I am not here to be an advocate for one side or the other with respect to the specific allegations which we will review, and it is my hope and belief that my colleagues here today share that view.

Achieving fairness in the atmosphere in which these hearings are being held may be the most difficult task I have ever undertaken in my close-to-nineteen years in the U.S. Senate.

Each of us in this committee has already stated how he will vote on Judge Thomas's nomination. The committee, as the Senate rules require, has already voted in this committee on whether or not Judge Thomas should be on the Court. Each of us has already said whether we think Judge Thomas should or should not be a Supreme Court Justice, for reasons related to or unrelated to charges we will listen to today.

In this setting, it will be easy and perhaps understandable for the witnesses to fear unfair treatment, but it is my job, as chairman, to ensure as best as I possibly can fair treatment, and that is what I intend to do, so let me make three ground rules clear for all of my colleagues:

First, while legal counsel sitting behind me has advised that the rules of evidence do not apply here, counsel has also advised the Chair that the Chair does have the power to rule out of order questions that are not relevant to our proceedings. Certain subjects are simply irrelevant to the issue of harassment, namely, the private conduct of out-of-the-workplace relationships, and the intimate lives and practices of Judge Thomas, Professor Hill, and any other witness that comes before us.

Thus, as Chairman, I will not allow questions on matters totally irrelevant to our investigation of the professional relationship of Judge Thomas and any woman who has been employed by him.

The committee is not here to put Judge Thomas or Professor Hill on trial. I hope my colleagues will bear in mind that the best way to do our job is to ask questions that are nonjudgmental and open-ended, in an attempt to avoid questions that badger and harass any witness.

Second, while I have less discretion than a judge in a trial to bar inappropriate or embarrassing questions, all of the witnesses should know that they have a right, under Senate Rule 26.5, to ask that the committee go into closed session, if a question requires an answer that is "a clear invasion of their right to privacy."

The committee will take very seriously the request of any witness to answer particularly embarrassing questions, as they view them, in private.

Third, the order of questioning: Because this is an extraordinary hearing, Democrats and Republicans have each taken the step of designating a limited number of Senators to question for the committee. On the Democratic side, our questioners will be Senators Heflin, Leahy, and myself. As I understand it, on the Republican side, the questioners will be the ranking member, Senator Hatch and Senator Specter. That is said to make sure that we do not mislead anyone as to how we will proceed.

In closing, I want to reiterate my view that the primary responsibility of this committee is fairness. That means making sure that we do not victimize any witness who appears here and that we treat every witness with respect. And without making any judgment about the specific witnesses we will hear from today, fairness means understanding what a victim of sexual harassment goes through, why victims often do not report such crimes, why they often believe that they should not or cannot leave their jobs.

Perhaps fourteen men sitting here today cannot understand these things fully. I know there are many people watching today who suspect we never will understand, but fairness means doing our best to understand, no matter what we do or do not believe about the specific charges. We are going to listen as closely as we can at these hearings.

Fairness also means that Judge Thomas must be given a full and fair opportunity to confront these charges against him, to respond fully, to tell us his side of the story and to be given the benefit of the doubt.

In the end, this hearing may resolve much or it may resolve little, but there are two things that cannot remain in doubt after this hearing is over: First, that the members of this committee are fair and have been fair to all witnesses; and, second, that we take sexual harassment as a very serious concern in this hearing and overall.

So, let us perform our duties with a full understanding of what I have said and of our responsibilities to the Senate, to the Nation and to the truth.

I yield now to my colleague from South Carolina.

OPENING STATEMENT OF HON. STROM THURMOND, A U.S. SENATOR FROM THE STATE OF SOUTH CAROLINA

SEN. THURMOND: Mr. Chairman, we have taken the unusual step of reconvening this committee in order to consider further testimony regarding the nomination of Judge Clarence Thomas to be a Justice of the Supreme Court of the United States.

We are here this morning to attempt to discern the truth in some rather extraordinary allegations made against this nominee, and because Judge Thomas has requested an opportunity to refute these allegations and restore his good name.

Mr. Chairman, before we begin, I want to emphasize that the charge of sexual harassment is a grave one and one that each Senator on this committee takes with the utmost seriousness. This is an issue of great sensitivity and there is no doubt in my mind that this is difficult for everyone involved.

Both Judge Thomas and Professor Hill find themselves in the unenviable position of having to discuss very personal matters in a very public forum. I want to assure them at the outset that they will be dealt with fairly. This will be an exceedingly uncomfortable process for us all, but a great deal hangs in the balance and our duty is clear, we must find the truth.

I would like to commend Chairman Biden, who worked with me to ensure that this hearing would be conducted fairly. After consulting with each member on my side, I have decided that Senator Hatch will conduct the questioning of Judge Thomas. I have also decided, after consultation, that Senator Specter will undertake the questioning of Professor Hill and the other witnesses. I reserve the privilege of propounding questions myself.

I want to make it clear that every Republican member of this committee has been deeply involved in this process from the day Judge Thomas was nominated by President Bush. However, in the interest of time and fairness to all the witnesses, I believe the procedures that have been outlined will work best for everyone involved.

Over one hundred days ago, when President Bush nominated Judge Thomas, this committee undertook a thorough and far-reaching investigation of his background. That investigation turned up nothing questionable about the judge, but, rather, showed him to be an individual of great character and accomplishment.

During the original confirmation hearings, this committee heard testimony from over one hundred witnesses, both for and against the nomination. Not one of these witnesses, even those most bitterly opposed to this nomination, had one disparaging comment to make about Clarence Thomas's moral character. On the contrary, witness after witness spoke of the impeccable character, abiding honesty and consummate professionalism which Judge Thomas has shown throughout his career.

In conclusion, I want to comment briefly about the allegations that have been raised by Professor Hill. The alleged harassment she describes took place some ten years ago. During that time, she continued to initiate contact with Judge Thomas in an apparently friendly manner. In addition, Professor Hill chose to publicize her allegations the day before the full Senate would have voted to confirm Judge Thomas.

While I fully intend to maintain an open mind during today's testimony, I must say that the timing of these statements raises a tremendous number of questions which must be dealt with, and I can assure all the witnesses that we shall be unstinting in our efforts to ascertain the truth.

Thank you, Mr. Chairman.

THE CHAIRMAN: Thank you.

Now, before I swear Judge Thomas, I ask that the police officer go to the front of that door while Judge Thomas is speaking, and prevent anyone from going in or out. He is entitled to absolute quiet in this room, no matter who wishes to enter.

Judge, would you stand to be sworn? Judge, do you swear to tell the truth, the whole truth, and nothing but the truth, so help you, God?

JUDGE THOMAS: I do.

THE CHAIRMAN: Judge, do you have an opening statement? Please proceed.

TESTIMONY OF HON. CLARENCE THOMAS, OF GEORGIA, TO BE ASSOCIATE JUSTICE OF THE U.S. SUPREME COURT

JUDGE THOMAS: Mr. Chairman, Senator Thurmond, members of the committee: as excruciatingly difficult as the last two weeks have been, I welcome the opportunity to clear my name today. No one other than my wife and Senator Danforth, to whom I read this statement at 6:30 a.m., has seen or heard the statement, no handlers, no advisers.

The first I learned of the allegations by Professor Anita Hill was on September 25, 1991, when the FBI came to my home to investigate her allegations. When informed by the FBI agent of the nature of the allegations and the person making them, I was shocked, surprised, hurt, and enormously saddened.

I have not been the same since that day. For almost a decade my responsibilities included enforcing the rights of victims of sexual harassment. As a boss, as a friend, and as a human being I was proud that I have never had such an allegation leveled against me, even as I sought to promote women, and minorities into non-traditional jobs.

In addition, several of my friends who are women, have confided in me about the horror of harassment on the job, or elsewhere. I thought I really understood the anguish, the fears, the doubts, the seriousness of the matter. But since September 25, I have suffered immensely as these very serious charges were leveled against me.

I have been wracking my brains and eating my insides out trying to think of what I could have said or done to Anita Hill to lead her to allege that I was interested in her in more than a professional way, and that I talked with her about pornographic or X-rated films.

Contrary to some press reports, I categorically denied all of the allegations and denied that I ever attempted to date Anita Hill, when first interviewed by the FBI. I strongly reaffirm that denial. Let me describe my relationship with Anita Hill.

In 1981, after I went to the Department of Education as an Assistant Secretary in the Office of Civil Rights, one of my closest friends, from both college and law school, Gil Hardy, brought Anita Hill to my attention. As I remember, he indicated that she was dissatisfied with her law firm and wanted to work in Government. Based primarily, if not solely, on Gil's recommendation, I hired Anita Hill.

During my tenure at the Department of Education, Anita Hill was an attorney-adviser who worked directly with me. She worked on special projects, as well as day to day matters. As I recall, she was one of two professionals working directly with me at the time. As a result, we worked closely on numerous matters.

I recall being pleased with her work product and the professional, but cordial relationship which we enjoyed at work. I also recall engaging in discussions about politics and current events.

Upon my nomination to become Chairman of the Equal Employment Opportunity Commission, Anita Hill, to the best of my recollection, assisted me in the nomination and confirmation process. After my confirmation, she and Diane Holt, then my secretary, joined me at EEOC. I do not recall that there was any question or doubts that she would become a special assistant to me at EEOC, although as a career employee she retained the option of remaining at the Department of Education.

At EEOC our relationship was more distant. And our contacts less frequent, as a result of the increased size of my personal staff and the dramatic increase and diversity of my day-to-day responsibilities.

Upon reflection, I recall that she seemed to have had some difficulty adjusting to this change in her role. In any case, our relationship remained both cordial and professional. At no time did I become aware, either directly or indirectly that she felt I had said or done anything to change the cordial nature of our relationship.

I detected nothing from her or from my staff, or from Gil Hardy, our mutual friend, with whom I maintained regular contact. I am certain that had any statement or conduct on my part been brought to my attention, I would remember it clearly because of the nature and seriousness of such conduct, as well as my adamant opposition to sex discrimination and sexual harassment.

But there were no such statements.

In the spring of 1983, Mr. Charles Kothe contacted me to speak at the law school at Oral Roberts University in Tulsa, Oklahoma. Anita Hill, who is from Oklahoma, accompanied me on that trip. It was not unusual that individuals on my staff would travel with me occasionally. Anita Hill accompanied me on that trip primarily because this was an opportunity to combine business and a visit to her home.

As I recall, during our visit at Oral Roberts University, Mr. Kothe mentioned to me the possibility of approaching Anita Hill to join the faculty at Oral Roberts University Law School. I encouraged him to do so. I noted to him, as I recall, that Anita Hill would do well in teaching. I recommended her highly and she eventually was offered a teaching position.

Although I did not see Anita Hill often after she left EEOC, I did see her on one or two subsequent visits to Tulsa, Oklahoma. And on one visit I believe she drove me to the airport. I also occasionally received telephone calls from her. She would speak directly with me or with my secretary, Diane Holt. Since Anita Hill and Diane Holt had been with me at the Department of Education they were fairly close personally and I believe they occasionally socialized together.

I would also hear about her through Linda Jackson, then Linda Lambert, whom both Anita Hill and I met at the Department of Education. And I would hear of her from my friend Gil.

Throughout the time that Anita Hill worked with me I treated her as I treated my other special assistants. I tried to treat them all cordially, professionally, and respectfully. And I tried to support them in their endeavors, and be interested in and supportive of their success.

I had no reason or basis to believe my relationship with Anita Hill was anything but this way until the FBI visited me a little more than two weeks ago. I find it particularly troubling that she never raised any hint that she was uncomfortable with me. She did not raise or mention it when considering moving with me to EEOC from the Department of Education. And she never raised it with me when she left EEOC and was moving on in her life.

And to my fullest knowledge, she did not speak to any other women working with or around me, who would feel comfortable enough to raise it with me, especially Diane Holt, to whom she seemed closest on my personal staff. Nor did she raise it with mutual friends, such as Linda Jackson, and Gil Hardy.

This is a person I have helped at every turn in the road, since we met. She seemed to appreciate the continued cordial relationship we had since Day One. She sought my advice and counsel, as did virtually all of the members of my personal staff.

During my tenure in the executive branch as a manager, as a policymaker, and as a person, I have adamantly condemned sex harassment. There is no member of this committee or this Senate who feels stronger about sex harassment than I do. As a manager, I made every effort to take swift and decisive action when sex harassment raised or reared its ugly head.

The fact that I feel so very strongly about sex harassment and spoke loudly about it at EEOC has made these allegations doubly hard on me. I cannot imagine anything that I said or did to Anita Hill that could have been mistaken for sexual harassment.

But with that said, if there is anything that I have said that has been misconstrued by Anita Hill or anyone else, to be sexual harassment, then I can say that I am so very sorry and I wish I had known. If I did know I would have stopped immediately and I would not, as I have done over the past two weeks, had to tear away at myself trying to think of what I could possibly have done. But, I have not said or done the things that Anita Hill has alleged. God has gotten me through the days since September 25 and He is my judge.

Mr. Chairman, something has happened to me in the dark days that have followed since the FBI agents informed me about these allegations. And the days have grown darker, as this very serious, very explosive, and very sensitive allegation or these sensitive allegations were selectively leaked in a distorted way to the media over the past weekend.

As if the confidential allegations, themselves, were not enough, this apparently calculated public disclosure has caused me, my family, and my friends enormous pain and great harm.

I have never in all my life felt such hurt, such pain, such agony. My family and I have been done a grave and irreparable injustice. During the past two weeks, I lost the belief that if I did my best all would work out. I called upon the strength that helped me get here from Pin Point, and it was all sapped out of me. It was sapped out of me because Anita Hill was a person I considered a friend, whom I admired and thought I had treated fairly and with the utmost respect. Perhaps I could have better weathered this if it were from someone else, but here was someone I truly felt I had done my best with.

Though I am by no means a perfect person, I have not done what she has alleged, and I still do not know what I could possibly have done to cause her to make these allegations.

When I stood next to the President in Kennebunkport, being nominated to the Supreme Court of the United States, that was a high honor. But as I sit here, before you, 103 days later, that honor has been crushed. From the very beginning charges were leveled against me from the shadows—charges of drug abuse, anti-Semitism, wife-beating, drug use by family members, that I was a quota appointment, confirmation conversion and much, much more, and now, this.

I have complied with the rules. I responded to a document request that produced over 30,000 pages of documents. And I have testified for five full days, under oath. I have endured this ordeal for 103 days. Reporters sneaking into my garage to examine books I read. Reporters and interest groups swarming over divorce papers, looking for dirt. Unnamed people starting preposterous and damaging rumors. Calls all over the country specifically requesting dirt. This is not American. This is Kafka-esque. It has got to stop. It must stop for the benefit of future nominees, and our country. Enough is enough.

I am not going to allow myself to be further humiliated in order to be confirmed. I am here specifically to respond to allegations of sex harassment in the workplace. I am not here to be further humiliated by this committee, or anyone else, or to put my private life on display for a prurient interest or other reasons. I will not allow this committee or anyone else to probe into my private life. This is not what America is all about.

To ask me to do that would be to ask me to go beyond fundamental fairness. Yesterday, I called my mother. She was confined to her bed, unable to work and unable to stop crying. Enough is enough.

Mr. Chairman, in my forty-three years on this Earth, I have been able, with the help of others and with the help of God, to defy poverty, avoid prison, overcome segregation, bigotry, racism, and obtain one of the finest educations available in this country. But I have not been able to overcome this process. This is worse than any obstacle or anything that I have ever faced. Throughout my life I have been energized by the expectation and the hope that in this country I would be treated fairly in all endeavors. When there was segregation I hoped there would be fairness one day or some day. When there was bigotry and prejudice I hoped that there would be tolerance and understanding some day.

Mr. Chairman, I am proud of my life, proud of what I have done, and what I have accomplished, proud of my family, and this process, this process is trying to destroy it all. No job is worth what I have been through, no job. No horror in my life has been so debilitating. Confirm me if you want, don't confirm me if you are so led, but let this process end. Let me and my family regain our lives. I never asked to be nominated. It was an honor. Little did I know the price, but it is too high.

I enjoy and appreciate my current position, and I am comfortable with the prospect of returning to my work as a judge on the U.S. Court of Appeals for the DC Circuit and to my friends there.

Each of these positions is public service, and I have given at the office. I want my life and my family's life back and I want them returned expeditiously.

I have experienced the exhilaration of new heights from the moment I was called to Kennebunkport by the President to have lunch and he nominated me. That was the high point. At that time I was told eye-to-eye that, Clarence, you made it this far on merit, the rest is going to be politics and it surely has been. There have been other highs; the outpouring of support from my friends of long-standing a bonding like I have never experienced with my old boss, Senator Danforth, the wonderful support of those who have worked with me.

There have been prayers said for my family, and me, by people I know and people I will never meet, prayers that were heard and that sustained not only me, but also my wife and my entire family. Instead of understanding and appreciating the great honor bestowed upon me, I find myself here today defending my name, my integrity, because somehow select portions of confidential documents dealing with this matter were leaked to the public.

Mr. Chairman, I am a victim of this process and my name has been harmed, my integrity has been harmed, my character has been harmed, my family has been harmed, my friends have been harmed. There is nothing this committee, this body or this country can do to give me my good name back, nothing.

I will not provide the rope for my own lynching or for further humiliation. I am not going to engage in discussions, nor will I submit to roving questions of what goes on in the most intimate parts of my private live or the sanctity of my bedroom. These are the most intimate parts of my privacy, and they will remain just that, private.

THE CHAIRMAN: Thank you, Judge. You will not be asked to.

Before I begin my questioning of Judge Thomas, I would remind the committee and the nominee that, with respect to one set of allegations, those pertaining to Professor Anita Hill, we are somewhat limited at this stage as to permissible questions. Professor Hill, as recently as late last night, continues to ask us to maintain the confidentiality of her statement to the committee.

So, Judge Thomas, at this stage of the hearing, without having heard Professor Hill's testimony and without using her statement, our questioning to you may not be complete. We may have to discuss some aspects of the allegations with you at the end of these hearings.

I would also note for the record that the choice of the order of these hearings was left to you. I asked whether or not you wished to go first or second, and you chose, as is your right, to speak first and then, if you so chose, to speak last.

Therefore, with respect to Professor Hill, I intend to focus on the general nature of your relationship with her, her responsibilities in your office and the environment in which she worked.

Judge, you have spoken to some of these issues in your opening statement, but let me ask you—

SEN. HATCH: Mr. Chairman.

THE CHAIRMAN: Yes.

SEN. HATCH: Mr. Chairman, I just want to say something for the record here. This is not the appointment of a justice of the peace. This is the nomination process of a man to become a Justice of the Supreme Court of the United States, and he has been badly maligned.

I might add that I have a lot of sympathy for Professor Hill, too, and I am not going to sit here and tolerate her attorneys telling you or me or anybody else that, now that she has made these statements in writing, with what is, if the judge is telling the truth—and I believe he is—scurrilous allegations, that that statement cannot be used, especially in this proceeding. It is a matter of fairness.

I might add that I have been informed that the reporter who broke this story has her statement and read it to her before she would even talk to her. Now, it would be the greatest travesty I have ever seen in any court of law, let alone an open forum in the nomination process of a man for Justice of the U.S. Supreme Court, to allow her attorneys or her or anybody on this committee or anybody else, for that matter, to tell us what can or cannot be used now that this man's reputation has been very badly hurt.

THE CHAIRMAN: Would the Senator yield?

SEN. HATCH: I am not finished.

I intend to use that statement, because it is fair to use it. I do not want to hurt—

THE CHAIRMAN: Senator, let me—

SEN. HATCH: Let me finish.

THE CHAIRMAN: No; I will not.

SEN. HATCH: Yes, you will. Yes, you will.

THE CHAIRMAN: Let me just make one—you are entitled to use the statement under the rule. No one, the Chair cannot stop you from using the statement.

SEN. HATCH: Well, Mr. Chairman, how can it be admissible to everybody? Everybody in this country is going to see it.

SEN. SIMPSON: Mr. Chairman, how can she request confidentiality at this point, when she said she—

THE CHAIRMAN: I can answer that question. Professor Hill says that she wants to tell her story. She did not release the statement, she says, and she wants her story told by her. Because we have given the opportunity to the judge to speak first, if he so chose, and he has, she wants to be able to present her thus far unreleased statement in her own words. She will not have spoken publicly when she comes and addresses the committee.

Now, why don't we get on with this process?

SEN. THURMOND: Mr. Chairman, let me say a word.

SEN. HATCH: I am not finished.

SEN. THURMOND: Wait just one minute.

SEN. HATCH: Okay.

SEN. THURMOND: Mr. Chairman, she has been on television telling her story. She has made it public, so therefore, I think the right to use that statement ought to be admitted.

SEN. KENNEDY: Mr. Chairman.

SEN. HATCH: Mr. Chairman, I did not release the floor. I did to the chairman, because the chairman—I want to finish my comments.

THE CHAIRMAN: The Senator from Massachusetts and then we will go back—

SEN. HATCH: Mr. Chairman.

THE CHAIRMAN: Everybody is going to get a chance to say what—

SEN. HATCH: All right, if you will come back to me, I would appreciate it.

SEN. KENNEDY: Mr. Chairman, it seems to me that you outlined a reasonable way of proceeding. I think it is entirely proper that Judge Thomas be able to make what statement that he so desires. And I thought it was a very moving statement, Judge.

It might be appropriate, if that is the desire, that at least we work out in terms of the committee and the committee's understanding the way that we are going to proceed on this. As I understand, the professor had indicated a willingness to testify first or go second, and now we are in the situation where Judge Thomas has spoken, and it seems to me that we ought to be able to work out at least the way that we are going to proceed that is going to be respectful both of Judge Thomas and the witness, without getting into a lot of back and forth up here, which is not really the purpose of the hearing.

What I might suggest, at least, is that we have a very brief recess, so that we can at least find out the way that we can proceed that is consistent with Judge Thomas, consistent with the others, and satisfactory to the committee.

SEN. HATCH: Mr. Chairman.

SEN. DECONCINI: Mr. Chairman.

SEN. HATCH: Mr. Chairman.

THE CHAIRMAN: The Senator from Utah.

SEN. HATCH: I object to a recess. The fact of the matter is, last Thursday, a substantial majority of the Senate frankly asked us to get to the bottom of this. The public deserves to know now, one way or the other, and the public is going to know, if I have anything to say about it.

Our colleagues demanded it. They did not ask us to just find out so much as the witness will allow us to ask, and I have no intention of pillorying or maligning Professor Hill. I feel sorry for both of these people. Both of them are going to come out of this with less of a reputation. It is pathetic and it would not have happened—

SEN. DECONCINI: Mr. Chairman.

SEN. HATCH: Let me finish, if I could.

If somebody on this committee or their staff had had the honesty and the integrity before the vote to raise this issue and ask for an executive session and say this has to be brought—nobody did, and then somebody on this committee or their staff, and I am outraged by it, leaked that report, an FBI report that we all know should never be disclosed to the public, because of the materials that generally are in them. They take it down as it is given. It has raw stuff in it, but it has been leaked. The media knows everything in it. I think the American people are entitled to know, if they want to.

What I am trying to say is that, to be frank, Mr. Chairman, there are inconsistencies in the statement of Anita Hill to the FBI, compared to her other statements. I do not particularly intend to go into that. She is entitled to explain these discrepancies, but Judge Thomas is entitled to point out these inconsistencies for their bearing on the credibility of the accuser in this instance, nice person though she may be, a good law professor though she may be, a fellow Yale law graduate though she may be, and the statements of—

THE CHAIRMAN: Senator—

SEN. DECONCINI: Mr. Chairman.

SEN. HATCH: If I could just finish. I promise to be shorter. The statements of the subsequent witnesses are also at variance with Professor Hill's statements with what she told the FBI. If she happens to testify differently today, we have to find out which of those statements are true, and if I—

THE CHAIRMAN: Senator, we are not at liberty to publicly discuss what is in the FBI report. Her statement is what—

SEN. HATCH: The heck we're not. This report has been leaked to the press, they know about it. Part of it has been read to the accuser in this case. I think it is time to be fair to the nominee. He has come this far. He is the one who is being accused. They have the burden of showing that he is not telling the truth here, and he has a right to face the accuser and everything that accuser says, and if he does not, then I am going to resign from this committee today. I am telling you, I don't want to be on it.

THE CHAIRMAN: The hearing is in recess for five minutes.

[Recess.]

THE CHAIRMAN: The hearing will come to order.

The committee has met and resolved the impasse the following way: Professor Hill indicated on the telephone that she was prepared to have her statement released.

In further discussion with the committee and others involved, it has been determined that we will excuse temporarily Judge Thomas and we will call momentarily as the witness Anita Hill. Anita Hill will be sworn and will make her own statement in her own words. At that time, we will begin the questioning of Professor Hill, after which we will bring back Judge Thomas for questioning.

Now, the committee will stand in recess until—and I imagine it is only momentarily, until Professor Hill arrives. We will stand in recess until she is able to take her seat, which should be a matter of a minute or so.

I am told that security is clearing the hall. She is in the hall, so that she can come down.

[Pause. Anita Hill enters the room.]

THE CHAIRMAN: [addressing Ms. Hill] I will tell you what the procedure will be, while your family and others are being seated. In a moment, I will ask you to stand to be sworn. When that is finished, we will invite you to make any statement that you wish to make, and then I will begin by asking you some questions. Senator Specter will ask you some questions, and then Senator Leahy will ask you some questions, and then I assume it will be Senator Specter again, but I am not certain of that.

Again, welcome. We are happy that you are here, and stand and be sworn, if you will: Professor, are you prepared to tell the whole truth and nothing but the truth, so help you, God?

MS. HILL: I do.

TESTIMONY OF ANITA F. HILL, PROFESSOR OF LAW, UNIVERSITY OF OKLAHOMA, NORMAN, OKLAHOMA

THE CHAIRMAN: Professor Hill, please make whatever statement you would wish to make to the committee.

MS. HILL: Mr. Chairman—

THE CHAIRMAN: Excuse me. I instruct the officers not to let anyone in or out of that door while Professor Hill is making her statement.

MS. HILL: Mr. Chairman, Senator Thurmond, members of the committee, my name is Anita F. Hill, and I am a Professor of Law at the University of Oklahoma.

I was born on a farm in Okmulgee County, Oklahoma, in 1956. I am the youngest of thirteen children. I had my early education in Okmulgee County. My father, Albert Hill, is a farmer in that area. My mother's name is Erma Hill. She is also a farmer and a housewife.

My childhood was one of a lot of hard work and not much money, but it was one of solid family affection as represented by my parents. I was reared in a religious atmosphere in the Baptist faith, and I have been a member of the Antioch Baptist Church in Tulsa, Oklahoma, since 1983. It is a very warm part of my life at the present time.

For my undergraduate work, I went to Oklahoma State University, and graduated from there in 1977. I am attaching to the statement a copy of my resume for further details of my education.

THE CHAIRMAN: It will be included in the record.

MS. HILL: Thank you.

I graduated from the university with academic honors and proceeded to the Yale Law School, where I received my J.D. degree in 1980.

Upon graduation from law school, I became a practicing lawyer with the Washington, DC firm of Wald, Harkrader & Ross. In 1981, I was introduced to now-Judge Thomas by a mutual friend. Judge Thomas told me that he was anticipating a political appointment and asked if I would be interested in working with him. He was, in fact, appointed as Assistant Secretary of Education for Civil Rights. After he had taken that post, he asked if I would become his assistant, and I accepted that position.

In my early period there, I had two major projects. First was an article I wrote for Judge Thomas's signature on the education of minority students. The second was the organization of a seminar on high-risk students, which was abandoned, because Judge Thomas transferred to the EEOC, where he became the chairman of that office.

During this period at the Department of Education, my working relationship with Judge Thomas was positive. I had a good deal of responsibility and independence. I thought he respected my work and that he trusted my judgment.

After approximately three months of working there, he asked me to go out socially with him. What happened next and telling the world about it are the two most difficult things, experiences of my life. It is only after a great deal of agonizing consideration and a number of sleepless nights that I am able to talk of these unpleasant matters to anyone but my close friends.

I declined the invitation to go out socially with him, and explained to him that I thought it would jeopardize what at the time I considered to be a very good working relationship. I had a normal social life with other men outside of the office. I believed then, as now, that having a social relationship with a person who was supervising my work would be ill advised. I was very uncomfortable with the idea and told him so.

I thought that by saying "no" and explaining my reasons, my employer would abandon his social suggestions. However, to my regret, in the following few weeks he continued to ask me out on several occasions. He pressed me to justify my reasons for saying "no" to him. These incidents took place in his office or mine. They were in the form of private conversations which would not have been overheard by anyone else.

My working relationship became even more strained when Judge Thomas began to use work situations to discuss sex. On these occasions, he would call me into his office for reports on education issues and projects or he might suggest that because of the time pressures of his schedule, we go to lunch to a Government cafeteria. After a brief discussion of work, he would turn the conversation to a discussion of sexual matters. His conversations were very vivid.

He spoke about acts that he had seen in pornographic films involving such matters as women having sex with animals, and films showing group sex or rape scenes. He talked about pornographic materials depicting individuals with large penises, or large breasts involved in various sex acts.

On several occasions Thomas told me graphically of his own sexual prowess. Because I was extremely uncomfortable talking about sex with him at all, and particularly in such a graphic way, I told him that I did not want to talk about these subjects. I would also try to change the subject to education matters or to nonsexual personal matters, such as his background or his beliefs. My efforts to change the subject were rarely successful.

Throughout the period of these conversations, he also from time to time asked me for social engagements. My reactions to these conversations was to avoid them by limiting opportunities for us to engage in extended conversations. This was difficult because at the time, I was his only assistant at the Office of Education or Office for Civil Rights.

During the latter part of my time at the Department of Education, the social pressures and any conversation of his offensive behavior ended. I began both to believe and hope that our working relationship could be a proper, cordial, and professional one.

When Judge Thomas was made Chair of the EEOC, I needed to face the question of whether to go with him. I was asked to do so and I did. The work itself was interesting, and at that time, it appeared that the sexual overtures, which had so troubled me, had ended.

I also faced the realistic fact that I had no alternative job. While I might have gone back to private practice, perhaps in my old firm, or at another, I was dedicated to civil rights work and my first choice was to be in that field. Moreover, at that time the Department of Education, itself, was a dubious venture. President Reagan was seeking to abolish the entire department.

For my first months at the EEOC, where I continued to be an assistant to Judge Thomas, there were no sexual conversations or overtures. However, during the fall and winter of 1982, these began again. The comments were random, and ranged from pressing me about why I didn't go out with him, to remarks about my personal appearance. I remember him saying that some day I would have to tell him the real reason that I wouldn't go out with him.

He began to show displeasure in his tone and voice and his demeanor in his continued pressure for an explanation. He commented on what I was wearing in terms of whether it made me more or less sexually attractive. The incidents occurred in his inner office at the EEOC.

One of the oddest episodes I remember was an occasion in which Thomas was drinking a Coke in his office. He got up from the table, at which we were working, went over to his desk to get the Coke, looked at the can and asked, "Who has put pubic hair on my Coke?"

On other occasions he referred to the size of his own penis as being larger than normal and he also spoke on some occasions of the pleasures he had given to women with oral sex. At this point, late 1982, I began to feel severe stress on the job. I began to be concerned that Clarence Thomas might take out his anger with me by degrading me or not giving me important assignments. I also thought that he might find an excuse for dismissing me.

In January 1983, I began looking for another job. I was handicapped because I feared that if he found out he might make it difficult for me to find other employment, and I might be dismissed from the job I had.

Another factor that made my search more difficult was that this was during a period of a hiring freeze in the Government. In February 1983, I was hospitalized for five days on an emergency basis for acute stomach pain which I attributed to stress on the job. Once out of the hospital, I became more committed to find other employment and sought further to minimize my contact with Thomas.

This became easier when Allyson Duncan became office director because most of my work was then funneled through her and I had contact with Clarence Thomas mostly in staff meetings.

In the spring of 1983, an opportunity to teach at Oral Roberts University opened up. I participated in a seminar, taught an afternoon session in a seminar at Oral Roberts University. The dean of the university saw me teaching and inquired as to whether I would be interested in pursuing a career in teaching, beginning at Oral Roberts University. I agreed to take the job, in large part because of my desire to escape the pressures I felt at the EEOC due to Judge Thomas.

When I informed him that I was leaving in July, I recall that his response was that now I would no longer have an excuse for not going out with him. I told him that I still preferred not to do so. At some time after that meeting, he asked if he could take me to dinner at the end of the term. When I declined, he assured me that the dinner was a professional courtesy only and not a social invitation. I reluctantly agreed to accept that invitation but only if it was at the very end of a working day.

On, as I recall, the last day of my employment at the EEOC in the summer of 1983, I did have dinner with Clarence Thomas. We went directly from work to a restaurant near the office. We talked about the work that I had done both at Education and at the EEOC. He told me that he was pleased with all of it except for an article and speech that I had done for him while we were at the Office for Civil Rights. Finally he made a comment that I will vividly remember. He said, that if I ever told anyone of his behavior that it would ruin his career. This was not an apology, nor was it an explanation. That was his last remark about the possibility of our going out, or reference to his behavior.

In July 1983, I left the Washington, DC area and have had minimal contacts with Judge Clarence Thomas since. I am, of course, aware from the press that some questions have been raised about conversations I had with Judge Clarence Thomas after I left the EEOC.

From 1983 until today I have seen Judge Thomas only twice. On one occasion I needed to get a reference from him and on another, he made a public appearance at Tulsa. On one occasion he called me at home and we had an inconsequential conversation. On one occasion he called me without reaching me and I returned the call without reaching him and nothing came of it. I have, at least on three occasions, been asked to act as a conduit to him for others.

I knew his secretary, Diane Holt. We had worked together both at EEOC and Education. There were occasions on which I spoke to her and on some of these occasions, undoubtedly, I passed on some casual comment to then-Chairman Thomas. There were a series of calls in the first three months of 1985, occasioned by a group in Tulsa which wished to have a civil rights conference. They wanted Judge Thomas to be the speaker and enlisted my assistance for this purpose.

I did call in January and February to no effect and finally suggested to the person directly involved, Susan Cahall, that she put the matter into her own hands and call directly. She did so in March 1985.

In connection with that March invitation, Ms. Cahall wanted conference materials for the seminar, and some research was needed. I was asked to try and get the information and did attempt to do so. There was another call about another possible conference in July 1985.

In August 1987, I was in Washington, DC and I did call Diane Holt. In the course of this conversation she asked me how long I was going to be in town and I told her. It is recorded in the messages as August 15, it was in fact August 20. She told me about Judge Thomas's marriage and I did say, congratulations.

It is only after a great deal of agonizing consideration that I am able to talk of these unpleasant matters to anyone, except my closest friends as I have said before. These last few days have been very trying and very hard for me, and it hasn't just been the last few days this week. It has actually been over a month now that I have been under the strain of this issue. Telling the world is the most difficult experience of my life, but it is very close to hav[ing] to live through the experience that occasioned this meeting. I may have used poor judgment early on in my relationship with this issue. I was aware, however, that telling at any point in my career could adversely affect my future career. And I did not want, early on, to burn all the bridges to the EEOC.

As I said, I may have used poor judgment. Perhaps I should have taken angry or even militant steps, both when I was in the agency or after I had left it, but I must confess to the world that the course that I took seemed the better, as well as the easier approach.

I declined any comment to newspapers, but later when Senate staff asked me about these matters, I felt that I had a duty to report. I have no personal vendetta against Clarence Thomas. I seek only to provide the committee with information which it may regard as relevant.

It would have been more comfortable to remain silent. I took no initiative to inform anyone. But when I was asked by a representative of this committee to report my experience, I felt that I had to tell the truth. I could not keep silent.

THE CHAIRMAN: Thank you, very much.

Professor, before I begin my questioning, I notice there are a number of people sitting behind you. Are any of them your family members that you would like to introduce?

MS. HILL: Well, actually my family members have not arrived yet. Yes, they have. They are outside the door, they were not here for my statement.

THE CHAIRMAN: We will make room for your family to be able to sit.

MS. HILL: It is a very large family, Senator.

THE CHAIRMAN: Well, we will begin but attempt to accommodate as quietly as we can what may be an unusual arrangement. I might ask, is everyone who is sitting behind you necessary? Maybe they could stand and let your family sit. I would assume the reason that—to make it clear—the reason that your family is not here at the moment is that you did not anticipate coming. If those who do not need to be seated behind Miss Hill could stand with the rest of our staffs, we could seat the family.

We will try to get a few more chairs, if possible, but we should get this underway. We may, at some point, Professor Hill, attempt to accommodate either your counsel and/or your family members with chairs down the side here. They need not all be up front here.

Fine, we can put them in the back, as well.

Now, there are two chairs on the end here, folks. We must get this hearing moving. There are two chairs on the end here. We will find everyone a seat but we must begin.

Now, Professor Hill, at the risk of everyone behind you standing up, would you be kind enough to introduce your primary family members to us.

MS. HILL: I would like to introduce, first of all, my father, Albert Hill.

THE CHAIRMAN: Mr. Hill, welcome.

MS. HILL: My mother, Erma Hill.

THE CHAIRMAN: Mrs. Hill.

MS. HILL: My mother is going to be celebrating her 80th birthday on the 16th.

THE CHAIRMAN: Happy birthday, in advance.

MS. HILL: My sister, my eldest sister, Elreatha Lee is here; my sister Jo Ann Fennell, my sister Coleen Gilcrist, my sister Joyce Baird.

THE CHAIRMAN: I welcome you all. I am sorry?

MS. HILL: My brother, Ray Hill.

THE CHAIRMAN: Thank you, Professor.

MS. HILL: I would also—I am sorry.

THE CHAIRMAN: Please?

MS. HILL: I would also like to introduce my counsel at this time.

THE CHAIRMAN: Yes; that would be appropriate.

MS. HILL: Mr. Gardner, Ms. Susan Ross, and Mr. Charles Ogeltree.

THE CHAIRMAN: Thank you.

Now, Professor, thank you for your statement and your introductions and I think it is important that the committee understand a little more about your background and your work experience before we get into the specific allegations that you have made in your statement.

I understand, as you have just demonstrated, you come from a large family and I have been told that you have indicated that you are the youngest in the family, is that correct?

MS. HILL: Yes, I am.

THE CHAIRMAN: Now, I assume, like all families, they have been a great help and assistance to you. Let me ask you, tell me again your educational background for the record?

MS. HILL: I went to primary, elementary and secondary school in Okmulgee County, and Morris High School, Morris Jr. High and Erim Grade School in reverse order. I went to Oklahoma State University starting in 1973 and graduated in 1977 from Oklahoma State University with a degree in psychology, and in 1977 I began attending Yale Law School. I graduated, received my J.D. degree from there in 1980.

THE CHAIRMAN: Now, what was your first job after graduation from law school?

MS. HILL: I worked at the firm of Wald, Harkrader & Ross.

THE CHAIRMAN: How did you acquire the job—that is a Washington law firm?

MS. HILL: That is a Washington, DC law firm.

THE CHAIRMAN: And how did you acquire that job?

MS. HILL: Through the interviewing process. The first interview took place at Yale Law School. I was interviewed for that job. I don't remember the names of the interviewers. I was called to Washington for an interview in the office of Wald, Harkrader & Ross, I was interviewed by a number of people and I accepted an appointment with them.

Now, I will say that that interview process was preceded by work that I had done with them as a summer associate, and so the interview process the second time around was really, actually I will say that the interview process took place before the summer associate and then at the end of that summer associateship I was asked to work there full time.

THE CHAIRMAN: Who was your immediate supervisor when you were at that law firm?

MS. HILL: Well, a number of individuals. I worked with a number of different attorneys on different projects.

THE CHAIRMAN: Now, what type of work did you do while you were at the law firm? Was it specialized, or did you do whatever was asked by any of the partners?

MS. HILL: Well, since I worked there for only one year, I was a fairly new associate, most of my work was basically what was available and when I had time available to do it. However, I did some Federal trade work, I did some environmental law work there, and I participated in the drafting of a manual on banking law while I was there.

THE CHAIRMAN: Now, did you decide you wanted to leave that law firm, or was it suggested to you?

MS. HILL: It was never—

THE CHAIRMAN: Did someone approach you and say there's another job you might like, or did you indicate that you would like to leave the law firm to seek another job?

MS. HILL: I was interested in seeking other employment. It was never suggested to me at the firm that I should leave the law firm in any way.

THE CHAIRMAN: How old were you at this time?

MS. HILL: At the time, I was twenty-four years old.

THE CHAIRMAN: Now, were you dissatisfied at the law firm? Why did you want to leave?

MS. HILL: Well, I left the law firm because I wanted to pursue other practice, in other practice other than basically the commercial practice, civil practice that was being done at the law firm. I was not dissatisfied with the quality of the work or the challenges of the work. I thought that I would be more personally fulfilled if I pursued other fields of the law.

THE CHAIRMAN: Now, again, were you approached as to the opportunity at the Department of Education, or were you aware that there was a potential opening and you sought it out?

MS. HILL: I spoke only with Clarence Thomas about the possibility of working at the—

THE CHAIRMAN: Excuse me. How did you get to Clarence Thomas, that is my question?

MS. HILL: I was introduced to him by a mutual friend.

THE CHAIRMAN: Was the mutual friend a member of the law firm for which you worked?

MS. HILL: Yes, and his name is Gilbert Hardy. He was a member of the firm for which I worked, Wald, Harkrader & Ross.

THE CHAIRMAN: You had expressed to Mr. Hardy that you would like to move into Government or move out of the practice? Were you specific in what you wanted to do?

MS. HILL: I told him only that I was interested in pursuing something other than private practice.

THE CHAIRMAN: Now, some of the activities of the Office of Civil Rights at the time were pretty controversial. We heard testimony, in fact, about the fact the Office was under court order to change its practice for carrying out its duties, and some have suggested that Mr. Thomas had done an exemplary job in changing things, and some have suggested otherwise.

Did the controversy surrounding the office detract from your interest in taking this job, or did you consider it?

MS. HILL: I certainly considered it. I considered the fact that there was talk about abolishing the office. I considered all of those things, but I saw this as an opportunity to do some work that I may not get at another time.

THE CHAIRMAN: Did you think this was a good job?

MS. HILL: Pardon me?

THE CHAIRMAN: Did you view this as a good job, or did you view this as an intermediate step?

MS. HILL: I viewed it as a good job, yes.

THE CHAIRMAN: Can you describe for the committee your duties, initial duties when you arrived at the Department of Education, in the civil rights area? What were your duties?

MS. HILL: My duties were really special projects and special research. A lot of the special projects involved commenting on Office for Civil Rights policies, it involved doing research on education issues as they related to socio-economic factors, and so forth.

THE CHAIRMAN: Was Judge Thomas your direct supervisor? Did you report to anyone else but Judge Thomas at the time?

MS. HILL: I reported only to Judge Thomas.

THE CHAIRMAN: So, the Department of Education, your sole immediate supervisor was Judge Thomas?

MS. HILL: Yes.

THE CHAIRMAN: And what was your title?

MS. HILL: Attorney adviser.

THE CHAIRMAN: Attorney adviser. Now, did you have reason to interact with Judge Thomas in that capacity very often during the day?

MS. HILL: We interacted regularly.

THE CHAIRMAN: Did you attend meetings with Judge Thomas?

MS. HILL: I would attend some meetings, but not all of the meetings that he attended.

THE CHAIRMAN: Perhaps you would be willing to describe to the committee what a routine work day was at that phase of your career in working with Judge Thomas.

MS. HILL: Well, it could—I am not sure there was any such thing as a routine workday. Some days I would go in, I might be asked to respond to letters that Judge Thomas had received, I might be asked to look at memos that had come from the various offices in the Office for Civil Rights.

If there was a meeting which Judge Thomas needed to attend, that he wanted someone there to take information or to help him with information, I might be asked to do that.

THE CHAIRMAN: Where was your office physically located relative to Judge Thomas's office?

MS. HILL: His office was set up down the hall from mine. Inside his set of offices, there was a desk for his secretary and then his office was behind a closed door. My office was down the hall, it was separated from his office.

THE CHAIRMAN: Can you describe to us how it was that you came to move over to the EEOC with Judge Thomas?

MS. HILL: Well, my understanding of—I did not have much notice that Judge Thomas was moving over to the EEOC. My understanding from him at that time was that I could go with him to the EEOC, that I did not have—since I was his special assistant, that I did not have a position at the Office for Education, but that I was welcome to go to the EEOC with him.

It was a very tough decision, because this behavior occurred. However, at the time that I went to the EEOC, there was a period—or prior to the time we went to the EEOC, there was a period where the incidents had ceased, and so after some consideration of the job opportunities in the area, as well as the fact that I was not assured that my job at Education was going to be protected, I made a decision to move to the EEOC.

THE CHAIRMAN: Were you not assured of that, because you were a political appointee, or were you not assured of it because—tell me why you felt you weren't assured of that.

MS. HILL: Well, there were two reasons, really. One, I was a special assistant of a political appointee, and, therefore, I assumed and I was told that that position may not continue to exist. I didn't know who was going to be taking over the position. I had not been interviewed to become the special assistant of the new individual, so I assumed they would want to hire their own, as Judge Thomas had done.

In addition, the Department of Education at that time was scheduled to be abolished. There had been a lot of talk about it, and at that time it was truly considered to be on its way out, and so, for a second reason, I could not be certain that I would have a position there.

THE CHAIRMAN: Now, when you moved over to EEOC, can you recall for us, to the best of your ability, how that offer came about? Did you inquire of Judge Thomas whether or not you could go to EEOC? Did he suggest it? Do you recall?

MS. HILL: I recall that when the appointment at the EEOC became firm, that I was called into his office, and I believe Diane Holt was there, too, and—

THE CHAIRMAN: Diane Holt, his personal secretary?

MS. HILL: Diane Holt was his secretary at Education. We were there and he made the announcement about the appointment and assured us that we could go to the EEOC with him.

THE CHAIRMAN: Now, when you went to EEOC, what were your duties there?

MS. HILL: Well, my duties were really varied, because it was a much larger organization, there were so many more functions of the organization, my primary duties were to be the liaison to the Office of Congressional Affairs and the Office of Review and Appeals, so that I reviewed a number of the cases that came up on appeal, to make certain our office had given proper consideration, I acted as a liaison to the press sometimes for the chairman's office, through Congressional Affairs and Public Relations.

I had some additional responsibilities as special projects came along.

THE CHAIRMAN: Did you have as much occasion to interact personally with Judge Thomas at EEOC as you had with him at the Department of Education?

MS. HILL: No, no. We were much busier. We were all much busier and the work that we did was work that did not necessarily require as much interaction. A lot of times, at the Education Department, the work required some—there were policy decisions that were to be made and we were trying to do an evaluation of the program, so there was more interaction at that time. At EEOC, there were just projects that had to get out, and so there was less of an opportunity for interaction.

THE CHAIRMAN: Who was your immediate supervisor at EEOC?

MS. HILL: At the EEOC, initially, Clarence Thomas was my immediate supervisor. After a period, Allyson Duncan was appointed to be the Director of the Staff. Initially, the staff consisted of two special assistants, myself and Carlton Stewart. The staff eventually grew to a larger number of assistants, and Allyson Duncan was brought up from the Legal Counsel's Office to take control of that situation.

THE CHAIRMAN: Now, how long were you at EEOC with Judge Thomas before Allyson Duncan became the chief of staff?

MS. HILL: I don't recall.

THE CHAIRMAN: Once she became the chief of staff, was she the person who gave you assignments most often and to whom you reported most often?

MS. HILL: That's right. Occasionally, at the staff meeting assignments would be given out, but that was held only one day a week, so during the rest of the week when things came up, Allyson was in charge of giving out assignments.

THE CHAIRMAN: Now, did the judge's chief of staff report directly to him, or did she have an intermediate supervisor?

MS. HILL: No, she reported directly to him, as I understand.

THE CHAIRMAN: Who prepared your performance evaluation?

MS. HILL: I understood that Judge Thomas prepared the performance evaluations.

THE CHAIRMAN: Did the chief of staff, to the best of your knowledge, have the power to fire you?

MS. HILL: Not to my knowledge.

THE CHAIRMAN: Who had that power?

MS. HILL: Judge Thomas.

THE CHAIRMAN: Was there anyone else at EEOC that you believe possessed that power?

MS. HILL: No; not for that office.

THE CHAIRMAN: Was Judge Thomas still then your ultimate boss and the boss of the entire office?

MS. HILL: Yes.

THE CHAIRMAN: Now, was there any routine workday at EEOC that you could describe for the committee?

MS. HILL: Actually, most of the work that we did, unlike at Education, most of the work was responding to internal memos, instead of responding to things that had come from outside. There were many more of those, because there were many more offices, and so each of us were responsible for a certain area, would respond to a memo or write up a memo to be sent to the chairman for his response.

We also had hearings and there was always a special assistant who was assigned to sit in the Commission hearings, and so some days, if we were having hearings, well, one of the special assistants—very often it was me—would sit in the hearing to provide the chairman with information.

During the days of the week that we were not having hearings, we had to prepare the chairman for the hearings themselves, so that we had to go through the files on the hearings and the records and brief the chairman on those or write memos that briefed the chairman on them.

THE CHAIRMAN: Professor, you have testified that you had regular contact with Judge Thomas at the Department of Education and you have just described the extent of your contact with Judge Thomas at EEOC, and you have described your professional interaction with him.

Now, I must ask you to describe once again, and more fully, the behavior that you have alleged he engaged in while your boss, which you say went beyond professional conventions, and which was unwelcome to you. Now, I know these are difficult to discuss, but you must understand that we have to ask you about them.

Professor, did some of the attempts at conversation you have described in your opening statement occur in your office or in his office?

MS. HILL: Some occurred in his office, some comments were made in mine. Most often they were in his office.

THE CHAIRMAN: Did all of the behavior that you have described to us in your written statement to the committee and your oral statement now and what you have said to the FBI, did all of that behavior take place at work?

MS. HILL: Yes, it did.

THE CHAIRMAN: Now, I would like you to go back—

MS. HILL: Let me clarify that. If you are including a luncheon during the workday to be at work, yes.

THE CHAIRMAN: I am just trying to determine, it was what you described and what you believe to be part of the workday?

MS. HILL: Yes.

THE CHAIRMAN: Now, I have to ask you where each of these events occurred? If you can, to the best of your ability, I would like you to recount for us where each of the incidents that you have mentioned in your opening statement occurred, physically where they occurred.

MS. HILL: Well, I remember two occasions these incidents occurred at lunch in the cafeteria.

THE CHAIRMAN: Do you remember which of those two incidents were at lunch, Professor?

MS. HILL: No.

THE CHAIRMAN: Let me ask this, as an antecedent question: Were you always alone when the alleged conversations would begin or the alleged statements by Judge Thomas would begin?

MS. HILL: Well, when the incidents occurred in the cafeteria, we were not alone. There were other people in the cafeteria, but because of the way the tables were, there were few individuals who were within the immediate area of the conversation.

THE CHAIRMAN: Of those incidents that occurred in places other than in the cafeteria, which ones occurred in his office?

MS. HILL: Well, I recall specifically that the incident about the Coke can occurred in his office at the EEOC.

THE CHAIRMAN: And what was that incident again?

MS. HILL: The incident with regard to the Coke can, that statement?

THE CHAIRMAN: Once again for me, please?

MS. HILL: The incident involved his going to his desk, getting up from a worktable, going to his desk, looking at this can and saying, "Who put pubic hair on my Coke?"

THE CHAIRMAN: Was anyone else in his office at the time?

MS. HILL: No.

THE CHAIRMAN: Was the door closed?

MS. HILL: I don't recall.

THE CHAIRMAN: Are there any other incidents that occurred in his office?

MS. HILL: I recall at least one instance in his office at the EEOC where he discussed some pornographic material and he brought up the substance or the content of pornographic material.

THE CHAIRMAN: Again, it is difficult, but for the record, what substance did he bring up in this instance at EEOC in his office? What was the content of what he said?

MS. HILL: This was a reference to an individual who had a very large penis and he used the name that he had referred to in the pornographic material—

THE CHAIRMAN: Do you recall what it was?

MS. HILL: Yes; I do. The name that was referred to was Long John Silver [*sic*].

THE CHAIRMAN: Were you working on any matter in that context, or were you just called into the office? Do you remember the circumstances of your being in the office on that occasion?

MS. HILL: Very often, I went in to report on memos that I had written. I'm sure that's why I was in the office. What happened generally was that I would write a note to Clarence Thomas and he would call me in to talk about what I had written to him, and I believe that's what happened on that occasion.

THE CHAIRMAN: Let's go back to the first time that you alleged Judge Thomas indicated he had more than a professional interest in you. Do you recall what the first time was and, with as much precision as you can, what he said to you?

MS. HILL: As I recall, it either happened at lunch or it happened in his office when he said to me, very casually, "You are to go out with me some time."

THE CHAIRMAN: You ought to or you are to?

MS. HILL: You ought to.

THE CHAIRMAN: Was that the extent of that incident?

MS. HILL: That was the extent of that incident. At that incident. I declined and at that incident I think he may have said something about, you know, he didn't understand why I didn't want to go out with him, and the conversation may have ended.

THE CHAIRMAN: Would you describe for the committee how you felt when he asked you out? What was your reaction?

MS. HILL: Well, my reaction at that time was a little surprised, because I had not indicated to him in any way that I was interested in dating him. We had developed a good working relationship; it was cordial and it was very comfortable, so I was surprised that he was interested in something else.

THE CHAIRMAN: With regard to the other incidents—and my time is running down, and I will come back to them—but with regard to the other incidents that you mentioned in your opening statement, can you tell us how you felt at the time? Were you uncomfortable, were you embarrassed, did it not concern you? How did you feel about it?

MS. HILL: The pressure to go out with him I felt embarrassed about because I had given him an explanation, that I thought it was not good for me, as an employee, working directly for him, to go out. I thought he did not take seriously my decision to say no, and that he did not respect my having said no to him.

I—the conversations about sex, I was much more embarrassed and humiliated by. The two combined really made me feel sort of helpless in a job situation because I really wanted to do the work that I was doing; I enjoyed that work. But I felt that that was being put in jeopardy by the other things that were going on in the office. And so, I was really, really very troubled by it and distressed over it.

THE CHAIRMAN: Can you tell the committee what was the most embarrassing of all the incidents that you have alleged?

MS. HILL: I think the one that was the most embarrassing was this discussion of pornography involving women with large breasts and engaged in a variety of sex with different people, or animals. That was the thing that embarrassed me the most and made me feel the most humiliated.

THE CHAIRMAN: If you can, in his words—not yours—in his words, can you tell us what, on that occasion, he said to you? You have described the essence of the conversation. In order for us to determine—well, can you tell us, in his words, what he said?

MS. HILL: I really cannot quote him verbatim. I can remember something like, you really ought to see these films that I have seen or this material that I have seen. This woman has this kind of breasts or breasts that measure this size, and they got her in there with all kinds of things, she is doing all kinds of different sex acts. And, you know, that kind of, those were the kinds of words. Where he expressed his enjoyment of it, and seemed to try to encourage me to enjoy that kind of material, as well.

THE CHAIRMAN: Did he indicate why he thought you should see this material?

MS. HILL: No.

THE CHAIRMAN: Why do you think, what was your reaction, why do you think he was saying these things to you?

MS. HILL: Well, coupled with the pressures about going out with him, I felt that implicit in this discussion about sex was the offer to have sex with him, not just to go out with him. There was never any explicit thing about going out to dinner or going to a particular concert or movie, it was, "we ought to go out" and given his other conversations I took that to mean, we ought to have sex or we ought to look at these pornographic movies together.

THE CHAIRMAN: Professor, at your press conference, one of your press conferences, you said that the issue that you raised about Judge Thomas was "an ugly issue". Is that how you viewed these conversations?

MS. HILL: Yes. They were very ugly. They were very dirty. They were disgusting.

THE CHAIRMAN: Were any one of these conversations—this will be my last question, my time is up—were any one of these conversations, other than being asked repeatedly to go out, were any one of them repeated more than once? The same conversation, the reference to—

MS. HILL: The reference to his own physical attributes was repeated more than once, yes.

THE CHAIRMAN: Now, again, for the record, did he just say I have great physical attributes or was he more graphic?

MS. HILL: He was much more graphic.

THE CHAIRMAN: Can you tell us what he said?

MS. HILL: Well, I can tell you that he compared his penis size, he measured his penis in terms of length, those kinds of comments.

THE CHAIRMAN: Thank you.

My time is up, under our agreement. By the way, I might state once again that we have agreed to go back and forth in half-hour conversation on each side; when the principals have finished asking questions, those members who have not been designated to ask questions, since all have been keenly involved and interested in this on both sides, will have an opportunity to ask questions for five minutes.

But let me now yield to my friend from Pennsylvania, Senator Specter.

SEN. SPECTER: Thank you, Mr. Chairman.

Professor Hill, I have been asked to question you by Senator Thurmond, the ranking Republican, but I do not regard this as an adversary proceeding.

MS. HILL: Thank you.

SEN. SPECTER: My duties run to the people of Pennsylvania, who have elected me, and in the broader sense, as a U.S. Senator to constitutional government and the Constitution.

My purpose, as is the purpose of the hearing, generally, is to find out what happened.

MS. HILL: Certainly.

SEN. SPECTER: We obviously have a matter of enormous importance from a lot of points of view. The integrity of the Court is very important. It is very important that the Supreme Court not have any member who is tainted or have a cloud. In our society we can accept unfavorable decisions from the Court if we think they are fairly arrived at.

THE CHAIRMAN: Senator, excuse me for interrupting but some of our colleagues on this end cannot hear you. Can you pull that closer? I know that makes it cumbersome.

SEN. SPECTER: I have tried carefully to avoid that.

THE CHAIRMAN: Well, it worked.

SEN. SPECTER: You can hear me all right, can you not, Professor Hill?

MS. HILL: Yes, I can.

SEN. SPECTER: Okay. But I was just saying, about the importance of the Court where there should be a feeling of confidence and fairness with the decisions, as we parties can take unfavorable decisions if they think they are being treated fairly. I think this hearing is very important to the Senate and to this committee, because by 20-20 hindsight we should have done this before. And obviously it is of critical importance to Judge Thomas, and you, whose reputations and careers are on the line. It is not easy to go back to events which happened almost a decade ago to find out what happened. It is very, very difficult to do. I would start, Professor Hill, with one of your more recent statements, at least according to a man by the name of Carl[ton] Stewart, who says that he met you in August of this year. He said that he ran into you at the American Bar Association Convention in Atlanta, where Professor Hill stated to him in the presence of Stanley Grayson, "How great Clarence's nomination was, and how much he deserved it."

He said you went on to discuss Judge Thomas and your tenure at EEOC for an additional thirty minutes or so. There was no mention of sexual harassment or anything negative about Judge Thomas. He stated that during that conversation [*sic*]. There is also a statement from Stanley Grayson corroborating what Carlton Stewart has said.

My question is, did Mr. Stewart accurately state what happened with you at that meeting?

MS. HILL: As I recall at that meeting, I did see Carlton Stewart and we did discuss the nomination. Carlton Stewart was very excited about the nomination. And said, I believe that those are his words, how great it was that Clarence Thomas had been nominated. I only said that it was a great opportunity for Clarence Thomas. I did not say that it was a good thing, this nomination was a good thing.

I might add that I have spoken to newspaper reporters and have gone on record as saying that I have some doubt and some questions about the nomination. I, however, in that conversation where I was faced with an individual who was elated about the probabilities of his friend being on the Supreme Court, I did not want to insult him or argue with him at that time about the issue. I was very passive in the conversation.

SEN. SPECTER: Excuse me?

MS. HILL: I was very passive in the conversation.

SEN. SPECTER: So that Mr. Stewart and Mr. Grayson are simply wrong when they say, and this is a quotation from Mr. Stewart that you said, specifically, "how great his nomination was, and how much he deserved it." They are just wrong?

MS. HILL: The latter part is certainly wrong. I did say that it is a great opportunity for Clarence Thomas. I did not say that he deserved it.

SEN. SPECTER: We have a statement from former dean of Oral Roberts Law School, Roger Tuttle*, who quotes you as making laudatory comments about Judge Thomas, that he "is a fine man and an excellent legal scholar." In the course of three years when Dean Tuttle knew you at the law school, that you had always praised him and had never made any derogatory comments. Is Dean Tuttle correct?

MS. HILL: During the time that I was at Oral Roberts University I realized that Charles Kothe, who was a founding dean of that school, had very high regards for Clarence Thomas. I did not risk talking in disparaging ways about Clarence Thomas at that time.

I don't recall any specific conversations about Clarence Thomas in which I said anything about his legal scholarship. I do not really know of his legal scholarship, certainly at that time.

SEN. SPECTER: Well, I can understand it if you did not say anything, but Dean Tuttle makes the specific statement. His words are, that you said, "the most laudatory comments."

MS. HILL: I have no response to that because I do not know exactly what he is saying.

SEN. SPECTER: There is a question about Phyllis Berry who was quoted in the *New York Times* on October 7, "In an interview Ms. Barry [*sic*] suggested that the allegations," referring to your allegations, "were the result of Ms. Hill's disappointment and frustration that Mr. Thomas did not show any sexual interest in her."

You were asked about Ms. Berry at the interview on October 9 and were reported to have said, "Well, I don't know Phyllis Berry and she doesn't know me." And there are quite a few people who have come forward to say that they saw you and Ms. Berry together and that you knew each other very well.

MS. HILL: I would disagree with that. Ms. Berry worked at the EEOC. She did

*Sen. Specter appears to be referring to Dean Charles Kothe.

attend some staff meetings at the EEOC. We were not close friends. We did not socialize together and she has no basis for making a comment about my social interests, with regard to Clarence Thomas or anyone else.

I might add, that at the time that I had an active social life and that I was involved with other people.

SEN. SPECTER: Did Ms. Anna Jenkins and Ms. J.C. Alvarez, who both have provided statements attesting to the relationship between you and Ms. Berry, a friendly one. Where Ms. Berry would have known you [*sic*], were both Ms. Jenkins and Ms. Alvarez co-workers in a position to observe your relationship with Ms. Berry?

MS. HILL: They were both workers at the EEOC. I can only say that they were commenting on our relationship in the office. It was cordial and friendly. We were not unfriendly with each other, but we were not social acquaintances. We were professional acquaintances.

SEN. SPECTER: So that when you said, Ms. Berry doesn't know me and I don't know her, you weren't referring to just that, but some intensity of knowledge?

MS. HILL: Well, this is a specific remark about my sexual interest. And I think one has to know another person very well to make those kinds of remarks unless they are very openly expressed.

SEN. SPECTER: Well, did Ms. Berry observe you and Judge Thomas together in the EEOC office?

MS. HILL: Yes, at staff meetings where she attended and at the office, yes.

SEN. SPECTER: Let me pick up on Senator Biden's line of questioning. You referred to the "oddest episode I remember," then talked about the Coke incident. When you made your statement to the FBI, why was it that that was omitted if it were so strong in your mind and such an odd incident?

MS. HILL: I spoke to the FBI agents and I told them the nature of comments, and did not tell them more specifics. I referred to the specific comments that were in my statement.

SEN. SPECTER: Well, when you talked to the FBI agents, you did make specific allegations about specific sexual statements made by Judge Thomas.

MS. HILL: Yes.

SEN. SPECTER: So that your statement to the FBI did have specifics.

MS. HILL: Yes.

SEN. SPECTER: And my question to you, why, if this was such an odd episode, was it not included when you talked to the FBI?

MS. HILL: I do not know.

SEN. SPECTER: I would like you to take a look, if you would, at your own statement in the first full paragraph of page 5, on the last line and ask you why that was not included in your statement to the FBI?

MS. HILL: Excuse me, my copy is not—would you refer to that passage again?

SEN. SPECTER: Yes, of course.

Referring to page 5 of the statement which you provided to the committee, there is a strong allegation in the last sentence. My question to you is, why did you not tell that to the FBI?

MS. HILL: When the FBI investigation took place I tried to answer their questions as directly as I recall. I was very uncomfortable talking to the agent about that, these incidents, I am very uncomfortable now, but I feel that it is necessary. The FBI agent told me that it was regular procedure to come back and ask for more specifics if it was necessary. And so, at that time, I did not provide all of the specifics that I could have.

SEN. SPECTER: Professor Hill, I can understand that it is uncomfortable and I don't want to add to that. If any of it—if there is something you want to pause about, please do.

You testified this morning, in response to Senator Biden, that the most embarrassing question involved—this is not too bad—women's large breasts. That is a word we use all the time. That was the most embarrassing aspect of what Judge Thomas had said to you?

MS. HILL: No. The most embarrassing aspect was his description of the acts of these individuals, these women, the acts that those particular people would engage in. It wasn't just the breasts; it was the continuation of his story about what happened in those films with the people with this characteristic, physical characteristic.

SEN. SPECTER: With the physical characteristic of—

MS. HILL: The large breasts.

SEN. SPECTER: Well, in your statement to the FBI you did refer to the films but there is no reference to the physical characteristic you describe. I don't want to attach too much weight to it, but I had thought you said that the aspect of large breasts was the aspect that concerned you, and that was missing from the statement to the FBI.

MS. HILL: I have been misunderstood. It wasn't the physical characteristic of having large breasts. It was the description of the acts that this person with this characteristic would do, the acts that they would engage in, group acts with animals, things of that nature involving women.

SEN. SPECTER: Professor Hill, I would like you now to turn to page 3 of your statement that you submitted to the committee, that we got just this morning. In the last sentence in the first full paragraph, you again make in that statement a very serious allegation as to Judge Thomas, and I would ask you why you didn't tell the FBI about that when they interviewed you.

MS. HILL: I suppose my response would be the same. I did not tell the FBI all of the information. The FBI agent made clear that if I were embarrassed about talking about something that I could decline to discuss things that were too embarrassing, but that I could provide as much information as I felt comfortable with at that time.

SEN. SPECTER: Well, now, did you decline to discuss with the FBI anything on the grounds that it was too embarrassing?

MS. HILL: There were no particular questions that were asked. He asked me to describe the kinds of incidents that had occurred as graphically as I could without being embarrassed. I did not explain everything. I agree that all of this was not disclosed in the FBI investigation.

SEN. SPECTER: Was it easier for you because one of the FBI agents was a woman, or did you ask at any time that you give the statements to her alone in the absence of the man FBI agent?

MS. HILL: No, I did not do that. I didn't ask to disclose. I just—I did not.

SEN. SPECTER: Well, I understand from what you are saying now that you were told that you didn't have to say anything if it was too embarrassing for you. My question to you is, did you use that at any point to decline to give any information on the ground that it was too embarrassing?

MS. HILL: I never declined to answer a question because it was too embarrassing, no. He asked me to describe the incidents, and rather than decline to make any statement at all, I described them to my level of comfort.

SEN. SPECTER: Well, you described a fair number of things in the FBI statement, but I come back now to the last sentence on page 3 in the first full paragraph, because it is a strong allegation. You have said that you had not omitted that because of its being embarrassing. You might have said even something embarrassing to the female agent. My question to you is, why was that omitted?

MS. HILL: Senator, at the time of the FBI investigation, I cooperated as fully as I could at that time, and I cannot explain why anything in specific was not stated.

SEN. SPECTER: Professor Hill, you testified that you drew an inference that Judge Thomas might want you to look at pornographic films, but you told the FBI specifically that he never asked you to watch the films. Is that correct?

MS. HILL: He never said, "Let's go to my apartment and watch films," or "go to my house and watch films." He did say, "You ought to see this material."

SEN. SPECTER: But when you testified that, as I wrote it down, "We ought to look at pornographic movies together," that was an expression of what was in your mind when he—

MS. HILL: That was the inference that I drew, yes.

SEN. SPECTER: The inference, so he—

MS. HILL: With his pressing me for social engagements, yes.

SEN. SPECTER: That that was something he might have wanted you to do, but the fact is, flatly, he never asked you to look at pornographic movies with him.

MS. HILL: With him? No, he did not.

THE CHAIRMAN: Will the Senator yield for one moment for a point of clarification?

SEN. SPECTER: I would rather not.

THE CHAIRMAN: To determine whether or not the witness ever saw the FBI report. Does she know what was stated by the FBI about her comments?

SEN. SPECTER: Well, Mr. Chairman, I am asking her about what she said to the FBI.

THE CHAIRMAN: I understand. I am just asking that. Have you ever seen the FBI report?

MS. HILL: No; I have not.

THE CHAIRMAN: Would you like to take a few moments and look at it now?

MS. HILL: Yes; I would.

THE CHAIRMAN: Okay. Let's make a copy of the FBI report. I think we have to be careful. Senator Grassley asked me to make sure—maybe you could continue—it only pertains to her. We are not at liberty to give to her what the FBI said about other individuals.

SEN. SPECTER: I was asking Professor Hill about the FBI report.

Obviously because the portion I am questioning you about relates to their recording what you said, and I think it is fair, one lawyer to another, to ask about it.

THE CHAIRMAN: No, I would continue, because you are not asking her directly. I just wanted to know whether or not her responses were at all based upon her knowledge of what the FBI said she said. That is all I was asking.

SEN. SPECTER: Well, she has asked to see it, and I think it is a fair request, and I would be glad to take a moment's delay to—

THE CHAIRMAN: This is the FBI report as it references Professor Hill, only Professor Hill.

SEN. SPECTER: May we stop the clock, Mr. Chairman?

THE CHAIRMAN: Yes we will. We will turn the clock back and give the Senator additional time. I will not ask how long to turn it back. I will leave that decision to Senator Simpson.

SEN. SIMPSON: I will be watching the clock. Thank you, Mr. Chairman.

[Pause. While Ms. Hill reads the report Sen. Biden uses the gavel.]

THE CHAIRMAN: That was not to hurry you along, Professor. That was to ask for silence in the room.

The only point I wish to make is that you know what is in the report and understand that the report is a summary of your conversation, not a transcription of your conversation.

[Pause.]

THE CHAIRMAN: While we have this momentary break, the Senator has ten or more minutes remaining, and at the conclusion of his questioning we will recess for lunch for an hour and then begin with Senator Leahy. . .

Have you had a chance to peruse it?

MS. HILL: Yes.

THE CHAIRMAN: Thank you.

MS. HILL: Thank you.

THE CHAIRMAN: Now I apologize to my colleague for the interruption.

SEN. SPECTER: Thank you, Mr. Chairman.

Professor Hill, now that you have read the FBI report, you can see that it contains no reference to any mention of Judge Thomas's private parts or sexual prowess or size, et cetera. My question to you would be, on something that is as important as it is in your written testimony and in your responses to Senator Biden, why didn't you tell the FBI about that?

MS. HILL: Senator, in paragraph two on page 2 of the report it says that he liked to discuss specific sex acts and frequency of sex. And I am not sure what all that summarizes, but his sexual prowess, his sexual preferences could have—

SEN. SPECTER: Which line are you referring to, Professor?

MS. HILL: The very last line in paragraph two of page 2.

SEN. SPECTER: Well, that says—and this is not too bad, I can read it—"Thomas liked to discuss specific sex acts and frequency of sex." Now are you saying, in response to my question as to why you didn't tell the FBI about the size of his private parts and his sexual prowess and "Long John Silver [*sic*]," that information was comprehended within the statement, "Thomas liked to discuss specific sex acts and frequency of sex"?

MS. HILL: I am not saying that that information was included in that. I don't know that it was. I don't believe that I even mentioned the latter information to the FBI agent, and I could only respond again that at the time of the investigation I tried to cooperate as fully as I could, to recall information to answer the questions that they asked.

SEN. SPECTER: Professor Hill, you said that you took it to mean that Judge Thomas wanted to have sex with you, but in fact he never did ask you to have sex, correct?

MS. HILL: No, he did not ask me to have sex. He did continually pressure me to go out with him, continually, and he would not accept my explanation as being valid.

SEN. SPECTER: So that when you said you took it to mean, "We ought to have sex," that that was an inference that you drew?

MS. HILL: Yes, yes.

SEN. SPECTER: Professor Hill, the *USA Today* reported on October 9, "Anita Hill was told by Senate staffers her signed affidavit alleging sexual harassment by Clarence Thomas would be the instrument that 'quietly and behind the scenes' would force him to withdraw his name."

Was *USA Today* correct on that, attributing it to a man named Mr. Keith Henderson,"a ten-year friend of Hill and former Senate Judiciary Committee staffer"?

MS. HILL: I do not recall. I guess—did I say that? I don't understand who said what in that quotation.

SEN. SPECTER: Well, let me go on. He said, "Keith Henderson, a ten-year friend of Hill and former Senate Judiciary Committee staffer, says Hill was advised by Senate staffers that her charge would be kept secret and her name kept from public scrutiny."

Apparently referring again to Mr. Henderson's statement, "they would approach Judge Thomas with the information and he would withdraw and not turn this into a big story, Henderson says."

Did anybody ever tell you that, by providing the statement, that there would be a move to request Judge Thomas to withdraw his nomination?

MS. HILL: I don't recall any story about pressing, using this to press anyone.

SEN. SPECTER: Well, do you recall anything at all about anything related to that?

MS. HILL: I think that I was told that my statement would be shown to Judge Thomas, and I agreed to that.

SEN. SPECTER: But was there any suggestion, however slight, that the statement with these serious charges would result in a withdrawal so that it wouldn't have to be necessary for your identity to be known or for you to come forward under circumstances like these?

MS. HILL: There was—no, not that I recall. I don't recall anything being said about him being pressed to resign.

SEN. SPECTER: Well, this would only have happened in the course of the past month or so, because all this started just in early September.

MS. HILL: I understand.

SEN. SPECTER: So that when you say you don't recall, I would ask you to search your memory on this point, and perhaps we might begin—and this is an important subject—about the initiation of this entire matter with respect to the Senate staffers who talked to you. But that is going to be too long for the few minutes that I have left, so I would just ask you once again, and you say you don't recollect, whether there was anything at all said to you by anyone that, as *USA Today* reports, that just by having the allegations of sexual harassment by Clarence Thomas, that it would be the instrument that "quietly and behind the scenes" would force him to withdraw his name. Is there anything related to that in any way whatsoever?

MS. HILL: The only thing that I can think of, and if you will check, there were a lot of phone conversations. We were discussing this matter very carefully, and at some point there might have been a conversation about what might happen.

SEN. SPECTER: Might have been?

MS. HILL: There might have been, but that wasn't—I don't remember this specific kind of comment about "quietly and behind the scenes" pressing him to withdraw.

SEN. SPECTER: Well, aside from "quietly and behind the scenes" pressing him to withdraw, any suggestion that just the charges themselves, in writing, would result in Judge Thomas withdrawing, going away?

MS. HILL: No, no. I don't recall that at all, no.

SEN. SPECTER: Well, you started to say that there might have been some conversation, and it seemed to me—

MS. HILL: There might have been some conversation about what could possibly occur.

SEN. SPECTER: Well, tell me about that conversation.

MS. HILL: Well, I can't really tell you any more than what I have said. I discussed what the alternatives were, what might happen with this affidavit that I submitted. We talked about the possibility of the Senate committee coming back for more information. We talked about the possibility of the FBI, asking, going to the FBI and getting more information; some questions from individual Senators. I just, the statement that you are referring to, I really can't verify.

SEN. SPECTER: Well, when you talk about the Senate coming back for more information or the FBI coming back for more information or Senators coming back for more information, that has nothing to do at all with Judge Thomas withdrawing. When you testified a few moments ago that there might possibly have been a conversation, in response to my question about a possible withdrawal, I would press you on that, Professor Hill, in this context: You have testified with some specificity about what happened ten years ago. I would ask you to press your recollection as to what happened within the last month.

MS. HILL: And I have done that, Senator, and I don't recall that comment. I do recall that there might have been some suggestion that if the FBI did the investigation, that the Senate might get involved, that there may be—that a number of things might occur, but I really, I have to be honest with you, I cannot verify the statement that you are asking me to verify. There is not really more that I can tell you on that.

SEN. SPECTER: Well, when you say a number of things might occur, what sort of things?

MS. HILL: May I just add this one thing?

SEN. SPECTER: Sure.

MS. HILL: The nature of that kind of conversation that you are talking about is very different from the nature of the conversation that I recall. The conversations that I recall were much more vivid. They were more explicit. The conversations that I have had with the staff over the last few days in particular have become much more blurry, but these are vivid events that I recall from even eight years ago when they happened, and they are going to stand out much more in my mind than a telephone conversation. They were one on one, personal conversations, as a matter of fact, and that adds to why they are much more easily recalled. I am sure that there are some comments that I do not recall the exact nature of from that period, as well, but these that are here are the ones that I do recall.

SEN. SPECTER: Well, Professor Hill, I can understand why you say that these comments, alleged comments, would stand out in your mind, and we have gone over those. I don't want to go over them again. But when you talk about the withdrawal of a Supreme Court nominee, you are talking about something that is very, very vivid, stark, and you are talking about something that occurred within the past four or five weeks, and my question goes to a very dramatic and important event. If a mere allegation would pressure a nominee to withdraw from the Supreme Court, I would suggest to you that that is not something that wouldn't stick in a mind for four or five weeks, if it happened.

MS. HILL: Well, Senator, I would suggest to you that for me these are more than mere allegations, so that if that comment were made—these are the truth to me, these comments are the truth to me—and if it were made, then I may not respond to it in the same way that you do.

SEN. SPECTER: Well, I am not questioning your statement when I use the word "allegation" to refer to ten years ago. I just don't want to talk about it as a fact because so far that is something we have to decide, so I am not stressing that aspect of the question. I do with respect to the time period, but the point that I would come back to for just one more minute would be—well, let me ask it to you this way.

MS. HILL: Okay.

SEN. SPECTER: Would you not consider it a matter of real importance if someone said to you, "Professor, you won't have to go public. Your name won't have to be disclosed. You won't have to do anything. Just sign the affidavit and this," as the *USA Today* report says, "would be the instrument that 'quietly and behind the scenes' would force him to withdraw his name." Now I am not asking you whether it happened. I am asking you now only, if it did happen, whether that would be the kind of a statement to you which would be important and impressed upon you, that you would remember in the course of four or five weeks.

MS. HILL: I don't recall a specific statement, and I cannot say whether that comment would have stuck in my mind. I really cannot say that.

SEN. SPECTER: The sequence with the staffers is very involved so I am going to move to another subject now, but I want to come back to this. Over the luncheon break, I would ask you to think about it further, if there is any way you can shed any further light on that question, because I think it is an important one.

MS. HILL: Okay. Thank you.

SEN. SPECTER: Professor Hill, the next subject I want to take up with you involves the kind of strong language which you say Judge Thomas used in a very unique setting, where there you have the chairman of the EEOC, the nation's chief law enforcement officer on sexual harassment, and here you have a lawyer who is an expert in this field, later goes on to teach civil rights and has a dedication to making sure that women are not discriminated against. If you take the single issue of discrimination against women, the chairman of the EEOC has a more important role on that question even than a Supreme Court Justice—a Supreme Court Justice is a more important position overall—than if you focus just on sexual harassment.

The testimony that you described here today depicts a circumstance where the chairman of the EEOC is blatant, as you describe it, and my question is: Understanding the fact that you are twenty-five and that you are shortly out of law school and the pressures that exist in this world—and I know about it to a fair extent. I used to be a district attorney and I know about sexual harassment and discrimination against women and I think I have some sensitivity on it—but even considering all of that, given your own expert standing and the fact that here you have the chief law enforcement officer of the country on this subject and the whole purpose of the civil rights law is being perverted right in the office of the chairman with one of his own female subordinates, what went through your mind, if anything, on whether you ought to come forward at that stage? If you had, you would have stopped this man from being head of the EEOC perhaps for another decade. What went on through your mind? I know you decided not to make a complaint, but did you give that any consideration, and, if so, how could you allow this kind of reprehensible conduct to go on right in the headquarters, without doing something about it?

MS. HILL: Well, it was a very trying and difficult decision for me not to say anything further. I can only say that when I made the decision to just withdraw from the situation and not press a claim or charge against him, that I may have shirked a duty, a responsibility that I had, and to that extent I confess that I am very sorry that I did not do something or say something, but at the time that was my best judgment. Maybe it was a poor judgment, but it wasn't dishonest and it wasn't a completely unreasonable choice that I made, given the circumstances.

SEN. SPECTER: My red light is on. Thank you very much, Professor Hill.
Thank you, Mr. Chairman.

THE CHAIRMAN: Thank you, Senator.

Thank you, Professor Hill.

We will adjourn until 2:15 p.m. We will reconvene at 2:15 p.m.

[Whereupon, at 1:10 p.m., the committee was recessed, to reconvene at 2:15 p.m., the same day.]

AFTERNOON SESSION

THE CHAIRMAN: The committee will come to order.

Welcome back, Professor Hill.

The Chair now yields to the Senator from Vermont, Senator Leahy, who will question for one half-hour, and then we will go back to Senator Specter.

SEN. LEAHY: Good afternoon, Professor Hill.

MS. HILL: Good afternoon, Senator.

SEN. LEAHY: Professor, we have had a number of discussions, almost shorthand discussions here, about things you are familiar with and which members of the committee are familiar with, but I would like to take you through a couple of the spots.

You have mentioned—and there were discussions and answers from you regarding the FBI investigation—would you tell us, was it one FBI agent, two FBI agents? How many spoke to you and where?

MS. HILL: There were two FBI agents who visited me in my home.

SEN. LEAHY: How was that arranged? Just focus on the mechanics, please.

MS. HILL: Well, it was arranged, as I understand it, through Senator Biden's office. I received a phone call from one of the staff members of Senator Biden and she informed me that she had—excuse me, the date was September 23—she informed me that she had received a fax from me of my statement and that I should expect a call from the FBI.

When the FBI called, they called me at home, left a message on my machine, I returned their phone call that evening after work and arranged for them to come over immediately from Oklahoma City, I believe, to talk with me.

SEN. LEAHY: That evening?

MS. HILL: That evening, on Monday, September 23.

SEN. LEAHY: About what time did they arrive?

MS. HILL: They arrived at about 6:30.

SEN. LEAHY: And who arrived?

MS. HILL: Inspector Luton and—there was one inspector named Inspector Luton, and I don't recall the name of the other individual.

SEN. LEAHY: One male and one female?

MS. HILL: And one female.

SEN. LEAHY: Now, was anybody else present for that interview?

MS. HILL: No, no one else was present.

SEN. LEAHY: It was just the three of you?

MS. HILL: The three of us; yes.

SEN. LEAHY: Did they tape record the interview?

MS. HILL: No; one inspector did take notes.

SEN. LEAHY: Now, what did they tell you they wanted?

MS. HILL: They told me that they had been contacted by the committee, the Judiciary Committee, and that they wanted information regarding the statement that I had made to the committee.

SEN. LEAHY: Did they have that statement with them?

MS. HILL: I do not believe that they had the statement with them. It was clear from the questioning that they had read the statement, and I believe at one point in the evening Inspector Luton did say that he had read the statement.

SEN. LEAHY: When you made that statement, you had it typed up and you signed it, is that correct?

MS. HILL: I typed it and I signed it.

SEN. LEAHY: You typed and signed it, and kept a copy for yourself?

MS. HILL: I only telefaxed a copy. I did keep a copy, the original.

SEN. LEAHY: And you still have that?

MS. HILL: I still have it.

SEN. LEAHY: Have you given copies of that, other than the copy you telefaxed, to anybody else?

MS. HILL: Well, I shared the statement with my counsel.

SEN. LEAHY: Let's make sure I have this well in mind: You have the original copy, correct?

MS. HILL: Yes.

SEN. LEAHY: And you telefaxed a copy which, in itself, made copies to the committee, is that correct?

MS. HILL: Pardon me?

SEN. LEAHY: You faxed a copy to the committee, is that correct?

MS. HILL: Yes.

SEN. LEAHY: You gave a copy to your council?

MS. HILL: Yes.

SEN. LEAHY: Did you give a copy to anybody else?

MS. HILL: Other than counsel? I don't believe that I gave a copy to anyone else.

SEN. LEAHY: You did not give a copy to the FBI agents?

MS. HILL: No; they told me that they had received a copy from the committee.

SEN. LEAHY: Did you give a copy to any member of the press?

MS. HILL: No; I did not.

SEN. LEAHY: And so your counsel, the faxed copy, and your own copy are the only ones that you have had control of, is that correct?

MS. HILL: Yes.

SEN. LEAHY: Now, did the FBI give any indication to you of how you should answer—in great detail, little detail? How was the interview done?

MS. HILL: Well, the interview was conducted, the indication that I had from the agents was that they would like to take as much information as they could, that they wanted as much as I felt comfortable giving. The questions that were asked were fairly general, in terms of what kinds of comments were made.

SEN. LEAHY: Did they—go ahead. I didn't mean to cut you off.

MS. HILL: No, that's fine.

SEN. LEAHY: Now, in your statement that they told you they had, in that statement you were fairly specific about the kind of sexual discussions that you said Judge Thomas had with you, is that correct, Professor?

MS. HILL: Yes, I felt that I was fairly specific.

SEN. LEAHY: Did they refer to that specificity when they talked with you?

MS. HILL: I'm sorry?

SEN. LEAHY: Did the FBI agents refer to that specificity when they talked with you?

MS. HILL: They simply said that if I got to any point with regard to being specific that made me uncomfortable, that I should withdraw from the conversation or I could perhaps give the information to the female agent who was there. They did not indicate that my comments were not specific enough or that they needed more information.

SEN. LEAHY: Did they say that they might come back and talk with you again?

MS. HILL: Yes, he almost assured me that he would come back.

SEN. LEAHY: But did they?

MS. HILL: In fact, they did not come back. I did receive a phone call the next day to verify two names of persons that I had given them, but they did not return for more information.

SEN. LEAHY: And has anybody come back to talk with you since then?

MS. HILL: From the FBI?

SEN. LEAHY: From the FBI.

MS. HILL: No, I have not spoken with the FBI since then.

SEN. LEAHY: Now, you had a chance to read their report about you this morning, did you not?

MS. HILL: Yes, I did.

SEN. LEAHY: If you could just bear with me a moment, I want to read—do you have that before you?

MS. HILL: Yes, I do.

SEN. LEAHY: Would you turn to the part of the FBI report— and someone is getting me a copy now, as I do not have one—turn to the part where you have reference to the last time or the time you went out to dinner with Judge Thomas. Do you know the one I am referring to?

MS. HILL: Yes.

SEN. LEAHY: I believe it is on the second—let's see, now—yes, on page 4, is a line that, according to the FBI report, "Hill stated that when she left EEOC, Thomas took her out to eat." Do you find that paragraph, Professor Hill?

MS. HILL: I'm sorry, what page are you referring to?

SEN. LEAHY: On page 3 of your report, you see the paragraph which begins—I think it is one, two, three, four, five paragraphs down, "Hill stated that when she left EEOC, Thomas took her out to eat."

MS. HILL: Yes.

SEN. LEAHY: Would you read the rest of that sentence, please?

MS. HILL: "Took her out to eat and told her that if she ever told anyone about their conversation, he would ruin her career."

SEN. LEAHY: Now, is that precisely the way it is in your statement?

MS. HILL: That is not precisely the way it is in my statement. That is not what I told the FBI agents.

SEN. LEAHY: And what did you tell the FBI agents?

MS. HILL: I told the FBI agent that he said that it would ruin his career.

SEN. LEAHY: Now, the FBI agents, did they ask you to give them any written statement of any sort?

MS. HILL: No, they didn't ask for any written statement.

SEN. LEAHY: Did they ask if you would be willing to come to Washington to talk with them?

MS. HILL: They didn't ask that.

SEN. LEAHY: Did they ask if there was anything else you might be willing to do?

MS. HILL: No, they didn't mention anything farther, except for coming back for additional questioning.

SEN. LEAHY: Did they ask you if you would be willing to take a polygraph?

MS. HILL: They asked if I would be willing to take a polygraph.

SEN. LEAHY: And what did you say?

MS. HILL: I answered, "yes."

SEN. LEAHY: Let us go to that last meal discussion. It is your statement that the FBI misunderstood you and, as you have said in each of your statements, that Judge Thomas said that if this came out, it would ruin his career, not that he would ruin your career?

MS. HILL: Exactly.

SEN. LEAHY: Thank you. Where did you go for dinner that time?

MS. Hill: I do not recall the restaurant, the name of the restaurant.

SEN. LEAHY: Was it nearby or—

MS. HILL: It was nearby work.

SEN. LEAHY: Do you remember the type of restaurant?

MS. HILL: No, I don't. It wasn't anything that was memorable to me, the type of food that we had.

SEN. LEAHY: Do you remember how you got there?

MS. HILL: I believe that the driver for Chairman Thomas or then-Chairman Thomas took us, Mr. Randall, and dropped us off at the restaurant.

SEN. LEAHY: And you went right from the office?

MS. HILL: Went from the office.

SEN. LEAHY: After dinner, how did you get home?

MS. HILL: I took the subway home, if I recall correctly. As I am recalling—I'm not sure how I got home.

SEN. LEAHY: Do you recall whether then-Chairman Thomas offered you a ride home?

MS. HILL: No, he did not offer me a ride home.

SEN. LEAHY: Do you know whether his car came to pick him up?

MS. HILL: I don't know how he got home, either.

SEN. LEAHY: Do you recall approximately how long a time this was? Was this a case where you had to stand in line a long time to get a table or anything like that?

MS. HILL: No, we walked right into the restaurant and sat down. I imagine that it was about an hour all-told.

SEN. LEAHY: Did you have cocktails?

MS. HILL: I did not have a cocktail.

SEN. LEAHY: Anything alcoholic?

MS. HILL: I don't recall having anything alcoholic.

SEN. LEAHY: How long into the meal did the conversation you discussed come up? How long were you into the meal before the conversation you have just described came up?

MS. HILL: I believe it was about—it was well into the meal, maybe mid-way, half-way or beyond.

SEN. LEAHY: And what did you say in response?

MS. HILL: My response was that I really just wanted to get away from the office and leave that kind of activity behind me.

SEN. LEAHY: Did he ask you if you intended to ever make this public?

MS. HILL: He did not ask me that.

SEN. LEAHY: You have discussed somewhat earlier here today why you did not come forward with these allegations before. Had you come forward with them, at the time of your employment, either at the Department of Education or at the EEOC, what would have been the mechanism to come forward with the allegations?

MS. HILL: I do not know of my own knowledge. I have been told or I have heard suggested that the oversight committee would have been the proper authority to deal with such an issue.

SEN. LEAHY: Oversight within the department or here on the Hill?

MS. HILL: No, here on the Hill, the congressional oversight committee that had oversight over the EEOC. But I don't know that, I just heard that.

SEN. LEAHY: Did you at any time consider going somewhere, wherever the appropriate place might be, to make this public?

MS. HILL: I considered it, but I really at the time did not clearly think out exactly where I would go.

SEN. LEAHY: Had you come forward, what do you think would have happened?

MS. HILL: Well, I can speculate that it might have been difficult—I can speculate that, had I come forward immediately after I left the EEOC, I can speculate that I would have lost my job at Oral Roberts.

SEN. LEAHY: Professor Hill, this morning, Judge Thomas testified before this committee—and I don't know if you saw his testimony or not—

MS. HILL: Yes, I did.

SEN. LEAHY: Let me read from his statement. He said:

> I cannot imagine anything that I said or did to Anita Hill could have been mistaken for sexual harassment. With that said, if there is anything that I have said that has been misconstrued by Anita Hill or anyone else to be sexual harassment, then I can say that I am so very sorry and I wish I had known. If I did know, I would have stopped immediately and I would not, as I have done over the past two weeks, had to tear away at myself trying to think what I could possibly have done, but I have not said or done the things that Anita Hill has alleged.

You are aware of that statement by Judge Thomas?

MS. HILL: I am aware.

SEN. LEAHY: Do you agree with that? Do you agree with his statement?

MS. HILL: Do I agree with his statement?

SEN. LEAHY: Yes.

MS. HILL: No, I do not.

SEN. LEAHY: Well, let us go through in summary. What are the things that you felt he should have known were sexual harassment?

MS. HILL: Well, starting with the insisting on dates, I believe that once I had given a response to the question about dating, that my answer showed him that any further insisting was unwarranted and not desired by me.

I believe that the conversations about sex and the constant pressuring about dating which I objected to, both of which I objected to, were a basis—there was enough for him to understand that I was unappreciative and did not desire the kind of attention in the workplace. I think that my constantly saying to him that I was afraid, because he was in a supervisory position, that this would jeopardize my ability to do my job, that that should have given him notice.

SEN. LEAHY: Did he ask you—well, you have said that he asked you for dates many times. By many, what do you mean? Can you give us even a ball park figure?

MS. HILL: Oh, I would say over the course of—

SEN. LEAHY: Of both the Department of Education and the EEOC.

MS. HILL: I would say ten times, maybe, I don't know, five to ten times.

SEN. LEAHY: And you said, no, each time?

MS. HILL: Yes.

SEN. LEAHY: With the exception of the departure dinner to which you have just testified here?

MS. HILL: That was not a date and I made clear that it was not considered to be a date.

SEN. LEAHY: And on that occasion, while you rode to the restaurant with him, you did not leave the restaurant with him? I mean you did not go—

MS. Hill: No, I did not.

SEN. LEAHY: You took the subway home.

Now, you said you made it clear to him about the discussions of pornography and all, that you did not like what he was saying, is that a fair statement of yours?

MS. HILL: Yes, it is.

SEN. LEAHY: Were these often or ever, these discussions of pornography or sexual acts, co-terminous with a request to go out on a date? I mean did they come up in the same conversation or was one of them one day and one of them the next?

MS. HILL: I cannot say that they came up in the same conversation.

SEN. LEAHY: Well, let's go back to this. You said that he had described pornographic movies to you, is that correct?

MS. HILL: Yes.

SEN. LEAHY: And explicitly described them?

MS. HILL: Yes.

SEN. LEAHY: When that happened, what would you say or what would you do?

MS. HILL: I would say, specifically with the pornographic movies or material, I would say that I am really not interested in discussing this, I am uncomfortable with your talking about this, the kind of material that is—I would prefer not to discuss this with you.

SEN. LEAHY: You would be that clear about it. Would the discussions end when you said that? I mean for that occasion?

MS. HILL: Yes, for that occasion, very often they would. Sometimes I would have to say it more than once. But, yes, they would.

SEN. LEAHY: Did you ever hear him say this to anybody else?

MS. HILL: These kinds of—

SEN. LEAHY: Yes.

MS. HILL: I did not hear it.

SEN. LEAHY: Did anybody ever tell you that he did?

MS. HILL: No, no one ever told me that he did the same with them.

SEN. LEAHY: Did he say these things to you in your office, at any time?

MS. HILL: There might have been some occasion when he said it in my office.

SEN. LEAHY: But you do recollect him saying it to you in his office?

MS. HILL: Yes.

SEN. LEAHY: Was that a big office or a small office, for either of the two jobs he had?

MS. HILL: Well, I think they were relatively, both were relatively large offices. I remember the EEOC setup a little bit more clearly. I was there longer, but they were both large offices.

SEN. LEAHY: Did you, at some time when he was saying it, say, "Look, I don't want to hear about this," and just walk out the door?

MS. HILL: There were times when I would just walk away. If I were in a situation, like I could get up from his office and just leave, yes.

SEN. LEAHY: Did he ever try to stop you from going out of the office?

MS. HILL: No, he did not, not physically.

SEN. LEAHY: In any fashion, like saying, "Don't go any further"?

MS. HILL: Oh, no, he might have said, don't go or, you know, okay.

SEN. LEAHY: What you mentioned happening in a cafeteria— were people within earshot? Was there anybody within earshot when it happened in the cafeteria?

MS. HILL: No, not that I could see anyway. There might have been somebody within earshot.

SEN. LEAHY: Now, you testified to this today. You have given a statement that we have referred to. You discussed it with the FBI. Let's go back more to a time contemporaneous with when this happened. Did you discuss it with anybody at that time?

MS. HILL: Yes, I did.

SEN. LEAHY: And with whom did you discuss it at that time?

MS. HILL: Well, Sue Hoerchner, I did discuss it with Sue Hoerchner, she was a friend of mine and someone I confided in. And I spoke of this to two other people also.

SEN. LEAHY: Let's talk about Ms. Hoerchner. Was that when you were at EEOC or the Department of Education?

MS. HILL: That was at Education, I believe.

SEN. LEAHY: And what was your relationship to her, was it as a co-worker or—

MS. HILL: No, she was not a co-worker at Education. We had never worked together. She was a friend from law school.

SEN. LEAHY: How often did you discuss it with her?

MS. HILL: Maybe once or twice. Not, we did not discuss it very often. I can't say exactly how many times.

SEN. LEAHY: What was the nature of your discussion with her?

MS. HILL: Well, I was upset about the behavior. And that's what I was expressing to her as a friend, that it was upsetting and that I wanted it to stop and maybe even asked for advice or something to help me out of the situation.

SEN. LEAHY: And did she offer advice?

MS. HILL: I don't recall her offering any advice. I am not sure, exactly sure, what she said. I think she offered more comfort, because she knew I was upset.

SEN. LEAHY: And did you discuss it with somebody else?

MS. HILL: Yes, I have discussed it with other people.

SEN. LEAHY: At that time?

MS. HILL: Yes, at that time.

SEN. LEAHY: And who was that, Professor?

MS. HILL: I discussed it, in passing, well, no, not in passing. I discussed it with Ellen Wells, who is another female friend. She and I were close during the time and we had a conversation, in particular, we were talking about what I should do, how I should respond to it, what might make it stop happening.

At the time, in addition, I was dating someone, John Carr, and we discussed it because I was, I was upset by it. And I wanted to let him know why I was upset and again, just trying to see if there might be some way that he could handle this differently.

SEN. LEAHY: And did he give you a recommendation?

MS. HILL: I don't recall whether he did.

SEN. LEAHY: You said when you talked to Ms.—was there anybody else that you recall?

MS. HILL: At this point, I don't recall.

SEN. LEAHY: You said when you talked with Ms. Hoerchner, you were very concerned and upset, and that is why you did. Describe to us how you felt when this happened.

MS. HILL: Well, I was really upset. I felt like my job could be taken away or at least threatened. That I wasn't going to able to work. That this person who had some power in the new Administration would make it difficult for me in terms of other positions. I, it really, it was threatening from the job, in terms of my job, but it was also just unpleasant and something that I didn't want to have to deal with.

And it wasn't as though it happened every day but I went to work, during certain periods, knowing that it might happen.

SEN. LEAHY: You said in your statement that at one point you were hospitalized for five days. Am I correct in understanding your statement, you felt it was related to this?

MS. HILL: Yes, I do believe that it was related to the stress that I felt because of this.

SEN. LEAHY: Had you ever had a similar hospitalization?

MS. HILL: I had never had a similar hospitalization.

SEN. LEAHY: Now, when you think back on this, you described how you felt at the time, how do you feel about it today?

MS. HILL: Well, I am a little farther removed from it in time, but even today I still feel hurt and maybe today I feel more angry and disgusted. I don't feel quite as threatened. The situation, I am removed from it. My career is on solid ground and so the threat is not there. But the anger and hurt is there.

SEN. LEAHY: In your statement you had said that between 1981 and 1983 you spoke to only one person about these incidents—Susan Hoerchner, and you have talked about two others now. Is there a contradiction there?

MS. HILL: Well, in my statement I do say that I only spoke with one person. That is all that I recalled at the time that I made the statement. I am finding that I am recalling more about the situation. I really am finding that I repressed a lot of the things that happened during that time, and I am recalling more, in more detail.

When I made the statement too, I might add, that I made it rather hurriedly and even though I had been thinking about the situation, I had not perhaps given all of the consideration in terms of who I had told that I should have for such a statement.

SEN. LEAHY: Since this began, for whatever series of reasons, there has been discussion and debate about how all of this came about, and this has become a most public matter. You cannot get much more public than the situation we are in right now.

And Judge Thomas has been up for confirmation on other occasions. Did you think, on any of those other occasions, about coming forward and giving, in effect, the same testimony that you are giving here today?

MS. HILL: I may have considered it, but I was not contacted in those confirmation hearings. And I did not come forward on my own in that confirmation hearing, the most recent one.

SEN. LEAHY: You mean this one?

MS. HILL: Not this one, but the prior one.

SEN. LEAHY: Had you been contacted in the prior one?

MS. HILL: I had not been contacted in the prior one.

SEN. LEAHY: But you were contacted in this one?

MS. HILL: I was contacted in this one, yes.

SEN. LEAHY: I realize—and my time is virtually up—this requires speculation and you can or cannot answer as you see fit, but had you not been contacted would you have come forward on this occasion?

MS. HILL: I cannot say that I would have.

SEN. LEAHY: Mr. Chairman, I have a lot more questions, but my time is up and I will stop there.

Thank you.

THE CHAIRMAN: We will give you an opportunity, Senator, to complete those.

SEN. LEAHY: Thank you.

THE CHAIRMAN: We now recognize the Senator from Pennsylvania, Senator Specter.

SEN. SPECTER: Thank you, Mr. Chairman.

Professor Hill, there is a report in the *Kansas City Star* of October 8, 1991, that says, "In an August interview with the *Kansas City Star*, Anita Hill offered some favorable comments regarding Clarence Thomas and some criticism." And then further on it says, quoting you, "Judicial experience aside, the Clarence Thomas of that period"—referring to his days in EEOC early—"would have made a better judge on the Supreme Court because he was more open-minded."

Now, how is it that you would have said that Judge Thomas, in his early days at EEOC would have made a better judge, at least an adequate judge, considering all of the things you have said that he told you about, at the Department of Education and also at EEOC?

MS. HILL: That opinion, Senator, was based strictly on his experience, his ability to reason. It was not based on personal information which I did not see fit to share with that reporter. I was trying to give as objective an opinion as possible and that's what that statement is based on.

In addition, very early on, I believe I was commenting on his time at Education. Very early on at Education I was not experiencing the kinds of things that I later experienced with Judge Thomas.

SEN. SPECTER: But when you make a statement in August 1991 and say that "Judicial experience aside, the Clarence Thomas of that period would have made a better judge on the Supreme Court because he was more open-minded" you are making a comparison as to what Judge Thomas felt judicially early on before he changed his views on affirmative action. So that is the reference to, at that period.

But when you say that Judge Thomas would have made a better Supreme Court Justice, you are saying that, at one stage of his career, he would have made an adequate Supreme Court Justice.

MS. HILL: Well, I am not sure that that's what I am saying at all. I am sure that what I was trying to give to that reporter was my assessment of him objectively without considering the personal information that I had. Now, if I had said to him, I don't think he would have made a good judge because of personal information that I have, then I think I would have had to explain that or at least created some innuendo that I was not ready to create.

In addition, I think as a university professor, quoted as a university professor, you have some obligation to try to make objective statements. And that's what I was doing. I was attempting to make an objective statement about the individual based on his record as a public figure and I was not relying on my own private understanding and knowledge.

SEN. SPECTER: Well, let's take it the way you have just re-explained it. An objective evaluation, without considering personal information, as a law school professor to make a comment on his record as a public figure. How could you conclude, in any respect, that he would be appropriate for the Court even if you say that was without considering the personal information, if you had all of this personal information?

MS. HILL: I did not say that he would be appropriate for the Court, Senator. I said that he would make a better judge. I did not say that I would consider him the best person for the Supreme Court.

SEN. SPECTER: Well, when you say he would have made a better judge at one point, are you saying that there is not an explicit recommendation or statement that, as you said earlier, on the basis of his intellect, aside from the personal information that you decided not to share, that he would have been a better Supreme Court Justice?

MS. HILL: I am sorry, would you rephrase that?

SEN. SPECTER: Sure. Isn't the long and short of it, Professor Hill, that when you spoke to the *Kansas City Star* reporter, that you were saying, at one point in his career he would have been okay for the Supreme Court?

MS. HILL: No.

[Pause.]

SEN. SPECTER: What were you saying as to Judge Thomas's qualifications for the Supreme Court when you spoke to the reporter in August?

MS. HILL: We were speaking in terms of his being open-minded. One of the comments that the reporter made was that some have complained that he has a set ideology and that he won't be able to review cases on their own. My comment went to whether or not he did have that set ideology and it was that now he did, whereas a few years ago, I did not find that to be so.

I found him to be more open-minded. So in that sense, I believe that he was better suited for a judicial position at that time, than now. And that's all that I was referring to, that particular comment or my concern about the nominee's qualifications for being on the Court.

SEN. SPECTER: Well, it is certainly true, Professor Hill, that your statement has a comparative that Judge Thomas would have been a better judge of the Supreme Court at an earlier point in his career, but if you stand on your statement that this interview does not contain a recommendation for Judge Thomas, so be it. Is that your position?

MS. HILL: Yes, it does, that is my position.

SEN. SPECTER: Did you ever maintain any notes or written memoranda of the comments that Judge Thomas had made to you?

MS. HILL: No, I did not.

SEN. SPECTER: In your statement and in your testimony here today, you have said that you were concerned that "Judge Thomas might take it out on me by downgrading me, or by not giving me important assignments. I also thought that he might find an excuse for dismissing me."

As an experienced attorney and as someone who was in the field of handling sexual harassment cases, didn't it cross your mind that if you needed to defend yourself from what you anticipated he might do that your evidentiary position would be much stronger if you had made some notes?

MS. HILL: No, it did not.

SEN. SPECTER: Well, why not?

MS. HILL: I don't know why it didn't cross my mind.

SEN. SPECTER: Well, the law of evidence is that notes are very important. You are nodding yes. Present recollection refreshed, right?

MS. HILL: Yes, indeed.

SEN. SPECTER: Prior recollection recorded, right?

MS. HILL: Yes.

SEN. SPECTER: In a controversy, if Judge Thomas took some action against you, and you had to defend yourself on the ground that he was being malicious in retaliation for your turning him down, wouldn't those notes be very influential if not determinative in enabling you to establish your legal position?

MS. HILL: I think they would be very influential, yes.

SEN. SPECTER: So, given your experience, if all this happened, since all this happened, why not make the notes?

MS. HILL: Well, it might have been a good choice to make the notes. I did not do it, though. Maybe I made the wrong choice in not making the notes. I am not a person—I was not interested in any litigation. I was not interested. If I had been dismissed, very likely I would have just gone out and tried to find another job. I was not interested in filing a claim against him, and perhaps that is why it did not occur to me to make notes about it.

SEN. SPECTER: Well, I am not on the point of your being interested in making a claim. What I am on the point of is your statement that you were concerned that he might take retaliatory action against you, and therefore the inference arises that the notes would have been something which would have been done by an experienced lawyer.

MS. HILL: One of the things that I did do at that time was to document my work. I went through very meticulously with every assignment that I was given. This was, this really was in response to the concerns that I had about being fired. I went through, I logged in every work assignment that I received, the date that it was received, the action that was requested, the action that I took on it, the date that it went out, so I did do that in order to protect myself, but I did not write down any of the comments or conversations.

SEN. SPECTER: Well, when you comment about documenting your work to protect yourself because of concern of being fired, wouldn't the same precise thought about documentation have led you to document Judge Thomas's statements to you?

MS. HILL: Well, I was documenting my work so that I could show to a new employer that I had in fact done these things. I was not documenting my work so that I could defend myself or to present a claim against him.

SEN. SPECTER: Well, why would you need to document with precision the time the assignment came in and the time you completed the work for a new employer? Wouldn't that kind of documentation really relate to the adequacy and speed of your work at EEOC, contrasted with a finished product which you could show to a new prospective employer?

MS. HILL: I'm sorry. I don't quite understand your question. Are you saying that the new employer would not be interested in knowing whether or not I turned my work around quickly?

SEN. SPECTER: What is the relevancy as to when you got the assignment and how fast you made it, for a new employer?

MS. HILL: Because it goes to whether or not I was slow in turning around the work product in a very fast-paced job situation.

SEN. SPECTER: Professor Hill, as you know, the statute of limitations for filing a case on sexual harassment is 180 days, right?

MS. HILL: Yes.

SEN. SPECTER: A very short statute of limitations because of the difficulty of someone defending against a charge of sexual harassment, right?

MS. HILL: Well, it is a short turnover time. I am not quite sure exactly why it is that short. That is one of the reasons that it is so short.

SEN. SPECTER: Well, you are an expert in the field. *Delaware State College v.*

Ricks, 101 Supreme Court Reporter, in 1980, *Johnson v. Railway Express Agency*, 421 U.S. Reports, comment about the short period of limitations because of the difficulty of defending against a charge of sexual harassment.

MS. HILL: Yes, but I don't believe either of those cases say that that is the only reason. And let me clarify something: I consider myself to be an expert in contracts and commercial law, not an expert in the field of sexual harassment or EEO law. I don't even teach in that area any more.

SEN. SPECTER: Well, you did teach civil rights law?

MS. HILL: Yes, at one point.

SEN. SPECTER: You taught civil rights law after 1980, right?

MS. HILL: Yes, I have.

SEN. SPECTER: Well, all right, it is one of the reasons for having a short period of limitations, to give someone an opportunity to defend himself against a charge of sexual harassment because they are hard to defend.

MS. HILL: Certainly.

SEN. SPECTER: The statute of limitations in a contract case is six years?

MS. HILL: Well, in some states.

SEN. SPECTER: Some states, six years?

MS. HILL: The statute of limitations is not set. It is not a set thing. It varies from state to state.

SEN. SPECTER: The Federal statute of limitations on crimes is five years?

MS. HILL: I am not a criminal expert. I don't know.

SEN. SPECTER: Do you know of any statute of limitations which is as short as six months, besides sexual harassment cases?

MS. HILL: Do I know of any?

SEN. SPECTER: Yes.

MS. HILL: No, not offhand.

SEN. SPECTER: Well, in the context of the Federal law limiting a sexual harassment claim to six months because of the grave difficulty of someone defending themselves in this context, what is your view of the fairness of asking Judge Thomas to reply eight, nine, ten years after the fact?

MS. HILL: I don't believe it is unfair. I think that that is something that you have to take into account in evaluating his comments.

SEN. SPECTER: I had asked you this morning, Professor Hill, about a statement which was made by Ms. Berry, and I had asked you then in the context of your saying that she didn't know you and you didn't know her. You then expanded that to say that she didn't know your social life, but you did say that she had an opportunity to observe you and Judge Thomas at EEOC. I want to come back to that for just a moment, because the *New York Times* says this: "In an interview, Ms. Barry [*sic*] suggested that the allegations were a result of Ms. Hill's disappointment and frustration that Mr. Thomas did not show any sexual interest in her."

Now, aside from saying that Ms. Berry doesn't know about you on the social side, what about the substance of what Ms. Berry had to say?

MS. HILL: What exactly are you asking me?

SEN. SPECTER: Well, I will repeat the question again.

Was there any substance in Ms. Berry's flat statement that, "Ms. Hill was disappointed and frustrated that Mr. Thomas did not show any sexual interest in her"?

MS. HILL: No, there is not. There is no substance to that. He did show interest, and I have explained to you how he did show that interest. Now she was not aware of that. If you are asking me could she have made that statement, she could have made the statement if she wasn't aware of it. But she wasn't aware of everything that happened.

SEN. SPECTER: Professor Hill, do you know a man by the name of John Doggett?

MS. HILL: Pardon me?

SEN. SPECTER: A man by the name of John Doggett?

MS. HILL: John Doggett?

SEN. SPECTER: John Doggett III.

MS. HILL: Yes, I have met him.

SEN. SPECTER: I ask you this, Professor Hill, in the context of whether you have any motivation as to Judge Thomas. What was your relationship with Mr. Doggett?

MS. HILL: I don't recall. I do not recall. We were friends, but I don't—it wasn't anything. I just don't know.

SEN. SPECTER: Well, before I pursue this question, I will give you a copy of his statement, give you an opportunity to read it before I ask you about that, and I will do that at a break.

MS. HILL: Thank you.

SEN. SPECTER: How close were you to Dean Charles Kothe of the Oral Roberts Law School?

MS. HILL: He was the dean of the law school. I was there for a year. I believe he was the dean for a year while I was there. We worked together.

SEN. SPECTER: One of the comments which was made by Dean Kothe related to your voluntarily driving Judge Thomas to the airport on an occasion when he came to speak at Oral Roberts Law School. My question is that in a context where you had responded to some people who asked you to make inquiries of Judge Thomas, in a context of his having said these things to you as you represent, being violations of the Civil Rights law, constituting sexual harassment, given that background, why would you voluntarily agree to drive Judge Thomas to the airport?

MS. HILL: I really don't recall that I voluntarily agreed to drive him to the airport. I think that the dean suggested that I drive him to the airport, and that I said that I would. But at any rate, one of the things that I have said was that I intended to —I hoped to keep a cordial professional relationship with that individual, and so I did him the courtesy of driving him to the airport.

SEN. SPECTER: Well, when you say you wanted to maintain a cordial professional relationship, why would you do that, given the comments which you represent Judge Thomas made to you, given the seriousness of the comments, given the fact that they violated the Civil Rights Act? Was it simply a matter that you wanted to derive whatever advantage you could from a cordial professional relationship?

MS. HILL: It was a matter that I did not want to invoke any kind of retaliation against me professionally. It wasn't that I was trying to get any benefit out of it.

SEN. SPECTER: Well, you say that you consulted with him about a letter of recommendation. That would have been a benefit, wouldn't it?

MS. HILL: Well, that letter of recommendation was necessary. The application asked for a recommendation from former employers.

SEN. SPECTER: Judge Thomas testified at some length this morning about his shock and dismay and anger, and specified a group of facts which he said in effect undercut your credibility: when you moved with him from the Department of Education to EEOC; when you went with him voluntarily, and I take it it was voluntary, to go to a speech which he made at Oral Roberts Law School; when you contacted him about the speech at the University of Oklahoma; when you asked him for his guidance and his advice.

Would you say, Professor Hill, that all of those contacts and the continuation of a cordial professional association, relationship, have no bearing at all on your representation that he made these disgusting comments to you and was guilty of sexual harassment in violation of the Civil Rights Act?

MS. HILL: I wouldn't say that they have no bearing, but I believe that I have explained a number of those factors. I talked to you about why I went to the EEOC. I talked to you about—would you list those again? I have forgotten what representations you are suggesting.

SEN. SPECTER: Well, I know that you have explained or given an explanation as to why you moved from the Department of Education to EEOC, and I know you have an explanation for the Oklahoma University invitation, but nonetheless you called him. I know you have an explanation for the Oral Roberts incident.

But in seeking to evaluate the credibility between you and Judge Thomas, I am asking, and I think you have already answered it, that it does have some relevancy as to whether you would maintain over a long period of time this cordial association if he had been so disgusting to you, had victimized you with sexual harassment and had violated the Civil Rights Act.

MS. HILL: Well, the things that occurred after I left the EEOC, occurred during a time—any matter, calling him up from the university—occurred during a time when he was no longer a threat to me of any kind. He could not threaten my job; I already had tenure there. He could not threaten me as he had, implicitly at least, at the EEOC; I was no longer working with him at the EEOC. So I was removed from the harassment at that point. I did not feel that it was necessary to cut off all ties or to burn all bridges or to treat him in a hostile manner.

Moreover, I think that if I had done that, I would have had to explain this, this whole situation that I have come for today. I think what one has to do is try to put oneself in the situation that I was in, and I think it is not an atypical situation. Perhaps all of those things, if you look at them without any explanation, might suggest that there was no harassment, but there is an explanation for each of those things. And given the judgment that I made at the time, that I did want to maintain some cordial but distant relationship, I think that there is no contradiction in what I am saying and those actions.

SEN. SPECTER: All right. I am prepared to leave it at that. There is some relevancy to that continuing association questioning your credibility, but you have an explanation. I will leave it at that.

I want to ask you about one statement of Charles Kothe, Dean Kothe, because he knew you and Judge Thomas very well. I want to ask you for your comment on it. There is a similar reference in the Doggett statement which I am not going to ask you about because you haven't read the Doggett statement and you say you do not remember him. Out of fairness I want to give you a chance to read that first, but you do know Dean Kothe and he does know Judge Thomas.

And this is his concluding statement: "I find the references to the alleged sexual harassment not only unbelievable but preposterous. I am convinced that such are the product of fantasy." Would you care to comment on that?

MS. HILL: Well, I would only say that I am not given to fantasy. This is not something that I would have come forward with, if I were not absolutely sure about what it is I am saying. I weighed this very carefully, I considered it carefully, and I made a determination to come forward. I think it is unfortunate that that comment was made by a man who purports to be someone who says he knows me, and I think it is just inaccurate.

SEN. SPECTER: Well, you have added, during the course of your testimony today, two new witnesses whom you made this complaint to. When you talked to the FBI, there was one witness, and you are testifying today that you are now "recalling more," that you had "repressed a lot." And the question which I have for you is, how reliable is your testimony in October 1991 on events that occurred eight, ten years ago, when you are adding new factors, explaining them by saying you have repressed a lot? And in the context of a sexual harassment charge where the Federal law is very firm on a six-month period of limitation, how sure can you expect this committee to be on the accuracy of your statements?

MS. HILL: Well, I think if you start to look at each individual problem with this statement, then you're not going to be satisfied that it's true, but I think the statement has to be taken as a whole. There's nothing in the statement, nothing in my background, nothing in my statement, there is no motivation that would show that I would make up something like this. I guess one does have to really understand something about the nature of sexual harassment. It is very difficult for people to come forward with these things, these kinds of things. It wasn't as though I rushed forward with this information.

I can only tell you what happened to the best of my recollection, what occurred, and ask you to take that into account. Now, you have to make your own judgments about it from there on, but I do want you to take into account the whole thing.

SEN. SPECTER: Well, I will proceed with the question of motivation on my next round, because the red light is now on.

THE CHAIRMAN: Thank you very much, Senator.

There is one-half hour still to use. I am going to yield the bulk of it to Senator Heflin, but I am going to ask for just a few minutes.

Would you prefer a break?

MS. HILL: No.

THE CHAIRMAN: Because you have been sitting there a long time.

MS. HILL: I will take a break. I need to read the statement from Mr. Doggett.

THE CHAIRMAN: Well, we are not going to go to Mr. Doggett now. Before we get back to Senator Specter, we will break and give you an opportunity to read that statement, which, I might add, we are reading for the first time ourselves.

MS. HILL: Okay.

THE CHAIRMAN: But we are not going to break now, so there will be order. Order in here. We will break after Senator Heflin and I ask our questions, and then we will give you time to read the statement, and, as I said, give all us time to read the statement, because the statement is news to me as well as the rest of the committee, other than Senator Specter.

Senator Specter and all of us acknowledge that there is a need to understand the nature of sexual harassment and the way in which people respond to that harassment.

One of the things that you have repeatedly said here, and you have said publicly prior to coming here, is that this was not your idea, you did not want to come here. You have stated, and it appears to be so, that you are a reluctant witness, not one who is out charging down the road. As Senator Specter acknowledged, and as every expert in the field acknowledges, that is not conduct inconsistent with someone who has been harassed.

Now, let me ask you this, though, because I am sure a lot of people, including me, are wondering about it. You indicated, and it is totally understandable, that you repressed a lot. Again, every expert over the years with whom I have spoken about this subject—not about you, not about this incident, but about the nature and the conduct of harassment and the response of the person harassed acknowledges that repression is not unusual.

MS. HILL: Yes.

THE CHAIRMAN: But I would like to ask you if, notwithstanding that fact, you can lay out for the committee what, in fact, was the sequence of events that did bring you forward?

You and I had a long discussion—relatively long discussion—the night that the Senate agreed—we meaning the members of the committee—the Senate agreed to put off the vote on Judge Thomas until 6 o'clock this coming Tuesday. I called to tell you that you would be receiving a subpoena so that you would not be alarmed when someone knocked at your door, and then you and I had a discussion about the sequence of events that brought you here. You have made reference to that sequence, directly and indirectly, on this record and off this record, but publicly.

Now, this is not something that you initiated, is that correct?

MS. HILL: No; it is not.

THE CHAIRMAN: And you were contacted by a staff person from the U.S. Senate, is that correct?

MS. HILL: Yes.

THE CHAIRMAN: And you indicated to me you thought that staff person—and it is perfectly understandable you would, in my view—you thought that staff person was a staff person from the Judiciary Committee, is that correct?

MS. HILL: Yes.

THE CHAIRMAN: And then you were contacted subsequently by two other staff persons?

MS. HILL: Yes. Let me clarify something. I thought that staff person was acting on behalf of a member of the committee—

THE CHAIRMAN: I see.

MS. HILL: [continuing]—with regard to their duties on the committee.

THE CHAIRMAN: I see. Which is I understand to be the case, and legitimately so.

MS. HILL: Yes.

THE CHAIRMAN: But as we talked, I had indicated to you that I, in my responsibilities as chairman, did not make known the allegations to the committee as a whole until after the committee had begun its meeting. That is not your responsibility, that is mine, but I want to get at this issue, because it seems to me it does go to explain your assertions here this morning as to how you got here.

What ultimately made you decide that you must go public, knowing that all this would occur?

MS. HILL: Well, I was presented with the information by a newspaper reporter.

THE CHAIRMAN: The information that you had submitted to me and I distributed to the committee?

MS. HILL: Yes.

THE CHAIRMAN: You were presented with that information and—

MS. HILL: Over the telephone, it was read to me verbatim by a member of the press.

THE CHAIRMAN: Now, the thing that was read to you verbatim was the statement that you had submitted and asked me to distribute to the committee, is that correct?

MS. HILL: Yes.

THE CHAIRMAN: So, in your view, you are here as a result of some unexpected events —

MS. HILL: Definitely.

THE CHAIRMAN: [continuing]—and events that turned out not to be within your control?

MS. HILL: Definitely.

THE CHAIRMAN: Do you consider yourself part of some organized effort to determine whether or not Clarence Thomas should or should not sit on the bench?

MS. HILL: No, I had no intention of being here today, none at all. I did not think that this would ever—I had not even imagined that this would occur.

THE CHAIRMAN: Now, as I listened to you today answer very direct questions by Senator Specter, fair and direct questions, you stated here—correct me if I am wrong—that you did not view what was happening to you as a situation in which you would need to have a record to be able to retaliate or sue. Your main objective was to try to stop what you alleged to be happening, from happening, is that correct?

MS. HILL: That is correct, that was my motive at the time, just to stop the activity.

THE CHAIRMAN: Is this what you anticipated?

MS. HILL: This? No, not at all. I would have never even dreamed, I just can't imagine.

THE CHAIRMAN: Is it reasonable to say that it was your hope and expectation that it would not come to this?

MS. HILL: It was exactly what I was trying to really very—I made greater effort to make sure that it did not come to this, and I was meticulous, I was making every effort to make sure that this public thing did not happen. I did not talk to the press. I was called by the press on July 1. I did not talk to the press. This is exactly what I did not want.

THE CHAIRMAN: And is it fair to say that attitude prevailed up until the moment the press person called you and read you your statement?

MS. HILL: Well, the attitude of not wanting this to happen?

THE CHAIRMAN: Yes.

MS. HILL: It prevails even today.

THE CHAIRMAN: Well, we are beyond that point, as you know.

MS. HILL: Yes, we are beyond that point, but it certainly prevailed up until that point.

THE CHAIRMAN: The reason I ask that is that it is important, it seems to me, for the committee to know why someone would move from one point to the next and still hope that she didn't have to reach an end point, with the end point being a situation like this one here. Am I misstating in any way your desires as you moved along in this process or were moved along in this process?

MS. HILL: The desire was never to get to this point. The desire— and I thought that I could do things and if I were cautious enough and I could control it so that it would not get to this point, but I was mistaken.

THE CHAIRMAN: I thank you very much.

I yield to my friend from Alabama, Senator Heflin.

SEN. HEFLIN: Professor Hill, we heard Judge Thomas deny that he had ever asked you to go out with him socially, dating, and deny all allegations relative to statements that allegedly he had made to you that involved sex, sex organs, pornographic films and materials and this type of thing.

You have testified that this occurred, and that he asked you to date and go out socially. You have testified here today concerning statements that he had made to you about pornographic films and materials and other things.

I, and I suppose every member of this committee, have to come down to the ultimate question of who is telling the truth. My experience as a lawyer and a judge is that you listen to all the testimony and then you try to determine the motivation for the one that is not telling the truth.

Now, in trying to determine whether you are telling falsehoods or not, I have got to determine what your motivation might be. Are you a scorned woman?

MS. HILL: No.

SEN. HEFLIN: Are you a zealoting civil rights believer that progress will be turned back, if Clarence Thomas goes on the Court?

MS. HILL: No, I don't—I think that—I have my opinion, but I don't think that progress will be turned back. I think that civil rights will prevail, no matter what happens with the Court.

SEN. HEFLIN: Do you have a militant attitude relative to the area of civil rights?

MS. HILL: No, I don't have a militant attitude.

SEN. HEFLIN: Do you have a martyr complex?

MS. HILL: No, I don't. [Laughter.]

SEN. HEFLIN: Well, do you see that, coming out of this, you can be a hero in the civil rights movement?

MS. HILL: I do not have that kind of complex. I don't like all of the attention that I am getting, I don't—even if I liked the attention, I would not lie to get attention.

SEN. HEFLIN: Well, the issue of fantasy has arisen. You have a degree in psychology from the University of Oklahoma State University.

MS. HILL: Yes.

SEN. HEFLIN: Have you studied in your psychology studies, the question of fantasies? Have you ever studied that from a psychology basis?

MS. HILL: To some extent, yes.

SEN. HEFLIN: What are the traits of fantasy that you studied and as you remember?

MS. HILL: As I remember, it would require some other indication of loss of touch with reality other than one instance. There is no indication that I am an individual who is not in touch with reality on a regular basis and would be subject to fantasy.

SEN. HEFLIN: The reality of where you are today is rather dramatic. Did you take, as Senator Biden asked you, all steps that you knew how to take to prevent being in that witness chair today?

MS. HILL: Yes, I did. Everything that I knew to do, I did.

SEN. HEFLIN: There may be other motivations. I just listed some that you usually look to relative to these. Are you interested in writing a book? [Laughter.]

MS. HILL: No, I'm not interested in writing a book.

SEN. HEFLIN: In the statement that was made which we refer to as an affidavit, on the—do you have a copy of that?

MS. HILL: Yes, I do.

SEN. HEFLIN: Mr. Chairman, just for part of the full record, I would move that that statement be made a part of the record.

THE CHAIRMAN: Without objection, it will be made part of the record.

SEN. HEFLIN: You describe on the second page, starting at the first paragraph there, about the working relationship and the various conversations, which you say were very vivid and very graphic, pertaining to pornographic materials and films and other statements of that nature.

Then you end that paragraph with these words: "However, I sense that my discomfort with his discussions only urged him on, as though my reaction of feeling ill at ease and vulnerable was what he wanted."

In other words, you are basically stating that that appeared to be his goal, rather than trying to obtain an intimate or sexual relationship with you. It may be that you also felt that, though that raises quite an issue.

"However, I sense that my discomfort with his discussions only urged him on as though my reaction of feeling ill at ease and vulnerable was what he wanted." What do you mean by that? How do you conclude that?

MS. HILL: Well, it was almost as though he wanted me at a disadvantage, to put me at a disadvantage, so that I would have to concede to whatever his wishes were.

SEN. HEFLIN: Do you think that he got some pleasure out of seeing you ill at ease and vulnerable?

MS. Hill: I think so, yes.

SEN. HEFLIN: Was this feeling more so than a feeling that he might be seeking some type of dating or social relationship with you?

MS. HILL: I think it was a combination of factors. I think that he wanted to see me vulnerable and that, if I were vulnerable, then he could extract from me whatever he wanted, whether it was sexual or otherwise, that I would be under his control.

SEN. HEFLIN: As a psychology major, what elements of human nature seem to go into that type of a situation?

MS. HILL: Well, I can't say exactly. I can say that I felt that he was using his power and authority over me, he was exerting a level of power and attempting to make sure that that power was exerted. I think it was the fact that I had said no to him that caused him to want to do this.

SEN. HEFLIN: You cite the instance of the Coke can and his statement of pubic hair on it. Do you feel that he was attempting to have some specific message by relating that? How did you interpret that?

MS. HILL: I did not have a clue as to how to interpret that. I did not know; it was just a very strange comment for me. I could not interpret it. I thought it was inappropriate, but I did not know what he meant.

SEN. HEFLIN: Now, was there an occasion when you were at the EEOC that you wanted a different job or a promotion or a higher job?

MS. HILL: I never sought a promotion with Clarence Thomas while at the EEOC. I never sought a promotion with anyone while at the EEOC.

SEN. HEFLIN: Well, did this Allyson Duncan, in effect, take over some position or became a supervisor of you, as opposed to what it had previously been, and was it a reorganization, or what were the facts pertaining to that?

MS. HILL: When Allyson Duncan took over her position—let me say this: Prior to when Allyson Duncan moved into the office of the Chair as an assistant, the assistants had basically been reporting directly to Thomas, and what I understood happened was that the work got too much for him to handle, to dole out to the assistants himself, so he reorganized the structure and appointed Allyson as the chief of staff for the special assistants in that office.

SEN. HEFLIN: Now, Senator Specter asked you about the *USA Today* report of October 9, 1991, in which it recites that Anita Hill was told by Senate staffers her signed affidavit alleging sexual harassment by Clarence Thomas would be the instrument which quietly and behind the scenes would force him to withdraw his name. "Keith Henderson, a ten-year friend of Hill's and a former Senate Judiciary Committee staffer, says Hill was advised by Senate staffers that her charge would be kept secret and her name kept from the public scrutiny."

Have you had a conversation with Keith Henderson during the period of time from when you were originally contacted by some staffers from the Senate and the time that this newspaper account occurred?

MS. HILL: Yes, I did.

SEN. HEFLIN: You did. All right. And what was your conversation with Mr. Henderson? What did you tell him?

MS. HILL: Well, my conversation was that I was really concerned about the situation involving this issue, that I had made the comments to the staff, that I had followed up on those comments with an affidavit and that I had gone through the investigation, all with the understanding that this was not going to be a public matter, and that I was concerned about whether or not the information would be made available to all the committee.

SEN. HEFLIN: Well, during any conversation with Keith Henderson, did you tell him that certain staffers had told you that if you went ahead and signed the affidavit, that that might be a way to get him to withdraw?

MS. HILL: No, I did not tell him that.

SEN. HEFLIN: Well, did you tell him that that was mentioned or that it would have been mentioned relative to this?

MS. HILL: No, I didn't tell him that.

SEN. HEFLIN: Do you know whether or not Keith Henderson talked to certain Judiciary Committee staffers?

MS. HILL: I did not—I don't know whether he did talk to Judiciary Committee staffers.

SEN. HEFLIN: Do you know whether in any conversation that he might have talked to Judiciary staffers, they might have said that is a possibility?

MS. HILL: Do I know of any conversation—

SEN. HEFLIN: Well, do you know whether or not there was a conversation between Keith Henderson and some staffer in which they were discussing the affidavit and saying that there were certain possibilities, which included the possibility that Clarence Thomas might withdraw his name?

MS. HILL: That might have happened, but I haven't talked with Keith Henderson about that.

SEN. HEFLIN: When you were at the EEOC, were you there on November 23, 1983? Would you have been there then?

MS. HILL: No, I was not there then. I had left for Oral Roberts University.

SEN. HEFLIN: When did you leave?

MS. HILL: I left in July 1983.

SEN. HEFLIN: Have you read a story in *The Washington Post*, today, Friday, October 11, in which there is mentioned a case involving allegations that Earl Harper, Jr., a regional attorney in the EEOC Baltimore office, had made unwelcome sexual advances to several women on his staff? When you were there at the EEOC, do you remember anything about a case being alleged involving Earl Harper, who was a trial attorney at the Baltimore office of the EEOC?

MS. HILL: I don't recall any case.

SEN. HEFLIN: All right. Since you graduated, your scholastic work, have you written any *Law Review* articles?

MS. HILL: Yes, I have.

SEN. HEFLIN: How many *Law Review* articles have you written?

MS. HILL: I've written six, seven, including a short *Law Review* article—if I may back up, I have written five *Law Review* articles, some shorter pieces in journals.

SEN. HEFLIN: Now, while you were at the Office of Civil Rights of the Department of Education, according to the way I read the statements, most of these instances pertaining to descriptions of pornographic films and materials was mentioned to you at the Department of Education, as opposed to the EEOC office?

MS. HILL: I think the more explicit statements probably did occur at Education more than later at EEOC.

SEN. HEFLIN: But they did occur some at EEOC?

MS. HILL: Yes.

SEN. HEFLIN: Now, how old were you at this particular time that you were at the Department of Education?

MS. HILL: I was twenty-five, I just turned twenty-five when I started the job.

SEN. HEFLIN: Did you have any family here in Washington?

MS. HILL: No, I did not.

SEN. HEFLIN: Did you have other than certain friends that you could turn to in times of difficulty and—

MS. HILL: I just had some friends. I did have some friends, but no family.

SEN. HEFLIN: Mr. Chairman, I believe that is all I have.

THE CHAIRMAN: Thank you very much.

We will recess for fifteen minutes—let's have order in here, please—and at that time we will come back and Senator Specter will question, and then we will move to Senators who have five minutes of questions and we hope that will be it. We will, in due course, call back Judge Thomas.

We are recessed for fifteen minutes.

[Recess.]

THE CHAIRMAN: The hearing will come to order.

Before we begin this next round of questioning, through what I know to be inadvertence, the affidavit that was given to Professor Hill was also for the first time made available to the committee at large; the Senator from Pennsylvania did not realize that we did not have it, either.

There has been an agreement from the outset of this proceeding—because, as I said, this is not a trial, this is a hearing to seek the facts—that everyone on the committee would have made available to them any and all documents that are produced, for whatever reason, before there is any introduction of such documents in the record or before there is any questioning on any documents. That applies to Professor Hill, that applies to Judge Thomas, and that applies to all our witnesses.

Again, I think in this case this was inadvertence. The Senate has indicated to us they want this very important and difficult matter resolved and they gave us essentially forty-eight hours to get ready for this, so there is going to be a lot that drops between the cup and the lip here, but one of the things that won't is any document that all members of the committee have not had in sufficient time to examine, read, and think about before it is even presented.

With that, while we are doing a bit of housekeeping here on such an important matter, let me suggest, again, the committee's intention in terms of timing: The committee intends to go back to Senator Specter. He indicates he may have more questions than his next half-hour, and Senator Leahy has indicated that he has some more questions. It is my sincere hope, Professor Hill, that we do not keep you much longer.

At the conclusion of Senator Leahy's questioning, we will then do what I indicated at the outset. Each member who has not asked questions, all of whom have a keen interest in this matter, will have up to five minutes to ask a question or questions.

We will then, God willing, excuse Professor Hill and call Judge Thomas back this evening, and I hope we will complete Judge Thomas's testimony tonight before we go tomorrow to other witnesses.

I thank you for your patience, Professor Hill. Again, as we have with all witnesses, if at any point during this process, as I indicated to Judge Thomas and to every witness before us, you desire to ask for a break, for whatever reason—you need not have any reason—you just indicate to the Chair and we will recess.

Now, with that, let me yield to my friend from Pennsylvania, Senator Specter.

SEN. SPECTER: Thank you, Mr. Chairman.

Mr. Chairman, as you have noted, I have not known you had not seen the Doggett statement, but, in any event, the interruption gave both Professor Hill and other members of the committee a chance to see that statement.

Professor Hill, a copy or copies of that statement, copies were made available to you over the break, and I ask you now if you would have any objection to answering questions about that statement.

MS. HILL: No.

SEN. SPECTER: All right. It may be that Mr. Doggett will appear as a witness. If he does, it would be appropriate to give you a chance to comment and, rather than have you come back after the fact, you can comment now. I had candidly some question in my mind about asking you about this statement at all, but our lines of inquiry at this kind of a proceeding are very different from any other kind of a proceeding. You have now had a chance to read it and you are willing to comment about it?

MS. HILL: Yes, I will.

SEN. SPECTER: I bring up the statement of Mr. Doggett, because of the statement which was made by Dean Kothe. You have already commented about where Dean Kothe of the Oral Roberts Law School made the statement about fantasy. I don't intend to repeat again, but that comes up in the Doggett statement.

Now, the Doggett statement is a long statement and I am going to summarize it by reading a portion of page 2. You, of course, Professor Hill, are free to bring up any other part of it you want, if you would like to go into any of the rest of it.

SEN. METZENBAUM: Mr. Chairman, may I ask a question?

THE CHAIRMAN: Yes, you may, Senator.

SEN. METZENBAUM: Mr. Chairman, it is my understanding that if I follow this procedure by accepting this affidavit and inquiring of the witness in connection with it, that you open up a little Pandora's box, because we can get all sorts of sworn statements—I see a number of them that were handed to me a little bit ago, and it seems that there is no end.

It is my understanding further that there were some limits as to the number of witnesses that would be called by Judge Thomas, that were interested in his confirmation; a number by Ms. Hill. And my question is what are the rules?

THE CHAIRMAN: The Senator makes a valid point. We had agreed to a witness list submitted on behalf of Judge Thomas by the minority, and a witness list that was submitted on behalf of Professor Hill. We were of the understanding that this was the totality of the witness list.

There was an agreement that there would be no witnesses called other than those witnesses, without the entire committee being informed of, and deciding on, whether or not to issue a subpoena to any witness that had not, heretofore, been mentioned.

Now, obviously Mr. Doggett's affidavit, it would seem to me, at a minimum, would require Mr. Doggett to come forward and be under oath. So, by implication, we have changed the ground rules of who would be witnesses and under what circumstances.

I would suggest that it may not be inappropriate to question Professor Hill on Mr. Doggett's statement, but not absent the opportunity of the majority to be able to question Mr. Doggett. I have insisted that both the majority counsel and the minority counsel simultaneously interview every person on the witness list so that they have an opportunity to listen to and question that potential witness.

In the case of Mr. Doggett that has not occurred. Now, unless my colleague from South Carolina would object, it seems to me that it is not appropriate at this moment to question Professor Hill, notwithstanding her willingness to be questioned, and I am told that Mr. Doggett is scheduled to be interviewed by majority and minority staff at 5 o'clock today.

SEN. THURMOND: Yes, this afternoon.

THE CHAIRMAN: I would respectfully suggest to my friend from Pennsylvania it would be more appropriate to question Professor Hill on Mr. Doggett's assertions after all parties on the committee have had an opportunity to speak with Mr. Doggett, so that other Senators will have an opportunity to intelligently question Professor Hill on Mr. Doggett's statement, and after the staff has spoken to Mr. Doggett.

So, unless my colleague from South Carolina objects, I would suggest we postpone any questioning on Mr. Doggett, although it may be totally appropriate to do so, until the full committee has had a chance, as per our agreement, to interview Mr. Doggett so we are all prepared, and are able to ask intelligent follow-up questions.

SEN. THURMOND: Mr. Chairman, I do not object, just provided that we have the opportunity to question Professor Hill after Mr. Doggett has testified.

THE CHAIRMAN: Professor Hill, this may mean that you have to come back. And I would leave the choice to you but I would respectfully suggest that it is better for us to have an opportunity, all of us, to question Mr. Doggett before you are questioned about whatever Mr. Doggett had to say.

Would you like time to confer with your counsel?

MS. HILL: Yes, just a moment, please.

I will agree to come back if necessary to respond on Mr. Doggett's statement.

THE CHAIRMAN: Well, it may be possible—I am not promising this—it may be possible that we can do this by interrogatories or sworn interrogatories, or by affidavit, but I do not make that commitment. The only commitment I am making now—it seems to me fair—is for the committee to be fully informed prior to your being questioned on this.

SEN. HATCH: Mr. Chairman?

THE CHAIRMAN: Yes?

SEN. HATCH: I haven't perhaps been privy to some of these agreements that have been made, but it seems to me there is nothing wrong—

SEN. LEAHY: Orrin, we cannot hear you down here.

SEN. HATCH: I am sorry, I apologize. It seems to me there is nothing wrong with while the witness is here, asking her about these questions about, you know, this particular statement. She was willing to answer it. And I think you save time by doing it. And, frankly, I don't see any problem with that. I think the Senator could have—

SEN. THURMOND: If she is willing to go ahead, we have no objections.

SEN. HATCH: He can ask any questions he wants, maybe we will not call Doggett. But at least he should be able to ask her if this is true, or if this is what happened? And she can answer.

SEN. LEAHY: Mr. Chairman?

THE CHAIRMAN: I will yield in a moment to my friend from Vermont. There is one simple reason why I would not like to go forward now. Quite frankly, it is not totally as a consequence of whether or not we are being fair to the witness, although I think it would be unfair to her.

It is simply that I don't know enough. I want to be able to question the witness on this issue when she returns for questioning and it seems to me that the best way to find out the truth is for everybody on this committee to have ample opportunity to review whatever is going to be introduced in evidence, so that we can all intelligently question on the matter.

I yield to my friend from Vermont.

SEN. LEAHY: Mr. Chairman, I really echo what you said, but I know that we have tried, in fairness to everybody involved—the Administration, Judge Thomas, Professor Hill and everybody else—we have worked out ground rules that you and Senator Thurmond and the rest of the committee have agreed to. And we have all had to develop whatever we were going to do within those ground rules. This would go outside them, and as one who has been designated to ask questions, I would find it very difficult to do any kind of a follow-up on this without having been able to at least delve into a statement of somebody who is not going to be a witness, but used almost as though they had been. And for the sake of a few hours' delay, whatever it might be, I would rather do it in a way that all of us—those asking questions based on the statement, those who may want to do follow-up questions based on the statement—at least know what the facts are.

SEN. HATCH: Well, Mr. Chairman, I don't know of these ground rules. I have not heard of this that you can't ask a witness questions. Now, admittedly we may decide that we do not call this man as a witness, but it is a verified statement, as I understand it, and she may agree or not agree with it, but she did read it, she said that she was willing to testify and I don't see any reason why we can't ask questions about it. It is relevant to the proceedings.

SEN. THURMOND: Mr. Chairman, I do not think we ought to attempt to require her, but if she is willing to go ahead, then we can save time, I think.

THE CHAIRMAN: Ms. Hill, would you prefer to wait until we or our staffs have had a chance to interview Mr. Doggett, or would you prefer to go now?

MS. HILL: That's a hard choice, if the committee needs—

THE CHAIRMAN: Then the Chair will make the choice. We will wait.

SEN. SIMPSON: I would like to hear her choice, if I might.

THE CHAIRMAN: Okay.

SEN. THURMOND: We'll give her the choice.

MS. HILL: I can comment on the statement now. I am not sure what the statement is supposed to mean.

THE CHAIRMAN: That's the problem.

MS. HILL: And it is really baffling me. I am really confused by it, but it is meaningless to me.

SEN. THURMOND: Do you prefer to go forward now or not?

MS. HILL: Excuse me, just a moment.

SEN. THURMOND: I think whatever she prefers.

THE CHAIRMAN: I agree, whatever the witness prefers, we will do.

SEN. LEAHY: Mr. Chairman, I might say that it is because the affidavit is so meaningless to me that I wanted to question it further, but whatever works.

MS. HILL: If the chairman recommends that we wait, I am perfectly happy to wait.

THE CHAIRMAN: I have no recommendation. [Laughter.]

MS. HILL: So you are going to make me decide, aren't you?

THE CHAIRMAN: If it were left to me I would want to abide by the established rules, but if the witness prefers to go, she may go.

MS. HILL: I would prefer that we abide by the rules that we have then.

THE CHAIRMAN: Then we will wait.

SEN. SIMPSON: Mr. Chairman, let me ask a question. We were all in the hall during the recess and the media has this affidavit and they are not going to wait for anything.

MS. HILL: That's true, they don't.

SEN. SIMPSON: And so you know that. And I just say that to you as a lawyer, that it will be circulated. It is now going out, and there is no response from you. I would think that obviously this man should come and testify. I would think that he automatically qualifies as a witness. The other witness, Angela Wright, I was told about yesterday afternoon. They took a deposition from her yesterday and I saw it last evening. And she said—although the headline was, "new and dazzling evidence," she said, "I am not stating a claim of sexual harassment against Clarence Thomas. It is not something that intimidated or frightened me. At the most it was annoying and obnoxious."

So, surely, if we are going to have fairness, and we have had fairness, but this is an extraordinary document and it is not, nor was yours, a notarized statement. It is a sworn statement. It is an affidavit. And so I think I am ready to do anything you wish but the feeding frenzy is on.

THE CHAIRMAN: There is no right answer, I expect, to this question. With regard to the person referred to by the Senator from Wyoming, as soon as we became aware that such a person existed we contacted all staff within twenty minutes, and any discussions that took place with that person were done jointly.

But I only say that to put them at rest. I want to end this. I see your counsel has indicated that it might be a good idea for you to go forward. And if that is your decision, we will go forward; from now on though, as I said, no document will be put in place until every member has had time to examine it and we will abide by your counsel's recommendation to you.

MR. GARDNER: Mr. Chairman, I want to explain that she is ready to answer questions. The issue of whether or not to bend the rules is not ours, it is yours.

THE CHAIRMAN: Yes, sir, and this is the last statement I am going to make on this. It is very easy for me to insist on the committee rules being followed, but you and Ms. Hill's other counsel may rightly conclude that Senator Simpson is correct, and that this will mean that this affidavit will be sitting out there for two, four, six, eight hours without a response. Since it is not a court of law, I am not prepared to make the judgment on whether or not Professor Hill is prejudiced by the fact that she cannot respond. That is why the Chair is not going to rule that the committee rules must be adhered to, especially as they are not the committee rules, but ground rules laid down in what is obviously an extraordinary, unusual, and unprecedented hearing.

So, ultimately, we must look to the witness and her counsel to determine what is in her best interests, not the committee's best interest. From the beginning, the interests at stake are those of Professor Hill and those of Clarence Thomas, not those of the committee.

MS. HILL: Will there be an opportunity to respond to the witness if he is called?

THE CHAIRMAN: Yes. You will have an opportunity to respond today, this moment if you wish, and to the witness if he is called.

MS. HILL: Then I am ready to go forward.

THE CHAIRMAN: Senator Specter.

SEN. SPECTER: Thank you, Mr. Chairman.

I think my time is up. [Laughter.]

Mr. Chairman, I would just like to say initially for the record that I did not make this statement available to the media or anyone.

THE CHAIRMAN: I understand that, Senator, I know you better than that.

SEN. SPECTER: And the election is to proceed.

THE CHAIRMAN: The election of the witness is to proceed knowing that we may call Mr. Doggett here to testify under oath if we so deem necessary.

SEN. SPECTER: Thank you, Mr. Chairman.

Professor Hill, I had started to question you about this affidavit. I had desisted in mid-sentence because I wanted you to have an opportunity to read it. There was a concern on my part about the document but I think it has sufficient value and since you are willing to respond to it, I am going to discuss it with you briefly.

This is an affidavit provided by a man who knew both you and Judge Thomas, and its relevancy, to the extent that it is relevant, arises on page 2 where Mr. Doggett says the following:

> The last time I saw Professor Anita Hill was at a going-away party that her friends held for her at the Sheraton Carlton Hotel on K Street, just before she left for Oral Roberts Law School. During this party she said that she wanted me to talk in private. When we moved to a corner of the room she said, "I am very disappointed in you. You really shouldn't lead on women and then let them down." When she made that statement I had absolutely no idea what she was talking about. When I asked her what she meant she stated that she had assumed that I was interested in her. She said that it was wrong for me not to have dinner with her or to try to get to know her better. She said that my actions hurt her feelings and I shouldn't lead women on like that. Quite frankly I was stunned by her statement and I told her that her comments were totally uncalled-

> for and completely unfounded. I reiterated that I had never expressed a romantic interest in her and had done nothing to give her any indication that I might be romantically interested in her in the future. I also stated that the fact that I lived three or four blocks away from her but never came over to her house or invited her to my condominium should have been a clear sign that I had no personal or romantic interest in her. I came away from her going-away party feeling that she was somewhat unstable and that in my case she had fantasied about my being interested in her romantically.

On page 3,

> It was my opinion at the time and it is now my opinion that Ms. Hill's fantasies about sexual interest in her were an indication of the fact that she was having a problem being rejected by men she was attracted to. Her statements and actions in my presence during the time when she alleges that Clarence Thomas harassed her were totally inconsistent with her current descriptions and are, in my opinion, of yet another example of her ability to fabricate the idea that someone was interested in her, when, in fact, no such interest existed.

My question to you, Professor Hill, is, is Mr. Doggett accurate when he quotes you as saying, "I am very disappointed in you. You really shouldn't lead on women and then let them down."

MS. HILL: No, he is not.

SEN. SPECTER: What, if anything, did he say to you?

MS. HILL: As I recall, before we broke I told you that I had very limited memory of Mr. Doggett. The event that he is talking about was a party where there were thirty or forty people. I was talking to a lot of people, they were people who I had known while I was here in Washington, and we might have had some conversation, but this was not the content of that conversation. I have very limited memory of him. I did not at any time have any fantasy about a romance with him.

SEN. SPECTER: In the earlier part of his affidavit he says that he met you in 1982 at a gathering of African-American lawyers on Capitol Hill, and that he had a number of contacts with you. Are his statements in that regard accurate, if you recall?

MS. HILL: As I said, my memory of him is limited. I do remember at some point seeing him jogging near my home, but beyond that I have a very limited memory of any interaction that I had with him or how I might have met him, anything like that.

SEN. SPECTER: I am shifting now, Professor Hill, to a key issue regarding your testimony that you moved with Judge Thomas from the Department of Education to EEOC because you needed the job. That is your testimony, correct?

MS. HILL: Well, I think that is your summary of my testimony.

SEN. SPECTER: Well, is my summary accurate?

MS. HILL: Well, I said that I moved to EEOC because I did not have another job. This position that—I was not sure whether I would have a position at the Department of Education. I suppose that could be translated into I needed the job.

SEN. SPECTER: Okay. I am informed, Professor Hill, that you were a Schedule A attorney and in that capacity could stay at the Department of Education. Is that incorrect?

MS. HILL: I believe I was a Schedule A attorney but, as I explained it, I was the assistant to the Chair of—oh, excuse me—assistant to the Assistant Secretary of Education, that I had not been interviewed by anyone who was to take over that position for that job. I was not even informed that I could stay on as a Schedule A attorney, as well as, as I stated before, the agency was subject to being abolished.

SEN. SPECTER: But as a Schedule A attorney, you could have stayed in some job?

MS. HILL: I suppose. As far as I know, I could have, but I am not sure because at the time the agency was scheduled to be abolished.

I want to add, too, that one of the things that I have made the point about before was that the activity had ended at that time, and I enjoyed the work. I wanted to do civil rights work, but I didn't know what work I would be doing if I could have even stayed at the agency, at the Department of Education. I moved on because I assumed that the issue of the behavior of Clarence Thomas had been laid to rest, that it was over, and that I could look forward to a similar position at the EEOC.

SEN. SPECTER: I understand that you have given that reason, that the behavior had ended, so that you have given a basis for not expressing a concern, but your statements in your earlier testimony involved your conclusion that you would have lost your job, and I am now—

MS. HILL: That was one of the factors.

SEN. SPECTER: Excuse me?

MS. HILL: That was one of the factors.

SEN. SPECTER: That was one of the factors, and I am now asking you about the correctness of that in light of the fact that you were a Schedule A attorney. While you would not have been Judge Thomas's assistant or perhaps the assistant of the Assistant Secretary, as a Class A attorney you could have in fact kept your job, had you wanted to stay there.

MS. HILL: That really was not my understanding, sir. At the time I understood that my job was going to be lost. That was my understanding.

SEN. SPECTER: Well, did you make an inquiry?

MS. HILL: With whom?

SEN. SPECTER: Anyone?

MS. HILL: I did not make an inquiry. I went on what I was told in my conversation with Mr. Thomas.

SEN. SPECTER: Well, Judge Thomas was replaced by Harry Singleton, and Harry Singleton in fact, according to an affidavit provided, was prepared to retain you as one of his attorney advisors. Now I pursue this in some detail, Professor Hill, because on your prior statements as well as your testimony here [*sic*]. In extensive newspaper accounts there has been a major question raised about why you would leave with Judge Thomas, considering your statements about his sexual harassment.

And I understand that you have given us part of your thinking, the cessation, so perhaps it wouldn't arise. But there has been a major basis for your leaving the Department of Education, because you would have lost your job and at twenty-five, as I recollect the press accounts and your statements, you needed a job. But on inquiry it is determined, number one, that as a Class A attorney you could have stayed at the Department of Education in an attorney's job; and, second that Harry Singleton, who took Judge Thomas's position, was ready to retain you as one of his attorney advisers, had you made an inquiry.

So that leads to the question, just how concerned were you about losing the job when you made no inquiry about your status to keep a job as a Class A attorney, or any inquiry with the successor Assistant Attorney General who was prepared to keep you?

SEN. METZENBAUM: Mr. Chairman, again I want to raise the question about the method of procedure. What we have now—within the last fifteen minutes we were presented five pieces of paper, some of which are notarized, some of which aren't—are various people making certain statements. And now we find that our friend, Senator Specter—and before that we had been presented the affidavit of Mr. Doggett—now we find that this lady is being called upon to respond to these statements, some of which are notarized, some of which aren't.

But what we are doing is, we are introducing a whole new element of testimony in this means by inquiring of her. And frankly, Mr. Chairman, I feel it violates the rules under which you told us this committee was operating and which I think we all agreed to. I think it is a back door way of approaching the question of how many witnesses each side will bring forth.

SEN. SPECTER: Mr. Chairman, if I may respond—

THE CHAIRMAN: Yes.

SEN. SPECTER: [continuing]—this is a key point as to why Professor Hill left one department and went to another. According to her statements, Judge Thomas had sexually harassed her at the Department of Education, and she went with him to EEOC in significant part, if not in major part, according to her statement, because she would have lost her job.

Now, Senator Metzenbaum may find that uncomfortable, but I frankly object to his interruption. The witness doesn't have any problem with the question.

SEN. METZENBAUM: I want to say I am not wanting to interrupt my friend in his line of inquiry. I am raising the question with the Chair with respect to the procedure. We were all told that there would be only so many witnesses, and unless there was agreement between the Chair and the ranking member, that is the number that would be had. But if you have witnesses come in through affidavits and then inquire about them to Ms. Hill, I think that it just is not following the procedures.

SEN. SPECTER: Mr. Chairman, this is a question which goes to the heart of the credibility of what the witness has testified to, as to her reason for a very critical move from the Department of Education to EEOC.

THE CHAIRMAN: There is no question that it is as represented. The question is whether the remainder of the committee had any opportunity to prepare, or even know whether this was going to happen. What I am afraid is going to happen now is, by the time that Judge Thomas gets here, there will be two, seven, ten, twelve, fifteen affidavits that no one will have had an opportunity to look at, and Judge Thomas will be questioned on things that could be totally scurrilous, could be in fact totally off the wall, without any of our staffs having had an opportunity to determine whether the person proffering the statement is in fact credible and whether that person should be called before the committee.

SEN. THURMOND: Mr. Chairman, may I make a statement?

THE CHAIRMAN: Yes.

SEN. THURMOND: I think the question is proper because without this affidavit, you don't need the Doggett affidavit. He could ask her the question that he did ask her, why she left when she could have stayed, without this affidavit. You don't need this affidavit. The question he asked is perfectly proper.

SEN. KENNEDY: But Mr. Chairman, just on this issue, it is being represented that Singleton had a job available for Professor Hill. I mean, I think it would be legitimate to find out when did Mr. Singleton indicate that Professor Hill might have a job. Did he have a conversation with her prior to the time that she left the agency? Here a Senator is saying, "Well, don't you know that Mr. Singleton," who happens to be one of Clarence Thomas's best friends, "had a job just out there, and why didn't you take it? And the fact you didn't take it must reflect something," and I think all of us know what is trying to be reflected.

And so I think it is perfectly appropriate for us, when we are going to talk about asking a witness about when that job was available, to know when that job—whether Mr. Singleton talked to Professor Hill, when he talked to her, when he indicated a job was going to be available, rather than just go ask the witness right here on an affidavit, "at some time Mr. Singleton concluded, based upon your standing over there, that you would have been available."

And I think that is the point the Senator from Ohio is making. I think it is a legitimate point.

SEN. SPECTER: Mr. Chairman, if I may respond just briefly—

THE CHAIRMAN: Yes.

SEN. SPECTER: [continuing]—the question is whether Professor Hill asked Mr. Singleton. She is in the process of leaving. She is concerned about her job, and the question which I asked goes to the issue of her inquiry as to her ability to stay because she is in a Class A status or, secondarily, to keep the same position as the Assistant Secretary's advisor. It goes to the issue of her state of mind, as to whether she felt she really had to move with Judge Thomas to keep a job.

SEN. HATCH: Well, Mr. Chairman—

THE CHAIRMAN: Wait a minute. Let me say something.

SEN. HATCH: Before you rule I would like to make a statement, though—

THE CHAIRMAN: Make it briefly, if you could.

SEN. HATCH: I will try.

It seems to me that these questions are relevant—

SEN. METZENBAUM: We can't hear you, Orrin.

SEN. HATCH: I'm sorry.

It seems to me that these questions are relevant. Last night we were trying to obtain all the knowledge we could from this so-called Angela Wright. Well, she gave so much testimony and then refused to talk after that. Now does that mean that she is going to be barred from testifying? I don't think anybody on your side is going to argue that.

He is entitled to ask her, in advance, what her recollection is of these things. And all that means is, if she will answer it, either she agrees with the statement or she doesn't. If she doesn't, she doesn't. Now if she doesn't and the Singleton statement says something else, we have an option of calling Singleton or not calling him. I mean, that doesn't take anybody's rights away from them, and I think if she wanted to, she would have an option of coming back if she didn't like what he said. So I think I never heard of this rule.

THE CHAIRMAN: I thank my friend, and—

SEN. LEAHY: Mr. Chairman, I do wish to make one point on this. How fair can it be to either Professor Hill or any other witness if any of us can sit up here and say, "I have this stack of affidavits, and in affidavit No. 5 in the third paragraph somebody says such-and-such. What do you have to say about that?"

I mean, at the very least, at the very least they ought to be able to see these affidavits. At the very least, they ought to have some idea of who the person is and if they are credible. Otherwise you could go down through a whole list and say, "Ah, affidavit No. 29, in the second sentence, they say that you were living in Japan at the time. Can you prove that you weren't?" I mean, this doesn't make much sense.

THE CHAIRMAN: I thank my colleagues for their advice. The Chair rules as follows.

SEN. SIMPSON: Mr. Chairman, may I? I have been—

THE CHAIRMAN: You have been very good. [Laughter.]

SEN. SIMPSON: I promise. It is a very difficult day for me.

Mr. Chairman, let me just say every one of us at this table is in anguish because what we are trying to deal with is the credibility of these two people, principally, and so anything that goes to their credibility we have to hear. Forget about Doggett. I am glad you responded. I think that was appropriate, because that thing would be splattered all over the place, and if you hadn't said anything, you would pay for it.

And so now you can't tell me what you are going to do when Clarence Thomas gets here and you bring up any questions impugning his credibility. Are we going to invoke this rule? I want to see it to believe it. This is about credibility.

SEN. SIMON: Mr. Chairman.

THE CHAIRMAN: Well, let me tell you what I am going to do, and then I will yield to my colleagues.

It is appropriate to ask Professor Hill anything any member wishes to ask her to plumb the depths of her credibility. It would be appropriate to ask her about Mr. Singleton, but it is inappropriate to represent what Mr. Singleton says via an affidavit. There is a distinction.

So you can ask anything you want. You can ask her what Santa Claus said or didn't say, whether she spoke to him or not, but it is inappropriate to introduce an affidavit from Santa Claus prior to every member on this committee having an opportunity to check it out, for the following reason: We may find out that Santa Claus is not real. Therefore, it may not be very relevant whether Santa Claus said something or not.

So, we are all lawyers on this committee, with one or two exceptions. There is a fundamental distinction between being able to ask a direct question, to determine the credibility of a witness, and representing what another individual said the witness said or what an individual said they thought about the motivation of the witness. There is a distinction.

So the Chair will rule that you can ask anything you want about credibility; you cannot represent, via an affidavit or a sworn statement or a statement, as to what the individual in question thinks. If that is the case, ask the committee to bring that witness forward, and then we will sit down and renegotiate among ourselves and with the White House how many witnesses we are going to have. But as pointed out here, this is another way of getting in two, five, seven, ten, twenty witnesses without allowing for an opportunity to cross-examine them.

Now that is the Chair's ruling. Did my friend want to say anything?

SEN. SIMON: I would just buttress that by saying there is one other reason, Mr. Chairman, and that is, if we don't abide by the rules, we are going to end up in these wrangles constantly every time a new affidavit is brought up.

THE CHAIRMAN: I assure my friend from Wyoming that I will impose the same exact rule on anyone questioning Judge Thomas.

Now, the Senator from Pennsylvania has the floor.

SEN. SPECTER: Mr. Chairman, am I accurate that I only have twenty-nine minutes left?

THE CHAIRMAN: You have whatever time was—let me ask. Let me ask Senator Simon.

SEN. SPECTER: Twenty-nine minutes on my thirty-minute round.

THE CHAIRMAN: Pardon me?

SEN. SPECTER: Is it accurate that I only have twenty-nine minutes left on my thirty-minute round?

THE CHAIRMAN: It is accurate you can have as much time as you want, Senator.

SEN. SPECTER: Thank you very much, Mr. Chairman.

Professor Hill, did you know that, as a Class A attorney, you could have stayed on at the Department of Education?

MS. HILL: No, I did not know at that time.

SEN. SPECTER: Did you make any effort to find out that, as a Class A attorney, you could have stayed on at the Department of Education?

MS. HILL: No, I relied on what I was told.

SEN. SPECTER: Sorry, I didn't hear you.

MS. HILL: I relied on what I was told by Clarence Thomas.

SEN. SPECTER: My question—

MS. HILL: I relied on what I was told by Clarence Thomas. I did not make further inquiry.

SEN. SPECTER: And what are you saying that Judge Thomas told you?

MS. HILL: His indication from him was that he could not assure me of a position at Education.

SEN. SPECTER: Was that when you were hired or when he was leaving?

MS. HILL: When he was leaving.

SEN. SPECTER: Did you make any inquiry of his successor, Mr. Singleton, as to what your status would be?

MS. HILL: No, I did not. I'm not even sure that I knew who his successor would be at the time.

SEN. SPECTER: Well, was Mr. Singleton on the premises for about four weeks in advance of Judge Thomas's departure as the—

MS. HILL: I don't—

SEN. SPECTER: May I finish the question?

MS. HILL: I don't—I'm sorry.

SEN. SPECTER: May I finish the question?

MS. HILL: I'm sorry.

SEN. SPECTER: Was Mr. Singleton on the premises for about four weeks prior to Judge Thomas's departure, for transition?

MS. HILL: I don't recall.

SEN. SPECTER: Did you make any effort at all with anybody in the Department of Education to find out whether you could stay on in a job there?

MS. HILL: As I said before, I did not make any further inquiries.

SEN. SPECTER: Well, how concerned were you on your decision to move with Judge Thomas to EEOC, notwithstanding your represented comments about retaining some job somewhere?

MS. HILL: I'm sorry, could you rephrase your question?

SEN. SPECTER: Well, I would be glad to repeat it. If you made no inquiry to see if you could stay at the Department of Education, perhaps even as the assistant to the Assistant Secretary of Education, how much of a factor was your need for a job to go along with Judge Thomas, even though he had made these reprehensible statements?

MS. HILL: It was part of what I considered.

SEN. SPECTER: Professor Hill, there has been disclosed in the public milieu the records of certain telephone logs as so much of the evidence or representations or comments about this matter, and you were quoted in *The Washington Post* as saying, " 'I'm terribly saddened and deeply offended by these allegations.' Ms.

Hill called the telephone logs garbage, and said that she had not telephoned Thomas, except to return his calls." Did you, in fact, say that you had not telephoned Thomas, except to return his calls?

MS. HILL: No, I did not say that.

SEN. SPECTER: *The Washington Post* is in error on that statement attributed to you?

MS. HILL: Well, I can tell you something about that conversation.

SEN. SPECTER: Please do.

MS. HILL: When that conversation was made, it was my indication that the reporter was saying to me that "we have information that you talked to Clarence Thomas ten or eleven times over this period of time that was described." That was my understanding of what she was telling me. I knew that I had not talked to Clarence Thomas, and I told her that. I said I haven't talked to Clarence Thomas ten or eleven times, and she said that there were telephone logs that indicated that I had.

SEN. SPECTER: Well, it is not a matter of talking to Judge Thomas, it is a matter of telephoning—

MS. HILL: I understand that.

SEN. SPECTER: May I finish the question—it is a matter of telephoning him. Did you tell the reporter for *The Washington Post* that you had not telephoned Thomas, except to return his calls?

MS. HILL: I said to her that I had not talked to Clarence Thomas ten or eleven times over that period of time.

SEN. SPECTER: So, she misunderstood you, to say that you had not telephoned Thomas ten or eleven times?

MS. HILL: I think there was miscommunication in the entire interview.

SEN. SPECTER: Did you call the telephone log issue "garbage"?

MS. HILL: I believe that the issue is garbage, when you look at what seems to be implied from the telephone log, then, yes, that is garbage.

SEN. SPECTER: Have you seen the records of the telephone logs, Professor Hill?

MS. HILL: Yes, I have.

SEN. SPECTER: Do you deny the accuracy of these telephone logs?

MS. HILL: No, I do not.

SEN. SPECTER: Then you now concede that you had called Judge Thomas eleven times?

MS. HILL: I do not deny the accuracy of these logs. I cannot deny that they are accurate, and I will concede that those phone calls were made, yes.

SEN. SPECTER: So, they are not garbage?

MS. HILL: Well, Senator, what I said was the issue is garbage. Those telephone messages do not indicate that—they are being used to indicate, that is, that somehow I was pursuing something more than a cordial relationship, a professional relationship. Each of those calls were made in a professional context. Some of those calls revolved around one incident. Several of those calls, in fact three, involved one incident where I was trying to act on behalf of another group, so the issue that is being created by the telephone calls, yes, indeed, is garbage.

SEN. SPECTER: Well, the issue which was raised by Senator Danforth, who disclosed this log in a press conference, was done so on the point that you had made repeated efforts to contact Judge Thomas. This bore on the issue as to whether he had sexually harassed you, on the approach that if he had victimized you by sexual harassment, you would not be calling him so many times. So, when you were quoted by *The Washington Post* as, number one, calling them garbage and denying that you had telephoned Thomas, it constituted your statement that you had, in fact, not made those efforts to contact him.

Now, my question to you is, since those calls were in fact made as you now say, doesn't that have some relevance as to whether the committee should accept your statements about Judge Thomas's sexual harassment in the context of your efforts to call him this many times over that period of time?

MS. HILL: No.

SEN. SPECTER: Okay.

Answer into the microphone, if you will, so we can hear you.

MS. HILL: I'm sorry. My response is no, that those are not relevant to the issue of whether or not there was harassment. My point is this—and I believe that these are completely consistent with what you have before you in my statement—my point is that I have stated to you that I continued, I hoped to continue to maintain a professional relationship, for a variety of reasons. One was a sense that I could not afford to antagonize a person in such a high position.

Those calls that were made, I have attempted to explain, none of them were personal in nature, they involved instances where I passed along casual messages or instances where I called to either find out whether or not the chairman was available for a speech, acting on behalf of someone else. No, they have very little, if any, relevance at all to the incidents that happened before those phone calls were made.

SEN. SPECTER: Very little relevance, but perhaps some?

MS. HILL: I believe they have none. We may differ on that.

SEN. SPECTER: You say that they were all professional and you have accounted for a number of them in your statement, but a number of them have not been accounted for. For example, the log on January 30, 1984, "Just called to say hello, sorry she didn't see you last week." May 9, 1984, "Please call." October 8, 1986, "Please call."

Taking the one, "Just called to say hello, sorry she didn't see you last week," first of all, is that accurate?

MS. HILL: As I indicated earlier, I do not deny the accuracy of these messages.

SEN. SPECTER: You had picked out one of the calls in your statement which appears on page 8, as follows: "In August of 1987 I was in Washington and I did call Diane Holt. In the course of this conversation, she asked me how long I was going to be in town, and I told her."

Now, the log says, "Anita Hill, 547-4500, 4:00 o'clock, in town until 8-15," is dated August 4. Now, if the log represents your making the statement "in town until August 15," from August 4, some might interpret that as a suggestion that you would be available to meet, maybe, maybe not, but some might suggest that.

If, on the other hand, Judge Thomas's secretary asked you how long you were going to be in town, the initiative would come from her. It would contain no possible suggestion of your availability to meet. My question to you is how do you know today that, on August 4, 1987, she asked you how long you were going to be in town, as opposed to your saying that you would be in town until August 15?

MS. HILL: That is my recollection of how the telephone conversation took place.

SEN. SPECTER: And your representation to this committee is that you have recollection at this moment that Judge Thomas's secretary asked you how long you were going to be in town, as opposed to your volunteering the statement to her? You have an active recollection of that?

MS. HILL: That is my recollection.

SEN. SPECTER: Okay.

MS. HILL: May I comment on that telephone call?

SEN. SPECTER: Sure.

MS. HILL: I was actually in town until the 20th of August, so at least this may be an accurate representation of what was written in the log, but that is not an accurate representation of my activities.

SEN. SPECTER: What relevance does that have?

MS. HILL: My point is you asked if these phone messages were accurate, and I said that I would not deny their accuracy, but I will deny the accuracy of that as a representation of my activities.

SEN. SPECTER: Let me return, Professor Hill, to the question as to how you first came to be contacted by the Senate, and I would appreciate it if you would tell us when the first contact was made, by whom and the circumstances?

MS. HILL: On September 4, a woman named Gail Laster called me and a message was left at my office.

SEN. SPECTER: On September 4?

MS. HILL: On September 4.

THE CHAIRMAN: What was the woman's name?

MS. HILL: September 4.

THE CHAIRMAN: Her name?

MS. HILL: Gail Laster.

THE CHAIRMAN: Thank you.

SEN. SPECTER: You say the person was who?

MS. HILL: Gail Laster, and I don't have the message in front of me, but the indication was that she was working with a Senate office and I can't—

SEN. SPECTER: And what happened next?

MS. HILL: At some point in between—on September 4, I must have returned her call or she on her own initiative called back on September 5 and I returned her call on that same day.

SEN. SPECTER: Now, on September 4, did you call back or on September 5 did she call you again?

MS. HILL: On September 4, I called back.

SEN. SPECTER: And did you talk to someone?

MS. HILL: I left a message.

SEN. SPECTER: What happened next?

MS. HILL: On September 5, she called me.

SEN. SPECTER: And what was the content of that conversation?

MS. HILL: I returned her call on September 5, and during that call she asked me if I knew anything about allegations of sexual harassment.

SEN. SPECTER: Do you have notes of these matters, Professor Hill? I see you reading from something there.

MS. HILL: Yes, I do, I have notes that I have made.

SEN. SPECTER: Did you make those notes contemporaneously with the event?

MS. HILL: No, I did not.

SEN. SPECTER: When did you make the notes?

MS. HILL: I made these notes yesterday.

SEN. SPECTER: Okay. What was the conversation that you had on September 5 with, you say, Gail Laster?

MS. HILL: G-a-i-l, Laster, L-a-s-t-e-r.

SEN. SPECTER: And what was the conversation which you had with Gail Laster?

MS. HILL: She asked me some general questions and then she asked me if I knew anything about allegations of sexual harassment or tolerance of sexual harassment at the Office of the EEOC, in particular as they related to Clarence Thomas.

SEN. SPECTER: And what was your response?

MS. HILL: My response was that I did not have any comment on either of those.

SEN. SPECTER: And what did she say when you told her that you had no comment, as opposed to no knowledge of any tolerance of sexual harassment?

MS. HILL: I believe we might have gone on to something more general about the nomination. I don't believe the conversation lasted very long after that.

SEN. SPECTER: Well, what was in the conversation?

MS. HILL: As I say, we went on to more general matters regarding the nomination, issues about—

SEN. SPECTER: You don't recall the specific contents of the conversation?

MS. HILL: Oh, we talked about general issues involving women in the workplace, what I thought of his views on that, on those issues.

SEN. SPECTER: What happened next?

MS. HILL: On September 6, Ricki Seidman called me. I returned the call on that day and she asked me some specific questions about some work that I had done at the Department of Education. We spoke about that work and she asked what role I played in doing it, and then she again asked me about rumors or did I know anything or had I heard any rumors while I was at the EEOC involving his tolerance, Judge Thomas's tolerance of sexual harassment—

SEN. SPECTER: And what response—

MS. HILL: [continuing] or whether I knew anything about his actually engaging in sexual harassment acts.

SEN. SPECTER: And what was your response?

MS. HILL: At that point, I told Ms. Seidman that I would neither confirm nor deny any knowledge of that.

SEN. SPECTER: Anything further in that conversation?

MS. HILL: At that point, I think again we might have moved on. She—

SEN. SPECTER: Might have moved on, or do you not recall the specifics of the conversation?

MS. HILL: I will complete my thought here. At that point, she said are you saying that you will neither confirm nor deny your knowledge, or are you saying that you will neither confirm or deny that the actual harassment existed, and I told her it was the latter.

SEN. SPECTER: What happened next?

MS. HILL: I told her that I wanted to think about it and that I would get back to her.

SEN. SPECTER: Think about what?

MS. HILL: Think about this issue of sexual harassment.

SEN. SPECTER: Did that conclude the conversation?

MS. HILL: That concluded the conversation.

SEN. SPECTER: What happened next?

MS. HILL: I think in the interim, on the weekend, over the weekend of September 7 or 8, I spoke to Ms. Seidman again. I did speak to her again and I asked her specifically, if I were to discuss this matter, where should I go? That I wanted to talk with someone who was knowledgeable about the issue before I proceeded to tell what I knew. At that point what I was trying to do was to really determine, get some sense of how the committee would approach this and give some—take some effort to weigh what I thought was valuable information, but I wanted to do it from a more objective viewpoint.

SEN. SPECTER: And what did Ms. Seidman tell you?

MS. HILL: At that point she told me that she knew someone who worked on the Senate Labor Committee, James Brudney, who would have information, who had worked in the area of sex discrimination, and that he would be able to give me some indication of the law. She also said that she had his telephone number.

SEN. SPECTER: Well, why would you need someone to give you an indication of the status of the law, considering your own knowledge of sexual harassment and the fact that you had been a civil rights professor at Oral Roberts Law School?

MS. HILL: I had not practiced in the area. I have never actually practiced in the area. I have taught in the area, but it has been—I haven't taught in the area since 1986, and I understand that this is a very fast-developing area of law. In addition, I wanted a more objective evaluation of my situation and I wanted to do it with someone who I could trust. I knew James Brudney and I wanted to talk with him so that I might be able to make that evaluation.

SEN. SPECTER: So Ms. Seidman recommended Mr. James Brudney?

MS. HILL: She gave me his name, and I indicated that he was someone who I knew and who I thought had integrity and who I could trust with confidential information.

SEN. SPECTER: Okay, and then you did talk to Mr. Brudney?

MS. HILL: Yes, we talked.

SEN. SPECTER: And when was that?

MS. HILL: Well, we talked on the weekend of September 7 and 8.

SEN. SPECTER: And what was the content of that conversation?

MS. HILL: Actually, I'm sorry, that is incorrect. We talked on September 9.

The content of the conversation was really, "Tell me something. What do you know about the development of sexual harassment? If I disclose to you certain facts, can you make an evaluation of some kind as to what kind of legal conclusion one might make?"

SEN. SPECTER: So that at that time there was a doubt in your mind as to whether Judge Thomas was, in fact, guilty of sexual harassment on the facts as you knew them?

MS. HILL: Well, I want to back up and say something here. In my statement to you I never alleged sexual harassment. I had conduct that I wanted explained to the committee. My sense was, my own personal sense was that yes, this was sexual harassment, but I understood that the committee with their staff could make that evaluation on their own. So I didn't have any doubts, but I wanted to talk with someone who might be more objective.

SEN. SPECTER: Well, you did call it sexual harassment in your extensive news conference on October 7, even though you did not so characterize it to the FBI or in your statement to this committee.

MS. HILL: But that news conference on August 7 had not taken place at the time —or, excuse me, on October 7—

SEN. SPECTER: October 7.

MS. HILL: [continuing]—on October 7 had not taken place at the time that this conversation was made.

SEN. SPECTER: Well, the statement to the committee and the statement to the FBI hadn't taken place, either.

MS. HILL: The statement to the FBI had not; you are right.

SEN. SPECTER: So that you made statements to the FBI during the week of September 23 and you furnished this committee a statement on September 23, both of which occurred after your conversation with Mr. Brudney, but in neither of those statements did you conclude that Judge Thomas was guilty of sexual harassment.

MS. HILL: I had reached—in either of which statements?

SEN. SPECTER: You did not tell the FBI that Judge Thomas was guilty of sexual harassment, did you?

MS. HILL: I don't recall telling them that he was guilty of sexual harassment, no. I didn't tell them that.

SEN. SPECTER: Or you didn't characterize his conduct as sexual harassment.

MS. HILL: I did or did not?

SEN. SPECTER: You did not characterize Judge Thomas's conduct as sexual harassment when you gave the statement to the FBI, correct?

MS. HILL: Senator, I guess I am not making myself clear. I was not raising a legal claim in either of my statements. I was not raising a legal claim. I was attempting to inform about conduct.

SEN. SPECTER: But you did raise a legal claim in your interview on October 7.

MS. HILL: No, I did not raise a legal claim then.

SEN. SPECTER: Well, I will produce the transcript which says that it was sexual harassment.

MS. HILL: Well, I would suggest that saying that it is sexual harassment and raising a legal claim are two different things. What I was trying to do when I provided information to you was not say to you, "I am claiming that this man sexually harassed me." What I was saying and what I state now is that this conduct that took place, you have your own legal staff and many are lawyers yourselves. You can investigate and determine whether or not it is sexual harassment, and that is one of the things that I want to get away from.

Were I filing a claim, if I were filing a complaint in court, this would be done very differently, but this does not constitute a legal complaint.

SEN. SPECTER: So that you are not now drawing a conclusion that Judge Thomas sexually harassed you?

MS. HILL: Yes, I am drawing that conclusion.

SEN. SPECTER: Well, then, I don't understand.

MS. HILL: Pardon me?

SEN. SPECTER: Then I don't understand.

MS. HILL: Well, let me try to explain again.

I brought this information forward for the committee to make their own decision. I did not bring the information forward to try to establish a legal claim for sexual harassment. I brought it forward so that the committee could determine the veracity of it, the truth of it, and from there on you could evaluate the information as to whether or not it constituted sexual harassment or whether or not it went to his ability to conduct a job as an Associate Justice of the Supreme Court.

SEN. SPECTER: But, Professor Hill, there is a big difference between your articulating your version of events, contrasted with your statement that Judge Thomas sexually harassed you. And in the transcript of your October 7 interview, you responded to a question saying that it was sexual harassment.

MS. HILL: In my opinion, based on my reading of the law, yes, it was. But later on, immediately following that response, I noted to the press that I did not raise a claim of sexual harassment in this complaint. It seems to me that the behavior has to be evaluated on its own with regard to the fitness of this individual to act as an Associate Justice. It seems to me that even if it does not rise to the level of sexual harassment, it is behavior that is not befitting an individual who will be a member of the Court.

SEN. SPECTER: Well, Professor Hill, I quite agree with you that the committee ought to examine the conduct or the behavior and make a factual determination of what you say happened and what Judge Thomas said happened. But when you say that you had not made the statement that he had sexually harassed you, that is at variance with your statement at the October 7 news conference.

MS. HILL: Senator, I would submit that what I said was, I have not raised a claim of sexual harassment in either of my statements and I will say again that in the news conference I was simply stating that yes, in my opinion, this does constitute sexual harassment.

SEN. SPECTER: Okay. Back to Mr. Jim Brudney. You consulted with him because you wanted some expert advice on what—

THE CHAIRMAN: Senator, I am not going to interrupt you, but your time is up. Go ahead, finish this line of questioning, and then we will move to our friend from Vermont, but I just wanted you to be aware.

SEN. SPECTER: I am sorry. I hadn't noticed.

THE CHAIRMAN: That is all right. There is no reason why you should have.

SEN. SPECTER: I had recollected your statement, "Take as much time as you want."

THE CHAIRMAN: That is true. Go ahead, finish this line, and then we will go to our friend from Vermont. I just wanted to alert you to start to wind down.

SEN. SPECTER: Well, this is not necessarily brief, because I think it is important to develop the facts as to the contacts, which end up with the issue as to whether the *USA Today* report is correct that, "Anita Hill was told by Senate staffers her signed affidavit alleging sexual harassment by Clarence Thomas would be the instrument that 'quietly and behind the scenes' would force him to withdraw his name."

THE CHAIRMAN: Well, I understand, and I assumed that is where the Senator was going. Since that will take a little more time, why don't we break here?

SEN. SPECTER: That is fine with me, Mr. Chairman.

THE CHAIRMAN: And let me ask, because there is a lot of pressure for any witness sitting under the lights this long, would you like to take a break now?

Now before everyone starts to get up and go, let me tell you what we are going to do from here on, if I can. It is our hope and intention that shortly we will take a break. We will then come back to Senator Leahy, and from that point will continue—although we agreed we would stop at this point, the purpose of this is fact-finding. We will allow time for any questions my friend from Pennsylvania has, or my friend from Vermont may have, speaking for me and for Senator Heflin.

But we are going to try to finish with the witness relatively soon, and then we will break for dinner. It is the intention of the Chair to have Judge Thomas return then. In fairness to him, he should have an opportunity to speak tonight and should not have to wait to respond to what has been asserted, and so that is how we will proceed.

We will recess for ten minutes.

[Recess.]

THE CHAIRMAN: Welcome back. Now again we are waiting to hear from Judge

Thomas, whether he wishes to—I know there are a few people in the press who are anxious to know what the schedule will be for tonight.

I have made a commitment, I think it is only fair, that Judge Thomas can come on whenever he wishes after Professor Hill finishes. He has not decided whether he wants to testify tonight. If he wishes to speak tonight, we will go tonight as long as is appropriate or is reasonable, and I can't guess what that would be at this moment.

So I apologize to those who are trying to set their schedules but again, as I said, this is not a trial. This is a fact-finding mission, and we are going to be as fair as we can to all parties.

As it appears now, we have, Professor Hill, two more principal questioners who will question you for roughly a half-hour apiece. Then we are going to yield, as I indicated at the outset, to any of our colleagues who wish to ask up to five minutes. It is my sincere hope that all the questions that they wish to have asked will have been asked.

So we will be a minimum of another hour and a maximum of another hour and forty minutes or thereabouts. We will then break for dinner. If Judge Thomas wishes to come back, we will break for roughly forty-five minutes to one hour for dinner. If he does not wish to come back, we will recess until tomorrow morning. We will have to decide on the time when I speak to the ranking member, whether it is 9 or 10 o'clock tomorrow morning.

I can see my friend from Wyoming seeking recognition.

SEN. SIMPSON: Mr. Chairman, I think that all should be aware that I feel rather positive that Judge Thomas does want to be here this evening. Whether it can be concluded or not I don't know, but—

THE CHAIRMAN: [continuing] I guarantee that he will be then.

SEN. SIMPSON: I know you will be fair. I know you will be.

THE CHAIRMAN: So thank you for your patience, Professor Hill and for everyone else's. Let us now turn to the Senator from Vermont, Senator Leahy.

SEN. LEAHY: Thank you, Mr. Chairman.

Professor Hill, let me go back to some of the areas we discussed earlier. I would like to refer first to a comment just made by the chairman, and then I want to go into a couple of the questions posed by Senator Specter.

The chairman said, and quite rightly, that this is not a trial. We are not having a trial on whether sexual harassment under the statute was committed or not, and whether or not the statute of limitations has run. We are trying to find out what the facts are.

And with that in mind, I turn to the questions Senator Specter was asking you. He talked about whether you had called your charges against Judge Thomas "sexual harassment" in your FBI statements. During your October 7 press conference in Norman, Oklahoma, you were asked, "Professor Hill, you said that you did not describe this as sexual harassment in your FBI statement." You answered, "I described the incidents. I did not use the term 'sexual harassment.'"

Let me go, if I might—and please just bear with me a couple of minutes on this—let me go to your earlier statement today, your sworn statement. You talked of Judge Thomas calling you into his office and then saying, and I quote from your statement on page 3,

> After a brief discussion of work, he would turn the conversation to discussions of sexual matters. His conversations were very vivid. He spoke about acts that he had seen in pornographic films involving such matters as women having sex with animals and films showing group sex or rape scenes. He talked about pornographic materials depicting individuals with large penises or large breasts involved in various sex acts.

Now without saying whether you felt that his conduct met a specific statutory definition of harassment, tell us in your own words, Professor Hill, after one of those conversations, how did you feel?

MS. HILL: I was embarrassed. I found this talk offensive, completely offensive. It was—I made the point that it was offensive and it was something that was thrust upon me. It was not something that I voluntarily entered into and, therefore, it was even more offensive. It was—just the nature of the conversation was very offensive and disgusting, and degrading.

SEN. LEAHY: Without going into a statutory description of what is or is not sexual harassment, how did you feel after—and I quote from your statement, "on several occasions Thomas told me graphically of his own sexual prowess."

How did you feel then?

MS. HILL: That was really embarrassing because I thought it even personalized it more to the individual who I was looking at. I mean it is one thing to hear about something that someone has seen, but it is another thing to be face to face with an individual who is describing to you things that they have done and that was very embarrassing and offensive and I did not like it. I felt—I just—it was just—I mean it is hard for me to describe. It just made me feel very bad about the whole situation.

SEN. LEAHY: And on page 5, without repeating it again, you spoke of discussions he had had with you, about himself and other women, is that correct?

MS. HILL: Yes.

SEN. LEAHY: Professor Hill, you spoke of us all being lawyers and we read the statute and the code words of the statute, let me just ask you one more time, did you consider that—at least as it involved you—harassment?

MS. HILL: Yes, I did.

SEN. LEAHY: Thank you.

Now, Professor, we have spoken in other questions of phone logs. Have you seen the phone logs that Senator Danforth released; I believe the *New York Times* and *The Washington Post* and others have had articles about them?

MS. HILL: Yes, I have seen that.

SEN. LEAHY: Now, you left EEOC in 1983. Is that correct?

MS. HILL: Yes.

SEN. LEAHY: Judge Thomas left EEOC in 1990. Is that correct?

MS. HILL: As far as I recall.

SEN. LEAHY: Approximately seven years there?

MS. HILL: Yes.

SEN. LEAHY: If you count up the phone calls that are shown on those phone logs —assuming that they are accurate—and that amounts to, in the seven years, what, a dozen phone calls?

MS. HILL: I think they were described as ten-to-twelve or ten-to-eleven phone calls.

SEN. LEAHY: About one and a half per year?

MS. HILL: Yes.

SEN. LEAHY: So assuming those phone logs are accurate, you were not exactly beating down the doors with phone calls there, were you?

MS. HILL: I was not at all.

SEN. LEAHY: Now, there was a question about Mr. Doggett. Do you have any strong and clear recollection of Mr. Doggett at all?

MS. HILL: No, not at all.

SEN. LEAHY: If you were asked to, would you be able to describe him accurately?

MS. HILL: I could not with any specificity describe him. I think I remember him as being tall.

SEN. LEAHY: It happens to a lot of us.

Who was the legal counsel at EEOC when you started there in the spring of 1982?

MS. HILL: Legal counsel was Constance Dupree.

SEN. LEAHY: I beg your pardon?

MS. HILL: The legal counsel was, I believe, Constance Dupree at the EEOC.

SEN. LEAHY: Did there come a time when there was a change made in this position? After you went to EEOC?

MS. HILL: After I went to the EEOC, I believe she retired from the Government service altogether, but she left that position.

SEN. LEAHY: Was it a short time after you arrived or a long time after you arrived? Do you recall?

MS. HILL: Oh, I believe it was about midway, maybe four or five months, it may have been shorter than that.

SEN. LEAHY: Who became legal counsel then, do you recall?

MS. HILL: I do not recall the individual's name.

SEN. LEAHY: Now, in one of the interviews this morning a witness stated—and this was an interview for which you have not seen the transcript but both the Republican and Democratic counsel were there—the witness said that you had expressed your desire to have the legal counsel's position. Had you done that, had you expressed such a desire at the time that the vacancy occurred, the one you just described?

MS. HILL: No. I did not express any desire for that position. I had no desire for such a position. I was just new to the EEOC.

SEN. LEAHY: So did you have conversations with an Armstrong Williams about getting that job, the job of legal counsel?

MS. HILL: No, I did not.

SEN. LEAHY: And you do not recall applying for the job of legal counsel?

MS. HILL: I did not.

SEN. LEAHY: Thank you.

Senator Specter questioned you at some length about following Judge Thomas from the Department of Education to the EEOC, is that correct?

MS. HILL: Yes, that is correct.

SEN. LEAHY: And am I correct in restating your testimony that those conversations, which you now describe as—just during these questions—have described as harassment, those conversations began at the Department of Education, is that correct?

MS. HILL: Yes, that is correct.

SEN. LEAHY: But notwithstanding that, you went to the EEOC when Judge Thomas went there?

MS. HILL: Yes.

SEN. LEAHY: Do you recall prior to going to the EEOC, how long before that had been the last conversation of the nature that you have described here with Judge Thomas? Of those conversations that you found offensive, how long prior to your transfer had one of those occurred?

MS. HILL: I would say four months or so, about four months.

SEN. LEAHY: Some time, in fact.

MS. HILL: Some time.

SEN. LEAHY: Now, did anybody tell you that you could stay and have a job at the Department of Education?

MS. HILL: Nobody told me that.

SEN. LEAHY: Had President Reagan pledged and campaigned on such a pledge that he would do away with the Department of Education, if elected?

MS. HILL: Yes, he had, and that was the understanding within the Department itself. The individuals who were working in the Department understood that to be the case.

SEN. LEAHY: And President Reagan was then President?

MS. HILL: Yes, he was.

SEN. LEAHY: And nobody told you that there would be a job in the Department of Education where you could still work in civil rights, is that correct?

MS. HILL: Nobody told me that.

SEN. LEAHY: But you did want to work in civil rights, according to your testimony?

MS. HILL: Yes, I did.

SEN. LEAHY: Now, walk me through again, please, what was the nature of the job that would be available to you at EEOC, how did you hear about it, what did you do to apply for it and so forth?

MS. HILL: I did not apply for it. I heard about it from Judge Thomas. He indicated to me that I could go with him to the EEOC and I would have the same type of position that I had at the Department of Education.

SEN. LEAHY: And that was?

MS. HILL: That of a special assistant who would be working directly under him, advising him on a number of projects and issues that came up.

SEN. LEAHY: Now, Professor Hill, you have told us of the conversations. In answering questions today you have elaborated even on the statement that you gave us early on, is that correct?

MS. HILL: Yes, I have.

SEN. LEAHY: Is there anything you would change, in either your statement or your answers that you have given us today about the kinds of conversations that you had with Judge Thomas that you say were so offensive?

MS. HILL: No, sir, I would not change anything.

SEN. LEAHY: How did you feel at the time that you had those conversations?

MS. HILL: During the time that I had those conversations I was very depressed. I was embarrassed by the type and the content of the conversations. I was concerned about whether or not I could continue in my position.

SEN. LEAHY: Now, that was years ago. As you recount them today, how do you feel today?

MS. HILL: Today I feel more angry about the situation. Having looked at it with hindsight I think it was very irresponsible for an individual in the position of the kind of authority as was Mr. Thomas, at the time, to engage in that kind of a conduct. It was not only irresponsible, in my opinion, it was in violation of the law. Now, I am much more divorced from it. I am less embarrassed by the fact that I went through that; after having gone through what I have gone through now, I am less embarrassed by it. It is still embarrassing. It is embarrassing that I did not say anything, but I am angrier about it and I think that it needs to be addressed by this committee.

SEN. LEAHY: Do you have anything to gain by coming here? Has anybody promised you anything for coming forth with this story now?

MS. HILL: I have nothing to gain. No one has promised me anything. I have nothing to gain here. This has been disruptive of my life and I have taken a number of personal risks. I have been threatened and I have not gained anything except knowing that I came forward and did what I felt that I had an obligation to do and that was to tell the truth.

SEN. LEAHY: And my last question: Would your life be simpler, quieter, far more private had you never come forth at all?

MS. HILL: Yes. Norman, Oklahoma is a much simpler, quieter place than this room today.

SEN. LEAHY: I have a good friend in Norman, Oklahoma and I have actually visited Norman, Oklahoma and I agree with you.

Mr. Chairman, that is all I have.

THE CHAIRMAN: Thank you.

SEN. THURMOND: Senator Specter, do you want to proceed?

SEN. SPECTER: Yes, thank you, Mr. Chairman.

When my time expired we were up to the contact you had with Mr. Brudney on September 9. If you could proceed from there to recount who called you and what those conversations consisted of as it led to your coming forward to the committee?

MS. HILL: Well, we discussed a number of different issues. We discussed one, what he knew about the law on sexual harassment. We discussed what he knew about the process for bringing information forward to the committee. And in the course of our conversations Mr. Brudney asked me what were specifics about what it was that I had experienced.

In addition, we talked about the process for going forward. What might happen if I did bring information to the committee. That included that an investigation might take place, that I might be questioned by the committee in closed session. It even included something to the effect that the information might be presented to the candidate or to the White House. There was some indication that the candidate or, excuse me, the nominee might not wish to continue the process.

SEN. SPECTER: Mr. Brudney said to you that the nominee, Judge Thomas, might not wish to continue the process if you came forward with a statement on the factors which you have testified about?

MS. HILL: Well, I am not sure that that is exactly what he said. I think what he said was, depending on an investigation,the Senate, whether the Senate went into closed session and so forth, it might be that he might not wish to continue the process.

SEN. SPECTER: So Mr. Brudney did tell you that Judge Thomas might not wish to continue to go forward with his nomination, if you came forward?

MS. HILL: Yes.

SEN. SPECTER: Isn't that somewhat different from your testimony this morning?

MS. HILL: My testimony this morning involved my response to this *USA* newspaper report, and the newspaper report suggested that by making the allegations that that would be enough that the candidate would quietly and somehow withdraw from the process. So, no, I do not believe that it is at variance. We talked about a number of different options. But it was never suggested that just by alleging incidents that that might, that that would cause the nominee to withdraw.

SEN. SPECTER: Well, what more could you do than make allegations as to what you said occurred?

MS. HILL: I could not do any more, but this body could.

SEN. SPECTER: Well, but I am now looking at your distinguishing what you have just testified to from what you testified to this morning. This morning I had asked you about just one sentence from the *USA Today* news, "Anita Hill was told by Senate Staffers that her signed affidavit alleging sexual harassment by Clarence Thomas would be the instrument that 'quietly and behind the scenes' would force him to withdraw his name."

And now you are testifying that Mr. Brudney said that if you came forward and made representations as to what you said happened between you and Judge

Thomas, that Judge Thomas might withdraw his nomination?

MS. HILL: I guess, Senator, the difference in what you are saying and what I am saying is that that quote seems to indicate that there would be no intermediate steps in the process. What we were talking about was process. What could happen along the way. What were the possibilities? Would there be a full hearing? Would there be questioning from the FBI? Would there be questioning by some individual members of the Senate?

We were not talking about or even speculating that simply alleging this would cause someone to withdraw.

SEN. SPECTER: Well, if your answer now turns on process, all I can say is that it would have been much shorter had you said, at the outset, that Mr. Brudney told you that if you came forward, Judge Thomas might withdraw. That is the essence as to what occurred.

MS. HILL: No, it is not. I think we differ on our interpretation of what I said.

SEN. SPECTER: Well, what am I missing here?

SEN. KENNEDY: Mr. Chairman, can we let the witness speak in her own words, rather than having words put in her mouth?

SEN. SPECTER: Mr. Chairman, I object to that. I object to that vociferously. I am asking questions here. If Senator Kennedy has anything to say let him participate in this hearing.

THE CHAIRMAN: Now, let everybody calm down. Professor Hill, give your interpretation to what was asked by Senator Specter. And then he can ask you further questions.

MS. HILL: My interpretation—

SEN. THURMOND: Speak into the microphone, so we can hear you.

MS. HILL: [continuing]—I understood Mr. Specter's question to be what kinds of conversation did I have regarding this information. I was attempting, in talking to the staff, to understand how the information would be used, what I would have to do, what might be the outcome of such a use. We talked about a number of possibilities, but there was never any indication that, by simply making these allegations, the nominee would withdraw from the process. No one ever said that and I did not say that anyone ever said that.

We talked about the form that the statement would come in, we talked about the process that might be undertaken post-statement, and we talked about the possibilities of outcomes, and included in that possibility of outcome was that the committee could decide to review the point and that the nomination, the vote could continue, as it did.

SEN. SPECTER: So that, at some point in the process, Judge Thomas might withdraw?

MS. HILL: Again, I would have to respectfully say that is not what I said. That was one of the possibilities, but it would not come from a simple, my simply making an allegation.

SEN. SPECTER: Professor Hill, is that what you meant, when you said earlier, as best I could write it down, that you would control it, so it would not get to this point?

MS. HILL: Pardon me?

SEN. SPECTER: Is that what you meant, when you responded earlier to Senator Biden, that the situation would be controlled "so that it would not get to this point in the hearings"?

MS. HILL: Of the public hearing. In entering into these conversations with the staff members, what I was trying to do was control this information, yes, so that it would not get to this point.

SEN. SPECTER: Thank you very much.

THE CHAIRMAN: Thank you, Senator.

Now, Professor Hill, with your continued indulgence, I will yield to my colleagues, alternating, and limit their questions to five minutes, if I may, and I would begin with my friend from Massachusetts, Senator Kennedy.

SEN. KENNEDY: Thank you, Mr. Chairman. I will just take a moment.

I know this has been an extraordinary long day for you, Professor Hill, and it obviously has been for Judge Thomas, as well, and I know for your family. I just want to pay tribute to both your courage in this whole procedure and for your eloquence and for the dignity with which you have conducted yourself, and, as is quite clear, from observing your comments, for the anguish and pain which you have had to experience today in sharing with millions of Americans. This has been a service and we clearly have to make a judgment. It certainly, I think, has been a very important service.

Let me just say, as far as I am concerned, I think it has been enormously important to millions of Americans. I do not think that this country is ever going to look at sexual harassment the same tomorrow as it has any time in its past. If we are able to make some progress on it, I think history books will show that, to a very important extent, it is because of your action.

The viciousness of harassment is real, it is experienced by millions of people as a form of sex discrimination, and I think all of us are hopeful that we can make progress on it, and I just want you to know that I believe that you have made an important contribution, if we do.

Thank you, Mr. Chairman.

MS. HILL: Thank you.

THE CHAIRMAN: Thank you, Senator.

Senator Thurmond.

SEN. THURMOND: Thank you, Mr. Chairman.

Mr. Chairman, I appointed Senator Specter to question Professor Hill and those supporting her, so I will now yield my time to him.

SEN. SPECTER: Well, with an additional yielding, Mr. Chairman, I would just join in thanking Professor Hill for coming forward. I would join in the comment that this proceeding has been illuminating to tell America what is the law on sexual harassment. That is something which had not been known. From what I have heard in the last few days, there has been a lot of change in conduct in the workplace in this country.

I just would have wished, in retrospect, that we had done this earlier and that this educational process had not come in this forum on a Supreme Court nominee at this stage. But you have answered the questions and I join in thanking you for that.

MS. HILL: Thank you.

THE CHAIRMAN: Senator Metzenbaum.

SEN. METZENBAUM: Ms. Hill, I could not help but think of my own four daughters, as you sat there, and thought to myself how much courage and commitment and concern, but even more, the valor you possess to come before the U.S. Senate and speak out in areas so sensitive, and I am sure are so difficult for you to talk about.

I do not know what impact your testimony will have on the confirmation process, but I know that your testimony will have a tremendous impact on this nation from henceforth. The women of this country, I am certain, owe you a fantastic debt of gratitude for bringing this issue of sexual harassment to the fore.

But as one of those ninety-eight men in the U.S. Senate, I think I speak for all of us when I say we owe you a debt of gratitude, as well, for bringing this issue up to the fore, in a more striking, more sympathetic, more concerned manner than ever before. I think you have made this nation, men and women alike, more enlightened, more aware, more sensitive, and the nation will never be the same, thanks to you.

Thank you.

THE CHAIRMAN: There will be order in the chamber. I am serious when I say that, any outburst at all, no matter how small, will result in police removing whomever does it from the chamber.

Senator Hatch.

SEN. HATCH: Thank you, Mr. Chairman.

I have been pleased to sit here and listen today, and I just want to say one thing, that I apologize to you on behalf of our committee that you had to be heard under these circumstances, because had the committee considered this matter—and I have to say that Chairman Biden and ranking member Thurmond, when they heard about this the first time, they immediately ordered this FBI investigation, which was the very right thing to do, it was the appropriate thing to do and they did what every other chairman and ranking member have done in the past, and the investigation was done and it was a good investigation.

Then Chairman Biden notified everybody on his side and many of us were notified, as well. Any member of the committee, before we voted, could have put this over for a week for consideration, if they were concerned. Any member could have insisted on at least an executive session, where neither of you would have had to have appeared in public, or any member could have insisted on an open session. The committee could have voted.

These FBI reports are extremely important and they have raw data, raw information. They take down what people tell them and that is why they are not to be leaked to the press or anywhere else, and that is why these rules are so important.

And had an appropriate, fair procedure been followed, you would not have been dragged through the media and through all of these other things that both of you have been dragged through, that both of you have suffered from, as you have.

I have to say that I hope I never see that happen again to anybody in any confirmation proceeding, let alone a confirmation for a Justice of the Supreme Court of the United States of America.

Having said that, I wish you well and I won't make any further comments at this time.

THE CHAIRMAN: Thank you very much.

Senator DeConcini.

SEN. DECONCINI: Thank you, Mr. Chairman.

Professor Hill, I join in realizing the difficulty of today's proceedings. It is very obvious and I appreciate that immensely. Sexual harassment is not as new as maybe some members seem to think it is. I just remember, as a young boy, my mother telling me about sexual harassment on her job and losing her job when she was twenty-two years old. So I grew up with that in my mind. She mentioned it several times as I grew in age.

I had dinner with her the night before last and she got choked up just telling me again about it sixty years later.

So, it is a subject that is very sensitive. Obviously, men have a more difficult time, I believe, of understanding it, but I do believe there are many men in this Senate, in the House of Representatives and other political offices that indeed are sensitive as much as a man can be.

Now, one of the areas that intrigued me today was Senator Heflin's questions of motives. I am not at all indicating any diminution of your motive, but I am interested in your answers to some of those.

Before I ask you that, do you see anything positive coming out of what you have been through here today and the last week or so of this ordeal, other than increasing the awareness of sexual harassment in the workplace? Is there any single thing you see more significant than that coming out of this?

MS. HILL: Yes, Senator.

SEN. DECONCINI: What do you see as the most significant public thing coming out of this unfortunate experience that you have had to go through now?

MS. HILL: Other than creating awareness, I see that the information is going to be fully explored, the information that I provided will be fully explored, it will be given a full hearing. In addition, I think that coming out, my coming forward, may encourage other people to come forward, other people who have had the same experiences who have not been able to talk about them.

SEN. DECONCINI: That would be raising the awareness of sexual harassment in the public.

MS. HILL: Raising the awareness, but also giving people courage.

SEN. DECONCINI: And giving people the courage to step forward and do what you did not do ten years ago or six years ago or even two years ago, but you are doing today?

MS. HILL: Yes.

SEN. DECONCINI: Is your motive also an attempt to clear your name from any degrading publicity that has occurred? Do you feel put upon? Do you feel exposed?

MS. HILL: Coming here today?

SEN. DECONCINI: Do you feel injured and damaged as a result of this, even though you obviously have committed yourself to proceed with it?

MS. HILL: You mean my motive in coming here today or something that I think will be a positive thing from coming here today?

SEN. DECONCINI: No, I mean is your motive also to help clarify to the public your own position on sexual harassment, due to the publicity that has resulted from this being brought up to the forefront? Is that one of your motives? Is that one of the reasons you came forward? In other words, was your reputation one of the reasons you came forward? Do you feel that your reputation was being degraded or impugned by the fact that this was printed all over the press and that people were making countercharges and questioning your motives, and what have you? Is that one of the reasons?

MS. HILL: I definitely—coming here today, yes, I did want to accomplish that. There were a number of very ugly and nasty things that have been said, and I did want to come forward and tell my side.

SEN. DECONCINI: Do you think, now having told your side and responded to these questions, that your reputation from your standpoint could ever be fully restored?

MS. HILL: Not in the minds of many, never, it will not be.

SEN. DECONCINI: And in your opinion, Professor Hill, is there any single group or entity that you think caused more damage to you? I am interested in your perception. It seems to me that those who leaked this information certainly caused damage. The press, in my opinion, should be on trial, because they did not have to print this, but they elected to do so. In this country, as we all know they can print anything they want, true or false. Then the committee made a judgment to not address these allegations, and I think that is certainly on trial.

Obviously, Judge Thomas is on trial, though this is not a trial. You are on trial, in the sense of credibility here. Is the committee more culpable for causing you to have to come forward, is the press more culpable, or is everyone equally culpable?

MS. HILL: I think it is just the reality, Senator, of this situation, the nature of this complaint and I cannot point my finger at any one entity and say you are responsible for it.

SEN. DECONCINI: But you said earlier—and correct me if I am wrong—that you did not want today to be what it is, that you had hoped that you could just get the information to this committee, and ultimately you agreed that your name could be used only among the committee members. You had hoped that that would be sufficient for the members to make a judgment, and that you would not have to do what you are doing today. Is that correct?

MS. HILL: Yes.

SEN. DECONCINI: Yes. Now, that did not happen or we would not be here today. Would you repeat why you think we are here? Why did you have to come forward and make this public presentation, when you had hoped just to bring this information to the committee, without having to do what you are doing today?

MS. HILL: Well, I think that there are a number of factors. I think that however the material was leaked, that was one factor. I believe that the press is a factor, but I think, in addition, that the information is just going before the public that wants to know and wants to know about this, and so I think, again, there is a variety of situations and factors that caused this to occur today.

SEN. DECONCINI: Let me ask you this, if I can, Professor Hill: If this information had not been leaked, would you have come forward in this public forum?

MS. HILL: No.

SEN. DECONCINI: If the press had not published or read your statement to you, and left you with the distinct impression that they were going to publish it, would you still have felt obligated to come forward in this public way?

MS. HILL: I do not believe that I would have come forward.

SEN. DECONCINI: You would not have come forward.

MS. HILL: I do not believe I would have.

SEN. DECONCINI: So, it is safe to say that because the information was first leaked and then made public, that you felt that you no longer could proceed with what you originally felt was proper, which was making the information available only to the committee and not in a public forum. Is that a fair statement?

MS. HILL: Yes.

SEN. DECONCINI: Thank you. I won't be very much longer.

Another concern I have is, when you were at the Department of Education and these, in my terms, God-awful things occurred—grotesque, ugly, I don't know how else I can depict them. Obviously they were extremely offensive, and you did not want them to continue, so you attempted to inform the person that you didn't want them to continue. I have a difficult time understanding, and it is obviously because I am not a woman and have not had that kind of personal experience, I have a difficult time understanding, but how could you tolerate that treatment, even though you didn't have another job? I realize that this is part of the whole problem of sexual harassment in the workplace, the fact that women tolerate it.

Maybe you explained this sufficiently, but if you wouldn't mind repeating to me what went through your mind: Why, number one, you would stay there after this happened several times; and, number two, even though it ceased for a few months, why you would proceed on to another job with someone that hadn't just asked you out and pressed you, but had gotten into the explanations and explorations of the anatomy with you?

MS. HILL: Well, I think it is very difficult to understand, Senator, and in hindsight it is even difficult for me to understand, but I have to take the situation as it existed at that time. At that time, staying seemed the only reasonable choice. At that time, staying was the way that—in a way, a choice that I made because I wanted to do the work. I in fact believed that I could make that choice to do the work, and that is what I wanted to do, and I did not want to let that kind of behavior control my choices.

So I attempted to end the behavior, and for some time the behavior did stop. I attempted to make that effort. And so the choice to continue with the same person to another agency involved a belief that I had stopped the behavior that was offensive.

SEN. DECONCINI: Is it safe to say, then, Ms. Hill—based on the readings that I have done in this area by professionals who counsel on it—that you were willing to stuff this inside you and go on with your life and keep it from exploding?

Is that a safe assumption? We all have done that under different circumstances. We stuff certain things in and don't explode or react. Is that one way of describing what you did?

MS. HILL: I did repress a number of my feelings about it, to allow myself to go on and to continue.

SEN. DECONCINI: Is it safe to say that you did this for a long period of time?

MS. HILL: Yes, I did.

SEN. DECONCINI: And you obviously saw Chairman Thomas move on to bigger and better positions, including being appointed to an appellate court judge, and still you did not take any action. Did you, at that time, again repress your feelings and have to keep it down? Do you recall going through that any other time?

MS. HILL: Well, at some point over the last few years, or at various points, I think that I have dealt with many of my repressed feelings about this. I have just dealt with them on my own.

SEN. DECONCINI: You didn't hire or solicit any counseling or any assistance. You just dealt with it on your own?

MS. HILL: Dealt with them on my own.

SEN. DECONCINI: And finally we are here today where it is all over, so to speak. It is all out, not that by any means there won't be repercussions, but you finally have let it all out.

MS. HILL: Well, that is my feeling, but one has to consider that even before this point, I had dealt with the feelings of humiliation, realizing that none of this was my fault, and had dealt with a sense that I was helpless to confront this kind of a situation again, so many of the feelings have been dealt with.

SEN. DECONCINI: And the fact that you admit that in retrospect maybe you should have done something, do you conclude that it is all someone else's fault, and not your own?

MS. HILL: Yes.

SEN. DECONCINI: Is that your frame of mind?

MS. HILL: That is my frame of mind.

SEN. DECONCINI: Thank you.

Thank you, Mr. Chairman, and thank you for the additional time.

THE CHAIRMAN: Thank you very much.

Senator Simpson.

SEN. SIMPSON: Thank you, Mr. Chairman.

Mr. Chairman, there are two additional documents here, and I am asking and take your advice, from the two FBI agents who are—if this has been furnished for over two hours under the rules—the affidavits from the two FBI agents indicating the inconsistencies as expressed by Professor Hill this morning. Is that not appropriate?

THE CHAIRMAN: It is appropriate. The inconsistencies are not of all that much consequence. At some point maybe we should read it. I think it may be helpful for you to read the entire thing in the record.

SEN. SIMPSON: I only have five minutes, Mr. Chairman.

THE CHAIRMAN: No, no. Well, you go ahead and put it in the record and I will read them, because they are not of much consequence, but—let me put it this way—I think people should know what they say.

SEN. SIMPSON: Well, I think that they should know that the witness did not say anything to the FBI about the described size of his penis, the description of the movie *Long Dong Silver*, about the pubic hair in the Coke story, and describing giving pleasure to women with oral sex. That is not part of the original FBI report. And the agents are simply saying that there was no pressure upon the witness, and they specifically say—the woman FBI agent particularly said that she was quite clear that she did not care whether it was general or specific.

The interviewing Special Agent, a woman, said that if the subject was too embarrassing, she did not have to answer, that was Professor Hill's statement, but the Special Agent said that she, the other agent, apologized for the sensitivity of the matter but advised Professor Hill that she should be as specific as possible and give details. She was further advised that if the questions were too embarrassing, Special Agent Luton would leave the room and she could discuss the matter with Special Agent Jameson.

I think that is appropriate only from the standpoint that you describe in your statement so poignantly that these were disgusting things, and yet they did not appear in the FBI report. That is enough. We will enter it into the record.

[The statement referred to follows:]

FEDERAL BUREAU OF INVESTIGATION

Date of transcript 10/11/91

Special Agent (SA) JOHN B. LUTON, Federal Bureau of Investigation, Oklahoma City, Oklahoma, watched the morning session of testimony by Professor ANITA FAYE HILL, before the U. S. Senate, Judiciary Committee, Washington, DC, on October 11, 1991. The following discrepancies were noted regarding her testimony when compared to the statement she provided Special Agents JOHN B. LUTON, and JOLENE SMITH JAMESON, September 23, 1991.

Professor HILL stated that she was advised by the interviewing Agent that she did not have to answer questions if they were too embarrassing as she would possibly be re-interviewed by FBI Agents at a later date. In fact, she was told by Special Agent LUTON to provide the specifics of all incidents. She was also told that it might be necessary to re-interview her at a later time regarding this matter, but that occurred at the end of the interview.

During Professor HILL's testimony before the Senate Judiciary Committee, she referred to numerous telephonic contacts with representatives of that Committee regarding her allegations prior to preparing the Signed Statement. On September 23, 1991, she was asked by the interviewing Special Agents as to what her motivation was for submitting her statement to the Judiciary Committee. She advised the interviewing Agents that she made the decision to prepare the statement after several telephone conversations with her personal friend, SUSAN HOERCHNER. The last telephone conversation between her and HOERCHNER was on a Sunday prior to her preparation of her statement. She did not mention the telephone conversation that she had had with representatives of the Judiciary Committee.

Professor HILL in her testimony identified a number of specific incidents in which Judge CLARENCE THOMAS made embarrassing comments to her about sexual activities. Among these was the reference to Judge Thomas's sexual prowess and size. She made reference to a pornographic movie in which an individual by the name of LONG DONG SILVER played a role. She cited an instance in which she was in his office and he referred to a Coke can and made the statement, "Who left their pubic hair on my Coke," or words to that effect. During the interview on September 23, 1991, Professor HILL did not mention any of the above incidents.

This document contains neither recommendations nor conclusions of FBI. It is the property of the FBI and is loaned to your agency; it and its contents are not to be distributed outside your agency.

FEDERAL BUREAU OF INVESTIGATION

Date of transcription 10/11/91

Special Agent (SA) JOLENE SMITH JAMESON observed the morning session of the testimony to the Senate Judiciary Committee by Professor ANITA HILLL as it was broadcast on CNN on October 11, 1991. During that broadcast, Professor HILL made comments that were in contradiction with statements she had made to SAs JAMESON and JOHN B. LUTON. Those contradictory comments are set forth as follows:

Professor HILL stated she did not discuss specific incidents in detail because the interviewing Special Agent had advised her that, if the subject was too embarrassing, she did not have to answer. In fact, SA LUTON apologized for the sensitivity of the matter, but advised Professor HILL that she should be as specific as possible and give details. She was further advised if the questions were too embarrassing, SA LUTON would leave the room and she could discuss the matter with SA JAMESON.

During the interview with the SAs, Professor HILL stated she could only recall specifics regarding the pornographic incidents involving people in sex acts with each other and with animals. Ms. HILL never mentioned Judge THOMAS saying how well endowed he was. HILL never mentioned or referred to a person named *Long Dong Silver* or any incident involving a Coke can, all of which she testified to before the Senate Judiciary Committee.

Professor HILL stated she had been advised early in the interview that SA LUTON would recontact her at a later time to obtain more specific details. In fact, SA LUTON advised Professor HILL, only at the termination of the interview,that a follow up interview might be necessary if further questions arose.

This document contains neither recommendations nor conclusions of FBI. It is the property of the FBI and is loaned to your agency; it and its contents are not to be distributed outside your agency.

THE CHAIRMAN: I realize that the way we are doing this is a bit unusual. My recollection was, that the witness had acknowledged that they did not appear in the report, and had acknowledged that she had not said that to the agents, as well.

MS. HILL: That is true.

SEN. SIMPSON: Mr. Chairman, you have your opportunity to—

THE CHAIRMAN: No, I just wanted to mention this now because this is unusual, and she hasn't had a chance to see it. Please continue.

SEN. SIMPSON: You are very fair.

Let me ask you, I think both of you say that you—both Judge Thomas and you say you never met each other until 1981. Is that correct?

MS. HILL: That is correct.

SEN. SIMPSON: Weren't you both members of the Black Republican Congressional Staff Association?

MS. HILL: No.

SEN. SIMPSON: You never were?

MS. HILL: No, I never was.

SEN. SIMPSON: Well, I don't have enough time to go into that one. I had heard you were, and that you knew him there, and other people stated that, and perhaps—that is what I was advised by a person who called me who knew you both, and was there with you both, but that is enough.

I am not leaving that out there as some sinister thing. I am just trying to find out if you knew each other before, because I heard that because he knew you there and respected you and enjoyed you there and found you very professional, that it was there he made the contact to then bring you to the Department of Education.

MS. HILL: Which group is this?

SEN. SIMPSON: The Black Republican Congressional Staff Association.

MS. HILL: No, I am not a member of that. I have never been a member of that group.

SEN. SIMPSON: In 1970, 1979, or 1980, some time in there.

MS. HILL: I was in law school in 1979 and 1980.

SEN. SIMPSON: Eighty and eighty-one?

MS. HILL: In eighty, I graduated from law school in 1980 and went to work in private practice here in Washington, DC.

SEN. SIMPSON: Okay, that's good. Thank you. That was presented to me.

Now I heard Howard Metzenbaum say, and you have presented yourself and your testimony in an extraordinary way [*sic*]. I did think that Senator Specter pointed out some inconsistencies. But like Howard, I thought too of my daughter, my rainbow of life, and I would be outraged if such alleged conduct occurred directed to her.

And then I have had the terrible pain of also thinking of my sons, raised by a very enlightened mother, responsive, still kiss their old man good night and things like that, and rather expansive, stalwart boys, and where that kind of conduct could lead them—very troubling for me. Because all we have heard for 103 days is about a most remarkable man, and nobody has come forward, and they scoured his every shred of life, and nobody but you and another witness, apparently who is alleging no sexual harassment, has come forward.

And so maybe, maybe, it seems to me you didn't really intend to kill him, but you might have. And that is pretty heavy, I don't care if you are a man or a woman, to know that forty-three years or thirty-five years of your life or sixty years of your life, where no one has corroborated what is a devastating charge, kind of a singular torpedo below the water line and he sinks, while 103 days of accumulated things never penetrated the armor.

So I guess I would just say it is a very troubling thing to me, it really is, and leave out who leaked what to who or what media person let it out. That all will be hashed. But let me tell you, if what you say this man said to you occurred, why in God's name, when he left his position of power or status or authority over you, and you left in 1983, why in God's name would you ever speak to a man like that the rest of your life?

MS. HILL: That is a very good question, and I am sure that I cannot answer that to your satisfaction. That is one of the things that I have tried to do today. I have suggested that I was afraid of retaliation, I was afraid of damage to my professional life, and I believe that you have to understand that this response—and that is one of the things that I have come to understand about harassment—that this response, this kind of response, is not atypical, and I can't explain. It takes an expert in psychology to explain how that can happen, but it can happen, because it happened to me.

SEN. SIMPSON: Well, it just seems so incredible to me that you would not only have visited with him twice after that period and after he was no longer able to manipulate you or to destroy you, that you then not only visited with him but took him to the airport, and then eleven times contacted him. That part of it appalls me. I would think that these things, what you describe, are so repugnant, so ugly, so obscene, that you would never have talked to him again, and that is the most contradictory and puzzling thing for me.

THE CHAIRMAN: Thank you, Senator.

Senator Simon.

SEN. SIMON: Thank you, Mr. Chairman.

First, Professor Hill, let me say to your parents, you have a daughter you ought to be very, very proud of. I am sure you are proud of your whole family.

I want to underscore what has been said by my colleagues. You have shown great courage and you have handled yourself with dignity, and you have lifted the level of consideration of this whole question of sexual harassment as no one has done before in the history of our country. No matter what happens on the nomination, I think you have performed a real public service.

On the question of sexual harassment, you and I know and the members of this committee know that physical contact is not necessary for sexual harassment, but I have had two people tell me over the phone that there couldn't have been sexual harassment because there was no physical contact. If I can use another analogy that I think people would understand, if you were to receive the kind of language over the telephone that you received in an office, would you consider that an obscene phone call?

MS. HILL: Yes.

SEN. SIMON: And I think everyone understands obscene phone calls.

Let me just ask two totally disconnected questions beyond this: You say in your statement, "In February, 1983 I was hospitalized for five days on an emergency basis for an acute stomach pain which I attributed to stress on the job." One of the things we have to do in this committee, and my colleagues in the Senate have to do, is to make an evaluation, who is telling the truth? This is something objective that happened out there. But when you say "which I attributed to stress on the job," did your physician also suggest this as a possibility?

MS. HILL: My physician suggested that it could be stress-related. They could not identify the nature of the illness. They couldn't give a medical diagnosis, so the physician did suggest that it might be stress-related.

SEN. SIMON: And then, finally—and this has been partially touched upon—but there are those who say the timing of this is all some kind of a plot. That is the term I hear over and over.

I recall calling you the day before our committee voted, when we talked about the possibility of distributing this, your statement, to members of the Senate, and I said, "You can't do that and keep it confidential, and keep your name confidential." I sensed that you were really agonizing on this whole thing, and I think I sensed correctly, for obvious reasons.

But this thing gradually built, from the time you first contacted or had contact with the members of the Senate staff and Senate committee. Was there at any point anyone who suggested, "If you hold this out until the last minute, you could have a great impact on this process"?

MS. HILL: No one ever suggested that, not at all.

SEN. SIMON: And then finally let me just make a suggestion. You are always giving assignments to students at the University of Oklahoma Law School.

If I could give you and your fellow faculty members at the University of Oklahoma Law School and your law students an assignment, we face a very difficult problem, and it is not just with the Thomas nomination. How do we deal with a charge that someone makes, that is a substantial charge, but that person says, "I don't want my name used publicly," or even "I don't want the charge made publicly"? We should not simply ignore it. On the other hand, how are you fair to a nominee?

This is the struggle that this committee has gone through and the Senate is going through. I would be interested in you and your colleagues taking a look at that, sending a letter to members of this committee. But again I thank you. I think you have performed a great public service.

MS. HILL: Thank you.

SEN. SIMON: Thank you, Mr. Chairman.

THE CHAIRMAN: Senator Grassley.

SEN. GRASSLEY: Professor Hill, let me at the outset be very candid and tell you that even though the issues that have been discussed here this afternoon and this morning are very, very important, if I had to ask some of these questions that were asked of you today, I would not be able to do that. It is just not my nature. But I have one question and a couple of comments.

This is in regard to your testifying that you were approached by Senate staff members about disclosing these allegations. My question is whether or not any other individuals or any other organizations other than those who you publicly stated today or otherwise, or Senator Specter stated, whether any other individuals or organizations have approached you about disclosing these matters to the Judiciary Committee any time since Judge Thomas was nominated by the President on July 1st?

MS. HILL: No. No other individual, no other organizations or individuals have approached me to disclose this to anyone. Do you mean prior to the contact from this or even after that?

SEN. GRASSLEY: Or any time during July, August, or September, other than all those names that have already been discussed here today?

MS. HILL: No. No one has urged me to do that or even approached me about it.

SEN. GRASSLEY: Okay.

Now, a couple of points that I would like to make and I suppose I am making these more for my colleagues than I am for anybody else. But one of the hardest parts of this discussion for me is the fact that if any Senate employee had a complaint of sex harassment, that individual would not have the same remedy that you had available to you, Professor Hill, when you were an employee of Government, particularly EEOC, although I know you chose not to pursue that remedy. Because, like so many laws that we pass, the U.S. Senate has exempted itself, as an employer, from the coverage of Title VII, including the EEOC rules governing sex harassment. That is a situation that I hope the Senate will soon change so that our employees will be treated fairly just like any other employees.

On another point there has been much said—and, of course, each of us on this committee have had to deal with this, as the press has asked us how come we did not consider all of these things prior to voting this out of committee. This concerns the process of the Judiciary Committee. People are asking how we could have let your statement slip past us? How could we have had the committee vote without airing this matter? Those are valid questions.

And let me say that I am going to work towards assuring that this never happens again. I realize, of course, that our committee gets hundreds, maybe even thousands of allegations in a nomination like this one. And we rely upon our chairman and ranking member to determine which ones need investigation and which ones might be coming from cranks and crackpots. They determined this one needed investigation and they called in the FBI. But somewhere along the process something broke down.

So I would like to work with the chairman and ranking member and other colleagues to establish a new ground rule. Whenever the FBI is dispatched, every committee member should be notified about the nature of the allegation. And when the FBI has completed its work, every committee member should be notified and have access to that report. And a determination by the committee should be made as to how we need to proceed with any allegations.

A rule like this should ensure, once and for all, that even an eleventh hour charge, like yours, has been fully considered.

I yield the floor.

You can comment if you want to.

MS. HILL: I would like, for a moment, to revisit your first question. I am keenly aware that I want to be certain of my answers. The first question was whether or not anyone had contacted me to urge me to come forward with this?

SEN. GRASSLEY: Yes.

MS. HILL: No. No one did that. Ms. Hoerchner did contact me and reminded me of the situation and we discussed the fact that we had talked about this in earlier years but she did not urge me to come forward at all.

SEN. GRASSLEY: Thank you, Mr. Chairman.

SEN. KENNEDY: [presiding]. Thank you, very much. Of course the state of the law actually is that women, even in these kinds of situations, don't have adequate remedies. All they have is an injunction. They are not permitted to get any damages which is one of the matters that is being addressed in the Civil Rights Bill.

The Senator from Wisconsin.

SEN. KOHL: Thank you, Mr. Chairman

Professor Hill, as you said, this has been a difficult time for you. You wanted to make the committee aware of your experiences with Clarence Thomas but you also wanted to preserve your privacy and that is understandable and we deeply regret that it has not worked out that way. But while the process may have failed you, Professor Hill, you certainly have not failed the process.

For without making, at this time, any judgments about the ultimate truth of your claims we can make a certain judgment about the value of the public discussions that your claims have created. All of us have learned a great deal about and become more sensitive to the problem of sexual harassment and inappropriate behavior. The issue is complex and our understanding may never be complete, but your perception of your relationship with Judge Thomas is clear in your own mind, and your courage in coming forward and the composure you have demonstrated since this issue became public all speak to your character.

I am sure this has been very painful for you, as it has been for all of us, but I believe the pain will vastly improve the way that men and women respond to this problem throughout our country.

Thank you, very much.

MS. HILL: Thank you, Senator Kohl.

SEN. THURMOND: Senator Brown is next on my side.

SEN. BROWN: Thank you, Mr. Chairman.

Professor Hill, you were kind enough to take my call earlier this week and you were very forthcoming and I appreciated that and the information you provided. I had a few additional questions that I thought might be helpful that I would bring up.

My impression was that calls from the staff that had originally prompted you to begin thinking about making a statement included not only questions about sexual harassment but had actually implied to you that there were rumors circulating about sexual harassment at the EEOC and even a suggestion that there might be rumors to sexual harassment related to you.

Now, could you share your view of what those rumors were or what they had suggested to you in those calls?

MS. HILL: Well, when I received the calls I assumed that someone had known about the incidents as they were occurring who I did not know, who might have contacted the offices that called me. So when the statements were made and the questions were asked, I assumed that it was someone who knew that these things had happened and that they had come forward to the committee or to the individuals who were calling and that they were following up on that.

SEN. BROWN: I guess what had occurred to me when I heard that description from you was that—at least the inference in my mind—was that the fact that there were stories or there could be stories circulating relating to sexual harassment, and perhaps the sexual harassment toward you, that that was one of the factors that encouraged you to come forward?

MS. HILL: That was definitely one of the factors. I did not want the committee to rely on rumors. I did not want the rumors to perhaps circulate through the press without at least considering the possibilities or exploring the possibilities through the committee process of coming forward. So, yes, that call, those calls and that raising the issue with me very much encouraged me to further explore the process to determine how and if I could come forward.

SEN. BROWN: You mentioned that you talked to several staffers and then eventually made a decision to come forward and you chatted with the committee and had a variety of conversations there. Were there others that you talked to after you talked to those two staffers and before you decided to speak to the commitee?

MS. HILL: I talked with personal friends. I talked with individuals who knew more about Title VII law than I did.

SEN. BROWN: But I take it none of these conversations included people who were actively opposing the nomination?

MS. HILL: No.

SEN. BROWN: On the employment question, I thought I would go back to it. I must tell you that my own impression is that I think if you have a job you are reluctant to leave it without some other offers, but I thought it might be helpful to put a cap on that. At the point that Judge Thomas was leaving the Department of Education and had invited you to accompany him or go with him in terms of a job assignment over to the EEOC, did you contact anyone in the private sector for a job? You have already talked about not exploring alternatives within the Education Department, but did you contact anyone about a job at that point?

MS. HILL: I did not contact anyone in the private sector. I had left the private sector nine months earlier and decided that I did not want to return at that point, to the private sector.

SEN. BROWN: At the point that the harassment, or at least the harassment was alleged to have taken place at the Department, Education Department, did you begin to explore job opportunities at that point? As I understand that was a point sometime before the decision to leave?

MS. HILL: No. I did not explore. I may have read Government printouts but I did not actively look for another job.

SEN. BROWN: With regard to the judge himself, you clearly, in working with him as you had, were familiar with a portion of his philosophy. Do you find you were in agreement with his philosophy on most issues proposed? What can you share with us on that?

MS. HILL: Well, I am not really sure what his philosophy on many issues is. And so I can't say that I am in agreement or disagreement. I can say that during the times that we were there, worked together, there were matters that we agreed on and some that we did not agree on and we had discussions about those matters.

But I am not really certain what his philosophies are at this point.

SEN. BROWN: Would that be the case with regard to, say, abortion or *Roe v. Wade?*

MS. HILL: That I am not sure of his philosophies?

SEN. BROWN: Sure of his philosophy or do you perceive a significant difference between the two of you in that area?

MS. HILL: Yes.

SEN. BROWN: Can you tell us what that might be? I don't mean to pressure you here. If you would prefer not to, please don't. But if there is something that you could share with us in that area, I think the committee would like to hear it.

THE CHAIRMAN: Senator, from Judge Thomas's position this was supposed to relate to issues of harassment, and was not intended to be an investigation of Judge Thomas's views on abortion.

SEN. BROWN: Mr. Chairman, you are perfectly correct. If there were something that wished to be offered there I thought it would be helpful.

I see the red light is on so I will conclude.

THE CHAIRMAN: Now, two of our primary questioners also want to take an additional five minutes. Senator Leahy and then Senator Specter.

SEN. LEAHY: I will be very brief. I know that everyone is tired. Professor Hill, you were asked questions by Senator Simpson this afternoon regarding the FBI report, which I believe you were shown, and about the question of whether there may be some inconsistencies. Everybody has to determine whether they feel there are or are not, I make no statement to that. Basically, the thrust was that you were less specific about these incidents—the language and the description of these two incidents—when you talked to the two agents than you were in your statement, here today.

Let me just ask three or four very quick questions and I think probably you could just answer, "yes" or "no".

The statement that you made here today was made under oath, is that correct?

MS. HILL: Yes.

SEN. LEAHY: And that statement was more specific than the conversation that you had with the FBI agents, is that correct?

MS. HILL: Yes, I agree.

SEN. LEAHY: And when specific questions were asked by different Senators about that, you went into even more specific details of the language that you say that Judge Thomas used, is that correct?

MS. HILL: Yes.

SEN. LEAHY: And if there had been even more questions going specifically conversation by conversation it would be safe to say that you would have had even more specific language?

MS. HILL: I would have attempted to.

SEN. LEAHY: It would be safe to say, also, that you found it uncomfortable repeating even the language that we elicited from you in the questions?

MS. HILL: Yes.

SEN. LEAHY: Thank you.

I have no further questions.

THE CHAIRMAN: Thank you.

Senator Specter.

SEN. SPECTER: Thank you, Mr. Chairman.

Just a word or two. Professor Hill, when you say that by hindsight—because I wrote this down, it is difficult for me to understand. In looking at the entire record, it is difficult for me to understand. You have substantially enlarged a testimony which I had expected based on the FBI report and your statement as to what you allege Judge Thomas had done. The critical move from the Department of Education to the EEOC is not understandable to me, where you make the statements about his offensive conduct. For an experienced lawyer not to inquire about standing, or even an inexperienced lawyer not to inquire about standing to stay at the Department of Education or not to make an inquiry of the people in charge.

The toll calls you characterized as garbage—which you admitted to in your interviews with the newspaper, although you denied other aspects—you now concede to be true, you did make those calls. It is one thing for you to say that you felt constrained to maintain some sort of an association with Judge Thomas in the face of this kind of conduct which you have represented, but why make the calls which you agreed to, the how are you doing, or I am in town, or tell the secretary you are in town? Why drive the man to the airport? Why maintain that kind of a cordial association in the face of this kind of conduct?

We have an office, equal opportunities, EEOC, to enforce the laws on sexual harassment. And we have here representations that the nation's chief law enforcement officer sexually harassed his attorney advisor. That attorney advisor is dedicated to enforcement of the law against sexual harassment and tells us that she moved from the Department of Education to EEOC because she wanted to protect the women of America. And conceding that this is an enormous educational experience, the question is why with an experienced lawyer in that position being concerned about women's rights, do you leave a man, Clarence Thomas, as chairman of the EEOC for years, when according to your testimony he has been guilty of sexual harassment himself?

Now, I do see explanations at every turn. And I have wondered about the quality of those explanations, candidly. But there is no description for this entire proceeding other than a tragedy. I do not know how Judge Thomas defends himself beyond stepping forward and saying that he is shocked, surprised, hurt, and saddened. And the shortest statute of limitations I have ever heard of is 180 days.

Until I got involved in this proceeding I did not know there was such a short statute of limitations. Contract cases are six years, tort cases are two years, criminal cases are five years, but the Federal law has put that into effect because it is so difficult to defend and to go back and to recollect all that has happened. And I appreciate the stark nature of the statements which have been made.

But I also see that your own statement that you prepared in your leisure—put aside the FBI statement—you were with two people, but no mention about the Coke bottle, no mention about sexual prowess, no mention about other major issues which are in your statement. So I conclude, from looking at this very complex day on our obligation to try to find out what happened between a man and a woman long ago, and nobody else was there, that I would agree with you, Professor Hill, it is very difficult for me to understand.

THE CHAIRMAN: Thank you, Senator.

The Senator from North Carolina—South Carolina, I beg your pardon.

SEN. THURMOND: Well, don't forget it. [Laughter.]

THE CHAIRMAN: I realize there are certain things I should never say to the Senator from South Carolina, and one of them is that he is from North Carolina.

SEN. THURMOND: Mr. Chairman, I just have one brief question.

Professor Hill, I understand you told the FBI that you had concerns about the political philosophy of Judge Thomas and that he may no longer be open-minded. Is that accurate?

MS. HILL: I told them that I did not quite understand, but as they had been represented, yes, that I did have some concerns.

SEN. THURMOND: I have the FBI report here, and I just wondered if you remember telling them that.

MS. HILL: I remember discussion about political philosophy and I remember specifically saying that I'm not quite sure that we understand his political philosophies. But based on what I understand, yes, there is some discomfort.

SEN. THURMOND: That is all, Mr. Chairman.

THE CHAIRMAN: Thank you.

Now, let me just say, Professor Hill, we have heard in a sense the half of this story today, all of your story, and we have not heard all of Judge Thomas's story.

But I, for one, can assure you that, assuming for the moment what you have said is true, there is nothing hard to understand. Having spent as many years as I have dealing with the issue of victimization and victimization of women, I have seen that every single psychiatrist and psychologist who considers himself or herself an expert in the field will point out that the nature of response is not at all atypical, assuming it to be true—and please do not be offended by my saying "assuming it to be true." I view myself again here as a finder of fact and we have yet to hear the whole story from Judge Thomas.

This is a tragedy; and people keep mentioning that, and my good friend from Iowa hopes that this will never happen again in the sense of the way the committee handled it.

I must be brutally frank with my colleagues and with everyone else involved: I do apologize to the women of America, if they got the wrong impression about how seriously I take the issue of sexual harassment, but I make no apologies for attempting to follow every one of your wishes, because everyone that I have spoken to, again, in the years that I have dealt with this subject indicate that the most unfair thing to do to a woman in your position is what was done to you, force you to do something that you did not intend to do.

So, I must tell you and I must tell everyone else, I take sexual harassment seriously, but I take your claim, and took your claim that you have reasserted here today half a dozen times that you did not want this to go public, as seriously as I possibly could. For those who suggest that there was some way to do it differently and still honor your commitment, I respond that I know of no such way to guarantee your anonymity, or to guarantee you would not have to be in this place on this day.

I must tell you, every instinct in me in the world wanted to say to the whole Senate and to the whole world that we should have a hearing on this. But again, we tend to look at large issues and forget individuals. You were the individual in the middle of this, and I will say again to anyone who will listen, as long as I am chairman of this committee, if a person comes to me in a similar circumstance and says repeatedly and in different ways that I have no authority to tell their story, to leak their story, to demand that their story be put in a context different than they wish, I will honor that commitment.

I appreciate the fact, and to be very, very blunt about it, I can't tell you how thankful I am, purely from a personal standpoint—and I should not say this, but I am going to say it anyway—that you were so straightforward and honest about the way in which this committee handled your request, and so straightforward and honest about, notwithstanding occasional confusion, how you did not decide to do what is being done here, and were it not for the fact that it was leaked to a press person, you would not be here today.

It seems to me, ultimately, in this great giant machine we call this Nation and this Government, that I don't know how we can call ourselves civil libertarians, I don't know how we can call ourselves people interested in the individual, if, in the name of a larger cause to justify the ends, we make a judgment for an individual that that individual chooses and has a right not to make.

So, I must tell you. I admire you. I admire the way you handled this matter once you were confronted with it. As I said to you very bluntly over the telephone, all of us up here choose to be in this business, we choose to be under these lights, we choose to be under the scrutiny of those ladies and gentlemen sitting behind you, we choose to go before the American public and say "judge me," but we have no right to make you choose to do that.

Once you chose to do that, because you had no choice, you handled it with such grace and such elan that I can't quite understand how you were able to pull it off in the sense of walking before all those press people in the press conference and handling it the way you did. I don't know three candidates in my whole life who could do that, and they have had twenty-seven handlers telling them how to do it. So, I don't want to kid anybody. If you came to me again in the same circumstance and said, "Senator Biden, keep this tight, do not make it go public," I would do the same thing again. I thank you for your honesty in laying out just what you did, because you could have very easily said, "Oh, no, I would have come forward no matter what, I was getting ready to do that," and, quite frankly, made me look like an idiot.

I thank you very, very much. We can all talk about the process, it is a cumbersome one, but, ultimately, it seems that the purpose of the process is to protect the rights of individuals.

I thank you for being willing to be here. I thank you for your testimony.

We will now recess—

SEN. HEFLIN: Mr. Chairman?

THE CHAIRMAN: I will yield in just a moment.

Judge Thomas has indicated he wants very much to come back on this evening, so we will reconvene this hearing at 9 o'clock to hear from Judge Thomas.

Before we do, I yield to my friend from Alabama, who wants to submit for the record some—well, I will let him say what he wants to do.

SEN. HEFLIN: Mr. Chairman, I want to submit certain newspaper articles that have appeared for the record.

These are from *The Washington Post*, October 11, 1991, and the headline is "Thomas's View Of Harassment Said to Evolve"; from *The Baltimore Sun*, dated October 11, 1991, "Thomas-Hill Disputes"; from *The New York Times*, on October 10, 1991, "Stark Conflict Marks Accounts Given by Thomas and Professor"; *The Washington Post*, of the same date, "Conflict Emerges Over A Second Witness"; from *The Washington Post*, October 11, 1991, "Charlotte Woman Details Thomas's Conduct"; from *The New York Times*, October 7, 1991, "Law Professor Accuses Thomas Of Sexual Harassment in 1980's"; and from *The U.S. News & World Report*, September 16, 1991, an article entitled "The Crowning Thomas Affair."

THE CHAIRMAN: Without objection, they will be made a part of the record.

Again, I thank your family—

MS. HILL: Mr. Chairman?

THE CHAIRMAN: Yes?

MS. HILL: I would just like to take this opportunity to thank the committee for its time, its questions and the efforts that it has put into this investigation on my behalf.

Thank you.

THE CHAIRMAN: Thank you.

We are adjourned until 9 o'clock.

[Whereupon, at 7:40 p.m., the committee was recessed, to reconvene at 9 p.m., the same day.]

EVENING SESSION

THE CHAIRMAN: The committee will please come to order.

Judge, it is a tough day and a tough night for you, I know. Let me ask, do you have anything you would like to say before we begin?

I understand that your preference is, which is totally and completely understandable, that we go one hour tonight, thirty minutes on each side. Am I correct in that?

JUDGE THOMAS: That is right.

FURTHER TESTIMONY OF HON. CLARENCE THOMAS, OF GEORGIA, TO BE ASSOCIATE JUSTICE OF THE U.S. SUPREME COURT

THE CHAIRMAN: Do you have anything you would like to say?

JUDGE THOMAS: Senator, I would like to start by saying unequivocally, uncategorically that I deny each and every single allegation against me today that suggested in any way that I had conversations of a sexual nature or about pornographic material with Anita Hill, that I ever attempted to date her, that I ever had any personal sexual interest in her, or that I in any way ever harassed her.

Second, and I think a more important point, I think that this today is a travesty. I think that it is disgusting. I think that this hearing should never occur in America. This is a case in which this sleaze, this dirt, was searched for by staffers of members of this committee, was then leaked to the media, and this committee and this body validated it and displayed it in prime time over our entire nation.

How would any member on this committee or any person in this room or any person in this country would like sleaze said about him or her in this fashion or this dirt dredged up and this gossip and these lies displayed in this manner? How would any person like it?

The Supreme Court is not worth it. No job is worth it. I am not here for that. I am here for my name, my family, my life and my integrity. I think something is dreadfully wrong with this country, when any person, any person in this free country would be subjected to this. This is not a closed room.

There was an FBI investigation. This is not an opportunity to talk about difficult matters privately or in a closed environment. This is a circus. It is a national disgrace. And from my standpoint, as a black American, as far as I am concerned, it is a high-tech lynching for uppity blacks who in any way deign to think for themselves, to do for themselves, to have different ideas, and it is a message that, unless you kow-tow to an old order, this is what will happen to you, you will be lynched, destroyed, caricatured by a committee of the U.S. Senate, rather than hung from a tree.

THE CHAIRMAN: We will have—

SEN. THURMOND: Mr. Chairman?

THE CHAIRMAN: The Senator from South Carolina.

SEN. THURMOND: I have named Senator Hatch to cross-examine the judge and those who are supporting him.

SEN. HATCH: As I understand it, it was—

THE CHAIRMAN: I think that is correct. I think we would start with Senator Heflin and then go to Senator Hatch.

SEN. HATCH: I think that is the way I was—I would be happy to do it, but I think that is the way I was told.

THE CHAIRMAN: Senator Heflin.

SEN. HEFLIN: Judge Thomas, in addition to Anita Hill, there have surfaced some other allegations against you. One was on a television show last evening here in Washington, Channel 7. I don't know whether you saw that or not?

JUDGE THOMAS: No.

SEN. HEFLIN: You didn't see it. It was carried somewhat in the print media today, but it involved a man by the name of Earl Harper, Jr., who allegedly was a senior trial lawyer with the EEOC at Baltimore in or around the early 1980's. Do you recall this instance pertaining to Earl Harper, Jr.?

JUDGE THOMAS: I remember the name. I can't remember the details.

SEN. HEFLIN: The allegations against Mr. Harper involved some twelve or thirteen women who claim that Mr. Harper made unwelcome sexual advances to several women on his staff, including instances in which Mr. Harper masturbated in the presence of some of the female employees. The allegations contain other aspects of sexual activity.

The information we have is that the General Counsel of the EEOC, David Slate, made a lengthy internal investigation and found that this had the effect of creating an intimidating, hostile and offensive working environment, and that on November 23, 1983, you wrote Mr. Slate a memo urging that Mr. Harper be fired. Mr. Slate eventually recommended dismissal. Then the story recites that you did not dismiss him, you allowed him to stay on for eleven months and then he retired.

Does that bring back to you any recollection of that event concerning Mr. Earl Harper, Jr.?

JUDGE THOMAS: Again, I am operating strictly on recollection. If I remember the case, if it is the one I am thinking of, Mr. Harper's supervisor recommended either suspension or some form of sanction or punishment that was less than termination.

When that proposal—the supervisor initially was not David Slate—when that proposal reached my desk, I believe my recommendation was that, for the conduct involved, he should be fired. The problem there was that if the immediate supervisor's decision is changed—and I believe Mr. Harper was a veteran—there are a number of procedural protections that he had, including a hearing and, of course, he had a lawyer and there was potential litigation, et cetera.

I do not remember all of the details, but it is not as simple as you set it out. It was as a result of my insistence that the General Counsel, as I remember, upgraded the sanction to termination.

SEN. HEFLIN: Do you know a Congressman by the name of Scott Kluge, a Republican Congressman who was defeated by Robert Kastenmeier of Wisconsin, who now serves in Congress, who back in the early 1980's, 1983 or something, was a television reporter for a channel here in Washington and that he at that time disclosed this as indicating that, after the recommendation of dismissal, that you did not move in regards to it for some eleven months and let him retire? Do you know Congressman Kluge?

JUDGE THOMAS: I do not know him. Again, remember, I am operating on recollection. There was far more to it than the facts as you set them out. His rights had much to do with the fact that he was a veteran and that we could not simply dismiss him. If we could, that was my recommendation, he would have been dismissed.

SEN. HEFLIN: There was no political influence brought to bear on you at that time to prevent his dismissal? Do you recall if any political—

JUDGE THOMAS: There was absolutely no political influence. In fact, it was my policy that no personnel decisions would in any way be changed or influenced by political pressure, one way or the other.

SEN. HEFLIN: Now, it is reported to me that Congressman Kluge, after your nomination, went to the White House and told this story and, I hear by hearsay, that the White House ignored his statement and that Congressman Kluge further came to the Senate Judiciary Committee and made it known here.

As far as I know, I attempted to check—I have not been able to find where it was in the Judiciary Committee, if it was, and I think the chairman has attempted to locate it—but the point I am asking is, in the whole process pertaining to the nomination and the preparation for it, were you ever notified that Congressman Kluge went to the White House in regards to this?

JUDGE THOMAS: I do not remember that, Senator.

SEN. HEFLIN: Nobody ever discussed that?

JUDGE THOMAS: No.

SEN. HEFLIN: Well, that is the way it has been reported to me and it is very fragmented relative to it, but I have asked that all the records of the EEOC be subpoenaed by *subpoena duces tecum* pertaining to that, in order that we might get to the bottom of it.

SEN. HATCH: Mr. Chairman, if I could interrupt Senator Heflin, I really think this is outside the scope, under the rules. I would have to object to it.

THE CHAIRMAN: I would have to sustain that objection. I do not—

SEN. HATCH: I hesitate to object, but I just think we ought to keep it on the subject matter.

THE CHAIRMAN: I do not see where it is relevant.

SEN. HEFLIN: Well, I think it is relevant in the issue pertaining to the period of time relative to the issue, particularly in regards to the responsibilities as head of the agency dealing with discrimination in employment.

SEN. HATCH: Mr. Chairman—

THE CHAIRMAN: If I may say—

SEN. HATCH: Mr. Chairman—

THE CHAIRMAN: If I may speak, let me say this is not about whether the judge administered the agency properly. The only issue here relates to conduct and the allegations that have been made, so I would respectfully suggest to my friend from Alabama that that line of questioning is not in order and I rule it out of order.

SEN. HEFLIN: All right, sir, I will reserve an exception, as we used to say.

Now, I suppose you have heard Professor Hill, Ms. Hill, Anita F. Hill testify today.

JUDGE THOMAS: No, I haven't.

SEN. HEFLIN: You didn't listen?

JUDGE THOMAS: No, I didn't. I have heard enough lies.

SEN. HEFLIN: You didn't listen to her testimony?

JUDGE THOMAS: No, I didn't.

SEN. HEFLIN: On television?

JUDGE THOMAS: No, I didn't. I've heard enough lies. Today is not a day that, in my opinion, is high among the days in our country. This is a travesty. You spent the entire day destroying what it has taken me forty-three years to build and providing a forum for that.

SEN. HEFLIN: Judge Thomas, you know we have a responsibility too, and as far as I am involved, I had nothing to do with Anita Hill coming here and testifying. We are trying to get to the bottom of this. And, if she is lying, then I think you can help us prove that she was lying.

JUDGE THOMAS: Senator, I am incapable of proving the negative that did not occur.

SEN. HEFLIN: Well, if it did not occur, I think you are in a position, with certainly your ability to testify, in effect, to try to eliminate it from people's minds.

JUDGE THOMAS: Senator, I didn't create it in people's minds. This matter was investigated by the Federal Bureau of Investigation in a confidential way. It was then leaked last weekend to the media. I did not do that. And how many members of this committee would like to have the same scurrilous, uncorroborated allegations made about him and then leaked to national newspapers and then be drawn and dragged before a national forum of this nature to discuss those allegations that should have been resolved in a confidential way?

SEN. HEFLIN: Well, I certainly appreciate your attitude towards leaks. I happen to serve on the Senate Ethics Committee and it has been a sieve.

JUDGE THOMAS: But it didn't leak on me. This leaked on me and it is drowning my life, my career and my integrity, and you can't give it back to me, and this committee can't give it back to me, and this Senate can't give it back to me. You have robbed me of something that can never be restored.

SEN. DECONCINI: I know exactly how you feel.

SEN. HEFLIN: Judge Thomas, one of the aspects of this is that she could be living in a fantasy world. I don't know. We are just trying to get to the bottom of all of these facts.

But if you didn't listen and didn't see her testify, I think you put yourself in an unusual position. You are, in effect, defending yourself, and basically some of us want to be fair to you, fair to her, but if you didn't listen to what she said today, then that puts it somewhat in a more difficult task to find out what the actual facts are relative to this matter.

JUDGE THOMAS: The facts keep changing, Senator. When the FBI visited me, the statements to this committee and the questions were one thing. The FBI's subsequent questions were another thing. And the statements today, as I received summaries of them, are another thing.

I am not—it is not my fault that the facts change. What I have said to you is categorical that any allegations that I engaged in any conduct involving sexual activity, pornographic movies, attempted to date her, any allegations, I deny. It is not true.

So the facts can change but my denial does not. Ms. Hill was treated in a way that all my special assistants were treated, cordial, professional, respectful.

SEN. HEFLIN: Judge, if you are on the bench and you approach a case where you appear to have a closed mind and that you are only right, doesn't it raise issues of judicial temperament?

JUDGE THOMAS: Senator? Senator, there is a difference between approaching a case objectively and watching yourself being lynched. There is no comparison whatsoever.

SEN. HATCH: I might add, he has personal knowledge of this as well, and personal justification for anger.

SEN. HEFLIN: Judge, I don't want to go over this stuff but, of course, there are many instances in which she has stated, but—and, in effect, since you didn't see her testify I think it is somewhat unfair to ask you specifically about it.

I would reserve my time and go ahead and let Senator Hatch ask you, and then come back.

THE CHAIRMAN: Senator Hatch?

SEN. HATCH: Judge Thomas, I have sat here and I have listened all day long, and Anita Hill was very impressive. She is an impressive law professor. She is a Yale Law graduate. And, when she met with the FBI, she said that you told her about your sexual experiences and preferences. And I hate to go into this but I want to go into it because I have to, and I know that it is something that you wish you had never heard at any time or place. But I think it is important that we go into it and let me just do it this way.

She said to the FBI that you told her about your sexual experiences and preferences, that you asked her what she liked or if she had ever done the same thing, that you discussed oral sex between men and women, that you discussed viewing films of people having sex with each other and with animals, and that you told her that she should see such films, and that you would like to discuss specific sex acts and the frequency of sex.

What about that?

JUDGE THOMAS: Senator, I would not want to, except being required to here, to dignify those allegations with a response. As I have said before, I categorically deny them. To me, I have been pilloried with scurrilous allegations of this nature. I have denied them earlier and I deny them tonight.

SEN. HATCH: Judge Thomas, today in a new statement, in addition to what she had told the FBI, which I have to agree with you is quite a bit, she made a number of other allegations and what I would like to do is—some of them most specifically were for the first time today in addition to these, which I think almost anybody would say are terrible. And I would just like to give you an opportunity, because this is your chance to address her testimony.

At any time did you say to Professor Hill that she could ruin your career if she talked about sexual comments you allegedly made to her?

JUDGE THOMAS: No.

SEN. HATCH: Did you say to her in words or substance that you could ruin her career?

JUDGE THOMAS: No.

SEN. HATCH: Should she ever have been afraid of you and any kind of vindictiveness to ruin her career?

JUDGE THOMAS: Senator, I have made it my business to help my special assistants. I recommended Ms. Hill for her position at Oral Roberts University. I have always spoken highly of her.

I had no reason prior to the FBI visiting me a little more than two weeks ago to know that she harbored any ill feelings toward me or any discomfort with me. This is all new to me.

SEN. HATCH: It is new to me too, because I read the FBI report at least ten or fifteen times. I didn't see any of these allegations I am about to go into, including that one. But she seemed to sure have a recollection here today.

Now, did you ever say to Professor Hill in words or substance, and this is embarrassing for me to say in public, but it has to be done, and I am sure it is not pleasing to you.

Did you ever say in words or substance something like there is a pubic hair in my Coke?

JUDGE THOMAS: No, Senator.

SEN. HATCH: Did you ever refer to your private parts in conversations with Professor Hill?

JUDGE THOMAS: Absolutely not, Senator.

SEN. HATCH: Did you ever brag to Professor Hill about your sexual prowess?

JUDGE THOMAS: No, Senator.

SEN. HATCH: Did you ever use the term "Long Dong Silver" in conversation with Professor Hill?

JUDGE THOMAS: No, Senator.

SEN. HATCH: Did you ever have lunch with Professor Hill at which you talked about sex or pressured her to go out with you?

JUDGE THOMAS: Absolutely not—

SEN. HATCH: Did you ever tell—

JUDGE THOMAS: [continuing]— I have had no such discussions, nor have I ever pressured or asked her to go out with me beyond her work environment.

SEN. HATCH: Did you ever tell Professor Hill that she should see pornographic films?

JUDGE THOMAS: Absolutely not.

SEN. HATCH: Did you ever talk about pornography with Professor Hill?

JUDGE THOMAS: I did not discuss any pornographic material or pornographic preferences or pornographic films with Professor Hill.

SEN. HATCH: So you never even talked or described pornographic materials with her?

JUDGE THOMAS: Absolutely not.

SEN. HATCH: Amongst those or in addition?

JUDGE THOMAS: What I have told you is precisely what I told the FBI on September 25 when they shocked me with the allegations made by Anita Hill.

SEN. HATCH: Judge Thomas, those are a lot of allegations. Those are a lot of charges, talking about sexual experiences and preferences, whether she liked it or had ever done the same thing, oral sex, viewing films of people having sex with each other and with animals, that maybe she should see such films, discuss specific sex acts, talk about pubic hair in Coke, talking about your private parts, bragging about sexual prowess, talking about particular pornographic movies.

Let me ask you something. You have dealt with these problems for a long time. At one time I was the chairman of the committee overseeing the EEOC and, I might add, the Department of Education, and I am the ranking member today. I have known you for eleven years and you are an expert in sexual harassment. Because you are the person who made the arguments to then-Solicitor General Fried that the Administration should strongly take a position on sexual harassment in the *Meritor Savings Bank v. Vinson* case, and the Supreme Court adopted your position.

Did I misstate that?

JUDGE THOMAS: Senator, what you have said is substantially accurate. What I attempted to do in my discussions with the Solicitor is to have them be aggressive in that litigation, and EEOC was very instrumental in the success in the *Meritor* case.

SEN. HATCH: Now, Judge, keep in mind that the statute of limitations under Title VII for sexual harassment for private employers is 180 days or six months. But the statute of limitations under Title VII for Federal employers and employees is thirty days.

Are you aware of that?

JUDGE THOMAS: Yes, Senator, I am generally aware of those limitations.

SEN. HATCH: And are you aware of why those statutes of limitation are so short?

JUDGE THOMAS: I would suspect that at some point it would have to do with the decision by this body that either memories begin to fade or stories change, perhaps individuals move around, and that it would be more difficult to litigate them.

I don't know precisely what all of the rationale is.

SEN. HATCH: Well, it involves the basic issue of fairness, just exactly how you have described it. If somebody is going to be accused in a unilateral declaration of sexual harassment, then that somebody ought to be accused through either a complaint or some sort of a criticism, so that that somebody can be informed and then respond to those charges, and, if necessary, change that somebody's conduct. Is that a fair statement?

JUDGE THOMAS: I think that is a fair statement.

SEN. HATCH: Now let me ask you something: I described all kinds of what I consider to be gross, awful sexually harassing things, which if you take them cumulatively have to gag anybody. Now you have seen a lot of these sexual harassment cases as you have served there at the EEOC. What is your opinion with regard to what should have been done with those charges, and whether or not you believe that, let's take Professor Hill in this case, should have done something, since she was a Yale Law graduate who taught civil rights law at one point, served in these various agencies, and had to understand that there is an issue of fairness here.

JUDGE THOMAS: Senator, if any of those activities occur, it would seem to me to clearly suggest or to clearly indicate sexual harassment, and anyone who felt that she was harassed could go to an EEO officer at any agency and have that dealt with confidentially. At the Department of Education, if she said it occurred there, or at EEOC, those are separate tracks. At EEOC, I do not get to review those, if they involve me, and at Department of Education there is a separate EEO officer for the whole department. It would have nothing to do with me. But if I were an individual advising a person who had been subjected to that treatment, I would advise her to immediately go to the EEO officer.

SEN. HATCH: An EEO office then would bring the parties together, or at least would confront the problem head-on, wouldn't it?

JUDGE THOMAS: The EEO officer would provide counseling—

SEN. HATCH: Within a short period of time?

JUDGE THOMAS:[continuing]—within a short period of time, as well as, I think, if necessary, an actual charge would be—

SEN. HATCH: So the charge would be made, and the charge would then—the person against whom it was made would have a chance to answer it right then, right up front, in a way that could resolve it and stop this type of activity if it ever really occurred?

JUDGE THOMAS:[continuing]. That is right.

SEN. HATCH: And you have just said it never really occurred.

JUDGE THOMAS: It never occurred. That is why there was no charge.

SEN. HATCH: You see, one of the problems that has bothered me from the front of this thing is, these are gross. Cumulative, I don't know why anybody would put up with them, or why anybody would respect or work with another person who would do that. And if you did that, I don't know why anybody would work with you who suffered these treatments.

JUDGE THOMAS: I agree.

SEN. HATCH: Furthermore, I don't know why they would have gone to a different position with you, even if they did think that maybe it had stopped and it won't start again, but then claimed that it started again. And then when they finally got out into the private sector, wouldn't somehow or other confront these problems in three successive confirmation proceedings. Does that bother you?

JUDGE THOMAS: This whole affair bothers me, Senator. I am witnessing the destruction of my integrity.

SEN. HATCH: And it is by a unilateral set of declarations that are made on successive dates, and differ, by one person who continued to maintain what she considered to be a "cordial professional relationship" with you over a ten-year period.

JUDGE THOMAS: Senator, my relationship with Anita Hill prior to September 25 was cordial and professional, and I might add one other thing. If you really want an idea of how I treated women, then ask the majority of the women who worked for me. They are out here. Give them as much time as you have given one person, the only person who has been on my staff who has ever made these sorts of allegations about me.

SEN. HATCH: Well, I think one of our Senators, one of our better Senators in the U.S. Senate, did do exactly that, and he is a Democrat, as a matter of fact, one of the fairest people and I think one of the best new people in the whole Senate.

This is a statement that was made on the floor of the Senate in this Record by my distinguished colleague, Senator Lieberman, a man I have a great deal of respect for. Senator Lieberman's staff conducted a survey of various women who have worked for you over the years. He was concerned. He has been a supporter of yours, and he was one who asked for this delay so that this could be looked into because he was concerned, too.

But as a result of the survey, Senator Lieberman made the following statement: He said, "I have contacted associates, women who worked with Judge Thomas during his time at the Department of Education and EEOC, and in the calls that I and my staff have made there has been universal support for Judge Thomas and a clear indication by all of the women we spoke to that there was never, certainly not a case of sexual harassment, and not even a hint of impropriety." That was put into the Congressional Record on October 8, 1991.

And I think Senator Lieberman has performed a very valuable service because he is in the other party. He is a person who looks at these matters seriously. He has to be as appalled by this type of accusation as I am, and frankly he wanted to know, "Just what kind of a guy is Clarence Thomas?" And those of us who know you, know that all of these are inconsistent with the real Clarence Thomas.

And I don't care who testifies, you have to keep in mind, this is an attorney, a law graduate from one of the four or five best law schools in this land, a very intelligent, articulate law professor, and the only person on earth other than you knowing whether these things are true—the only other person. I don't blame you for being mad.

JUDGE THOMAS: Senator, I have worked with hundreds of women in different capacities. I have promoted and mentored dozens. I will put my record against any member of this committee in promoting and mentoring women.

SEN. HATCH: I will put your record against anybody in the whole Congress.

JUDGE THOMAS: And I think that if you want to really be fair, you parade every single one before you and you ask them, in their relationships with me, whether or not any of this nonsense, this garbage, trash that you siphoned out of the sewers against me, whether any of it is true. Ask them. They have worked with me. Ask my chief of staff, my former chief of staff. She worked shoulder to shoulder with me.

SEN. HATCH: Well, I think we should do that.

Now, Judge, what was Professor Hill's role in your office at the Education Department and at the EEOC?

JUDGE THOMAS: Senator, as I indicated this morning, at the Department of Education Ms. Hill was an attorney-adviser. I had a small staff and she had the opportunity to work on a variety of issues.

SEN. HATCH: She was your number one person?

JUDGE THOMAS: By and large, on substantive issues, she was.

SEN. HATCH: How about when you went to the EEOC?

JUDGE THOMAS: At EEOC that role changed drastically. As I indicated, my duties expanded immensely. EEOC, as you remember, had enormous management problems, so I focused on that. I also needed an experienced EEO staff, and my staff was much more mature. It was older. It was a more experienced staff.

As a result, she did not enjoy that close a relationship with me, nor did she have her choice of the better assignments, and I think that as a result of that there was some concern on her part that she was not being treated as well as she had been treated prior to that.

SEN. HATCH: At any time in your tenure in the Department of Education, did Professor Hill ever express any concern about or discomfort with your conduct toward her?

JUDGE THOMAS: No.

SEN. HATCH: Never?

JUDGE THOMAS: No. The only caveat I would add to that would be that from time to time people want promotions or better assignments or work hours, something of that nature, but no discomfort of the nature that is being discussed here today.

SEN. HATCH: Now I note that Professor Hill alleges improper conduct on your part during the period of November, 1981 to February or March of 1982. Now isn't it true that both you and Professor Hill moved from the Education Department to the EEOC in April of that same year?

JUDGE THOMAS: Senator, that is an odd period. The President expressed his intent to nominate me to become Chairman of EEOC in February 1982, and during that very same period, to the best of my recollection, she assisted me in my nomination and confirmation process. I did in fact leave actual work at the Department of Education, I believe in April, and started at EEOC in May 1982, and she transferred with me.

SEN. HATCH: So, in other words, Professor Hill followed you to the EEOC no more than two or three months, possibly only one month after she claims this alleged conduct occurred.

JUDGE THOMAS: Precisely.

SEN. HATCH: Isn't it true, Judge Thomas, that Professor Hill could have remained in her job at the Education Department when you went to the EEOC?

JUDGE THOMAS: To the best of my recollection, she was a Schedule A attorney. I know she was not cleared through the White House, so she was not a Schedule C. She was not a political appointee. As a result, she had all the rights of Schedule A attorneys, and could have remained at the Department of Education in a career capacity.

SEN. HATCH: And even if she might not have remained the number one person to the head of the Civil Rights Division, which you were, she would have been transferred to another equivalent attorney's position.

JUDGE THOMAS: If she had requested it.

SEN. HATCH: Did you tell her anything to the contrary?

JUDGE THOMAS: Not to my knowledge. In fact, I don't think it ever came up.

SEN. HATCH: She didn't even ask you?

JUDGE THOMAS: I don't think it ever came up. I think it was understood that she would move to EEOC with me if she so desired.

SEN. HATCH: If I could just button it down, in other words, Judge Thomas, if instead of following you to the EEOC, Professor Hill had remained at the Department of Education as a Schedule A attorney, she would have had as much job security as any other civil service attorney in the Government. And this is especially true, isn't it, because of your friendship with Harry Singleton?

JUDGE THOMAS: That is right. If she was concerned about job security, I could have certainly discussed with Harry Singleton what should be done with her. He is a personal friend of mine. He is also, or was, a personal friend of the individual who recommended Anita Hill to me, Gil Hardy. Gil Hardy of course drowned in 1988, but both of us or all three of us had gone to Yale Law School and knew each other quite well.

SEN. HATCH: Now, Judge Thomas, I understand that on occasion, and you correct me if this is wrong, but I have been led to believe that on occasion Professor Hill would ask you to drive her home, and that on those occasions she would sometimes invite you into her home to continue a discussion, but you never thought anything—you never thought of any of this as anything more than normal, friendly, professional conversation with a colleague. Am I correct on that, or am I wrong?

JUDGE THOMAS: It was not unusual to me, Senator. As I remember it, I lived in southwest Washington, and would as I remember—and again, I am relying on my recollection, she lived someplace on Capitol Hill—and I would drive her home, and sometimes stop in and have a Coke or a beer or something and continue arguing about politics for maybe forty-five minutes to an hour, but I never thought anything of it.

SEN. HATCH: When Professor Hill worked for you at the EEOC, did she solicit your advice on career development or career opportunities?

JUDGE THOMAS: Senator, as I discuss with most of the members of my personal staff, I try to advise them on their career opportunities and what they should do next. You can't always be a special assistant or an attorney adviser. And I am certain that I had those discussions with her, and in fact it would probably have been based on that that I advised Dean Kothe that she would be a good teacher and that she would be interested in teaching.

SEN. HATCH: Did she treat you as her mentor at the time, in your opinion?

JUDGE THOMAS: Pardon me?

SEN. HATCH: Did she treat you as though you were a mentor at the time?

JUDGE THOMAS: She certainly sought counsel and advice from me.

SEN. HATCH: Now at any time during your tenure at the EEOC, did you ever discuss sexual matters with Professor Hill?

JUDGE THOMAS: Absolutely not, Senator.

SEN. HATCH: At any time during your tenure at the EEOC, did Professor Hill ever express discomfort or concern about your conduct toward her?

JUDGE THOMAS: No, Senator.

SEN. HATCH: From your observations, what was the perception of Professor Hill by her colleagues at the EEOC? What did they think about her?

JUDGE THOMAS: Senator, some of my former staffers I assume will testify here, but as I remember it there was some tension and some degree of friction which I attributed simply to having a staff. As I have had two weeks to think about this and to agonize over this, and as I remember it, I believe that she was considered to be somewhat distant and perhaps aloof, and from time to time there would be problems that usually involved—and I attributed this to just being young—but usually involved her taking a firm position and being unyielding to the other members of the staff, and then storming off or throwing a temper tantrum of some sort that either myself or the chief of staff would have to iron out.

SEN. HATCH: What was your opinion of the quality of Professor Hill's work at the EEOC, as her administrator and as the head of the EEOC?

JUDGE THOMAS: I thought the work was good. The problem was that—and it wasn't a problem—was, it was not as good as some of the other members of the staff.

SEN. HATCH: While Professor Hill worked for you at the EEOC, did she ever seek a promotion?

JUDGE THOMAS: I believe she did seek promotions. Again, most of that was done through the chief of staff at that time.

SEN. HATCH: Well, if so, to what position?

JUDGE THOMAS: She may have sought a promotion. In 1983, my chief of staff left and I was going to promote someone to my executive assistant/chief of staff, which is the most senior person on my personal staff, and I think that—again, I am relying on my memory—she aspired to that position and, of course, was not successful and I think was concerned about that.

SEN. HATCH: I see. When did Professor Hill leave the Equal Employment Opportunity Commission?

JUDGE THOMAS: In 1983.

SEN. HATCH: In 1983. Why do you think she decided to leave the agency at that time?

JUDGE THOMAS: Senator, I thought that she felt at the time that it was time for her to leave Washington and also to leave Government. She had, I believe, expressed an interest in teaching and the opportunity at Oral Roberts University provided her both with the opportunity to be in Oklahoma and to teach and, as I remember, she did not lose any salary or any income in the bargain, and that was attractive.

SEN. HATCH: Did you assist her in getting that job at Oral Roberts University?

JUDGE THOMAS: Yes, Senator, I discussed her with Dean Charles Kothe, both informally and provided written recommendation, formal recommendation for her.

SEN. HATCH: All right. Have you had any contacts with Professor Hill since she left the EEOC in 1983?

JUDGE THOMAS: Senator, from time to time, Anita Hill would call the agency and either speak to me or to my secretary and, through her, she would leave messages. They had been friends, Diane Holt. On a number of occasions, I believe, too, I am certain of one, but maybe two, when I was in Tulsa, Oklahoma, I spent time with her, I saw her, and I believe on one occasion she drove me to the airport and had breakfast with me.

SEN. HATCH: Mr. Chairman, with unanimous consent, I would introduce into the record at this point excerpts from Judge Thomas's telephone logs from 1983 to 1991, if I could.

THE CHAIRMAN: Without objection.

[The information was entered into the record.]

SEN. HATCH: Judge Thomas, do you have—

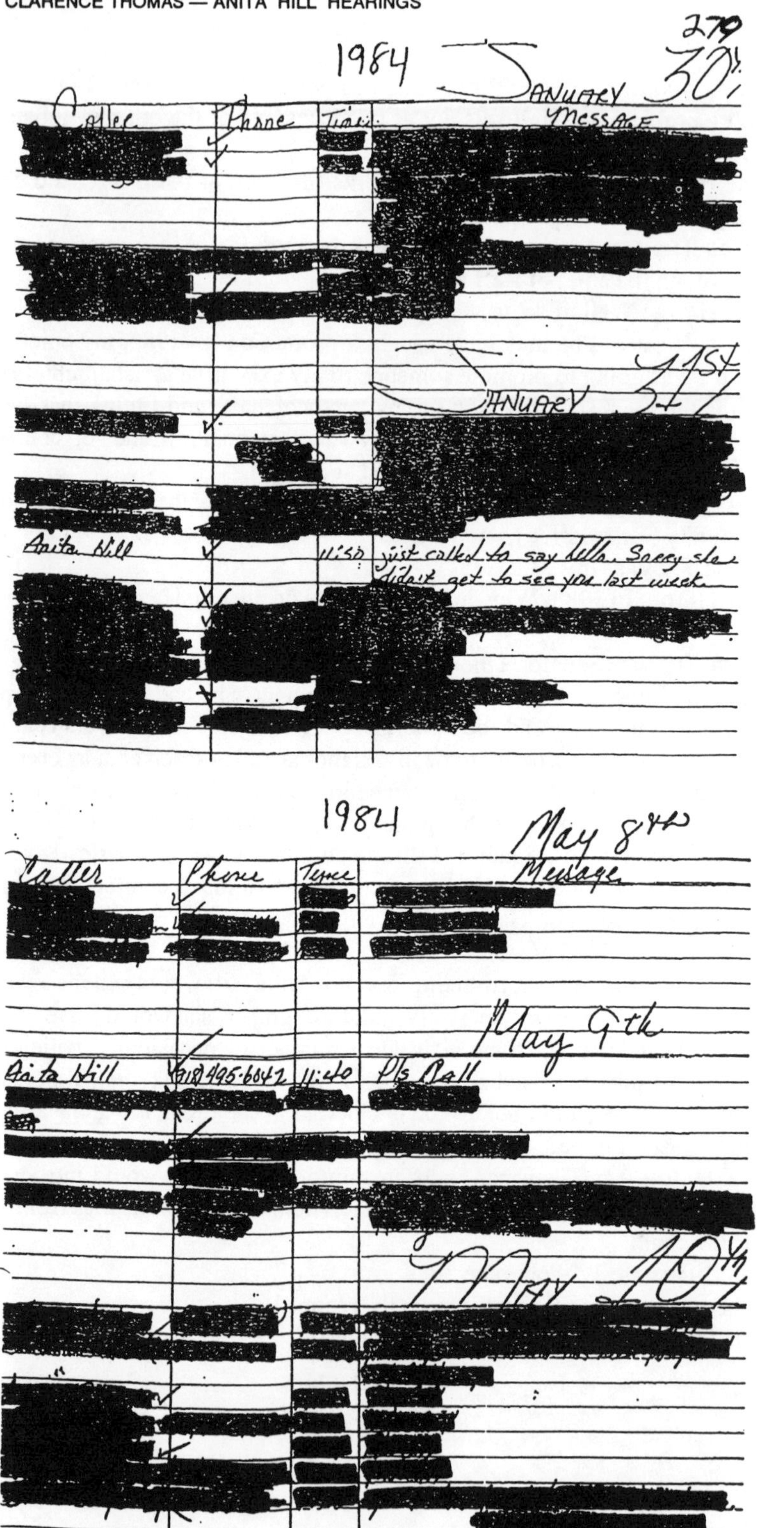
270

1984 January 30th

Caller	Phone	Time	Message

January 31st

Caller	Phone	Time	Message
Anita Hill	✓	11:50	just called to say hello. Sorry she didn't get to see you last week.

1984 May 8th

Caller	Phone	Time	Message

May 9th

Caller	Phone	Time	Message
Anita Hill	(918) 495-6042	11:40	Pls call

May 10th

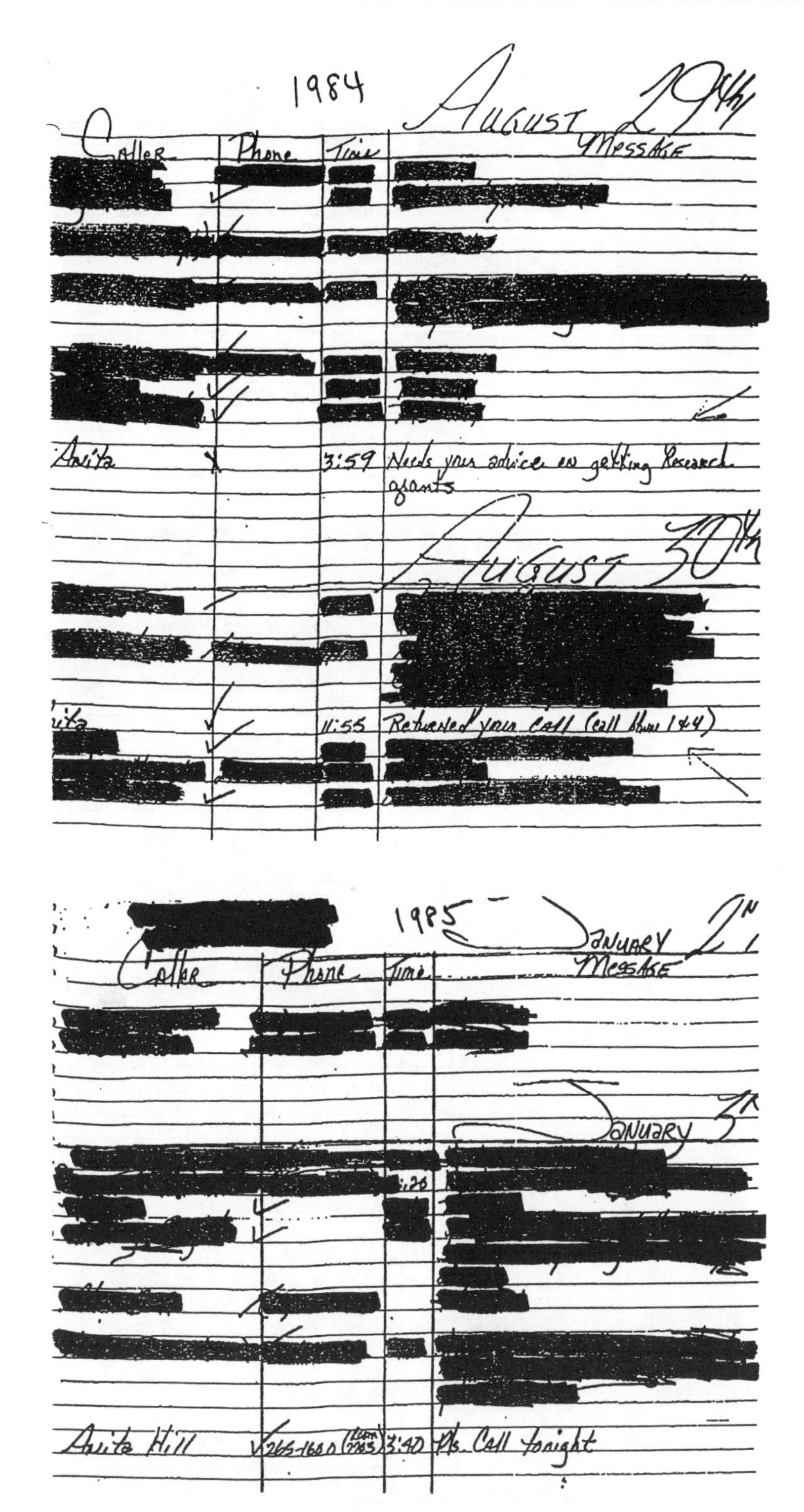

1984 August 29th

Caller	Phone	Time	Message
Anita		3:59	Needs your advice on getting Research grants

August 30th

Caller	Phone	Time	Message
Anita		11:55	Returned your call (call thru 1&4)

1985 January 2nd

Caller	Phone	Time	Message

January 3rd

Caller	Phone	Time	Message
Anita Hill	265-1600	3:40	Pls. Call tonight

1985 February 25th

Caller	Phone	Time	Message
nita Hill	✓	5:50	Pls. Call

February 26th

1985 March 1st

Caller	Phone	Time	Message

March 4th

Caller	Phone	Time	Message
nita Hill	✓	11:15	Pls. Call re: Research Project
isan Cahall	✓ (918) 588-7365	11:25	w/ Tulsa EEO ofc. Referred by Anita + see if you would come to Tulsa on 3/22 Speak at the EEO conference

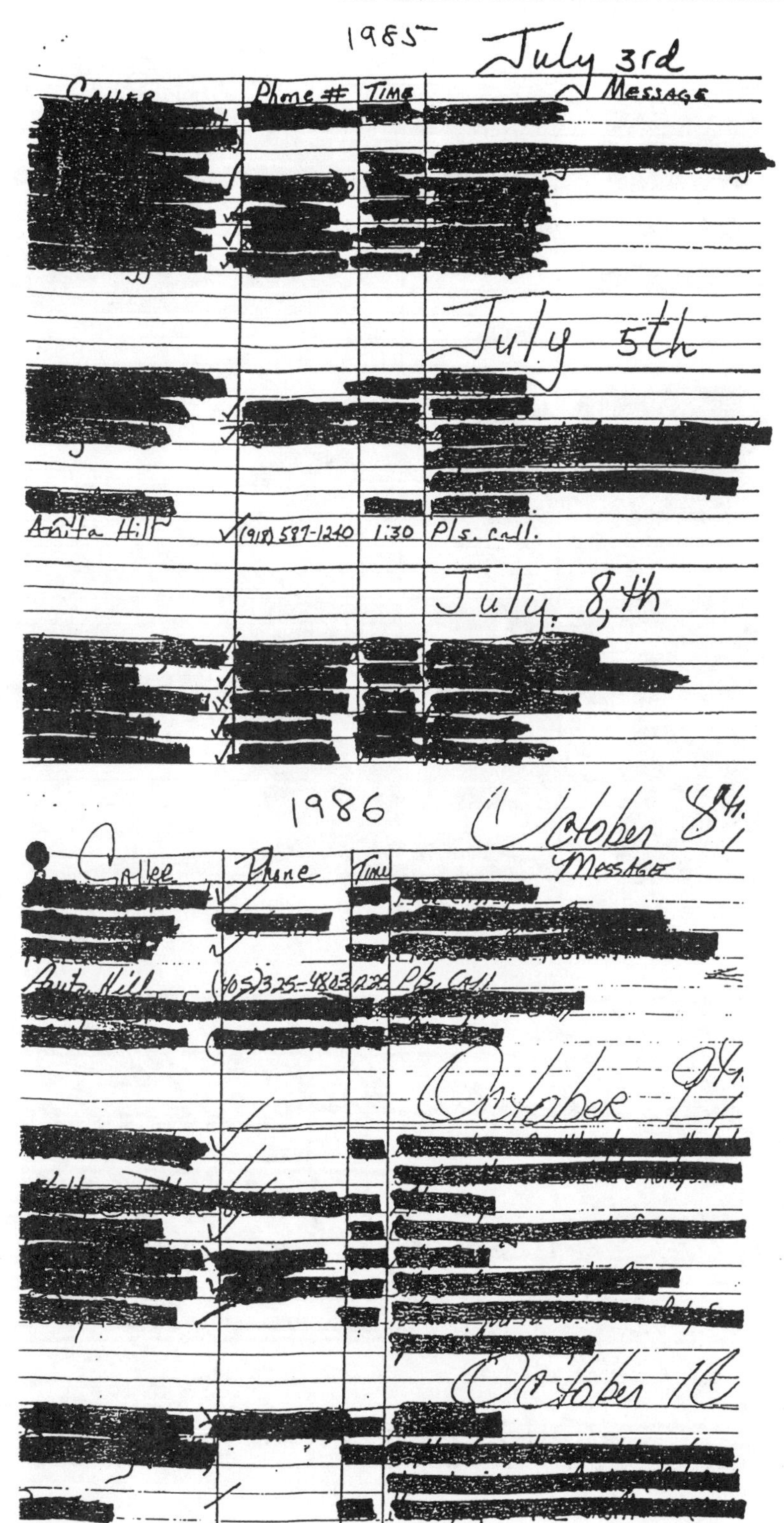
1985 July 3rd

Caller	Phone #	Time	Message

July 5th

Caller	Phone #	Time	Message
Anita Hill	(918) 587-1240	1:30	Pls. call.

July 8th

1986 October 8th

Caller	Phone	Time	Message
Anita Hill	(405) 325-4803	2:25	Pls. call

October 9th

October 10

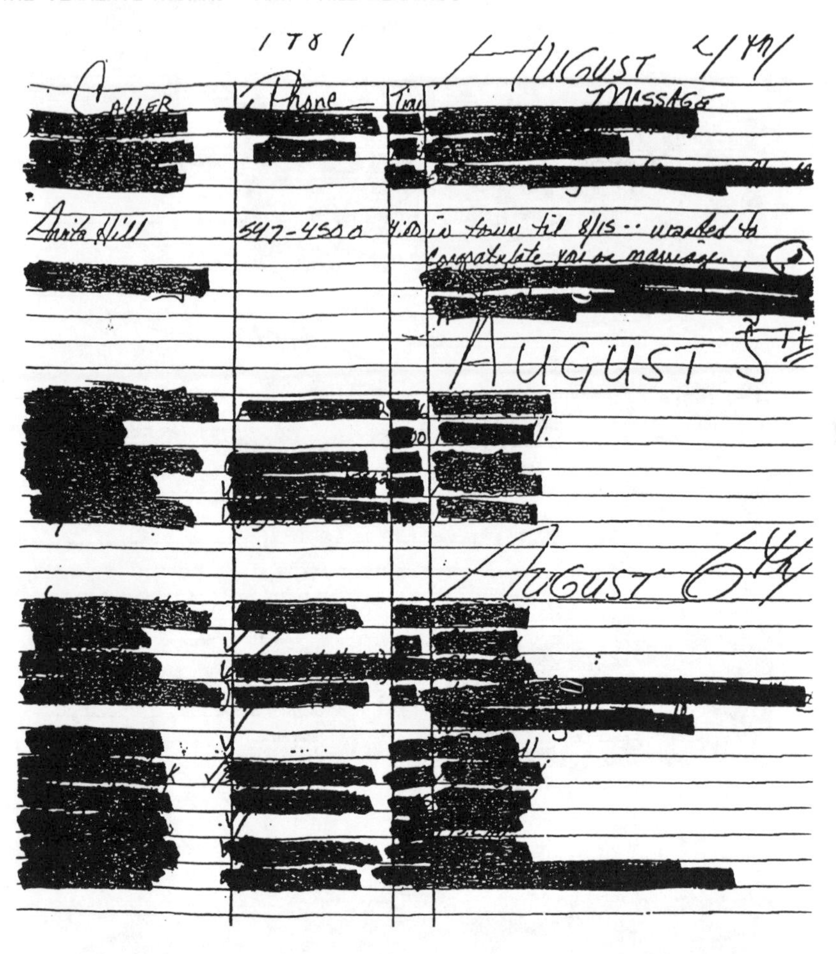

1981 — AUGUST 4TH

Caller	Phone	Time	Message
Anita Hill	547-4500	4:00	in town til 8/15 -- wanted to congratulate you on marriage.

AUGUST 5TH

AUGUST 6TH

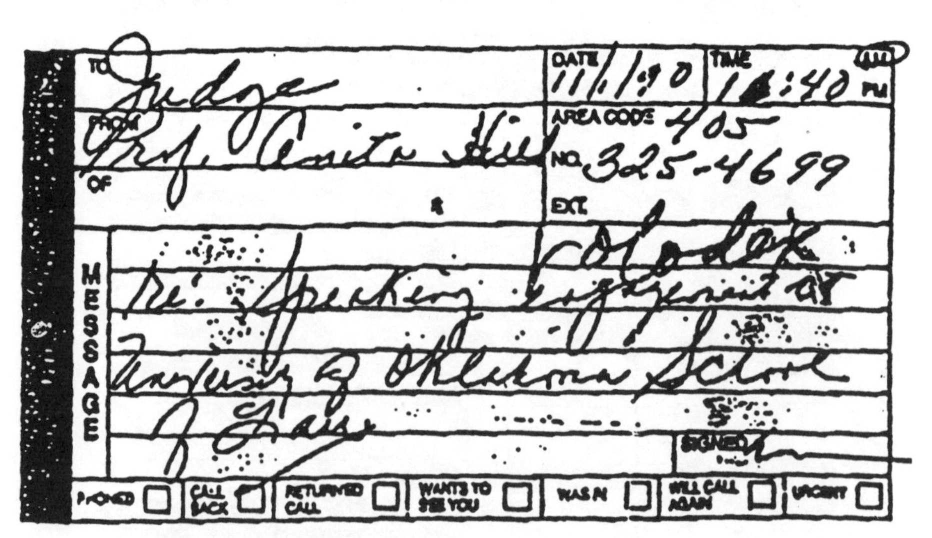

TO Judge

DATE 11/1/90 TIME 11:40 AM

FROM Prof. Anita Hill

OF

AREA CODE 405

NO. 325-4699

EXT.

MESSAGE rolodex

Re: Speaking Engagement at University of Oklahoma School of Law

SIGNED

PHONED ☐ CALL BACK ☐ RETURNED CALL ☐ WANTS TO SEE YOU ☐ WAS IN ☐ WILL CALL AGAIN ☐ URGENT ☐

THE CHAIRMAN: These are the same excerpts that he has had.

SEN. HATCH: [continuing]. These are the same ones that you have had. Now, Judge Thomas, are you familiar with these?

JUDGE THOMAS: I have seen those logs, Senator.

SEN. HATCH: Do you recall any of the telephone conversations with Professor Hill reflected by these particular messages?

JUDGE THOMAS: I do, Senator.

SEN. HATCH: For instance, on January 31, according to these logs—and I think I have got them correct, I am quite sure—on July 31, 1984, at 11:30 a.m., a message from Anita Hill, "Just called to say hello, sorry she didn't get to see you last week." Is that accurate?

JUDGE THOMAS: Yes, that was I think one instance when she had come to town, either on personal business or because of her job, and my schedule conflicted with any opportunity to meet with her and simply called to—that was a call from her, I think, to reflect that.

SEN. HATCH: Number two, on May 9, 1984, at 11:40 a.m., Anita Hill was the caller. The message was "Please call," and she left her phone number, 718 et cetera. Do you remember that?

JUDGE THOMAS: Yes, Senator.

SEN. HATCH: Number three, on August 29, 1984, at 3:59 p.m., Anita called, and the message was "Need your advice in getting research grants." Do you recall that?

JUDGE THOMAS: I remember that, Senator.

SEN. HATCH: What was that call about?

JUDGE THOMAS: I can't remember exactly what the project was, but she wanted some ideas as to how she could get I think some grants, either from EEOC or some other agency, to do some research I believe at Oral Roberts, and I believe we discussed that and I may have put her in contact with someone. Again, my recollection of that is vague, but we did have a discussion.

SEN. HATCH: Did you help her?

JUDGE THOMAS: I tried.

SEN. HATCH: You tried.

Number four, on August 30, 1984, at 11:55 a.m., Anita was the caller, the message "Returned your call (call between 1 and 4)." Do you remember that?

JUDGE THOMAS: I don't remember the specifics of the call, but I remember that on the log, Senator.

SEN. HATCH: Was she calling you or were you calling her?

JUDGE THOMAS: She was calling me. My secretary, when I placed the call and someone returned it, my secretary noted "returned your call."

SEN. HATCH: On January 3, 1985, at 3:40 p.m., Anita Hill was the caller, "Please call tonight," and then left a phone number and a room number. Do you remember that?

JUDGE THOMAS: I remember that. I think she must have been in town on a trip and that was her hotel room number. I don't know which hotel. I again may have been out of town, either on a business trip or somehow for some other reason inaccessible or unavailable.

SEN. HATCH: Number 6, February 6, 1985, 5:50 p.m., Anita Hill was the caller, again it said, "Please call." Another call from her to you?

JUDGE THOMAS: That's right.

SEN. HATCH: Number seven, on March 4, 1985, at 11:15 a.m., Anita Hill called again, "Please call re research project." Do you remember that?

JUDGE THOMAS: I remember that, Senator.

SEN. HATCH: Did you help her?

JUDGE THOMAS: I did. I think the—I can't remember the details, but I think she and Dean Charles Kothe were involved in some research in a fairly large project and wanted some data from EEOC, and I think we provided them with that data.

SEN. HATCH: Number eight, March 4, 1985, at 11:25 a.m., call from Susan Cahall, "With Tulsa EEO office referred by Anita to see if you would come to Tulsa on 3/27 to speak at the EEO Conference." Do you remember that?

JUDGE THOMAS: Yes, I remember the message. I think that was—she would not have otherwise gotten through to me and used Anita's name in order to gain access to me and perhaps receive a positive response.

SEN. HATCH: Mr. Chairman, I notice that my time is about up—

THE CHAIRMAN: You go right ahead.

SEN. HATCH: [continuing]—but I just want to finish this one line, if I can.

THE CHAIRMAN: No, you take all the time you want.

SEN. HATCH: Thank you. I really appreciate that.

Number nine, is July 5, 1985, at 1:30 p.m., Anita Hill is the caller, "Please call," with a number clearly out of town. Do you remember that?

JUDGE THOMAS: Again, I remember it being in my log, Senator.

SEN. HATCH: Okay. Number ten, October 9, 1986, at 12:25 p.m., Anita Hill called, message, "Please call, leaving at 4:05," and an area code number. Do you remember that?

JUDGE THOMAS: Yes, I do.

SEN. HATCH: Number eleven, August 4, 1987, 4:00 p.m., Anita Hill, caller, "In town until 8:15, wanted to congratulate you on your marriage." Do you remember that?

JUDGE THOMAS: I remember that, Senator, because one of the—my wife and I were on a delayed honeymoon in California when she came to town.

SEN. HATCH: Number twelve, November 1, 1990, 11:40 a.m., Anita Hill, caller, "Re speaking engagement at University of Oklahoma School of Law." Do you remember that?

JUDGE THOMAS: That was since I have been on the Court of Appeals, Senator.

SEN. HATCH: There are twelve phone calls between 1983 and 1990. Did you try to call her back each time?

JUDGE THOMAS: Senator, I tried, whenever I received calls from her or from others, I attempted to return those calls. Although, as I indicated before you started through those series of calls, I remember the messages in the log themselves, but I don't remember the nature of each call. It would be my practice to return those calls, especially from someone such as Anita.

SEN. HATCH: So, each and every time she called you, you tried to call her back and tried to help her?

JUDGE THOMAS: Senator, the log reflects only those calls where she was unsuccessful in reaching me.

SEN. HATCH: Did you ever call her, other than to return these calls?

JUDGE THOMAS: Senator, I may have. Again, Anita Hill was someone that I respected and was cordial toward and felt positive toward and hopeful for her career, and I may have on occasion, and I can't remember any specific occasion, picked up the phone just to see how she was doing. Again, the calls that you have there are the calls that are reflected or that reflect her inability to get in touch with me when she had called, as opposed to the instances in which she was able to contact me successfully.

SEN. HATCH: Judge Thomas, before this day, have you seen Professor Hill on various occasions since she left the Equal Employment Opportunity Commission?

JUDGE THOMAS: Yes, Senator. As I indicated, I recall seeing her I am certain one time and perhaps twice in Tulsa, Oklahoma, and on one of those occasions it is my recollection that we had dinner with Charles Kothe, we also had—

SEN. HATCH: She was there?

JUDGE THOMAS: [continuing]— Charles Kothe, the Dean of—

SEN. HATCH: Was she there at that dinner?

JUDGE THOMAS: [continuing]—she was at the dinner. We also had—we being Anita and myself—breakfast with Charles Kothe at his house. I usually slept at Charles Kothe's house, and I believe she drove me to the airport, and for some reason I seem to remember that she had a Peugeot.

I may be wrong on that, but I remember her being very proud of it, because, to my recollection, she did not have a car in Washington.

SEN. HATCH: I see. In addition to all the phone calls, you had these contacts and these meetings. How would you describe these meetings?

JUDGE THOMAS: Very cordial, positive, always one—as I treat my other special assistants, I tend to be the proud father type who sees his special assistants go on and become successful and feels pretty good about it. It would be that kind of a contact, as well as her telling me how her teaching assignments were going. Indeed, that was similar to the conversation, again, that I would have with my other special assistants or former special assistants.

SEN. HATCH: Overall, how would you characterize the nature of your contacts with Professor Hill since she left the EEOC in 1983?

JUDGE THOMAS: They have always been very cordial and very positive, Senator.

SEN. HATCH: Any unpleasantness?

JUDGE THOMAS: Never.

SEN. HATCH: Any problems ever raised?

JUDGE THOMAS: No, Senator.

SEN. HATCH: Any questions about your conduct?

JUDGE THOMAS: No, Senator.

SEN. HATCH: Can you think of any reason for her efforts to continue to try to be associated with you?

JUDGE THOMAS: Senator—could you repeat the question, Senator?

SEN. HATCH: Can you think of any reason why she would want to continue this cordial professional relationship with you?

JUDGE THOMAS: Senator, I would hope it would have been for the same reasons that all of my other special assistants did, that I was very supportive of them. The people, some of whom you will hear from today, who have flown in, certainly at their own expense, they feel warmly toward me and have a sense of loyalty and feel that I will help them and that I will assist them as best I could, and I believe that was a part of the reason and we certainly enjoyed a cordial and professional relationship.

SEN. HATCH: Before you first heard of Professor Hill's allegations during this confirmation process, did you have any reason to believe that she was unhappy with you?

JUDGE THOMAS: Senator, on Tuesday, September 24, the day before I heard from the FBI, I would have told you, if you asked me, that my relationship with Anita Hill was cordial, professional and that I was very proud of her for all she had done with her life and the things that she had accomplished.

SEN. HATCH: Judge Thomas, this is your fourth confirmation in nine years, isn't that correct?

JUDGE THOMAS: Yes, Senator. It is either my—yes, Senator, it is.

SEN. HATCH: In fact, three of those confirmations occurred during the time of the allegations by Professor Hill.

JUDGE THOMAS: Actually this, Senator, would be the fourth.

SEN. HATCH: That's right, this would be the fourth.

So she actually has known you through four Senate confirmations, four of them. No, this is the fourth. So four Senate confirmations, right?

JUDGE THOMAS: That's right.

SEN. HATCH: And none of those have been very easy, have they?

JUDGE THOMAS: That's right, now that I think about it, none of my confirmations, aside from the first one, was easy.

SEN. HATCH: And you had your critics in each and every one of them, didn't you?

JUDGE THOMAS: That is right.

SEN. HATCH: Do you remember the details of each of those calls that were made that we went over?

Or do you just remember them generally?

JUDGE THOMAS: I remember the calls generally, Senator. I don't remember the specifics of each call. That has been quite some time.

SEN. HATCH: Well, let me just say this. I have kept everybody too long and I know we can continue tomorrow, but I would like to ask this question just to end the day with and I think it is an important question. I have to say, cumulatively, these charges, even though they were made on all kinds of occasions, I mean they are unbelievable that anybody could be that perverted. I am sure there are people like that but they are generally in insane asylums. What was your reaction when you first heard of these allegations against you, just the first allegations, not all the other ones, and then you can tell me your reaction when you heard of these ones that were brought forth for the first time today?

JUDGE THOMAS: Senator, when the FBI informed me of the allegation, the person first, there was shock, dismay, hurt, pain, and when he informed me of the nature of the allegations I was surprised, there was disbelief and again, hurt. And I have reached a point over the last two weeks, plus, I have reached a point where I can't go over each and every one of these allegations again.

As I said in my statement this morning, that when you have allegations of this nature by someone that you have thought the world of and felt that you have done the best for it is an enormously painful experience and it is one when you ask yourself, you rip at yourself, what could you have done? And why could this happen or why would it happen?

SEN. HATCH: How do you feel right now, Judge, after what you have been through?

JUDGE THOMAS: Senator, as I indicated this morning, it just isn't worth it. And the nomination is not worth it, being on the Supreme Court is not worth it, and there is no amount of money that is worth it, there is no amount of money that can restore my name, being an associate Justice of the Supreme Court will never replace what I have been robbed of, and I would not recommend that anyone go through it.

This has been an enormously difficult experience, but I don't think that that is the worst of it. I am forty-three years old and if I am not confirmed I am still the youngest member of the U.S. Court of Appeals for the DC Circuit. And I will go on. I will go back to my life of talking to my neighbors and cutting my grass and getting a Big Mac at McDonald's and driving my car, and seeing my kid play football. And I will live. I will have my life back. And all of this hurt has brought my family closer together, my wife and I, my mother, but that is not—so there is no pity for me. I think the country has been hurt by this process. I think we are destroying our country. We are destroying our institutions. And I think it is a sad day when the U.S. Senate can be used by interest groups, and hatemongers, and people who are interested in digging up dirt to destroy other people and who will stop at no tactics, when they can use our great political institutions for their political ends, we have gone far beyond McCarthyism. This is far more dangerous than McCarthyism. At least McCarthy was elected.

SEN. HATCH: Judge, I have a lot of other questions to ask you and I think they are important questions. I think you deserve the opportunity to tell your side of this and you have done it here so far. And I have to tell you this has come down to this, one woman's allegations that are ten years old against your lifetime of service over that same ten-year period. I have known you almost eleven years. And the person that the good professor described is not the person I have known.

We are going to talk a little bit more about this tomorrow and about what went on there and about how this could have happened. How one person's uncorroborated allegations, could destroy a career and one of the most wonderful opportunities for a young man from Pin Point, Georgia.

JUDGE THOMAS: Senator, I repeat what I said, I have been hurt by this deeply, and nothing is worth going through this. This has devastated me and it has devastated my family. It is untrue. They are lies. I have hundreds of women who work with me and you can call them, dozens who worked closely with me on my personal staff. You can call them. You can bring them up and give them as much air time as you have given this one, one person, with uncorroborated scurrilous lies and allegations. Give them as much time and see what they say.

SEN. HATCH: I hope we will do that.

JUDGE THOMAS: It is not just that, Senator, it is more than that. You are ruining the country. If it can happen to me it can happen to anybody, any time over any issue. Our institutions are being controlled by people who will stop at nothing. They went around this country looking for dirt, not information on Clarence Thomas, dirt. Anybody with any dirt, anything, late night calls, calls at work, calls at home, badgering, anything, give us some dirt. I think that if our country has reached this point we are in trouble. And you should feel worse for the country than you do for me.

SEN. HATCH: I feel bad for both.

Mr. Chairman, I am sorry I have kept us over a little bit. I wish I could proceed further tonight but I think we will wait until tomorrow morning. I know everybody is dead tired, and I am sure you are dead tired, I know that.

So, thank you for giving me this extra time. You have always been courteous and decent, and frankly, you have run this committee through this whole process in a courteous and decent way, including the way in which you ran it with regard to the FBI report, as well. We, on this side, know that but thank you.

THE CHAIRMAN: Let me, before we go—Judge Heflin reserved some of his time.

SEN. HEFLIN: Judge Thomas, you describe Anita Hill and your relationship with her up until you heard, on September, I believe you said the 24th, as cordial, positive, had no trouble with her, in any way. Now, you make rather strong statements. Do you think that Anita Hill is lying?

JUDGE THOMAS: Senator, I know that what she is saying is untrue.

SEN. HEFLIN: Now, what do you think that her motivations are to come here and testify?

JUDGE THOMAS: Senator, I have agonized over that. I have thought about it. I have thought about why she would say these things, why she would come here, why it would keep changing. I don't know.

SEN. HEFLIN: Well, if you don't know, see we, in the committee, have a responsibility to figure out if she is not telling the truth, why? When you worked with her did you feel that she was a zealous civil rights supporter who was willing to consider and be only a one-interest individual?

JUDGE THOMAS: Senator, I cannot characterize her that way. I have not thought about her that way. But I would like to address what you said before that. I think you have more than an obligation to figure out why she would say that. I think you have an obligation to determine why you would allow uncorroborated, unsubstantiated allegations to ruin my life.

SEN. HEFLIN: Well, she has testified, that you, in effect, act as a character witness for her. You have testified here about the relationship, her work, and her reputation and here we are trying to get to the bottom of what the facts are. And we want to know what the truth is, and you knew her probably better than any one of us.

JUDGE THOMAS: Senator, there are others that you could bring as witnesses. I have suggested to you there are dozens of people who work there. And—

SEN. HEFLIN: I think you have made a point and I hope they are brought here.

THE CHAIRMAN: We are, we have agreed already to do that.

SEN. HEFLIN: But we are still faced with the fact, Judge, that if she is lying, why? We are still faced with the fact that if she is telling a falsehood, what is the motivation?

Now, we have watched her testify today and she is a meek woman.

JUDGE THOMAS: That is not as I remember Anita. Anita is, I can't say that and you can ask others who visit here, Anita would not have been considered a meek woman. She was an aggressive debater. She stood her ground. When she got her dander up, she would storm off and I would say that she is a bright person, a capable person. Meek is not a characterization that I would remember.

SEN. HEFLIN: Well, you say when she got her dander off she would stalk off.

JUDGE THOMAS: Well, she was a good debater. She fought for her position. I don't remember her as being someone who was a pushover.

SEN. HEFLIN: Well, was she a vindictive woman?

JUDGE THOMAS: I think, Senator, that she argued personally for her position, and I took it as a sign of immaturity, perhaps, that when she didn't get her way, that she would tend to reinforce her position and get a bit angry. I did not see that as a character flaw or vindictiveness.

SEN. HEFLIN: Did she give any indication to you that she wanted to be a martyr in the civil rights movement?

JUDGE THOMAS: Senator, I can't answer all those questions. What I have attempted to do here is simply say to you that—you indicated that she was meek and suggesting that she was not an aggressive, strong person. I remember Anita as aggressive, strong and forceful and advocating the positions that she stood for. Again, there are others who worked with her and I suggest that you have them come before this committee and you ask them.

With respect to why, as I saw through my own memory and my own recollection of what could possibly have happened, particularly at EEOC, the change in position, where she was no longer my top assistant or my top aide and she became one of many, and certainly not the most senior and not the one who received the better assignments and later not becoming the top assistant, that could have been a basis for her being angry with me, but that doesn't seem to be too much of a basis.

I don't know, Senator. If I knew, I would not have been as perplexed as I am.

SEN. HEFLIN: Well, did she ever show signs of being resentful?

JUDGE THOMAS: I can't remember, Senator. I know that she has shown signs that she was upset when she did not get her way. Again, I am not going to sit here and attempt to criticize her character. I can only say that during the time that she worked with me, she was not perfect, but there seemed to me nothing that would suggest that she would do this to me.

SEN. HEFLIN: Well, did she at any time during the time that she worked with you at the EEOC, which most of—I mean at the Department of Education, where most of the charges that she makes against you pertaining to remarks about pornographic films and pornographic materials, and then she says they continued some, but that there were more at that time, she was your attorney assistant, as I understand it.

JUDGE THOMAS: Attorney adviser.

SEN. HEFLIN: All right. Did you at that time ever notice anything about her that would indicate to you that she was out of touch with reality?

JUDGE THOMAS: Senator, again, that is ten years ago and my working relationship with her, she was professional and cordial, as I suggested this morning. It did not involve, as I have indicated, any discussion of pornographic material or any attempt to ever date Anita. I view my special assistants as charges of mine. They are students, they are kids of mine and I have an obligation to them. It is the same way I feel toward interns and individual co-ops or stay-in-school students.

SEN. HEFLIN: Well, we are still left in a great quandary and we are trying to get to the bottom of it. After she went to EEOC with you, did she show any signs at that time of being out of touch with reality?

JUDGE THOMAS: Senator, again, I am not a psychologist or psychiatrist, and at EEOC, I can tell you, I was enormously busy and spent an enormous amount of time at the office, involved in any number of activities. At EEOC, the assignments, as I remember them, the individual in charge of the office, I had a chief of staff at the time who would take care of the assignments and would be more involved with the special assistants.

My suggestion to you, as I have indicated, would be that this committee spend some time with the people who worked there. This committee has spent I think an inordinate amount of time with someone making uncorroborated allegations against me, and should have people who have worked with me, who have not seen any such activity, who did not corroborate these allegations and who had opportunities to work with and observe Anita Hill.

SEN. HEFLIN: I believe Chairman Biden adds to that, saying that they will come and be available. But, now, at the Department of Education and at the EEOC, did any fellow employee of hers, did any supervisor of hers or anybody else indicate to you that she was out of touch with reality?

JUDGE THOMAS: The only one employee who indicated very strongly to me during my tenure at EEOC that she was, I believe—and I believe this may be a quote—my enemy, and I refused to believe that and argued with him about that and refused to act in accordance with that.

SEN. HEFLIN: Well, did he tell you any of the facts surrounding how he arrived at the opinion that she was your enemy?

JUDGE THOMAS: Senator, as I said, I ignored it. Loyalty is something that was important to me and I paid no attention to it and he in recent days reminded me of what he told me.

SEN. HEFLIN: All right. Now, was there any other information that came out while you were working with her that would indicate to you that she lived in a fantasy world or anything?

JUDGE THOMAS: Senator, again, I don't know, I am not a psychiatrist or psychologist. I was a busy chairman of an agency.

SEN. HEFLIN: Well, here we are in a perplexed situation trying to get to the bottom of it. I will ask you again, do you know of any reason why she might purposely lie about these alleged incidents?

JUDGE THOMAS: Senator, I don't know why anyone would lie in this fashion.

SEN. HEFLIN: I believe that is all.

THE CHAIRMAN: Judge, just because we take harassment seriously doesn't mean we take the charges at face value. You have pointed out that when you worked with Anita Hill and up until the moment that the charge was made available to you through an FBI agent, you thought her to be a respected, reasonable, upstanding person. When a respectable, reasonable, upstanding person, a professor of law, someone with no blemish on her record, comes forward, this committee has the obligation to do exactly what you would have done at EEOC, investigate the charge.

You are making a mistake, if you conclude that because this is being investigated before all the evidence is in, the conclusion has been reached by this committee.

You have said some things tonight that are new information to us. Assuming them to be true, it is the first time I've heard that you were ever invited, drove home and/or were invited into Professor Hill's apartment to have a Coke or a beer. You have told us things that are new. You should not in your understandable anger refuse to tell us more. We have to figure this out.

For us to have concluded, when faced with a person of Professor Hill's standing and background that this is something we were not going to look at would have been irresponsible.

I don't disagree with you, it was irresponsible, the way in which Professor Hill ended up before us. I understand that, and if I had had anything to do with it, I would apologize for it, but in a very much smaller fashion, I was at the other end of that one myself.

So, do not in your anger refuse to tell us more tomorrow. This is not decided. Witnesses are going to be coming forward, the witnesses that you and your attorneys have asked us to hear, and people we want to hear from.

SEN. HATCH: Mr. Chairman, could I just make one last comment?

THE CHAIRMAN: You may.

SEN. HATCH: I hope that nobody here, either on this panel or in this room, is saying that, Judge, you have to prove your innocence, because I think we have to remember and we have to insist that Anita Hill has the burden of proof or any other challenger, and not you, Judge.

The fact of the matter is, the accuser, under our system of jurisprudence and under any system of fairness, would have to prove their case.

Judge, we will go into some things tomorrow, and I look forward to questioning again tomorrow, and we wish you a good night's rest and we look forward to seeing you tomorrow.

SEN. SIMPSON: Mr. Chairman.

THE CHAIRMAN: I have been asked by one of my colleagues to clarify one thing. I don't think you misunderstood it, but no one else should. What I was referring to, that—

SEN. HATCH: I wasn't referring to you.

THE CHAIRMAN: I know you weren't. I am just referring to my comment. I was referring to the fact that Professor Hill testified here today that her statement, which we have attempted to keep confidential, was leaked to the press. That is what I am referring to as an injustice.

SEN. HATCH: Right.

SEN. SIMPSON: Mr. Chairman, just a moment, because Howell Heflin and I came here to the Senate together in the class of 1978. I have great respect for him and I see this terrible quandary that he is in, because I have watched him work.

Intimately we have worked together on a lot of things, and it is the same thing we all feel, but there is a big difference here, and Orrin has just touched on it, and that is what you said this morning, Mr. Chairman, in your very fair way, and I quote from your statement, and I think we must not forget this, and this is a quote from our Chairman this morning: "Fairness also means that Judge Thomas must be given a full and fair opportunity to confront these charges against him, to respond fully, to tell us his side of the story and to be given the benefit of the doubt."

Now, that's what we are doing here, and if there is any doubt, it goes to Clarence Thomas, it does not go to Professor Hill.

THE CHAIRMAN: I made the statement and I stand by the statement. That is why I—not that you need my recommendation, Judge, but tell us what you know. We are trying to determine what happened. It is as simple as that. And the mere fact, as I said, that we take the allegation seriously does not mean that we assume the allegation is correct.

SEN. THURMOND: Mr. Chairman, I believe you mentioned Clarence Thomas's attorneys. So far as I know, he has no attorneys. He doesn't need any.

THE CHAIRMAN: Tomorrow, we will reconvene—I assume, Judge, it is your choice, I assume you wish to come back tomorrow. The committee is not demanding you come back tomorrow. Do you wish to come back tomorrow?

JUDGE THOMAS: I think so, Senator. I would like to finish this.

THE CHAIRMAN: We will reconvene at 10 o'clock.

[Whereupon, at 10:34 p.m., the committee recessed, to reconvene on Saturday, October 12, 1991, at 10 a.m.]

NOMINATION OF JUDGE CLARENCE THOMAS TO BE ASSOCIATE JUSTICE OF THE SUPREME COURT OF THE UNITED STATES

SATURDAY, OCTOBER 12, 1991

U.S. SENATE,
COMMITTEE ON THE JUDICIARY
Washington, DC

The committee met, pursuant to notice, at 10:14 a.m., in room SR-325, Russell Senate Office Building, Hon. Joseph R. Biden, Jr. (chairman of the committee) presiding.

Present: Senators Biden, Kennedy, Metzenbaum, DeConcini, Leahy, Heflin, Simon, Kohl, Thurmond, Hatch, Simpson, Grassley, Specter, and Brown.

THE CHAIRMAN: The committee will come to order.

Good morning, Judge.

FURTHER TESTIMONY OF HON. CLARENCE THOMAS, OF GEORGIA, TO BE ASSOCIATE JUSTICE OF THE U.S. SUPREME COURT

THE CHAIRMAN: The Chair yields for the next round of questioning to the Senator from Vermont, Senator Leahy.

SEN. LEAHY: Thank you, Mr. Chairman.

Good morning, Judge. Judge, yesterday, you said—in answer, I believe, to a question—that you had not watched or listened to the six or seven hours of Professor Hill's testimony. You are obviously under no requirement to do so, but I wonder if, since then, you have had either an opportunity to read or be briefed about what she said?

JUDGE THOMAS: Senator, prior to coming here last night, I was briefed about much of what she said. Of course, my wife watched significant portions of it and talked about some of the things that she had to say.

SEN. LEAHY: The reason I ask, is that you may have followed a part of the testimony in which she spoke about going to dinner with you at the time when you—when she, rather, was leaving the EEOC. Are you familiar with that part of her testimony?

JUDGE THOMAS: Senator, I am familiar that she said that. I didn't see it. I was briefed that she said that.

SEN. LEAHY: Was there such a dinner?

JUDGE THOMAS: Senator, I do not recall such a dinner. It was not unusual for me, when a staffer was leaving, to go to lunch or to— dinner would be more unusual, but not out of the question, but it was not unusual to take them out and just simply say "thank you." In later years, I know we had much bigger dinners. We would have many members of the staff go out and be a cause for great celebration. But I don't specifically recall such a dinner.

SEN. LEAHY: Do you recall any time ever taking Professor Hill out to dinner?

JUDGE THOMAS: No, Senator.

SEN. LEAHY: Now, Judge, in her testimony, in which she speaks of this dinner, she said that you had driven her to the restaurant—she did not recall the restaurant. You have heard, I am sure, the conversation that she recounts as taking place. And then after you left and went on to wherever you went, she took the subway home, again according to her testimony. She said that the two of you went there in your car. You were assigned, I believe, a car and driver in your position. If that was so, would there be a log that the driver keeps of where he might drive you?

JUDGE THOMAS: No, Senator, we did not keep logs. I used my driver more frequently in the early years and less frequently in my later years at EEOC, but we didn't have logs.

SEN. LEAHY: Even though if drivers work late, they get paid overtime, they don't keep logs of where they go?

JUDGE THOMAS: Senator, my driver at that time worked with me later. He was on my personal staff. I don't think the driver today is on the personal staff. But the driver at EEOC was assigned to the chairman's office when I went on board and would still have been assigned to the chairman's office.

SEN. LEAHY: At the time that Professor Hill was talking about, just at the time that she was leaving the office, who would have been the driver?

JUDGE THOMAS: Mr. Randall, James Randall, who has since retired.

SEN. LEAHY: Mr. James Randall?

JUDGE THOMAS: Randall.

SEN. LEAHY: I'm sorry, between the sound of the cameras clicking, Judge, I still didn't hear the last name.

JUDGE THOMAS: Mr. James Randall.

SEN. LEAHY: Randall. Thank you. But the bottom line is that—well, let me make sure I understand this. Professor Hill said the two of you went out to dinner as she was leaving. Professor Hill, of course, further alleges—and this would be a major and explosive matter—that you said something to her to the effect, "If you ever tell about this, it will damage or destroy my career." Now, that was her statement. I want you to have a chance to give yours. Am I correct in understanding your testimony now that you have no recollection of ever having such a conversation at any time? Is that correct?

JUDGE THOMAS: No, I have no recollection of having dinner with her as she left, although I do not think that it would be unusual for me to have gone either to lunch or to particularly an early dinner with a member of my staff who was leaving. I would categorically deny that, under any circumstances, whether it is breakfast, lunch or dinner, that I made those statements.

SEN. LEAHY: Then, would it be safe to say your testimony is: At any time, whether in a social, business or any other setting, you never made the statement, "If this comes out, it would ruin my career," or anything even relating to that kind of a statement. Is that correct?

JUDGE THOMAS: That's right.

SEN. LEAHY: Thank you.

Now, I just want to make sure I understand this and then we will move on to another subject. Do you recollect ever going to dinner with Professor Hill? I understand your saying it would not be unusual to go with a member of the staff, but do you ever recollect going to dinner with her at all?

JUDGE THOMAS: I don't recall, other than the once I believe we had dinner, perhaps, with Charles Kothe in Oklahoma subsequent to her leaving EEOC, I don't recall ever having gone to dinner with Professor Hill.

SEN. LEAHY: I understand that, and you have stated that before, but I am just talking about the time when she was working there. You did not have any such—

JUDGE THOMAS: I do not recall. Let me add one thing, Senator.

SEN. LEAHY: Certainly.

JUDGE THOMAS: I occasionally, with my personal staff as well as with my personnel, when I am going out to lunch, I will grab the first person available and say is anybody ready for lunch and walk out to either a local place or perhaps just a deli to grab a sandwich. That is customary with me, so I don't want to suggest that there wasn't an occasion when I would do something like that.

SEN. LEAHY: Judge Thomas, I can't imagine a member of the Senate who doesn't do the same thing and say to some of the staff, "Let's grab a sandwich, let's grab lunch," something like that, and continue discussion of whatever might be going on. I don't think you speak of something unusual, nor do I suggest you do.

Tell me, Judge, you said yesterday that there were a couple of occasions when you would go by Professor Hill's apartment, probably have a beer, and continue discussions. Do you recall? I forget which Senator you had responded to.

JUDGE THOMAS: That's not the way I said it, Senator. What I said—

SEN. LEAHY: Would you restate it the way you said it?

JUDGE THOMAS: What I said was, when we were at the Department of Education, there were, as I recall, a number of instances in which I gave her a ride home and she asked me just to drop in to continue discussion, and I would have a Coke or a beer or something and leave. That was, again, nothing, I thought nothing of it. It was purely innocent on my part and nothing occurred with respect to that, other than those conversations.

SEN. LEAHY: I'm not suggesting by the question that there was anything that was not. I just wanted to make sure I understand this. That was only when you were at the Department of Education, is that correct?

JUDGE THOMAS: That's the reason I recall that, is because I lived in Southwest, and for a significant part of her tenure at EEOC, I did not have a personal car, and she lived nearby on Capitol Hill. The Switzer Building is in Southwest, and I would just simply give her a ride to the other side of the Hill.

SEN. LEAHY: Do you recall where on the Hill she lived?

JUDGE THOMAS: No, I do not.

SEN. LEAHY: Do you recall anything at all about the apartment, big, little, old, new?

JUDGE THOMAS: She had a roommate, of course, and the area that I remember was just a small living room-type area, where there was a TV and I think a small couch or something.

SEN. LEAHY: Okay. Do you remember whether it was an old building, a new building or—

JUDGE THOMAS: I remember it as an old building or an older building, and a duplex, for some reason a duplex in my mind.

SEN. LEAHY: Now, Judge, you have spoken eloquently in the past of the kind of racial harassment and racial discrimination you've faced growing up—a lesson perhaps for everybody, realizing that these are not some ancient things, that a man your age is speaking within a generation of it.

Let me ask you, since you have been in the work force for about twenty years since leaving law school, have you ever witnessed sexual harassment first-hand?

JUDGE THOMAS: Senator, I have witnessed incidents that I would consider sexual harassment and inappropriate conduct. As Chairman of EEOC, particularly, in the work force there, I was adamant that this conduct would not take place, and anyone who has worked with me understands that, I was adamant that it would not take place.

SEN. LEAHY: In being adamant, how did you translate that to staff or the people who worked for you? In statements, speeches, memos, personnel—how would you do it, Judge?

JUDGE THOMAS: If you engage in it, you will be fired, simple.

SEN. LEAHY: The easiest way to have it.

JUDGE THOMAS: If you engage in it, you will be fired.

SEN. LEAHY: We have a similar rule in my office for drug abuse and sexual harassment: If you do it, you're gone.

JUDGE THOMAS: Anyone who, and you will have witnesses who have worked with me, you ask them what my statements were. It was very simple. That is particularly easy on a personal staff and it is particularly easy with Schedule C appointees.

SEN. LEAHY: Judge, you said you have witnessed sexual harassment first-hand. What was the nature of—can you just give me some idea of the type that you have seen?

JUDGE THOMAS: Well, the types of things are, again, people using graphic language to subordinates who are female, women, there would be individuals who would expect certain conduct on the part of women, that they expect to stay in the work force or to prosper. Those kinds of things I have seen either when I was not in the position to do anything about it and I've heard about when I was in a position to do something about it, and in the latter instance, I did something about it.

SEN. LEAHY: Judge, it is a very difficult thing to do here, under the circumstances, but could you just step out of the role for a moment of being a Supreme Court nominee and think back to being head of the EEOC? You get a call from an investigator in a district office who has just had a woman come in with a claim of sexual harassment. He relays the claim to you and you look at it and say, "Yes, this fits on all fours within the regulations and statutes." And he says, "But, Mr. Chairman, it was five years ago, the statute has run out." What would you say to him?

JUDGE THOMAS: Senator, that is certainly something that never occurred during my tenure. There were instances in which there were older charges of that nature. What we would generally find would be that the person involved would have engaged in a pattern of that kind of practice.

To give you an instance, if that person is a manager that we are talking about, you could find a pattern and you can find more recent occurrences, to my knowledge—again, this may not always be the case, but when you have a person who is engaged in grotesque conduct or harassing conduct, you will find more than one person. If the person has a habit of harassing secretaries, you will find a series of secretaries. If the person has a habit of harassing professionals, subordinates, or other employees, you will find a series of those. You will not find generally just one isolated instance, and I think that would be the trigger to look for more instances of them.

SEN. LEAHY: Would it be unusual, though, to have the initial allegation be something that happened sometime back? I understand what you are saying about the pattern, that you didn't reconstruct later, but would it be unusual to have the initial allegation of sex harassment be of some time past?

JUDGE THOMAS: To my knowledge, Senator, based on just what I have seen personally, it would be unusual.

SEN. LEAHY: Thank you.

JUDGE THOMAS: Usually, what you would have is you would have a recent occurrence that would trigger an instance, and then you would look back and you will see a pattern.

SEN. LEAHY: Going back to the charges that Professor Hill made yesterday, one was of your discussing pornographic films with her. She stated this happened on a number of occasions and that she had found it uncomfortable and asked you not to. Let me ask you—she has been asked whether this happened—let me ask you: Did you ever have a discussion of pornographic films with Professor Hill?

JUDGE THOMAS: Absolutely not.

SEN. LEAHY: Have you ever had such discussions with any other women?

JUDGE THOMAS: Senator, I will not get into any discussions that I might have about my personal life or my sex life with any person outside of the workplace.

SEN. LEAHY: I'm not asking—

JUDGE THOMAS: I will categorically say I have not had any such discussions with Professor Hill.

SEN. LEAHY: Please don't misunderstand my question, Judge. I am confining it to the workplace. I have no interest in what might be your personal life. That is yours. What I am asking about is within—as she alleges—within the workplace. Let me make sure I fully understand—I am asking you this question, so that you can give the answer.

Am I correct in understanding your answer that within the workplace with Professor Hill, you never had such a discussion?

JUDGE THOMAS: Right.

SEN. LEAHY: You never had such discussions within the workplace with any other women?

JUDGE THOMAS: That's right.

SEN. LEAHY: Or anyone, for that matter?

JUDGE THOMAS: That's right.

SEN. LEAHY: Thank you.

Now, were you interviewed—you were interviewed by the FBI, you have talked about that. Were you interviewed on—there seems to be some confusion —on September 28 by the FBI?

JUDGE THOMAS: I don't know which dates in September. I was interviewed on Wednesday, I believe, September 25, I'm not sure.

SEN. LEAHY: I think we have some confusion. In your affidavit, it says, "I told the Federal Bureau of Investigation on September 28, 1991, I categorically deny"—

JUDGE THOMAS: Well, it's Wednesday.

SEN. LEAHY: I've got—it says "date of transcription," the FBI, it says 9-28-91. It was faxed on September 25, 1991, and I am just wondering—we have in about five different places on here—if the FBI has made a typographical error and has the dates off by three days. It was on a Wednesday, which is—

JUDGE THOMAS: It was on a Wednesday.

SEN. LEAHY: When you had that discussion with them, did they ever mention or did you ever mention to them going to her apartment at any time, going to Professor Hill's apartment at any time?

JUDGE THOMAS: I think I may have mentioned that I dropped her off at home and I may have mentioned that I had been in her apartment. I can't remember. I don't think they were focusing on that. I think they were focusing more on whether or not I—the allegations that she made.

SEN. LEAHY: I understand. You said yesterday in your statement that,

> I cannot imagine anything that I said or did to Anita Hill that could have been mistaken for sexual harassment. With that said, if there is anything that I have said that has been misconstrued by Anita Hill or

anyone else to be sexual harassment, then I can say that I'm so very sorry, I wish I had known; if I did know I would have stopped immediately, and I would not, as I have done over the past two weeks, tear away at myself trying to think of what I could have possibly done, but I have not said or done the things Anita Hill has alleged.

I have heard people say was there something further to that. Can you think of anything—I mean, you say if there was anything, then you're very sorry, but you are also saying you cannot think of anything that could approach this, is that correct?

JUDGE THOMAS: That's right, Senator. I have agonized over this. This has not been an easy matter for me, and I don't know how or why she would say these things. I don't know what I could have done that would have resulted in this, and that is just to simply make that point, that if I did anything to anyone that would bring them to a point to suggest or to think that I engaged in sexual harassment, then I am sorry, because it is certainly conduct that I would not approve and conduct that I would not engage in.

SEN. LEAHY: Well, let me follow up on that a bit, since you searched your mind for why she would do this. Now, if I understand your testimony, I am trying to give a summary—and please correct me if I am inaccurate in the summary—you feel that you gave Professor Hill opportunities in Government service, as you have others, is that correct?

JUDGE THOMAS: That's right.

SEN. LEAHY: And you have stated that you felt a particular responsibility—you spoke of them really basically almost as family—to the people that have worked for you and for bringing them forward and giving them these opportunities, is that correct?

JUDGE THOMAS: Yes, Senator. In Professor Hill's case—and it is important to me that this be understood—I believe that when I have assistants or interns, that I have a personal responsibility for them, as teacher, advisor, not employer. I am the employer, also, but they are my personal charges for whom I have responsibility.

Anita Hill came to me through one of my dearest, dearest friends—he was the best man at my wedding, we were at Holy Cross College together, we were at Yale Law School together, we were the two slowest guys on the track team, we spent a lot of time together, we lived across the way from each other in law school, we lived together during the summer when my marriage broke up, I slept at his apartment—this was my dearest friend, and when he brought her to my attention, it was a special responsibility that he asked me to take on, and I felt very strongly that I could discharge that in the way that I did, and that was to be careful about her career, to make sure she had opportunities, to be there to offer advice and counsel, and that is something that I continued with my other special assistants. They are family. My clerks are my family. They are my friends.

SEN. LEAHY: Well, then, having done all this for Professor Hill, and knowing now what she has said here, and what you have read, and hearing her statement, under oath, explicit as it was—a statement that you have categorically denied, to use your term— why would she do this?

JUDGE THOMAS: Senator, you know, I— I have asked myself that question, as I told you. I have not slept very much in the last two and a half weeks. I have thought unceasingly about this, and my wife simply said, "Stop torturing yourself."

I don't know why family members turn on each other. I don't know why a son or a daughter, or a brother or sister would write some book that destroys a family. I don't know. All I can tell you is that from my standpoint I felt that I did everything I could toward Professor Hill in the same way that I would do with my other special assistants to discharge my responsibilities. I don't know. I do not have the answer.

SEN. LEAHY: Have you had any conversation with her since this began? I mean, since these charges came out?

JUDGE THOMAS: No, Senator.

SEN. LEAHY: I am not trying to be facetious, Judge, I am just—I mean, was there any attempt, not by you, but was there any attempt by Professor Hill—did she make any attempt to reach you?

JUDGE THOMAS: No, not to my knowledge. Senator, I have had no conversations with her since, to my knowledge, November 1991.

SEN. LEAHY: So, when did you first hear of these allegations?

JUDGE THOMAS: When the FBI walked—I first heard that there had been, in a call from the White House, allegations of an unspecified nature which needed to be—and the FBI would be sent out. That was Wednesday morning, the 28th or 25th. And that I was to contact the FBI agent or the FBI and set up an appointment. I did that and the agent came out, I think one and a half or two hours later. The first I heard of the nature of the allegations was when the FBI agent, after identifying himself, informed me.

SEN. LEAHY: At your home?

JUDGE THOMAS: At my home.

SEN. LEAHY: And were you there alone meeting with him or—

JUDGE THOMAS: I was there alone with two FBI agents.

SEN. LEAHY: Judge, what was your reaction? I mean when you heard this—you are saying you heard this for the first time—what was your reaction?

JUDGE THOMAS: Senator, my reaction initially, I was stunned. I was hurt. I was confused. I was pained. I did not know what happened, I did not know where it came from. I did not know what the basis of it was. I couldn't believe it and when he said there is an allegation by Anita Hill, I think my words to him were, "Anita?" And then when he told me what the nature of the allegations was, I said, "You can't"—something, like you have got to be kidding. This can't be true.

I can't remember. All I can tell you, it was painful.

SEN. LEAHY: There was no flash, could she have misconstrued—

JUDGE THOMAS: No.

SEN. LEAHY: Fill-in-the-blank that?

JUDGE THOMAS: No, it is just like this is incredible, I can't believe it.

SEN. LEAHY: Have you now—I don't want to go through repetition of them here —but have you now heard the specific charges that Professor Hill made yesterday during her six or seven hours of testimony against you?

JUDGE THOMAS: Senator, I have heard the initial charges through the FBI agent and I have been briefed on the specific charges from yesterday that were different from the previous statements.

SEN. LEAHY: And, Judge, what is your response to those specific charges again?

JUDGE THOMAS: Senator, my response is that I categorically, unequivocally deny them. They did not occur.

SEN. LEAHY: Incidentally, somebody just handed me a note, and I missed this, too, but you said your last contact with Professor Hill was November 1991.

JUDGE THOMAS: 1990, I am sorry, 1990. I would have to be clairvoyant I guess. [Laughter.]

SEN. LEAHY: Judge, I think that you and I may disagree on a number of things, but I think both of us would agree on one thing. Neither of us have been clairvoyant in these hearings or in this process. But you meant 1990?

JUDGE THOMAS: 1990.

SEN. LEAHY: Have you spoken with any of the witnesses of this hearing within the last week, the witnesses who are going to be at this hearing?

JUDGE THOMAS: I don't know. You would have to give me each of the witnesses, Senator. I have spoken with friends of mine who were at EEOC and maybe some of the witnesses. I have spoken to them in the halls here, they have called to wish me well. These are people who are like family to me. These are not—these are former special assistants, I believe, and individuals who were in the inner confines of my office. And again, as I indicated, my staff and I are family.

SEN. LEAHY: Do you know whether personnel from the White House have talked to the witnesses who are going to appear here?

JUDGE THOMAS: I would assume they coordinated their appearance here, Senator, so I would assume the conversations did occur to make sure they were here and the timing, et cetera.

SEN. LEAHY: Thank you, Judge.

My time is up and I know that Senator Hatch and Senator Biden have time and I will come back later on.

THE CHAIRMAN: Thank you.

Senator Hatch.

SEN. HATCH: Thank you, Chairman Biden.

Judge, there are a lot of things in Anita Hill's testimony that just don't make sense to me. I liked her personally. I thought she presented herself well. There is no question she is a very intelligent law professor. She has graduated from one of the finest schools in the land, law schools that is, and her undergraduate work was exemplary.

She is clearly a very intelligent woman. And I think everybody who listened to her wants to like her and many do. But, Judge, it bothers me because it just doesn't square with what I think is— some of it doesn't square with what I think is common experience, and just basic sense, common sense.

I hesitate to do this again but I think it is critical and I know it outrages you, as it would me, as it would anybody who is accused of these type of activities.

In her first statement on this issue, given to the FBI she said that "about two or three weeks after Thomas originally asked her for a date, he started talking about sex. He told her about his experiences and preferences and would ask her what she liked or if she had ever done the same thing. Hill said that he discussed oral sex between men and women. Thomas also discussed viewing films of people having sex with each other and with animals. He told her that he enjoyed watching the films and told her that she should see them. He never asked her to watch the films with him. Thomas liked to discuss specific sex acts and frequency of sex."

That is allegation number one, given in what I consider to be a pretty decent FBI investigation, pretty thorough, by a man and a woman, FBI agent.

In the four-page statement that she issued, which of course was leaked to the press by somebody on this committee, in violation of law, in violation of the Senate ethics, in violation of a stringent rule formulated because these FBI reports contain raw data. And information from the FBI report was released and this statement was given, in fact, the reporter who broke the story read the statement to her, according to her own remarks.

She then said in this statement—this is the second one—"after brief discussion about work he would turn the conversation to discussions about sexual interests. His conversations were very vivid. He spoke about acts that he has seen in pornographic films involving such things as women having sex with animals and films involving group sex or rape scenes. He talked about pornographic materials depicting individuals with large penises or breasts involved in various sex acts."

That is the second statement which is considerably different from the first and adds some language in. And you denied each and every one of these allegations last night.

So I won't go through that again today, although if you want to say anything about it further, I would be happy to have you do it.

Then, yesterday, she appeared before this committee and in her statement yesterday, her written statement of which I have a copy that was distributed to the press and everybody else, she said, "His conversations were very vivid. He spoke about acts that he had seen in pornographic films involving such matters as women having sex with animals and films showing group sex and rape scenes. He talked about pornographic materials depicting individuals with large penises or large breasts involved in various sex acts. On several occasions, Thomas told me graphically of his own sexual prowess." Three different versions, each expansive, each successively expansive.

Now, Judge Thomas, anybody who made all of those cumulative statements—

if you take one of them out of context, they are so graphic and so crude, and so outrageous, and I think so stupid, that would be enough, in my opinion, to find sexual harassment against anybody, if it happened. But if you have all of those cumulatively together the person who would do something like that, over a period of time, really a short period of time according to her, and in two different separate agencies, we will put it that way, that person, it seems to me, would not be a normal person. That person, it seems to me, would be a psychopathic sex fiend or a pervert.

Now, Judge, you have had to have thought about this, I know you are outraged by it, and you have denied all of these things, and you said, these things did not happen, they are simply untrue.

And you have had an evening to think about it, do you have anything further to say about it?

JUDGE THOMAS: Senator, my reaction to this has been, over the last two weeks, has been one of horror. I can't tell you what I have lived through. I can't tell you what my wife has lived through or my family. I can't tell you what my son has lived through. I don't know what to tell him about this. If I were going to date someone outside of the workplace, I would certainly not approach anyone I was attempting to date, as a person, with this kind of grotesque language.

SEN. HATCH: I have to interrupt you here, Judge, but there was an implication that you not only repetitively asked her for dates—I don't know, I guess that can be construed as sexual harassment, repetitively asking a woman for dates—but the implication was, and the clear implication which she spoke about was that you wanted more than dates, if her allegations were true.

JUDGE THOMAS: Senator, I did not ask her out, and I did not use that language. One of the things that has tormented me over the last two and a half weeks has been how do I defend myself against this kind of language and these kind of charges? How do I defend myself? That's what I asked the FBI agent, I believe, for the first time. That's what I have asked myself, how do I defend myself?

If I used that kind of grotesque language with one person, it would seem to me that there would be traces of it throughout the employees who worked closely with me; there would be other individuals who heard it, or bits and pieces of it, or various levels of it.

SEN. HATCH: Don't worry, Judge, probably before the week end's out they will find somebody who will say that.

JUDGE THOMAS: Well, the difficulty also was that, from my standpoint, is that in this country when it comes to sexual conduct we still have underlying racial attitudes about black men and their views of sex. And once you pin that on me, I can't get it off. That is why I am so adamant in this committee about what has been done to me. I made it a point at EEOC and at Education not to play into those stereotypes, at all. I made it a point to have the people at those agencies, the black men, the black women to conduct themselves in a way that is not consistent with those stereotypes, and I did the same thing myself.

SEN. HATCH: When you talk in terms of stereotypes, what are you saying here?

I mean I want to understand this. First of all, let me go back to your first spot.

You said that if you wanted to date somebody or even if you wanted to seduce somebody—you didn't say that—but just put yourself in the mind of this, if you had wanted to seduce her, is this the kind of language you would use? Is this the kind of language a reasonable person would use, is this the kind of language that anybody would use who wanted a relationship?

JUDGE THOMAS: Outside of the work force, or outside of the workplace, that is not certainly the way I would approach someone I would want to date. Whether I would date that person for a long time or just go to dinner, that is not my approach. I think that—and I have to reiterate this—that for someone in the work force to use that kind of grotesque language it has to show up with other staff members. When we looked at sex harassment cases, when we looked at cases of people involved in unacceptable conduct of this nature, there was always a pattern. The other point that I am making that is of great concern to me is that this is playing into a stereotype.

SEN. HATCH: Before we get to that, Judge, I am going to get to that, that's an interesting concept that you have just raised, and I promise I will get back to it. You are a very intelligent man, there is no question about it. Anybody who watches you knows that. You could not have risen to these high positions in Government, been confirmed four times by the august U.S. Senate, three times by the Labor Committee—upon which a number of us here on this committee serve, and whose staff members were used in this investigation—and I might add, once now before the Judiciary Committee, august committees.

She is an extremely intelligent woman and from all appearances a lovely human being. Do you think an intelligent African-American male, like you, or any other intelligent male, regardless of race, would use this kind of language to try and start a relationship with an intelligent, attractive woman?

JUDGE THOMAS: Senator, I don't know anyone who would try to establish a relationship with that kind of language.

SEN. HATCH: Unless they were sick.

JUDGE THOMAS: I don't know of anyone.

SEN. HATCH: I don't even know of people who might have emotional disturbances who would try this. Now, I want to ask you about this intriguing thing you just said. You said some of this language is stereotype language? What does that mean, I don't understand.

JUDGE THOMAS: Senator, the language throughout the history of this country, and certainly throughout my life, language about the sexual prowess of black men, language about the sex organs of black men, and the sizes, et cetera, that kind of language has been used about black men as long as I have been on the face of this Earth. These are charges that play into racist, bigoted stereotypes and these are the kind of charges that are impossible to wash off. And these are the kinds of stereotypes that I have, in my tenure in Government, and the conduct of my affairs, attempted to move away from and to convince people that we should conduct ourselves in a way that defies these stereotypes. But when you play into a stereotype it is as though you are skiing downhill, there's no way to stop it.

And this plays into the most bigoted, racist stereotypes that any black man will face.

SEN. HATCH: Well, I saw—I didn't understand the television program, there were two black men—I may have it wrong, but as I recall—there were two black men talking about this matter and one of them said, she is trying to demonize us. I didn't understand it at the time. Do you understand that?

JUDGE THOMAS: Well, I understand it and any black man in this country—Senator, in the 1970's I became very interested in the issue of lynching. And if you want to track through this country, in the 19th and 20th centuries, the lynchings of black men, you will see that there is invariably or in many instances a relationship with sex—an accusation that that person cannot shake off. That is the point that I am trying to make. And that is the point that I was making last night that this is high-tech lynching. I cannot shake off these accusations because they play to the worst stereotypes we have about black men in this country.

SEN. HATCH: Well, this bothers me.

JUDGE THOMAS: It bothers me.

SEN. HATCH: I can see why. Let me, I hate to do this, but let me ask you some tough questions. You have talked about stereotypes used against black males in this society. In the first statement of Anita Hill she alleges that "he told her about his experiences and preferences and would ask her what she liked or if she had ever done the same thing." Is that a black stereotype?

JUDGE THOMAS: No.

SEN. HATCH: Okay. Anita Hill said that "he discussed oral sex between men and women." Is that a black stereotype?

JUDGE THOMAS: No.

SEN. HATCH: "Thomas also discussed viewing films of people having sex with each other and with animals." What about that?

JUDGE THOMAS: That's not a stereotype about blacks.

SEN. HATCH: Okay. "He told her that he enjoyed watching the films and told her that she should see them." Watching X-rated films or pornographic films, is that a stereotype?

JUDGE THOMAS: No.

SEN. HATCH: "He never asked her to watch the films with him, Thomas liked to discuss specific sex acts and frequency of sex."

JUDGE THOMAS: No, I don't think so. I think that could—the last, "frequency"—could have to do with black men supposedly being very promiscuous or something like that.

SEN. HATCH: So it could be partially stereotypical?

JUDGE THOMAS: Yes.

SEN. HATCH: In the next statement she said,"His conversations were very vivid. He spoke about acts that he had seen in pornographic films involving such things as women having sex with animals and films involving group sex or rape scenes.

He talked about pornographic materials depicting individuals with large penises or breasts involved in various sex acts." What about those things?

JUDGE THOMAS: I think certainly the size of sexual organs would be something.

SEN. HATCH: Well, I am concerned. "Thomas told me graphically of his own sexual prowess," the third statement.

JUDGE THOMAS: That is clearly—

SEN. HATCH: Clearly a black stereotype.

JUDGE THOMAS: [continuing]—stereotypical, clearly.

SEN. HATCH: Do you think that—well, what do you feel about that?

JUDGE THOMAS: Senator, as I have said before, this whole affair has been anguish for me. I feel as though I have been abused in this process, as I said last night, and I continue to feel that way. I feel as though something has been lodged against me and painted on me and it will leave an indelible mark on me. This is something that not only supports but plays into the worst stereotypes about black men in this society. And I have no way of changing it, and no way of refuting these charges.

SEN. HATCH: Now, let me just—people hearing yesterday's testimony are probably wondering how could this quiet, you know, retired, woman know about something like "Long Dong Silver"? Did you tell her that?

JUDGE THOMAS: No, I don't know how she knows.

SEN. HATCH: Is that a black stereotype, something like Long Dong Silver?

JUDGE THOMAS: To the extent, Senator, that it is a reference to one's sexual organs, and the size of one's sexual organs, I think it is.

SEN. HATCH: There is an interesting case that I found called *Carter v. Sedgwick County, Kansas*, a 1988 case, dated September 30. It is a Tenth Circuit Court of Appeals case. It is a district court case. It is a district court case within the tenth circuit. And do you know which circuit Oklahoma is in?

JUDGE THOMAS: My guess would be the tenth circuit. I remember serving on a moot court panel with a judge from the tenth circuit and I believe she was from Tulsa.

SEN. HATCH: Well, I have to tell you something, I believe Oklahoma is in the tenth circuit, and Utah is also.

An interesting case and I am just going to read one paragraph, if anybody wants to read it. I apologize in advance for some of the language, I really do. It is a civil rights case, an interesting civil rights case. And again I apologize in advance for the language. I just want to read one paragraph. "Plaintiff testified that during the course of her employment she was subjected to numerous racial slurs" —by the way, this is an extremely interesting case because the headnote says, "Black female brought suit against county and county officials contending she suffered sexual harassment and was unlawfully terminated from her employment with county on the basis of her race and sex." Now, anybody who wants it, we will make copies for you or you can get it. I will give the citation, as a matter of fact. The citation is 705 F.Supp 1474, District Court Kansas, 1988.

Let me just read the one paragraph."Plaintiff testified that during the course of her employment she was subjected to numerous racial slurs and epithets at the hands of the Defendant Brand. And was sexually harassed by Defendant Cameron. Specifically as to Plaintiff's claim of race discrimination. Plaintiff testified that Defendant Brand referred to Plaintiff on several occasions as John's [Cameron] token—" I apologize for this word, but it is in here—"nigger." That is certainly racist.

"And at other times, would tell Plaintiff that it was 'nigger pick day'. Plaintiff claims that Defendant Brand kept a picture of a black family in his office, and when Plaintiff questioned Brand about the picture he boasted of his own—"And the word is used again—"blood and of his sexual conquests of black"—and I am not going to say that word, it is a pejorative term, it is a disgusting term. So, this man was claiming sexual conquests. "Plaintiff further testified that on one occasion Defendant Brand presented her with a picture of Long Dong Silver—a photo of a black male with an elongated penis."

I apologize again. Well, it goes on, it gets worse, maybe not worse, but it goes on. That is the public opinion that's available in any law library. I have to tell you I am sure it is available there at the law school in Oklahoma and it is a sexual harassment case.

I am really concerned about this matter. Because, first of all, I really don't believe for one instant, knowing you for eleven years, sitting in on four confirmation processes, having them pick at you, and fight at you, and find fault all the way through—and it is fair game with regard to what you did and what you tried to do, what your excesses were with regard to your job, what your failures were, what your successes were—all of that is fair game and it happened. And you went through it and you held your dignity and answered all the questions. You were confirmed three times in a row. This is your fourth time. And you should be confirmed here. Never once were you attacked like this by anybody and I know you, and the people who know you the best and that involves hundreds of people, think the world of you. They know you are a good man. They know this woman's a good woman. And this is not consistent with reality. And I am not going to find fault beyond that with Professor Hill. I liked her, too, she presented herself well.

I will tell you the Juan Williams piece in *The Washington Post* telling how all these interest groups have scratched through everything on Earth to try and get something on you, all over the country, all over this town, all over your agency, all over everybody. And there are a lot of slick lawyers in those groups, slick lawyers, the worst kind. There are some great ones, too, and it may have been a great one who found the reference to "Long Dong Silver", which I find totally offensive.

And I find it highly ironic that you have testified here, today, that used against you by one who taught civil rights, who came from one of the five best law schools in the country, who is an intelligent, apparently decent African-American, used against you, a bunch of black stereotype accusations.

What do you think about that?

JUDGE THOMAS: Senator, as I have indicated before and I will continue to say this and believe this, I have been harmed. I have been harmed. My family has been harmed. I have been harmed worse than I have ever been harmed in my life. I wasn't harmed by the Klan, I wasn't harmed by the Knights of Camellia, I wasn't harmed by the Aryan Race, I wasn't harmed by a racist group, I was harmed by this process, this process which accommodated these attacks on me. If someone wanted to block me from the Supreme Court of the United States because of my views on the Constitution, that is fine. If someone wanted to block me because they felt I was not qualified, that is fine. If someone wanted to block me because they don't like the composition of the Court, that is fine. But to destroy me, Senator, I would have preferred an assassin's bullet to this kind of living hell that they have put me and my family through.

SEN. HATCH: Let me just give you one more. Everybody knows that the worst nightmare for any trial lawyer is to have a person who has an impeccable background, a good appearance and appears to believe everything that person is saying, testifying. And it happens in lots of trials, lots of them.

I have been there, believe it or not. I have lost a lot of the skills, but I have been there. Sixteen years here causes you to lose a lot of things. You almost lose your mind sometimes, and some have suggested that I have, from time to time. But I am just going to give you one more because it really offends me, maybe it doesn't anybody else, maybe I am wrong. But I don't think so. I have been through this a lot of times. I have been through this, only usually—Senator Biden, I am really going to have to take more time than a half hour, if you will let me, I have got to finish this and I have got to finish my line of questions.

THE CHAIRMAN: Without objection, you can take the time you want and then we will just reallocate the rest of the time.

SEN. HATCH: Thank you. I really appreciate that.

She testified:

"One of the oddest episodes I remember was an occasion in which Thomas was drinking a Coke in his office, he got up from the table, at which we were working, went over to his desk to get the Coke, looked at the can and asked, 'Who has put pubic hair on my Coke?'"

That's what she said. Did you ever say that?

JUDGE THOMAS: No, absolutely not.

SEN. HATCH: Did you ever think of saying something like that?

JUDGE THOMAS: No.

SEN. HATCH: That's a gross thing to say, isn't it?

Whether it is said by you or by somebody else, it is a gross thing to say, isn't it?

JUDGE THOMAS: As far as I am concerned, Senator, it is and it is something I did not nor would I say.

SEN. HATCH: Ever read this book?

JUDGE THOMAS: No.

SEN. HATCH: *The Exorcist*?

JUDGE THOMAS: No, Senator.

SEN. HATCH: Ever see the movie?

JUDGE THOMAS: I have seen only the scene with the bed flapping.

SEN. HATCH: I am going to call your attention, and keep in mind, Juan Williams said, this great journalist for *The Washington Post*, I differ with him, but he is a great journalist. I don't differ with him on everything, we agree on a lot of things.

We certainly agree in this area. But he wrote down what they have tried to do to smear you, he wrote down that they have the whole country blanketed trying to dig up dirt, just like you have said it, just like you have said it. And let me tell you these are not itty-bitty tort attorney investigators. These are the smartest attorneys from the best law schools in the land, all paid for at the public interest expense, that is what is ruining our country, in large measure because some of these groups not all of them—many of these public interests are great, I don't mean to malign them all—but a number of them are vicious. We saw it in the Bork matter and we are seeing it here.

You said you never did say this, "Who has put pubic hair on my Coke." You never did talk to her about "Long Dong Silver." I submit, those things were found.

On page 70 of this particular version of *The Exorcist*, "'Oh, Burk,' sighed Sharon. In a guarded tone, she described an encounter between the Senator and the director. Dennings had remarked to him, in passing, said Sharon, that there appeared to be 'an alien pubic hair floating around in my gin.'"

Do you think that was spoken by happenstance? She would have us believe that you were saying these things, because you wanted to date her? What do you think about that, Judge?

JUDGE THOMAS: Senator, I think this whole affair is sick.

SEN. HATCH: I think it's sick, too.

JUDGE THOMAS: I don't think I should be here today. I don't think that this inquisition should be going on. I don't think that the FBI file should have been leaked. I don't think that my name should have been destroyed, and I don't think that my family and I should have been put through this ordeal, and I don't think that our country should be brought low by this kind of garbage.

SEN. HATCH: These two FBI agents told her to be as specific as she could possibly be, and yet she never said anything about Long Dong Silver or pubic hair to them. She didn't say it in her statement, her four-page statement, which is extensive, single-spaced, four pages. But she said it yesterday.

I don't know whether you noticed, but I noticed that whole entourage—not her family, they looked beautiful, they look like wonderful people to me. Look at her parents, they are clearly good people, clearly, her sisters, clearly good people. But I saw the entourage come in, and I'm not saying they did this, but you can bet your bottom dollar that someone found every possible stereotype, to use your terms—but I never fully understood that—every possible stereotype that could be dug up.

Judge Thomas, I just have to finish another short line of questions. I will have others later.

THE CHAIRMAN: Senator, you are welcome to do that. Can you give us an idea how long you are going to go?

SEN. HATCH: If you could give me another ten minutes, I would appreciate it.

THE CHAIRMAN: Sure, just so we have an idea.

SEN. HATCH: First of all, I would like to put Juan Williams's article into the record at this point.

THE CHAIRMAN: Without objection.

[The article was entered into the record.]

SEN. HATCH: "The phone calls came throughout September," Juan Williams said:

> Did Clarence Thomas ever take money from the South African government? Was he under orders from the Reagan White House when he criticized civil rights leaders? Did he beat his first wife? Did I know anything about expense account charges he filed for out-of-town speeches? Did he say that women don't want equal pay for equal work? And finally, one exasperated voice said, "Have you got anything on your tapes we can use to stop Thomas?" The calls came from staff members working for Democrats on the Senate Judiciary Committee.

I didn't say that. I am just repeating it, but I know it's true.

> They were calling me, because several articles written about Thomas have carried my byline. When I was working as a White House correspondent in the early 1980's, I had gotten to know Thomas as a news source and later wrote a long profile of him. The desperate search for ammunition to shoot down Thomas has turned the 102 days—

This is just a few days ago—

> —102 days since President Bush nominated him for a seat on the Supreme Court into a liberal's nightmare. Here is indiscriminate, mean-spirited mudslinging supported by the so-called champions of fairness: liberal politicians, unions, civil rights groups and women's organizations.

All of whom Juan Williams has regard for, or at least did up until this article. I am just reading excerpts.

> Now the Senate has extended its attacks on fairness, decency and its own good name by averting its eyes, while someone in a position to leak has corrupted the entire hearing process.—

It couldn't have been said better in one paragraph, somebody on this committee—

> By releasing a sealed affidavit containing an allegation that had been investigated by the FBI, reviewed by Thomas's opponents and supporters on the Senate committee and put aside as inconclusive and insufficient

to warrant further investigation to stop the committee's final vote.

It is an interesting article. I commend it to everybody.

Judge Thomas, I have a copy of a November 14, 1984, memorandum concerning sexual harassment that you issued within the EEOC. The memo emphasizes the importance of an earlier EEOC order issued shortly before your arrival at that agency.

Judge Thomas, before I get into that memo, I would just like to say this to you, and I wrote it down, because I wanted to say it right: I have to tell you, Judge Thomas, I have reflected on these hearings—this is my handwriting—and what has unfolded this past week is terrible. One of the things that I find most ironic is that many have tried to turn this issue into a referendum on sexual harassment.

Well, let me say, this is not a referendum on sexual harassment. We all deplore sexual harassment. We all deplore the type of conduct articulated here by Professor Hill. But the most ironic thing to me is, it is easy for us on this committee to say that we deplore sexual harassment, and many on this committee have said so in the past and during these proceedings and before the media.

But you, Judge Thomas, you have spent your career doing something about it, a heck of a lot more than deploring sexual harassment. You and your people at the EEOC have been directly involved and have done a lot about it, I know that, because, along with Senator Kennedy and the other members of the Labor Committee, we oversee what you do.

Now, the memo that you issued at the EEOC on sexual harassment, this emphasizes the importance of an earlier EEOC order issued shortly before your arrival at the agency, and that memo stated in unequivocal terms that sexual harassment is illegal.

The final paragraph of the memo, which was signed by you, reads as follows:

> I expect every Commission employee to personally insure that their own conduct does not sexually harass other employees, applicants or any other individual in the workplace. Managers are to take the strongest disciplinary measure against those employees found guilty of sexual harassment. Sexual harassment will not be tolerated at the agency.

Underlined.

Now, Judge Thomas, does this memo reflect a major policy commitment of yours?

JUDGE THOMAS: It expresses my strong attitude and my adamant attitude that sex harassment was not to take place at EEOC.

SEN. HATCH: Judge Thomas, I also have a copy of an EEOC plan for the prevention of sexual harassment issued in 1987, while you were chairman of the Equal Employment Opportunity Commission, which clearly states that sexual harassment includes "unwelcome sexual teasing, jokes, remarks or questions." Now, is this consistent with the views that you personally have believed in and have abided by during your lifetime?

JUDGE THOMAS: Yes.

SEN. HATCH: Or certainly during these last ten or eleven years—

JUDGE THOMAS: Yes, Senator.

SEN. HATCH: [continuing]—which are the years in question. Was sexual harassment tolerated within the EEOC by you, as chairman, or while you were chairman?

JUDGE THOMAS: Absolutely not.

SEN. HATCH: Did you make clear your views to those around you or who were working with you on sexual harassment?

JUDGE THOMAS: Yes, on many occasions.

SEN. HATCH: I would like to just bring up briefly, to ask you what your experience was in handling sexual harassment charges within the EEOC itself while you were the chairman of the EEOC. I realize that most of the relevant information is contained in confidential employee files, but a few general questions would be in order at this point. You have been asked about this already, but this I think needs to be clarified.

There were a number of such charges brought and processed within the EEOC while you were there, were there not?

JUDGE THOMAS: That's right, Senator.

SEN. HATCH: And these—

THE CHAIRMAN: Excuse me, let me interrupt, not on your time. I made a ruling yesterday—you are fully within your rights and if the judge would like to go on it, we can continue—that the conduct at EEOC on sexual harassment was not at issue. Now, you have made it an issue again, which I understand. It is pretty hard—

SEN. HATCH: I agree it is not an issue, but it was made an issue.

THE CHAIRMAN: No, I ruled it out of order yesterday, it was not allowed to be an issue. Now, it seems to me that Senator Heflin has a right to go back and question now on that issue.

SEN. HATCH: On this particular issue, I have no problem with that.

THE CHAIRMAN: Fine. Yesterday I cut Senator Heflin off and I still think it is beyond the scope of this hearing. I do not think he should have to answer questions about his conduct at EEOC in terms of what his policies were. If that's the case, however, then it is going to be hard for me to fairly sit here and rule that one Senator can ask questions regarding an issue and another Senator cannot ask countervailing questions.

I just want to make that point.

SEN. HATCH: I appreciate it, but the real purpose of this is not to go into the matter any deeper than Senator Heflin did, but just to rebut what was said in his questioning, and that's the only reason I am doing this. I don't want to go any further, I don't want to particularly open up the whole issue, although I am sure that he would be happy to discuss it.

I think, frankly—let me just do this and I think you will see why it is relevant under the circumstances. I did not object—

THE CHAIRMAN: No, I think it is relevant. I just want to make sure you understand.

SEN. HATCH: But I mean as a rebuttal to what was said.

THE CHAIRMAN: There is no rebuttal. I cut the Senator from Alabama off. Go ahead.

SEN. HATCH: After a number of comments were made, I want it clarified. Maybe I should have objected earlier, but I didn't and I think this needs to be clarified.

Again, I repeat, I believe most of the relevant information is contained in confidential files there at the EEOC. I think the EEOC maintains its confidentiality, unlike the Senate Judiciary Committee.

There were a number of such charges brought and processed, you have just said, within the EEOC. You handled these matters, right?

JUDGE THOMAS: That's right.

SEN. HATCH: And these cases would have been investigated by the General Counsel's Office, with disposition recommended by that office and then approved by yourself, as chairman of the Commission itself, is that correct? Is that a fair statement?

JUDGE THOMAS: It would be approved by the whole Commission.

SEN. HATCH: Now, just to the specific point, I want to give you a chance to speak on it. Now, reference was made earlier today or last night to the Harper case. In November of 1983, the very time relevant to today's charges, you sent a memorandum to the General Counsel of the EEOC, David Slate, in which you concurred in a recommendation to terminate Mr. Harper's employment, because of sexual harassment charges, and that you specifically noted your view, your individual view that termination, as severe a punishment as it is, was in that case "too lenient" punishment.

JUDGE THOMAS: I generally remember either handwriting that on the memo [*sic*], I felt very strongly that he should have been fired, and that was my view. I felt and continue to feel that individuals engaged in this conduct should be fired, and that's the approach I took at the EEOC.

SEN. HATCH: Well, there are a lot of other things that I could go into to show that you have been a champion in this area for women. You have been a champion in many ways for a lot of us.

I have taken way over the allotted time, but I thought it was essential, because I really am starting to become, more than I have been, outraged about the way you have been treated. I have been outraged over the way this committee has treated you, and I think Senator Biden and Senator Thurmond did everything they should have done. They handled it like every prior difficult decision. The chairman, I have great respect for him for that.

But somebody on this committee has abused the process, and I am not going to be happy with just an Ethics investigation. I don't think anybody is.

THE CHAIRMAN: I am going to order one, though.

SEN. HATCH: I want you to order an FBI investigation. I want an investigation by real appropriate, non-Senate staffers. I want some people who are not affiliated with the Senate to look into this matter, because I think that is the only way we even have the slightest chance, anyway, of getting to the bottom of it, and then we probably will not.

But if we are fair, this is not, as I said at the beginning, the nomination of a justice of the peace to some small county in some small state. This involves the very integrity of and fabric of our country.

I also want to say that the burden of proof is certainly not on Judge Thomas. This is America. The burden of proof is on those who use statements that are stereotypical statements. I thought when we were talking about stereotypes, that we were talking about *The Exorcist* and some of these things that apparently some very bright minds out there have found to help make this dramatic in a destructive way to these good people.

Mr. Chairman, I will come back again and try to ask the rest of my questions.

THE CHAIRMAN: Thank you.

Let me make one thing clear, there will be an investigation of this matter, because I believe that not only has the judge been wronged, but Anita Hill has been wronged, and the process has been wronged.

I think it is appropriate to take a break in a moment, but I would like to ask my colleagues to caucus with me for a minute. I want to make it clear to the press, that there is nothing of any consequence in the caucus. I want to try to figure out the schedule for the rest of the day.

While we recess for fifteen minutes I would like my colleagues to caucus across the hall with me for a few minutes.

[Recess.]

THE CHAIRMAN: The hearing will come to order.

In order to accommodate the schedules of the committee and the nominee, we are going to adjourn—this is a committee decision— for lunch until 1:30.

[Whereupon, at 12:13 p.m., the committee recessed, to reconvene at 1:30 p.m., the same day.]

AFTERNOON SESSION

THE CHAIRMAN: The hearing will come to order.

Judge, I will begin with a few questions. I will be asking questions off and on during the day. Both Senators Leahy and Heflin may have questions, so we will go for roughly forty or forty-five minutes with questions on this side, and then yield back to our friend from Utah, and then maybe start to wind this down, hopefully.

SEN. THURMOND: I may have a few myself.

THE CHAIRMAN: As pointed out by the ranking member, other Senators may have questions, as well.

Judge Thomas, yesterday and today, we heard about the obviously sharp and stark contrast between Professor Hill's testimony and yours. You have indicated that you have no desire or willingness, and I have agreed, to go into aspects other than those that have been alleged in your personal life.

We had a witness before us who is a tenured professor at a law school and whom, prior to her coming forward, you viewed as a credible person. We have two very credible people, with very, very diverse positions on an issue. I know of no way to make this process enjoyable.

Rather than ask you to go through her allegations, which you have categorically denied and my colleagues, Senators Hatch and Heflin and Leahy, have already questioned you about, I would like to try to find out where there is agreement in the testimony, not disagreement. Hopefully we can determine whether or not there is any place from which we can logically begin to make the cut on who is telling the truth. Obviously, someone is not.

Again, I go back to the point that you have made time and again, and admirably, that you had not second-guessed the professor's credibility until now. It came as a shock to you.

So, if you are willing, I would like to decide where there is agreement between the testimony given by you and given by her. You testified that Professor Hill was your attorney advisor at the Education Department. Is that correct?

JUDGE THOMAS: That's right, Senator.

THE CHAIRMAN: How many such attorney advisors did you have?

JUDGE THOMAS: Senator, there was one other more senior professional on my staff, but she was not an attorney at the time—she was going to law school, in fact —on whom I relied for some policies as well as some management work. She would have been the only other professional on my personal staff.

THE CHAIRMAN: So, on your personal staff, there were only two people at the Department of Education—

JUDGE THOMAS: That's right.

THE CHAIRMAN: [continuing]—Professor Hill and this other person who was going to law school at the time.

JUDGE THOMAS: That's right. Two professionals, and there was also a secretary.

THE CHAIRMAN: And a secretary.

JUDGE THOMAS: That's right, Diane Holt.

THE CHAIRMAN: Now, I take it that it was not uncommon for you to talk one on one with Professor Hill, while at the Department of Education?

JUDGE THOMAS: That's true. That was also true with the other person.

THE CHAIRMAN: With regard to both of these persons, I assume conversations with either or both would take place fairly frequently. Let me not assume anything. Would they take place fairly frequently? Would you see them more than once a day, for example in the conduct of your affairs at the Department of Education?

JUDGE THOMAS: It would not be uncommon, but I would not assign a number to it. It may be that some days I may see them none and other days I might see them once.

THE CHAIRMAN: Up here, for example, as you know from working with Senator Danforth's staff, the chief of staff, the head of the committee, the person in charge of the legislative operation, those people, generally speaking, have media access to Senators Danforth, Thurmond, Biden. I mean that is kind of how it works up here, but I don't want to confuse how it works here with how it worked there. I assume that if Professor Hill wanted to see you, she would have essentially the same kind of access that you observe the chief of staff would have here, on the Hill, to the office in which you worked?

JUDGE THOMAS: No.

THE CHAIRMAN: No?

JUDGE THOMAS: That's not an accurate comparison.

THE CHAIRMAN: Then I would like to hear what yours was.

JUDGE THOMAS: The Deputy Assistant Secretary would have that kind of access.

THE CHAIRMAN: The Deputy Assistant Secretary would have that access to you.

JUDGE THOMAS: That's right.

THE CHAIRMAN: I see. Would you describe the type of access that Professor Hill, in her professional responsibilities at Education, had to you?

JUDGE THOMAS: I think it was my secretary who normally made those kinds of judgments. If I were available, if I were not busy, if I were not in the middle of something and the matter merited it, she certainly didn't have to make an appointment.

THE CHAIRMAN: Now, this other person who worked in the capacity similar to Professor Hill, as you described it, what was his or her name?

JUDGE THOMAS: Her name was Tricia Healey.

THE CHAIRMAN: Healey, H-e-a-l-e-y?

JUDGE THOMAS: I think so, but she perhaps had more access, because I believe—and that has been ten years ago—we met at the beginning and at the end of the day routinely. She was the person who followed the list of assignments that I had within the organization, people who needed to be involved in certain projects, people with whom I needed to touch base, projects that were finished and unfinished, evaluations that needed to be done, and those kinds of things.

THE CHAIRMAN: Now, either at the Department of Education or at EEOC, when Professor Hill would have access to you, either at her initiative or your initiative, in the performance of your duties, was it unusual for those conversations or exchanges to take place alone, just with the two of you?

JUDGE THOMAS: It wasn't unusual, just as it wasn't unusual for Tricia Healey, but normally I have basically an open door and my secretary Diane would guard that door, basically.

THE CHAIRMAN: So, like the conduct of any business, usually, not all decisions or all judgments that are brought to you by staff require you to call in all the staff. Many of those decisions are made, as they are here, one on one?

JUDGE THOMAS: No, I think that's going too far. I made those kinds of decisions one on one, generally with the Deputy Assistant Secretary.

THE CHAIRMAN: I see.

JUDGE THOMAS: There were any number of problems that we had within the agency, and I believe that when I made those kinds of decisions, it would have been with him. I would have spent a significant amount of time with Tricia Healey, I think, going through the assignments, and that would be one on one, but it would usually be more going through a list of things to get done.

THE CHAIRMAN: Now, in your discussions, conversations, and meetings with Professor Hill, you have indicated to the committee or I have gotten the impression that you viewed yourself as her mentor, the same role you have with all people who have been on your personal staff. Is that correct?

JUDGE THOMAS: I looked out for the members of my personal staff. I made sure that I tried to be aware of their careers and aware of their progress, et cetera, not just a mere employer-employee relationship. Again, that was true in the case of my other assistant, who was I believe at that time either finishing night law school and/or studying for the bar exam, and it was simply an effort to make some accommodation. I thought it was a good idea and she was doing very well.

THE CHAIRMAN: In attempting to find out where there is agreement, were there ever occasions that you would have an opportunity or occasion to be speaking with Professor Hill, in either capacity, EEOC or as her boss at Education, where you would discuss matters, either as her mentor, or in any other capacity, where you would discuss matters other than business matters?

JUDGE THOMAS: I think that there may be occasions when we would debate politics, as I indicated. She was from Yale Law School and, of course, I was interested in what had happened to the law school. There were some people I think who had clerked on the Supreme Court who had been in her class, and that sort of thing, similar to what I do with my clerks. They have their own friends, they have their ideas about the world, and occasionally they will chat with me about those or if they have problems. I think Anita Hill had some health problems from time to time. I can't remember exactly what they were, but I believe either back or allergies or something like that. It would be those sorts of things.

THE CHAIRMAN: Professor Hill testified, for example, that you sometimes discussed how your son was doing.

JUDGE THOMAS: No, I don't remember that. I brought my son to the office quite a bit. He was a young kid then and my wife and I were separated and he would be in the office, and—

THE CHAIRMAN: I am not going anywhere in terms of your son. I am just trying to get a sense of the flavor of the conversation.

JUDGE THOMAS: I am trying to tell you, I don't remember that. I discussed my son perhaps and the problems that I was having from a financial standpoint, I may have mentioned it to my secretary, but I don't remember mentioning that to Professor Hill. What I am suggesting to you now is that my son, because he was living with his mother, came to the office fairly frequently and was around.

THE CHAIRMAN: I understand that. Once when we were having a full committee meeting over here, there was a knock on the door. We had asked not to be disturbed, and in walked my ten-year-old daughter, so I understand about children being at work.

SEN. DECONCINI: It raised the IQ of the whole meeting, didn't it? [Laughter.]

THE CHAIRMAN: How can I disagree with that? [Laughter.]

Now, Judge, you testified that you never asked out the professor on a date, is that correct?

JUDGE THOMAS: That's right.

THE CHAIRMAN: Now, I am sure it was pointed out to you, if you don't know, that everything that is reported isn't true, not because it is intentionally meant to mislead, but because sometimes there is a miscommunication. It was reported in the *New York Times*, on October 7, on page A13, that "Judge Thomas told the investigators"—meaning the paper's investigators—"that he had asked the woman out a few times and, after she declined, eventually dropped all advances." I assume that is a misunderstanding?

Would someone rapidly running back tell me, without my glasses, did I misread it? What's this say? I don't have my glasses. What does that say?

SEN. THURMOND: Do you want to borrow mine?

THE CHAIRMAN: Yes. [Laughter.]

Thank you. You are only twice my age, too.

SEN. THURMOND: We are young otherwise.

THE CHAIRMAN: That's exactly right.

It says: "Senator Biden said in a statement today that the allegations were investigated by the Federal Bureau of Investigation, at the request of the Judiciary Committee. Judge Thomas"—this did not come from Senator Biden—"Judge Thomas told the Bureau's investigators that he had asked the woman out a few times and, after she declined, eventually dropped all advances." That is incorrect?

JUDGE THOMAS: That is wrong.

THE CHAIRMAN: Wrong.

JUDGE THOMAS: I had the occasion to be re-investigated by the FBI agents prior to this hearing. In fact, I believe that it would have been on Thursday afternoon, and the FBI agent, in my living room, stated that it was wrong, the very same FBI agents who interviewed me, and indicated that he was distressed that this matter had been reported that way. At no time did I ever indicate that I ever asked her out. I categorically deny that I ever asked her on a date.

THE CHAIRMAN: That is why I ask you the question, Judge, to confirm on the record what you said. I thought that is what you had said, but it has been sitting out there. Let me return to your discussions, if any, with Professor Hill that may have been of a non-work nature.

JUDGE THOMAS: Pardon me?

THE CHAIRMAN: You indicated, there were some discussions you have had with her about Yale Law School, discussions, conversations or exchanges at work that did not relate to what was going on at work, which would be almost impossible for anyone in the whole world to not have in a business setting. I want to make it clear that you don't every time, and we don't, always talk to our staff about business only. So, you have indicated that you have had some discussions with her about Yale Law School, how it was going, how it has changed.

JUDGE THOMAS: Mutual friends, frankly, Gil Hardy, it may have been current events, those sorts of things, the things I talk with my clerks about or the other members of my staff.

THE CHAIRMAN: Did you ever inquire about or did she ever volunteer, to the best of your recollection, anything about her social life. Such as, "I can't stay late tonight, I've got a date, yeah, that fellow you mentioned at the Supreme Court from Yale, I'm dating him," or anything? Was there any discussion ever that you recall about her social life?

JUDGE THOMAS: Someone might—she may have said. "I've got to leave tonight, because I'm going out to dinner." I can't recall a specific, nor would there be any reason for me. It would be simply a reason for her not being at work. There may have been an indication of what she was doing. There could be no extensive discussion about that. I don't see any reason why that would happen. I mean, today, what my clerks would simply do is, "I'm having dinner with a couple of friends of mine from law school."

The only thing that I can remember, and this is very general, was that I believe —and I could be misrecalling this—was that she had dated someone in Oklahoma who came to New England or something and they weren't together, or something like that. That's really vague.

THE CHAIRMAN: It is kind of hard for anybody to remember anything of a passing topic from a while ago.

And again, we are all trying to find out what could be the motivation, if, in fact, what you say is true and what she says is not true. How has this happened?

You indicated, today, that a friend of yours who was your Holy Cross classmate, law school classmate, summer roommate, is now deceased.

JUDGE THOMAS: That's right.

THE CHAIRMAN: This friend had referred Anita Hill to you—and I do not have the transcript from this morning, so please correct me if I am wrong—so you said you believed you had a special obligation as a consequence of his referral.

Now, did that special obligation result in any additional impact on your relationship, professional or otherwise, with Anita Hill in a way any differently than it has with any other person that has worked for you? Let me make it clear now, okay, for the moment I am not talking about the allegations, I am trying to figure the relationship that you and Professor Hill had. Did you feel a special obligation to look out for her? She was a young woman, so did you say,"Be careful what you do because certain parts of this city are dangerous." Or, you know, "You have to be careful who you date," or "Make sure you call your mother." Or "Have you called"—was his name Gil?

JUDGE THOMAS: Yes.

THE CHAIRMAN: "Have you called Gil, he is concerned about you, you need to keep in touch,"— or anything of that nature?

JUDGE THOMAS: I don't recall anything of that nature, Senator. What I was referring to was to make sure that I looked out for her career, that she got solid work, to make sure that everything was okay at work, that she got her promotions, those kinds of things. The kind of relationship that you are talking about, in your examples, those are the kinds of things I look out for with young interns, who work with me during the summer, or individuals who are in coop programs, those individuals.

I have had some who were nineteen or twenty years old who I would treat more like my own son or daughter.

THE CHAIRMAN: So there would be no reason for anyone, including Professor Hill, to assume that you were asserting and/or you were taking on a role, any other role, other than an employer who was concerned about the work product. This is as opposed to what all of us have when young interns, from our states, are sent down here to work for us. We have unpaid interns in my office. A friend will say, "Can my son or daughter come work for you?" and the first thing I say is "They can't come down unless I know where they are going to live. Is there a relative down here? I am not taking responsibility for a seventeen-year-old kid to come, not just to this city, but to any city." So, all of us, I am sure at one time or another have talked to young women or men who are in college and in town to work as interns. We have said,"How are you doing in school? Or tell me what you are doing?" Was there any reason for Anita Hill to think that there was that kind of relationship between you and her?

JUDGE THOMAS: I can't think of a reason for her to think that. As I indicated, Senator, or Mr. Chairman, there are any number of younger kids that have worked for me that I would be concerned about, individuals who are not from this city and who do not understand the city; individuals who occupy themselves after work with other kids their age, again, without the guidance, I would be concerned about them not knowing the rules of the city, but certainly not in her case.

THE CHAIRMAN: Now, you said yesterday something that I don't dispute—I don't know so I can't dispute it. When one of the committee members said that Professor Hill was a meek professional woman, and she came across as a meek person, you replied "Well, I would call her anything but meek."

Can you elaborate on that a little bit more for me today?

JUDGE THOMAS: Well, the point that I was making, Senator, if you asked me to describe the Anita Hill who worked for me, "meek" would not be the word. She was very bright. And she would argue for, particularly with the other special assistants, argue for her position and sometimes to a fault. And by that, I simply mean that she would become entrenched in her own point of view and not understand the other point of view. And she was certainly capable of storming off and going to her office, and that happened on any number of occasions.

So," meek" would not be the word. She was also a forceful debater on the issues that she was involved in.

THE CHAIRMAN: Was there any change between the Anita Hill that first started to work for you at the EEOC and the Anita Hill— I beg your pardon, at Education —who eventually worked for you at EEOC? Just before she left, was it basically the same person, same modus operandi, same professional relationship relative to you?

JUDGE THOMAS: No. The relationship, as I indicated in my opening statement, Mr. Chairman, changed primarily because my job changed and the staff went from those two professionals to maybe ten, twelve, fifteen professionals with a chief of staff, office directors of fourteen individuals, and a chief of staff being in charge of my personal staff, as opposed to the staff having direct access. So even the special assistants could not see me on an as-available basis.

The chief of staff could see me on that basis, but she could not.

THE CHAIRMAN: When you saw her, though, was it essentially the same professional woman in terms of her professional attitude? Did she seem more confident, less calm? Was there any difference in the Anita Hill, not necessarily in terms of access, but in terms of the professional lawyer who worked for Clarence Thomas? Was she the same woman in terms of when you were with her?

JUDGE THOMAS: Senator, I can't—all I can say is this, that I can't tell you that there was a specific change. What I can say is that she was having more of a difficulty, I thought, from my perspective, she was having more difficulty in the role at EEOC because there were so many more staffers. And there were so many different levels of communications.

For example, on—or responsibilities—for example, I would rely on individuals with more experience to work on projects that were of great significance to me. There were routine assignments that would be what I could call grunt work, much more than we had at Education. There was sort of a pecking order and I don't think that she, in that role, at EEOC was very high on the pecking order because of experience.

THE CHAIRMAN: Well, you said yesterday, when you first appeared, that you can't imagine what you could have said that would have caused Anita Hill to say what she has said. But if there was anything she misunderstood—I don't know this exact quote—then you are sorry.

Now, let me ask you this. On its face that seems to me to be a completely reasonable statement for one to make. I think—I will speak for myself—that things I might say, or jokes that I might tell with a male trusted aide that I have been with for twenty years, might not be the same joke that I would be willing to tell with the female members of my staff. And I suspect that, were I a woman, there are certain things that I could say to the females on my staff that I couldn't say to the males on my staff. Among the men on your staff did you ever kid about, make reference to, say you saw, or deal with any of the subjects that Anita Hill says you dealt with, spoke to, and mentioned to her?

JUDGE THOMAS: No. Let me go back a second. There are a couple of comments I would like to make about that.

THE CHAIRMAN: Sure.

JUDGE THOMAS: I attempted to conduct myself in a way with my staff so that there were no jokes that I would listen to or tell to men that I could not listen to or tell to women. There were no jokes that I found acceptable that I could not listen to or tell to any ethnic group.

The other thing. When I was speaking about on something I may have missed, I was talking about a kind of insensitivity—let me give you an example.

THE CHAIRMAN: That's what I am trying to drive at.

JUDGE THOMAS: And it doesn't mean mean-spirited and it's not in the area we are talking about. A former member of your staff came to work for me in 1982,

Barbara Parris.

THE CHAIRMAN: One of the best people who have ever worked for me.

JUDGE THOMAS: That's right, and one of the best who has ever worked for me and who is familiar with me.

THE CHAIRMAN: She has made me aware of just how familiar she is.

JUDGE THOMAS: That's right and she understands about why I feel so strongly about being here. Barbara Parris, my offices were on the fifth floor and the elevator panel, button panel, panel of buttons was at a level that Barbara Parris could not reach because she is a short person. She did not tell me. And I was insensitive to it because I could reach the panel. So someone had to inform me that she was climbing up four or five flights of stairs because she could not reach the panels.

It is that kind of insensitivity, oversight, and I made it a point to tell my staffers, if I do something, let me know what it is. If you see something, tell me what it is so that we can correct it. If you hear something, tell me what it is. My grandfather used to have a statement, "I can read your letter, but I can't read your mind."

And the point is, let me know if I am overlooking something, and I think that the totality, the other component of my statement was that if something happened, if I had known, I could have corrected it. That has been my attitude.

THE CHAIRMAN: I was just referring to your comment, I think you said, if there was anything I did or said.

JUDGE THOMAS: That's right.

THE CHAIRMAN: I was referring to the "said" part. I was not referring to telling ethnic jokes, but let's say that you and I are sitting and watching a football game and you watch some 280-pound tackle blow away a 158-pound flankerback. You and I might describe that in a way, sitting with one another and both having played football, that we would not describe in the same way if there were five women sitting in the room. I may be wrong, maybe you would not.

JUDGE THOMAS: Senator, this may sound unusual to you, but I would describe it the same way.

THE CHAIRMAN: Well, that's interesting. Maybe that is because you were closer to the 280-pound lineman and I was closer to the 130-pound flankerback. [Laughter.]

JUDGE THOMAS: Senator, my attitude was, in my work environment, my staffs were almost invariably predominantly women. The senior person on my staff was a woman. I could not tolerate individuals making that environment uncomfortable or hostile. I could not tolerate individuals who had to segregate their language or conduct in order to get along. The conduct had to be purged of offensive attitudes and I made that a constant effort, and that's something that I was proud of and it was something I am sure the people who worked with me felt comfortable with and understood.

THE CHAIRMAN: In order to attempt to seek the truth, I am accepting, for the sake of this discussion, the assertions that you never said anything in the workplace or out of the workplace to Ms. Hill. Let's, as we lawyers say, stipulate to that for the moment.

JUDGE THOMAS: Senator, you stipulated to my character earlier.

THE CHAIRMAN: I did, and I have again. All right, now let me ask you this question. We are trying to find out why we are here. An incredibly credible woman, who thus far has not had her character or her integrity impugned, sat before us and, at a minimum, impressed this committee on both sides. Now, we both know that employees form opinions about the person with whom they work not based totally upon that person in the working environment.

For example, no matter how well your boss treats you, if you knew, from observation or you heard from outside, that he did not treat his children well, then you would not necessarily have a universally high regard for him. You treat your children well, I am not making any innuendo. The point I am trying to make is how can we figure out, if we can, why this very credible woman might, as you are asserting, be telling a lie?

JUDGE THOMAS: No, she is asserting that I did something. I am not asserting anything about her.

THE CHAIRMAN: I understand that. Well, she is asserting you did something, and you are denying you did what she asserted. We have two very credible people in front of us. Now, all I am asking you is, if there is anything outside of the workplace that would reasonably, unreasonably, or even remotely lead a person to form an opinion of you different than they had of you in the workplace?

JUDGE THOMAS: Senator, my relationship with my staff, although I care about them, is in the workplace.

THE CHAIRMAN: I understand that, but opinions—

JUDGE THOMAS: No, Senator, it is in the workplace. I did not make these statements or do these things. And I cannot get into or determine how she arrived at whatever it is that influenced her. I am simply saying that I don't know what her motivation was. These things did not happen. I did not allege anything, or I did not say anything to her or I did not attempt to date her.

THE CHAIRMAN: I understand that. Let me give you an example of what I am thinking of and maybe you can think of something that relates to this. If not, we will drop the whole subject.

I can think of specific employees with whom I have worked. Their working relationship with me and with everyone in my office has been exemplary. I have gone—I can think of a specific incident—to lunch with this person and several others, in this case the person was a man. We ordered lunch and the lunch was late. We are out of the work environment. This person berated the waitress at which time I said, "You don't work for me here, and you are not going to work for me anywhere if you treat people that way." Now, this occurred out of the work environment. After about five or six years working with this person, I had never seen him this way, and yet I watched this person just read the riot act to a waitress because she brought the wrong meal. So my opinion of that person was colored by something totally unrelated to the workplace.

This is the last time I will ask you this and then I will drop it. Is there anything you can think of outside the workplace that Professor Hill would have heard of, or witnessed, that might have shaded her opinion of you?

JUDGE THOMAS: Senator, or Mr. Chairman, I attempt to conduct myself with my staff, at lunch or walking down the street or whatever, in a way that they could be, or think, or feel was admirable. I do not and did not co-mingle my personal life with my work life nor did I co-mingle their personal life with the work life.

I can think of nothing that would lead her to this.

THE CHAIRMAN: Okay. I accept your statement. Let me ask you another question. Did you inform the FBI that you had, on occasion, driven Professor Hill home or that you had, on occasion, gone in for a Coke or a beer after work?

JUDGE THOMAS: I think I did, Senator, again these events have unfurled very rapidly. And I don't think that was a particular issue. Their response was, or their questioning went to specific allegations.

THE CHAIRMAN: I am not suggesting if you didn't—

JUDGE THOMAS: I am just saying, I don't remember but I think I did.

THE CHAIRMAN: Okay, now, having asked you that, I have another area I am confused about. I don't know whether it was Senator Hatch, Senator Leahy, or Senator Specter, that asked these questions, but I am confused about cars.

SEN. LEAHY: About?

THE CHAIRMAN: Cars, automobiles. Now, I thought I heard you say you did not own an automobile when you were at the Department of Education. I thought I heard you say that you did not have a driver assigned to you when you were at the Department of Education. Did I miss that? What are the facts? Did you own an automobile when you were at the Department of Education, and/or did you have a driver assigned to you or an automobile available to you through the Government?

JUDGE THOMAS: At the Department of Education I owned a car.

THE CHAIRMAN: So you would drive to work?

JUDGE THOMAS: No. Some days—I lived in Southwest—and the Department of Education is in Southwest, the Switzer Building, and I would walk to work some days and other days I would drive depending on what I needed the car for. My point was that I would work late often, and if it was late or if for some reason she may have needed a ride, I would give her a ride. Or if I were headed in that direction or if I were leaving.

THE CHAIRMAN: So you would drive her in your own automobile is the point.

JUDGE THOMAS: Yes, but it wasn't—I don't remember a large number of times, but it has happened.

THE CHAIRMAN: Can you give us any sense of how often it happened that you would go in and have a Coke or a beer after work?

JUDGE THOMAS: Oh, it couldn't have happened any more than maybe twice or three times. Nothing, there was no, it was nothing major. It was just a matter of, you know, we may have been arguing about something, debating something, a policy or something.

THE CHAIRMAN: What are the kinds of things you would argue about?

JUDGE THOMAS: I think we debated affirmative action, we debated busing, those sorts of things, black colleges.

THE CHAIRMAN: Now, you said she had a roommate. Did you ever meet her roommate when you—

JUDGE THOMAS: Yes. To my knowledge, those were the only times I have seen her. She was, as I remember, a basketball player, I think she was in a basketball league. And occasionally she would walk by in her sweats or be there in her sweats.

THE CHAIRMAN: At the apartment?

JUDGE THOMAS: That's right.

THE CHAIRMAN: So you would be in the apartment with both—

JUDGE THOMAS: In an open area, yes, that's right.

THE CHAIRMAN: Okay.

I am almost finished here. I just want to make sure that I have covered the things that I had questions about or that I misunderstood.

JUDGE THOMAS: Let me make one point. I did not have a driver assigned to me at Education. There was a carpool at the Department of Education. I had a driver assigned to me as chairman of EEOC. After I arrived at EEOC, the car that I had, it was a Fiat Spider, was recalled. And—

THE CHAIRMAN: Was what? I am sorry?

JUDGE THOMAS: Was recalled.

THE CHAIRMAN: Oh, rehauled.

JUDGE THOMAS: Defective.

THE CHAIRMAN: Recalled?

JUDGE THOMAS: Yes.

THE CHAIRMAN: Oh, because it was defective. I am sorry. Fiat will appreciate that.

JUDGE THOMAS: And I used the money to pay my son's tuition so I didn't have a car.

THE CHAIRMAN: Gotcha. At Education?

JUDGE THOMAS: At EEOC.

THE CHAIRMAN: At EEOC.

JUDGE THOMAS: And I, subsequently, I believe in 1983, got a car a year or so later.

THE CHAIRMAN: Another area where you both agree is that occasionally, or at least on one or more occasions, you had lunch with Professor Hill in the cafeteria.

JUDGE THOMAS: I don't think I said that. I just—

THE CHAIRMAN: No, I think she said it. I'm not sure what you said.

JUDGE THOMAS: No, I don't think I said that. I don't recall ever having lunch with her in the cafeteria.

THE CHAIRMAN: I see.

JUDGE THOMAS: I would rarely, at the Department of Education, almost never, at EEOC, go to the cafeteria with the exception of breakfast. That may not have been a good thing, but I rarely went there in the early years. In the later years—

THE CHAIRMAN: This was at EEOC?

JUDGE THOMAS: At EEOC, in the later years I went more frequently.

THE CHAIRMAN: Did you ever have breakfast with her at EEOC in the cafeteria?

JUDGE THOMAS: No, not to my knowledge. I am trying to finish up with Education.

THE CHAIRMAN: I am sorry.

JUDGE THOMAS: At the Department of Education, my habits for eating lunch usually consisted of—and I am giving my normal pattern—my normal pattern was to work out at the NASA gym at noon and then to run and then to grab takeout or have my secretary grab takeout and eat at my desk. That was my normal pattern. I rarely remember eating at the Department of Education cafeteria.

THE CHAIRMAN: Okay.

JUDGE THOMAS: That does not mean I didn't, it just wasn't—

THE CHAIRMAN: No, I understand what you are saying. The one, two, or three occasions that you drove Professor Hill home and went into her apartment to have a Coke or continue a debate, were they all at Education or did any of them also occur at EEOC?

JUDGE THOMAS: To my knowledge, it only occurred at Education because it was very convenient for me. My car was parked right outside of my office and easy just to drive over and drop her off.

THE CHAIRMAN: All right. Now, are there other employees, such as this other person who had more access to you at EEOC, that you were in a position to offer a ride home? The one going to night school or law school or the bar exam, I apologize, but I forget the name.

JUDGE THOMAS: Her husband worked at the agency so they commuted together.

THE CHAIRMAN: I see.

JUDGE THOMAS: So that was not the problem. I have, over time, with other members of my staff dropped them off someplace if they needed it, at a Metro station or if we were headed, I was headed in the same direction.

THE CHAIRMAN: Judge, there has been a lot of reference to the telephone logs. We went through them in detail with Professor Hill, but we did not spend much time discussing them with you. And do you have the original telephone logs, by any chance?

JUDGE THOMAS: I have the originals in my chambers, yes.

THE CHAIRMAN: You have the originals, because EEOC doesn't have them nor does Ms. Holt?

JUDGE THOMAS: I have the originals in my chambers. I was advised, I believe, and I could be wrong, that those were my property when I left the EEOC.

THE CHAIRMAN: I am not suggesting they are not. I just wonder where they are, that's all.

Well, Judge, that's all. I have used up enough time. Now, I may have a few more questions later, as I digest this, but thank you very much.

I yield to the ranking member, who indicates that he has a question.

SEN. THURMOND: Mr. Chairman, in my opening statement I appointed Senator Hatch and Senator Specter to question the witnesses. However, I reserved the right, if I saw fit now and then, to ask a question. I do care to ask a question at this time.

Judge, we have your testimony and we have Ms. Hill's testimony. Some of the press have asked me outside and some people, too, what was the motivation? This question was raised by Senator Heflin earlier and Senator Biden touched on it—the motivation for these charges.

In other words, why did she make these charges? In talking with several people, some of them the press, and other people, various reasons have been assigned. I just want to ask you if you care to comment on any of them.

One is she failed to get a promotion under you. Another is because you didn't date her she felt rejected. Another is she said in her own statement to the FBI about differences in political philosophy. Another is stated by the dean of the law school, Charles A. Kothe, under whom she taught at the Oral Roberts University Law School, he made this short paragraph and it covers that. He said,

> I have come to know Clarence Thomas quite intimately over the last seven years and have observed him and his relationship with members of his staff as well as his conduct at social gatherings, and never once was there any hint of unacceptable conduct with respect to women. In fact, I have never heard him make a coarse remark or engage in any off-color conversation.

And he makes this statement, "I find the references to the alleged sexual harassment not only unbelievable, but preposterous. I am convinced that such is the product of fantasy." And I have had several other people mention that as a possible reason. Then, as a fifth reason that has been mentioned by someone is instability.

Now, those things have come to me from other people, and I just want to ask you if you care to comment on any of those?

JUDGE THOMAS: Senator, I don't know what the motivation is and, as I indicated, any of those may or may not be correct. I can't speculate. But I think that the appropriate individuals to ask that are the staffers who were involved in leaking this information and who made contacts with her.

SEN. THURMOND: That is all, Mr. Chairman.

THE CHAIRMAN: Thank you. I understand that you still have time. Whom do you wish to yield it to?

SEN. HATCH: I am happy to defer the balance of my time to Senator Specter.

THE CHAIRMAN: Senator Specter has the remainder of this half hour.

SEN. SPECTER: Thank you, Mr. Chairman.

Judge Thomas, at the start of my participation in today's hearings I repeat what I said yesterday. I do not view this as an adversary proceeding, and I do not represent anyone in this proceeding except the people of Pennsylvania who elected me. I took on the job of questioning at the request of Senator Thurmond, the ranking Republican, but that is not intended by me to mean that I am taking sides.

The questioning yesterday of Professor Hill was obviously difficult from many, many points of view. And I attempted with her, as I attempted with you during the earlier part of these proceedings, to be scrupulously polite and professional and non-argumentative.

The purpose of my questioning her and the purpose of the round that I am about to undertake with you is to deal with the issue of credibility. We have a situation here where many have characterized it as two very believable witnesses. And I had searched for a long while to see if there was a way to reconcile the testimony here, so that it would be possible to believe both of the critical witnesses and that has not been possible to do.

The next step, as I have seen it, is to try to make an analysis on credibility from what we have. It would be fine to go out and conduct a very extensive investigation but we have been given the charge here from last Tuesday to come to a conclusion so that the Senate can vote on this matter by this coming Tuesday. We are trying to do that. In the questions that I am about to ask you, which relate to Professor Hill's testimony yesterday, it is not with any intention of impugning Professor Hill at all, but in an effort to see what indicators there are as to credibility here.

The problem is a hard one because none of us wants to discourage women from coming forward with charges of sexual harassment. And I have been working for the past year and a half to get the civil rights bill which would improve the issue for women on sexual harassment. The fellow who is sitting behind you is Senator Danforth. It is obviously true that this hearing has raised the consciousness of America on this issue of sexual harassment, but the generalizations have to be put aside.

We have to make a determination as to whether you did or did not engage in the kind of conduct which is being charged. And with that brief introduction what I would like to cover with you in this round relates to questions on credibility, on four specific subjects.

First, the *USA* article; second, her move from Education to EEOC; third, her testimony on not documenting the alleged comments; and four, the inferences on credibility arising from the telephone logs.

The issue of the article in *USA Today*, I think is a very compelling one because I believe—and I am going to ask you about this— that Professor Hill testified in the morning and demolished her testimony in the afternoon. What I want to examine with you for the next few minutes is an extremely serious question as to whether Professor Hill's testimony in the morning was or was not perjury.

I do not make that statement lightly. But we are searching here for what happened. And nobody was present with a man and a woman when this tragedy arose. The quality of her testimony and the inferences are very significant on the underlying question as to credibility.

I am going to read you extensive extracts from the testimony which I re-read this morning and I think it ought to be noted that we proceed here on a very short timetable. Senator Thurmond asked me to undertake this job on Wednesday. I started on it with Thursday. We are in hearings on Friday and are reading overnight text this morning.

And the start of it was my question to Professor Hill about the *USA* article on October 9, "Anita Hill was told by Senate staffers her signed affidavit alleging sexual harassment by Clarence Thomas would be the instrument that would 'quietly, and behind the scenes,' would force him to withdraw his name."

Now, I am about to go through the transcript where I asked Professor Hill about this repeatedly. At one point she consulted her attorney and throughout an extensive series of questions yesterday morning flatly denied that any Senate staffer had told her that her coming forward would lead to your withdrawal. In the afternoon she flatly changed that by identifying a Senate staffer who she finally said told her that she was told that if she came forward you would withdraw or might withdraw your nomination.

The transcript, which is prepared overnight, does not reveal the part where she consulted with her attorney, but I asked my staffers to review the tape, because I recollected that and they did find the spot, which I shall refer to, but I want to make that plain that it is not in the written transcript.

I start, Judge Thomas, at page 9 of the record, where I questioned Professor Hill, that *USA Today* reported on October 9:

> Anita Hill was told by Senate staffers her signed affidavit alleging sexual harassment by Clarence Thomas would be the instrument that, 'quietly and behind the scenes,' would force him to withdraw his name.

I am not reading all of it, because I cannot in the time we have here, but if anybody disagrees with anything I read, they are at liberty to add whatever they choose.

On page 80:

> Question: Did anybody ever tell you that by providing the statement that there would be a move to request Judge Thomas to withdraw his nomination? MS. HILL: I don't recall any story about using this to press anyone.

Later, on page 80:

> MS. HILL: I don't recall anything being said about him being pressed to resign.

Page 81:

> SEN. SPECTER: Well, aside from 'quietly and behind the scenes pressing him to withdraw,' any suggestion that just the charges themselves in writing would result in Judge Thomas withdrawing and going away? MS. HILL: I don't recall that at all, no.

Skipping ahead to page 82—this is in the middle of one of my questions:

> You have testified with some specificity about what happened ten years ago. I would ask you to press your recollection as to what happened within the last month.
>
> MS. HILL: And I have done that, Senator, and I don't recall that comment. I do recall there might have been some suggestion that if the FBI did the investigation, that the Senate might get involved, that there may be that a number of things might occur, but I really, I have to be honest with you, I cannot verify the statement that you are asking me to verify. There is not really more that I can tell you on that.

Then skipping ahead to page 84:

> SEN. SPECTER: Would you not consider a matter of real importance, if someone said to you, Professor, you won't have to go public, your name won't have to be disclosed, you won't have to do anything, just sign the affidavit, and this, as *USA Today* reports, would be the instrument that, quietly and behind the scenes, would force him to withdraw his name. Now, I am not asking you whether it happened. I am asking you now only, if it did happen, whether that would be the kind of a statement to you which would be important and impressed upon you that you could remember in the course of four or five weeks.

Now, it is at this time that she consulted with her attorney, according to my recollection and according to my staff's, looking at the tape. And then she says: "I don't recall a specific statement and I cannot say whether that comment would have stuck in my mind, I really cannot say this."

In the afternoon session, I asked Professor Hill—

SEN. SIMON: What page are you referring to?

SEN. SPECTER: Page 203—to "begin, if you could, and proceed from there to account who called you and what those conversations consisted of as it led to your coming forward to the committee."

Then, on a long answer inserted at the end, which was not responsive, because I wasn't asking about the *USA Today* article any more, she says—and this appears at the bottom of 203—

> It even included something to the effect that the information might be presented to the candidate and to the White House. There was some indication that the candidate—excuse me—the nominee might not wish to continue the process.

Then, on the following page, 204, continuing in the middle of the page: "SEN. SPECTER: So, Mr. Brudney did tell you that Judge Thomas might not wish to continue to go forward with his nomination, if you came forward? MS. HILL: Yes."

Now, Judge Thomas, what do you make of that change of testimony?

JUDGE THOMAS: Senator, I think that the individuals such as Jim Brudney, Senator Metzenbaum's staffer on the Education and Labor Committee, should be brought to hearings like this to confront the people in this country for this kind of effort, and I think that they should at some point have to confront my family.

SEN. METZENBAUM: I would like to just make a statement. Yesterday, I called for the Ethics Committee to investigate the matter of the leak and anything else they consider appropriate. Jim Brudney was performing his responsibilities as a member of my staff.

SEN. THURMOND: Mr. Chairman, I might make this statement, that today I have called for an FBI investigation. I think that is the one that will count, and the Republicans on this side of the aisle, all I have talked with have agreed to sign it, all down the line, I believe, and—

SEN. SPECTER: Wait a minute. I am not getting into any collateral issues at this time. I have not discussed signing anything. I do not want to have any attention diverted from this issue, which is the nomination of Judge Thomas, and the point we are on now is where the credibility is. When Senators want to interrupt, that is part of the process around here, but I am not going to discuss that issue at this time.

Judge Thomas, I went through that in some detail, because it is my legal judgment, having had some experience in perjury prosecutions, that the testimony of Professor Hill in the morning was flat-out perjury, and that she specifically changed it in the afternoon when confronted with the possibility of being contradicted, and if you recant during the course of a proceeding, it is not perjury, so I state that very carefully as to what she had said in the morning.

But in the context of those continual denials and consulting the attorney and repeatedly asking the question, with negative responses, that, simply stated, was false and perjurious, in my legal opinion. The change in the afternoon was a concession flatly to that effect.

In searching for credibility, let me add that I am not representing that it is conclusive or determinative, but it certainly is very probative and very weighty.

Let me now move to another issue of credibility, which is an issue very central to this proceeding. That is the factors relating to Professor Hill's moving from the Department of Education to EEOC, and whether she would have moved with you, had you said the outrageous things which have been attributed to you.

In her statement, on page 4, she states, among other reasons, "I also faced the realistic fact that I had no alternative job." She then quotes you in her testimony —I want to be precise, so I will cite the reference, page 172, at the top of the page:

> MS. HILL: I was relying on what I was told by Clarence Thomas. I did not make any further inquiry. SEN. SPECTER: And what are you saying that Judge Thomas told you? MS. HILL: His indication from him was that he could not assure me of a position at Education. SEN. SPECTER: Was that when you were hired or when he was leaving? MS. HILL: When he was leaving.

Question, Judge Thomas: Did you tell her that you could not assure her of a position at Education, when you made the move to EEOC?

JUDGE THOMAS: Senator, I do not recall that conversation, and as I reflect back, there would be no reason for me to tell her that. Anita Hill was a graduate of Yale Law School, was performing well, and was a career employee. She was a Schedule A. She was not a political employee, so she could remain in the department in other capacities. There were a significant number of attorneys, both in the Department of Education, generally, and in the Office of Civil Rights, specifically.

In addition, my successor was a close personal friend of mine, Harry Singleton, also a Yale Law School graduate, and if she wanted to stay at the Department of Education, it would have been a simple matter of bringing it to the attention of Harry.

In addition to that, Gil Hardy was not only a personal friend of mine, he was a personal friend of Harry's. We were all at Yale Law School at the same time. So, there would have been no reason for me to have said that she could not remain at the Department of Education.

SEN. SPECTER: Judge Thomas, Professor Hill later said or at one point said, as it appears on page 160 of the record, "I was a Schedule A attorney." Now, based on your knowledge of her as an attorney herself, is it credible that she would not know, as a Schedule A attorney, that she could stay on at the Department of Education?

JUDGE THOMAS: Senator, it would seem more likely to me that someone of her intellect and her capabilities would know what her classification was and would certainly find out, when there is a question of whether or not you are going to have a job during a transitional period. Those are not complicated matters and they are not hard to find out. Indeed, the other assistant who was on my staff would have been knowledgeable in the area of personnel.

SEN. SPECTER: I want to now move to the issue of the record-keeping relating to my questioning of Professor Hill on keeping a record on the comments which she has said you made.

At page 114 of the record, I asked her—let me back up for just a minute to set the groundwork for what I had asked her, and I read her this, as well. In her statement, at page 5, she said, "I began to be concerned that Clarence Thomas might take it out on me by downgrading me or not giving me important assignments. I also thought he might find an excuse for dismissing me."

Now, in the context of that statement, I asked Professor Hill this question, which appears at page 114 of the record:

> In a controversy, if Judge Thomas took some action against you and you had to defend yourself on the ground that he was being malicious in retaliation for turning him down, wouldn't those notes be very influential, if not determinative, in enabling you to establish your legal position? MS. HILL: I think they would be very influential yes. SEN. SPECTER: So, given your experience, if all this happened, since all this happened, why not make the notes? MS. HILL: Well, it might have been a good choice to

make the notes. I did not do it, though.

Now, my question to you is, knowing Professor Hill as you do and based on your evaluation of her as an attorney, is it credible with these kind of things having been said and her being concerned contemporaneously about possible dismissal, that she would not make notes of these kinds of comments?

JUDGE THOMAS: Senator, it is not credible that any career employee would be concerned that one individual could effectuate a dismissal. It would be a much better case, if this were a Schedule C employee who can be dismissed summarily. Nor can you summarily downgrade an employee. The employees in the Federal system have an array of rights and opportunities for hearings, so that could not occur.

I think you are also right that it is reasonable for any employee who is faced with the possibility or fear of downgrading or dismissal to document any adverse conduct that has resulted in that that is in some way not appropriate conduct. That happens in many instances in which you have employees against whom actions have been taken.

SEN. SPECTER: When I pursued the question about making the notes, Professor Hill responded in a collateral way, which I think is relevant. I want to ask you about, on the issue of credibility, and this appears at page 115 of the record:

> MS. HILL: One of the things that I did do at that time was to document my work. I went through very meticulously with every assignment that I was given. This really was in response to the concerns that I had about being fired. I went through, I logged in every work assignment that I received, the date that it was received, the action that was requested, the action that I took on it, the date that it went out, and so I did do that in order to protect myself, but I did not write down any of the comments or conversations.

My question to you is this, Judge Thomas: Where she says she is concerned about being fired and she says that she is taking precautions and writes down the details of work assignments, if she is looking for retaliation from you, is it credible that, having statements been made, that she would not make a written notation of those statements in the context where— she writes down notes on all of these other matters?

JUDGE THOMAS: Senator, it does not sound credible to me, but I think there is further point. Oftentimes, when individuals are concerned about their ratings, they will document their work product, the quality of their work product or copies of their work product and the speed with which they turn around the work product, so that they can then argue during the rating period that they should receive a higher rating. That is not unusual, particularly if there have been some complaints that the work was not being done in a timely fashion.

I was not aware of that and don't know that that was the case in her situation, but it is not unusual for individuals who are concerned about their ratings to document their work. I think it would be unusual for someone who is thinking that they were going to be dismissed to be documenting the work that they received.

SEN. SPECTER: Well, I raise these issues and I ask you to amplify as to your view, knowing Professor Hill as you did, about the documentation which she testified to and the absence of documentation on these comments on the question of credibility.

Judge Thomas, a final subject matter on this round is a matter of the telephone logs, and I began this subject matter on the question as to how many times Professor Hill called you. The evidence already adduced demonstrated that there were eleven calls recorded, ten at EEOC and one at the Court of Appeals for the DC Circuit. My first question to you on this subject is: Were there other calls which got through, where you talked to Professor Hill on calls initiated by her, which, because they got through, would not have been recorded in the logs?

JUDGE THOMAS: Senator, there could well have been. If I were available when the calls were received, they would have gotten through and would not have been logged in. The purpose of our telephone log was only to log messages, so that I could return calls. So, there could have been any number of instances in which I spoke directly to her, without having returned her call.

SEN. SPECTER: Judge Thomas, *The Washington Post* reported on this issue that, "Ms. Hill called the telephone logs garbage, and said that she had not telephoned Thomas, except to return his calls." I questioned her about that at pages 173 and 174 of the record.

Then, to abbreviate this, when confronted with the logs, I asked her, and this appears at page 175 of the record, "Then you now concede that you had called Judge Thomas eleven times?" Answer, following some other material, "I will concede that those phone calls were made, yes."

My question to you, Judge Thomas, is what impact do you think that has on her credibility?

JUDGE THOMAS: Senator, I think it is another of many inconsistencies that have occurred in her testimony.

SEN. SPECTER: Judge Thomas, I was a little disappointed, maybe more than a little disappointed, that you did not watch the proceedings yesterday, in terms of seeing precisely what Professor Hill had to say, both from the point of view of wanting to know what it was and from the point of view of being in a better position to defend yourself. Why didn't you watch those hearings?

JUDGE THOMAS: Senator, the last two and a half weeks have been a living hell and there is only so much a human being can take, and as far as I was concerned, the statements that she sent to this committee and her statements to the FBI were lies and they were untrue, and I didn't see any reason to suffer through more lies about me. This is not an easy experience.

SEN. SPECTER: Judge Thomas, I can understand that it is not an easy experience for you. It hasn't been an easy experience for anybody. But in the context where she comes forward and she is testifying, and the fact is she said much more in her statement here than she had in either her written statement to the committee on September 23rd or what she said to the FBI, and there was a good bit of exchange above and beyond what she said, and it just struck me a little peculiarly that you had not wanted to see what she had said, realizing the difficulty, but also focusing on the question of being able to respond. It is a little hard to ask you questions, if you haven't seen her testimony. It requires going through a lot of the record. I just was concerned that you had taken that course, in light of the seriousness, the importance, and the gravity of the matter.

JUDGE THOMAS: Senator, I wish there was more for me to give, but I have given all I can.

THE CHAIRMAN: Senator, your time has expired, but we will come back.

SEN. SPECTER: Okay. Thank you very much. Thank you, Judge Thomas.

Thank you, Mr. Chairman.

THE CHAIRMAN: Before I yield to my colleagues to question, I must point out that reasonable people can differ and we certainly do on this committee. I would just like to make sure, I say to my friend from Pennsylvania, that the remainder of the record on page 204, 205, and 206 appear in the record with regard to Mr. Brudney. Senator Specter says:

> Mr. Brudney said to you that the nominee Judge Thomas might not wish to continue the process, if you came forward with a statement on the factors which you have testified about. MS. HILL: Well, I am not sure of exactly what he said. I think what he said, depending on the investigation of the Senate, whether the Senate went into closed session and so forth, it might be that he might not wish to continue the process. SEN. SPECTER: So, Mr. Brudney did tell you that Judge Thomas might not wish to continue to go forward with his nomination, if you came forward? MS. HILL: Yes. SEN. SPECTER: Isn't that somewhat different from your testimony this morning? MS. HILL: My testimony this morning involved my response to this *USA* newspaper report, and the newspaper report suggested that, by making the allegations, that would be enough, that the candidate would quietly and somehow would withdraw from the process, so, no, I do not believe that it is at variance. We talked about the matter of different options, but it was never suggested, just by telling incidents that might, that would cause the nominee to withdraw. SEN. SPECTER: Well what more could you do to make allegations as to what you said occurred? MS. HILL: I could not do any more, but this body could. SEN. SPECTER: Well, but I am now looking at your distinguishing what you just testified to, from what you testified this morning. This morning, I had asked you about just one sentence from *USA Today*. I emphasize that —Just one sentence from *USA Today*, "Anita Hill was told by Senate staffers that her signed affidavit alleging sexual harassment by Clarence Thomas would be the instrument that quietly and behind the scenes would force him to withdraw his name.

Skipping:

> MS. HILL: I guess, Senator, the difference in what you are saying and what I am saying is that that quote seems to indicate that there would be no intermediate stages in the process. What we were talking about was the process, what would happen along the way, what were the possibilities, would there be a full hearing, would there be questioning from the FBI, would there be questioning by some individual members of the Senate. We are not talking about or even speculating that simply alleging this would cause someone to withdraw.

At the bottom of page 206: "Ms. Hill"—

SEN. SPECTER: Why don't you continue reading, Senator Biden, if you are—

THE CHAIRMAN: I will read the whole thing, then:

> SEN. SPECTER: Well, if your answer now turns on process, all I can say is that it would have been much shorter, had you said at the outset that Mr. Brudney told you that if you came forward, Judge Thomas might withdraw. That is the essence of what occurred. MS. HILL: No, it is not. I think we differ on interpretation of what I said. SEN. SPECTER: Well, what am I missing here? SEN. KENNEDY: Mr. Chairman, can we let the witness speak her own words, rather than having words put in her mouth? SEN. SPECTER: Mr. Chairman, I object to that. I object to that vociferously. I am asking questions here. If Senator Kennedy has anything to say, let him participate in this hearing. THE CHAIRMAN: Now, let everybody calm down. Professor Hill, give your interpretation of what was asked by Senator Specter, and then we can ask you further questions. MS. HILL: My interpretation—. SEN. THURMOND: Speak into the microphone, so that we can hear you. MS. HILL: I understood Senator Specter's question to be what kinds of conversations did I have regarding this information. I was attempting, in talking to the staff, to understand how the information would be used, what I would have to do, what might be the outcome of such use. We talked about a number of possibilities, but there was never any indication that, by simply making these allegations, the nominee would withdraw from the process. No one ever said that, and I did not say that anyone ever said that.

Let me make sure I read that correctly:

> No one ever said that, and I did not say that anyone ever said that. We talked about the form that the statement would come in. We talked about the process that might be undertaken post-statement. We talked about the possibilities of outcomes, and included in that possibility of outcomes was the committee could decide to review the point and that the nominee, the vote could continue as it did. SEN. SPECTER: So that, at some point in the process, Judge Thomas might withdraw? MS. HILL: Again, I

> would have to respectfully say that is not what I said, that was one of the possibilities, but it would not come from my simply making an allegation.

Do you want me to keep reading?
SEN. SPECTER: Yes, please.
THE CHAIRMAN:

> SEN. SPECTER: Professor Hill, is that what you meant, when you said earlier, at best I could write it down, that you could control it so that it would not get to this point? MS. HILL: Pardon me? SEN. SPECTER: Is that what you meant, when you responded earlier to Senator Biden that the situation would be controlled so that it would not get to this point in the hearing? MS. HILL: Of a public hearing? In entering into these conversations with the staff members, what I was trying to do was control this information, yes, so that it would not get to this point. SEN. SPECTER: Thank you very much. THE CHAIRMAN: Thank you, Senator.

SEN. KENNEDY: Mr. Chairman?
SEN. METZENBAUM: Mr. Chairman?
THE CHAIRMAN: The Senator from Massachusetts.
SEN. KENNEDY: If I could be recognized, just in one other part of the record that was just referenced with regard to the telephone calls, on page 175, it will just take a moment, because there was reference about inconsistency and the use of "garbage," as Ms. Hill used it:

> SEN. SPECTER: Did you call the telephone log issue garbage? MS. HILL: I believe the issue is garbage, when you look at what seems to be implied from the telephone log, then, yes, that is garbage. SEN. SPECTER: Have you seen the records of the telephone logs? MS. HILL: Yes, I have. SEN. SPECTER: Do you deny the accuracy? MS. HILL: No, I don't. SEN. SPECTER: Then you now concede you have called Judge Thomas eleven times? MS. HILL: I do not deny the accuracy of the logs. I cannot deny they are accurate. I will concede that those phone calls were made, yes.
>
> SEN. SPECTER: So, they are not garbage? MS. HILL: Well, Senator, what I said was the issue is garbage. Those telephone calls do not indicate what they are being used to indicate, that somehow I was pursuing something more than a cordial relationship or a professional relationship. Each of those calls were made in a professional context. Some of those calls revolved around one incident. Several of those calls, in fact, three involved one incident where I was trying to act in behalf of another group. So, the issue that is being created by the telephone calls, yes, indeed, is garbage.

SEN. METZENBAUM: Mr. Chairman?
THE CHAIRMAN: The Senator from Ohio.
SEN. METZENBAUM: Mr. Chairman, there seems to be some issue made as to the

conduct of Mr. Brudney, who is the director of my Labor Subcommittee. Mr. Brudney is as honorable and able and dedicated as any person on my staff.

Mr. Brudney was performing his responsibilities in that connection by inquiring into the background of the nominee to be an Associate Justice of the Supreme Court. That came about by reason of the fact that Mr. Brudney and his staff had considerable knowledge concerning Judge Thomas when he was up for confirmation by reason of his activities at the Equal Employment Opportunity Commission. There is no secret about the fact, on the basis of those conclusions, this Senator decided not to vote for Judge Thomas's confirmation to the Circuit Court of Appeals.

But Mr. Brudney was inquiring into what facts were concerning the thoughts of your former employees. He and his staff were doing it. The first call was actually made in September—earlier than September 9. When Mr. Brudney was informed that there were certain allegations concerning the possibility of sexual harassment, he did exactly what any other staffer should have done.

He performed his responsibilities and performed them well. He reported them to me and I told him to immediately turn them over to the Judiciary Committee staff. That is what he did. The fact that Ms. Hill and he had a conversation as to what might develop by reason of her speaking out has already been spoken to in the transcript.

Now, Judge Hill, I have a lot of respect for you—Judge Thomas, excuse me —I apologize—Judge Thomas, I have to say to you that these are important allegations. These are allegations concerning the issue of sexual harassment, and I can only say this to you: Mr. Brudney would have been irresponsible had he not brought the matter to my attention, and I would have been irresponsible if I did not direct him to bring it to the attention of the Judiciary Committee, in order that the Judiciary Committee might investigate the matter. Mr. Brudney did not arrive at any conclusion, I did not arrive at any conclusion, and the subject of this hearing has not, as yet, arrived at any conclusion, and I doubt very much that it will arrive at any specific conclusion.

But I want to make it clear that Mr. Brudney was doing what he should have done, and had he done less he would have been irresponsible. And had this Senator and this committee done less, it would have been irresponsible. Sexual harassment is too important an issue to sweep under the rug.

JUDGE THOMAS: Senator, it was not swept under the rug. This issue was investigated by the FBI and then leaked to the press, and I do not share your view that this was not concocted. This has caused me great pain—and my family great pain, and God is my judge, not you, Senator Metzenbaum.

SEN. BROWN: Mr. Chairman, the Senator from Ohio has brought up the subject of his staffer and I understand his interest in defending him—

THE CHAIRMAN: If I may—

SEN. BROWN: [continuing]—why can't this committee hear from Mr. Brudney?

THE CHAIRMAN: If you will just yield for just a second.

We are going a half hour and a half hour. The subject of Mr. Metzenbaum's staff was not brought up by Mr. Metzenbaum. It was brought up, appropriately, by Senator Specter. It was appropriate for Senator Specter to bring it up.

Now, on the half-hour time we have on this side, it was appropriate for the Senator to respond. When we go back, it will be appropriate for you to pursue it, if you would like.

It is true, Judge Thomas, that God is your judge and all our judges, we all know that. But in the meantime, under the rules, we have to make a vote, and we have to judge. We are not God and none of us thinks we are, and none of us like this. Some of us have been in a situation similar to yours, not many of us, but some of us, and it is not very comfortable, but, unfortunately, there is a question of judgment.

Now, before I yield the remainder of our time, which is probably only about twenty minutes. How much time is left? Fifteen minutes. Before I yield the remainder of the time to either Senator Heflin or Senator Leahy—

SEN. HEFLIN: I believe it is Senator Leahy.

THE CHAIRMAN: Before I yield to Senator Leahy, let me ask a question, if I may, and that is: Did you, when the nominee first moved into her apartment, help her and her roommate install a stereo and a turntable, her roommate is the basketball player whose name I don't remember? Did you—

JUDGE THOMAS: Sonia Jarvis is her name.

THE CHAIRMAN: [continuing]—Ms. Jarvis, her roommate. There is nothing wrong with this, but did you help her install a stereo and a turntable that took about a half hour or an hour or so? Did that occur? I'm just trying to find out where we agree.

JUDGE THOMAS: Senator, I don't recall that at all.

THE CHAIRMAN: I thank you.

Now, I yield the remainder of the time to my friend from Vermont.

SEN. LEAHY: Judge, you said that you remember seeing her housemate there. I understand you don't remember the name of her housemate?

JUDGE THOMAS: Sonia Jarvis.

SEN. LEAHY: That was Sonia Jarvis?

JUDGE THOMAS: She is on my phone logs, also.

SEN. LEAHY: And if Anita Hill were to say that you came to her house once to install stereo equipment and a turntable, and that was the only time you were in her home, would that be accurate?

JUDGE THOMAS: No, it would have been—I don't remember helping her install a stereo or turntable. I do remember several times just dropping in after I had driven her home, just to chat, but that was it. It was no significant—it was nothing of great moment. But I do not recall helping her install a—I don't know when she moved into her apartment.

SEN. LEAHY: Of the times that you brought her home or to her apartment, how many times was Sonia Jarvis there, if you recall?

JUDGE THOMAS: I think each time. She would have wandered in or came by or something like that. I just simply remember her being in sweats, from a basketball game or something. That's the only time I can remember seeing her, I think.

SEN. LEAHY: But you think that she was there each time?

JUDGE THOMAS: That's right.

SEN. LEAHY: And if—

JUDGE THOMAS: That's my recollection.

SEN. LEAHY: I understand. And if Anita Hill said that—other than that stereo and turntable, which you say you do not recall—if she said other than that time, that Judge Thomas never drove her home and never came in to visit and talk politics or any other thing, that would not be accurate?

JUDGE THOMAS: Not to my recollection, Senator.

SEN. LEAHY: And if Sonia Jarvis said that she saw you there only once and it was to help install stereo equipment and that is the only time that she ever saw you in the house, that would be inaccurate?

JUDGE THOMAS: That would not be my recollection, Senator.

SEN. LEAHY: It would be contrary to what you just testified to. That is, your recollection was that she was there each time you were there?

JUDGE THOMAS: My recollection was, as I stated this morning, again, we are talking ten years ago, Senator.

SEN. LEAHY: I understand.

But I am talking about what you stated just one minute or two ago.

JUDGE THOMAS: That she would have been there, yes, that would have been my recollection.

SEN. LEAHY: Judge, I want to yield to Senator Heflin, but I have tried throughout all of this to ask very short questions and to stay away from the speechmaking. But bear with me just for a moment.

A robbery takes place, an armed robbery say, and two people are standing there, two witnesses see it. And one says, "That robber was tall." The other one says, "No, that robber was short." Well, the fact is, the robbery took place. Everybody, including the victim, agrees the robbery took place, but you have two people, honest people, standing there and one says, "By God, it was a tall robber," and the other one says, "No, it was a short robber," but the robbery takes place. We can understand that. And we can understand the difference of view in how two people might observe an event.

But here, it is like two ships in the night. I mean you seem to be diametrically opposed, certainly, in your testimony and Anita Hill's. I think we would both agree that, on the basic substance of what we are talking about here, you are diametrically opposed, is that correct?

JUDGE THOMAS: Senator, I just simply said that I deny her allegations categorically.

SEN. LEAHY: I understand. If her allegations were correct, if what she has stated under oath was so, that would be sexual harassment, would it not?

JUDGE THOMAS: Senator, I think it would be.

SEN. LEAHY: But, at the same time, you categorically deny that those events ever took place?

JUDGE THOMAS: I categorically deny, Senator, in the strongest terms.

SEN. LEAHY: It would be sexual harassment if they happened, but you say they did not happen?

JUDGE THOMAS: That's right.

SEN. LEAHY: Then we have one of two possibilities, obviously. One of you is not telling the truth. Or is there any possibility that both of you are seeing the same thing, both of you seeing the same robbery but seeing it entirely differently? Which is it? Is it that one of you absolutely is not telling the truth or one of you—or both of you, rather, are viewing the same events differently?

JUDGE THOMAS: Senator, I am not going to get into analyzing that. I will just simply say that these allegations are false. They were false when the FBI informed me of them, when they were subsequently changed to additional allegations they were false. And they continue to be false.

SEN. LEAHY: And there is nothing in her testimony of these allegations, in your mind, where the two of you could be seeing the same thing?

JUDGE THOMAS: Senator, my relationship with Anita Hill was cordial and professional, just as it was with the rest of my special assistants. And I maintain that that is all there was. My other special assistants are available for you to talk to them to determine exactly how I treated them.

SEN. LEAHY: Thank you.

SEN. HEFLIN: Judge, Senator Hatch brought up the issue of the tenth circuit case pertaining to Long John [*sic*] Silver, and in your responsibility as head of the EEOC, do you keep up with cases involving discrimination and sexual harassment that the circuit court of appeals may decide?

JUDGE THOMAS: Senator, the way that that is normally done is that if there is a significant case, I did not read specific cases, but if there were a significant case the general counsel would summarize that, would analyze it, and if necessary, would simply provide us with a copy of it.

I would not normally read circuit court opinions unless it was breaking new ground.

SEN. HEFLIN: In the field of employment discrimination, how many circuit court of appeals opinions have been written, per year over the last several years?

JUDGE THOMAS: Senator, I don't know.

SEN. HEFLIN: Now, let me ask you, did you read this case of the tenth circuit that involved this Long John [*sic*] Silver?

JUDGE THOMAS: Senator, this is the first I have heard of it, and I have not read it.

SEN. HEFLIN: I have been told that there is a pornographic movie in regards to "Long John [*sic*] Silver". Have you ever heard of that name?

JUDGE THOMAS: No, Senator.

SEN. HEFLIN: Now, this issue of pubic hair in the Coke—did you read the book, *The Exorcist*?

JUDGE THOMAS: No, Senator.

SEN. HEFLIN: Quite a few people have read it, from what I understand. I haven't read it, but—

JUDGE THOMAS: I don't know. I can't testify. I think the publisher would have to tell you that, Senator.

SEN. HEFLIN: All right, have you seen the deposition of Angela Wright that has been taken in this case?

JUDGE THOMAS: No, Senator.

SEN. HEFLIN: Well, then I will wait on that. It has some reference to your relationship with Juan Williams. I suppose Angela Wright is going to testify and the proper time would be to ask then.

You, in your opening remarks, made a statement about the lack of corroborating witnesses. I had some discussion with two other people and we were talking about how unusual this case was and how it has attracted attention nationally because of its unusualness. And one of them remarked it is not unusual that this occurs and the type of situation we are in today occurs in almost every date rape case—that there are no witnesses.

Usually in regard to the prosecution and the defense of those cases, a somewhat wider latitude is allowed relative to background pertaining to it.

SEN. HATCH: Mr. Chairman, excuse me, Senator, I have to object to this line of questioning. I don't know of anybody who has accused him of date rape. Is that what you are driving at?

SEN. HEFLIN: Well, it is a common term as I understand it. Date rape is where people go out on dates and rape occurs.

SEN. HATCH: What does that have to do with this?

SEN. HEFLIN: Well, the analogy between the two is that in the trial of such cases, a broader leeway is given relative to investigations of people that have a past history of such tendencies. And the only thing I am asking you, Judge, is whether or not you refuse to answer any questions other than what may have occurred in employment. Do you continue to do that?

JUDGE THOMAS: Oh, absolutely, Senator. I will not be further humiliated by this process. I think I have suffered enough, my family has suffered enough. I think that I have attempted to address all of the questions with respect to my relationship with Ms. Hill in the work force and I think enough is enough.

SEN. HEFLIN: I had an old trial lawyer tell me one time, Judge, that if you've got the facts on your side, argue the facts to the jury. If you've got the law on your side, argue the law to the judge. If you've got neither, confuse the issue with other parties.

SEN. HATCH: You mean like date rape?

SEN. HEFLIN: That's a statement. I don't simply ask questions. You have been asked questions that really have been asked for the purpose of making speeches. After a long period of time they would ask you a question.

And they would ask you questions about whether that is credible, which, in effect, is asking a participant if such occurred. Let me just ask you these other things. This might have some bearing and it might not.

But I think it should be asked. What was the date of your divorce?

JUDGE THOMAS: I think it is irrelevant here, Senator. I was separated during—I will only answer during the relevant time period. All of that material is in my FBI file and was available to the committee before. I will only discuss the allegations in this case. My family, Senator, has been humiliated enough. I have been humiliated enough. I was separated from my former wife, once in January of 1981; we reconciled during the summer; and then we separated again in August of 1981.

SEN. HEFLIN: All right, I will respect you. Whatever you want to state and however you want to answer it.

There was a question that I believe was asked of Ms. Hill or she brought it out, or I have seen it in files, affidavits, or somewhere, that Professor Hill said you made a statement to her, "You know if you had any witnesses, you would have a good case against me."

Did any such thing like that ever happen?

JUDGE THOMAS: That's nonsense, Senator. I never made any statement like that. I never made the statements that she has alleged.

SEN. HEFLIN: Well, we get back to the issue of who is telling the truth, and what the motives are. Has any thought come to your mind as to what her motive might be?

JUDGE THOMAS: Senator, as I said before, I think you should ask the people who helped concoct this and the people who leaked it to the press what the motives were.

SEN. HEFLIN: That is when we talk about other issues of both parties.

JUDGE THOMAS: I understand.

SEN. HEFLIN: We are still left with a quandary as to where we are. And as I stated in the first hearing, what is the real Clarence Thomas like? I think an issue now is what is the real Anita Hill like? And we have to make the decisions relative to those issues.

SEN. LEAHY: I wonder if I just might—if the Senator would yield on that—I wonder if I might follow on the last, when Senator Heflin spoke to the question of motivation, Judge, and asked what could be her motivation? And you said, we ought to ask the people who concocted this. I think I am accurately restating what you said, is that correct? I don't want to put words in your mouth.

JUDGE THOMAS: Yes.

SEN. LEAHY: I am not sure that that's an answer that many might accept. Let's think about this just for a moment. You have Anita Hill, a woman who has gone to Yale Law School, certainly one of the finest law schools in this country and I am sure, as a graduate, you accept that.

She is obviously quite bright, and you have certainly stated in the past a high regard for her. You have hired her in two positions of significant trust and responsibility. She went through the bar exam, and all of that, not an easy task for anyone.

She held those two positions of high trust and responsibility, both at the Department of Education and at the EEOC, and she then went to a university where she is a law professor and has done well enough to become tenured. Holding that, not only the law degree, but a license to practice law, something she has worked extremely hard for four years, protected and nurtured all this way through, as well as her experience. Why would she come here and perjure herself, throw away all of that? For what? What would she possibly get out of throwing all of that away?

JUDGE THOMAS: Senator, I don't know. I know the Anita Hill that worked for me and the relationship that I have had with her from time to time on the intermittent calls or the few visits over the years. I don't know what has happened since 1983. All I know is that the allegations are false and that I don't have a clue as to why she would do this.

SEN. LEAHY: Do you know Angela Wright?

JUDGE THOMAS: Angela Wright?

SEN. LEAHY: Yes.

JUDGE THOMAS: Yes. She was a Schedule C employee at EEOC.

SEN. LEAHY: Would she have any reason to attack you or—

JUDGE THOMAS: Yes.

SEN. LEAHY: And what would that be?

JUDGE THOMAS: I terminated her very aggressively a number of years ago. And very summarily.

SEN. LEAHY: Not with extreme prejudice, as the term is sometimes used?

JUDGE THOMAS: It was summarily.

SEN. LEAHY: Thank you. I just realized, I have been handed a note that says my time is up.

Thank you, Mr. Chairman.

THE CHAIRMAN: First of all, Judge, would you like to break for a moment?

JUDGE THOMAS: Yes, my back is giving me some problems.

THE CHAIRMAN: I am sorry I have been out of the room for a few moments. The Senator from Ohio is asking unanimous consent to speak for two minutes. Is there an objection to that?

SEN. THURMOND: I have no objection.

SEN. HATCH: I have no objection.

SEN. METZENBAUM: Mr. Chairman, I thank you and I thank my colleagues on the other side. There has been continued discussion and suggestions with respect to the matter of how this matter was leaked to the press. One Senator actually made a public statement that was carried in the *New York Times* indicating that this Senator or my staff had been responsible for the leak.

I went to the floor of the Senate and demanded an apology from that Senator and said I had not leaked it, neither had my staff. I am pleased to say that he acknowledged that and indicated a correction. But I want to make it clear today to you, Judge Thomas, and to any of the rest of the world that neither this Senator nor any of my staff have been the source of any leaks to the press on this subject.

Thank you.

THE CHAIRMAN: Judge, fifteen, ten, twenty? How much time do you want? You are the guy under the gun, how much time do you want?

JUDGE THOMAS: Ten is fine.

THE CHAIRMAN: We will recess for ten minutes.

SEN. KENNEDY: Mr. Chairman, if I could just ask the judge, I was not aware that the Senator from Ohio was going to make the comment, but I, too, want to indicate here, before this committee and in this forum that neither I nor my staff were involved in any of these leaks. I regret that we all have to get into a situation where we have to deny these matters, but I want to give that assurance in this forum, in this committee to the judge

SEN. HATCH: Mr. Chairman, I would like to speak on behalf of all of the Republicans, none of us did it, I will guarantee you that.

JUDGE THOMAS: Somebody did it, Senator.

SEN. LEAHY: Well, obviously nobody did it.

THE CHAIRMAN: The chair will recess for ten minutes.

[Recess.]

JUDGE THOMAS: Senator, I would like to correct something. I was just informed by someone who is more informed than I was about my staff at Education. Again, this has been quite some time. I had two attorney advisors and I think two or three Schedule C appointees who also reported to me.

THE CHAIRMAN: I am sorry, I could not hear the last part, Judge.

JUDGE THOMAS: Senator, I indicated that I only had two professional staffers.

THE CHAIRMAN: Correct.

JUDGE THOMAS: It appears that I had two attorney advisors, one other than in addition to Anita Hill, as well as a second professional, and then, in addition to those, two political appointees, two or three political appointees on my personal staff, so that is six.

THE CHAIRMAN: Judge, I am not sure it is relevant, but can you—

JUDGE THOMAS: Well, the—

THE CHAIRMAN: No, no, I appreciate you correcting it. Do you recall the names of the two attorney advisors?

JUDGE THOMAS: Well, Anita Hill and Kathleen Flake, I think was the second.

THE CHAIRMAN: Kathleen?

JUDGE THOMAS: Flake.

THE CHAIRMAN: F-l-a—

JUDGE THOMAS: [continuing]—k-e, I think.

THE CHAIRMAN: You also had two or three political appointees.

JUDGE THOMAS: Whom I can't remember. That's easy enough to check.

THE CHAIRMAN: Okay, and then you mentioned one other person, the woman who was in law school at the time?

JUDGE THOMAS: Right. That's right.

THE CHAIRMAN: She was not an attorney advisor, but she was one who was in frequent contact.

JUDGE THOMAS: Exactly.

THE CHAIRMAN: Okay. Thank you for correcting the record.

I think we are pretty well ready to wind up here, Judge, but it is now the opportunity of Senator Hatch to question, and he says he would like to have thirty minutes and he is entitled to that.

SEN. HATCH: I hope I don't have to take the whole thirty minutes, Judge, but I do want to cover just one or two other points before we are through here today.

Judge Thomas, yesterday Senator Heflin repeatedly asked you to ascribe some motivation to Professor Hill's allegations, and I think, from the way I look at this record, there are some profound differences in political philosophy between you and her.

I am about to read an excerpt of one of her statements that I think is worth putting in the record:

> Hill said that her initial impression of Thomas was very favorable and she respected him for his accomplishments and concern for others. She said that she also came from a poor family, so she related closely to his circumstances. She said that when she started working for Thomas, he supported quotas for minorities in employment and Federal sanctions against employers who did not comply with the quotas, and then went on.

That is the relevant part.

> Later, Hill said that she has also seen Thomas change his political philosophy since 1981 to the present from supporting quotas for minorities in employment with sanctions for non-compliance to no quotas. She is concerned that these may be changed for personal political expediency and may not represent his true philosophy. If that is the case, he may no longer be open-minded, which is essential for an Associate Justice of the United States Supreme Court.

THE CHAIRMAN: Senator, what are you reading from?

SEN. HATCH: I am reading from her statements made to the FBI agents.

THE CHAIRMAN: So, you are reading from the FBI report?

SEN. HATCH: That's right.

THE CHAIRMAN: Senator, we agreed that we would not violate the committee rules and read from the FBI report. You and I agreed with the remainder of the committee in the room across the hall two hours ago. It is incredible to me that you would walk in here and read from an FBI report, when we all know it is against the committee rules to read from FBI reports.

SEN. HATCH: Now we are concerned with FBI reports. I didn't agree to that. If you will recall, I stepped out to use the men's room—[Laughter.]—which I do with regularity at my age, I have to say. But to make a long story short, how does that hurt anything?

THE CHAIRMAN: Senator, let me tell you how it hurts. It is beyond the issue related to here. I may be mistaken, but I thought you were one who said in the other room that having dealt with these reports as much as any of us have, that they are full of nothing but hearsay on most occasions. The reason why I have worked so hard to keep FBI reports totally secret is because they have little or no probative weight, because they are hearsay. The FBI does their interviews by walking up to person A and saying will you speak to us, and the guarantee is anonymity. That is what the FBI tells the person, and the FBI speaks to the person.

Now, for us to summarily go back and say, as a matter of policy, that we are going to break the commitment the Federal Government makes to an individual, in order to get that individual to cooperate in an investigation, is disastrous.

SEN. HATCH: That is exactly my point, Senator. You just made the best argument in the world against why this is the most unfair process for Judge Thomas we have ever had. But if you listened in that meeting, I said yes, in the future, let's abide by that rule, there is a very good reason for it, but we have to be able to use it here, because there has to be some evidence of motivation, and I told you at the beginning of this hearing I was going to use it, because there are inconsistencies with Professor Hill's testimony and statements. Now, let's be fair. I mean these are not hearsay statements. These are statements made by her. Let me back it up further with a statement she made to the press, because it says the same thing, basically.

THE CHAIRMAN: Precisely. Why don't you ask from that? Ask him the FBI report, without—

SEN. HATCH: Senator, listen, I refuse to accept a process where someone on this committee releases her statement and materials from the FBI report for all the world to see and the newspapers to print and the media to show, that are tremendously damaging to the judge, because they have been brought up in open forum that had to occur, because somebody in a sleazy way broke the rules.

THE CHAIRMAN: Senator—

SEN. HATCH: Now, wait, let me just finish.

THE CHAIRMAN: I'm going to let you finish and then I'm going to cut you off real quick.

SEN. HATCH: Well, if you think you're going to cut me off, I think you're wrong. I'm going to listen to you and I'm going to pay attention to you, Mr. Chairman, but let me just finish. This is all I'm going to say about it and I won't read any more from that particular report, but I am going to read from the newspaper.

Let me tell you something, this never had to occur if whoever did this was honest. They could have brought this up before the vote, we could have decided this matter, we could have determined to have an executive session here, and you know that and you would have done it. I don't find any fault with you and I don't find fault with you feeling this way now, but I felt this way from the beginning and I know you did.

But those are fair comments. These matters have been leaked. I don't know that people out there don't have every aspect of the report, and I think some of them probably do and others, and to prevent me from bringing this up, when it is an important point at the last minute of this I think would be a travesty under the circumstances. I have never, never leaked an FBI report.

THE CHAIRMAN: You just did, Senator.

SEN. HATCH: Oh, no, I didn't. Oh, no, I didn't. I used an FBI report under very fair circumstances, and they couldn't be more fair. Like I say, this is no longer, this is not some insignificant appointment. This is one of the most important appointments in our country.

THE CHAIRMAN: Are you finished, Senator?

SEN. HATCH: This is not the Soviet Union. This is the United States of America. And let me tell you, let me tell you something— well, I didn't mean it quite that way—[Laughter.]

Let me go on. I won't—

THE CHAIRMAN: Senator—

SEN. HATCH: Go ahead, I will listen to you, but if I can, I would like to go ahead.

THE CHAIRMAN: No one has worked harder or has been more diligent in the nineteen years I have been in the Senate about keeping confidential anything that was sent to me as confidential. No one on this committee has been more damaged by the leak by an unethical person than me. I fully understand.

SEN. HATCH: I agree.

THE CHAIRMAN: Now to turn around and decide that because somebody was unethical about releasing not an FBI report, not an affidavit, but a memorandum from a woman who asked that it be confidential, is justification for discussing, from that point on, anything that appears in an FBI report, including the FBI report matters that had to do with Mr. Thomas or any of the witnesses who were spoken to, is totally inappropriate. I sincerely hope we won't go through this again.

Senator DeConcini.

SEN. HATCH: I did not have my time.

SEN. DECONCINI: Mr. Chairman?

THE CHAIRMAN: The Senator from Arizona.

SEN. DECONCINI: Mr. Chairman, let me say a word, because I agree with what you just said.

SEN. HATCH: I do, too.

SEN. DECONCINI: I also agree that this is most unfair, and I think the Senator from Utah has pointed that out, I think a number of us have pointed that out, even members who have already taken a position in opposition to Judge Thomas, that this thing is unfair because of the unauthorized leak.

But I do not believe that old saying "Two wrongs make a right", and to do it again I think is improper, and the only thing that I differ with you, Mr. Chairman, in your statement is that no one has been hurt more than you, an unauthorized leak, because that—

THE CHAIRMAN: No, no, I mean on this matter in this committee.

SEN. DECONCINI: No, I understand. I just take exception to that personally, and I can—

THE CHAIRMAN: Whether or not—

SEN. SIMPSON: Mr. Chairman?

THE CHAIRMAN: It is irrelevant, whether I was hurt the most. Let me just make this point. If we began to read from FBI reports, the ability of the FBI to conduct further investigations with witnesses will come to a screeching halt.

SEN. DECONCINI: I agree.

SEN. HATCH: Mr. Chairman, let me just—

SEN. SIMPSON: May I?

SEN. HATCH: Surely.

SEN. SIMPSON: Mr. Chairman, may I just say—

THE CHAIRMAN: Yes, please.

SEN. SIMPSON: [continuing]—I think we have done that already. To say that we haven't done that here, I think more than several of us, particularly with Ms. Hill, have referred continually—the record is full of references—to her FBI report; as comparing it with her second version with more explicit sexual material, and to her third version with ever-more vivid sexual material. We have used that several times by various members of this committee.

SEN. HATCH: Yes.

THE CHAIRMAN: If the Senator from Wyoming would yield to—

SEN. SIMPSON: I am ready to do what you suggest. I would concur with what you are doing and I support that, but it is a difficult thing. We have injected this entire record with quotes from FBI reports, not the report, but a paragraph, a sentence. I have heard it now for three—

SEN. HATCH: Everybody has. Everybody has. Now, if I could—

THE CHAIRMAN: I yield now to the Senator from South Carolina.

SEN. THURMOND: Mr. Chairman, how would it do to just eliminate the words "FBI" from the report and let him go ahead? [Laughter.]

SEN. HATCH: Let me say this: Mr. Chairman, I said at the beginning, when I raised my voice at the beginning of these hearings, that now that the FBI report has been leaked, it is not fair for the media to have it and not the general public.

On the other hand, I agree with your statement, it should never have been leaked—

THE CHAIRMAN: Senator, do you have evidence that the press has the FBI report? You keep saying that. Do you have evidence that the press or anybody has the report? Is there any place it has been printed, is there any place it has been quoted from?

SEN. HATCH: Senator, why don't you let me finish my statement? I will—you just let me do that—I respect you as chairman, I have stood up for you as chairman, I have said this hasn't been your fault, it hasn't been your doing, and I believe it, and I believe what you are saying is true now, and I hope in the future nobody will leak any of these reports or use them in any untoward manner.

SEN. THURMOND: Just check the newspaper, it is in there, the same thing. Go ahead with that.

SEN. HATCH: Let me just say what I intended to say. That is what I intend to do from here on in.

I will tell you, to sit here and say that something that is relevant, when I told you I was going to do what I wanted to do at the beginning, because of the unfairness of it, because I want the judge to have a square shake, and I made it clear, I didn't mince any words, I said that's going to happen and nobody really disagreed with me at that time—

THE CHAIRMAN: Senator—

SEN. HATCH: [continuing]—and I apologize, if you think I had agreed in that room, but I made it clear to you that, in this context, with the unfairness that has gone on, that I thought that it could be used. Now, I won't use it from here on out.

SEN. THURMOND: Mr. Chairman, aren't we wasting time?

THE CHAIRMAN: We are now, [Senator]. Let's move ahead.

SEN. THURMOND: Let's move ahead.

SEN. HATCH: Well, you people think you are wasting time, but I don't. I think he has been getting—

SEN. THURMOND: Use the newspaper, it's the same thing.

SEN. HATCH: I will use what I will.

SEN. THURMOND: Well, use the newspaper and you will be—

SEN. KENNEDY: Can you get them to stop fighting over there? [Laughter.]

THE CHAIRMAN: Will the Senator proceed, and proceed under the rules, please.

SEN. HATCH: I always follow Senator Kennedy's advice.

So, I will use the newspaper: "Anita Hill, a former special assistant to"—I think this is in *The Washington Post*, dated Monday September 9, 1991, just shortly after she was contacted—

> Anita Hill, a former special assistant to Thomas at the Education Department and the EEOC, was particularly disturbed by Thomas's repeated public criticism of his sister and her children for living on welfare. "It takes a lot of attachment to publicize a person's experience in that way and a certain kind of self-centeredness not to recognize some of the programs that benefited you," said Hill, now an Oklahoma law professor. "I think he doesn't understand people, he doesn't relate to people who don't make it on their own."

Then it says in this article, "If liberals consider him a traitor, conservatives within the Administration suspect that he was a closet liberal, Thomas said in a 1987 speech."

Now, the reason I brought that up, Judge, is because, basically, what Hill said in that article and what I have brought up was that she thought you had changed your political philosophy and that had been for quotas and now you are against them.

Now, my question is, just the day before the committee hearings began she was one of your opponents, and that was before any of the charges were aired. Now, is political philosophy part of this problem?

JUDGE THOMAS: Senator, as I have indicated about other motives, I have no reason to believe that it is not a basis for what has happened to me. It is obvious—there is another comment, though, that I would like to make, and that is that there is no record, to my knowledge, and I have no recollection of ever making a statement about my sister in any speeches. That was in one news article on December 16, 1981.

The references with respect to changing my position on quotas, my position on quotas has been pretty much the same, from a policy standpoint, since the mid-1970's.

SEN. HATCH: And what is that—well, I can let that go. Judge Thomas, I take it that she disagrees with you on your stand on quotas?

JUDGE THOMAS: She disagreed with me when she was on my personal staff on that issue, Senator.

SEN. HATCH: Was that a matter of some contention between you?

JUDGE THOMAS: I think in the instances she would get a bit irate on that particular issue, as I remember it.

SEN. HATCH: Because she took the opposite position?

JUDGE THOMAS: That's right.

SEN. HATCH: She was for quotas?

JUDGE THOMAS: I think she was adamant about that position.

SEN. HATCH: Okay. Well, I think that—

JUDGE THOMAS: That is my recollection, Senator.

SEN. HATCH: Well, I think that needed to be brought up.

Judge, when the President asked you at Kennebunkport whether you and your family could take what would follow in the process, did you have any idea what you were going to have to "take"? Could you have guessed that some people, including people on this committee, people in the media and others would dredge up stories about drug use, wife-beating, advocating Louis Farrahkan's anti-Semitism, lying about your neutrality in *Roe v. Wade,* sexual harassment, maybe even implications of other things? Did you think you would have to face scurrilous accusations like those, which you have refuted?

JUDGE THOMAS: Senator, I expected it to be bad and I expected awful treatment throughout the process, I expected to be a sitting duck for the interest groups, I expected them to attempt to kill me and, yes, I even expected personally attempts on my life. That is just how much I expected.

I did not expect this circus. I did not expect this charge against my name. I expected people to do anything, but not this. And if by going through this, another nominee in the future or another American won't have to go through it, then so be it, but I did not expect this treatment and I did not expect to lose my name, my reputation, my integrity to do public service. Again, I did not ask to be nominated, I did not lobby for it, I did not beg for it, I did not aspire to it.

I was perfectly happy on the U.S. Court of Appeals for the DC Circuit, which is a lifetime appointment. I did not expect to lose my life in the process.

SEN. HATCH: A *Washington Post* article just today said that you said—and I recall you saying—you told of "reporters sneaking into my garage, interest group lobbyists swarming over divorce papers looking for dirt." I remember you said this is not the American dream, this is Kafka-esque, it has got to stop, enough is enough.

The *Post* article goes on to say "some activists were unmoved by Thomas's emotional plea, dismissing it as a last-ditch effort to salvage his nomination. 'The major groups don't have anything to apologize for,' said one of the civil rights activists. He went on to say, 'The battle has been fought on policy and philosophy,' although he acknowledged 'it has taken a distressing turn.'"

The article goes on to say,

> That turn illustrates the increasingly symbiotic relationship between committee staffers, liberal interest groups and the news media. It is a phenomena that accelerated with the Reagan Administration's attempts to insure conservative domination of the judiciary in the 1980's. Many thought it reached its ultimate expression in the battle over the nomination of Robert H. Bork to the Supreme Court in 1987. But within days after President Bush announced Thomas's nomination, liberal activist groups began the search for ammunition they hoped could defeat him. An informal coalition that included Cropp—

I suppose he is with People for the American Way.

> —Kate Michelman of the National Abortion Rights Action League, Nan Aaron of the Alliance for Justice, and others began holding almost daily strategy sessions, at first restricting their probes to exposing what they viewed as his track record as a rigid Reagan Administration ideologue. Cropp said that his organization, which had played a pivotal role in the Bork fight—

I might add that they put ads in the paper and I accused them of 99, as I recall, errors in the ad, and they never answered the accusations, they could not, really.

> Cropp said that his organization, which had played a pivotal role in the Bork fight, assigned four full-time staffers, several interns and four other field organizers to anti-Thomas activities. The group also filed Freedom of Information requests for copies and videotapes of all his public speeches and videotapes while he headed the Equal Employment Opportunity Commission and the Office of Civil Rights in the Department of Education.

Naturally, they can do that if they want to, but these are only a few groups that are mentioned, and there are literally hundreds, if not thousands, of groups in this area, and the groups, many feel, have taken over the process.

And in the process the ideology becomes more important than truth, it becomes more important than integrity, it becomes more important than ethics, it becomes more important than preserving people's reputations, it becomes more important than simple, basic decency to human beings.

I think it was said best, again I cite Juan Williams's statement, he said:

"This desperate search for ammunition to shoot down Thomas has turned the 102 days since President Bush nominated him for a seat on the Supreme Court into a liberal's nightmare."

Now, this is a journalist who is not particularly conservative, but nevertheless a great journalist. [Laughter.]

"Here is indiscriminate"—didn't quite mean it the way that some have taken it, he is a great journalist and I mean that. I don't know how people take that implication but I mean that.

SEN. THURMOND: Tell them the name.

SEN. HATCH: Juan Williams. "Here is indiscriminate"—he is describing, he is describing this desperate search for ammunition.

> Here is indiscriminate mean-spirited mud-slinging supported by the so-called champions of fairness. Liberal politicians, unions, civil rights groups, and women's organizations, they have been mindlessly led into mob action against one man by the Leadership Conference on Civil Rights. Moderate and liberal Senators operating in the proud tradition of men, such as Hubert Humphrey and Robert Kennedy, have allowed themselves to become sponsors of smear tactics that have historically been associated with the gutter politics of a Lee Atwater or crazed right-wing self-promoters like Senator Joseph McCarthy. During the hearings on his nomination, Thomas was subjected to a glaring double standard.

Now, for those of you who laugh, why is it that Juan Williams is one of the few who has pointed out this glaring double standard? Laugh at that, laugh at that. That's what I am talking about here. I am not talking about liberal and conservative politics. I am talking about decency. I am talking about our country, America.

Thomas was subjected to a glaring double standard. I have never seen it worse, never. When he did not answer questions that former nominees David Souter and Anthony Kennedy did not answer, he was pilloried for his evasiveness. One opponent testified that her basis for opposing him was his lack of judicial experience.

She did not know that Supreme Court Justices, such as liberal icons Earl Warren and Felix Frankfurter, as well as current Chief Justice William Rehnquist, had no judicial experience before taking a seat on the high court.

There is a lot more that could be said. But he says a very interesting paragraph and I think it does sum it up, he said: "This slimy exercise orchestrated in the form of leaks of an affidavit to the Leadership Conference on Civil Rights is an abuse of the Senate confirmation process, an abuse of Senate rules, and an unforgivable abuse of a human being named Clarence Thomas."

Laugh at that. Everybody here knows what I am talking about, everybody here. People have tried to make this, have tried to make sexual harassment the only issue here. Now, sexual harassment is ugly, it is unforgivable. It is wrong. It is extremely destructive, especially to women, but to men, too. Sexual harassment should not be allowed.

I would like you to describe now, for this gathering, what it is like to be accused of sexual harassment. Tell us what it feels like. And let me add the word, unjustly accused of sexual harassment.

JUDGE THOMAS: Senator, as I have said throughout these hearings, the last two and a half weeks have been a living hell. I think I have died a thousand deaths. What it means is living on one hour a night's sleep. It means losing fifteen pounds in two weeks. It means being unable to eat, unable to drink, unable to think about anything but this and wondering why and how? It means wanting to give up. It means losing the belief in our system, and in this system, and in this process. Losing a belief in a sense of fairness and honesty and decency. That is what it has meant to me.

When I appeared before this committee for my real confirmation hearing, it was hard. I would have preferred it to be better. I would have preferred for more members to vote for me. But I had a faith that at least this system was working in some fashion, though imperfectly.

I don't think this is right. I think it's wrong. I think it's wrong for the country. I think it's hurt me and I think it's hurt the country. I have never been accused of sex harassment. And anybody who knows me knows I am adamantly opposed to that, adamant, and yet, I sit here accused. I will never be able to get my name back, I know it.

The day I get to receive a phone call on Saturday night, last Saturday night, about 7:30 and told that this was going to be in the press, I died. The person you knew, whether you voted for me or against me, died.

In my view, that is an injustice.

SEN. HATCH: Now, Judge—

JUDGE THOMAS: As I indicated earlier, it is an injustice to me, but it is a bigger injustice to this country. I don't think any American, whether that person is homeless, whether that person earns a minimum wage or is unemployed, whether that person runs a corporation or small business, black, white, male, female, should have to go through this for any reason.

The person who appeared here for the real confirmation hearings believed that it was okay to be nominated to the Supreme Court and have a tough confirmation hearing. This person, if asked by George Bush today, would he want to be nominated would refuse flatly, and would advise any friend of his to refuse, it is just not worth it.

SEN. HATCH: Judge, you are here, though. Some people have been spreading the rumor that perhaps you are going to withdraw. What is Clarence Thomas going to do? What is Clarence Thomas going to do?

JUDGE THOMAS: I would rather die than withdraw. If they are going to kill me, they are going to kill me.

SEN. HATCH: So, you would still like to serve on the Supreme Court?

JUDGE THOMAS: I would rather die than withdraw from the process. Not for the purpose of serving on the Supreme Court but for the purpose of not being driven out of this process. I will not be scared. I don't like bullies. I have never run from bullies. I never cry uncle and I am not going to cry uncle today whether I want to be on the Supreme Court or not.

SEN. HATCH: Well, Judge, I hope next Tuesday you make it and I believe you will, and I believe you should. And I believe it is important for every American that you do.

Because I think in your short forty-three years of life that you have just about seen it all and if anybody's in a position to help their fellow men and women under the Constitution, then I have to say you are. And I am proud of you. I am proud of you for not backing down.

That's all I have, Mr. Chairman.

THE CHAIRMAN: Thank you.

Now, we are down to Senators having five minutes and I will begin to yield back and forth. Judge, let me make sure I understand one thing. Do you believe that interest groups went out and got Professor Hill to make up a story or do you believe Professor Hill had a story, untrue from your perspective, that groups went out and found. Which do you believe?

JUDGE THOMAS: Senator, I believe that someone, some interest group, I don't care who it is, in combination came up with this story and used this process to destroy me.

THE CHAIRMAN: A group got Professor Hill to say or make up a story?

JUDGE THOMAS: I believe that in combination this story was developed or concocted to destroy me.

THE CHAIRMAN: With Professor Hill? I mean it is a critical question. Are you saying a group concocted a story with Professor Hill and then went out—

JUDGE THOMAS: That's just my view, Senator.

THE CHAIRMAN: I know, I am trying to make sure I understand it.

JUDGE THOMAS: There are no details to it or anything else. The story developed. I do not believe—the story is not true. The allegations are false and my view is that others put it together and developed this.

THE CHAIRMAN: And put it in Professor Hill's mouth?

JUDGE THOMAS: I don't know. I don't know how it got there. All I know is the story is here and I think it was concocted.

THE CHAIRMAN: Well, Judge, I know you believe that and I am not going to be able to or attempt to, at this moment, refute that. There has been an assertion that has just been made and I want to know whether you would agree with it. It is important for us to keep our eye on the ball here. There are two versions of this story. Either Professor Hill had a story that she told someone and it was taken advantage of by being leaked, or a group sat down, decided to make up a story and found a willing vessel willing to speak out in Professor Hill.

Professor Hill suggests the first version. I want to know what you believe.

Now, they are fundamentally different things in terms of culpability.

JUDGE THOMAS: Senator, those distinctions are irrelevant to me. The story is false. And the story is here and the story was developed to harm me.

THE CHAIRMAN: Thank you.

JUDGE THOMAS: And it did harm me.

THE CHAIRMAN: Let me go down the line here. Senator Kennedy?

SEN. KENNEDY: No, Judge, we just thank you for coming under extraordinary difficult circumstances.

THE CHAIRMAN: Senator Thurmond?

SEN. THURMOND: I believe he is coming back to answer any other charges and I will wait until then.

THE CHAIRMAN: Senator Metzenbaum?

SEN. METZENBAUM: I have no comment.

THE CHAIRMAN: Senator Simpson.

SEN. SIMPSON: Well, it has been a powerful presentation by a powerful person. And I have known you for several years and I have known Ginny before I knew you. I think it is very well that you were not here to hear the testimony of Ms. Hill. That was a good step, whosever idea that was that you did not, of course, you were not here, but you didn't watch it. It would have driven you—

JUDGE THOMAS: Thank you.

SEN. SIMPSON: [continuing]—in a way I do not think would have been appropriate. And here we are. You have been before us for 105 days. We have seen everything, known everything, heard every bit of dirt, as you call it so well. And what do we know about Professor Hill? Not very much. I am waiting for 105 days of surveillance of Ms. Hill and then we will see, you know, who ate the cabbage, as we say out in the Wild West. This is an impossible thing.

And now, I really am getting stuff over the transom about Professor Hill. I have got letters hanging out of my pockets. I have got faxes. I have got statements from her former law professors, statements from people that know her, statements from Tulsa, Oklahoma, saying, watch out for this woman. But nobody has the guts to say that because it gets all tangled up in this sexual harassment crap.

I believe sexual harassment is a terrible thing. I had a bill in a year ago, doubling the penalties on sexual harassment. I don't need any test. I don't need anybody to give me the saliva test on whether one believes more or less about sexual harassment. It is repugnant, it is disgusting in any form. And the stuff we listened to, I mean, you know, come on—from the moon.

And it is a sexual stereotype. Just like asking you sexual stereotype questions about your personal life, any woman would be offended by that—about your divorce, you did this, you did that. Talk about in reverse. There is not a woman alive who would take the questions you have had to take, would be just repelled by it. That's where the watershed is here.

It is a good thing that this awareness goes up. It is a terrible, tragic, thing that it should bruise you. And if we really are going to do it right, we are all mumbling about how do you find the truth? I will tell you how you find the truth, you get into an adversarial courtroom and everybody raises their hand once more and you go at it with the rules of evidence and you really punch around in it. And we can't do that. It is impossible for us to do that in this place.

The chairman knows it and he has been exceedingly fair. And so here we are and we will not get to the truth in this process. But there is truth out there and that is in the judicial system. Thank God that there is such a system. It has saved many, many a disillusioned person who was, you know, headed for the Stygian pits.

So, if we had 104 days to go into Ms. Hill and find out about her character, her background, her proclivities, and all the rest, I would feel a lot better about this system. And I am talking about the stuff I am getting from women in America who are sending me things and especially women in Oklahoma. That will all become public. I said, at the time it would be destructive of her and some said, well, isn't that terrible of Simpson, a menacing threat. It was not menacing. It is true.

That she would come forward and she would be destroyed. She will, just as you have been destroyed. I hope you can both be rehabilitated. I have a couple of questions, if I may, Mr. Chairman.

THE CHAIRMAN: Yes.

SEN. SIMPSON: I have not taken time and I will get to that. Angela Wright will soon be with us, we think, but now we are told that Angela Wright has what we used to call in the legal trade, cold feet. Now, if Angela Wright doesn't show up to tell her tale of your horrors, what are we to determine about Angela Wright?

Did you fire her and if you did, what for?

JUDGE THOMAS: I indicated, Senator, I summarily dismissed her and this is my recollection. She was hired to reinvigorate the public affairs operation at EEOC. I felt her performance was ineffective, and the office was ineffective. And the straw that broke the camel's back was a report to me from one of the members of my staff that she referred to another male member of my staff as a faggot.

SEN. SIMPSON: As a faggot?

JUDGE THOMAS: And that is inappropriate conduct, and that is a slur, and I was not going to have it.

SEN. SIMPSON: And so you just summarily discharged her?

JUDGE THOMAS: That is right.

SEN. SIMPSON: That was enough for you?

JUDGE THOMAS: That was more than enough for me. That is my recollection.

SEN. SIMPSON: That is kind of the way you are, isn't it?

JUDGE THOMAS: That is the way I am with conduct like that, whether it is sex harassment or slurs or anything else. I don't play games.

SEN. SIMPSON: And so that was the end of Ms. Wright, who is now going to come and tell us perhaps about more parts of the anatomy. I am sure of that. And a totally discredited and—we had just as well get to the nub of things here—a totally discredited witness who does have cold feet.

Well, Mr. Chairman, you know all of us have been through this stuff in life, but never to this degree. I have done my old stuff about my past, and shared those old saws.

But I will tell you, I do love Shakespeare, and Shakespeare would love this.

This is all Shakespeare. This is about love and hate, and cheating and distrust, and kindness and disgust, and avarice and jealousy and envy, all those things that make that remarkable bard read today.

But boy, I will tell you, one came to my head, and I just went and got it out of the back of the book. *Othello*, read *Othello*, and don't ever forget this line: "Good name in man and woman, dear my Lord"—do you remember this scene? "— is the immediate jewel of their souls. Who steals my purse, steals trash. 'Tis something, nothing. 'Twas mine, 'tis his, and has been slave to thousands. But he that filches from me my good name, robs me of that which not enriches him, and makes me poor indeed."

What a tragedy. What a disgusting tragedy.

THE CHAIRMAN: Senator DeConcini?

SEN. DECONCINI: Mr. Chairman, I have some questions, and it may take more than five minutes. I hope I could just follow them up and get this over with, rather than waiting around. Judge I have great empathy with what you have been through. I happen to have a little experience, going through an awful process. I think this is atrocious. I went through an atrocious process that I thought I would never get over, but I did. Just like you, I had a strong family, I believed in myself, and I did not do the things I was accused of, so I have a kind of a feeling of what you have gone through. Mine was not a sexual harassment charge, but I felt just about as bad as you did. I thought I was going to die. Thanks to my wife and family and some good friends, that didn't happen.

And when the leaks came toward this Senator, I must say there wasn't a howl except from the chairman of the Ethics Committee, who stood up on the floor of the Senate, and the Majority Leader, and very few other people stood up on the floor of the Senate, as they did when the leaks came about you. So if nothing else, at least for this Senator, somebody gives a damn about leaks and breaking the rules, and maybe we will finally put an end to leaks, which I think caused you to go through what you have had to go through.

Now, Judge Thomas, I think the question that chairman Biden asked you, and you answered it in such a manner that it really is irrelevant, was how all this happened. The fact is that it happened, no matter whether Ms. Hill plotted it, whether she was paid to do it, whether her conscience drove her to do it. The fact is that it has, in your judgment, ruined your name, and that you died two weeks ago.

Is that fair, to restate your position?

JUDGE THOMAS: It is fair.

SEN. DECONCINI: Now, Judge, based on that—and I think that the circumstances that give rise to these allegations against you are—I can't believe I am here myself. I can't believe that this process is taking place, to a U.S. Appellate Court Judge who has been confirmed three times by this body, a life appointment, I can't believe you are even here and I am even here. I am ashamed to be part of this process.

But nevertheless, that is my job, and I am here because the Senate said, "Go back and do it again." We did it. We did it right, I believe. I think the chairman protected Ms. Hill, as she wanted to be protected, and he did it with the spirit of protecting her rights. And now, I won't go into the press any more, I have beat up on them enough I guess, but we are here because it was leaked and the press released it.

I don't think Professor Hill will ever fully recover from what she has gone through, regardless of what happens to you, and I don't know whether you will. And my question to you is, do you think you can recover from dying a thousand deaths, having your name and your reputation ripped from you through this process? Can you recover as an individual and serve on the Supreme Court?

JUDGE THOMAS: Senator, there is also a positive side of this.

SEN. DECONCINI: Tell me what it is, except raising the awareness of sex harassment, and I don't say that is minimal, but I think that awareness is out there and has been out there for a long time, if I may say myself, and I didn't need this experience to raise it for me, but please don't let me interrupt what you say is the positive side. Believe me, I am looking for one; I am praying for one.

JUDGE THOMAS: During this process, the last 105 days, and the last two and a half weeks especially, I have never had such an outpouring of love and affection and friendship in people who know me, not people making these scurrilous assertions but people who know me, supporting me and caring for me, helping me to recover from it and survive it—my wife; my son, whose reaction is just to be terribly angry.

I think it showed me just how vulnerable I am as a human being, and any American, that these kinds of charges can be given validity in a process such as this, and the destruction it can do. It has given me that sense.

I think it has also shown people in our country what is happening. I didn't want them to see what happened to me. I didn't want my personal life or allegations about my sexual habits or anything else broadcast in every living room in the United States. But they see this process for what it is, and I think that is good, and hopefully it never happens to another American.

Yes, I can heal. As I said in my opening remarks, I will simply walk down the Hill, if I am not confirmed, that will be it, and continue my job as Court of Appeals Judge, and hopefully live a long life, enjoy my neighbors and my friends, my son, cut my grass, go to McDonald's, and drive my car, and just be a good citizen and a good judge and a good father and a good husband. Yes, I will survive. My question was, will the country survive, and hopefully it will.

SEN. DECONCINI: And if you are confirmed?

JUDGE THOMAS: I will survive, a different person. I would have hoped, Senator, when I was nominated, that it would have been an occasion for joy. There has never been a single day of joy in this process. There has never been one minute of joy in having been nominated to the Supreme Court of the United States of America.

SEN. DECONCINI: Judge Thomas, you said—correct me if I am wrong—after ten days or whatever it was, ninety witnesses and your five days, I thought you were not just being gracious but being sincere, where you thanked the chairman and this committee and, as you said today, you would have liked to receive more votes here but you didn't, and that was the process. As I remember your words, you said, "I think I have been treated fairly, and I have no quarrel or no ill feelings." Am I restating that correctly, how you felt after your formal hearing?

JUDGE THOMAS: That is right, Senator.

SEN. DECONCINI: And I can understand that you don't feel that way today, and my question continues to go to the sense of you being confirmed. What does it do to somebody? Does it affect their ability to approach cases, as you indicated, and satisfactorily so to this Senator, approach cases as a Supreme Court Judge? Can you be reborn in the sense of the loss that you have had to suffer here in the last two weeks? And how do you cope with it, if you care to say? And if you don't, I will understand.

JUDGE THOMAS: Senator, there is one thing that I have learned over my life, and that is that I will be back.

The other thing that I have learned in this process are things that we discussed in the real confirmation hearing, and that is our rights being protected, what rights we have as citizens of this country, what constitutional rights, what is our relationship with our Government. And as I sit here on matters such as privacy, matters such as procedures for charges against individuals in a criminal context or a civil context, this has heightened my awareness of the importance of those protections, the importance of something that we discussed in theory —privacy, due process, equal protection, fairness.

SEN. DECONCINI: Judge, is it safe to say that—what a way to have to come to it, and this Senator was satisfied you didn't have to come to it, that you met the threshold for my vote—what you are now saying to us is that through this God-awful experience you will be more sensitive towards the rights of the accused, and that is because your rights have been violated. Is that correct?

JUDGE THOMAS: I have been an accused.

SEN. DECONCINI: And your rights—

JUDGE THOMAS: Were violated, as far as—

SEN. DECONCINI: [continuing]—were violated?

JUDGE THOMAS: I think strongly so.

SEN. DECONCINI: Thank you, Judge Thomas.

Thank you, Mr. Chairman.

THE CHAIRMAN: The Senator from South Carolina.

SEN. THURMOND: Mr. Chairman, it has been mentioned here about he has been confirmed three times. My recollection is four times, as the assistant in the Civil Rights Division, and twice in EEOC, wasn't it?

JUDGE THOMAS: That is right, Senator.

SEN. THURMOND: And then in the civil court. Four times.

JUDGE THOMAS: That is right.

SEN. THURMOND: So this will be the fifth time.

JUDGE THOMAS: That is right, Senator.

SEN. THURMOND: I just want to make the record straight.

JUDGE THOMAS: Thank you, Senator Thurmond.

SEN. GRASSLEY: Judge Thomas, the thing that keeps going through my mind is, all fourteen of us sit here, while you are being questioned all the time. I am reminded of the verse that says, "He who is without sin, let him be the first to cast the stone." I know you have gone through a lot of things. I have sinned; I can't cast that stone. And there isn't anybody perfect on this side, either. As you stare at us, I keep hoping you know that at least half of the members of this committee voted for you, and that not everybody on this side of the aisle is your enemy.

I heard something on one of the commentaries on television, more than once. I want to bring it up for you to give a response to, because I think it has put a very unfair message out there. I don't think it has come from anchor people; I think it has come from people that have appeared to make commentary, other than politicians.

They contrast you and Professor Hill, saying, why would she come forward? She doesn't have anything to gain by coming forward and didn't have to come forward, so she obviously would have to be telling the truth, while in your case it is considered implicit that you are lying because you have everything to lose.

I would like to have you tell the American people your reaction to that comparison.

JUDGE THOMAS: Senator, I think that people can rationalize just about anything. I have learned through this process that people have fit square pegs into round holes, and they do it very well and have no problem with that inconsistency. I don't know what Anita Hill has to gain; I don't know. I don't know what goes on in her mind. But I have already lost. I have lost my name.

As I said before, I never aspired to the Supreme Court. I am on the Court of Appeals. I love my job. I love what I do every day. I have lost everything in this process. I am here not to be confirmed; I am here to get my name back. All I have to gain from this process is to salvage a little bit of my integrity and a little bit of my name. Nothing more.

SEN. GRASSLEY: You haven't mentioned your grandfather at all this particular sitting. I would like to have you tell me what advice you think he would give to you if he were advising you today.

JUDGE THOMAS: Well, Senator, in 1983—and this is something that I said during my real confirmation hearings—when I was getting hammered in the public and getting criticized, and I complained to him, he told me to stand up for what I believe in. That is what he would tell me today: not to quit, not to turn tail, not to cry uncle and not to give up until I am dead. He had another statement: "Give out but don't give up." That is what he would say to me.

SEN. GRASSLEY: Mr. Chairman, I yield. Thank you.

THE CHAIRMAN: Senator Simon.

SEN. SIMON: Thank you, Mr. Chairman.

Judge Thomas, most of us have made the decision on the basis that you have asked for. There are, I think it is safe to say, a few members of the Senate who have not made the decision yet, and what is happening here may be the decisive factor. I read in one of the morning newspapers where Senator Brown was quoted as saying, "We have two very credible witnesses." I think there are those who, whether they are reporters in this room or people viewing it on television, have come away with a good impression of both of you; but obviously one person is telling the truth and one is not, and it is difficult to determine that.

And you look at factors that weigh on either side that, in a small way, may be measurable. Let me just outline for you some of these factors, and if you would correct me if I am leaving out anything on your side of the fact. First, that she followed you from one job to another. I understand her statement that the harassing ceased and she needed the job, but she did follow.

Second, the phone calls, eleven phone calls in seven years. Some of them can be explained, maybe all of them can be, I don't know. And some additional contact with you, limited, but some additional contact. While psychiatrists say for those who have sexual abuse, this is not an uncommon occurrence, nevertheless, it seems to me those weigh on your side.

On the other side is, first of all, the much-discussed question of motivation. She is clearly a reluctant witness and, as I sense it, her motivation may be public service. It is very difficult. You can stretch, but it is hard to find other motivation.

Second, the detailed facts that she comes up with could be created, but it is difficult to imagine that. I don't happen to be a fan of lie-detectors, but she volunteered to the FBI that she would take a lie-detector test. I don't find generally that people who are not telling the truth volunteer to take lie-detector tests.

Finally, she experienced stomach pains only one time in her life, due to job stress, she says, and her physician at least apparently partially confirms, and that was during this period that she was working for you.

Now, none of these factors alone is enough, and maybe in combination they are not enough. But what would you say to my colleagues in the Senate who are trying to weigh this thing and say what are some more objective criteria that can be used, as you weigh this?

JUDGE THOMAS: Senator, I don't think there are objective criteria in weighing evidence. That is why you have rules of evidence and procedures in courts of law. This is not a court of law. That is why you have judges and finders of fact. That is why you have a careful review process. That is why you have statutes of limitations. That is why you have cross-examination by experienced trial counsel. That is why you have precedents. That is why you have a judicial system.

SEN. SIMON: Let me ask you another question about the process. If you were on this committee and we came up with another similar situation, would we be better off having such a hearing in executive session, without cameras, without reporters, without television sets in executive session?

JUDGE THOMAS: Senator, I think you should in these instances trust the FBI or experienced investigators. If you don't like their reports, I think you should stop relying on them. I don't think that this body can serve as a judicial system.

SEN. SIMON: But we have to make judgments.

JUDGE THOMAS: I don't think that this body can serve—this is a political body, I don't think it can serve as a judicial system.

SEN. SIMON: I guess, again, the FBI does not draw conclusions, as you know, as you have seen FBI reports, and we have to make judgments and I don't think the —I don't know how we are going to improve the process.

JUDGE THOMAS: I think that this is clearly wrong.

SEN. SIMON: I think we are in agreement that the process has to be improved.

JUDGE THOMAS: No, Senator, in the strongest terms, this process can only go in one direction and that is improvement. This is clearly wrong.

SEN. SIMON: I have no further questions, Mr. Chairman.

THE CHAIRMAN: The Senator from Colorado, Senator Brown.

SEN. BROWN: Thank you, Mr. Chairman.

THE CHAIRMAN: Senator Specter has already asked questions. If he has any more, we will go to him later.

SEN. BROWN: In trying to review what we have had before us, it strikes me that we have taken on a question that, by any measure, is very difficult. It is not just that we have had two very persuasive people before us, but I have tried to make some notes as to what it is we are looking at. We are looking at a very serious charge. We are looking at a charge about activities, about very repugnant statements of an extreme nature, and the case is one where there are no witnesses.

Normally, when you have a disagreement, you have got some witnesses, but we don't have any witnesses here. There is no documentation here. There is nothing we can check, in terms of the documents, because there are no documents that were made up at the time. There was no notification. Normally, with an event like this occurred, someone would bring a charge and there would be a notice to the person who is accused. There is no notification here.

We are looking at a charge that is ten years old. It wasn't done yesterday, it wasn't done last week, it wasn't done six months ago or five years ago, it was done ten years ago. That is some twenty times beyond the statute of limitations. The statute of limitations, as I understand it, is a number of days, or in some events as long as six months. This is twenty times the statute of limitations. Basically, what we are called upon to prove or you are called upon to prove is a negative. You are called upon to prove that ten years ago you didn't do something. I am not sure how you do that. I am not sure how you prove a negative.

One thing I guess that does come to mind is that you could call in every woman that has worked closely with you and show this committee whether or not you have exhibited that type of activity with others. That is, it is difficult to prove a negative, but that is one thing to do. As I understand our rules, we have requested that those women be called in, and the committee has not allowed that. I don't fault the chairman with that. I believe the chairman has tried very hard to be fair. We do have time limitations. Nevertheless, we are faced with trying to prove this question and not be able to listen to them.

Now, I also followed up with a letter to ask that we at least require the FBI to take statements from these women who we don't have time to hear, and that request was turned down by this committee. I think that evidence is important and should be taken, but that evidence was turned down by this committee. I have asked and the chairman has agreed to allow statements, if these women want to make them, to be entered in the record, and I think that will be helpful.

I have also asked that the staffers who there is reason to believe [have] evidence to offer here be called. In talking with Professor Hill and in listening to her testimony, it became very clear that the reason she came forward with these charges is because these staffers told her there were rumors about sexual harassment and there was an implication that she was involved in those rumors, and part of the reason I believe she came forward was in response to the stories they told her, and to not take that testimony I just think is wrong. We have made that point and that request has been turned down.

The bottom line I think is it is tough to decide this case. I think there are two avenues that we can look at: One, if the event took place, what kind of conduct would it have engendered in her and what kind of conduct would it have engendered in you. I haven't got a complete list, but I think there is a possibility, if the very severe conduct took place, that it could have resulted in a complaint from her. It did not. No complaint was made. Is that determinate? No. There are certain reasons that complaints would not be brought forth, but it is one question to look at.

No notes were made of the incident. There was no effort at the time of the incident to find another job. There was no effort at the time of moving to the EEOC to find another job. Even though she indicated that she didn't want to continue on, she made no effort to check for another job at the Department of Education or in the private sector.

Even after the incident, there was no effort to cut off contacts, either in terms of finding another job or in terms of even, after having left the job, contacts continued. Now, it strikes me that the incident, as vile as it is described, took place, that there may well be a reason to not continue contacts.

There was no mention of these charges when you were up for confirmation in 1982. There was no mention of these charges when you were up for reconfirmation in 1984. No one came forward. There was no mention of these charges when you were up for confirmation for the Circuit Court of Appeals.

There are even some reports that have come of her praise of you after the incidents. Now, none of these by themselves determine the issue, but all of them I think bear on the question of whether or not it happened. Because if it did happen, as vile conduct as is described, it surely must have affected these nine specific examples, and I suspect more.

That brings me to what I hope you will search your mind for: It strikes me, if this incident happened, it would not only affect her conduct toward you, but it would affect your conduct toward her. What is alleged is that you repeatedly asked her out and she refused. What is alleged is that you uttered very vile words, and she did not react the way you wished her to.

I would like you, if you are willing, to itemize for us decisions you had to make about Professor Hill in terms of job references, in terms of retention for jobs, in terms of pay, in terms of evaluation, in terms of references, and in terms of assistance, what did you do in terms of your conduct after this alleged event took place.

JUDGE THOMAS: Senator, my treatment of Anita Hill was consistent throughout. As I have indicated, her allegations are false. She repeatedly received promotions as scheduled, as far as I can remember. In fact, she may have been promoted on an accelerated basis. Her assignments, for her age and experience at that time, I think were fairly aggressive.

I certainly made sure that when she decided to leave, that I assisted her and I have kept contact with her, not on a regular basis, but certainly returned her calls and, whenever she needed help, responded to that. That is during and after. My conduct is consistent with my treatment of all of my special assistants, particularly those who do a good job. There is nothing in my conduct toward her that would indicate any negative events.

Her conduct toward me over the years has been precisely the same, it has always been warm and cordial, professional. This is the first I have heard of any allegations and, certainly, as I have indicated, or two and a half weeks ago, certainly as I indicated, it did not occur. But my conduct toward her is the same as my conduct toward my other special assistants who were successful or who performed well.

I would look for, if these events had happened, some disparity in that, and there is no disparity in that. My relationship with her I think at this time or prior to this event was pretty much the same as my relationship with my other former special assistants.

SEN. BROWN: Is there anything you can think of in your conduct that would suggest you retaliated?

JUDGE THOMAS: Absolutely not, Senator.

SEN. BROWN: I yield back. Thank you.

THE CHAIRMAN: Senator Kohl.

SEN. KOHL: Thank you very much, Mr. Chairman.

Judge, all of our hearts and our concerns and our sympathies go out to you and your family, for the travail which you have undergone here, and I think it is important to recognize that it is a collective travail—that extends to institutions of government, the American people and Anita Hill. This has been a very damaging affair and many, many people have gotten hurt. I don't know as there is anybody in our country who has been helped by this unhappy situation.

I would like to offer the observation and get your response to it that, regardless of all the other reasons that brought us here—including things like leaks which should not have occurred—there is a single most important reason without which we would not be here today, and that is Professor Hill, an African-American, hired by you, trained by you, promoted by you, a person that you have described repeatedly as smart, tough-minded, resilient, and effective.

That person leveled a charge against you of sex harassment, a charge that you have said is a very, very serious charge and cannot be taken lightly. And Anita Hill and all that she represents in the relationship that you had with her is what brings us here today. Do you have a comment on that, sir?

JUDGE THOMAS: I don't agree with that, Senator. I have been exposed to this process for 105 days—105. I wasn't nominated last week and confirmation hearings set for this week. I think this is wrong.

SEN. KOHL: But at the—

JUDGE THOMAS: I think this is wrong.

SEN. KOHL: [continuing]—but at the end of the nomination process, you said—you said to Senator DeConcini and he repeated back to you—you said that you had been treated fairly up to that point.

JUDGE THOMAS: I was treated fairly, Senator, but this is 105 days. That is a month ago. That is a month ago.

SEN. KOHL: That's thirty days ago.

JUDGE THOMAS: Yes.

SEN. KOHL: Right.

JUDGE THOMAS: This process is wrong, Senator. There is no way, as far as I am concerned, that you can validate it.

SEN. KOHL: I don't want to—

JUDGE THOMAS: The allegations, anyone can make an allegation. I deny those allegations. I have always cooperated with the FBI. Think about who you are talking to. I have been a public figure for ten years. I have been confirmed four times. I have had five FBI background checks. I have had stories written about me, I have had groups that despise me, looking into my background.

I have had people who wanted to do me great harm. You are talking about a person who ran an agency—two agencies to fight discrimination, who, if I did anything stupid like this, gross like this, had everything to lose, who adamantly preached against it. It just seems as though I am here to prove the negative in a forum without rules and after the fact.

I think that all this has done is give a forum to people who can make terrible charges against individuals who have to come here for confirmation. I think this is all this has done and it has harmed me greatly, Senator.

That is not to say that sex harassment is not serious. My record speaks for itself on that. But there is a forum for that. You have agencies for that. You have courts for that to deal with those. You cannot deal with those in this process in this manner.

What you are doing is you are inviting and validating people making very serious charges against other individuals who do not have the capacity to extricate themselves from it.

SEN. KOHL: I think you are absolutely right. I still would like to make the point, if I may, very respectfully, that the charge was brought not by somebody who was a stranger to you but by somebody who was very close to you in a very important job with you, for a very long time.

JUDGE THOMAS: She was not there a very long time, Senator, and it was in 1983 that she left.

SEN. KOHL: Okay.

Finally, I would like to say, Judge Thomas, and to all of us who are here today and listening that this is obviously not what America ought to be. And while we want to get to the truth in this particular case, the truth will be well-served if all of us stop and think long and hard about what we are doing to our nation.

We simply have to restore civility and decency to the public debate.

Thank you, Mr. Chairman.

THE CHAIRMAN: Thank you, Senator Kohl.

SEN. SPECTER: Mr. Chairman?

THE CHAIRMAN: Senator Specter and then to you. I hope the principals will limit their questions to five minutes or less. They have had plenty of time to question.

SEN. SPECTER: Thank you, Mr. Chairman, just a couple of more questions.

Judge Thomas, the visits which you have testified about to the home of Professor Hill had not been known, at least to me, and my question to you is, how do you square that with your policy of not socializing or not dating anybody in the office? Was there any element of socializing at all in the visits which you have described to Professor Hill's apartment?

JUDGE THOMAS: Senator, I did not consider it socializing. It was, of course, it would be more the nature of my talking to my clerks or my talking to my special assistants outside of the office. I did not consider it anything other than a professional cordial talk or chat. And, of course, she has indicated, I guess, in some communications with the committee that I went over to help her with a stereo, but I would not have considered it socializing.

SEN. SPECTER: Judge Thomas, when I met with you on the morning of September 27, before the Judiciary Committee voted, I had asked you at that time about these charges, having seen the FBI report the night before.

And I was asking you about the question of motivation. You made some comments to me at that time, although they are somewhat sensitive, I think they are worth exploring for just a moment now. That was the comment you made about a possible concern that Professor Hill might have had regarding your dating a woman who was of a lighter complexion. Would you amplify what had happened, respond, and testify as to what had happened in that regard?

JUDGE THOMAS: Senator, I think it is sensitive, and I think enough sensitive matters have been discussed here. I would reluctantly discuss it but I was merely speculating and groping around for some rationale. And the point I was making to you was that there seemed to be some tension between, as a result of the complexion, the lighter complexion of the woman I dated and the woman whom I chose to be my chief of staff, or my executive assistant and some reaction, as I recall it, to my preferring individuals of the lighter complexion.

SEN. SPECTER: Did Professor Hill not get a promotion that she was working for within your staff?

JUDGE THOMAS: Again, I can't remember the exact details of it, but I think she wanted to have that position, the executive assistant position. But that's again,

Senator, that is speculation as to what the motivation would be and I hesitate to even mention it here.

SEN. SPECTER: Finally, you mentioned that there had not been any detailing given to the comment about an associate of yours who classified Professor Hill as your enemy which you had disregarded because of your overall view of the generalized loyalty of your staff. Can you amplify what happened in that regard?

JUDGE THOMAS: Well, there were some members of my—at least one member of my staff who felt that she did not have my best interests at heart and he would continue to, as I remember it, articulate that point of view, and I would, again, dismiss it.

SEN. SPECTER: Well, did he tell you why he felt that way?

JUDGE THOMAS: It must have been based on specific things at that time. I don't recollect the bases of his conclusion nor his statements, but he would say it repeatedly when he saw evidence of it.

SEN. SPECTER: Thank you, very much, Judge Thomas. I am glad to conclude before the red light went on.

THE CHAIRMAN: Thank you, very much. Senator Heflin.

SEN. HEFLIN: Mr. Chairman, I will just take thirty seconds. I want to clarify one thing. One member of my staff thought there might be some misunderstanding about it. I accused no one of rape. And the only reason I was using it as a comparison is because when you have date rape offenses you seldom have any witnesses, any corroborating witnesses. I was using that analogy in this instance because we don't have any witnesses or any corroborating witnesses, that's all.

THE CHAIRMAN: Senator Leahy.

SEN. LEAHY: Thank you, Mr. Chairman.

Mr. Chairman, I will be brief. We can go around and around and we will be back basically at the same position. Judge, when you and I left off, I think we agreed on the fact that there is irreconcilable conflict in the testimony. I know you feel strongly about which way that should come down.

I am not at all happy with the whole process. This is my third term here and I have sat on four different committees that have had confirmation processes. We have spent more time on this one than any other nomination in nearly eighteen years. I can only gather how difficult it has been for you, and your family, your wife, son, others. You are here with a good friend of all of ours, and a tower of integrity in the U.S. Senate, Senator Danforth. I know how difficult it has been for him, I chatted briefly with him this morning.

As a U.S. Senator—I do not like at all the way we have been brought here. The chairman stated and virtually everybody on the committee has supported the position that he took about how we got here. I was glad to hear the chairman and the ranking member state that an investigation will be made of where this material came from. I assume that is going to be completed and we will find out.

I especially want to know because I got to see that FBI report about three days after it was in the newspapers for the first time. I would like to read them in a little bit different sequence. But we were sent by the Senate to try and find an answer and this is a very difficult process.

I suspect that everybody watching this is trying to figure out what the answer is, just like we are. Telephone calls, I have just been advised, into my office are absolutely split down the middle. I would hope that nobody would decide this by polls but that we would do it by our best independent judgment.

And I would hope that we might find a way where we are sure that when we do a confirmation process, we are always dealing with the facts. I don't know the answer to this one. We still have a long time to go. You can think of a hundred places you would rather be, I can think of at least one hundred places I would rather be—all in my home state.

And we may never come to the final conclusion we want. We may never come to the final conclusion of what has happened here. And you know, if that happens, it is even a greater tragedy than many think.

Thank you, Mr. Chairman.

THE CHAIRMAN: Thank you.

Let me, Judge, say a couple of things and we will let you go.

First of all, this unfortunately is not the first time this committee has been presented with a situation like this. It has been the first time we have been presented one that involved a Supreme Court Justice. We have other people nominated before this Court where there are allegations by former wives of mistreatment and wife beating. There is no appropriate forum to resolve that, as you point out.

Now, we have an option in that particular case to say, well, we will send it to the court first. Before we decide whether to confirm this particular person, have the court decide that issue. Believe me, I would like that. I did not sign onto this job or run for it to be a judge. If I wanted to do that, I would be a judge now in my home state. I don't want to be a judge. I hate this job.

But all my colleagues here were telling everybody how awful the process is. Let me be completely blunt about it. It is like democracy. It is a lousy form of government, except that nobody has figured out another way.

Now, I can turn around and I can say to this particular person whose wife has come forward and said, I have been abused, I can say, I will tell you what, we are going to disregard that and we are going to confirm you anyway. Or I can say I don't believe it and therefore, I am not going to tell these fellows, which I have done on other matters unrelated to wife beating.

There has been more nominees sent up here in the last two administrations that have had drug problems, and I never even told these folks about, because it happened ten, twenty, thirty years ago.

So I take the heat and I take the responsibility and I will continue to do it as long as I am chairman, no matter what these guys think of this process, okay? Number one.

Number two, when an allegation of consequence comes forward I do not have the recourse to send it to the courts. I have the recourse only to send it to my colleagues. There is no other institutional way of doing it. I made a judgment on this one. My trust was violated by somebody. And then the fat was in the fire. And we would be in the same position if the day before the hearing began Ms. Hill, unrelated to any statement of this committee, stood up and held a press conference and said, as I spoke with counsel, as the possibility could happen, from the White House and just held a press conference. We would be in the same spot. We could say we are not going to resolve that, let's put this nomination on hold and send it to the courts.

Not a possibility. Not able to do that no matter what my colleagues who are now telling everybody how wrong this process is. And let me say another thing. This isn't over. Your grandfather is right, you have no right to give up. There are compelling arguments to be made for you and they may end up being made by me and others.

For example, one of the arguments made against you constantly by those who opposed your nomination is here is a guy who sought this. He has suckered it. He has gone out and he has laid down for people for it and he is not dumb. A guy who wanted this in the beginning. I heard people coming to us and testifying and saying you wanted this and planned this since the late 1970's. Well, if you planned this in the late 1970's and you did this you are one of the dumbest people I have ever run across in my life.

And you don't impress me as being dumb. Your defenders here are not even smart enough to figure out to make that defense for you. My job is not to defend you or to prosecute you. It is to see to it that you get a fair shot in a system that is imperfect but it is a good system.

Now, everybody points out what hasn't been made here. Every expert that has ever testified before me in this committee on an issue that I do know something about and I have spent—with the exception than maybe one person on this committee—more time dealing with abuse against women and the surrounding circumstances than anybody else in the Senate.

And every expert comes forward and says, there's a pattern. It doesn't happen in isolated instances. It is a pattern. If there is not a pattern, to me that is probative. That has some dispositive weight. No one has proved a pattern here of anything. We are not finished yet. But no one has proved a pattern.

Again, these people have decided already, once and for all, they are for you or against you. You need better lawyers. You need to hire me.

I am getting fed up with this stuff about how terrible this system is. I hear everybody talking about how terrible the primary system is. We are big boys. I knew when I ran for President that everything was free game. Anybody who runs for the Supreme Court or who is appointed to the Supreme Court, to be more precise, should understand, this is not Boy Scouts, it is not Cub Scouts. In the case of the President and the right to be leader of the free world, well, no one ever said it would be easy. And whoever goes to the Supreme Court is going to determine the fate of this country more than anybody. For the next twenty years we are going to have people scrupulous and unscrupulous respond and react. And this is not a referendum on whether or not, whether or not sexual harassment is a grave offense. I said from the beginning, this is about whether or not sexual harassment occurred.

And lastly, Judge, with me, from the beginning and at this moment, until the end, the presumption is with you. Now we are going to hear more witnesses. They are going to come in and corroborate your position and hers. And we will find out whether they are telling the truth or not as best as we are capable of doing, just like you as a judge are when you look them in the eye and make a judgment.

So, Judge, this is less directed at you, than it is to my pontificating colleagues, Democrat and Republican alike, so, Judge, I have not made my judgment, based upon this proceeding, because we have not heard all the evidence.

And the last thing I will point out, the next person who refers to an FBI report as being worth anything, obviously doesn't understand anything. FBI explicitly does not, in this or any other case, reach a conclusion, period, period. So, Judge, there is no reason why you should know this.

The reason why we cannot rely on the FBI report, you would not like it if we did because it is inconclusive. They say "he said, she said, and they said," period.

So when people wave an FBI report before you, understand they do not, they do not reach conclusions. They do not make, as my friend points out more accurately, they do not make recommendations.

Judge, it is no fun, but there are certain things in our society that have occurred that the nature of the offense is an offense that it almost always takes place [where] there can be and will be no corroborating evidence, and all of us are susceptible to that errant charge [*sic*].

And if you don't think that we are going to see individuals up here charged, individuals in the Senate, individuals in the workplace charged, maybe even not without merit charged.

But Judge, everybody says, "We know how you feel." No one can know how you feel. That always excites me, when I hear people tell me how it feels.

"Oh, you lost family. I know how it feels."

"Oh, you lost this. I know how it feels."

"You went through that, and they ruined your reputation by it. I know how it feels."

No one knows how it feels, but I hope we stop this stuff. The press did nothing wrong; it is not their fault. It is the nature of what happens here when something goes public. This is not a right and wrong, until it comes down to a decision about you, and the presumption is with you. With me, the presumption is with you, and in my opinion it should be with you until all the evidence is in and people make a judgment.

So, Judge, I don't know exactly how you feel, but you have clearly demonstrated how you feel, and some of us, not all of us here, have an inkling how you feel. And like I said, I ran for this job to affect foreign policy, to affect domestic policy, not to be a judge. If I wanted to be a judge, I would have arranged for that a long time ago.

Judge, wait until it is over—it will be over in the next two days—to make your judgment. You will not be unaffected by this, no matter what happens. Nobody goes through the white hot glare of this process, any level, for any reason, and comes out unaffected. But, Judge, nobody's reputation, nobody's reputation is a snapshot. It is a motion picture, and the picture is being made, and you have made the vast part of it the last forty-three years.

SEN. THURMOND: Can I say just a word?

Judge, the chairman is a good man. He frequently votes with me.

THE CHAIRMAN: Judge, I voted against you. It had nothing to do with this. I voted against you, and you and I disagree, like you said, on philosophy, as I can best understand it.

Judge, go home, do whatever you are going to do. Thank you for being here. You are entitled to come back any time you want to come back, after we hear the rest of the witnesses, and no one should make any judgment about anybody until we hear the rest of the witnesses.

We are recessed for fifteen minutes.

[Recess.]

THE CHAIRMAN: The committee will please come to order.

I apologize for keeping the witnesses waiting, and as the old saying goes, we have got good news for you and bad news for you. After a caucus of the committee, the full committee, Democrats and Republicans, in deciding how we would meet our responsibilities to the full Senate to be able to conduct and conclude this hearing in as fair a way to everyone involved, and particularly to the nominee, it has been concluded as follows, and essentially unanimously concluded:

That we will reconvene tomorrow at noon; that the reason why we are not going to go forward with this panel tonight, is that if we go forward with this panel tonight, under the agreed procedures we would be required to, understandably, go forward with the next panel tonight. The likelihood of that occurring and finishing in any remotely reasonable hour is incredibly unlikely.

So if the witnesses are able, and we sincerely hope they are, we will ask them to come back, this panel, Ms. Hoerchner, Ms. Wells, Mr. Carr, Mr. Paul, tomorrow at noon. It is our hope, although not full expectation, to finish this hearing tomorrow, to give our colleagues in the Senate, as we were charged, an opportunity to contemplate and mull over the record and what they have heard and seen on Monday and Tuesday, and to vote Tuesday.

There is no question, as I informed the leadership when they asked if we could conduct this hearing fully by the vote Tuesday night and still give the Senate time to fully consider every aspect of it, my unequivocal answer was no, we could not. And the Senate decided that we were going to do it within that time, so that there would be a final vote in order to lift the unanimous consent agreement from last week. So we are operating under some limitations. Our goal continues to be to find the truth. We believe that a full night's sleep may help elucidate that goal somewhat—not for the panel, but for the committee and the staff—and so we will reconvene tomorrow at noon and go hopefully as long as it takes to finish.

[Whereupon, at 6:30 p.m., the committee recessed, to reconvene at 12 p.m., Sunday, September 13, 1991.]

AP/Wide World Photos

Washington, October 11, 1991—Anita Hill testifies in the Caucus Room of the Russell Senate Office Building on Capitol Hill before the Senate Judiciary Committee.

Reuters/Bettmann

From left to right: Chairman Sen. Joseph Biden, Sen. Howard M. Metzenbaum, Sen. Paul Simon, and Sen. Ted Kennedy.

AP/World Wide Photos

From left to right: Sen. Charles Grassley , Sen. Alan Simpson, Sen. Arlen Specter, Sen. Orrin Hatch, and Sen. Strom Thurmond.

AP/World Wide Photos

From left: Judge Susan Hoerchner, Ellen Wells, John Carr, and Joel Paul

Reuters/Bettmann

From left: J.C. Alvarez, Nancy Fitch, Diane Holt, Phyllis Berry Myers.

AP/World Wide Photos

From left: Sen. Hank Brown, Sen. Strom Thurmond, Sen. Alan Simpson, Sen. Joseph Biden (Chairman), Sen. Howell Heflin, and Sen. Edward Kennedy.

Senator DeConcini

Senator Leahy

Senator Kohl

AP/Wide World Photos

From left to right: Stanley Grayson, Carlton Stewart, John N. Doggett III, and Charles Kothe.

UPI/Bettmann

John N. Doggett, III.

Reuters/Bettman

From left: Counsel Charles Ogeltree, and Professor Anita Hill

AP/World Wide Photos

Judge Clarence Thomas and his wife, Virginia, sitting behind him.

NOMINATION OF JUDGE CLARENCE THOMAS TO BE ASSOCIATE JUSTICE OF THE SUPREME COURT OF THE UNITED STATES

SUNDAY, OCTOBER 13, 1991

The committee met, pursuant to notice at 12:04 p.m. in room SR-325, Russell Senate Office Building, Hon. Joseph R. Biden, Jr. (Chairman of the Committee) presiding.

Present: Senators Biden, Kennedy, Metzenbaum, De Concini, Leahy, Heflin, Simon, Kohl, Thurmond, Hatch, Simpson, Grassley, Specter, and Brown.

U.S. SENATE,
COMMITTEE ON THE JUDICIARY
Washington, DC

THE CHAIRMAN: The committee will come to order.

I thank the witnesses, the first panel and others, for doing what they obviously believe to be their civic duty and step into the breech. It is not comfortable for anyone at all involved in this process.

I would like to begin, prior to introducing the panel, by indicating how we are going to proceed. The designated questioners will proceed for fifteen minutes per questioner, and then non-designated Senators will have an opportunity to question for up to five minutes.

In addition, I want to make it clear that we thought it best to come back with clear heads this morning and start this morning. That was the only reason for us not going into the night last night. Third, we are going to try our best to accommodate the truth emerging in this process, but it is hard to do that in this process.

One senior correspondent said to me on the way into the building today, as I saw him, "You know, this criticism of the process of this all being done in the cold light of day or the hot lights of television," he said, "when I got here, I spent the first so many years of my professional career criticizing all these hearings that were held closed."

So, the only thing I want to emphasize, if there is any witness anywhere along the process today who wishes to have their comments made in closed session, because they believe it would be embarrassing to say something or repeat something, we will do that. We will do that.

Finally, last night, as I defended the process as the only one we have, I want to make it absolutely clear, I am not defending, have not defended, will not defend, and will pursue to determine who caused us to have to defend this whole matter and leaked this information. Whoever leaked this information did something that I believe to be totally unethical, if not illegal.

But we here, we will pursue this question and we will attempt to end the process today, although I must say at the start what I said at the start of this entire process: We could go on legitimately for another ten days, seeking out corroborators of corroborators, seeking out additional information, further investigating.

That is not a luxury that we have, and it is not the condition upon which this vote was postponed. The postponement, I might add, was called for by the nominee, as well as by the Senate as a whole when this information was leaked to the press.

Having said that, let me introduce our panel today, our first panel, who includes the following witnesses:

The Honorable Susan Hoerchner, a Worker's Compensation Judge in Norwalk, California. Thank you for coming all the way across the country, Judge.

Ellen Wells, project manager for the American Welfare Association, in Washington, DC.

John Carr, a partner in a law firm in New York City.

And Joel Paul, an associate professor of law at the Washington College of Law, at the American University, in Washington, DC.

Now, would you each prepare to proceed in the order in which you were called. Prior to that, I am going to yield to my colleague, the Senator from South Carolina, to see if he has anything he would like to say at the outset of today's hearing.

SEN. THURMOND: Mr. Chairman, as I understand it, we are going to stay in session now until we finish all of the witnesses. It will be completed when we end today or tonight, whenever it is?

THE CHAIRMAN: Will you all stand and be sworn—I beg your pardon. We are going to attempt to finish this this evening. I have learned, after almost nineteen years in the Senate, not nearly however many it has been for you, Senator, that I never predict what the Senate can do, and as has been observed by everyone, I cannot control what any one Senator on this committee will or will not do, or I cannot predict what is going to happen in terms of the desire on the part of the nominee or anyone else to have additional witnesses. But it is my sincere hope that we will bring this matter to a close in terms of the public hearing this evening.

Now, will the witnesses stand to be sworn: Do you swear to tell the whole truth and nothing but the truth, so help you, God?

MS. HOERCHNER: I do.

MR. PAUL: I do.

MS. WELLS: I do.

MR. CARR: I do.

THE CHAIRMAN: Now, we will begin with Ellen Wells. Ms. Wells, if you will proceed.

TESTIMONY OF A PANEL CONSISTING OF:

ELLEN M. WELLS, Project Manager, American Welfare Association, Washington, DC.

JOHN W. CARR, ESQ., New York, New York

SUSAN HOERCHNER, Worker's Compensation Judge, Norwalk, California

JOEL PAUL, Associate Professor, American University Law School, Washington, DC.

TESTIMONY OF ELLEN M. WELLS

MS. WELLS: Thank you, Senator. Good afternoon, Senators. My name is Ellen M. Wells—

THE CHAIRMAN: Please do not have anyone in or out the door during the testimony of these four witnesses, during their statements, I mean.

SEN. THURMOND: If you will speak into the machine, so as we can hear.

THE CHAIRMAN: Unfortunately, this is an old room and you have to pull the microphone very close, if you could.

Thank you.

MS. WELLS: Good afternoon, Senators.

My name is Ellen M. Wells. I am a project manager at the American Public Welfare Association, in Washington, DC.

I received a master's degree in public affairs and a jurisdoctorate from the George Washington University.

I met Professor Hill in 1981 at a social gathering, and we developed a friendship. I was also acquainted with Judge Thomas during the late 1970's and early 1980's, as a result of our joint membership in the Black Republican Congressional Staff Association.

In the fall of 1982, Professor Hill shared with me, in confidence, the fact that she considered Judge Thomas's behavior toward her in the office—

SEN. HEFLIN: Mr. Chairman, if I might interrupt, I don't mean to, but if there are prepared statements that they are reading from, I think it would be helpful to the members of the committee if they had copies of the—I don't have one. If there is a copy of the prepared statement, I would like to follow it in writing, as well as by ear.

THE CHAIRMAN: While Ms. Wells is doing her statement, if the—do we have statements? The statements have not been provided, Senator. It is too late now.

SEN. HEFLIN: All right.

MS. WELLS: I can—

THE CHAIRMAN: No, it is not your fault. Just proceed.

MS. WELLS: All right.

In the fall of 1982, Professor Hill shared with me, in confidence, the fact that she considered Judge Thomas's behavior toward her in the office to be inappropriate. Professor Hill did not at that time nor in subsequent conversations provide exact details about the actions she found inappropriate conduct. She did tell me they were sexual in nature.

I should note that I did not ask for details, for two reasons: Neither Professor Hill nor I would have been comfortable discussing such matters. Women typically don't talk in sexually explicit terms. Second, she appeared to simply need a sympathetic ear and as her friend, that is what I tried to provide.

I believed the statements made by my friend, Professor Hill. As she told me of the situation, she appeared to be deeply troubled and very depressed, and later I remember talking to her by telephone while she was in the hospital, and she explained to me that what she was suffering from appeared to be job related, job-stress related.

I think it is important for me to state that Professor Hill did not contact me in connection with this hearing. In fact, because of the way our lives have been proceeding, I have not seen or spoken to Professor Anita Hill in two years.

I called the law school and left a message of support and willingness to be of assistance, if needed. My call jogged her memory of what she had said to me. As a consequence, Professor Hill asked her attorneys to get in touch with me.

Finally, Senators, I would like to say that I am not a party to any effort to derail Judge Thomas's confirmation to the Supreme Court by any interest group or by individuals who may not agree with his political philosophy. I am here as an individual simply as a matter of conscience to tell you what I was told by Anita Hill, and I believe this information relevant to the decision that you are called upon to make.

Thank you.

THE CHAIRMAN: Thank you very much.

Mr. Carr.

TESTIMONY OF JOHN W. CARR

MR. CARR: Mr. Chairman, Senator Thurmond, members of the committee: My name is John William Carr. I reside in the city of New York. I am an attorney by profession, and a partner at the law firm of Simpson, Thatcher & Bartlett.

I met Anita Hill in the spring of 1981. At the time, we were introduced by a mutual friend, while they both were employed at the law firm of Wald, Harkrader & Ross, in Washington, DC.

I was a student at the time at Harvard University, where I was simultaneously pursuing a law degree at the Harvard Law School and an MBA degree at the Harvard Business School. During the final semester of the 1982-83 academic year, I developed a social relationship with Anita Hill.

I lived in Cambridge, MA, and she lived in Washington, DC, which made seeing one another very difficult. However, during this particular period, we spoke several times at length on the telephone.

During one of these telephone conversations, Anita Hill revealed to me that her supervisor was sexually harassing her. I recall that she did not initially volunteer this information. Rather, during the telephone conversation, it quickly became clear to me that she was troubled and upset. In response to my expressions of concern about her feelings, Anita Hill told me that she was upset, because her boss was making sexual advances toward her. I recall that she was clearly very disturbed by these advances and that she cried during the telephone call.

I knew that Anita Hill worked for Clarence Thomas at the Equal Employment Opportunity Commission. In this telephone conversation, it was immediately clear to me that she was referring to Judge Thomas.

I asked her to tell me what he had done. It is my recollection that she told me that Clarence Thomas had asked her out on dates and showed an unwanted sexual interest in her. She was very uncomfortable talking about these events, and said that she did not want to go into any detail about the actions that so upset her. I do recall, however, that she said these sexual advances had taken place before.

It was clear to me at that time that she found this very painful to talk about, and I did not push her to speak of it further. At this point, the conversation turned to how appalling it was that the head of the EEOC would engage in sexual advances toward one of his own employees.

I thought it was outrageous and, in a perverse sort of way, ironic that the person in charge of fighting discrimination in the workplace could harass an employee in this way. This portion of the conversation I dominated with my own repeated expressions of outrage. It is because of this outrage and irony that I recall our conversation today.

It was clear that Anita Hill did not want to continue to dwell on these incidents, and the conversation moved to other subjects. Later in the spring of 1983, my relationship with Anita Hill subsided. We did not have the opportunity to see one another and lost touch. I believe we last spoke prior to my graduation in June 1983. Except for seeing her at these proceedings, I have not seen or spoken to Anita Hill since 1983.

On Sunday evening, October 6, I saw television reports that Professor Hill had accused Judge Thomas of sexual harassment. I immediately remembered that she had told me of his sexual advances. The next day, Monday, October 7, I discussed with colleagues at my office that these conversations had taken place with Professor Hill and her comments about Judge Thomas.

As I discussed these conversations, my recollection of them became clearer. On the following day, Tuesday, October 8, I discussed my recollections with a few of my partners, whose experience and judgment I respect. Later that day, I sent Professor Hill an overnight letter in which I stated that I remember our conversation about sexual harassment. In my letter, I also expressed my admiration for the public stance she had taken, particularly in light of the pain it might cause her.

The next day, Wednesday, October 9, I received a telephone call from a man who identified himself as a friend of Anita Hill at the University of Oklahoma. He said that Professor Hill had received my letter, and he and I discussed its contents briefly. I also spoke that day about my recollections of our 1983 telephone call with an attorney representing Ms. Hill in Washington.

On Thursday morning, October 10, I traveled to Chicago on business, where I received a message to call another attorney, Janet Napolitano, who I was told was also representing Professor Hill. Ms. Napolitano asked me if I would be willing to come before the Senate Judiciary Committee and tell of my 1983 telephone conversation with Anita Hill. I agreed to come.

Later that evening, I was interviewed over the telephone by various members of the staff of the Judiciary Committee. After this interview, I immediately flew to Washington, where on Friday, October 11, I received a subpoena to appear before this committee.

THE CHAIRMAN: Thank you.

Judge Hoerchner.

TESTIMONY OF JUDGE SUSAN HOERCHNER

JUDGE HOERCHNER: Mr. Chairman, Senator Thurmond and members of the committee: My name is Susan Hoerchner.

I am here testifying pursuant to this committee's subpoena. I have not seen any FBI report or any other written record of any information I have supplied in the course of this investigation. Neither have I seen Anita's affidavits.

I am a Workers' Compensation Judge in California. I have known Anita Hill for about thirteen years. We met when she was my editor for a project at Yale Legislative Services, when we were first-year law students. We soon became friends.

While at Yale, Anita had good friends across every spectrum: men and women, black and white, conservative and liberal. Reasons for her popularity were apparent. It's not just a question of my never having known her to lie—I have never known Anita even to exaggerate. I have never known her to express anger. I have never known her to condemn a person, rather than particular behavior. I have never known her to use profane or offensive language.

In law school, Anita was always gracious and generous with her understanding and her time. Many times, she would invite me and other of her harried law student friends to her apartment for a delicious home-cooked dinner, which she somehow found time to prepare, even though she was a busy and hard-working law student herself. Perhaps most important of all to me personally, Anita was always somebody to whom I could talk and with whom I could laugh.

When Anita and I graduated from law school, both of us, as it happened, came to Washington for our first jobs. We lived in different parts of the city. We were both busy with our new jobs, so we did not get together with great frequency. What we did do, however, was keep in touch by telephone. Those conversations would often last as much as an hour.

I remember, in particular, one telephone conversation I had with Anita. I should say, before telling you about this conversation, that I cannot pin down its date with certainty. I am sure that it was after she started working with Clarence Thomas, because in that conversation she referred to him as her boss, Clarence.

It was clear when we started this conversation that something was badly wrong. Anita sounded very depressed and spoke in a dull monotone. I asked Anita how things were going at work. Instead of a cheery "Oh, just busy," her usual response, this time she led me to understand that there was a serious problem.

She told me that she was being subjected to sexual harassment from her boss, to whom she referred by name. That boss was Clarence Thomas. Anita's use of the words "sexual harassment" made an impression on me, because it was the first time I had heard that term used by a friend in personal conversation.

Anita said that Clarence Thomas had repeatedly asked her out. She told me she had, of course, refused, but that he wouldn't seem to take "no" for an answer. He kept pressing her and repeating things like "I'm your time" and "You know I'm your kind of man, but you refuse to admit it."

One thing Anita told me that struck me particularly and that I remember almost verbatim was that Mr. Thomas had said to her, "You know, if you had witnesses, you'd have a perfect case against me."

She told me that she was very humiliated and demoralized by Mr. Thomas's behavior and that it had shaken her faith in her professional ability.

At the end of the conversation, Anita seemed more depressed than when it began. Contrary to my hope, talking things out did not seem to have given her any relief or comfort.

After our conversation, I was both saddened about my friend. Because it had been so painful for Anita to talk about the matter, I did not try to pull information out of her. In subsequent conversations with Anita, I learned that the problem continued, but I do not recall in detail further conversations about this matter.

Mr. Chairman, in conclusion, as a result of the high esteem in which her law school classmates hold her, sixty-five members, over sixty-five members of Anita's law school class have been contacted and have signed the following statement:

> It has been our privilege to know Anita Hill, professionally and personally, since the late 1970's, when we were in law school together. The Anita Hill we have known is a person of great integrity and decency. As colleagues, we wish to affirm publicly our admiration and respect for her.
>
> She is embroiled now in a most serious and difficult controversy, which we know is causing her great pain. We make no attempt to analyze the issues involved or to prejudge the outcome. We do, however, wish to state emphatically our complete confidence in her sincerity and good-faith, our absolute belief in her decency and integrity. In our eyes, it is impossible to imagine any circumstances in which her character could be called into question. We are dismayed that it has been. We know that it could not be by anyone who knows her.
>
> Anita has imperiled her career and her peace of mind to do what she felt was right. We know we are powerless to shield her from those who will seek to hurt her out of ignorance, frustration or expediency in the

days ahead, but we will have failed ourselves, if we did not at least raise our voices in her behalf. She has our unhesitating and unwavering support.

Thank you, Mr. Chairman.

THE CHAIRMAN: Thank you very much.

Mr. Paul.

TESTIMONY OF JOEL PAUL

MR. PAUL: Mr. Chairman, Senator Thurmond and members of the committee: I am an associate professor of law at the Washington College of Law at American University here in Washington. Before joining the faculty at American University in 1986, I practiced banking and corporate law in California. I presently teach international business and trade and foreign relations law.

I am here to give my account of what I was told in the summer of 1987 by Professor. Anita Hill —

THE CHAIRMAN: The summer of when?

MR. PAUL: The summer of 1987.

THE CHAIRMAN: Thank you.

MR. PAUL: [continuing]—and to give my impressions of her character and credibility.

As soon as I read Professor Hill's allegations in *The Washington Post*, on Monday morning, I realized that I had a duty to come forward and to give my account, because I knew that Professor Hill's allegations were not an eleventh-hour fabrication, as some have said, but, rather, a more specific description of the events she related to me more than four years ago.

I first met Professor Hill at a ten-day conference of the Association of American Law Schools, in June 1987, at the University of New Mexico Law School. I was impressed by her intellect and her professional achievements.

At that time, she was interested in coming to Washington to research an article she was then writing. I suggested to her that she might want to spend some time at the Washington College of Law, since we are always looking for good teachers and scholars to join our faculty.

Subsequently, I arranged for Professor Hill to come to our school during July 1987, where she was given an office, secretarial support, and use of our library facilities for the summer.

At that point, a number of our faculty were very interested in encouraging Professor Hill to apply for a visiting professorship at the American University. During the course of her research at our school, we had a number of occasions to talk about her interest in the American University and our interest in having her join the faculty.

During one such occasion, over lunch in the university cafeteria, I asked Professor Hill why she had left the EEOC. This was a logical question to ask in the course of discussing with her her employment history. Professor Hill responded, reluctantly and with obvious emotion and embarrassment, that she had been sexually harassed by her supervisor at the EEOC.

I was shocked and astonished by her statement, which is why I remember the incident so vividly. I do not recall whether she went on to say the name Clarence Thomas, but if she had said it, the name would not have meant anything to me at that time, because I had no idea who Judge Thomas was. I asked Professor Hill if she had sought any recourse for her situation, and she said no. When I asked her why not, she said that she felt she had no effective recourse in that situation.

I believe that Professor Hill's statement to me was truthful. Professor Hill at that time had no reason to claim sexual harassment as an explanation for leaving the EEOC. Many people leave government jobs for teaching positions. Thus, I concluded then and I still believe that she was telling the truth.

On Monday morning, after I read the news of Professor Hill's allegations, I phoned some of my colleagues from my home to ask their advice about what to do with this information that I had.

When I arrived at school later that morning, another colleague, Ms. Susan Dunham, on her own initiative, came to me, having read the article in the *Post*—

THE CHAIRMAN: What day was this, again?

MR. PAUL: This was on Monday morning, sir—and she reminded me, that is, Ms. Susan Dunham reminded me of the fact that I had communicated to her the substance of my conversation with Professor Hill shortly after it occurred.

I then recalled that, indeed, right after my lunch conversation with Professor Hill, I went to Ms. Dunham, who had some practical experience in the field of employment discrimination, and told her of Professor Hill's problems at the EEOC. Ms. Dunham said at that time that this was the case of the fox guarding the henhouse. That phrase stuck in my mind. I was pleased that Ms. Dunham independently could confirm my memory of these events.

I had at that time, and I have now, no reason to question the facts as Professor Hill related them to me. I always regarded her as having the highest integrity. I know her to be a deeply religious person.

Moreover, I cannot believe that she could be politically motivated. I know from numerous conversations with her that she served faithfully in the Reagan Administration, that she was generally in sync with the goals of that Administration, and that she did not disagree with the overall policies of theAdministration.

Indeed, when Judge Robert Bork was nominated to the Supreme Court in the summer of 1987, I remember vividly that Professor Hill supported his nomination and told me that she held him in extremely high esteem, as a former teacher of hers at Yale. Her strong support of Judge Bork led to a number of loud lunch table disagreements between Professor Hill and other colleagues of mine. Thus, I cannot accept the conclusion that her statements have been motivated by political ideology.

In closing, I would reemphasize that I am here simply to aid the Senate Judiciary Committee in its efforts to determine these facts. I have not taken any position with regard to Judge Thomas's nomination prior to these allegations. Indeed, a national petition of law professors opposing his nomination was circulated at my law school several weeks ago. I was asked to sign it and I refused, despite the fact that 18 of my colleagues signed that petition, as well as many others from other law schools.

I came forward on my own initiative to recount what I was told by Professor Hill. I have not spoken to Professor Hill since some time prior to the nomination of Judge Thomas. I have never discussed my testimony or any aspect of these hearings with Professor Hill or any person representing Professor Hill, or with any organization or anyone representing any organization.

Mr. Chairman, I am here to help you get to the facts. Thank you.

THE CHAIRMAN: Let me begin by asking you again, for the record, just go down the line starting with the judge, if you will, tell me your college education, your post-graduate education and what jobs you have held since your graduation from post-graduate school, please.

JUDGE HOERCHNER: I have a Bachelor of Arts degree from the University of the Pacific, and, more specifically, from their honors college, Raymond College, which has since been re-absorbed into the university. I have a Ph.D. in American studies from Emory University. I have a J.D. from Yale University Law School.

THE CHAIRMAN: A J.D. law degree.

JUDGE HOERCHNER: Right.

THE CHAIRMAN: And upon graduating, was Yale Law School, your last formal education?

JUDGE HOERCHNER: That is correct.

THE CHAIRMAN: So, you graduated with honors from undergraduate school, you went on to get a Ph.D. from Emory University, and then you went on to get a law degree from Yale University.

JUDGE HOERCHNER: That is almost correct. We did not have the classification, I believe, of graduating with honors.

THE CHAIRMAN: I see.

JUDGE HOERCHNER: It was an honors college.

THE CHAIRMAN: An honors college, excuse me. Now, upon graduating from Yale, where did you go to work?

JUDGE HOERCHNER: I went to work for the National Labor Relations Board, in Washington.

THE CHAIRMAN: And from there—

JUDGE HOERCHNER: And from there to Littler, Mendelssohn, Baskiff & Tiche.

THE CHAIRMAN: And from there—

JUDGE HOERCHNER: And thereafter, I was self-employed and worked as an independent contractor. Thereafter, I went into teaching—I skipped one point.

After I had accepted a teaching position at Valparaiso University School of Law in Indiana, I worked on a temporary basis for an elected city auditor in the city of Berkeley. I taught at Valparaiso University School of Law and at Chase Law School in Northern Kentucky University. Thereafter, I returned to California, where I worked for the State Compensation Insurance Fund for about three and a half years, before becoming a Workers Compensation Judge, a little bit more than a year ago.

THE CHAIRMAN: Thank you. I think it is important we establish each of your backgrounds, because this is all coming down to background and credibility, the credibility of everyone involved in this matter. I am not questioning your credibility. I want to establish for the record who you are, before I question you.

Now, let me ask you, Judge Hoerchner, you indicated you had numerous conversations, as I understand it, with Professor Hill during the period of the alleged harassment, while she was working at EEOC and the Department of Education. Is that correct?

JUDGE HOERCHNER: That is not exactly correct, Senator. I have said that I remember mainly one conversation. I believe there were other conversations in which she led me to understand that the problem was continuing, but I do not have any detailed recollection—

THE CHAIRMAN: All I am trying to establish now is the nature of the relationship you had with Anita Hill when you were both in Washington during that period.

JUDGE HOERCHNER: Okay.

THE CHAIRMAN: Was it an unusual thing for you to talk to Professor Hill during that period, or was that a fairly normal undertaking? Did you keep in contact with one another?

JUDGE HOERCHNER: Yes, we did, we kept in contact, namely by telephone, due to our busy schedules.

THE CHAIRMAN: And how often during this period, would you estimate, you spoke to Professor Hill, either on a weekly basis, a monthly basis or during the entire period? Did you speak to her once a week, once a month? Did you see her frequently? Can you give us some estimation of the frequency?

JUDGE HOERCHNER: I believe that while I was living in Washington, we spoke at least once a week.

THE CHAIRMAN: And how long were you living in Washington?

JUDGE HOERCHNER: I left Washington in late November, late November 1981.

THE CHAIRMAN: And you arrived when?

JUDGE HOERCHNER: In early June 1980.

THE CHAIRMAN: So, you were there about a year and four months or five months?

JUDGE HOERCHNER: Approximately.

THE CHAIRMAN: So, it is fair to say you spoke to her more than a couple dozen times during that period?

JUDGE HOERCHNER: Oh, yes. I would like to clarify: In September and October 1981, I was on a temporary assignment in California.

THE CHAIRMAN: Now, let me ask you further: You recalled for our committee minority and majority staff, you have recalled in other inquiries made of you officially, and you have recalled today, one specific conversation where Professor Hill said to you that she was being harassed, that she was being repeatedly asked out on dates.

Now, you said you did not ask her for any detail and she did not offer any detail.

In light of the frequency with which you spoke to her, did you find it unusual that she would not tell you more about this? It sounds like you had an ongoing close relationship, at least by telephone. Did it surprise you?

JUDGE HOERCHNER: Not after hearing the tone of her voice when she initially told me how depressed and demoralized she was. In addition, as I mentioned in my statement, I have never known Anita to use offensive language. The situation was to me too clearly painful to her for me to try to pull out any further information.

THE CHAIRMAN: Did you advise her to take any action? Did she seek your counsel? Did—

JUDGE HOERCHNER: She did not ask for advice.

THE CHAIRMAN: Did you say, you should complain. Did you give her any advice?

JUDGE HOERCHNER: She did not ask for advice, and I did not give her any advice.

THE CHAIRMAN: Why did you think she was calling you then to tell you this?

JUDGE HOERCHNER: I have not said that she telephoned me. I don't remember who called whom.

THE CHAIRMAN: Why did you think she initiated this with you?

JUDGE HOERCHNER: I believe she initiated this part of the conversation in response to a question about how things were going at work.

THE CHAIRMAN: Now, you said, in your testimony, that you knew the problem continued after that conversation. How did you know that the problem continued after first being made aware of it in the conversation that you related to us, here today?

JUDGE HOERCHNER: In telephone conversations I asked and she led me to understand that it was happening, and often would say, she didn't want to talk about it at that time.

THE CHAIRMAN: Mr. Carr, you were dating Anita Hill. I assume that's what you meant by having a—we use a lot of euphemisms in this town and an old-fashioned word—you were dating Professor Hill at some point in the past, is that correct?

MR. CARR: I think that's close.

THE CHAIRMAN: Okay. Well, maybe—

MR. CARR: Let me explain, if I may? When you say "dating" I think of a relationship that was going on.

THE CHAIRMAN: I admit that I find it difficult—I mean these phrases, my sons are twenty-one and twenty-two and I use phrases like "dating" and they look at me like I—did you go out alone with her from time to time? [Laughter.]

MR. CARR: Yes. I would characterize it that we met, we dated, and the bulk of our relationship was on the telephone getting to know one another.

THE CHAIRMAN: I see. Now—

MR. CARR: I guess I would say we didn't get but so far.

THE CHAIRMAN: I understand that. [Laughter.]

All right. Seriously, I am not trying to get into anything, the details of your relationship. I just want to get a sense of what this is. Because the reason I ask, I would like you to tell me, Mr. Carr, you said that—please correct me if I am wrong; I am paraphrasing— that you were angry or outraged when you heard from her on the telephone that her boss was doing what?

MR. CARR: She said her boss was making sexual advances.

THE CHAIRMAN: Making sexual advances. Now, would you characterize your response, again, for us. When she told you that, at the time, do you recall—

MR. CARR: I was outraged.

THE CHAIRMAN: Now, did you give her any advice?

MR. CARR: I don't recall giving her any advice, other than to calm down and to try to—

THE CHAIRMAN: To what? I m sorry.

MR. CARR: To calm down and to try to cheer up. I don't think I gave her any advice about what to do.

THE CHAIRMAN: Your testimony, in case she didn't mention to you—did she mention to you any other form of harassment, and it can be harassment, any other form of harassment other than repeatedly being asked out? Did she indicate to you the nature of the harassment, beyond being asked out?

MR. CARR: My recollection is that she did not go into detail as to the nature of the harassment, but I have a clear recollection that the advances toward her were sexual in nature and something beyond merely, "Would you go out with me?"

THE CHAIRMAN: Now, you indicated you spontaneously contacted Professor Hill via a letter when this all broke.

MR. CARR: That's correct.

THE CHAIRMAN: You were then contacted by several of her attorneys, or you ended up speaking to several of her attorneys. Now, have you spoken to any interest group, have you been contacted by anyone other than members of this committee or the Federal Government that have called you to encourage you to do, say, or characterize anything at all?

MR. CARR: No.

THE CHAIRMAN: Ms. Wells, you were quite emphatic about not being—I'm not sure it's your phrase—a tool of or pushed by or any—

MS. WELLS: A party to—

THE CHAIRMAN: [continuing]—any interest group. Let's go back, if I may. Again, would you tell me the dates or the approximate dates of the conversation you had with the professor. Just tell me the date, and I will follow it from there.

MS. WELLS: It was in the fall of 1982. And that, I know, well, I have a recollection that we had other conversations concerning the situation, but the one that stands out and is most vivid for me is that initial conversation when she made the disclosure.

THE CHAIRMAN: Now, what makes you remember that you had other conversations relative to her displeasure with her boss and how he was treating her relative to sexual advances?

MS. WELLS: My—well, because of the way we operated, we were in frequent contact. We were a support mechanism for one another. I mean we shared the good news and we shared the bad news.

THE CHAIRMAN: Did you ever see her, or was this merely a telephone relationship?

MS. WELLS: Oh, no, she told me this in person.

THE CHAIRMAN: She told you that in person?

MS. WELLS: Yes.

THE CHAIRMAN: Give me a sense of the relationship that you had with her at the time. Did you go to dinner with her? Did you meet her for lunch? Would you visit each other in your apartments or homes? I mean, what was the nature of your social relationship?

MS. WELLS: Senator, we had a very warm and close relationship. I would not say that we were best friends, we had other friends, but she and I shared certain values, and outlook about life. She would come to my home and have dinner. She would go on shopping sprees with my mother and sister.

We went out, did a lot of things together.

THE CHAIRMAN: Now, you seem like a very strong-willed person?

MS. WELLS: My friends say so.

THE CHAIRMAN: Why did you not give her any advice, during this period when you knew she was unhappy. I mean did you not pull her aside, at any point, and say, hey, look, Anita, whatever? Or, did you do it at all? Did you ever raise the subject with her or did it only come up from her to you?

MS. WELLS: It was something that came up from her. If I—to open the conversation—if I were to do something like that, I would say, well, you know, how are things going? I know Professor Hill as a very private person. And I am a very private person. And I do not believe, and it is my experience that she shares this, that you don't walk around carrying your burden so that everyone can see them. You are supposed to carry that burden and try to make the best of it.

Now, if you need to talk about it, you need a good ear for that, then I am there for you. And if you want my advice, and you let me know that you want that, then I will give it to you.

THE CHAIRMAN: Did it surprise you that she stayed?

MS. WELLS: No, it did not, because I think that is something that a woman in that situation would do. I know, in my situation, when confronted with something not quite as of a long-term nature as Professor Hill's experience, I stayed.

THE CHAIRMAN: Right. Now, Mr. Paul, you are corroborating that you were told about Professor Hill's displeasure with her boss and his sexual advances. Let me not characterize; what did she say to you? Did she use the term that she was harassed or sexual advances or uncomfortable? What was the term that she used to you when you asked her why she left EEOC?

MR. PAUL: Senator, the specific terms that I recall were, that she said that she was sexually harassed by her supervisor at the EEOC.

THE CHAIRMAN: Now, who is Susan Duncan that you refer to?

MR. PAUL: Susan Dunham, D-U-N-H-A-M—

THE CHAIRMAN: I am sorry.

MR. PAUL: [continuing]—is the head of the legal methods program at our law school, Washington College of Law.

THE CHAIRMAN: So she teaches at law school as well?

MR. PAUL: Yes, she does. She teaches courses on legal methods and she also runs the legal methods program.

THE CHAIRMAN: Why would you go from the lunch table to the—I assume that's where you were told this—

MR. PAUL: Susan's office at the time was adjacent to mine. Susan had a practice prior to working on the faculty which involved employment discrimination cases. I was shocked and disturbed by what Professor Hill had told me. I did not know anything about that area of the law, as I have testified. My area of expertise is business law and corporate law. So I went to Susan to sort of ask her, you know, what could have been done? Why wasn't any recourse taken, and that was how we had this conversation.

THE CHAIRMAN: Were you going to her in the expectation or hope that there might still be recourse that could be taken? Were you thinking of going back and advising—

MR. PAUL: No, Senator, no.

THE CHAIRMAN: Now, you say, well, I am still curious. If you were not doing it for that reason, to see if there was still a cause of action to go back and try to convince Professor Hill to do something, did it surprise you that she—I mean why—what was the motivation of going to your fellow colleague?

MR. PAUL: My motivation was to try to understand better the position that women may be in, in that situation. It was simply a matter of academic—

THE CHAIRMAN: What were you told—

MR. PAUL: [continuing] —curiosity.

THE CHAIRMAN: What were you told?

MR. PAUL: I am sorry?

THE CHAIRMAN: What were you told by your colleague as to why women stay in that situation, or did she volunteer anything?

MR. PAUL: Ms. Dunham said—and this is all that I really can say that I recall on my own—is that she said that this was a case of the fox guarding the hen house. That portion of the conversation I can recall on my own. I believe Ms. Dunham has had a conversation with the Judiciary Committee staff, but I don't recall.

THE CHAIRMAN: She has. I just want to ask one last question. I realize my fifteen minutes are up. Judge, I would like to ask you, you read a letter from your classmates at the law school. Now, were they classmates who were from the same graduating class, or were they people who were contemporaneously at Yale Law School at the time that Professor Hill was at Yale Law School? Do you know?

JUDGE HOERCHNER: I believe that they were from the same graduating class.

THE CHAIRMAN: How many were in your graduating class, do you recall, roughly?

JUDGE HOERCHNER: I believe 131 people graduated and I am not sure whether or not that included people who were getting degrees other than the J.D.

THE CHAIRMAN: Now, the last question; how did this letter materialize? Did you circulate this letter?

JUDGE HOERCHNER: No. Due to the last-minute nature of these proceedings, I have not at all been involved in the letter.

THE CHAIRMAN: How did it come to be placed in your hand then?

JUDGE HOERCHNER: When I came to the hearings, Friday, I saw a copy of it.

THE CHAIRMAN: Who gave you the letter?

JUDGE HOERCHNER: I think my attorney, Ron Allen, had a copy and he passed it over.

THE CHAIRMAN: Judge, help me out here. Do you know where the devil the letter came from? That's what I am trying to find out.

JUDGE HOERCHNER: I am not quite sure—

THE CHAIRMAN: Fair enough.

JUDGE HOERCHNER: [continuing]—what you are asking.

THE CHAIRMAN: All right, my time is up.

SEN. THURMOND: Mr. Chairman, I yield to Senator Specter, who will examine the witnesses supporting Anita Hill.

SEN. SPECTER: Thank you, Mr. Chairman.

I begin today with a statement that I made before that I have been asked to raise the questions by Senator Thurmond. But I do so in the context of I do not believe this is an adversarial proceeding. I do not represent anyone except Pennsylvania, and what we are trying to do here is to find out what the facts are.

Judge Hoerchner, you said when you were questioned by staff members, there had been a brief questioning of you a few days ago, back on October 10, and this appears on page 14 of the record."Question: Did she ever relate to you that you were the only person that knew about these allegations or these problems she was having at work? Answer: I think she told me that more recently. Question: More recently that you were the only person that knew? Answer: Yes."

When was it that Professor Hill told you that you were the only person she had told about this incident?

JUDGE HOERCHNER: I do not have a copy of the transcript, but I know that very shortly after that, I corrected that statement. The agent—

SEN. SPECTER: In the transcript, Judge Hoerchner?

JUDGE HOERCHNER: I do not have a copy of the transcript.

SEN. SPECTER: Are you saying that you corrected that at the time that you were questioned about other people?

JUDGE HOERCHNER: Right. That it was the FBI agent who told me that there were only three names mentioned, and now that was either in her original statement or in her FBI interview. Those names were Anita Hill, Clarence Thomas, and Susan Hoerchner. And from that I concluded, I understand wrongly, that I was the only one she had told.

SEN. SPECTER: Well, let us make a copy of the transcript available to you, Judge Hoerchner. May we have an extra copy presented to the judge, so that she can have it while she responds to the questions, please?

Judge Hoerchner, the first reference that I made was at page 14, where I had read to you the short exchange beginning in the fourth line down: "Did she ever relate to you that you were the only person that knew about these allegations or these problems she was having at work?Answer: I think she told me that more recently. Question: More recently that you were the only person that knew? Answer: Yes."

Do you find that on page 14?

JUDGE HOERCHNER: Yes; I do.

SEN. SPECTER: Now, there is a later reference in the transcript to the FBI. It appears on page 24 of the record. About the middle, Ms. Hoerchner:

> Okay, I recently came to the conclusion that I was the only one that she had told at the time and I believe that the basis for the conclusion was that I was told by the FBI agent who interviewed me that there were only three names on, either the affidavit, or stemming from her FBI interview, I am not sure which, I think the affidavit, and that my name was the only one she had listed as a corroborating witness.

Is that the reference that you had to what you said to the FBI?

JUDGE HOERCHNER: Yes.

SEN. SPECTER: Well, did the FBI tell you that anything other than that you were the only person that she was supposed to have told about this?

JUDGE HOERCHNER: I am not sure that the FBI actually said that I was the only corroborating witness. I know he told me that there were only three names listed on one or another of the documents that he had.

SEN. SPECTER: May I ask you to refer now to the bottom of page 21 of the transcript, the last three lines?

You said, you were the only person Anita Hill told. You were the only person who knew about the allegations of sexual harassment, and you said that she reiterated that recently to you. "Was this in one of those phone conversations? Answer: No, she never told me until recently. Question: That you were the only person who knew? Answer: Right. Question: When did she tell you that? Answer: It may have been around the time that she wanted to know if I would talk to the FBI? Question: So we are talking about the last couple of weeks of September? Answer: Very recent, yes."

Is that accurate, Judge Hoerchner?

JUDGE HOERCHNER: No, that was my mistake. I corrected that, as you have noted, on page 24 of the transcript.

SEN. SPECTER: Well, on the part that I read?

JUDGE HOERCHNER: I beg your pardon?

SEN. SPECTER: On the part that I read about the FBI?

JUDGE HOERCHNER: Yes.

SEN. SPECTER: Well, the part about the FBI says this:

> JUDGE HOERCHNER: Okay. I recently came to the conclusion that I was the only one she had told at the time, and I believe that the basis for the conclusion was that I was told by the FBI agent who interviewed me that there were only three names on either in the affidavit or stemming from her FBI interview—I'm not sure which, I think the affidavit—and my name was the only one she had listed as a corroborating witness.

Is that what you are referring to that you told the FBI?

JUDGE HOERCHNER: No, I did not tell the FBI that. That is what the FBI agent told me, and I drew a conclusion.

SEN. SPECTER: Well, in your statement about what the FBI told you, on the part I just read to you, that's the same thing as in your two prior segments of testimony, and you conclude in that sentence—and this is at the bottom of that paragraph— "and that my name was the only one she had listed as a corroborating witness."

Are you saying, Judge Hoerchner, that you—as I read these three statements, they all say the same thing to me, that it was recently that—where they all say that you thought you were the only person she had told about this, and the extract that I read at page 22 said that it was very recently that she had told you that, within the last couple of weeks of September.

JUDGE HOERCHNER: And on page 24, which is my better recollection, it was the FBI agent who said that to me, and not Anita.

SEN. SPECTER: Well, where on page 24 does it say that it was the FBI agent who —well, on page 24, it does say that the FBI agent told you that your name was the only one. But you're saying that your prior reference to—well, let me ask you this: Did you say anywhere in this interview that when you had said Professor Hill told you that you were the only one she had told this about, that you were incorrect on that?

JUDGE HOERCHNER: I don't think that I explicitly retracted that. I do believe that that was incorrect.

SEN. SPECTER: Let me move to another point, Judge Hoerchner, and that is when did Professor Hill tell you about this incident, Judge? And I ask you this, because in a couple of parts of your testimony you said it was in September 1981, and at page 28, the following question-and-answer session occurred: "Question: Can you give us maybe how that came up, why she talked to you about Judge Thomas" — are you with me there, Judge?

JUDGE HOERCHNER: Not yet.

SEN. SPECTER: Okay. It is about two-thirds of the way down: "Question: Can you give us maybe how that came up, why she talked about Judge Thomas to you?"

JUDGE HOERCHNER: Okay. Is that a question? I'm sorry.

SEN. SPECTER: Well, I want to refer to the transcript.

JUDGE HOERCHNER: Yes, line sixteen, page 28?

SEN. SPECTER: Right. It reads as follows: [Question] 'Can you give us maybe how that came up, why she talked about Judge Thomas to you?' [Answer]: 'She said she was changing jobs and going to work for him in the Office of Civil Rights, Department of Education and how excited she was.' Question: 'Do you remember roughly when you all may have had that conversation, when that came up?' Answer: 'Have to be that it was before the part where we talked about his behavior. I don't really know.'"

Now, my question to you is, when you said that it "have to be that it was before the part where we talked about his behavior," did she change jobs before she told you about this incident as you testified, where she said that he sexually harassed her?

JUDGE HOERCHNER: She changed jobs from her law firm to go to work for Clarence Thomas in the Department of Education before she mentioned any problems with sexual harassment.

SEN. SPECTER: Well, did she tell you about the sexual harassment after she moved from the Department of Education to EEOC?

JUDGE HOERCHNER: I have made clear to the FBI and in the staff interview that I simply cannot pin down the date with certainty.

SEN. SPECTER: Judge Hoerchner, you called, according to the information you have given us before, you called Professor Hill the day of the appointment of Judge Thomas to the Supreme Court of the United States. Is that correct?

JUDGE HOERCHNER: Yes, I did.

SEN. SPECTER: And what was the purpose of that call?

JUDGE HOERCHNER: I called to ask her whether she had heard about the nomination, and she said she had been contacted by telephone by the press and she heard about it that way and that her stomach turned. I asked her whether she was going to say anything. She did not give me a direct answer.

SEN. SPECTER: Why did you ask her whether she was going to say anything? Was there some thought in your mind that she should come forward?

JUDGE HOERCHNER: I had no thought of should or shouldn't. I wanted to see what she was going to do.

SEN. SPECTER: And what was her response to you at that time?

JUDGE HOERCHNER: She replied that she was appalled at the treatment of Professor-then Judge Bork in his confirmation hearing, and from that I concluded that she did not intend to step forward.

SEN. SPECTER: And did she tell you at that time that she thought that both Judge Bork and Judge Thomas should stand or fall on their ideas?

JUDGE HOERCHNER: I believe she did.

SEN. SPECTER: At page 21 of the transcript, looking at the top, the first line, you said, "And she said that she was told that her only option was to be investigated by the FBI, and we both thought it was odd and I thought that there should have been some alternative where she could make a statement with her name being used as some sort of an intermediate measure, so I guess some days later the phone started ringing."

When did that conversation with Professor Hill occur, Judge Hoerchner?

JUDGE HOERCHNER: That was after she had made a statement to a member of the chairman's staff and I had made a statement to the member of the chairman's staff.

SEN. SPECTER: Was there a thought that you had expressed that it might be possible for Professor Hill to come forward, is that the alternative that you were referring to, where there would be an intermediate measure, or just what did you mean by that?

[Pause.]

SEN. SPECTER: I ask this, Judge Hoerchner, because there has been a good bit of testimony as to whether Professor Hill might have come forward, without having these public hearings, and had Judge Thomas withdraw, and my question to you is: When you had that discussion with her about some alternative and some sort of intermediate measure, whether you were discussing with her at that time the possibility that there could be some action taken to have Judge Thomas withdraw, without having these proceedings?

JUDGE HOERCHNER: Neither she nor I had ever used the term "withdraw," nor had that thought ever occurred to me, until I appeared here and listened to the committee hearings.

SEN. SPECTER: Well, what did you mean, when you said "alternative and intermediate measure"?

JUDGE HOERCHNER: I was under the impression that the information had not been disseminated to the committee, and I understood that we both had requested confidentiality. I'm not sure that even today I know exactly what "confidentiality" entailed.

SEN. SPECTER: But you know what it doesn't entail?

JUDGE HOERCHNER: I am beginning to think I am learning.

SEN. SPECTER: Well, what I am getting at is did you have some thought that your identity and her identity could have been kept confidential, and had the matter concluded without coming forward, and if so, in what way?

JUDGE HOERCHNER: Senator, I am a judge. My job is to look at evidence and apply the law and make a decision. When I first made my statement to a member of the chairman's staff, that is what I expected the Senate to do. I still expect the Senate to do that, and at this point I have no idea what the result will be. My concern is simply telling the truth.

SEN. SPECTER: I see that my time is up, Mr. Chairman. Thank you.

THE CHAIRMAN: Thank you. Senator Leahy?

SEN. LEAHY: Thank you, Mr. Chairman. Judge, you live in California now, correct?

JUDGE HOERCHNER: Yes, I do.

SEN. LEAHY: Judge, let me ask you, you have not testified before Senate committees before, have you?

JUDGE HOERCHNER: I certainly have not.

SEN. LEAHY: Would it be safe to say that has never been high on your agenda of things that you might want to do on a Sunday afternoon? [Laughter.]

JUDGE HOERCHNER: That would be extremely high or very near the top.

SEN. LEAHY: Judge, we have had a number of discussions in answer to Senator Specter's questions about the transcript of your interview, and I ask you to turn to page 4 of that transcript. Would you read lines fifteen through eighteen, please?

JUDGE HOERCHNER: "I remember, in particular, one statement that I am remembering almost verbatim, but not completely verbatim. That was that he said to her, you know, if we had any witnesses, you would have a perfect case against me."

SEN. LEAHY: Now, who was it who made that statement to you, and who was that person talking about?

JUDGE HOERCHNER: Anita Hill was quoting to me what her boss Clarence had said to her.

SEN. LEAHY: And by Clarence, did you understand Clarence Thomas?

JUDGE HOERCHNER: I understood Clarence Thomas.

SEN. LEAHY: Thank you.

Would you turn to page 11 of your transcript, please. On page 11, there is a question asked of you, and let me read the question to you. It begins on page 10, and then I would ask you to read your answer: "Let me get back to a comment you made about the first telephone call you related. You said that Anita Hill had related to you that there had been sexual harassment at work by my boss. I may be paraphrasing part of that, except that I know the words 'sexual harassment' were used in your quote. Do you specifically recall her using those two words?"

Judge, would you please read on lines eighteen and nineteen what your response was to the question, whether you specifically recall Anita Hill using the words "sexual harassment"?

JUDGE HOERCHNER: "Yes, I do. I think they were the first time I had ever heard them on a personal basis from a friend."

SEN. LEAHY: Then, last, would you turn to page 29, please, Judge. There is a question that begins on line eleven, and I will read the question to you. The question was, "Did she give specific details, or how specific did she get?" Judge, what was your answer?

JUDGE HOERCHNER:"Well, my memory, I remember two specific aspects about his behavior, and that was the repetitive pushing himself upon her as a social partner and his statement,'if we had any witnesses, you would have a great case against me.'"

SEN. LEAHY: Lastly, in your statement this morning, you say, "It's not just a question of my never having known her to lie, I've never known Anita to even exaggerate."

Judge, on each of these statements, the ones that you have just read and, of course, the one I just referred to from this morning's statement, is that your testimony here today?

JUDGE HOERCHNER: Yes, that is correct.

SEN. LEAHY: Now, did the FBI agents at one point in their discussion with you tell you that in the FBI report they could keep your name anonymously, if you requested that?

JUDGE HOERCHNER: I believe we finished the interview, with the understanding that the agent would have interviewed Susan Hoerchner, who would have said "No comment," and that my interview, the interview that I gave him would go out under something like L.A. No. 1.

SEN. LEAHY: Judge, you were given the opportunity, if you just wanted to stay anonymous, not to have to testify here, to be in California this afternoon. Why did you come forth?

[Pause.]

JUDGE HOERCHNER: I think my reasons were similar to those of Anita and the sense that I have a duty, as a citizen, to tell the truth.

SENATOR LEAHY And what you have told me here today is the truth?

JUDGE HOERCHNER: Yes, it is.

SEN. LEAHY: I will just ask you one more question about Professor Hill. Is she, in your estimation, a woman who suffers from fantasies in any way, or is she pretty level-headed?

JUDGE HOERCHNER: She is one of the most level-headed people I have ever known. Her feet are firmly on the ground. She has never conveyed any fantasy to me whatsoever.

SEN. LEAHY: Thank you, very much.

Ms. Wells, in speaking of Anita Hill, you said, "we are both very private persons." Is that a fair restatement of what you said?

MS. WELLS: Yes, Senator.

SEN. LEAHY: But you said something else and I think maybe it's important—especially for this panel to hear, and probably a lot of other people to listen to—you said, you weren't surprised that she stayed.

I am sorry to delve into your privacy and everybody else's—tell me, why do you say that?

MS. WELLS: Well, when you are confronted with something like that, you feel powerless and vulnerable. And unless you have a private income, you have no recourse. And since this is generally done in privacy, there are no witnesses, and so it is your word, an underling, against that of a superior, someone who is obviously thought well of or they would not have risen to the position that they hold. And so if you hope to go forward, and by going forward, move out from under their power and control, you sometimes have to put up with things that no one should be expected to put up with.

SEN. LEAHY: No one should be expected to put up with—but, Ms. Wells, it's your experience that this is something that goes on?

MS. WELLS: Yes, it is my experience.

SEN. LEAHY: And Ms. Wells, sitting here today do you feel that this is what Anita Hill experienced?

MS. WELLS: Yes, I do, Senator.

SEN. LEAHY: Thank you.

Now, Mr. Carr, thinking back on it, you said that you did not give her any advice on filing a complaint or anything else. Now that you have thought about it, and listened to all that has happened, if you had it to do over again, what do you think you might have given for advice?

MR. CARR: I think I would have advised her to leave her job. I just, I have no recollection that I gave her any advice or didn't give her any advice, and we may have discussed that. I mean she may have told me that she was planning to leave her job at some point. I just don't recall it.

SEN. LEAHY: Mr. Carr, would it not be right to say if a friend comes to you and says, "Look, I've got this problem"—well, let's do it in the abstract: A friend comes to you with a problem. What is going to be your first reaction? Interrogate the heck out of them on the problem? Or, if they are troubled, offer them comfort?

MR. CARR: I am sorry, the first choice was?

SEN. LEAHY: Interrogate the heck out of them on the problem or offer them comfort?

MR. CARR: I think my first inclination is going to be to try to find out exactly what they are talking about, but I think I will be very hesitant to push to find out too much information if they are reluctant.

And realizing that they are reluctant and I think I would certainly worry about comforting them.

SEN. LEAHY: And Ms. Wells, I want to deal with one point you said. And correct me if I am not restating your testimony correctly. You said that if somebody not independently wealthy, needs a job, and hopes that maybe if they stay at that job they might advance to a different job, that's one reason for not just walking away. Is that correct?

MS. WELLS: That is correct.

SEN. LEAHY: Was Anita Hill somebody who was independently wealthy who could just say, "I will take my trust fund or whatever and walk out of here"?

MS. WELLS: By no means. If she was, she certainly never disclosed it to me. One of the things we liked to do was to bargain hunt.

SEN. LEAHY: Would it be fair to say that your impression of her was of the single woman in the workplace living on her salary?

MS. WELLS: Precisely, Senator.

SEN. LEAHY: Now, Mr. Paul, account again what Professor Hill's demeanor was when she told you about this?

MR. PAUL: We were sitting in the university cafeteria. It was in the course of an informal conversation about her employment opportunities. She was obviously embarrassed that I had asked the question. She was reluctant to answer the question. She was emotional, hesitant.

SEN. LEAHY: You remember that attitude on her part?

MR. PAUL: I remember quite vividly because I felt embarrassed, Senator, that I had asked what may have been an inappropriate question with no intention of asking an inappropriate question.

SEN. LEAHY: Did you have any reason to doubt what she was saying to you?

MR. PAUL: Absolutely not.

SEN. LEAHY: Now, back to you, Judge Hoerchner. You have come here and you have testified under oath about a conversation some years ago. The conversation, because of its nature, apparently stands out strongly in your mind. Is that correct?

JUDGE HOERCHNER: There are certain aspects of the conversation that stand out in my mind. They are the fact that her boss's name was Clarence. He repeatedly asserted to her that he was her kind of man, she would not admit it, he said, and that if she had any witnesses she would have a great case against him.

SEN. LEAHY: Judge, has anybody forced you or enticed you to come forward here?

JUDGE HOERCHNER: Absolutely not. In fact, Anita has never asked me to come forward.

SEN. LEAHY: Ms. Wells, I will ask you the same question. Has anybody enticed you, forced you to come forward here?

MS. WELLS: No, they have not, Senator.

SEN. LEAHY: Is this a process you would have just as soon passed up?

MS. WELLS: Oh, yes, I—oh, yes, I would not be here if I could have, you know, done something else.

SEN. LEAHY: Mr. Carr, you are a partner in a law firm in New York City, is that correct?

MR. CARR: That's correct.

SEN. LEAHY: And would it be safe to say that this type of a Sunday afternoon testifying is not the sort of thing that the partners in your law firm normally do?

MR. CARR: That's true, Senator. I would tell you that I am a corporate lawyer. I represent clients in business transactions that we try to keep quiet and confidential and discreet. I do not believe any client I have represented would be pleased to know that their lawyer was before you or before the cameras. It is something that I have been concerned about and worried about and was very hesitant to do this.

But I think it is—I think it is important to speak the truth when you know it, and I felt that I had an obligation to do this.

SEN. LEAHY: And, Mr. Paul, you stated earlier that when many of your colleagues signed a letter or petition or whatever opposing Judge Thomas for confirmation to the Supreme Court, you declined to sign that, that you did not join with the others.

Mr. Paul, did anybody force you to come forward here?

MR. PAUL: Absolutely not, Senator.

SEN. LEAHY: And why are you here?

MR. PAUL: I am here because I read the reports in the newspaper on Monday and credibility and character of a professional colleague of mine was called into question. I felt that it was my duty to come forward. My duty both with respect to my colleague and also, more importantly, with respect to the U.S. Senate.

SEN. LEAHY: Thank you very much.

Mr. Chairman, I see the red light is on.

THE CHAIRMAN: Thank you, very much, Senator.

Now, we will have one more, an additional fifteen-minute round for Senator Specter.

SEN. SPECTER: Thank you, Mr. Chairman.

Judge Hoerchner, turning now to page 7 of the previous deposition which you have given on line four, the question was, the last part of the question: "You tried to talk to her about it later; did you have any idea about when your attempt was? Answer: I think it would have been once or twice when we spoke on the phone. It was very unsuccessful and I just know that it was after the one time we talked about it at length."

JUDGE HOERCHNER: I am sorry, Senator, we are page 7, line?

SEN. SPECTER: No, we are on page 13, line four.

And the question is: "You tried to talk to her about it later; did you have any idea when your attempt was? Answer: I think it would have been once or twice when we spoke on the phone and it was very unsuccessful and I just know that it was after the one time that we talked about it at length."

And my question to you is, Why did you think or was there any indication given to you by Professor Hill why she wouldn't talk about it again?

JUDGE HOERCHNER: The reason would have been apparent to me from her initial pain and humiliation when she told me about it the first time. I agree with Ms. Wells, that Anita is a very private person. She has no desire to discuss these things, particularly in a public forum.

SEN. SPECTER: Well, my question goes to her having talked to you about it once and her declining to talk to you about it again, and whether there was any thought in your mind as to what had actually happened on her unwillingness to talk about it when you had asked her about it on one or two occasions after that?

JUDGE HOERCHNER: As I mentioned in my statement, to my surprise at the end of the conversation she did not seem to be cheered or comforted in any way. Apparently talking about it was of absolutely no help to her.

SEN. SPECTER: Let me turn now, Judge Hoerchner, to the question about a couple of the job changes. You had commented in your deposition, which appears at page 7, line four—picking up at the end of line four—

JUDGE HOERCHNER: Just a moment.

SEN. SPECTER: [continuing]—"She was going to leave because of that, whether or not she had another job." And that was in response to the question of her reasons for leaving her job at EEOC.

Were you aware of the fact that she did not leave her job at EEOC, or that the circumstances as represented to you did not cause her to leave the job at EEOC without finding another job first?

JUDGE HOERCHNER: I believe after she left she told me—I met her at a professional conference—and it was clear that she did have another job. In that conversation she did not say that she was going to leave her job and refuse to get another job. She just said that she would give herself some time and then she would leave no matter what.

SEN. SPECTER: Well, my question to you goes to the point as to whether when you said that she was going to leave EEOC whether she had another job or not. Whether from the conversation which you had with her, you thought that she was so upset that she would leave EEOC even if she couldn't find another job? It goes to the issue of how upset she was on the conversation that she had with you when she did not leave immediately, but did not leave until she found another job?

JUDGE HOERCHNER: At the time that we spoke, she was very upset.

SEN. SPECTER: Let me move on then, Judge Hoerchner. You talked, on page 30 of your deposition, about your view of Judge Thomas. And it starts on page 30, line five, I will skip up to line two, where it said:

> Question: And you based, you said an attitude toward power. Where did that come from? Why would you think that Judge Thomas had an attitude about power, where did that come from?
>
> Answer: It came from the idea that most of the positions that he had, that I knew about were in civil rights, equal employment opportunity and that his behavior really showed a disregard for general principles of equal opportunity or the rights of individuals and it led me to believe that he possibly thought that the law was for other people.

My question, Judge Hoerchner, did you ever consider in the light of Professor Hill telling you that Judge Thomas had sexually harassed her and he was the chairman of the EEOC, which was the nation's chief law enforcement officer on this issue, did you ever consider giving Professor Hill advice that she ought to come forward and expose him so that he would not be in the position to thwart appropriate enforcement of equal rights, and laws against sexual harassment?

JUDGE HOERCHNER: No, Senator, I did not. I believe that the tremendous inequity in power between them would have been dispositive.

SEN. SPECTER: On page 37, Judge Hoerchner, you refer to a conversation with Mr. James Brudney, would you tell us what the circumstances were of that, please?

JUDGE HOERCHNER: A conversation between Anita and Jim Brudney?

SEN. SPECTER: Between you and Jim Brudney.

JUDGE HOERCHNER: Between myself and Jim Brudney. Yes. After I was interviewed by the FBI, we left, I left the interview, I believe, with the understanding that a pseudonym, a number LA-1, would be used instead of my name. The next day I was in a training class with other judges and the presiding judge of the board where we were being trained pulled me out of class because I had a telephone call from the FBI. It was the FBI agent who had interviewed me. He said that the people in Washington wanted me to give my name. He led me to understand that because there were only three names involved everyone would know who LA-1 was. At that point, I was still unsure whether I wanted to give my name.

The state court system that I work in is part of the executive branch under a Republican administration. I feared retaliation. I knew that there was one person on the Hill, I knew of the name of one person who was at Yale at the same time that I was, who was a member of my brother's class. I wished to speak with him about the ramifications of having my name used in the FBI report.

SEN. SPECTER: Did Mr. Brudney urge you to come forward?

JUDGE HOERCHNER: Absolutely not. He refused to give me any advice. He repeated many times very kindly that he understood my reluctance.

SEN. SPECTER: Judge Hoerchner, have you heard Ms. Hill's testimony about details as to what she said Judge Thomas said to her, without repeating them now?

JUDGE HOERCHNER: I believe I heard almost all of it.

SEN. SPECTER: Did she give you any details at all, except for saying that he pushed himself on her and tried to date her and the statement about if they had a witness, it would be a good case? But did she tell you about any of the other materials, about the films, about the rest of it?

JUDGE HOERCHNER: About that—I'm sorry?

SEN. SPECTER: About the films and about the rest of what she had testified here, which you say you think you heard?

JUDGE HOERCHNER: I do not have a specific memory of that and that would be very much in keeping with her reserved character.

SEN. SPECTER: Let me ask you about one final part of the transcript, and it appears at page 12, line fourteen. The question is:

> Is it possible, Judge Hoerchner, that she was referring to—again, I understand the comments you made about your recollection—is it possible that she was referring to the same time period in which she worked at EEOC?
>
> Answer: Well, I was trying to remember all of this at first. At one point, I thought it was EEOC, but I was drawing conclusions based on other parts of my memory. I really don't know which it was, and, again, I really don't know if it was 1981 versus another time.

I was concerned, when I saw this reference that you said that "I was drawing conclusions based on other parts of my memory," and my question to you is what did you mean by that?

JUDGE HOERCHNER: Well, I did know that Clarence Thomas became the Chair for the EEOC. Now, whether I knew that at the time I spoke to Anita and we had the most memorable conversation or not, I can't really say.

SEN. SPECTER: Well, what was there that you were drawing from other parts of your memory, though?

JUDGE HOERCHNER: I think I mentioned to the staff member that I have a vague memory of something about education films that they had reviewed for civil rights, sexual harassment-related issues, and that is a very vague memory.

SEN. SPECTER: Judge Hoerchner, did Professor Hill ever have any discussion with you about her move from the private law firm to the Department of Education? She has testified that one of the reasons she left the Department of Education to go with Judge Thomas to EEOC, notwithstanding the incidents, was that she was fearful that the Department of Education would be abolished, because that was one of the planks in President Reagan's program. Did you ever have any conversation with her or any insight into any of her thinking, when she left the law firm to go to the Department of Education, any concern that that might be insecure, because the department might be abolished?

JUDGE HOERCHNER: I don't remember anything about the abolition of the department. The only thing I remember her saying about her desire to go to the Department of Education was that she was very interested in working in a policy-making position.

SEN. SPECTER: Mr. Carr, you have testified that Professor Hill told you about comments during the course of the telephone conversation. How did they happen to arrive during the course of a telephone conversation?

MR. CARR: My recollection is that we spoke periodically and that it was natural in those conversations to inquire about how we were each doing. In this conversation, it was clear that she was not doing very well, and I asked her why she was upset or what was bothering her, and this is what she explained.

SEN. SPECTER: When you say it was clear from your conversation that she was not doing very well, can you amplify that? I ask, because it is rather unusual, obviously, to bring up the subject of sexual harassment, and I am interested to know what there was in the conversation that would have led you to that inquiry and would have led her to that disclosure.

MR. CARR: Well, my recollection is that, in response to a generalized "How are you doing," that the tone of her voice was a little different, that she was trying not to express something, that she was holding something in, that she could not make the standard and sort of normal affirmative declaration that things were fine, and then I inquired further as to what was wrong.

SEN. SPECTER: In response to Senator Biden's questions and also in your deposition, you were precise on both occasions in saying that she said that her boss was making sexual advances toward her. Did she specify what those advances were?

MR. CARR: I don't recall that she did, no.

SEN. SPECTER: And in the deposition, at page 3—and I don't think you will need the transcript, but we can give you one—the question was, "Did she identify who her boss was? Answer: I knew she worked for the EEOC and that it was Clarence Thomas."

And in your testimony here today, you said that it was clear to you that she was referring to Judge Thomas, but she did not identify Judge Thomas by name, did she?

MR. CARR: I don't recall that she identified him by name. I do recall, though, that I spoke very strongly about the irony, I guess, in how I guess disgusting it was that the head of the EEOC should be making sexual advances toward her. There's no question in my mind—in fact, I think of how do I remember this, and the reason I remember this is because it was the chairman of the EEOC.

SEN. SPECTER: Well, aside from what is clear in your mind, my question to you is did she say it was Clarence Thomas?

MR. CARR: I don't recall.

SEN. SPECTER: I see that my time is up, Mr. Chairman.

THE CHAIRMAN: Thank you very much.

We are going to go now to five-minute rounds. Mr. Carr, let me ask you, before I yield to—

SEN. SPECTER: Mr. Chairman, I have some more questions.

THE CHAIRMAN: Well, we agreed we can do this, but we are going to have to begin to change the ground rules here. We will confer on this.

SEN. SPECTER: Well, there was no agreement as to a total length of time.

THE CHAIRMAN: No, but we will go to five-minute rounds. You can have your questions in five-minute rounds like other Senators.

SEN. SPECTER: Okay. Fine.

THE CHAIRMAN: Mr. Carr, how would you know someone was upset on the telephone? Are you married?

MR. CARR: No.

THE CHAIRMAN: Is there anyone you have had a relationship with for an extended period of time?

MR. CARR: Yes.

THE CHAIRMAN: Did you ever have any doubt when you picked up the phone and say how are you, whether or not you know whether they are all right or not?

I wonder if any man or woman in the world has ever picked up the phone and called someone with whom they had a relationship and said how are you, and heard that silence on the other end of the phone and not wondered whether something was wrong. The inability to know whether someone on the other end of the phone is upset seems to me to be an experience every American has probably shared at one time or another.

MR. CARR: I would agree that it is very easy with anyone that you have even the slightest of relationship, to be able to tell whether they are happy or sad with the slightest of cues over the phone.

THE CHAIRMAN: Were you surprised that—did you find it unusual at all that, notwithstanding the fact that the relationship had not—whatever your phrase was—not matured, not gone forward, that she would discuss or raise the subject of sexual harassment?

The Senator from Pennsylvania said it was rather unusual to bring up the subject of sexual harassment. Did you find it unusual that she would confide in you to the extent that she would tell you she was upset and she was being harassed? What did you think when she told you? Did you say well, our relationship just hit a new high? What did you think?

MR. CARR: If someone would have asked me, sort of in the abstract, whether Anita Hill would have shared such a thing with me at that point in our relationship, I would not have been able to say yes. I would have wondered whether she would have. But as I think about it, my recollection is that Anita Hill is a very honest and forthright person, and maybe, in a simplistic sense, when asked the question, she was visibly upset, she could not—she did not think to avoid telling me.

THE CHAIRMAN: I yield to my friend from Alabama.

SEN. HEFLIN: Judge Hoerchner, you are a Workman's Compensation Judge, and in the experience that you have had relative to judging, have you found that when confronted with an issue of fact, that the recollection process, where the fact occurred several years previous, that recollection of the incident and the details of the incident do not always come to mind in the witness's recital of them and his recollection, the continuing process, particularly if these events, incidents, facts and conversations occurred a number of years ago?

JUDGE HOERCHNER: Yes, Senator, I definitely believe that is the case.

SEN. HEFLIN: Do conversations with people who bring back to your memory certain instances help in regard to trying to comprehensively refresh your memory?

JUDGE HOERCHNER: I believe that is the case, as well. I do wish to say, though, that I have never discussed with Anita since that main conversation that I remember, the substance of that conversation or when it took place.

SEN. HEFLIN: Now, we are faced with the issue here between two people, both Yale Law School graduates, both who appear to have had prior to all of this arising, good reputations among people that had worked with them. We have the problem of trying to sift through all of the facts and come up with some decision, if it is humanly possible—and it may not be humanly possible—of who is telling the truth.

The issue of motivation as to someone coming forward and making a statement that was untrue arising—now, we have gone into various elements that people might think of in regard to motivation, and I want to ask you, and all of you and each of you can answer it: Was she, in your observation, a zealous-cause person, whether it be in civil rights, the feminist movement, or whatever? Did she ever indicate to you that she was a zealous-cause person, who was willing to do great things, move forward, and take drastic steps in order to advance whatever her cause would be?

JUDGE HOERCHNER: Most definitely not, Senator. I know that she worked under the Reagan Administration. To this day, I have no idea how she votes. I have very little sense of where she would fit on a political spectrum. Further, due to the quiet and gentle strength of her nature, she is not someone who seeks a public forum.

SEN. HEFLIN: Certainly, you wouldn't use the word "militant" in any degree?

JUDGE HOERCHNER: I think she would be very offended by that word.

SEN. HEFLIN: All right. Ms. Wells?

MS. WELLS: I would agree with the judge. In all the time that I have known Professor Hill, we have not had a conversation that would indicate a militant viewpoint about current affairs or any particular philosophy. She is very even-tempered, in my estimation.

SEN. HEFLIN: Mr. Carr?

MR. CARR: Your characterization of her as militant I found—

SEN. HEFLIN: Well, I don't mean to necessarily use "militant." It is probably the extreme word to use.

MR. CARR: Well, just to respond to that, I am a corporate, sort of a Wall Street lawyer, my profession, and I would consider myself militant compared to Anita Hill. [Laughter.]

SEN. HEFLIN: Mr. Paul.

MR. PAUL: I recall on one occasion asking her specifically about whether she agreed with the policies of the Reagan Administration specifically on civil rights issues, and I remember her saying that she didn't have any disagreements with them.

The only time I remember her being at all animated in a political discussion was the lunch table discussion that I referred to in my testimony, where she very strenuously defended her former mentor-teacher Judge Robert Bork.

SEN. HEFLIN: I am limited to five minutes, and I will sort of go over these and ask each of you to make comments on it: Vindictiveness, a martyr-type complex, desire to be a hero, write a book, spurned woman or scorned woman in regard to romantic interests, and then the issue of whether or not she has any fantasy or out of touch with reality.

I suppose most of you have heard what we have attempted to go over to find motivation, and if you would comment on those, each one of you.

JUDGE HOERCHNER: Is that to start with me, Senator?

SEN. HEFLIN: Yes.

JUDGE HOERCHNER: On vindictiveness, I have never known Anita to express a desire for revenge in any context. I will address the characteristics that I remember, and then I hope you can refresh my memory.

She was not a spurned woman, and I am unaware of any context in which she has ever felt herself to be a spurned woman.

And what are the other qualities?

SEN. HEFLIN: Well, I don't know if I remember them all. I will have to go back and read them—martyr complex—you could look at it from a group basis and give them—because my time is up— just an overall response relative to these matters and give us a thumbnail viewpoint.

JUDGE HOERCHNER: They all sound like the product of fantasy, frankly, Senator. As we have all commented, she is a very private, reserved person, whose personal style is that of gentleness, dignity, and understatement. She is very uncomfortable with the prospect of being in the public eye.

SEN. HEFLIN: All right.

Ms. Wells.

MS. WELLS: The answer would be in the nature for all of the qualities, if you will, that you listed, Senator. I would say that the thing that attracted me to Professor Hill, made me feel I want to know this person, is the fact that she is a very sweet-natured person, and yet you can feel from within her a wonderment, a sense of joy about life, and I love to hear her laugh and she loves to laugh. She is a happy person, a very giving person and one of the best friends anyone could hope to have.

SEN. HEFLIN: Mr. Carr.

MR. PAUL: You have to remember that my recollections of Anita Hill are, I guess, nine years ago. I can't remember any of those characteristics being particularly applicable to her. I heard earlier this characterization as a spurned woman, and for a moment I tried to recall whether I had spurned her or she had maybe spurned me, but I don't recall. [Laughter.]

Professor, I don't know Professor Hill in the same personal way as these other individuals. I know her as a professional colleague and she has always struck me as a person with two feet very firmly planted on the ground. The only book, Senator, I could conceive of her wanting to write would be a book on the Uniform Commercial Code. [Laughter.]

THE CHAIRMAN: Again, we are going to continue this going back and forth for five minutes. I have indicated to Senators on both sides that, as we get to the end of the process and people have no questions, but if one Senator continues to have questions, he will have an opportunity to ask those questions. We will alternate, so that every Senator gets an opportunity to participate this way. I will just recognize the ranking member each time and he can determine who will move next.

I recognize the Senator from South Carolina.

SEN. THURMOND: Mr. Chairman, I am going to yield my five minutes to Senator Specter and suggest to other members that they yield their time to him such as they don't need.

I now yield to Senator Hatch.

SEN. HATCH: I would be happy to yield my five minutes to Senator Specter, as well.

SEN. THURMOND: Senator Simpson?

SEN. SIMPSON: Mr. Chairman, I would like to ask a couple of questions.

THE CHAIRMAN: The Senator from Wyoming.

SEN. SIMPSON: Thank you, Mr. Chairman.

Because the anguish of the committee is just encompassed in the immediate remarks of Ellen Wells saying those things about Ms. Hill in a beautiful way is just exactly what Jack Danforth said about Clarence Thomas, that he was a man of joy, you said, and laughter and a great friend to be around, and that was said the first day, and now you add to it this day and that is the anguish of the moment for us.

We are, you know, trying our best. We really are not open-minded, but trying, because we have had a vote here already. The vote was seven to seven, and when you hear people speak, the two speaking from that side of the aisle, they are speaking on the basis that they voted against Judge Clarence Thomas to confirmation to the U.S. Supreme Court, and when you hear Senator Specter and Senator Hatch, they voted for his confirmation.

So, this is really not—we are not here as judges, as our chairman has so clearly reminded you, and it becomes ever more clear every day. But we are doing our best, and they can chuckle and giggle and laugh about the process and be cynical, but cynics have no heroes and they never will. Something terribly, something terribly bad has happened here. I don't know that we will ever find it.

I just wanted to ask—just to be sure that I have—Mr. Paul just one question. In your statement, you said when she told you of this, you did not recall whether she went on to say the name Clarence Thomas. You have been very frank about that. You don't remember that?

MR. PAUL: I don't recall that she did, Senator. She may have, but it would have meant nothing to me.

SEN. SIMPSON: And then you said, "If she said it, the name would not have meant anything to me, since I would not have recognized it at the time."

MR. PAUL: That's correct, Senator.

SEN. SIMPSON: You know, part of this terrible process has been about sexual harassment, a great deal of it, but some of it has been about leaks, a lot of it, too. So,

I looked in your testimony here in the transcript of proceedings, and on page 18, you name a person who spoke with you who told you that you were going to be subpoenaed later that day.

That person is on Senator Biden's staff and a very reputable man. His name I do not bring up. He is a senior staff person, and that would have been his job, for him to call you and say you are going to be subpoenaed. But I was interested in your comment only because I had my old bald dome battered in the other day by this person.

It says here on page 18 that Mr. Biden's person spoke to you to say that "I was going to be subpoenaed later today, although I had already learned that from Nina Totenberg."

MR. PAUL: Senator, I should explain—

SEN. SIMPSON: Would you tell me how that came to pass? I just have a passing interest.

THE CHAIRMAN: I would like to know the answer to that, too.

MR. PAUL: Senator, I apologize. I didn't mean to take sides between you and Ms. Totenberg.

SEN. SIMPSON: No, no, we are both able to do that. [Laughter.]

MR. PAUL: I was being perhaps too glib there. I've never spoken to Ms. Totenberg. What I meant was that I had been woken up by my clock radio going off and I heard Ms. Totenberg say my name, as I woke up, saying that I had been subpoenaed to appear before this committee.

SEN. SIMPSON: I see.

MR. PAUL: It was quite a wake-up call, Senator. [Laughter.]

SEN. SIMPSON: That saved us a further round. [Laughter.]

Now, wait until I tell you what she told me. [Laughter.]

I have it here before me, but it is Sunday in America, so I shall leave it out. [Laughter.]

One final question, and here it really is. You are speaking with passion and with truth, and this is my question: Does it seem odd to any of you here that these universally crude and obscene things which we have all heard, it is all that is out there, and we know that they took place, according to Ms. Hill, between 1981, 1982, 1983, and 1984, somewhere in all that pattern, perhaps, that is what we are told, and that she has stated to this panel that pressure, that this man was exerting power over her, authority, status, a threat of a loss of a job.

Those things are all in this record, and yet others have said that, because she was a Schedule A attorney, there was never any fear of that and that she knew that or should have known that, and others have given us information that there was plenty of budget there and she would have been taken care of, and that will come in later in the next panel.

So, here is this foul stack of stench, justifiably offensive in any category, that she was offended, justifiably, embarrassed, justifiably, and that she was repelled, justifiably. And I ask you why, then, after she left his power, after she left his presence, after she left his influence and his domination or whatever it was that gave her fear—and call it fear or revulsion or repulsion—why did she twice after that visit personally with him in Tulsa, Oklahoma, had dinner with him in the presence of others, had breakfast with him in the presence of others, rode to the airport alone with him in the presence of no one, and we have eleven phone calls initiated by her from 1984 through the date of Clarence Thomas's marriage to Ginni Lamp, and then it all ended and not a single contact came forward.

What does that say about behavior? Because Ms. Hill is not alleging sexual harassment—go back and look, go back and look at her press conference, go back and look at all of it—she is alleging behavior.

We are here today because of behavior. If we are here today because of behavior, may I please have a summary from you of what this says about her behavior? I would ask each of you—and I will defer my next round—I just think it is critical. We are talking about behavior. As human beings, I would like you to respond to this as behavior.

MR. PAUL: Senator, I am not an expert in the field of sexual harassment and I think I probably should defer to someone who has had a bit more experience in the area.

SEN. SIMPSON: Thank you. Mr. Carr?

MR. CARR: Neither am I an expert in sexual harassment or, for that matter, behavioral sciences. However, I do know that in looking forward as a young professional at my career, I am concerned that I will be on good terms with the people who have a say or an impact or are in a position to judge my career, and I would be extremely, extremely hesitant to say anything to offend or cut them off, for fear that in the future they might adversely impact my career.

I may need them for a reference or anything of that sort, and it may well be that Anita Hill—and I am just telling you, this is my own view on the way people act—it may well be that a good portion of Anita Hill's, so to speak, professional claim to fame was due to her experiences with Clarence Thomas, and it may well be that to categorically cut off that relationship would have been detrimental to her career going forward.

SEN. SIMPSON: Even in the face of this stuff. Now, may I ask Ms. Wells?

MS. WELLS: Yes, Senator, I think Mr. Carr has stated the case very well, and even in the face of that, you would, until she got to be in a position that would be, shall we say, higher, she would not wish to find herself on less than cordial terms with him. It is something that—I know my mother told me, and I am sure Anita's mother told her, when you leave, make sure you leave friends behind, because you don't know who you may need later on, and so you at least want to be cordial.

I know I get Christmas cards from people that I don't see from one end of the year to the other and, quite frankly, do not wish to, and I also return their cards and will return their calls, and these are people who have insulted me and done things which perhaps have degraded me at times, but they are things that you have to put up with, and, being a black woman, you know, you have to put up with a lot, and so you grit your teeth and you do it.

SEN. SIMPSON: Judge.

JUDGE HOERCHNER: Senator, I believe Anita has testified very credibly in response to the issues that you raised. I would like to add my voice to what Mr. Carr has said, that simply the realities of business and professional life are such that she could not afford to burn that particular bridge behind her, particularly, to extend the metaphor, when that bridge is the highest person in her field and her claim to fame.

And to that, I would add the understanding of her character, that she, in my impression, only wanted the behavior to stop. She has no desire to get even or to harm him.

SEN. SIMPSON: Mr. Chairman, I thank you. I am afraid that will remain a puzzlement for me forever, as to how that can be, where one would continue a relationship with a person that had done this foul, foul presentation of verbiage, verbal garbage to him or her, and I shall never understand that, and it remains one of my great quandaries. Another thing that puzzles me deeply, she was in Washington, DC, where there would have been a very fertile ground for her complaint. It might not have been out in the land. It might not have been in some other state of the Union, but she was in Washington, DC, at a time of public consciousness and awareness, and it just seems to me impossible to believe that something that happened ten years or eight years ago can come out of the night like a missile and destroy a man, after forty-three years of exemplary life.

SEN. THURMOND: Senator Grassley.

THE CHAIRMAN: Senator, we go to this side, if we could.

SEN. THURMOND: Excuse me.

THE CHAIRMAN: Senator Metzenbaum next.

SEN. METZENBAUM: I address these comments to the two ladies on the panel. These hearings have brought forth comments from women, and I am not sure we men totally appreciate the significance of sexual harassment.

During these hearings, one lady came to me and told me that when she was sixteen years old, she was fondled by a male, a friend of the family, and she never told her parents, never told anybody about it for twenty-seven years, until the night before she spoke to me, she had told her husband. And all during that entire twenty-seven years she had felt that she was somehow guilty, that she had done something wrong, but she hadn't done anything, nothing. She was in the presence of this person and it occurred.

Another lady told me that she had worked at a company where the chief executive had made numerous approaches to her, and she said, "I didn't quit talking to him, I didn't quit having a relationship if he gave me a ride home, I didn't create a chasm between us, because I, as a black woman, was concerned about my future."

I just want to ask you, Judge and Ms. Wells, if you can maybe explain to us fourteen men and the balance of our colleagues in the Senate and maybe the rest of the country, what it is to experience sexual harassment or how a woman feels and the repression that she places upon herself not to talk about it or do anything about it or to sever the relationship with the person who has harassed her, either one of you.

MS. WELLS: I think one of the first things you would ask yourself is what did I do. You blame yourself, you say is it something I'm wearing. I have been in this sort of situation. Okay, perhaps it's the perfume I have on.

I went to a Catholic school, and the nuns certainly taught me to be careful in my dress. I remember one sister telling us that you had to be careful of the perfume that you wore, because the title indicated the kind of emotions you would generate in a gentleman. [Laughter.]

I laughed, but, I will tell you, Sr. Ganier, the advice you have given me has held me in good stead, so I paid attention to that. But you do ask yourself what did I do, and so you try to change your behavior, because it must be me, I must be the wrong party here.

Then I think you perhaps start to get angry and frustrated, but there is always that sense of being powerless and you are also ashamed. I mean, what can you tell your friends and family, because they ask you, well, what did you do, and as you keep it in, you don't say anything. Or someone says, well, you should go forward, you have to think again, well, how am I going to pay the phone bill, if I do that. Yes, perhaps this job is secure, but maybe they will post me in an office in a corner with a telephone and *The Washington Post* to read from nine to five, and that won't get me anywhere. So, you are quiet and you are ashamed and you sit there and you take it.

JUDGE HOERCHNER: Senator, I agree that there is a tremendous tendency toward self-blame in women who are subjected to this sort of experience. It goes so far back into our history, even in the Garden of Eden, who was the bad person there who offered the apple to Adam and had to suffer for that for the rest of eternity or for the rest of human history.

I believe that most women who are in a situation of sexual harassment really only desire cessation of the problem. They have, very often, I believe, little desire for revenge. If the behavior stops, then they are much more comfortable, I believe, but I think the pain remains. I think it is indelible.

THE CHAIRMAN: Let me reiterate here that there are two distinct issues here. One is the response of those victimized and the other is whether or not someone was victimized here. This is relevant testimony, what we just heard.

I always find it difficult as to why men can't understand it. I wonder how many tens of thousands of millions of men in this country work for a boss who treats them like a lackey, tells them to do certain things and they stay on the job. We never ask why does that man stay on the job.

I wonder how many men there are, if in fact they are approached by a man on the job who had a different preference than they do, I wonder how ready they would be to go open and say, "By the way, my boss, that fellow up there, approached me." A lot would, just like a lot of women do go forward, and a lot wouldn't.

I don't know why we have so much trouble understanding the pattern of the victimized person, but that is not the issue here today. The issue here today is whether or not there was victimization, whether or not there was harassment. Although this is relevant, I want to keep bringing it back.

The only reason it is brought up now is because those who are making, as they should, Judge Thomas's case, keep coming forward and saying, "Why would you stay?" I have not brought forward, as was suggested, "expert testimony" on the pattern of victimization, the pattern of behavior that people would engage in.

I have held numerous hours of hearings on that subject, but we are here again, please, as a fellow I used to talk for, a great trial lawyer in Delaware, used to say, please keep our eye on the ball, and the ball is not the overall pattern of harassment in America, but whether or not Anita Hill was harassed. This will only continue to be brought up as long as we continue to ask the question "Why would she stay?" There are both legitimate questions but let's keep our eye on the ball as best we can.

Now I yield to my friend from South Carolina.

SEN. THURMOND: Senator Grassley.

SEN. GRASSLEY: None of you have claimed close friendship with Anita Hill. What bothers me in this whole hearing is the fact that these allegations, as serious as they are and as serious as she felt about them to come forward at this time, it seems to me would also be told to close friends who would come and want to testify, and I don't have any indication that we have any close friends who are willing to come and testify.

Do you know that she is a person who has close friends, or does this bother you that you have not had this close friendship with her, and yet you come forward and other people don't come forward?

JUDGE HOERCHNER: Senator Grassley, I believe that you are laboring under a misapprehension. I consider Anita Hill a very close friend and one of my very best friends from law school.

SEN. GRASSLEY: You do consider her a close friend?

JUDGE HOERCHNER: Yes.

SEN. GRASSLEY: Okay, what about for the other three?

MS. WELLS: I consider myself a close friend. In my comments at the start of this session, I mentioned that I had not seen or spoken to her in two years, but that was scheduling problems, shall we say. We kept in contact occasionally through correspondence, and one of the reasons I will—and that is just the last two years—one of the reasons I know that we are close is, because the moment the phone rings and I hear her voice or she hears my voice, we pick up as though the conversation had just ended an hour before.

So I have these ties to her, this invisible tie to her that exists across the miles that separate us.

SEN. GRASSLEY: But not close enough in either one of your two cases, although you say you were close friends to her, to offer her any advice. If she is a close friend, why would you not offer advice in a time of trial and tribulation like she evidently was going through?

MS. WELLS: In my case it was because the situation was so personal and painful, it would have been very presumptuous of me to try to tell her what to do. I would like to add that there are other very close friends of her under subpoena to testify before this committee.

SEN. GRASSLEY: Wouldn't your friendship, the more trying the situation is, demand your help, the closer that relationship is?

MS. WELLS: My feeling seems to have been pretty much what Mr. Carr said that his was, that I wanted to listen and to comfort, and it is very painful to me that my listening apparently did not provide comfort.

MR. CARR: I would just say that you may find this difficult to understand, but the limitations on our relationship had to do with time. It began and it ended, but during that period of time I would have considered us close. I would have considered us very close.

MS. WELLS: Senator, on that point of why I would not have offered her advice, as I indicated, she wanted a sympathetic ear, and the nature of the complaint is such that you have to be very careful what you suggest to someone in terms of how they ought to proceed, because of the very serious ramifications. And quite frankly, although I may very well have said something that sounded like advice, I am afraid I would have told her to do exactly what she did. I would have been wrong, but that is what I would have done.

MR. PAUL: Senator, as I have testified, I am not a close personal friend of Professor Hill's. I am a professional colleague of hers who has always been very impressed by her, and so my recollections are not colored by a personal relationship to her.

SEN. GRASSLEY: Mr. Chairman, I will yield the rest of my time to Senator Specter.

THE CHAIRMAN: Well, since there are only a few seconds left of that time, we will give Senator Specter more time.

SEN. THURMOND: Senator Brown?

THE CHAIRMAN: No, no. I'm sorry. We are going back to this side again.

SEN. THURMOND: Well, that is what I was thinking. Did you change your mind?

THE CHAIRMAN: No, I didn't. I misled you. I'm sorry. We will not go to Senator Specter now. We will go to Senator Kennedy, and then we will go to Senator Brown, and then we will go to Senator DeConcini, then back to Senator Specter. And if he needs more than five minutes, we will do more than five minutes.

Senator Kennedy?

SEN. KENNEDY: Thank you very much, Mr. Chairman.

I am sure I want to join in welcoming the panel, and I am sure in their own minds they must be wondering why they are being so questioned about what they understand were conversations that took place over a period of years. And I commend them for the honesty of their comments and for the helpfulness that they have provided this committee. I think it has been a very important service.

Some people just don't want to believe you. You have to understand that. They just don't want to believe you, and they don't want to believe Professor Hill. That is what the fact of the matter is, and you may be detecting some of that in the course of the hearing and the questions this afternoon.

But I hope, Mr. Chairman, that after this panel we are not going to hear any more comments, unworthy, unsubstantiated comments, unjustified comments about Professor Hill and perjury, as we heard in this room yesterday. I hope we are not going to hear any more comments about Professor Hill being a tool of the various advocacy groups, after we have heard from Ellen Wells and John Carr and Joe Paul, all of whom have volunteered to come forward after they heard about this in the newspapers—comments about individual groups and staffers trying to persuade her.

I hope we are not going to hear more about politics. You can imagine what Professor Hill would have gone through if she had been a Democrat, and we hear this afternoon she was a Bork supporter; worked in a Republican Administration. I hope we are not going to hear a lot more comments about politics.

I hope we are not going to hear a lot more comments about fantasy stories picked out of books and law cases, after we have heard from this distinguished panel, or how there have been attempts in the eleventh hour to derail this nomination. I hope we can clear this room of the dirt and innuendo, that has been suggested [about] Professor Hill as well, about over-the-transom information, about faxes, about proclivities. We heard a good deal about character assassination yesterday, and I hope we are going to be sensitive to the attempts of character assassination on Professor Hill. They are unworthy. They are unworthy.

And, quite frankly, I hope we are not going to hear a lot more about racism as we consider this nominee. The fact is that these points of sexual harassment are made by an Afro-American against an Afro-American. The issue isn't discrimination and racism. It is about sexual harassment, and I hope we can keep our eye on that particular issue.

I want to thank the panel for their testimony, for their response to questions. I found it enormously enlightening. I think the members of the Senate will. It is very clear from your presence here, the comments you have made, the way you have responded to questions, that you are doing this as a matter of responsibility and justice—justice to an individual who has had the courage in very difficult and trying times, and everyone who has seen the attempts to go after her over the period of the last three days has to understand her hesitancy, but your presence here I think has been enormously helpful to this committee and to the Senate, and I thank you for responding.

THE CHAIRMAN: Senator Brown.

SEN. BROWN: I think your coming today is not only appreciated but very helpful for us to understand the state of mind of Anita Hill, and I think very helpful in giving some verification to her thoughts at the times that you all had conversations with her.

As I review the various comments that each of you have made, it strikes me that you have given verification to the fact that she indeed talked about being asked out, talked about inappropriate actions. I believe one of you or several of you used the term "sexual harassment."

I want to try and get a feel, if there were other things besides these involved in what she related to you. Specifically, did she relate to you that there was any touching, any physical contact initiated by Clarence Thomas? Anyone have that conversation?

JUDGE HOERCHNER: No, Senator, she did not relay that to me.

MS. WELLS: Nor to me, Senator.

MR. CARR: She never told me that, I don't believe. I don't recall.

MR. PAUL: I don't recall.

SEN. BROWN: We have heard some comments about very gross language being used, with extremely descriptive terms being used. Were those terms related to any of you?

MS. WELLS: I beg your pardon? I don't think I understood.

SEN. BROWN: We have heard comments that Judge Thomas used very gross language, very explicit terms. Were those specific terms related to any of you, in the conversation you had with her?

MR. PAUL: I don't recall.

MR. CARR: My recollection is that I attempted to find out more about what had happened, briefly, but that she did not want to talk about it.

MS. WELLS: She did not relay those terms to me. As I said, it would have been a use of sexually explicit language, and neither she nor I engage in such conversation.

JUDGE HOERCHNER: I do not recall her use of such terms with me, either.

SEN. BROWN: Well, thank you. I appreciate your very straightforward responses. I will give the balance of my time to Senator Specter, as well.

SEN. THURMOND: Senator Specter.

SEN. DECONCINI: Wait a minute.

SEN. THURMOND: I beg your pardon.

SEN. DECONCINI: Thank you.

SEN. KENNEDY: [presiding]. He does have remaining time. We will go to Senator DeConcini.

SEN. DECONCINI: Thank you, Mr. Chairman.

SEN. KENNEDY: Is that okay?

SEN. THURMOND: If he can pick that up, when Specter questions, just go ahead.

SEN. KENNEDY: Senator DeConcini.

SEN. DECONCINI: Thank you, Mr. Chairman, and I am sure that Senator Specter is going to have all the time.

I want to thank you, too, for coming forward. We all have some judgments that we all took here on Judge Thomas before we had to come back, so we all have staked out a position. The other eighty-four Senators, some have and some haven't. So all of us here, as you may know, have already taken a position, but our job is to listen, and I have listened, and I thank you for coming forward.

My questions I hope are really observations, first of all. Mr. Carr, it just really got to me when you said that—or did you say this?— that your appearance here, not only would you much rather be doing something else, but it was not going to enhance your career, and that your corporate clients wouldn't like this. Is that what you said, or did I misinterpret you?

MR. CARR: I don't know the political views of my corporate clients, per se, Senator. What I meant was that I doubted that any of them would find it a positive thing.

SEN. DECONCINI: They wouldn't?

MR. CARR: I don't think so.

SEN. DECONCINI: You don't think so?

MR. CARR: Although I don't know whether they would find it a negative thing.

SEN. DECONCINI: Just out of curiosity, and it has nothing to do with the proceedings, and you don't have to do this, I would like to know, just if you would call me sometime, if your corporate clients really do object to you coming forward and doing this, and you don't even have to tell me who they are. But it just struck me funny, I think any corporate client would be proud of you, that you are that kind of a man, but maybe I am wrong. I haven't practiced law for fifteen years, and so maybe corporations and corporate clients are different than they were when I practiced.

The other thing is, Mr. Carr, did you say that no outside group or anybody contacted you, that you came forward on your own?

MR. CARR: I saw the accusations on the television. I remembered them. I wrote a letter to Anita Hill, telling her that I remembered our conversation, and then I was contacted by people working with her and asked if I would testify.

SEN. DECONCINI: If you would, and your lawyer is Janet Napolitano? Or is that—

MR. CARR: No, she is, I assume she is Anita's lawyer.

SEN. DECONCINI: She is Anita's lawyer. I didn't know if she also represented you. She is a very fine lawyer. I happen to know her.

Ms. Wells, let me ask you this: I appreciate your explanation of why a woman—and perhaps this applies to men, too, in different senses—why a woman would stay on under sexual harassment, and you said you would have done that, and you would have advised her to stay, even though now you say that was wrong, and I appreciate that honesty.

If Professor Hill had told you the explicits that she told this committee, number one, would you have felt obligated to give her advice? And would that advice have been, as you said it would have been, to stay on?

MS. WELLS: If I had learned of the actual nature of the behavior, I would—well, I was stunned, first of all, just to hear the news without details. To hear the details, I think I would have been so outraged that I perhaps would have said, "Well, we have to do something. You cannot live through this."

SEN. DECONCINI: Do something. And personally, you know, nobody can really get inside someone else's moccasins or shoes, but if that had happened to you, would you have stayed on and moved on in the job—given the explicitness of the testimony given yesterday?

MS. WELLS: Without getting into details, Senator, and I say this only to try to help you understand what I think went on here, I would be unsure, simply because I was touched in the workplace, not merely on one occasion, and I stayed in that position.

SEN. DECONCINI: And you stayed on.

MS. WELLS: So therefore, I really can't say what I would have done with words.

SEN. DECONCINI: And, Judge, did Professor Hill at any time in your conversations mention to you her desire to be advanced in the EEOC, of another position she would like to have had or was seeking?

JUDGE HOERCHNER: No, not to my recollection.

SEN. DECONCINI: There was never any discussion, in that hour-long conversation, of her aspirations or her disappointment or her ambitions?

JUDGE HOERCHNER: No, but let me clarify, if I may. I don't know how long that conversation lasted. I do know that we often spoke for up to an hour.

SEN. DECONCINI: And none of those conversations, whether they were ten minutes or up to an hour, ever contained any discussion about her ambitions or her desires to move on and what she thought her chances were, or any discussions along that line?

JUDGE HOERCHNER: No, absolutely no. The only thing I clearly remember her saying about the nature of the work was that she liked being—

SEN. DECONCINI: Excuse me. I didn't hear your answer.

JUDGE HOERCHNER: She made no comments about moving upward or—

SEN. DECONCINI: Thank you. I did hear your answer.

Judge Hoerchner, did you have to hire a lawyer to come here today?

JUDGE HOERCHNER: No.

SEN. DECONCINI: You didn't? Do you have a lawyer representing you here?

JUDGE HOERCHNER: I have a lawyer who was my moot court director at Yale Law School. His name is Ron Allen.

SEN. DECONCINI: And he is a pro bono lawyer, or are you paying him?

JUDGE HOERCHNER: He has not submitted a bill yet. [Laughter.]

SEN. DECONCINI: Lots of luck, Mr. Allen.

Thank you.

And just lastly, Dean Paul, you don't consider yourself a friend of Professor Hill. A professional acquaintance, is that fair to say?

MR. PAUL: I would say that we were professional colleagues.

SEN. DECONCINI: Professional colleagues.

MR. PAUL: We are on friendly terms. I see Professor Hill typically once or twice a year at the annual meetings of the Association of American Law Schools.

SEN. DECONCINI: Yes. Do you think you fall into the category, then, in her statement where she said: "It is only after a great deal of agonizing consideration, that I am able to talk of these unpleasant matters to anyone but my closest friends."

She must consider you a friend, don't you think?

MR. PAUL: I think that she considers me a friendly professional colleague. I don't know why she chose to relate the story to me. I don't know if she remembers relating the story to me. As I say, I haven't spoken to Professor Hill since prior to the Thomas nomination.

SEN. DECONCINI: Thank you.

And thank you, Chairman, for the additional time. I appreciate it.

SEN. THURMOND: Senator Specter?

SEN. SPECTER: Thank you, Mr. Chairman.

Ms. Wells, let me pick up with your statement as I wrote it down, when you heard the details as to what Professor Hill had said that Judge Thomas said to her, "so outraged you would have to do something." The issue which we have before us is one of credibility, as to whom to believe. We have gained substantial insights in a lot of testimony which has been given as to the view of a woman in a position of this sort.

You did not know the details. You only knew that it was inappropriate and sexual in nature, as to what Professor Hill had told you. That is what your testimony has been here today.

When you get the details and, as you say, you were outraged that you thought something would have to have been done, we have a situation where Professor Hill went from the Department of Education to the EEOC, and she was a classification attorney where she could have kept her job, and then she went with him voluntarily on a trip to Oral Roberts. I am not suggesting any impropriety, but she went with him. And after that she called him on many occasions. There are eleven in a log, and we will have a witness later who will testify that she called him on many other occasions that weren't written down in the log because they got through to Judge Thomas.

And we have an astute professor, a law professor, a lawyer, who was concerned about being fired by Judge Thomas, so that when he gave her work assignments she wrote them all down, the date she received them, the nature of the work, how long it took her to finish them.

But in the context of that kind of concern, and she testifies about these outlandish statements having been made, she doesn't write any of them down.

And we are trying to figure out what really happened. If it is sexual harassment, the man ought not be on the Court. Ought not be on any court. He ought not be the head of EEOC.

And the testimony has been that, I think it was, that he was her claim to fame, should not burn that bridge. But, even considering all of that and knowing Professor Hill as you do, and in the light of your statement "so outraged, have to do something," what would that something have been? Would it have been to follow him from one job to another? To call him up? To drive him to the airport? Or would it at least have been not to maintain that kind of an association?

MS. WELLS: Well, Senator, as I believe I indicated earlier, one of the reasons that I would be hesitant to offer advice on this kind of issue is because of the ramifications, and it is such a personal thing. So, yes, if she had something like that, sitting outside of the situation I would have said, "Oh, this is terrible. Yes, you must do something."

But what could I actually expect her to do? When I told a close friend about my occurrence, in terms of being touched, I was told immediately, "Oh, you should file a suit." I wasn't going to do that. I couldn't do that. First of all, who saw it? Nobody. But I would tell you this: I didn't need to write it down because I remember the places on my body that he touched, just as she did not need to write down the words he used because they are burned indelibly into her brain.

And so, yes, it may seem strange that you maintain contact, but I think it is something that you just school yourself to do. And I understand that that seems difficult, but that is what happens oftentimes.

And it takes a great deal of strength and courage to not maintain some kind of a cordial relationship, if you will, because we are all told about networking. I mean, my goodness, gracious! You can open up any women's magazine and you go to seminars on how women are supposed to learn to network since we don't have the old boys club."Take up golf, ladies. Take up tennis. Learn to get out there so you can do these things to maintain these contacts." And so you don't burn your bridges.

SEN. SPECTER: So, in essence, you are saying that even though you were so outraged you would have to do something, that ultimately you would have done nothing?

MS. WELLS: I think that is the case.

SEN. SPECTER: And would she have maintained that kind of a friendly relationship, called him up, drive him to the airport, et cetera?

MS. WELLS: I don't know all those—all the circumstances, but given the kind of work—I am sorry?

SEN. SPECTER: Well, Professor Hill has said that she made those calls. She admits to eleven calls.

MS. WELLS: Yes.

SEN. SPECTER: I think the record is plain that she did drive him to the airport. And it is, of course, very plain that she moved with him from one agency to another and that she went to Oral Roberts. She accompanied him on a trip.

We are interested in your perspective, and interested if you would have maintained all of those kinds of activities, given the feelings that were involved with the reprehensible statements alleged to have been made.

MS. WELLS: Well, over the course of, let's see, what—I am not sure. I think it was 1983 when she started at Oral Roberts and we are at 1991. I don't see eleven calls, some of them on behalf of other people, as a lot of contact. It is business in nature.

SEN. SPECTER: Well, there were more calls than that eleven which were recorded where he was not present.

Mr. Carr, you said that you found the comments outrageous. Did you give any thought, at the time you had this telephone conversation with Professor Hill, to saying to her, "What are you going to do about it; let's consider taking some action; here you have a man who is the head of the EEOC, chief law enforcement of the country on sexual harassment"?

Did the thought cross your mind, whether or not she did anything, that these outrageous comments should at least warrant some consideration of some action?

MR. CARR: I don't recall that we discussed that or that we did not discuss it. I— it may well be that at that point she had decided to leave his employ and she told me that. I just don't recall.

SEN. SPECTER: Well, my question to you is did you give her any such advice? Are you saying that you might have given her that advice or am I to consider it if it were simply now? Do you not recall?

MR. CARR: I am saying I don't recall today. That is right.

SEN. SPECTER: Professor Paul, you testified about a comment made by an associate of yours, the fox in the hen house, and I believe as you characterized it you were shocked and astonished by what Professor Hill had told you.

Did you give any thought to any suggestion about her taking some action given the fact that this happened at EEOC, the agency which was charged with enforcing laws against sexual harassment?

MR. PAUL: As I testified, Senator, I asked her if she had taken any recourse and she said no. And I asked her why not and she said that she felt that she had no recourse. I don't recall more than that conversation.

SEN. SPECTER: Your testimony was that she said she had been sexually harassed by her supervisor. I am advised, and we have to have testimony on this, but I am advised reliably that she had two supervisors besides Judge Thomas, who was her ultimate supervisor as the chairman of the EEOC.

Would the statement she made to you about a supervisor comprehend as well a supervisor other than the chairman of the EEOC?

MR. PAUL: Well, Senator, she said that she had been sexually harassed by her supervisor. From what I know of Professor Hill, it is not conceivable to me that she would now be blaming Judge Thomas for the actions of another man. So I would have to conclude that no, Senator, I believe that she was talking about Judge Thomas.

SEN. SPECTER: Well, I am not asking you for a conclusion. I am asking you about what she said in terms of supervisor and whether that, aside from any other inferences which you may make whether the category "supervisor" or whatever it was she said, would comprehend other supervisors, if, in fact, there were? And we have to hear about that.

MR. PAUL: I don't know, Senator.

SEN. SPECTER: Judge Hoerchner, let me come back to a couple of points which have been asked, that I asked you about by some other people. I turn to page 5 of the notes and testimony, and line six.

SEN. KENNEDY: Repeat the page, please.

SEN. SPECTER: Page 5, line six.

SEN. KENNEDY: Thank you.

THE CHAIRMAN: Senator, I am not going to cut you off. But again, there are some who haven't asked over here, so you are beyond the five minutes.

SEN. SPECTER: That is fine. Thank you, Mr. Chairman.

THE CHAIRMAN: We are going back and forth.

SEN. SPECTER: Glad to yield?

THE CHAIRMAN: Why don't we do that? And you will have an opportunity to ask again.

Now, Senators Simon and Kohl have not had an opportunity to ask, as I understand it. So, Senator Simon?

And again, any member of the panel who continues to have questions, we will allow them the opportunity to question. But I just want to make sure everybody gets a shot first.

SEN. SIMON: Thank you, Mr. Chairman.

First, not to the panel, but on a talk show this morning one of the commentators said that I was the source for the leak of the affidavit. That is just absolutely false. I don't operate that way. I have seen how leaks have damaged people, our colleagues. Senator DeConcini suffered a great injustice because of a leak. And I just want everyone to know that there is simply no truth to that. Neither I nor my staff leaked the documents.

THE CHAIRMAN: Senator?

SEN. SIMON: Yes, sir?

THE CHAIRMAN: I am sorry. If it is on that matter, continue. But before you get to questioning I want to ask the panel a question about—

SEN. SIMON: Go ahead.

THE CHAIRMAN: You have been on for a while now. Would you all like to break—yes. I can see the heads shaking.

Senator, would you rather continue your questioning now or give them a break and then question? How would you like to do it?

SEN. SIMON: The panel would like to take a break right now. I will take my five minutes after the break, Mr. Chairman.

THE CHAIRMAN: We will recess for fifteen minutes.

[Recess.]

THE CHAIRMAN: The hearing will come back to order.

To explain to the witnesses what we are doing, we are trying to figure out the remainder of the schedule. I emphasize again that Senator Thurmond and I are under strict time constraints placed on us, understandably, by the entirety of the Senate, the leadership in the Senate and the remainder of the Senate, to resolve this entire matter in time for all of our colleagues to be able to consider all the testimony here and make a judgment.

As I have indicated at the outset, were this a trial, which is not, all of you who are sitting as the panel members here know that there would be a legitimate reason for this trial to go on for another week or more. We do not have that luxury.

The nominee insists on a resolution of it. The White House insists on a resolution of it. And the Senate insists on a resolution of it. So what we are attempting to do is work out not only a time when we are going to vote on this on the Senate floor,which is done six o'clock Tuesday night, but an agreement on an absolute end time when these hearings will end.

And I assure this panel, you will not have to be here till the end. We are about to do that with you all now, and we will probably recess very briefly after this panel is completed, to discuss the final witness list and the time frame within which each witness or panel will be coming before the committee.

I thank the panel and I thank everyone in this room for their indulgence, and I hope they understand. But based upon the knowledge of the arcane processes of the Senate, I am sure no one will understand. But nonetheless, that is where we are.

Now, where were we in questioning? Who was next?

Senator Simon has five minutes.

SEN. SIMON: Mr. Chairman, first, if I may comment on something said by Senator Specter just before my time came up. He said, and I wrote it down, there were more than eleven calls, that only eleven were documented. To my knowledge, that is an inaccurate statement.

We know Judge Thomas—

SEN. SPECTER: Mr. Chairman, I said we would produce a witness who would testify to that. That there were other calls, that eleven were documented when he wasn't there, but we would produce a witness.

So, if Senator Simon is going to quote me, please be accurate.

SEN. SIMON: Well, perhaps you know that there were more. So far there has been nothing entered into the evidence suggesting that there were more than eleven calls.

THE CHAIRMAN: Let me ask the Senator from Pennsylvania, has the name of that witness been made available to the Committee as a whole?

SEN. SPECTER: Yes, that is Ms. Holt, who is the custodian of the records—

THE CHAIRMAN: Ms. Holt. All right. Fine.

SEN. SPECTER: [continuing]. —and also the secretary, who is prepared to testify that there were many more calls made by Professor Hill which got through to Judge Thomas, so there was not a notation.

THE CHAIRMAN: But it is Ms. Holt we are talking about?

SEN. SPECTER: That is right.

THE CHAIRMAN: Thank you.

SEN. SIMON: And let me just add that one or more of those calls were made with great reluctance. We have evidence on that also. Now, getting to the panel, and we will get to you here. Judge Hoerchner, you said in your deposition you were asked:

> *Question*. Did you see her press conference on television?
> *Answer.* Yes, I did.
> *Question*: Did you find her to be credible?
> *Answer.* I saw most of it. Absolutely. If you knew Anita you couldn't doubt her word on anything. I've never known her even to exaggerate. As you can tell from what you've seen of her on television and in person, her style is understatement in everything she does.

Now, yesterday it was suggested by one of the members of the Senate that the fact that she did not document what was happening to her questions her credibility. I would be interested in any reflections you might have, all four witnesses, on whether or not—on the matter of documentation in that kind of a situation, and does the fact that she did not document this in any way diminish her credibility in your mind? Judge, if we can call on you first.

JUDGE HOERCHNER: Absence of documentation could never diminish Anita's credibility to those of us who have known her since 1977 and 1978. Documentation is usually in my experience something that someone would do who is contemplating a lawsuit. It was always my impression that Anita had no intention to sue then-Mr. Thomas and that she has had no agenda vis-a-vis Judge Thomas.

SEN. SIMON: Ms. Wells?

MS. WELLS: The lack of documentation does not trouble me, Senator, because I think, as I tried to indicate to Senator Specter earlier, I don't see what a record would have accomplished. She knew what was done to her. And furthermore, to put it down on paper, to say he said X to me on Thursday, would have been no more evidence for us today than anything else.

SEN. SIMON: And, of course, she didn't anticipate anything

MS. WELLS: No. So there was no reason. As the judge said. She wasn't thinking of bringing a suit.

SEN. SIMON: And, if I could relate it, it says to me that she didn't intend to prosecute or carry on in that way.

You have mentioned your own experience. Did you document that in any way, writing it down in a diary or anything?

MS. WELLS: No, I did not. It is just something that will always be with me and so I have no need to write it down. I would like to forget it and I cannot. So I would not want it to be anywhere where it could be picked up and read by anyone.

SEN. SIMON: Mr. Carr?

MR. CARR: I would echo that, I guess. But in addition, my recollection of discussing these things with Anita Hill is that they were very painful for her, and I think she did not want to, certainly, talking about them with me, and she may well have wanted to forget them, and that writing them down may, in fact, in and of itself have been additionally painful for her.

SEN. SIMON: Mr. Paul?

MR. PAUL: Senator, I would have to say as a lawyer that the absence of documentation is completely consistent with my recollection of her reluctance in wanting to discuss it and her statement that she felt she had no recourse.

SEN. SIMON: If I may ask one more question, Mr. Chairman?

THE CHAIRMAN: Briefly.

SEN. SIMON: Each of you has explained why you are here. Why do you think Anita Hill came forward and testified?

JUDGE HOERCHNER: She has said that she came forward out of a sense of her obligation as a citizen. I think the incidents that occurred those many years ago have raised a serious question of character in someone who has been nominated for one of the most important positions in the country.

I know that she was very reluctant to come forward. I think she felt she had a duty to her country.

SEN. SIMON: Ms. Wells?

MS. WELLS: Well, I can only echo what the judge has said. Anita, Professor Hill, is a very loyal person and therefore she is loyal to what she believes she ought to do, and so therefore she has come forward only because she felt that that was the right thing to do.

SEN. SIMON: Mr. Carr?

MR. CARR: Senator, I can really only, I guess, speculate on it, on why she has come forward. I would think my recollections of her personality are that while she would like to come forward in this manner she would be terrified of the invasion of privacy and she would have been extremely hesitant.

At the same time, I have the recollection that she is a forthright person and when asked a question she feels compelled to give an honest answer. And I would think here that she has somehow found herself on the sort of proverbial slippery slope. That she has felt obligated to make some statement when asked and that that has snowballed totally out of control to the point where she had no alternative but to come forward in a total and fulsome way.

SEN. SIMON: And, if I could ask you, and then I want to hear from Mr. Paul, she is both a lawyer and a law professor. I assume she has a very elevated feeling, as we all do, for the Supreme Court. Do you think this was a factor in coming forward also?

MR. CARR: It may well have been that when she looked at the price she would have to pay to do this, that because it was the Supreme Court she viewed it as of such great importance that she was willing to pay that price.

SEN. SIMON: Mr. Paul.

MR. PAUL: Of course, I haven't discussed with Professor Hill, Senator, her reasons for coming forward, but I would imagine that if I were in her situation, when asked the question by an agent of the FBI, I would feel compelled to answer the question honestly as a servant to the court.

I cannot imagine anything that Professor Hill could think to gain as a legal academician by coming forward. I think her career has, frankly, probably suffered as a result of her coming forward. I think that she had a very bright career. I think that if someone had asked me a few weeks ago, I would say that I could imagine Professor Hill coming before this committee in a very different capacity, as a judicial nominee herself. I think her opportunities for that now have been destroyed. I think she paid a big price for her conscience.

SEN. SIMON: I thank you. And I thank all four of you for coming forward. Thank you, Mr. Chairman.

SEN. KENNEDY: [presiding]. Senator Thurmond.

SEN. KOHL: Thank you very much, Mr. Chairman. And thank you for being here today, folks.

SEN. KENNEDY: I think it goes Senator Thurmond, and then, Senator Kohl, I will recognize you.

SEN. KOHL: Oh, I am sorry.

SEN. THURMOND: I would like to ask you this question. From your testimony, it appears that none of you four witnesses have any personal knowledge of the charges made by Professor Hill against Judge Thomas, and that all you know about the matter is what Professor Hill told you. Is that correct?

JUDGE HOERCHNER: I was not a precipitate witness, Senator.

SEN. THURMOND: What was that?

JUDGE HOERCHNER: I was not a precipitate witness.

SEN. THURMOND: What did she say?

JUDGE HOERCHNER: I said that is correct.

SEN. THURMOND: Ms. Wells.

MS. WELLS: That is correct, Senator.

SEN. THURMOND: Mr. Carr.

MR. CARR: It is correct. I was not in the room.

SEN. THURMOND: Mr. Paul.

MR. PAUL: That is true, Senator.

SEN. THURMOND: That is all. Thank you very much. I yield the rest of my time to Senator Specter.

SEN. SPECTER: Thank you, Mr. Chairman.

When my time last expired, Judge Hoerchner, I was asking you to refer to page 5 of your prior testimony before the staff. A question where you said, at line six, on page 5, "I did run into her very briefly at a professional conference in 1984, late December."

My question to you is did you, at that time, ask Professor Hill anything about these alleged statements made by Judge Thomas?

JUDGE HOERCHNER: I did not remember asking her that.

SEN. SPECTER: Judge Hoerchner, can you be any more specific than you have been about where you were at the time this conversation occurred where you say Professor Hill made these statements about Judge Thomas's comments? We have been trying to fix the date. It would be helpful if you were able to at least say where you lived at that time, in an effort to try to pin that down. Can you help us on that?

JUDGE HOERCHNER: Unfortunately as I have explained to the FBI and here, I really cannot pin the date down. The one thing I can be absolutely certain about is the fact that she was working for Clarence Thomas at the time because she stated that she was experiencing sexual harassment from her boss, Clarence.

SEN. SPECTER: Can you, at least, tell us whether you were living in Washington at the time you had that conversation with her?

JUDGE HOERCHNER: I cannot pin down the date with any further specificity.

SEN. SPECTER: Judge Hoerchner, shifting over to the contacts you had with other people at or about the time you called Professor Hill on the day of Judge Thomas's nomination for the Supreme Court, have you received a call from anyone prior to the time you called Professor Hill asking her what she was going to do?

JUDGE HOERCHNER: Absolutely not.

SEN. SPECTER: When did you have the first call, if any, from any member of the news media?

JUDGE HOERCHNER: I am trying to remember who called whom. The first person from the news media with whom I spoke was Nina Totenberg from National Public Radio and PBS.

SEN. SPECTER: What did she say to you?

JUDGE HOERCHNER: That was after Anita had already spoken to her. She just briefly asked me the same types of things that I had been asked by the staff member of the chairman.

SEN. SPECTER: And what did you respond?

JUDGE HOERCHNER: I responded with essentially the same information that I had given in my statement. I also asked her not to use my name.

SEN. SPECTER: Judge Hoerchner, you are not in a position to corroborate Professor Hill's statement that Judge Thomas spoke about acts that he had seen in pornographic films, are you?

JUDGE HOERCHNER: I do not have an explicit memory of that.

SEN. SPECTER: Judge Hoerchner, are you in a position to corroborate Professor Hill's statement that Judge Thomas talked to her about such matters as women having sex with animals?

JUDGE HOERCHNER: I do not have a memory of references of women having sex with animals. But I do have a memory of her telling me that he said to her, if we had any witnesses, you would have a perfect case against me.

SEN. SPECTER: I understand that. What I am trying to do now is to go through the real essence or gravamen or testimony which Professor Hill gave against Judge Thomas to be sure that we understand you. Because as I understand it, you do not, but I want to be sure, that you said you don't have, you can't corroborate her claim that Judge Thomas spoke to her about pornographic films. You can't corroborate Judge Thomas's statement about women having sex, et cetera, as I just said. Can you corroborate her claim that Judge Thomas spoke about pornographic materials depicting individuals with large sex organs?

JUDGE HOERCHNER: No.

SEN. SPECTER: Can you corroborate her claim that Judge Thomas spoke to her graphically about his own sexual prowess?

JUDGE HOERCHNER: No.

SEN. SPECTER: Can you corroborate her claim that Judge Thomas spoke to her about the odd episode, or Judge Thomas participated in the odd episode about drinking a Coke with the allegation of the pubic hair?

JUDGE HOERCHNER: No.

SEN. SPECTER: Ms. Wells, are you in a position to corroborate Professor Hill's testimony that Judge Thomas spoke to her about pornographic films?

MS. WELLS: No, I am not.

SEN. SPECTER: Are you in a position to corroborate Professor Hill's claim that Judge Thomas spoke to her about women having sex, et cetera, with others than men?

MS. WELLS: No.

SEN. SPECTER: Are you in a position to corroborate that he talked about pornographic materials with large private parts?

MS. WELLS: No, I am not.

SEN. SPECTER: Are you in a position to corroborate that Judge Thomas talked to her about his own sexual prowess?

MS. WELLS: No, I am not.

SEN. SPECTER: Or about the Coke incident?

MS. WELLS: No, I am not.

SEN. SPECTER: Mr. Carr, are you in a position to corroborate any of that?

MR. CARR: Those are all consistent with the things she has told me but I am not in a position to corroborate them specifically.

SEN. SPECTER: And, Professor Paul, are you in a position to corroborate that Judge Thomas talked to Professor Hill about pornographic films?

MR. PAUL: No.

SEN. SPECTER: About any of the specifics I have asked Ms. Wells and Judge Hoerchner about?

MR. PAUL: All of that, Senator, would be consistent with sexual harassment, but she did not talk to me—I don't recall that she talked to me about any of those particulars.

SEN. SPECTER: Professor Paul, did you know prior to the time these hearings started, that when Professor Hill accompanied Judge Thomas from the Department of Education to EEOC that as a matter of fact she had a classification at the Department of Education that she could have stayed there?

MR. PAUL: No, Senator.

SEN. SPECTER: Professor Paul, did you know that prior to the time that this hearing started that Professor Hill had made at least eleven calls which were recorded to Judge Thomas, and others unrecorded?

MR. PAUL: No, Senator.

SEN. SPECTER: Did you know, Professor Paul, that Professor Hill drove Judge Thomas to the airport and was with him alone on that occasion in Oklahoma City or Tulsa?

MR. PAUL: No, Senator.

SEN. SPECTER: Did you know any of that, Mr. Carr?

MR. CARR: No.

SEN. SPECTER: Did you know any of that, Ms. Wells?

MS. WELLS: No, Senator.

SEN. SPECTER: Did you know any of that, Judge Hoerchner?

JUDGE HOERCHNER: I didn't hear her testify about driving him to the airport.

SEN. SPECTER: So you didn't know about that?

JUDGE HOERCHNER: No, I did not know about that.

SEN. SPECTER: Judge Hoerchner, if you had to vote on Judge Thomas, yes or no, what would it be?

JUDGE HOERCHNER: Senator, I don't have a vote here.

SEN. SPECTER: Ms. Wells, if you had to vote yes or no on Judge Thomas, what would it be?

MS. WELLS: Senator, the hearings are not over and you have more witnesses for Anita Hill to hear and I think then you would have a better understanding of her and why we are here saying that her allegations are true.

SEN. SPECTER: Mr. Carr, if you had to vote yes or no on Judge Thomas, what would it be?

MR. CARR: Senator, I have not followed the hearings earlier before the Senate decided to delay, and so I can't make an informed decision based on that, but I do believe the sexual harassment charges, and I think he would have to be one incredible jurist to get over my view that those are true. So I would vote, no.

SEN. SPECTER: Would you want to hear the rest of the testimony?

MR. CARR: I think if I was in the official position to make that choice, then I would definitely hear the rest of the testimony.

SEN. SPECTER: Professor Paul, you have already testified that when they came to you, you wouldn't sign the letter.

MR. PAUL: That's correct, Senator.

SEN. SPECTER: Do you have an opinion today, would you vote yes or no on Judge Thomas?

MR. PAUL: If these allegations are proved true, Senator, I would say that he is not fit for the Supreme Court.

SEN. SPECTER: But you would want to hear the rest of the evidence?

MR. PAUL: Yes, Senator.

SEN. SPECTER: So that none of you is in a position, sitting there today without hearing the rest of the evidence to reject Judge Thomas solely on the basis of what Professor Hill has said?

MR. CARR: Sir, I am in a position to do that.

SEN. SPECTER: I thought you wanted to hear the rest of the evidence, Mr. Carr.

MR. CARR: I said that I would—I think it would be incumbent upon me to review all of the evidence, but that I have great difficulty imagining that he could be such a great jurist as to justify being confirmed in light of my belief that there was sexual harassment.

SEN. SPECTER: No further questions, Mr. Chairman.

THE CHAIRMAN: Thank you.

Senator Kohl.

SEN. KOHL: Thank you, very much, Mr. Chairman.

Just to follow up on what Senator Specter has been asking you. You are in a position, do I understand it, on the basis of your testimony today, to state as a matter of fact that Professor Hill informed you in a way that satisfied you that she was being sexually harassed by Judge Thomas, by Clarence Thomas? Is there any question in your mind about the clarity of the information that she provided to you? The sense that she provided to you?

Judge Hoerchner.

JUDGE HOERCHNER: There is no question in my mind that that happened.

SEN. KOHL: In specific, did she tell you and corroborate to you that he had asked her out on numerous occasions in a manner that made her very uncomfortable and felt that she was being harassed?

JUDGE HOERCHNER: Yes, she did.

SEN. KOHL: Ms. Wells.

MS. WELLS: She did not get into that detail. She helped me to understand that she was the recipient of inappropriate and offensive behavior in the office.

SEN. KOHL: Mr. Carr.

MR. CARR: My recollection, at the time, is that I believed her and I believed her without question. Since recalling that conversation and listening to and hearing much of the testimony here, I have rethought that view, and I have racked my brain trying to understand it. Having done that, I nonetheless come back to the same position that I believe her.

MR. PAUL: There is no question in my mind, Senator, that she told me she was sexually harassed by her supervisor at the EEOC and I believed her then and I believe her still.

SEN. KOHL: Has she ever discussed with you being sexually harassed by anybody else, any other supervisor?

MR. PAUL: No, Senator.

SEN. KOHL: Any other evidence except this evidence with respect to Clarence Thomas?

Judge Hoerchner.

JUDGE HOERCHNER: She has never done so. She has been very poised in dealing with men and has had little trouble in laughing off or brushing off unwelcome advances, but in a situation like this where there is such a gross inequity in power she was not able to do so to her satisfaction.

SEN. KOHL: Ms. Wells, did she ever discuss with you sexual harassment from anybody else?

MS. WELLS: No, never, just concerning Judge Thomas.

SEN. KOHL: Mr. Carr.

MR. CARR: No, she didn't, but to be fair, we only discussed for a brief period of time. Our contact was over a limited period of time. No.

SEN. KOHL: Judge Hoerchner, we have discussed today the pain and suffering that Anita Hill has endured. I would like to ask you from your vantage point, as a judge, do you have any comment to make on the pain and the suffering that has been endured by Judge Thomas's family here?

Can you give us some insight, offer some words?

JUDGE HOERCHNER: Yesterday Judge Thomas spoke here very eloquently about the pain that he has experienced. There is only one person to blame for that pain, and I know no one who takes any joy in his suffering. His suffering is very apparent. There is, however, only one person to blame. It is not the press. It is not the person or persons who leaked the information. It is not Anita Hill. He is suffering as a result of his own actions. And there is another person who has been suffering much, much longer. She is suffering now, she was suffering ten years ago, and she is not suffering as a result of her actions. And that person is Anita

Hill.

SEN. KOHL: Anybody else wish to comment on that?

[No response.]

SEN. KOHL: One more question. This is 1991, that was 1981. Do you have any comment on how you think that sexual harassment might be approached in our society today compared to ten years ago?

Are we ten years further ahead, or are we in the same place?

How do you imagine a woman might handle a similar situation today, Judge?

JUDGE HOERCHNER: Senator, even today, a woman who is twenty-three, twenty-four years old, as Anita was, just out of law school, working in a situation of such tremendous inequity of power, I really could not realistically advise her that she would have adequate protection were she to make a complaint.

SEN. KOHL: Ms. Wells.

MS. WELLS: I think there is, to a certain extent, a greater sensitivity among men about this, not overwhelming, but there is a greater one. And so I have seen some progress to that extent. But if there is anything that will help women deal with this, I think it is the fact that women seem to rely so much more on one another and have a better understanding that you can come together and talk about this and the best thing to do is to talk about it and to try to work together to resolve it, and to realize that you are not the guilty party. And the sooner that you throw off that idea, the sooner that you can get some healing and some closure to it.

SEN. KOHL: Mr. Carr, anything different today from ten years ago? If she would have called you today, versus ten years ago and discussed her problem with you, what might you have recommended differently today from ten years ago?

MR. CARR: I am not sure how I would have differed today from then. I may well, at this point, being ten years older and having a better sense of how my own career has gone and how careers do go, on the one hand been extremely cautious in advising her about the risk. On the other hand, upon reflection, I may have been more supportive of her to take the risk.

MR. PAUL: Senator, as you know, the Supreme Court did not establish hostile work environment as a cause of action until 1987, I believe, so that in that sense perhaps we have made some progress in our understanding of the law. But I must admit, as a person who does not teach in this area and is not familiar with the law in this area, that four years ago when Anita Hill came to me and told me this story and said that she felt she had no recourse at the EEOC, I did not understand why. I think now, when I see what has happened to Professor Hill as a result of these hearings, as a result of coming forward, I can better understand why victims of sexual harassment don't feel that they have any recourse.

SEN. KOHL: Well, I, too, want to thank you for coming here today. I think you have given us dramatic evidence of what it is like in our society today to be female and not powerful and not wealthy, and still make an attempt to try and get by what the difficulties are in many cases. In that respect, you have been very enlightening to me, I would like to hope to my colleagues, and to many millions of Americans, so I thank you for being here today.

Thank you, Mr. Chairman.

THE CHAIRMAN: Thank you very much. Senator Simpson.

SEN. SIMPSON: Mr. Chairman, I really will be much less than five minutes.

It is a very puzzling thing here for me. You are all lawyers, and you are all lawyers telling us that the system does not work for sexual harassment. What a curious and extraordinary thing. It is 1991, and these laws have been on the books for years, and Joe Biden, our chairman, has been involved deeply in these issues. So have many of us.

Sexual harassment is talked about all over America, and you are telling us as four lawyers that the system doesn't work, and this is very troubling to me. Obviously we have a great deal to do. I thought it worked. I thought if you went forward, that things took place. A consultation takes place, supervisors; anonymous; and these things take place. And you are saying just—it is like saying the process doesn't work.

I can understand why the chairman bridles. The process does work, but you are telling us it doesn't, and I don't understand that, in this day, in this city, that sexual harassment claims aren't done in the way the statute was drawn, in the sense of a way to get them expressed to protect both—both the victim and the harasser. Because here is a pattern—if there is a pattern, we are told that—psychologically, of the victim and their response, and there is also a pattern of the harasser. It is seldom a singular thing. And that is the way it is, and that is what we are dealing with.

And my question is this. I understood Ellen Wells very effectively and passionately describes sexual harassment. Did you say—and I am asking you, if I didn't hear with all this going on—you said you had been touched. Did you bring a claim of sexual harassment? No, you said not. Okay. I'm sorry.

Judge Hoerchner, have you ever brought a claim of sexual harassment?

JUDGE HOERCHNER: There was an incident of sexual harassment where I now work, and the main victim of this contained it through the internal system, and an investigation was done. I spoke to the investigator and I wrote a statement which was not sent to the decision-maker in that instance, because the perpetrator and his attorneys had worked out a settlement, the terms of which are secret.

SEN. SIMPSON: But you were involved in that in some way?

JUDGE HOERCHNER: I was involved in a very minor way.

SEN. SIMPSON: Well, I am not trying to be sinister. I was just thinking if you were involved in it or you were helping someone else with a sexual harassment charge, either as a counsel or friend, I am wondering why you didn't help your closest friend, Anita Hill, when she was faced with the same information, and why you didn't give her that same counsel, and that is, "Do something."

JUDGE HOERCHNER: You are making an unwarranted assumption.

SEN. SIMPSON: I am not trying to; I am just asking.

JUDGE HOERCHNER: In this more recent situation I did not counsel the person, and as I said, I did try to help Anita. I tried to help her by listening and providing comfort, and apparently there was no comfort to be found.

SEN. SIMPSON: Would you have done it differently now, knowing what you know, than what you did then?

JUDGE HOERCHNER: If I were dealing with Anita at her present age, confidence, professional status, I would consider advising her to do something or say something. To be frank, I don't remember ever giving Anita advice about anything in my life.

SEN. SIMPSON: I thank you, Mr. Chairman.

THE CHAIRMAN: Thank you very much.

I have a few questions, and there are still some more, if you are prepared. Let me ask each of you to answer each of these questions, if you would.

Did Professor Hill ever complain to you that any other employer she had or anyone else other than the nominee had harassed her or had made unwanted sexual advances toward her, had asked her for a date, anything? Can anyone? Let's just go down the list. Judge?

JUDGE HOERCHNER: I will just repeat essentially the same thing that I said the last time I was asked that question. No, she has never complained of that. She was very poised and very capable of brushing off or laughing off unwanted sexual advances. In this situation, in part I am sure because of the great disparity in power, she was not able to successfully do that.

THE CHAIRMAN: Ms. Wells.

MS. WELLS: She has never described to me a situation similar to this or any way remotely similar to this, in terms of a work situation where a supervisor or a superior was making unwelcome advances.

THE CHAIRMAN: Mr. Carr.

MR. CARR: No, Senator.

THE CHAIRMAN: Mr. Paul.

MR. PAUL: No, Senator.

THE CHAIRMAN: Now have any of you ever known, under any circumstances—and you are under oath—has there been any circumstance in your relationship at any time with Professor Hill where you have known her to lie? Judge?

JUDGE HOERCHNER: Absolutely not.

MS. WELLS: Never.

MR. CARR: Never.

MR. PAUL: Absolutely not.

THE CHAIRMAN: And it is an obvious question, but do any of you have any reason to believe, because there have been a lot of notions proffered here as to whether Professor Hill, who has obviously made an impression of sincerity on the committee as well as many other people, is doing anything other than simply telling the truth? Judge Thomas has come across as very forceful and sincere in his denials. Do you have any reason to believe that any of the reasons that have been offered here, raised here, suggested here over the last several days as you have watched this, amount to anything other than she is simply telling the truth and the facts as they occurred? Anyone?

MR. PAUL: Senator, if there were any desire on the part of Professor Hill for some sort of advancement in the profession of legal education, this whole proceeding was not the way to advance her career. She had tremendous opportunities. I feel confident that there were many law schools in this country that would have been happy to have offered Professor Hill a position, prior to this proceeding. She chose to stay where she was because she wanted to be close to her family.

THE CHAIRMAN: Do any of you, anyone else, have any reason? For example, does anybody have any reason to believe—and again, you are under oath—that, as has been suggested by some here, there is a possibility that Professor Hill is fantasizing? Is there anything in her background or character, in any aspect of your relationship with her, that would lead you to believe—and remember, you are under oath—that she is possibly fantasizing about what happened?

MS. WELLS: She is one of the most truthful people that I know. She is not one subject to bouts of fantasy. At best, she might be a little sentimental, but to make up a story, for what purpose? To bring this kind of public exposure to herself, it would not be in character.

MR. CARR: Senator, I certainly would echo that there is absolutely nothing in her character, as I recall, and that the things in her character that I do recall would not support the notion that she would fantasize.

THE CHAIRMAN: What in her character do you recall that would not support the notion that she would fantasize?

MR. CARR: My recollection is that she is a very level-headed and factual person.

THE CHAIRMAN: There has been suggested here the possibility that—and I know this has been raised, but I want it on the record—that she might be so ambitious that although, Professor Paul, she would not be looking to advance her career this way, she might be looking to advance her financial situation by being able to turn this into a book or a movie. That has been suggested by some here. Is there anything in her character that would lead you to believe that is a possibility?

MR. PAUL: Senator, as I said earlier, I believe that the only book Professor Hill has any interest in writing would be a book on the Uniform Commercial Code. She is a private person, as has been testified already. I can't imagine her wanting to reopen this episode. She was so reluctant in her discussions with me. And, moreover, once again going back four years ago in our discussion, there is no conceivable, possible gain or advantage she could have imagined four years ago, in a discussion in a university cafeteria about her coming to work at my university, in telling me then that she left the EEOC because she was sexually harassed by her supervisor.

THE CHAIRMAN: I would like each of you to answer the question.

MR. CARR: I can only imagine that the rationale for wanting to write a book would be fame or money, and I do not think those are significant motivations for Anita Hill. I don't believe she would have made the career choices she has made with the hope of somehow cashing in at some late date in her life. I think if she was motivated by money, she would have made different career choices.

THE CHAIRMAN: Are you a partner in your law firm?

MR. CARR: I am.

THE CHAIRMAN: Without naming your law firm, how large is your law firm?

MR. CARR: About 430 lawyers; about 100 partners.

THE CHAIRMAN: Would Anita Hill have any difficulty getting a job with your law firm?

MR. CARR: Today she might, but I think that is a reference to the economic times, but I have no doubt she would have—I don't think she would have any difficulty getting a job at a major law firm either in New York or in some other city.

THE CHAIRMAN: Ms. Wells, with regard to the question of writing a book, is there anything in her background? Did she ever indicate to you that, "Boy, I saw such-and-such a story, they could turn that into a mini-series," or anything?

MS. WELLS: There is nothing. I wouldn't even be tempted to say that she was particularly romantic in outlook. By that I mean, she is not even the type, as I know her, to want to sit down and talk about the latest best-seller, and get into the characterizations there and talk about how this character appeals to you, as though that individual were real. I don't even think she likes soap operas.

THE CHAIRMAN: Does she enjoy, like some men and women do, gossip?

MS. WELLS: We never gossip. She and I never gossip, so I can't speak to that. I mean, we knew many of the same people, and we never sat around talking about them and gloating over juicy tidbits. That wasn't in her nature.

THE CHAIRMAN: Judge, it has been suggested by some as well, that she may just be a very malleable person. It was clearly suggested yesterday, at least as one possibility, that she had an ideological bent that was inconsistent with the nominee, she felt strongly about that, and that she found herself placed in the hands of interest groups who used her like putty to accomplish this ideological end that she felt was important to accomplish and they felt was important to accomplish.

Is she that malleable a person, or is there anything in her character—and again you are under oath—in your knowledge of her, to indicate to you that she is someone that is that malleable or so inclined?

JUDGE HOERCHNER: Well, as I testified just a moment ago, I have never given her advice, and the reason is that she is so independent and that I respect her judgment so much that I would not presume to advise her. I cannot imagine a force that could take her and use her as a malleable object.

THE CHAIRMAN: I say to my colleagues, I know my time is up, I only have two more questions. It may be useful for me to finish them, if that is all right, and then move on to anyone else who may have questions.

I would like to ask a question of Mr. Carr and Mr. Paul. Mr. Paul, Professor Paul, at the university, did you find her one that was malleable, that shrank from intellectual combat, that was easily able to have her opinions formed? I mean, is there any evidence of that?

MR. PAUL: I would not describe her as shrinking from an argument, no, Senator.

THE CHAIRMAN: How would you describe her?

MR. PAUL: My impression is that she is a very strong person. I think my impression of her is that she feels very deeply about her own being. She has a strong sense of roots, a strong sense of who she is and what she is, perhaps based on her religious upbringing, and she doesn't shrink from anything.

THE CHAIRMAN: Notwithstanding the fact that maybe a more senior professor who is sitting having a discussion on a legal point, she is not the kind who would yield her opinion to an *ad hominem* argument?

MR. PAUL: That is correct, Senator. The summer that she was visiting at our school was the summer of Judge Bork's nomination to the Supreme Court. If you recall, that was a very controversial nomination.

THE CHAIRMAN: I had forgotten that. [Laughter.]

I would like to forget that.

MR. PAUL: Members of my faculty were, I would say, mostly opposed to the nomination, and in defending Judge Bork as she did at that time, she could not have thought she was advancing her opportunities to return to our school. She did so. She did so eloquently. She did so with tremendous force and conviction.

THE CHAIRMAN: Mr. Carr, on the same point, is she strong willed? Is she malleable? Was she someone who yielded to intellectual or any other kind of pressure?

MR. CARR: I would not call her malleable. I don't recall strenuous intellectual debate with her.

THE CHAIRMAN: I guess that wasn't what you had in mind. [Laughter.]

I don't mean that in a bad way. I wasn't trying to be facetious. I mean, there was a different relationship you had. I should drop this. [Laughter.]

SEN. HATCH: Yes, you should drop that.

THE CHAIRMAN: I should drop that part. You understand what I mean. I am being very serious. I mean, was there anything in her character that would lead you to believe that groups or individuals could use her for their advantage, to promote another cause? That is what I am trying to get at because that is what has been raised here. It has been flatly suggested that is what happened.

MR. CARR: I don't believe that that would be possible. My recollections of Anita are that she had some fundamental, basic beliefs about what was right and what was wrong, and I would venture to guess that these kinds of sexual accusations were clearly wrong, and that she was not expedient or willing to subvert or change her views inconsistent with the way they in fact were.

THE CHAIRMAN: I have one last area to cover. Did any of you attend her going-away party that was, we have heard testified to here, at the EEOC when she decided she was going to leave?

MS. WELLS: I attended a going-away party at the Sheraton-Carlton.

THE CHAIRMAN: Was that the going-away party, do you recall? What was the purpose of the going-away party?

MS. WELLS: Well, she was saying good-bye to her friends here.

THE CHAIRMAN: To go to where?

MS. WELLS: To Oral Roberts.

THE CHAIRMAN: To go to Oral Roberts University. Were there anyone else at that party among the four of you?

JUDGE HOERCHNER: No, she did tell me about it later.

THE CHAIRMAN: Do any of you know a Mr. Doggett, John Dog—

JUDGE HOERCHNER: No.

MS. WELLS: No.

MR. CARR: I went to business school with John Doggett, and I would consider him a friend.

THE CHAIRMAN: Do you know, did John Doggett ever indicate to you that he went out with, wanted to go out or thought that Ms. Hill wanted him to go out with her?

MR. CARR: No, I don't.

THE CHAIRMAN: I have no further questions now.

SEN. THURMOND: On our side, I don't believe anyone else except Senator Grassley.

THE CHAIRMAN: Senator Brown?

SEN. BROWN: Senator Specter had none and Senator Brown had none, and the rest of them have none, except Senator Grassley.

SEN. GRASSLEY: Well, maybe it is more of a comment than a question. The lawyers on the committee refer to you folks as corroborating witnesses, and I guess, as I understand it, you are supposed to confirm what Professor Hill has alleged about Judge Thomas. There is no doubt in my mind that you folks are telling the truth, so I don't raise any fault with that, that you are telling us what Professor Hill told you.

But it seems to me that, in this role, you do not confirm any sexual harassment by Judge Thomas of Professor Hill. Of course you couldn't give any details about what Professor Hill says happened to her, because she didn't give you any of these details. I have sat here and listened to you, I haven't heard of any details, so it would be very helpful to us, if you could provide confirmation of details that she discussed Friday.

I also find it surprising that you didn't really offer any advice to her, but Senator Simpson covered that point.

It seems to me that someone as forthright and independent as Professor Hill would have given some details, if they really had them. It just doesn't make sense that she simply told her friends or acquaintances that she was being harassed at work, and that's it, that's it. It just doesn't seem to fit.

I have one question, which does not follow up on that. Senator Specter asked —and I guess I would ask everybody but Mr. Carr this. Senator Specter asked if you would vote for Judge Thomas. I want to know if you want to see Judge Thomas on the Supreme Court. And I would start with you, Judge Hoerchner.

JUDGE HOERCHNER: Senator, I am only here to tell the truth about what I was told back in the early 1980's. You have heard the truth today, and it is up to you to decide what to do with it.

SEN. GRASSLEY: Ellen Wells?

MS. WELLS: I echo what the judge says. I am here to give you this information that I know to be the truth, and for me to sit here and to say what my personal opinions may be about Judge Thomas's qualifications for the Supreme Court, I think would not be appropriate, it would not answer to what I am here for.

SEN. GRASSLEY: Professor Paul?

MR. PAUL: Senator, as a legal scholar and an attorney, I have been asked the question many times prior to these allegations, whether or not Judge Thomas should be confirmed. I did not take a position then, I am not taking a position now. I am simply here to tell the truth about what I was told by Professor Hill four years ago, that she was sexually harassed by her supervisor at the EEOC.

SEN. GRASSLEY: Well, you said you didn't sign the letter. I am kind of puzzled. If you have reason to believe that Judge Thomas is a sexual harasser or guilty of sexual harassment, why wouldn't you sign a letter against him?

MR. PAUL: First of all, Senator, I was asked to sign a letter prior to these allegations. Second of all, Senator, I believe that Professor Hill told me the truth in 1987, but I believe that you, Senator, and the other members of this committee sitting here trying to determine the facts should wait to hear all the evidence, before making a determination.

As I said in response to Senator Simpson's question, if Judge Thomas, in fact, committed the acts alleged, then I don't think he should be confirmed. If he did not commit the acts alleged, I have no position.

SEN. GRASSLEY: I guess maybe I can't go any further and ask you further, if you don't want to answer my questions, but I can at least tell you why I asked. As I understand lawyers, you take an oath to uphold the Constitution in practicing your profession, Professor Paul. You are a student of the Constitution and of the Supreme Court decisions. It seems to me like people in your position ought to have a personal view of whether or not Judge Thomas ought to be on the Supreme Court and that you would welcome an opportunity to express it, and that you would think that, for a nonlawyer like me, it would be important for me to know it to determine whether or not you have got any bias.

MR. PAUL: Senator, I didn't have the opportunity during the original round of hearings to review the record, but if you would like me to review the record, I will be happy to come back and present you with my opinion. [Laughter.]

SEN. GRASSLEY: Mr. Chairman, I have no further questions.

SEN. LEAHY: Mr. Chairman?

THE CHAIRMAN: Senator Leahy.

SEN. LEAHY: Mr. Chairman, I would note, on the question of whether Mr. Paul, because he is a lawyer and has taken an oath as a lawyer, should be able to tell us how to vote on this. There are only 100 people in this country who have taken an oath that requires them to vote on this confirmation, and fourteen of them are here. We are the only ones who must state an opinion. I don't want to leave any kind of impression out there that, simply because somebody is a lawyer, they must have an opinion on whether Judge Thomas goes on the Supreme Court or not. There are only 100 people who have taken the oath of office that requires them to vote on it.

Judge Hoerchner, without going into everybody's testimony, you said you came here to tell the truth and that we should use that truth. None of you said you saw the activity. The nature of the activity is such that nobody would have. But each of you has testified that, years ago, Anita Hill came to you and told you of that. I just remind everybody who is watching these proceedings that corroboration is this: The woman who is sexually harassed is not going to go and tell you people about it, so that some day, nine or ten years later, you would be in this room to tell about it. But you are, and we will use your testimony.

Thank you, Mr. Chairman.

SEN. HATCH: Mr. Chairman?

THE CHAIRMAN: Senator—

SEN. THURMOND: Mr. Chairman, Senator Hatch wants to say something.

THE CHAIRMAN: Senator Hatch.

SEN. HATCH: Let me just ask you, Professor Paul—I have deliberately stayed out of asking any questions, but I have been intrigued—when Professor Hill chatted with you, did she seem upset when she was chatting with you?

MR. PAUL: Yes, Senator.

SEN. HATCH: Bitter?

MR. PAUL: No, I wouldn't describe her as bitter.

SEN. HATCH: But upset?

MR. PAUL: Yes, Senator, she was embarrassed.

SEN. HATCH: And she was not very happy with the person who did this to her, whoever it was?

MR. PAUL: I would hesitate to express an opinion on that, Senator.

SEN. HATCH: Well, how would you appraise her demeanor?

MR. PAUL: I would appraise it by saying that she was embarrassed that I had raised the subject by asking her why she had left the EEOC, and she responded to my direct question, I guess honestly—that is my assessment—and she was embarrassed that I had brought it up.

SEN. HATCH: This was in 1987?

MR. PAUL: Correct, Senator.

SEN. HATCH: Okay. That's all.

SEN. THURMOND: I guess we are through with the panel, Mr. Chairman.

THE CHAIRMAN: No, we're not, we have two over here that wish to ask questions.

SEN. SIMON: Mr. Chairman, if I could have the attention of Senator Specter here, there was a discussion about how many phone calls were made, and he said Ms. Holt's deposition indicates that more than eleven calls were made. If he will look at the deposition, on page 32, line fifteen, the question is asked, "Do you recall any other time that Anita Hill called, where you did not note that on the telephone log? Answer: I don't."

On page 44, line twenty: "You mentioned the Vice Chairman showed you three or maybe more pages. Do you have a recollection of Ms. Anita Hill calling Clarence Thomas any more times than may have sporadically shown up on three such pages? Answer: I would not even guess about that. I don't know."

Thank you, Mr. Chairman.

SEN. SPECTER: Mr. Chairman, I am advised that Ms. Holt will appear as a witness and testify that there were other calls made by Professor Hill. On the first citation where Senator Simon has read the record, which I am having pulled and will review, it was related to recordings which I think referred to occasions when Judge Thomas was not present. But she is up in the next panel, and we will soon see.

SEN. SIMPSON: Mr. Chairman?

THE CHAIRMAN: The Senator from Wyoming.

SEN. SIMPSON: I have one further question of Judge Hoerchner.

THE CHAIRMAN: Excuse me, does the Senator yield?

SEN. KOHL: I yield.

SEN. SIMPSON: Oh, I'm sorry.

THE CHAIRMAN: I apologize. The interruptions—they are not interruptions. The reason that I am occasionally turning around is because of this constant administrative question as to who comes on next and how in timing, and that is why the minority and majority staff, when I turn around, it is not for lack of input from my colleagues questioning.

The Senator from Wyoming.

SEN. SIMPSON: Judge Hoerchner, I asked you if you had ever filed a charge of sexual harassment. I don't think you indicated to me that you had.

JUDGE HOERCHNER: That's correct.

SEN. SIMPSON: I have a record from California, in Norwalk County or Norfolk County, California, that you did file a claim against a fellow judge, a man named Judge Foster. Is that correct?

JUDGE HOERCHNER: I was not sure how far in the proceedings that went. It was my understanding that he had negotiated a settlement. I was told that my statement was never taken up to the home office of our board, so—

SEN. SIMPSON: But you did file a claim of sexual harassment against a fellow judge within your system?

JUDGE HOERCHNER: I cannot say that I didn't. I did not fill out any papers. It's possible that the result of my having spoken to the investigator was taken as filing a claim within our system, and in that case it would be correct.

SEN. SIMPSON: But he did eventually resign and the process of his resignation and the activities around that were rather widely publicized within that county, weren't they?

JUDGE HOERCHNER: The terms of the settlement were secret, were supposed to be secret. I am not aware of the full extent of them.

SEN. SIMPSON: Again, I am interested only in your intent to do those things and you feel strongly about it, and I am wondering why that counsel was not given to your friend.

THE CHAIRMAN: Senator Kohl, did you have—

SEN. KOHL: Yes, just one quick question.

Yesterday, Judge Thomas said that there was a plot afoot in this country to derail his nomination to the Supreme Court. As I hear your comments today, it is obvious to me that if there was a plot afoot, it must have originated ten years ago. So, do you think that Anita Hill plotted for as long as ten years ago to derail Judge Thomas's nomination to the Supreme Court?

JUDGE HOERCHNER: I think that would have been impossible.

MS. WELLS: The same, Senator, that would have been impossible and unthinkable.

MR. CARR: I don't think that is possible.

MR. PAUL: No, Senator, she would be not only deserving of an Academy Award, but she would be a prophet.

SEN. KOHL: But he yesterday did, as you know, if you followed his testimony, he made a very, very big point of stating that what was happening here was that there was a huge plot among Anita Hill and others to see to it that he never achieved his nomination. Are you saying that you regard that sort of an analysis on his part to be almost out of the question?

MS. WELLS: Senator, I would like to point out that the members of this panel met when they walked into this room, so in order for us to have been part of a conspiracy or a plot, we needed to have met one another at some point to get our facts straight and whatever, and we did not have that opportunity.

MR. PAUL: That's correct, Senator.

JUDGE HOERCHNER: That is correct.

MR. CARR: I agree with that.

MR. PAUL: That's correct, Senator, we don't know each other.

SEN. KOHL: You've never met before you met here today?

MR. PAUL: I've never met any of these people before.

MR. CARR: We met yesterday.

JUDGE HOERCHNER: Yesterday, when we walked into the hearing room.

SEN. KOHL: Yesterday was the first time?

MS. WELLS. That's correct.

JUDGE HOERCHNER: Right.

SEN. KOHL: Thank you very much.

Thank you, Mr. Chairman.

THE CHAIRMAN: Mr. Chairman, any other questions?

SEN. THURMOND: No.

THE CHAIRMAN: There being none, I want to thank this panel very, very much. We kept you a long time, over five hours.

We are now going to recess for five minutes, but I want to call the next panel witnesses to come forward while we do this. The next panel will be J.C. Alvarez, Nancy Fitch, Diane Holt and Phyllis Berry-Myers.

We will reconvene in five minutes

[Recess.]

THE CHAIRMAN: Ladies and gentlemen, I thank the panel. I know they had to take a little break while we were taking a break, we had them sitting there so long. Let me indicate what the committee has agreed upon as to how we are going to proceed from now to the moment we end this hearing. And let me reiterate the constraint under which the Senate has placed this committee.

For those who don't know the Senate rules, which are, hopefully, 100 percent of the American people, there has been essentially a motion to recommit here; that is,we have been instructed by the Senate as a whole to take this matter back to the full committee, given a specific time constraint that we report back to the Senate as a whole on this specific issue, the allegation relating to sexual harassment; we have all our testimony in and concluded, so that there are twenty-four hours in which our colleagues can have time to reconsider or consider this matter; and there is a vote scheduled, by unanimous consent of the Senate, to take place at six o'clock on Tuesday night.

What we were taking our time doing a moment ago is deciding on how we were going to specifically accommodate the rights and interests of all the parties, in particular the nominee, and meet the requirement of the Senate. And this is what we have agreed upon, majority and minority.

We are going to proceed tonight with potentially all of the following panels, but with no more than, no one additional other than the people I am about to read. The distinguished panel that sits before us, and has been sitting before us very patiently.

When that panel is finished, there will be a panel that will be made up of up to three people, maybe fewer—made up of David Swank, Kim Taylor, and Sonya Jarvis. It may be fewer than that, but it can be up to those three people.

The next panel after that will be made up of Stanley Grayson, Carlton Stewart, John N. Doggett III, or Charles Kothe, the Dean of Oral Roberts. That is the maximum number of people who will appear on the panel. None of them have to appear. But that is the maximum that can appear.

And then there will be an additional panel of nine individuals, all of whom worked for Clarence Thomas, all women who wish to come and testify to how he related to them: Patricia Johnson, Pamela Talkin—T-a-l-k-i-n, Janet Brown, Ricky Silberman, Connie Newman, Linda Jackson, Nancy Altman, Anna Jenkins, Lori Saxon. They will each have three minutes to make whatever statement they wish to make on behalf of the nominee. There will be thirty-two minutes remaining in the time they will be allowed to be on the stand. Sixteen minutes will be divided on each side for cross-examination, if there is any cross-examination.

Then we will bring forward, if it is the decision of the witness to want to come forward, and that is not fully decided yet, Ms. Angela Wright. We are talking with Ms. Wright now, the committee as a whole, majority and minority. Ms. Angela Wright.

After Ms. Angela Wright there will be, if it is decided by any member of the committee to call this individual, a Ms. Rose Jourdain, who allegedly—I emphasize allegedly—can corroborate the testimony of Angela Wright. Staffs have taken her deposition. It will be reviewed by members of the committee, majority and minority. If the deposition taken by the majority and minority is sufficient, that will suffice. If not, any member can call that individual forward for cross-examination.

We will then end tonight. If that takes till nine, eleven, twelve, or four in the morning, that will be done.

Tomorrow we will reconvene at ten o'clock. Professor Anita Hill will have the right, if she so chooses, to come back at ten a.m. She will be able to testify and/or be cross-examined up until two p.m. Whether or not her statement is finished, whether or not the cross examination is finished, we will politely excuse her. She cannot remain beyond two o'clock.

At two o'clock the nominee, if he so chooses, will come forward. He will be able to say whatever he wishes and/or be cross-examined or examined on direct up until six o'clock.

At 6 o'clock p.m. tomorrow this committee shuts down. Period. There is no requirement, as a matter of fact, we are explicitly asked by the Senate as a whole not to vote on this matter. It will be left to the Senate. This committee has already voted on Clarence Thomas. The transcripts of this committee proceeding will be made available almost immediately to every member of the U.S. Senate. They will have twenty-four hours to make any judgment they wish to make and determine whether or not what has transpired here the previous four days influences their vote one way or another.

Any Senator can go to the Senate floor after six p.m., if the Senate is in, and I don't know whether it is in or not—but if the Senate is in, up until six p.m. on Tuesday, for as long as the Senate is in up to that point, and say anything they want about anything having to do with this matter, whether they wish to go in and say Cock Robin told them the following happened or a little bird dropped in from the blue and gave me this affidavit. But that is not the business of the committee. So, I want to turn to my distinguished colleague from South Carolina and ask him whether or not what I related is in fact what the majority, overwhelming majority of the committee voted to do?

SEN. THURMOND: Mr. Chairman, I think you have stated it correctly. The only thing, if you wish to bring Ms. Wright here, you have that right. And we will have a chance to cross-examine her.

THE CHAIRMAN: That is absolutely correct.

SEN. THURMOND: But we object to any statement by her, or affidavit, being put in the record without cross-examination.

THE CHAIRMAN: That is absolutely correct. No affidavits at all will be placed in this record from now until the time the committee completes its responsibility. Is there anyone on the committee that has heard what I have said that disagrees with what I laid out as being the majority will of the committee?

SEN. SIMPSON: Mr. Chairman?

THE CHAIRMAN: Yes?

SEN. SIMPSON: I believe there was one further addendum. That there would be no closing statements.

THE CHAIRMAN: That is correct. There will be no closing statements by any member on the committee.

SEN. SPECTER: Mr. Chairman?

THE CHAIRMAN: The Senator from Pennsylvania?

SEN. SPECTER: I would just like the record to note my dissent.

THE CHAIRMAN: The record will note the dissent of the distinguished Senator from Pennsylvania as to the manner in which we have otherwise I believe unanimously—

SEN. BROWN: Mr. Chairman?

THE CHAIRMAN: Yes?

SEN. BROWN: I would also like my dissent noted.

THE CHAIRMAN: Dissent as to all of it or—well, never mind. It doesn't matter. Senator, I don't mean that flippantly. I mean it is not worth going back into—

SEN. BROWN: Sure.

THE CHAIRMAN: The committee voted twelve to two to proceed as I have outlined, with the dissents noted. Obviously, everyone else other than Senator Specter and Senator Brown, voted affirmatively to proceed as I have stated.

Now, thank you all for your patience. That is the unanimous consent agreement that has just been agreed to. Ladies and gentlemen, let us proceed.

I thank this panel for their absolute patience here. You have been very gracious. And there will be no dinner break, I say to our friends in the press. There will be no break, other than occasionally requiring, if the witnesses are here longer than their constitutions would warrant, we will break for that purpose.

And I say to the panel, if you have any preferred order of proceeding—why don't we begin by first swearing you all in?

Do you all swear the testimony you are about to give is the truth and the whole truth, so help you, God.

MS. ALVAREZ: I do.

MS. FITCH: I do.

MS. HOLT: I do.

MS. BERRY: I do.

THE CHAIRMAN: I was just, as usual, properly corrected by my colleague. I should have said instead of the truth and the whole truth, the truth and nothing but the truth. But we understand what you all just swore to.

Now, why don't we begin then, if you have no preferred order, with Ms. Alvarez and work our way across. Or either way. Do you have a preference? There being none, we will start with Ms. Alvarez. And welcome back. I know you were here, it seems like 100 years ago, but not too long ago.

I have been instructed by my colleague from South Carolina to ask you if you can keep your statements to three minutes because there is going to be a lot of questions of you.

SEN. THURMOND: Well, Mr. Chairman, that was your—I think that it was agreed that there would be a three-minute limit.

THE CHAIRMAN: I think that is correct. Five minutes.

SEN. THURMOND: That was the last panel. Excuse me. I was in error on that.

THE CHAIRMAN: Keep your statements to five minutes, if you would, and then we will begin the questions.

MS. ALVAREZ: I will do the best I can.

THE CHAIRMAN: Thank you very, very much.

TESTIMONY OF A PANEL CONSISTING OF:
J.C. ALVAREZ, River North Distributing, Chicago, Illinois
NANCY E. FITCH, Philadelphia, Pennsylvania
DIANE HOLT, Management Analyst, Office of the Chairman, Equal Employment Opportunity Commission, Washington, DC
PHYLLIS BERRY-MYERS, Alexandria, Virginia

TESTIMONY OF J.C. ALVAREZ

MS. ALVAREZ: My name is J.C. Alvarez. I am a businesswoman from Chicago. I am a single mom, raising a fifteen-year-old son, running a business. In many ways, I am just a John Q. Public from Middle America, not unlike a lot of the people watching out there and not unlike a lot of your constituents. But the political world is not a world that I am unfamiliar with. I spent nine years in Washington, DC. A year with Senator Danforth, two years with the Secretary of Education, a short stint at the Federal Emergency Management Agency, and four years as Special Assistant to Clarence Thomas at the EEOC.

Because of this past political experience, I was just before this committee a couple of weeks ago speaking in support of Clarence Thomas's nomination to the Supreme Court. I was then and I still am in favor of Clarence Thomas being on the Supreme Court.

When I was asked to testify the last time, I flew to Washington, DC, very proud and happy to be part of the process of nominating a Supreme Court Justice. When I was sitting here before you last time, I remember why I had liked working in Washington, DC, so much—the intellectual part of it, the high quality of the debate. Although I have to admit when I had to listen to some of your questioning and postulating and politicking, I remembered why I had left. And I thought at that point that certainly I had seen it all.

After the hearings, I flew back to Chicago, back to being John Q. Public, having a life very far removed from this political world and it would have been easy to stay away from politics in Washington, DC. Like most of your constituents out there, I have more than my share of day-to-day challenges that have nothing to do with Washington, DC, and politics. As I said before, I am a single mom, raising a teenager in today's society, running a business, making ends meet—you know, soccer games, homework, doing laundry, paying bills, that is my day-to-day reality. Since I left Washington, DC, I vote once every four years for President and more frequently for other state and local officials. And I could have remained outside of the political world for a long, long time and not missed it. I don't need this. I needed to come here like I needed a hole in the head. It cost me almost $900 just for the plane ticket to come here, and then there is the hotel and other expenses. And I can assure you that especially in these recessionary times I have got lots of other uses for that money.

So why did I come? Why didn't I just stay uninvolved and apolitical? Because, Senators, like most real Americans who witness a crime being committed, who witness an injustice being done, I could not look the other way and pretend that I did not see it. I had to get involved.

In my real life, I have walked down the street and seen a man beating up a woman and I have stepped in and tried to stop it. I have walked through a park and seen a group of teenage hoodlums taunting an old drunk man and I have jumped in the middle of it. I don't consider myself a hero. No, I am just a real American from Middle America who will not stand by and watch a crime being committed and walk away. To do so would be the beginning of the deterioration of society and of this great country. No, Senators, I cannot stand by and watch a group of thugs beat up and rob a man of his money any more than I could have stayed in Chicago and stood by and watched you beat up an innocent man and rob him blind. Not of his money. That would have been too easy. You could pay that back. No, you have robbed a man of his name, his character, and his reputation.

And what is amazing to me is that you didn't do it in a dark alley and you didn't do it in the dark of night. You did it in broad daylight, in front of all America, on television, for the whole world to see. Yes, Senators, I am witnessing a crime in progress and I cannot just look the other way. Because I am John Q. Public and I am getting involved.

I know Clarence Thomas and I know Anita Hill. I was there from the first few weeks of Clarence coming to the Commission. I had the office next to Anita's. We all worked together in setting and executing the goals and the direction that the chairman had for the EEOC. I remember Chris Roggerson, Carlton Stewart, Nancy Fitch, Barbara Parris, Phyllis Berry, Bill Ng, Allyson Duncan, Diane Holt —each of us with our own area of expertise and responsibility, but together all of us a part of Clarence Thomas's hand-picked staff.

I don't know how else to say it but I have to tell you that it just blew my mind to see Anita Hill testifying on Friday. Honest to goodness, it was like schizophrenia. That was not the Anita Hill that I knew and worked with at EEOC. On Friday, she played the role of a meek, innocent, shy Baptist girl from the South who was a victim of this big, bad man.

I don't know who she was trying to kid. Because the Anita Hill that I knew and worked with was nothing like that. She was a very hard, tough woman. She was opinionated. She was arrogant. She was a relentless debater. And she was the kind of woman who always made you feel like she was not going to be messed with, like she was not going to take anything from anyone. She was aloof. She always acted as if she was a little bit superior to everyone, a little holier than thou. I can recall at the time that she had a view of herself and her abilities that did not seem to be based in reality. For example, it was sort of common knowledge around the office that she thought she should have been Clarence's chief legal advisor and that she should have received better assignments.

And I distinctly remember when I would hear about her feeling that way or when I would see her pout in office meetings about assignments that she had gotten, I used to think to myself, "Come on, Anita, let's come down to Earth and live in reality." She had only been out of law school a couple of years and her experience and her ability couldn't begin to compare with some of the others on the staff. But I also have to say that I was not totally surprised at her wanting these assignments because she definitely came across as someone who was ambitious and watched out for her own advancement. She wasn't really a team player, but more someone who looked out for herself first. You could see the same thing in her relationships with others at the office.

SEN. KENNEDY: [presiding]. Excuse me. Ms. Alvarez, we had the five minutes, you know, for the other panel. But we have very extensive questionings. I don't want to cut you off when you have been waiting a long time.

MS. ALVAREZ: Well, Senator, if you would just give me a few more minutes.

SEN. THURMOND: Mr. Chairman, I would like to make a statement. The other panel has been on all day long. This is a panel in reverse now. And the only limitation was the nine, number nine, for one hour, and that is the last panel to come on.

I object to cutting these people off. They are entitled to speak.

SEN. LEAHY: Mr. Chairman, we made an agreement just about ten minutes ago and it is already being broken. Let's stick to the agreement.

SEN. THURMOND: There is no agreement on this panel at all. It was the last panel of nine people that we agreed to take one hour on and no more. This panel is answering the first panel that has been on here for hours and hours, and they are entitled to speak, and we are going to contend for it.

SEN. KENNEDY: Well, I think the record will show that there were as many questions focused on the other panel from that side as it was from this side. I distinctly heard the chairman say that they were going to be five minutes and then it is unlimited.

SEN. THURMOND: Well, he suggested five minutes.

SEN. KENNEDY: All right. Let's make it seven.

SEN. THURMOND: No, we don't want to limit them.

SEN. KENNEDY: Let's make it seven.

SEN. THURMOND: You didn't limit this morning. You didn't limit all day long. They were in Ms. Hill's favor. Here are some in Judge Thomas's favor. They are entitled to speak.

SEN. HATCH: And they read their full statements, the last panel.

SEN. KENNEDY: I will ask the clerk to read back what Chairman Biden said about this panel.

SEN. THURMOND: Well, send it to Chairman Biden.

SEN. KENNEDY: I will ask the clerk to read back what was agreed to.

SEN. THURMOND: There was no agreement.

SEN. LEAHY: It was agreed to.

SEN. THURMOND: He just said he suggested five minutes.

SEN. SIMPSON: Mr. Chairman? Mr. Chairman?

SEN. KENNEDY: Go ahead, Ms. Alvarez. Continue.

SEN. SIMPSON: Mr. Chairman, if I—

SEN. KENNEDY: Ms. Alvarez is going to continue.

SEN. SIMPSON: Mr. Chairman, if I could, I think we all concurred on the one panel with three minutes and that is separate and apart from this.

SEN. THURMOND: The last panel.

SEN. SIMPSON: And this is the regular panel and the regular time that we did this morning with the other group. And we just ask for the same courtesies here.

SEN. KENNEDY: That is exactly, the Senator has stated, whatever time was given to the earlier panel ought to be given to this panel.

I am glad the Chair is back. [Laughter.]

Good to see you, Joe.

THE CHAIRMAN: [presiding]. Please go on.

MS. ALVAREZ: If I could finish.

THE CHAIRMAN: I know I don't know, and I don't want it repeated. Did you all settle it? Are we all square?

MS. ALVAREZ: It is settled. I am going to finish.

THE CHAIRMAN: There is no limit on this panel. What is the motion?

SEN. THURMOND: There is no motion at all. Just let them speak till they get through.

THE CHAIRMAN: Speak.

MS. ALVAREZ:. Please. I made an awful lot of effort to come here. I would like to just finish saying what I have to say.

THE CHAIRMAN: Yes. You go right ahead.

MS. ALVAREZ: You could see that Anita Hill was not a real team player, but more someone who looked out for herself. You could see this even in her relationships with others at the office. She mostly kept to herself, although she would occasionally participate in some of the girl-talk among the women at the office, and I have to add that I don't recall her being particularly shy or innocent about that either.

You see, Senators, that was the Anita Hill that we all knew and we worked with. And that is why hearing her on Friday was so shocking. No, not shocking. It was so sickening. Trust me, the Anita Hill I knew and worked with was a totally different personality from the Anita Hill I heard on Friday. The Anita Hill I knew before was nobody's victim.

The Clarence Thomas I knew and worked with was also not who Anita Hill alleges. Everyone who knows Clarence, knows that he is a very proud and dignified man. With his immediate staff, he was very warm and friendly, sort of like a friend or a father. You could talk with him about your problems, go to him for advice, but, like a father, he commanded and he demanded respect. He demanded professionalism and performance, and he was very strict about that.

Because we were friends outside of the office or perhaps in private, I might have called him Clarence, but in the office he was Mr. Chairman. You didn't joke around with him, you didn't lose your respect for him, you didn't become too familiar with him, because he would definitely let you know that you had crossed the line.

Clarence was meticulous about being sure that he retained a very serious and professional atmosphere within his office, without the slightest hint of impropriety, and everyone knew it.

We weren't a coffee-klatching group. We didn't have office parties or Christmas parties, because Clarence didn't think it was appropriate for us to give others the impression that we were not serious or professional or perhaps working as hard as everyone else. He wanted to maintain a dignity about his office and his every behavior and action confirmed that.

As his professional colleague, I traveled with him, had lunch and dinner with him, worked with him, one on one and with others. Never did he ever lose his respect for me, and never did we ever have a discussion of the type that Ms. Hill alleges. Never was he the slightest bit improper in his behavior with me. In every situation I have shared with Clarence Thomas, he has been the ultimate professional and he has required it of those around him, in particular, his personal staff.

From the moment they surfaced, I thought long and hard about these allegations. You see, I, too, have experienced sexual harassment in the past. I have been physically accosted by a man in an elevator who I rebuffed. I was trapped in a xerox room by a man who I refused to date. Obviously, it is an issue I have experienced, I understand, and I take very seriously.

But having lived through it myself, I find Anita Hill's behavior inconsistent with these charges. I can assure you that when I come into town, the last thing I want to do is call either of these two men up and say hello or see if they want to get together.

To be honest with you, I can hardly remember their names, but I can assure you that I would never try and even maintain a cordial relationship with either one of them. Women who have really been harassed would agree, if the allegations were true, you put as much distance as you can between yourself and that other person.

What's more, you don't follow them to the next job—especially, if you are a black female, Yale Law School graduate. Let's face it, out in the corporate sector, companies are fighting for women with those kinds of credentials. Her behavior just isn't consistent with the behavior of a woman who has been harassed, and it just doesn't make sense.

Senators, I don't know what else to say to have you understand the crime that has been committed here. It has to make all of us suspicious of her motives, when someone of her legal background comes in here at the eleventh hour, after ten years, and having had four other opportunities through congressional hearings to oppose this man, and alleges such preposterous things.

I have been contacted by I think every reporter in the country looking for dirt. And when I present the facts as I experienced them, it is interesting, they don't print it. It's just not as juicy as her amazing allegations.

What is this country coming to, when an innocent man can be ambushed like this, jumped by a gang whose ringleader is one of his own proteges, Anita Hill? Like Julius Caesar, he must want to turn to her and say, "Et tu, Brutus? You too,

Anita?"

As a mother with a child, I can only begin to imagine how Clarence must feel, being betrayed by one of his own. Nothing would hurt me more. And I guess he described it best in his opening statement on Friday. His words and his emotions are still ringing in all of our ears and all of our hearts.

I have done the best I could, Senators, to be honest in my statement to you. I have presented the situation as it was then, as I lived it, side by side, with Clarence and with Anita.

You know, I talked with my mom before I came here, and she reminded me that I was always raised to stand up for what I believed. I have seen an innocent man being mugged in broad daylight, and I have not looked the other way. This John Q. Public came here and got involved.

SEN. KENNEDY: [presiding]. Ms. Fitch.

TESTIMONY OF NANCY E. FITCH

MS. FITCH: Mr. Chairman, Senator Thurmond, members of the committee: My name is Dr. Nancy Elizabeth Fitch. I have a BA in English literature and political science from Oakland University, which was part of Michigan State University at the time—

SEN. THURMOND: Would you please pull the microphone closer to you, so that the people in the back can hear you.

MS. FITCH: [continuing] —and a Masters and Ph.D. in history from the University of Michigan in Ann Arbor. I have taught at Sangamon State University in Illinois, was a social science research analyst for the Congressional Research Service of the Library of Congress, have been a special assistant and historian to the then-Chairman of the U.S. Equal Employment Opportunity Commission, Clarence Thomas, an assistant professor of history at Lynchburg College in Virginia, and presently assistant professor of African-American Studies at Temple University, in Philadelphia.

From 1982 to 1989 I worked as a special assistant historian to then-Chairman Clarence Thomas of the U.S. Equal Employment Opportunity Commission. I worked for and with him seven years and have known him for nine. I researched the history of African-Americans, people of color and women and their relationship to issues, including employment, education and training. These were used for background on speeches, special emphasis programming at the Commission and for policy position papers.

I reported only to Judge Thomas, and my responsibilities also included outreach efforts to local colleges and universities and to the DC public schools. Judge Thomas was interested in his staff and himself being mentors and role models, especially, but not only to young people of color.

In these nine years, I have known Clarence Thomas to be a person of great integrity, morally upstanding, professional, a decent person, an exemplary boss. Those years spent in his employ as a Schedule C employee, a political appointee, were the most rewarding of my work life to that time. My returning to higher education I attribute to his persuading me to return to what I loved, not continuing as a bureaucrat, but returning to teaching.

I would like to say Judge Thomas, besides being a person of great moral character, I found to be a most intelligent man. Senator Biden was correct yesterday, when he indicated that the Republican side of the panel might have overlooked its easiest defense, that of dealing with the judge's intelligence.

If these allegations, which I believe to be completely unfounded and vigorously believe unfounded, were true, we would be dealing not only with venality, but with abject stupidity with a person shooting himself in the foot, having given someone else the gun to use at any time.

There is no way Clarence Thomas—C.T.—would callously venally hurt someone. A smart man, concerned about making a contribution to this country as a public official, recognizing the gravity and weightiness of his responsibilities and public trust, a role model and mentor who would, by his life and work, show the possibilities in America for all citizens given opportunity, well, would a person such as this, Judge Clarence Thomas would never ever make a parallel career in harassment, ask that it not be revealed and expect to have and keep his real career. And I know he did no such thing.

He is a dignified, reserved, deliberative, conscientious man of great conscience, and I am proud to be at his defense.

As I told the FBI agent who interviewed me on Tuesday, October 1, I trust Judge Thomas completely, he has all of my support and caring earned by nine years of the most positive and affirmative interacting, not only with me, but with other staff and former staff, men and women, and I know he will get back his good name.

Thank you.

SEN. KENNEDY: Thank you very much.

Ms. Holt.

TESTIMONY OF DIANE HOLT

MS. HOLT: Mr. Chairman, Senator Thurmond, and members of this committee: My name is Diane Holt. I am a management analyst in the Office of the chairman of the Equal Employment Opportunity Commission.

I have known Clarence Thomas for over ten years. For six of those years, I worked very closely with him, cheek to cheek, shoulder to shoulder, as his personal secretary. My acquaintance with Judge Thomas began in May 1981, after he had been appointed as Assistant Secretary for Civil Rights at the Department of Education.

I had been the personal secretary to the outgoing Assistant Secretary for several years. Upon Judge Thomas's arrival at the Department, he held a meeting with me, in which he indicated that he was not committed to bringing a secretary with him, and had no wish to displace me. Because he was not familiar with my qualifications, he made no guarantees, but gave me an opportunity to prove myself.

That is the kind of man he is.

In May 1982, Judge Thomas asked me to go to the EEOC with him, where I worked as his secretary until September 1987.

I met Professor Hill in the summer of 1981, when she came to work at the Department of Education as attorney adviser to Judge Thomas.

After about a year, Judge Thomas was nominated to be chairman of the EEOC. He asked both Professor Hill and myself to transfer with him.

Both Ms. Hill and I were excited about the prospect of transferring to the EEOC. We even discussed the greater potential for individual growth at this larger agency. We discussed and expressed excitement that we would be at the right hand of the individual who would run this agency.

When we arrived at the EEOC, because we knew no one else there, Professor Hill and I quickly developed a professional relationship, a professional friendship, often having lunch together.

At no time did Professor Hill intimate, not even in the most subtle of ways, that Judge Thomas was asking her out or subjecting her to the crude, abusive conversations that have been described. Nor did I ever discern any discomfort, when Professor Hill was in Judge Thomas's presence.

Additionally, I never heard anyone at any time make any reference to any inappropriate conduct in relation to Clarence Thomas.

The Clarence Thomas that I know has always been a motivator of staff, always encouraging others to grow professionally. I personally have benefited from that encouragement and that motivation.

In sum, the Chairman Thomas that I have known for ten years is absolutely incapable of the abuses described by Professor Hill.

SEN. KENNEDY: Thank you very much.

Ms. Berry-Myers?

TESTIMONY OF PHYLLIS BERRY-MYERS

MS. BERRY: You can call me Phyllis Berry, since that was my name that I used throughout my professional life, and that's probably what most people are going to refer to me as.

Mr. Chairman, Senator Thurmond and members of the committee, I am Phyllis Berry.

I know and have worked with both Clarence Thomas and Anita Hill. I have known Judge Thomas since 1979, and Anita Hill since 1982. Once Clarence Thomas was confirmed as the chairman of the Equal Employment Opportunity Commission and had assumed his duties there, he asked me to come and work with him at the Commission.

I joined his staff as a special assistant in June of 1982. At the Commission, Chairman Thomas asked that I assume responsibility for three areas: I was to, one, assist in assessing and reorganizing his personal staff, scheduling, speech writing, and those kinds of things; two, to assist in professionalizing the Office of Congressional Affairs, as that office was called then; and, three, assist in reorganizing the Office of Public Affairs, as that office was called then.

Anita Hill was already a member of Clarence Thomas's staff when I joined the Commission.

There are several points to be made:

One, many of the areas of responsibilities that I had been asked to oversee were areas that Anita Hill handled, particularly congressional affairs and public relations. We, therefore, had to work together. Chris Roggerson was the director of Congressional Affairs at that time, and Anita Hill worked more under his supervision than Clarence Thomas's.

Two, Clarence Thomas's behavior toward Anita Hill was no more, no less than his behavior toward the rest of his staff. He was respectful, demanding of excellence in our work, cordial, professional, interested in our lives and our career ambitions.

Three, Anita Hill indicated to me that she had been a primary advisor to Clarence Thomas at the Department of Education. However, she seemed to be having a difficult time on his EEOC staff, of being considered as one of many, especially on a staff where others were as equally or more talented than she.

Four, Anita Hill often acted as though she had a right to immediate direct access to Mr. Chairman. Such access was not always immediately available. I felt she was particularly distressed when Allyson Duncan became chief of staff and her direct access to the chairman was even more limited.

Five, I cannot remember anyone, except perhaps Diane Holt, who was regarded as personally close to Anita. She was considered by most of us as somewhat aloof.

In addition, I would like to make these comments:

In her press conference on October 7, 1991, Anita Hill indicated that she did not know me and I did not know her. However, in her testimony before this committee, she affirmed that not only did we know one another, but that we enjoyed a friendly, professional relationship.

Also, she testified that I had the opportunity to observe and did observe her interaction with Clarence Thomas at the office.

Two, I served at the Department of Education at the same time that Anita Hill and Clarence Thomas were there. One aspect of my job was to assist with the placement of personnel at the department, particularly Schedule C and other excepted service appointments, such as Schedule A appointments.

Excepted Service means those positions in Federal civil service excepted from the normal competitive requirements that are authorized by law, Executive order or regulation.

The Schedule C hiring authority is the means by which political appointees are hired. The Schedule A hiring authority is the means by which attorneys, teachers in overseas dependent school systems, drug enforcement agents in undercover work, et cetera, are hired.

The office that I worked in was also responsible for reviewing any hiring that the department's political appointees made under the excepted service hiring authority. Therefore, in that capacity, I was aware of any excepted service hiring decisions made in the Office of Civil Rights, and that is the office that Clarence Thomas headed at that time, and Anita Hill was hired in that office as a Schedule A employee.

Federal personnel processing procedures require a lot of specific knowledge and a lot of paperwork, and I do not profess to be a Federal personnel expert. But I can attest to the procedures required by our office and the Office of Personnel at the Department of Education at that time.

At the end of such procedures, a new employee would have no doubt whatsoever regarding their status, their grade, their pay, their benefits, their promotion rights, employment rights and obligation as a Federal employee and as an employee in the department.

A new employee would know whether their employment is classified as permanent or temporary, protected or nonprotected, and those kinds of things. Each new employee must sign a form that contains such information, before employment can begin.

The Personnel Department at the Department of Education is a fine one, and it takes pride in thoroughly counseling new employees.

SEN. HATCH: Let me start with you, Ms. Holt. You were here in what we would call, in a true trial, in the capacity of really a personal witness as well as a custodial witness. You can help us, it seems to me, figure out the significance and relevance of the telephone log records of the messages received by Clarence Thomas.

Also, since the testimony of Anita Hill on Friday, the issue of whether Professor Hill's telephone calls to Judge Thomas might in fact have been telephone calls to you has been interjected, because she indicated some of them were just calls to you. Is that so?

MS. HOLT: She did call me on occasion.

SEN. HATCH: Are they ones you have listed in these logs?

MS. HOLT: They are not, no.

SEN. HATCH: They are not?

MS. HOLT: No.

SEN. HATCH: And this is your handwriting on these logs, primarily?

MS. HOLT: Primarily.

SEN. HATCH: With regard to these phone calls involving Anita Hill?

MS. HOLT: Right.

SEN. HATCH: Each and every one of them?

MS. HOLT: Each and every call? No.

SEN. HATCH: But I am talking about the ones involving Anita Hill only.

MS. HOLT: That is what I am saying. No, there is one call on here that—

SEN. HATCH: Well, we will go through it. Yes, one call, but all the others are your handwriting.

MS. HOLT: Right.

SEN. HATCH: Now there are ten messages recorded by you in the telephone log book which I had entered into the record yesterday. Now do these represent all of the times that Anita Hill called or might have called Judge Thomas during the seven years that you worked for Judge Thomas?

MS. HOLT: There were other times she called and he was available to take the call, which would mean that there was no indication in the phone log.

SEN. HATCH: So there were a number of other times besides the at least ten that you wrote down, mentioned in these logs?

MS. HOLT: Right.

SEN. HATCH: Were they frequent or were they just sporadic?

MS. HOLT: They were sporadic.

SEN. HATCH: But they were more than one, two, three? Could you give us an estimate?

MS. HOLT: I would say maybe another five or six.

SEN. HATCH: Another five or six, so at least fifteen or sixteen calls that you received over these years, during the seven years you worked for Judge Thomas. Is that right?

MS. HOLT: Right.

SEN. HATCH: Were these always cordial calls?

MS. HOLT: They were always cordial.

SEN. HATCH: Was her voice always basically the same? Was it friendly?

MS. HOLT: It was always friendly.

SEN. HATCH: Okay. If she called and Judge Thomas were in and available to take the call, that would be put through on most occasions, right?

MS. HOLT: It would be put through.

SEN. HATCH: That you wouldn't write down?

MS. HOLT: I'm sorry?

SEN. HATCH: You would not write those calls down?

MS. HOLT: I would not write that down, no.

SEN. HATCH: Okay. Now as you have said, these ten calls are in your handwriting. So is there any other reason to dispute their correctness?

MS. HOLT: No, sir.

SEN. HATCH: Are you sure of their correctness?

MS. HOLT: I am, sir.

SEN. HATCH: As I mentioned, Professor Hill spoke of you this last Friday as a friend and, you know, attempts to diminish the significance of these messages, it seems to me, were made by her, at least at the one press conference, by claiming that many were calls placed to you and not to Judge Thomas, or Clarence Thomas at the time; that the messages to Judge Thomas were only accidental developments from her conversations with you. Have you heard that?

MS. HOLT: I heard that, yes.

SEN. HATCH: Is that true?

MS. HOLT: That is not true. Had Anita Hill called me and even asked that I pass on a hello to Judge Thomas, I would have done just that, but it would not have been an official message in his phone log.

SEN. HATCH: I see. Now I know it is a long time ago, but can you recall any tension or strain in her voice during any of these calls that she made to you and through you to Judge Thomas?

MS. HOLT: Never.

SEN. HATCH: So these particular questions that she would leave with you, or these particular statements that she made with you, they were basically unremarkable as far as any emotion or any other—

MS. HOLT: They were unremarkable to me.

SEN. HATCH: And they were all friendly?

MS. HOLT: They were all friendly.

SEN. HATCH: And they were all friendly toward Judge Thomas?

MS. HOLT: They were.

SEN. HATCH: Did you sense any animosity or any hostility or any aggravation or—

MS. HOLT: Never.

SEN. HATCH: Never. Is that true during the whole time that you knew her while she worked there?

MS. HOLT: That is true of the entire time.

SEN. HATCH: You were the gatekeeper, weren't you?

MS. HOLT: I was, yes.

SEN. HATCH: Nobody could get in or out without you?

MS. HOLT: If I was there, that is true.

SEN. HATCH: I bet you were a good one. I bet you were a good one.

Now I would like you to go back even further, to the time when all three of you worked at the EEOC. After any meeting or lunch between Anita Hill and Clarence Thomas, did you ever notice anything about Ms. Hill—or Professor Hill, excuse me—and her behavior, her moods or simply the way she looked, that ever led you to believe that anything unusual had really taken place between her and Clarence Thomas?

MS. HOLT: No, never.

SEN. HATCH: Never once?

MS. HOLT: I never noticed anything.

SEN. HATCH: Is it fair to say that their relationship was entirely professional?

MS. HOLT: I would say that, yes.

SEN. HATCH: How about the rest of you? Consider the same questions. Is there anything that would have indicated to you that the relationship was anything less than entirely professional? Ms. Alvarez?

MS. ALVAREZ: No, sir. They always appeared to be very professional with one another. That was the way Clarence demanded it.

SEN. HATCH: Ms. Fitch?

MS. FITCH: Always professional. The times that Anita Hill and I went out together, and that might be no more than three times in a little over a year's period, we would leave work and we were talking about the job, talking about him, felt that he was going places and wanted to make sure that we, as his personal staff, were in the position to help him do what he needed to do to get there, so no.

SEN. HATCH: Ms. Berry-Myers?

MS. BERRY: I don't remember any time them having anything that was more than professional, cordial, friendly. She always indicated that she admired and respected the man.

SEN. HATCH: Always?

MS. BERRY: Always.

SEN. HATCH: Right up to the day she left to go to Roberts University?

MS. BERRY: To my knowledge, yes.

SEN. HATCH: Now, Ms. Holt, in your opinion, or any of the others of you, is there any other person in the EEOC or any other person in this country who might have been in a better position to know whether or not Clarence Thomas and Anita Hill had anything other than a strictly professional relationship?

MS. BERRY: I don't think anyone could say that they had anything other than the professional relationship.

SEN. HATCH: Now, Ms. Holt, as I read this log, there are four messages in 1984, five messages in 1985, and then only one message in 1986, and then one in 1987, and then there follows a more than three-year gap without any messages. What is the last message before that three-year gap, in fact, the last message in the log book itself? What is the message of August 4, 1987?

MS. BERRY: On August 4?

SEN. HATCH: 1987.

MS. HOLT: "Anita Hill. In town until 8:15. Wanted to congratulate you on marriage."

SEN. HATCH: So for each of the years there were a number of calls that you have in the log here, and there were a number of calls outside of the log—

MS. HOLT: Right.

SEN. HATCH: [continuing] —that were passed through because he was there, but the log calls stop in August of 1987. Is that correct?

MS. HOLT: As far as I know.

SEN. HATCH: Were there any other calls made after that, other than the two for law schools?

MS. HOLT: I left the chairman's office in September, immediately after that.

SEN. HATCH: Okay. Well, as of that date in August of 1987, what was the message that was in that log?

MS. HOLT: I'm sorry, Senator?

SEN. HATCH: As of the date that I mentioned, on August 4, 1987, in your handwriting, what is the message that was left by Anita Hill?

MS. HOLT: On August 4?

SEN. HATCH: Yes.

MS. HOLT: "In town until 8:15. Wanted to congratulate you on marriage."

SEN. HATCH: And to your knowledge, that was the last one that you ever took, then?

MS. HOLT: To my knowledge, yes.

SEN. HATCH: Now you have independent knowledge, do you not, of Anita Hill's job title while at the Office of Civil Rights. Is that correct?

MS. HOLT: Right. She was attorney-advisor.

SEN. HATCH: She was an attorney-advisor?

MS. HOLT: Yes.

SEN. HATCH: Now do you know how that position is classified by the government?

MS. HOLT: Right. I know it is a Schedule A position.

SEN. HATCH: Schedule A. What does that mean?

MS. HOLT: It means that it doesn't have to go through the normal competitive process.

SEN. HATCH: It means that job is permanent, doesn't it?

MS. HOLT: Right.

SEN. HATCH: In other words, even though she may not be able to keep that first assistant to the—

MS. HOLT: Assistant Secretary.

SEN. HATCH: [continuing] —the secretary that she had with Clarence Thomas, she would be able to go in any other area as an attorney-advisor.

MS. HOLT: And even if Clarence Thomas's replacement had not wanted to keep her as his attorney-advisor, he could have placed her someplace else within the agency.

SEN. HATCH: Now she told this committee that she felt like she had to go along with Chairman Thomas over to the EEOC, if I recall this correctly—you correct me, if you saw it—but that she was afraid that she might not have a job. Do you think—

MS. HOLT: To my knowledge, I mean, she never asked me what her options were. I didn't think there was any indecision on her part. We were both enthusiastic about going to EEOC.

SEN. HATCH: She was enthusiastic?

MS. HOLT: She was.

SEN. HATCH: Well, wasn't that, though, because she wanted to serve in this particularly stronger civil rights area?

MS. HOLT: We discussed that this man was a rising star and we wanted to be there with him.

SEN. HATCH: But wasn't that just you feeling that way?

MS. HOLT: No, that was her feeling that way also.

SEN. HATCH: That he was a rising star, and that she wanted to be part of that rising—

MS. HOLT: We both wanted to be a part of that.

SEN. HATCH: You did, too?

MS. HOLT: Yes.

SEN. HATCH: I understand you because you have expressed your loyalty and your feelings toward Chairman Thomas, Judge Thomas now, but you are sure that that is the way she felt?

MS. HOLT: I am sure.

SEN. HATCH: You took her to lunch; you two went to lunch on a regular basis, didn't you?

MS. HOLT: We did.

SEN. HATCH: I mean, you knew each other real well. You went many times, didn't you?

MS. HOLT: We went to lunch often.

SEN. HATCH: Quite often. Well, what did you and Professor Hill like to talk about? Any particular subject or conversation that is more prominent in your memory than any other? And if you could kind of tie it into—

MS. HOLT: There was never any particular subject. We talked about men. We didn't talk about sex in any vivid sense, but we talked about it in a very general sense, as indeed many of my women friends and I do.

SEN. HATCH: Another other particular—

MS. HOLT: We talked about work, and we talked about what she did on the weekend or what I did on the weekend, just general conversations.

SEN. HATCH: Well, and you never saw anything that would indicate that she had animosity toward then-Chairman Thomas?

MS. HOLT: Never.

SEN. HATCH: Or even at the prior job as Assistant Secretary of Education?

MS. HOLT: None whatsoever.

SEN. HATCH: And you were just about as close to Judge Thomas as anybody could have been, right?

MS. HOLT: We were—we are very close, yes.

SEN. HATCH: You have heard—let me just throw this out to all of you—I am not going to repeat the cumulative charges that would fill a whole page, of what she said Judge Thomas told her as he was pursuing her for dates and, as she implied, maybe pursuing her for something more than dates. Now each of you have heard those, so there is no reason for me to repeat them, but cumulatively they are pretty awful. Would you all agree?

MS. FITCH: Yes.

MS. HOLT: They are.

SEN. HATCH: Could that have happened? Let's start with you, Ms. Alvarez. Could he have used that language with her?

MS. ALVAREZ: Knowing Clarence Thomas, it is impossible.

SEN. HATCH: It is impossible?

MS. ALVAREZ: In the work environment, he was so professional, he was so—and, you know, I considered myself a friend of his, and I could never be friendly with him in the office. He drew that line. We were friends, and he was my boss, and when I was in the office he was professional, as well as we knew each other.

SEN. HATCH: All right.

Ms. Fitch?

MS. FITCH: Yes, the probability of that happening, whether in the workplace or outside of it, in my best knowledge is nil, is zero. The probability is just not there. When I heard those things, I knew they didn't come from him.

SEN. HATCH: So you are saying you know that it is zero, the chances of him doing that?

MS. FITCH: The probability of his doing that is zero, Senator.

SEN. HATCH: So it really isn't even a probability. It just means it would not have happened.

MS. FITCH: Yes, sir.

SEN. HATCH: How about you, Ms. Holt?

MS. HOLT: In my opinion, he would never, ever subject any woman to that kind of language.

SEN. HATCH: Ms. Berry-Myers.

MS. BERRY: When I first met with Clarence Thomas in 1982, there was no—we sat in his office. He had a desk, a chair, and the chair I was sitting in. That was all that the EEOC employees left in the chairman's office. That is how much they welcomed him there.

And we sat down, and from my political background, usually the first thing that you ask a candidate is, "Okay, if I open up your closet, what skeletons are going to come falling out? I need to know right now." So I talked to Clarence Thomas about the need to comport himself in a way that there could be absolutely no taint on his reputation, on his character, on his honor, because we were about to embark upon an arduous task.

There wasn't anybody in this town, except perhaps Senator Hatch, that supported that man in the position that he had assumed, so I knew that everything that we did—public policy, program, firing people, anything that we did—he was going to be under microscopic scrutiny because he was a black Republican conservative in an agency that was overwhelmingly neither and in a town that is tough, and he was about to undertake a tough job. And with all the other things that we had to do, we didn't have any time to be dealing with anything that might besmirch his character.

SEN. HATCH: Well, do you have any concerns he might do otherwise?

SEN. METZENBAUM: [presiding]. Senator Hatch, your time has expired.

SEN. HATCH: Let me just finish. This line only takes a—

MS. BERRY: None whatsoever, and not only would he not, but he instructed his personal staff about the need for us to comport ourselves in such a way as to not disgrace his office.

SEN. HATCH: Okay. Thank you. My time is up, but I wanted to finish that and allow you to at least finish that thought, and we will come back to you in the next round.

MS. BERRY: Thank you.

SEN. METZENBAUM: Senator Heflin.

SEN. LEAHY: Mr. Chairman, would Senator Heflin yield to me just for one question?

Ms. Holt, just so we are not confused, could I ask one of the staff just would you let me take that just for a moment? We will give it right back to you. I just want to make sure we are all reading from the same choir book here, or log book.

Let me ask you, while he is bringing that up, just these questions: Each time that the log book shows Anita Hill calling, did she connect with Clarence Thomas every single time she called, to your knowledge?

MS. HOLT: I don't understand.

SEN. LEAHY: I mean, did she get through to him? A lot of these are messages. Does the fact that a message was there, does that mean that she—

MS. HOLT: The fact that a message was taken meant that she didn't get to him right away.

SEN. LEAHY: It does not mean she got to him each time?

MS. HOLT: It means she didn't get to him at that time.

SEN. LEAHY: Okay, and you don't know whether she ever did?

MS. HOLT: She did. The check mark beside the call indicates that the call was successfully returned.

SEN. LEAHY: And how do you know that?

MS. HOLT: It was my system. I devised it.

SEN. LEAHY: Okay, but do you know it because you placed the call back?

MS. HOLT: I placed the call, got them on the line, and I checked it off that the call had been successfully returned.

SEN. LEAHY: Senator Hatch asked you if there might have been a lot of other calls, and you were asked once before by the Republican and Democratic staff of this committee, "Do you have a recollection of Ms. Anita Hill calling Clarence Thomas any more times than may have sporadically shown up on three such pages?" And your answer was, "I would not even guess about that. I don't know." Is that correct?

MS. HOLT: I was saying that I would not even guess about any particular dates, any particular times, or any particular year.

SEN. LEAHY: Thank you very much.

Senator Heflin, thank you for your courtesy.

SEN. HEFLIN: Ms. Holt, you knew Anita Hill quite well socially.

MS. HOLT: We were professional friends.

SEN. HEFLIN: Professional friends, all right. You went out to lunch together and things like that. Did you ever go out in the evening together, for dinner or something?

MS. HOLT: Only on one occasion.

SEN. HEFLIN: On one occasion. All right. If Anita Hill is telling a falsehood, do you have any explanation why she would be telling it?

MS. HOLT: I have no idea, sir. She is the only one, I believe, that can answer that question.

SEN. HEFLIN: Now, you went from the Department of Education to EEOC with Judge Thomas, Clarence Thomas the director?

MS. HOLT: He went over two or three weeks before I did, yes.

SEN. HEFLIN: And then you followed him?

MS. HOLT: Right.

SEN. HEFLIN: And Anita Hill was also one of those that followed him from the Department of Education to the EEOC?

MS. HOLT: Right.

SEN. HEFLIN: Was there anybody else?

MS. HOLT: That is it, as far as I know, at that time.

SEN. HEFLIN: Did he ask you all to come?

MS. HOLT: He did.

SEN. HEFLIN: He did. All right. Now, at that particular time when that move was made was there a good deal of discussion that the Reagan Administration wanted to abolish the Department of Education?

MS. HOLT: I had heard that, Senator.

SEN. HEFLIN: You had heard it. Was there any discussion at that particular time that the Reagan Administration wanted to abolish the EEOC?

MS. HOLT: I had not heard that.

SEN. HEFLIN: You had not heard that.

Now, did you take dictation from Director Thomas?

MS. HOLT: Not in the traditional sense of the word. When Judge Thomas wanted to dictate, he stood at my desk and I typed.

SEN. HEFLIN: He didn't use a dictaphone?

MS. HOLT: He did on occasion.

SEN. HEFLIN: On occasion. And sometimes he would, in effect, dictate to you letters standing at your desk?

MS. HOLT: He did.

SEN. HEFLIN: He would. All right.

Did you open his mail?

MS. HOLT: If his mail was marked "personal," I opened it. We had an Office of Executive Secretariat that was responsible for opening all mail addressed to the chairman.

SEN. HEFLIN: To the chairman. But if it was personal you would open it?

MS. HOLT: I would open it; yes.

SEN. HEFLIN: All right. Do you know whether or not he received mail at his home?

MS. HOLT: I have no way of knowing that, Senator.

SEN. HEFLIN: You don't know about that.

What was the age of his son at that time in 1982?

MS. HOLT: I think six, seven.

SEN. HEFLIN: In the mail that you might have opened, did you ever open any mail that contained pornographic materials?

MS. HOLT: I did not.

SEN. HEFLIN: You did not. All right.

Now, did you hear of or know of anyone by the name of Earl Harper at the Washington office?

MS. HOLT: I am not familiar with him, no.

SEN. HEFLIN: You are not familiar with him. All right.

Did any of you?

MS. FITCH: No, Senator.

SEN. HEFLIN: Did you, Ms. Berry?

MS. BERRY: Yes.

SEN. HEFLIN: We went into this and then it was reopened later. It is my information that I now believe may have been incorrect.

Was he in the Washington office?

MS. BERRY: I am sorry. I don't know for sure which office he was assigned to.

SEN. HEFLIN: You don't know that. Well, what do you know about him?

MS. BERRY: What I know is, and I don't recall all of the facts of the case, I just understand that Earl Harper was alleged to have been a sexual harasser.

SEN. HEFLIN: Do you remember, Ms. Holt, dictating, any dictation by Clarence Thomas to the General Counsel pertaining to this man Harper?

MS. HOLT: I don't remember any specific letters; no.

SEN. HEFLIN: Now, Ms. Berry, have you made any statements that suggested that the allegations of Anita Hill were the result of Ms. Hill's disappointment and frustration that Mr. Thomas didn't show any sexual interest in her?

I am talking to Ms. Phyllis Berry-Myers.

MS. BERRY: That is what I said.

SEN. HEFLIN: You said that to a newspaper?

MS. BERRY: Yes, I did.

SEN. HEFLIN: What were the facts pertaining to that?

MS. BERRY: Just my observations of Anita wishing to have greater attention from the chairman. I think she was used to that at the Department of Education. Wanting to have direct access to his office, as though she had a right to have access to his office. Speaking in just highly admirable terms for the chairman, in a way sometimes that didn't indicate just professional interest.

Those were my impressions.

SEN. HEFLIN: Now, what you are relating to me relates to a sexual interest?

MS. BERRY: Pardon me?

SEN. HEFLIN: What you just related, are you saying that those set of circumstances made you to believe that she had a sexual interest?

MS. BERRY: That she had a crush on the chairman? Yes.

SEN. HEFLIN: She had a crush on the chairman?

MS. BERRY: Yes.

SEN. HEFLIN: And would you recite those statements and things that you observed again?

MS. BERRY: It is in my written testimony, sir.

SEN. HEFLIN: Well, I am asking you now, if you would, in order to recite those again as to that. I didn't understand anything that you said there had any effect relative to sexual relations. They appeared to be more professional and an attempt to have greater access to him from a professional viewpoint. I just would like for you to recite them again, if there is something that is your impression.

MS. BERRY: My impression was that Anita wished to have a greater relationship with the chairman than just a professional one.

SEN. HEFLIN: And so you say that the fact that she didn't have as much access and other things that they indicate a sexual interest, as opposed to a professional or a work interest?

MS. BERRY: Exactly.

SEN. HEFLIN: And that is what you are saying. How would you distinguish between the two?

MS. BERRY: How would I distinguish between the two?

SEN. HEFLIN: Yes. What you recited to me did not appear to be anything other than a work interest. But I would just like for you to go ahead and recite how that is a sexual interest, as opposed to a work interest.

MS. BERRY: To have in a working environment, in a busy office, part of my responsibilities coming to the EEOC was to help structure access to the chairman.

There was a lot of work to do helping setting up scheduling, helping organize the work flow of a product, determining staff positions, things of that nature. That was one of my responsibilities when I first came there.

To think that you should at any hour of the day, anytime that you want to be able to walk in, have time with him, indicated to me more of a proprietary interest than a professional interest.

SEN. HEFLIN: Were you conversant or did you know what the relationship had been at the Department of Education relative to access with her boss there?

MS. BERRY: Only from her indications. That she was a primary, and whatever that meant, a primary adviser to the chairman. And I would assume a primary adviser, such as myself or J.C. or Diane, meant someone that had readily—could be readily available to the chairman.

SEN. HEFLIN: Now, we went into this somewhat, Senator Leahy but also Senator Specter in his examination of Ms. Hill went into this question about whether or not she knew Phyllis Berry, and I assume—I don't know how—did the paper refer to you as Phyllis Berry or Phyllis Barry?

MS. BERRY: Yes, as far as I know. It wasn't a paper. It was a press conference.

SEN. HEFLIN: I mean, well whatever it was, was it Barry or Berry?

MS. BERRY: That was my understanding, that they said do you know Phyllis Berry?

SEN. HEFLIN: Is it Berry or Barry?

MS. BERRY: Berry—B-e-r-r-y.

SEN. HEFLIN: All right. Now, Senator Specter asked these questions, and I will read the questions and the answer: "SEN. SPECTER. There is a question about Phyllis Barry, B-a-r-r-y, who was quoted in the *New York Times* on October the 7th, 'In an interview Ms. Barry suggested that the allegation—referring to your allegation—was a result of Ms. Hill's disappointment and frustration that Mr. Thomas did not show any sexual interest in her.'

"You were asked about Ms. Barry at the interview on October the 7th and were reported to have said, 'Well, I don't know Phyllis Barry and she doesn't know me.' And there were quite a few people who have come forward to say that they saw you and Ms. Barry and that you knew each other very well."

Then Ms. Hill answered.

"I would disagree with that. Ms. Berry worked at EEOC. She did attend some staff meetings at EEOC. We were not close friends. We did not socialize together and she had no basis for making a comment about my social interest with regards to Clarence Thomas or anyone else. I might add at the time that I had an active social life and that I was involved with other people."

Then later Senator Specter asked her: "So that when you said Ms. Barry doesn't know me and I don't know her you weren't referring to just that, but to some intensity of knowledge."

And Ms. Hill answered: "Well, this is a specific remark about my sexual interest and I think one has to know another person very well to make those kind of remarks unless they are very openly expressed."

Now, I am asking, you don't have any question in your mind that Anita Hill knew you. It is a question as to the degree of intensity she knew you relative to whether or not you could form an opinion as to whether or not she had a sexual interest with Mr. Thomas?

MS. BERRY: Senator, as I indicated in my statement, I worked very closely with Anita and I think that—I don't have the record before me, but I do believe that Senator Specter asked her also, "And she had the opportunity to observe you and Clarence Thomas at the office?" and she indicated that yes, not only did I have the—yes, I did have the opportunity to observe them. And I did have that opportunity.

And my opinion is that Anita had more than a professional interest in Clarence Thomas.

SEN. HEFLIN: Well, did he ever indicate any return of it?

MS. BERRY: No. And, if you continue reading the *New York Times* article, that is exactly what I said. And I said that "And because of that I think her feelings were hurt."

SEN. HEFLIN: Now, Ms. Holt, in regard to telephone calls other than those that you logged, do you have a recollection as to whether there were any additional phone calls that came in from Anita Hill to Mr. Thomas?

MS. HOLT: What I recall, Senator, is that there were occasions when Ms. Hill would call the office and would be put directly through to Clarence Thomas.

SEN. HEFLIN: You have taken a deposition in this case where people asked you questions, and a question was asked you, "Do you have a recollection"—on page 44—"of Anita Hill calling Clarence Thomas any more times than may have been sporadically shown up on these three other pages?" And the answer: "I would not even guess about that. I don't know."

Have you had changes in recollection since giving that deposition?

MS. HOLT: As I just indicated to Senator Leahy, I was saying that I would not fathom a guess about any particular day or time or year that she had called him without it being in the log.

SEN. HEFLIN: So you are saying that he could have called, or do you know that she called or what?

MS. HOLT: I know, Senator, that there were occasions when she called and was put directly through to Judge Thomas.

SEN. HEFLIN: But those were not recorded and no record is made, is that what you are saying?

MS. HOLT: Exactly.

SEN. HEFLIN: Do you know how often they occurred?

MS. HOLT: No, I don't. But there weren't that many of them.

SEN. HEFLIN: Wasn't that many of them. And over a period of how many years are these phone—that is from 1984, these logs are 1984, 1985, 1986, 1987. Would there have been as many as two or three?

MS. HOLT: Four or five. Six, maybe.

SEN. HEFLIN: It would have probably been what, in the neighborhood of no more than one a year?

MS. HOLT: Possibly, sir.

SEN. HEFLIN: Well, my time has run out.

SEN. KENNEDY: [presiding]. Senator Hatch.

SEN. HATCH: Thank you. Now, let me go back to you, Ms. Berry. If I can call you Ms. Berry for the purposes of this hearing.

MS. BERRY: That is fine.

SEN. HATCH: Did you hear Anita Hill's press conference last Monday?

MS. BERRY: Pardon me?

SEN. HATCH: Did you see Anita Hill's press conference last Monday, or hear it?

MS. BERRY: Last Monday? Was that October—I don't know dates anymore.

SEN. HATCH: Whenever it was, the first press conference.

MS. BERRY: October 7? No, I did not see her press conference. Reporters starting calling my home asking me had I seen Anita Hill's press conference where she indicated that she was responding to my quotes in the *Times* article and she indicated that she did not know me and that I did not know her.

And so I issued a statement saying that this is in response to Anita Hill's statement at an October 7 press conference indicating that she did not know me and I did not know her, that is not true. And then I went on to explain how it is that I did, in fact, know Anita Hill.

SEN. HATCH: Well, when you heard Professor Hill claim "I don't know Phyllis Berry and she doesn't know me," did you think, as Professor Hill claimed on Friday, that her remark was only meant to indicate that you were not in a position to speculate about her private life or did you give those words what I would call their natural meaning and think that she was not telling the truth?

MS. BERRY: When I heard it I thought she wasn't telling the truth. Obviously, she knew me. We worked together for many years, and we worked closely together, particularly in the Office of Congressional Affairs, particularly on the chairman's staff, and I knew of her at the Department of Education. So I had no idea what she was talking about, except that I took her at face value. She said she didn't know me.

SEN. HATCH: Well, after Professor Hill denied that she knew you the press conference erupted in applause, which is the largest ovation of the day. What were you thinking at that moment?

MS. BERRY: I didn't see her press conference.

SEN. HATCH: You didn't see it?

MS. BERRY: I am sorry. I was working on Little League stuff and I wasn't watching television.

SEN. HATCH: Well, you have indicated that the reason why Professor Hill has been so reluctant to acknowledge your existence appears to be the fact that you have advanced a theory for why Professor Hill is making these allegations, and your theory is, to say the least, unflattering to her in her position.

Can you repeat that theory as you gave it to the *New York Times*, and tell us if it still seems accurate to you?

MS. BERRY: It still seems accurate to me.

SEN. HATCH: And what was your theory?

MS. BERRY: Because Clarence Thomas did not respond to her heightened interest, didn't respond to her in that way. He treated her just like he treated everybody else on the staff. That her feelings were hurt.

And I think opportunities that she thought that she ought to have, access that she ought to have and she didn't receive. I mean it was competitive. We were a tough, strong group of women around Clarence Thomas and he based—we had to perform. We had strict performance agreements, and you had to perform. And, if you couldn't hang, if you couldn't perform, you got his wrath. If you performed, you got his praise.

I think because she was at EEOC not treated special that she didn't feel comfortable there.

SEN. HATCH: Okay. Ms. Fitch, I was impressed by your statement, as I have been of all of your statements. I am impressed with each and everyone of you, and I think Judge Thomas was very lucky to have you working with him.

But I particularly notice you used the term "decent"—

MS. FITCH: I'm sorry.

SEN. HATCH: I particularly noticed you the used the term "decent" in describing Clarence Thomas.

MS. FITCH: Yes.

SEN. HATCH: Do you use that very often?

MS. FITCH: Yes. If you talk to the people who talked to me even before I left the Commission, when I went to Lynchburg, Virginia, when I went to Temple, even at the time that he was nominated for the Supreme Court, I've always used that term about the judge, and it kicked out for me some time ago, at least a year or two ago, if not longer, that I don't use that term for everybody, and it's not that there aren't other decent people, because there certainly are.

But what intrigues me about him is that I always paid a great deal of attention to his character, this man that I felt had a conscience that operated all the time, that realized the gravity of his position, and I found that impressive and that has a lot to do with my use of that term, and I still don't throw it around indiscriminately and I still call him a decent person.

SEN. HATCH: Did you consider yourself a friend of Anita Hill's, and did you have a relationship with her outside of Washington?

MS. FITCH: Anita Hill and I did not spend a lot of time together. We did not go to lunch, because I don't go to lunch often. We maybe went out three times after work for dinner. We were not prowling Washington or anything. I went to her house on one occasion. When she was in the hospital, I visited her there. At her farewell party at the Sheraton, I was in attendance and I believe I was the only person from the Commission who was there.

After she left the Commission, I stayed in touch with her. We did meet once when she came into town. Subsequently, we tried to get together. I had a housewarming gift for her, but we never caught up with each other.

SEN. HATCH: I see. Did you ever hear her mention any problems with Clarence Thomas?

MS. FITCH: Never. Never. Never, even after she left the Commission.

SEN. HATCH: So, both during the time she was there and after she left?

MS. FITCH: Yes, Senator.

SEN. HATCH: Okay. Now, your statement mentions that you knew both Anita Hill and Phyllis Berry while you were at the EEOC.

MS. FITCH: Yes.

SEN. HATCH: Is it possible, in your view, that Anita Hill was telling the truth at this press conference on Monday, when she stated, "I don't know Phyllis Berry and she doesn't know me"?

MS. FITCH: Senator, when I heard that, I was very surprised. I don't know what she meant by it. I took it to mean that she was unaware of Ms. Berry's existence, and I knew that not to be the case.

SEN. HATCH: Have you ever heard or ever known Anita Hill to lie on any other occasion?

MS. FITCH: No, I haven't, Senator.

SEN. HATCH: Okay.

Ms. Alvarez, did you know Phyllis Berry and Professor Hill at the EEOC?

MS. ALVAREZ: Yes, sir, I did.

SEN. HATCH: So, you knew they worked together?

MS. ALVAREZ: Yes.

SEN. HATCH: In your statement, you noted that Professor Hill was "not a team player," and "appeared to have her own agenda." Could you elaborate on that?

MS. ALVAREZ: Well, there seemed to be all of us in the group kind of working toward the same goal, and I think we got along with each other, we would occasionally talk, and Anita mostly kept to herself. She was very strong-willed, she liked to do things her way, and that was always the way she—that was the way she gave the impression, that she kind of had her own agenda, her own way of doing things. So, no matter what the rest of the team was doing, she was going to do it Anita's way.

SEN. HATCH: Now, you say you knew Judge Thomas well.

MS. ALVAREZ: Yes.

SEN. HATCH: Did you ever hear him ask Anita Hill for a date, the whole time you knew both of them?

MS. ALVAREZ: No, never.

SEN. HATCH: And you knew her well.

MS. ALVAREZ: I knew her at the office.

SEN. HATCH: Okay. Did you ever see any indication that either of them had a romantic interest in the other?

MS. ALVAREZ: No.

SEN. HATCH: Did you ever hear of Judge Thomas discussing sex with anybody, including Anita Hill?

MS. ALVAREZ: At the office, never, sir.

SEN. HATCH: Again, I am going to ask you this question. You are his close friend and you worked closely with him. Is it conceivable that Clarence Thomas, the Clarence Thomas you have known and worked with for the past thirteen years, that he could have made the perverted statements that Professor Hill said he did?

MS. ALVAREZ: Not a chance, sir.

SEN. HATCH: Did you ever hear Professor Hill express any dissatisfaction with then-Chairman Thomas or the way he treated her?

MS. ALVAREZ: No. No, not at all.

SEN. HATCH: If you had a young daughter in her early twenties, would you want her to work with Judge Thomas?

MS. ALVAREZ: Absolutely. Absolutely.

SEN. HATCH: From your experience of working with Professor Hill and Judge Thomas at the EEOC, did Professor Hill think that she had some sort of a special relationship with Judge Thomas?

MS. ALVAREZ: Yes, she used to give that impression. She used to like to tout the fact that she had worked with him before. You know, when we would get into debates on how we were going to handle an issue, she would say, "Well, I know how he thinks, I know how he likes his papers written or I know the position he wants to take," or something like that. That was something she always sort of held out in front of everyone at the staff, that she had this sort of inside track to him.

SEN. HATCH: What I would like to ask each and every one of you is, rack your brains, as people who were around both of them who have known both of them during that period of time, who really have had a close working relationship professionally and even a friendship relationship with Judge Thomas. How could she have testified the way she did here?

MS. FITCH: Senator, to me it was incredible. I don't know. I can't answer that. I was dumb-struck. I have no idea.

SEN. HATCH: Ms. Holt?

MS. HOLT: I have no idea, Senator.

SEN. HATCH: Well, let me ask you this: Do any of you believe her testimony here?

MS. HOLT: I do not believe a word, not one word.

MS. FITCH: Senator, I don't believe it, either.

SEN. HATCH: I didn't hear you.

MS. FITCH: I'm sorry. Senator, I do not believe a word of it either.

SEN. HATCH: You don't believe a word of it.

MS. FITCH: No, I don't.

SEN. HATCH: How about you, Ms. Myers?

MS. BERRY: When she could stand up in front of the world and say "I did not know Phyllis Berry and Phyllis Berry does not know me"? I can imagine she probably would say anything. I mean, I exist and I existed then. I worked very closely with her, and that wasn't the truth, so it seems to me that if she could not tell the truth on one thing, she could not tell the truth on another.

SEN. HATCH: Ms. Alvarez?

MS. ALVAREZ: I cannot believe one word of her testimony. That is not the Clarence Thomas I know. That is not the Clarence Thomas I worked with.

SEN. HATCH: You heard Chairman Thomas's testimony with regard to the allegations that she made on three successive occasions? Once to the FBI, once in her four-page single-spaced typewritten statement? And another one when she appeared here before this committee last Friday, and you heard Judge Thomas's response to that.

MS. FITCH: Yes, Senator, he said he categorically denied her allegations.

SEN. HATCH: He did deny them.

MS. FITCH: Yes.

SEN. HATCH: Did you hear his response on the negative stereotypes?

MS. FITCH: I heard most of it, Senator.

SEN. HATCH: What do you think of those comments made by her attributed to him and his comments back about those comments?

MS. FITCH: As a historian, I know those comments to be stereotypical.

SEN. HATCH: Why would you think she would say that?

MS. FITCH: Senator, I have no idea. I don't know, but they are certainly kind of pat formulaic statements that people have historically made about black men in this country.

SEN. HATCH: Don't they play on white prejudices about black men?

MS. FITCH: Of course they do, Senator.

SEN. HATCH: Of course they do, but why would she use that language? And why would he use it?

MS. FITCH: Senator, I think what I am trying to say is that it is incomprehensible that she would say these things, incomprehensible that she might believe them. I do not know. I have not talked to her in three years. I don't know.

SEN. HATCH: Would those kind of statements, had they been—would those kind of statements, as they are, would they tend to turn some people in this country against Clarence Thomas?

MS. FITCH: Senator, I have been in the street a lot lately listening to people's conversations, and they have been talking about this process and about this man, and I am finding that most people are concerned about the seriousness of the allegations, they take the issue of sexual harassment seriously. They are not discounting that. They do not believe the things that are being said about this man. They are too pat, they don't—even for people who don't know him—don't think they seem to hang very well together.

SEN. HATCH: Now, have any of you women ever heard of any male using that type of language, in order to obtain a date with a woman?

MS. FITCH: Senator, this was not to obtain a date with me, but when I taught at Sangamon State University in Illinois, in a room with four other people, including an older man who was old enough to be my father, a Federal contract compliance officer said some things like that to me, and nobody said anything in response. I was very hurt by that. I stayed away from him. He had no jurisdiction or authority over me. It's possible for people to say things like that. It is improbable that this man said those things.

SEN. HATCH: Well, what do the rest of you feel about that?

MS. HOLT: I agree that it's impossible for Clarence Thomas to have said those things.

SEN. HATCH: Ms. Alvarez.

MS. ALVAREZ: I agree that it is absolutely impossible for Clarence to have said it.

SEN. HATCH: Ms. Berry.

MS. BERRY: It's impossible and not a great deductive method in my way of thinking. [Laughter.]

SEN. HATCH: Well, you know, I hate to tell you this, but I agree with that. You know, people all over this country are trying to figure out how somebody could testify in such a believable manner and say the cumulative total of those awful, ugly, terrible sexual things and expect a woman to date him or expect some form of a relationship with a woman.

It bothers me, because she appears to believe everything that she said, and I myself don't want to call her a liar. But as an old trial lawyer, I have seen witnesses just like that who believe every word they say and every word is absolutely wrong and we have proven it wrong and they still believe it.

I am highly offended, having been the co-author, along with Senator Kennedy, of the Polygraph Protection Act to protect employees from being forced to go through polygraphs, that this group of handlers of Professor Hill have had her undergo a polygraph.

I can tell you right now, you can find a polygraph operator for anything you want to find them for. There are some very good ones and there are some lousy ones, and a whole raft in between. And to do that and interject that in the middle of this is pathetic, as if it has any relevance whatsoever. It wouldn't even be admissible in a court of law.

Now, I just want to ask you this last question. I have known Judge Thomas for eleven years. I have sat in on all five of his confirmation proceedings. I presided over three of them, as chairman of the Labor Committee. And I have never seen anything to indicate that he would treat any human being like this woman says he treated her.

I am going to ask you to search your minds one last time: Is there anything that could have been misconstrued or construed, in your opinion, that could have caused anyone, including Anita Hill, to say what she did here to the whole world?

MS. HOLT: Senator, since these allegations surfaced, that is all I've really done, is wonder why—

SEN. HATCH: Me, too.

MS. HOLT: [continuing] —why would she want to tell these lies, and I haven't come up with an answer yet. But I can certainly say that I don't believe a word of it.

SEN. HATCH: I think that sums it up pretty well.

Thank you very much.

THE CHAIRMAN: Thank you.

SEN. THURMOND: Mr. Chairman, I have one question I would like to propound.

THE CHAIRMAN: I could ask a couple, too, but you go right ahead, Senator. Instead of going back, we will go to you.

SEN. THURMOND: Is it possible that Professor Hill had a crush on Judge Thomas and felt rejected, because he would not date her? Any of you care to answer that?

MS. BERRY: Since I am the one who said that, you have got to understand, I guess, what kind of man Clarence Thomas is. In many ways, I think he is atypical in his treatment of women. He is respectful of our abilities and our talents and expertise, allowed us to have opportunities that ordinarily women did not have at the Commission.

My own title, as the Director of the Office of Congressional Affairs, is a good example. That is usually the purview of a man. He allowed us to do things that women ordinarily did not have the opportunity to do. He made sure that women were included in almost every aspect of Commission life as it related to job opportunities.

He is courteous, he is generous, he is caring, and I can understand any woman responding to a man that has those kinds of attributes.

MS. FITCH: Senator, as I said before, on the three occasions—and I don't think it was more than that—that Anita Hill and I did go out after work, from work, it was clear to me that she had very friendly feelings towards now-Judge Thomas and that she felt that they were returned.

I knew that she had been with him at the Department of Education. I knew that they had met through a mutual friend, and I knew that she had friendly feelings for him. That made it all the more surprising to me, therefore, that she made these allegations. I never got any sense from her that she had any romantic interest in him at all. From my experience with her, that was not what she was concerned about. As I said before, she saw him as a person who was going places and was going to make a contribution in this country, and both of us felt that we wanted to do whatever we could to help him do that.

In my case, at least, it was not to follow a rising star, necessarily and I can't say that that was her intention, either. I don't know. We did not talk about him in those terms, but we did talk about him when we went off together, and we talked about work and how we could make him almost perfect. I think it was unreasonable, the things that we wanted him to do, to be completely flawless, to be 100 percent perfect. No human being is that way, and when I was in my twenties I was very judgmental and wanted people to be perfect, too, and I think that was part of the problem. But I don't see that that would have led to this kind of an allegation.

SEN. THURMOND: Any other comments?

[No response.]

SEN. THURMOND: Thank you very much.

THE CHAIRMAN: Just for the record, as the Senator said, I appreciate your direct answer, Ms. Fitch, and yours, Ms. Myers. But I could ask you, for example, is it possible that there is life in outer space? Is it possible there is life in outer space?

MS. FITCH: Of course, it's possible, Senator.

THE CHAIRMAN: Ms. Myers, is it possible there's life in outer space?

MS. BERRY: It's possible.

THE CHAIRMAN: Thank you. Now, let me ask you another question, if I may. Before I ask you the question, let me make it clear that there has been a lot of discussion about records here and the testimony taken, when you were giving testimony over the telephone or in person or to the FBI, and I am not reading from the FBI. There are things that are said here that seem inconsistent.

I am not accusing you of inconsistency here, but I just want to make sure I understand. You said in a question from staff, in the staff interview—and it is only one thing so I don't think you have to have the whole page, but if you need it, I would be happy to give it to you, page 57—the staff person asked you, "Did you see Anita Hill's press conference on television?" And your answer was yes.

Then the next question asked you, "Did you find her credible?" Your answer was, "She sounded credible."

Now, that is not necessarily inconsistent with what you said today, but I want to make sure I understand. Today, you said that you believed that you don't believe one word of Anita's Hill testimony. Can you make a distinction between your saying "She sounded credible" and what you said here?

I might point out, before you answer it, I think that other Senators who question for the record should be able to understand that there are these kinds of discrepancies that aren't nearly the discrepancies they are made out to be, but go ahead.

MS. HOLT: What I meant was, if someone did not know Anita Hill, she sounded credible. I know Anita Hill and I know Clarence Thomas, and I know Clarence Thomas is not the kind of person that would do those things.

THE CHAIRMAN: So, notwithstanding the fact you said she sounded credible, in response to the staff—

MS. HOLT: Right, if I did not know her—

THE CHAIRMAN: [continuing]—you really meant to say, if you did not know her, you thought she sounded credible?

MS. HOLT: She sounded credible. She presents herself well.

THE CHAIRMAN: And you just failed to say the first part, if you did not know her, she sounded credible, is that correct?

MS. HOLT: That's correct.

THE CHAIRMAN: I accept that. I just want to make two points, one, to clear up the discrepancy, and, two, to point out that witnesses can appear to have discrepancies in these records, and there would be no discrepancy at all, in fact.

Now, let me ask you, Ms. Fitch, you have been extremely precise in your answers. I think you have been extremely precise, you made it absolutely clear that you think Clarence Thomas is an incredibly admirable man, an admirable person and one whom you don't believe said this.

For example, in response to my good friend from Utah, you pointed out what I think everyone in America does know, and that is that there are men who do say things like that alleged to have been said by the judge.

Now, you don't believe that the judge said that, but you explained to us that you believe—

MS. FITCH: Yes.

THE CHAIRMAN: From other men, not from the judge.

MS. FITCH: Not from Judge Thomas, and I do not believe he would say those things.

THE CHAIRMAN: I understand that, and I want to make it clear. You do not believe that. You believe he is totally credible.

MS. FITCH: Yes.

THE CHAIRMAN: You believe everything he is saying, but I want the record to show what I think every woman in America knows, that there are men who do say things exactly like what Judge Thomas is accused of saying, notwithstanding my friend from Utah's research creating the impression that it is so unusual that it never happens.

SEN. HATCH: Not as a cumulative whole, though.

MS. FITCH: Oh, no.

SEN. HATCH: Well, see, that is what he is trying to get you to say.

MS. FITCH: Yes.

SEN. HATCH: The fact is, he said one statement, but a cumulative whole, if you hung around that fellow—

MS. FITCH: Well, there might be two or three statements strung together, but no, it is not a whole litany like that.

THE CHAIRMAN: Let me put it another way, Ms. Fitch. And I was very fastidious about never interrupting my friend from Utah, and I assume he won't interrupt me again.

Now what do you think, let me ask you, that man who said those things to you, do you think if you had been in his company the next seven days, he might not have said similar things to you again and again?

MS. FITCH: Senator, I was very sure he would say those things to me in private if I was in his orbit, so I stayed away from him.

THE CHAIRMAN: Thank you very much. That is cumulative.

Now let me make another point, if I may. I want to make it clear, because I understand and I believe everything that all of you are saying. It is clear that you truly believe what you say to be correct and to be a legitimate and accurate characterization of Clarence Thomas. I don't doubt that for a minute. You are under oath and it is clear that you all believe that. I am not suggesting anybody has been put up to anything by anybody. I believe you believe it.

Now one of the things that has been indicated here is this notion of maybe that the witness, Professor Hill, really was basically the woman scorned, that she really had this romantic interest in Clarence Thomas and that she was spurned, and after being spurned she took up the role in the way that Shakespeare used the phrase, "Hell hath no fury like . . . " and that is what is being implied here.

Now, Ms. Fitch, you said you have no doubt, as I understand it, that the professor wanted very much to see the judge move on and do great things for America.

MS. FITCH: Be successful in his career, yes.

THE CHAIRMAN: Be successful. But I want the record to note— and correct me if I am wrong—that in those conversations with the professor where you drew that conclusion, that she wished to see him succeed.

MS. FITCH: Yes.

THE CHAIRMAN: You also went on to say, unless I misunderstood you, that you did not believe there was any romantic element to that.

MS. FITCH: Oh, no, Senator, and we both said the same things about him, and for neither one of us was there any romantic talk about him at all.

THE CHAIRMAN: Thank you.

Now, Ms. Alvarez, in a statement that you issued after Professor Hill's allegations became public, you observed, and I quote: "Ms. Hill was not a team player and appeared to have her own agenda. She always attempted to be aloof from the staff, constantly giving the impression she was superior to others on the staff."

Then your statement goes on to conclude that Professor Hill had a "penchant for being self-serving and condescending toward others," and that the allegations she made "are absurd and are clearly an attempt on her part to gain notoriety." You also said the charges are "outrageous, ridiculous and totally without merit."

Now, Ms. Alvarez, my question to you is this: Could there be a different conclusion drawn from your observation that during her tenure at EEOC, Professor Hill appeared "aloof from the staff"? You draw the conclusion from that that she was self-serving and condescending. Could Professor Hill's aloofness have resulted from feeling uncomfortable around the chairman of the Commission?

MS. ALVAREZ: No, it was not her aloofness that made me feel like she was condescending. She was aloof, and she has been described that way by a number of people. The way she made me feel, she acted condescending towards others, was that she would say she had this inside track, she knew the chairman better than anyone else, and therefore she had some sort of rights, because she had worked with him before, because she was close to him, because she knew how he thought and that sort of thing. So she condescended to others in that way.

THE CHAIRMAN: Well, how about the aloofness part. Could the aloofness be—

MS. ALVAREZ: Well, she was not aloof from him. She was aloof from the rest of the staff.

THE CHAIRMAN: I see. Now how do you know she wasn't aloof from him?

MS. ALVAREZ: Just in the dealings that I saw. She never seemed to avoid him. She never seemed to try and stay away—

THE CHAIRMAN: I see.

MS. ALVAREZ: [continuing] —or she didn't respond to him in a staff meeting or anything like that. I am saying that with the other staff she was very stand-offish.

THE CHAIRMAN: I see.

Ms. Holt, did you find her condescending and aloof? You dealt with her probably more than anybody.

MS. HOLT: She wasn't condescending to me, Senator.

THE CHAIRMAN: She was not?

MS. HOLT: No.

THE CHAIRMAN: I can understand why. She wanted to get in that door, right?

MS. HOLT: That could have been it.

THE CHAIRMAN: Ms. Myers—and my apologies, do you wish me to refer to you as Ms. Berry-Myers or would you prefer—

MS. BERRY: It doesn't matter, Senator.

THE CHAIRMAN: All right.

MS. BERRY: I know who you are talking to, either way.

THE CHAIRMAN: All right. Ms. Myers, did you find her to be aloof and condescending?

MS. BERRY: I found her to be aloof, and a woman scorned can mean not just in the romantic context, but if your ideas are no longer the ones that are considered the ones that the chairman adopts, if your point of view is not given more weight than some one else's, if your—there are many ways, and not just in the romantic sense, but in the ways that—

THE CHAIRMAN: I'm sorry. How did you mean them, then?

MS. BERRY: Pardon me?

THE CHAIRMAN: How did you mean?

MS. BERRY: I meant it with both of those contexts.

THE CHAIRMAN: You mean both romantic and in terms of being rejected professionally, in a sense?

MS. BERRY: Yes. Those were my observations of Anita and the situation.

THE CHAIRMAN: I see. Can you give me an example?

MS. BERRY: Of what?

THE CHAIRMAN: Of where she was either rejected and you observed the reaction to her rejection, either in terms of romantic entre or an intellectual entre?

MS. BERRY: Or an intellectual entre? That was my job, as I said, to be the political eyes and ears, and that sometimes meant that I had to advise the chairman to take a position that was in his best interest and that of the Commission, and not ofttimes a position that was in the best interests of the bureaucracy or of one side or the other. We had to do what was best in terms of enforcing the law, administering and managing the agency, et cetera, et cetera, and sometimes there were ideological conflicts in that way.

And I have heard Anita characterized in the press as a conservative, and I guess I have a different opinion of what that means. At the Commission I would not have characterized Anita as a conservative. I would have characterized her more as a moderate person or a liberal, and there were times when it was necessary that the conservative view prevail, in my opinion, on some positions that the chairman took that she adamantly disagreed with.

THE CHAIRMAN: How would you characterize yourself, Ms. Myers?

MS. BERRY: I would characterize—

THE CHAIRMAN: As conservative or liberal, I mean, or moderate or whatever.

MS. BERRY: Now that's a good question. On some issues I am very conservative; on some issues I am not.

THE CHAIRMAN: I see that.

SEN. LEAHY: Aren't we all?

THE CHAIRMAN: Is that not also the case for the professor?

MS. BERRY: Obviously, yes.

THE CHAIRMAN: I see, so she is just like you, then?

MS. BERRY: No, she is not. I haven't alleged that Clarence Thomas—

THE CHAIRMAN: No, no, no. I mean—

MS. BERRY: So she is not like me. [Laughter.]

THE CHAIRMAN: No, no. I mean in terms of her political ideology.

MS. BERRY: On some things, perhaps.

THE CHAIRMAN: Does anybody else want to ask a question?

SEN. LEAHY: This is not a question. I just would like to note something for the record, if I might, Mr. Chairman. And that is that Senator Hatch referred in just the last few minutes to Anita Hill's handlers somehow, Svengali-like—my term, not his—sending her out to take a polygraph.

I would just note for the record, according to her sworn testimony, the first suggestion of a polygraph came when the Administration sent the FBI to talk to her. According to what she stated here, she told us that the FBI asked her if she would be willing to take a polygraph and she said—again according to her testimony here—that indeed she would.

I have no idea of the qualifications of whomever administered it or anything else. I have just heard about it. It would not be admissible in a court of law. Nobody is required to take a polygraph, but I just wanted to note, for the record, that the first suggestion of that came not from somebody advising Professor Hill but from, according to her testimony, the people the Administration sent out on the investigation that was requested by the White House and this committee.

SEN. HATCH: If the Senator would yield on that point, as the co-author along with Senator Kennedy of the Polygraph Protection Act, we did a lot of study of this, and there is no question that polygraphs should only be given under certain circumstances, with the approval of both sides, and not unilaterally by one side that may be very biased. You can find a polygraph operator to do anything you want them to do, just like you can find a pollster. Some pollsters in this country, not many, but some will do anything. They will find any conclusion you want, just by changing the questions.

Then again, polygraph operators, there are circumstances where people really believe what they are doing. They really believe it. It is totally false, but they believe it. She may very well be in that category, and might even pass a real polygraph examination.

So to throw that in the middle of a Supreme Court nomination as though it is real, legitimate evidence is highly offensive, that is my only point, and highly political, and again, too pat, too slick, exactly what a two-bit slick lawyer would try to do in the middle of something as important as this. Now that is the point I was raising.

SEN. LEAHY: Mr. Chairman, the point to be made is that it was the FBI, sent by the White House, who first suggested the polygraph.

SEN. HATCH: No, that is not true. That is not true. It was this committee, not the White House. It was this committee.

SEN. LEAHY: Is that why the report first goes to the White House?

THE CHAIRMAN: Will the Senator withhold?

The FBI was asked by the Majority and the Minority to investigate. The White House, the Administration, has to authorize that when we request it.

SEN. LEAHY: That's right.

THE CHAIRMAN: It was in the FBI—

SEN. LEAHY: I am referring to the sworn testimony here.

SEN. HATCH: It's a terrible thing, I'll tell you.

SEN. LEAHY: The sworn testimony—

SEN. HATCH: You only use it when it benefits her.

SEN. LEAHY: The sworn testimony of Professor Hill was that she said that she was prepared to take an FBI polygraph.

SEN. SPECTER: Mr. Chairman, might I be heard for one minute?

THE CHAIRMAN: Yes, you may.

SEN. SPECTER: I think on this subject it ought to be said that lie detector tests are not generally admissible in court—

THE CHAIRMAN: That is correct.

SEN. SPECTER: [continuing]—because they do not have the requisite reliability. I have extensive experience, being the Assistant Counsel to the Warren Commission, which I was present when Jack Ruby's lie detector test was taken, and that is a very different circumstance. But notwithstanding the fact that Jack Ruby passed it all without any indication of deception, when J. Edgar Hoover forwarded the report to the Warren Commission, it was his statement that the polygraph ought not to be accepted because it wasn't sufficiently reliable. And while we talk about it, it is generally accepted, a general principle of law, that a polygraph lie detector test is not admissible in court because of the lack of requisite reliability.

THE CHAIRMAN: The Senator is correct, and this is one Senator, and I think most believe that lie detector tests are not—are not—the appropriate way to get to the truth. That wasn't the issue I thought that was being raised here. The issue I thought being raised here was whether or not some slick lawyer cajoled or coerced this particular individual into taking a lie detector test. Now let me—

SEN. METZENBAUM: Mr. Chairman?

THE CHAIRMAN: Yes?

SEN. METZENBAUM: I don't know anything at all about polygraphs or lie detectors, but as I understand it there is a reference paper indicating the credentials of the company or of the man who took the polygraph test. I think it would be appropriate—I think the CIA does use polygraph tests, I don't know that for sure, but I think they do—and I would just suggest that whatever the credentials are of the individual or company that took the test, that that be included in the record at this point.

THE CHAIRMAN: I would object to that. I believe that the admission in the record of a lie detector test this committee had nothing to do with ordering, and cannot vouch for the credentials. And even if they could vouch for the credentials of the person issuing the lie detector test, if we get to the point in this country where lie detector tests are the basis upon which we make judgments and insist upon people having them, and by inference of those who don't have them that they did something wrong, we have reached a sad day for the civil liberties of this country.

That does not go to the issue of whether the individual is entitled to, on their own, ask for a lie detector test. People can make of it what they wish.

Now let me—

SEN. THURMOND: Mr. Chairman, I commend you for that stand.

SEN. HATCH: So do I, Mr. Chairman.

SEN. LEAHY: I happen to agree with it too, Mr. Chairman, while we are passing out kudos here.

THE CHAIRMAN: Well, I am flattered. Let's move on. Thank you very much. Now let's move on.

Ms. Fitch, I want to clarify something in the record, again an apparent inconsistency; it may not be.

I have been in and out of the room trying to accommodate some administrative requirements, and I apologize for not being here. Correct me if I am wrong.

I am under the impression that you told Senator Hatch that you did not go to lunch with Anita Hill.

MS. FITCH: I did. And I said it because I tend not to go to lunch. Period.

THE CHAIRMAN: Now, is the letter that you—I don't want to misstate anything. Hang on.

I would like to ask staff to give you this letter, the original of this letter. The letter I am referring to is a letter written by you, allegedly written by you to Ms.

Hill. The members of the committee have a copy of this letter.

Again, this may not be an inconsistency. I just want to be sure I understand. This letter, I might add, was submitted to the committee, to me and to Senator Thurmond, on October 12, from Warren W. Gardner, counsel for Anita Hill.

Just so people—while you are reading it, there is nothing salacious in it. There is nothing outrageous. There is nothing, other than for you to explain to me and for the record.

MS. FITCH: I did, this is my handwriting. Yes.

THE CHAIRMAN: Now, will you read—this sounds like a trial. Would you explain the first three or four sentences to us?

MS. FITCH: Should I read it?

THE CHAIRMAN: If you would like. I just want you to explain what appears to be an inconsistency.

MS. FITCH: Senator, ask anybody, I rarely went to lunch.

THE CHAIRMAN: No, I am not suggesting—read the first sentence or the first two sentences. Unless you think that it is too private to read.

MS. FITCH: Oh. All right. Read it out loud?

THE CHAIRMAN: Yes, would you read it out loud, please.

MS. FITCH: "Life is dull without you. I keep looking for someone to go to lunch with or sneak out to an early movie with."

THE CHAIRMAN: That is sufficient.

MS. FITCH: "Now there is nobody."

THE CHAIRMAN: That is sufficient.

Now, would you just explain for the record what you mean when you say "I keep looking for someone to go to lunch with," "without you," and your statement that you didn't go to lunch with Anita Hill?

MS. FITCH: I don't remember ever going to lunch with Anita Hill. It is probably just hyperbole, Senator. Really.

THE CHAIRMAN: I see. I don't doubt you.

MS. FITCH: I may have gone into her office with a sandwich that I got from the snack bar and sat in her office and eaten it. But I was not in the office that often.

THE CHAIRMAN: Sufficient. I am not being accusatory. I just want, because it is in the record and every Senator has this—

MS. FITCH: I don't see any inconsistency, what I just said and what is actually the truth. Yes.

THE CHAIRMAN: I just want to make the point again that honorable, decent people like you can say things that seem inconsistent, and I hope we understand that other people on the record can say things in the record that appear to be inconsistent and in fact are not inconsistent.

SEN. THURMOND: Mr. Chairman, I want to call your attention.

THE CHAIRMAN: Sure.

SEN. THURMOND: She says "I keep looking for someone to go to lunch with." She didn't say she went to lunch with her.

THE CHAIRMAN: No, I agree with that. That is why I just asked. But most people would assume, if I wrote you a letter, Senator, after I retired, which would be long before you will, and I said, "Dear Strom, it's really dull not being in the Senate, I keep looking for someone to go to lunch with," any reasonable person would assume that you and I went to lunch based on that. I don't say we went to lunch, but reasonable persons would assume that. And that is all I wanted to clear up.

SEN. THURMOND: I wouldn't say "would" to him. I would say "could."

MS. FITCH: I think I was writing her a cheery letter. I did miss her. She was one of the first people that I met when—

THE CHAIRMAN: Let me make it clear, Ms. Fitch, I totally believe you. I think it is a totally clear explanation. I don't doubt it for a moment, and I don't doubt your credibility.

But, again, I would point it out for my colleagues on the committee who are trying to be very precise. If I wanted to make the case—

MS. FITCH: Yes.

THE CHAIRMAN: [continuing]—I could have very easily made the case, and all the press to the best of their ability would write down, I suspect, and say, "Geez. Biden just tripped her up. Biden just showed that she really did go to lunch with her." And you didn't. I believe you didn't. I accept it.

MS. FITCH: Senator, I said that I may very well have gone to the snack bar and gotten a sandwich and eaten in her office.

THE CHAIRMAN: I understand. I understand.

Now, let me move on—and I sincerely do not question your credibility.

Ms. Myers, and I only have a few more questions—well, as a matter of fact, you have been on a long time. I won't ask any more questions.

Anyone else have any more questions? Whomever, Senator Thurmond I recognize.

SEN. THURMOND: I recognize Senator Simpson.

SEN. SIMPSON: Well, thank you very much. You have been very impressive, and the night wears on and we have got a lot more to do. But I, since we are putting statements and things in the record about polygraphs, I want to get in the record a statement by Larry Thompson, Esquire, former U.S. attorney, with regard to the issue of the total unreliability of a polygraph test, and thank Senators Kennedy and Hatch for the Polygraph Protection Act which protects people from this kind of stuff.

This is a real, you know, bush league kind of a thing in the midst of these type of activities. And most of us practiced law here or somewhere, and it really is quite extraordinary. And then, you know, if the resources of the handlers have been directed to this letter, which is a simple letter of friendship from Ms. Fitch to Anita Hill with nothing in it at all, then it does continue to get to be a longer night.

Whether you had lunch with anybody or nobody, there is nothing in this letter. There is nothing even to be gained from that letter.

THE CHAIRMAN: If the Senator would yield?

SEN. SIMPSON: I certainly will, because I am commenting.

THE CHAIRMAN: It was only offered, not to purport that there was anything in there that was—

SEN. SIMPSON: My time is not running. Go ahead. I just want to be sure about my time.

THE CHAIRMAN: Your time won't run.

SEN. SIMPSON: Okay.

THE CHAIRMAN: It was only offered, not to purport that there was anything extraordinary in it, as I said even before I showed it to the witness. It was done, I assume, by not her handlers, by her lawyers. Now, if we are calling handlers, then I assume everybody has handlers out there.

SEN. SIMPSON: Mr. Chairman, let's be quite honest here as to what is going on. When Ms. Hill came here to testify the other day, this whole front row was filled with people. I thought they were family. They were not. They were attorneys. Some were friends. Some were paid. And Ms. Hill has a public relations firm which she has hired, or someone has hired for her, and that is public record. So let's get that in to the American people, and know that in these extraordinary activities she does have what anyone would call, could call handlers. A public relations firm for a witness is unheard of during my time here, plus handlers.

THE CHAIRMAN: Senator, I am not arguing with that. It is no different than Mr. Duberstein who has a public relations firm that has been hired by the White House to "handle the nominee."

All I am saying is there is nothing wrong with any of that. Nothing about it is pejorative, on either side. I don't think we should make it that.

I assume the reason the letter was sent to the Senator and myself—the ranking member—was because there was concern about the testimony being given. I guess why we were given the letter, might come up and be something totally inconsistent with the relationship.

It was not inconsistent. But that is the reason I assume the letter was there.

MS. FITCH: And it was as I stated, that we were friendly.

THE CHAIRMAN: You did. I say for the 400th time.

MS. FITCH: No. I understand, Senator.

THE CHAIRMAN: I am not questioning your integrity. I do not question it. I believe you are telling the truth as you know it, as you have observed it. I believe you.

SEN. THURMOND: In fact, you would believe all of them, wouldn't you?

THE CHAIRMAN: Yes. I don't question any of them. I do not question any of them as to the facts. I question their judgment some times as to being able to make these leaps of faith. Ms. Myers is a wonderful woman. I question her instinct that says that there was romantic interest. I don't know it to be true or not true. That is pure speculation on the part of Ms. Myers. I don't question anything else that Ms. Myers testified to as the facts.

SEN. THURMOND: You might ask her why she said that, if you want to.

THE CHAIRMAN: You did. We did. I did.

SEN. THURMOND: That is why I said it.

THE CHAIRMAN: And now let's go back to the Senator from Wyoming, whose time it is.

SEN. SIMPSON: Thank you, Mr. Chairman, and I do appreciate your unfailing patience as we grind on. But I did want that statement of Larry Thompson to appear in the record which, of course says, as I indicated, that they are not admissible in the workplace. And thanks to Senators Kennedy and Hatch, employers are not allowed to use that as a club over their employees.

Furthermore, Mr. Thompson goes on to say, "In the context of these proceedings I understand, based on information from reliable scientific sources, that if a person suffers from a delusional disorder he or she may pass a polygraph test. Therefore, a polygraph examination in this context has absolutely no bearing on whether the events at issue are true or untrue."

That is not my quote. That is his. And now let's go to some questions. Just a few, please.

The calls, the logger of the calls. I have heard about you, Ms. Holt, and I would like to have someone like you as my gatekeeper. But I do, and they are very good. Let me ask you this.

The last call from Ms. Hill, after maybe fifteen or sixteen calls, some logged, some not logged, some just talking to you as a friend, or if she would talk to Nancy Fitch as a friend, or Phyllis Berry-Myers as a friend, or J.C. Alvarez, she was someone you knew and I assume, you know—in all the ways I leave it to you. You have described your relationship. I won't embellish that. But, in any event, there were no more calls to you after the last one about the marriage. Isn't that the last one we have recorded for our records?

MS. HOLT: That is right, Senator.

SEN. SIMPSON: In other words, the calls came from 1984 to 1988, 1987—August of 1987, by a woman who had heaped a garbage of verbiage upon her in her life. And the calls continued to come, fifteen or sixteen of them, and then they ended on that August 4 day in the afternoon when she found—and did you tell her that Clarence had married?

MS. HOLT: I don't recall that, Senator.

SEN. SIMPSON: You remember that conversation?

MS. HOLT: Not really. I don't.

SEN. SIMPSON: In any event, she left the message, which is of the record, congratulations, and that was that.

SEN. THURMOND: On the marriage.

SEN. SIMPSON: On the marriage. And so that is the last call that Ms. Hill ever made to your knowledge to the agency?

MS. HOLT: That is the last one to my knowledge, yes.

SEN. SIMPSON: Let me ask—you made a statement, Ms. Alvarez, on page 4. A rather powerful comment about Ms. Hill and your alarm as to what she had done and said. It was something to the effect—you have your statement there?

MS. ALVAREZ: Um-hum.

SEN. SIMPSON: It was page 4. I quote from page 4, at the top: "I don't know how else to say it, but it blew my mind to see Anita Hill testifying Friday. Honest to goodness, it was like schizophrenia. That was not the Anita Hill I knew and worked with at the EEOC. On Friday, she played the role of a meek, innocent, shy Baptist girl from the South who was a victim of this big bad man." That is quite a powerful statement.

Why did you say this reference to schizophrenia?

MS. ALVAREZ: Because there were two different personalities.

SEN. THURMOND: Speak out so we can hear you, please.

MS. ALVAREZ: There were two different personalities. When I worked with Anita Hill and I knew her, as I said, she was not a victim. She was a very tough woman. She stood her ground. She didn't take a lot of anything from anyone, and she made sure you knew it.

And the person who was here Friday was somebody who played a totally different role. Who was, "I am meek, I am shy, I am overwhelmed, I am victimized." And that was not the Anita Hill I knew. It was two different personalities.

SEN. SIMPSON: Well, based upon the years that you have known her, all of you, and worked with Anita Hill, have any of you ever known her to exaggerate small slights that you might have seen, make a big deal out of something that didn't warrant it?

MS. ALVAREZ: Well, the exaggeration that I saw in her probably most often was about her relationship with the chairman. You know, that she knew how he thought, she had some sort of special insight into him, that sort of thing. That was the exaggeration that I saw.

SEN. SIMPSON: And so, and I am going to conclude. So have you ever known her to focus on an injustice of some sort that she felt should be remedied? Have any of you seen that? You do. I just asked you because you used that phrase. And I wonder if any of you have ever witnessed in her some exaggeration of a slight or focusing on an injustice of some sort. Do you recall that?

MS. HOLT: I don't recall, Senator.

MS. FITCH: There was once an overreaction that stuck out in my mind. It wasn't important, but I thought it was clearly an overreaction. But it was not about anything terribly important.

SEN. SIMPSON: Did you notice anything like that, Ms. Myers?

SEN. METZENBAUM: [presiding]. Senator, your time is up, and I have tried to be patient. It has gone over for several minutes.

SEN. SIMPSON: I know but I haven't—just the final witness, if I might. Did you notice anything like that in what I asked?

MS. BERRY: Not that I remember. Not that I can remember.

SEN. SIMPSON: Thank you, Mr. Chairman.

SEN. METZENBAUM: Thank you.

Ms. Berry or Berry-Myers, you made one statement that I found quite interesting. You said that, "In that capacity I have been privy to the most intimate detail of his life," meaning, of course, Judge Thomas.

Were you familiar with the details of his family life?

MS. BERRY: Somewhat. What I meant by that was having to go through the confirmation process I am witness to like—FBI documents, letters for or against, background checks, you know, those sorts of things. That is what I meant by that.

SEN. METZENBAUM: Those are the professional parts. You were saying the most intimate details of his life. Did you know, for example, of his relationship with his son?

MS. BERRY: Yes. His son and my son were friends, and are friends.

SEN. METZENBAUM: And did you know the ladies he dated, if any? I am not even sure if he was married at the time you made that statement.

MS. BERRY: Yes, I know.

SEN. METZENBAUM: You knew the ladies he went out with socially?

MS. BERRY: Some, yes. Yes. I know of them. Some I know. And I knew his wife, yes. His first wife, Kathy.

SEN. METZENBAUM: Do you know about personal problems that he had, if any?

MS. BERRY: I know how, I know the struggle that it was when he was separating from his wife, what impact that had on his life and his son's life.

SEN. METZENBAUM: The reason I asked the question is because Judge Thomas said in his statement, "I do not and will not commingle my personal life with my work life, nor did I commingle their personal life with the work life. I can think of nothing that would lead her to this," was the last sentence. It is not relevant to this point.

But the point is he says that he kept his personal life extremely private. You seem to indicate that it was sort of public.

Let me just ask—

MS. BERRY: There is not an inconsistency in that or what—what he has said or what I am saying. In the professional contact that I had with this man I also got to know of his private life, his private travails and things. Because that was part of my job in preparing him for processes like this one.

SEN. METZENBAUM: Let me just ask each of you a question which can be answered yes or no. Each of you has testified as to the qualities of Judge Clarence Thomas and with a great deal of respect, and one of the—a major issue in this matter relates to Anita Hill's testimony about certain claims of sexual harassment.

I ask you yes or no. Could Clarence Thomas have made such remarks to Anita Hill, whatever those remarks, absent your presence and you would never have known anything about it?

MS. BERRY: Of course, Senator, if we weren't there we wouldn't know anything about it.

SEN. METZENBAUM: Pardon?

MS. BERRY: If we weren't present, we wouldn't know anything about it.

SEN. METZENBAUM: Correct. Would each of you answer? Isn't that the fact for each of you? That you actually would—it would be normal if a man were making such remarks at the workplace or any other place that other workers would not be familiar with those remarks?

MS. ALVAREZ: Senator, I don't think any of us could account for his time twenty-four hours a day, even in the office. But we know the man that he is and we know that he is not capable of making those remarks.

MS. FITCH: Senator, I had said, I think carefully, that I was talking about probability in terms of the judge, not possibility. Anything is possible, but the probability for me was nil.

SEN. METZENBAUM: Thank you, Ms. Fitch.

Ms. Holt, do you care to comment?

MS. HOLT: It is true that those comments could have been made in private, a private moment between he and Ms. Hill. However, I do feel that if this were going on I would have discerned something at some point, and I did not.

SEN. METZENBAUM: Thank you, Mr. Chairman.

THE CHAIRMAN: Thank you.

Senator Thurmond?

SEN. THURMOND: Senator Grassley will inquire.

SEN. GRASSLEY: Taking off on a point that Senator Metzenbaum just raised, and following an axiom of politics—or maybe it's one that even ought to be practiced in everyday life—if you always tell the truth, then you don't have to worry about what you told somebody else and you won't be in a mode of lying to cover up another lie. So always tell the truth and you won't get in trouble.

As a practical matter, if Mr. Thomas was doing all of the things that Professor Hill accuses him of, he wouldn't have been doing them just with her. It would be a weakness that would come out in conversations and with activities with other people that surely there is no way that this could have been covered up.

I mean it would have come out someplace if a person had a weakness like this.

MS. BERRY: That's my belief.

SEN. GRASSLEY: I primarily ask the question, not based on your understanding of personal behavior, but rather in your office. In your office environment could anything like this have been kept secret?

MS. FITCH: Senator, no. My office was not in the suite of the chairman. It was on staff floors and I heard all kinds of things about things that were happening in the Commission, about other people. There were never any stories floating around about the chairman in a negative or of this kind of nature is what I am saying.

SEN. GRASSLEY: And especially in Washington, DC If two people know about something it is no longer a secret in this town.

MS. BERRY: And there were no secrets at the EEOC, believe me.

SEN. METZENBAUM: There were no secrets at the EEOC?

MS. BERRY: No secrets.

SEN. GRASSLEY: So I mean there is no way, given how people are, especially in this town, that an activity like this could have been a secret?

MS. HOLT: No.

MS. BERRY: No.

SEN. GRASSLEY: Okay. I have just kind of a comment about something that Senator Leahy asked you folks. He asked if you had any information about why Anita Hill would jeopardize her career by coming forward with public allegations about Judge Thomas.

Now, I am not sure that this is a relevant question. Professor Hill admits that she never expected her allegations to be made public, so the possibility of public disclosure must not have been a factor in her decision to accuse Judge Thomas. And by making secret allegations behind closed doors she would not have to worry about jeopardizing her career or reputation.

Does that sound reasonable to you?

MS. FITCH: I have said previously that I have no idea of motivation. I can't ascribe motivation to other people, only to myself.

MS. BERRY: And I am not a mind reader, Senator, so I have no idea what was going through her mind.

MS. HOLT: I have no ideas.

MS. ALVAREZ: I have no explanation.

SEN. GRASSLEY: There has been some suggestion by Ms. Alvarez that there may be two Anita Hills, because you never knew the one that you saw on television. I want to ask the other three of you, while you were working with Anita Hill, did you see that she could have been two different people? You saw her as an aggressive lawyer arguing for her position very vocally, fighting for her position, etc.

Did you ever see another side to her, so that there could be some reason to believe that she was other than just this aggressive person? Any hint of that in any way?

MS. HOLT: I never saw another side.

MS. FITCH: I saw her as a smart person and also as a reserved one and that is pretty much what I saw the other day, except the story was something I had never heard before. No, so the answer is, no.

SEN. GRASSLEY: Okay. Ms. Berry?

MS. BERRY: No.

SEN. GRASSLEY: Let me also ask you about Professor Hill: you know the old saying that a certain individual would even walk on their grandmother to get ahead. Is she the sort of a person? Did you ever see her as being that sort of a person that would do anything just to get ahead?

MS. FITCH: No, Senator.

MS. HOLT: No, I did not.

SEN. GRASSLEY: Ms. Berry.

MS. BERRY: To have ambition, to be ambitious, yes, but to do anything? I don't know.

MS. ALVAREZ: I also saw her as quite ambitious and I have said so. To take it to the extent that she has, I think it kind of got out of hand, maybe before she even realized it.

SEN. GRASSLEY: My time is up.

THE CHAIRMAN: If you need more time, Senator, go ahead, take a few more minutes. You have been very patient, extremely patient.

SEN. GRASSLEY: Given your expertise as a historian, Professor Fitch, I wondered if I might ask you to draw on that background for a moment. You heard

Judge Thomas testify Friday comparing his treatment here to a lynching. I would like to have you explain or elaborate on that comparison for us.

Why is this ordeal, defending against a charge of sex harassment, similar to a lynching, as he put it?

MS. FITCH: I haven't talked to the judge since he made those comments, but when he made those comments I felt that I understood them. I have a student who is working on lynching right now, so I have been thinking about this. Lynching was something that was done to intimidate people, that was done to control them, as well as kill them. And I think, if I understand what the judge was saying, was that this was an attempt to do that to him; that the process, the subsequent confirmation hearings process, this process was patently unfair, that it was a way to neutralize and control and intimidate not just him, but possibly through him, any person that was considered, as he put it, uppity.

When black soldiers came back from World War I, they felt that they had proved themselves to the country and to their fellow citizens; and wore their uniforms down South and that was a sure way to get yourself lynched, because they were wrapped, so to speak, in the American flag. That was to tell these people that they were not Americans. I see a connection and understood what he meant by that. He said electronic lynching, I believe.

SEN. GRASSLEY: Well, do you sense then that there has to be a larger group of people that see him or people who think like him as a threat that must be put down right now or worry about what will happen if they are not put down right now?

MS. FITCH: Senator, I have talked to a colleague who worked with us on personal staff who you may have a statement from, I am not sure, and we talked about this on the phone and his words, subsequently, I think used in the press were character assassination. For me the operative word there is assassination. And the other word is neutralization and I felt and some of us do feel that any person of color in this country who goes against the stream of what people think black people in this country should be thinking and feeling and doing by so distinguishing themselves, put themselves at great risk.

This is not something that my colleague and I felt only because of the last few weeks. This is something we talked about years ago and tried to talk to the judge about, and in a comment to a friend last evening, I said, if he didn't understand what we were trying to say then—and obviously we were not beating him over the head with it, because it is a very uncomfortable thing to say to someone—I was assured that after his testimony of the last two days he understood it now.

SEN. GRASSLEY: Yes. I had a black leader in my state advise me to be against him, saying. "He doesn't even speak our language."

What is meant by that? I honestly don't know.

MS. FITCH: Senator, I don't know what the person who said that meant, but I think it means that that person is somehow perceived to be outside the group, is not in some perceived lock-step. And I think if you look at the history of black people in this country you see that people have always had diverse views. We are not a monolithic community in thought. And I think that is a huge mistake for the dominant society to think and for us to buy into.

And I suppose that—I don't know the situation you are talking about—but that is probably what that meant.

SEN. GRASSLEY: Well, have you ever heard other black American leaders use the expression, "he doesn't even speak our language"?

MS. FITCH: I don't know if I have heard the exact words, but I have gotten the distinct impression from working and watching Judge Thomas and how he seems to be perceived by black leaders, some of them, that that is something that they are saying, in effect, if they are not using those exact words. So I understand what that means.

SEN. GRASSLEY: Well, it is almost like denouncing the individuality that we worship in America.

MS. FITCH: I think, Senator, the problem is that when you are a community under siege it is very difficult for people to want to allow diversity of opinion. It is understandable. I don't like it but it is understandable and I don't think in any situation where you have communities that are considered minority and where there are a majority community around them that you are going to find this kind of attitude [*sic*].

SEN. GRASSLEY: In other words, we are all going to hang together or hang separately?

MS. FITCH: That, I think that is one way of explaining it, yes, Senator. That may be a simplistic way of doing it. I am sure there are other things involved, but, certainly that is one way of putting it. And I don't think it is just true in this country, it's probably true in South Africa, and in other places where there are communities under siege within the countries that they live in, and the societies that they live in.

SEN. GRASSLEY: So you intellectually lynch the people who do want to—

MS. FITCH: That's one way of doing it, Senator. That is probably the lesser of many evils.

SEN. GRASSLEY: Okay, I am done.

THE CHAIRMAN: Thank you, very much.

Let me clear up two facts and you have been here a long time. We are not going to hold you much longer. But Ms. Holt, on the last page of the transcript that you have in front of you of your logs, there is an insertion or an addition, an addendum, that has one message on it, the very last page. And it is in a different form than the others are and it says, "Judge, 11-1-90, 1:40", etc.

And the handwriting seems to be different from all the other handwriting.

MS. HOLT: It is different.

THE CHAIRMAN: Is it yours?

MS. HOLT: No, it isn't. This was probably taken at the court.

THE CHAIRMAN: I want the record to show that this is not admissible as part of your telephone logs and it is not admissible in the record. Ms. Holt cannot testify as to whether or not this is true, is that correct, Ms. Holt?

MS. HOLT: That is correct, yes.

THE CHAIRMAN: So, therefore, it is not admissible as a part of the record. Now, let me ask one other thing. Do any of you know Sukari Hardnett?*

MS. HOLT: I knew her, Senator.

MS. FITCH: Yes, Senator.

THE CHAIRMAN: Do you, Ms. Alvarez?

MS. ALVAREZ: No.

THE CHAIRMAN: Ms. Fitch, you know her?

MS. FITCH: Yes.

THE CHAIRMAN: Ms. Holt, you know her?

MS. HOLT: Yes.

THE CHAIRMAN: Ms. Myers, do you know her?

MS. BERRY: No, I don't know her.

THE CHAIRMAN: Now, can Ms. Fitch and Ms. Holt tell me who she is? Ms. Holt?

MS. HOLT: She was a legal intern in the office of the chairman.

THE CHAIRMAN: At EEOC?

MS. HOLT: At EEOC. What happens is that we hire legal interns while they are still in law school. When they graduate law school they have a certain period, and I don't know what that is, to pass the bar. Their titles are then changed to attorney.

Ms. Hardnett completed law school but she failed the bar so she had to be dismissed from her position.

THE CHAIRMAN: I see. Do you know who she is?

MS. FITCH: Yes.

THE CHAIRMAN: What do you know of her?

MS. FITCH: Senator, the same thing.

THE CHAIRMAN: Did you work with her at all?

MS. FITCH: I vaguely remember that I might have been involved in some project or she might have been involved in some project I was working on. I remember her but I can't tell you what that project might have been about and I don't recall that she was there more than maybe nine months.

THE CHAIRMAN: More than maybe—

MS. FITCH: I don't think she was there more than nine months, if possibly that long. That's my recollection.

THE CHAIRMAN: What is your recollection, Ms. Holt?

MS. HOLT: No more than a year, at any rate.

THE CHAIRMAN: Did you hear the chairman's testimony last night?

MS. HOLT: I did.

THE CHAIRMAN: The judge's testimony and the judge will have an opportunity to come back and he can clarify this, but maybe you can help me. Remember when I was asking him about legal assistants, you may remember I asked him who his legal assistants were and he corrected the record and he said, "I had more than one legal assistant"?

MS. HOLT: I think he was referring to the Department of Education.

THE CHAIRMAN: Thank you. That was my question.

I also want the record to show that my friend from Wyoming, in an attempt to

*See page 471

save me from myself, has suggested to me that it was not William Shakespeare who said, "Hell hath no fury." I still thought Shakespeare may have said it as well, but he says William Congreve said it, and the phrase was, "Heaven hath no rage like love to hatred turned, nor hell fury like a woman scorned."

I want the record to show that and thank him for that. [Laughter.]

I also must tell you that I have my staff researching Shakespeare to see if he said it, not that I think Mr. Congreve would ever plagiarize Shakespeare. [Laughter.]

Does anybody have any further questions?

SEN. SPECTER: Could I inquire, Mr. Chairman?

SEN. THURMOND: Senator Specter.

SEN. SPECTER: Thank you, Mr. Chairman.

I welcome the chance to talk to you ladies because you are an unusual panel here which is testifying on behalf of Judge Thomas, but knows Professor Hill very well. What we have been searching for in this long proceeding is some way to understand the issue of motivation and each of you has testified very forcefully that you think Judge Thomas is correct that the charges are false.

Let me start with you, Ms. Holt, because you seem to know Professor Hill very well. Were you surprised when these charges were leveled?

MS. HOLT: I was absolutely surprised, I was in shock.

SEN. SPECTER: Well, knowing—I expected that to be your answer—knowing Professor Hill as you do and being confident that Judge Thomas is in the clear, do you have any insight to shed on what Professor Hill may be doing, what her motivation is, if you think she is not telling the truth?

MS. HOLT: I know, I mean the allegations she has made are not even in character with Clarence Thomas.

SEN. SPECTER: But is it in character with Professor Hill to make such charges?

MS. HOLT: I never thought so, sir.

SEN. SPECTER: So you have it out of character for Judge Thomas to do this and you have it out of character for Professor Hill to make the charges.

MS. HOLT: Right.

SEN. SPECTER: Then why is she making the charges?

MS. HOLT: I have no idea, Senator.

SEN. SPECTER: No speculation?

MS. HOLT: None whatsoever, but I hope they find out.

SEN. SPECTER: Well, I think that with you four women we have as good a chance to find out as any way.

Ms. Fitch, you were very friendly. You didn't go to lunch with her, but you knew her very well.

MS. FITCH: We might have had lunch, Senator.

SEN. SPECTER: I am sorry, I can't hear you.

MS. FITCH: We might have had lunch together, Senator, I am not—

SEN. SPECTER: But at any rate, you were close to her, you were friendly with her?

MS. FITCH: Yes, exactly.

SEN. SPECTER: And when you first heard of these charges against Judge Thomas what was your reaction?

MS. FITCH: I was stunned. I was absolutely stunned.

SEN. SPECTER: Stunned?

MS. FITCH: Yes, and I still am.

SEN. SPECTER: Still stunned?

MS. FITCH: Yes.

SEN. SPECTER: Was it in character for Professor Hill to make false charges like this?

MS. FITCH: I have never known Professor Hill to make false charges. And as I said—

SEN. SPECTER: Well, you knew her very well for how long?

MS. FITCH: We were together from July 1982 to whenever she left in 1983, and I stayed in touch with her for possibly two years and I called maybe once every other month.

SEN. SPECTER: Lots of contacts?

MS. FITCH: Excuse me?

Well, when I was in the office and she was in the office we saw each other.

SEN. SPECTER: Talked to her a great deal?

MS. FITCH: Yes, I did because—

SEN. SPECTER: Got to know her pretty well?

MS. FITCH: [continuing] —I felt she was kind of the person I could of relate to since I was new on the staff and she had been with the chairman for some time, and I just felt that she was somebody I kind of gravitated to, to kind of get—

SEN. SPECTER: But no idea, not any speculation?

MS. FITCH: No speculation because there was no basis in the conversations that we have had and we had many at work.

SEN. SPECTER: Ms. Berry, you have testified that your relationship was barely speaking professionally and we have already had extensive—

MS. BERRY: With Angela Wright, but not with Anita Hill.

SEN. SPECTER: [continuing] —No, no, I am coming with Professor Hill. Oh, your relationship with Professor Hill was—

MS. BERRY: She has described it, and it was so, that it was a cordial, friendly, professional relationship.

SEN. SPECTER: [continuing]—so, were you surprised when you read her statement in the news conference on October 7 that referring to you, that she doesn't know me and I don't know her?

MS. BERRY: Yes.

SEN. SPECTER: When you first heard of the charges by Professor Hill against Judge Thomas, what was your reaction?

MS. BERRY: I was devastated and I was angry. I couldn't understand how someone—for a man who helped nurture her career, on the word of a good friend of his and hers, gave her a job at the Department of Education, subsequently asked her to join him at the EEOC, come to the EEOC, gave her responsibilities there, supported her, acted as her mentor, gave her recommendations to go to Oral

Roberts, helped her to secure that job—

SEN. SPECTER: But is she the kind of a person to make false charges, prior to the time that these were made?

MS. BERRY: [continuing] —I hadn't known her to be such.

SEN. SPECTER: How well did you know her?

MS. BERRY: I knew her professional. I'm not much of a socializer, but I didn't socialize.

SEN. SPECTER: But over how long a period did you know her professionally?

MS. BERRY: I knew her from 1982 until the time that she left the Commission.

SEN. SPECTER: Did you talk to her fairly often?

MS. BERRY: Yes, it was part of my responsibility.

SEN. SPECTER: But no idea at all why she would be motivated to make false charges?

MS. BERRY: No idea whatsoever.

SEN. SPECTER: How about you, Ms. Alvarez, how well did you know her?

MS. ALVAREZ: No, I knew her professionally. I did not know her as well as some of these others did.

SEN. SPECTER: How long did you know her?

MS. ALVAREZ: From the first time, my first day at the Commission until she left.

SEN. SPECTER: What was your reaction, when you heard these charges by Professor Hill against Judge Thomas?

MS. ALVAREZ: I was shocked. I was absolutely shocked, and I was sickened by it, because, likewise, I knew that he had helped her on lots of occasions, and I just felt like it was a betrayal.

SEN. SPECTER: Ms. Holt, this committee has to make a judgment. We have heard people of the panel before you four women came on, who said that they had total confidence in Professor Hill. You women have said you have total confidence in Judge Thomas. Can you give any clue, any clue at all as to how this committee can break that deadlock?

MS. HOLT: Senator, I guess for all of us—again, we were talking about probability, we are talking about patterns of behavior that we have not witnessed—we are talking about the fact that up to the time of these allegations, we never heard anyone else make such allegations in our presence, talk about such things. We never heard rumors flying about this Chairman, Clarence Thomas—

SEN. SPECTER: But how about the behavior or patterns of behavior of Professor Hill?

MS. HOLT: Senator—

SEN. SPECTER: You never heard her make a false charge, did you?

MS. HOLT: No, I haven't, but I guess my focusing on constructive looking at people—my focus has been on Judge Thomas. I cannot—

SEN. SPECTER: Why not put a focus on Professor Hill?

MS. BERRY: On October 7, I made—

SEN. SPECTER: You first, Ms. Fitch, and then you, Ms. Berry.

MS. HOLT: Well, I have been out of touch with Professor Hill for three years, so

I may have written her lately about my last position, but I have not heard back from her. I can't say what she may be doing or thinking since the last three years that I last spoke to her. I have periodically run into the judge and talked to him, stayed in touch with his mother whom I met when I was in Savannah, so it is not the same thing.

SEN. SPECTER: What did you want to add, Ms. Berry?

MS. BERRY: Well, on October 7, I heard a false charge, "I do not know Phyllis Berry and she does not know me."

SEN. SPECTER: Let me ask one other question for response by all of you, and it is this: Is it possible that Professor Hill could think this happened and it did not? We have explored that possibility, and you are not professionals and I don't know how much insight the professionals can provide, but each of you women knew her rather well, especially Ms. Holt and Ms. Fitch.

One of the questions that has been going through my mind that I started out with was some effort to reconcile the testimony of these two people who appear to be so credible. I had thought that it might be possible to reconcile them, frankly, until I heard Professor Hill's testimony and the expanded nature of the charges which were made at that time—very different from what she put in her statement and very different from what she had told the FBI, and when I saw those expanded charges, it didn't seem possible to reconcile them.

But we have a situation here where you have a pattern of conduct toward Judge Thomas, which is admitted to by Professor Hill where she has a very cordial relationship, no indication of anger, moves with him from one job to another, she does tell one friend and tells that friend that she has only told her, and then three more people come up today, which I hadn't heard about until yesterday, and the charges are expanded and Ms. Berry has speculated about the spurned woman approach.

But can you women shed any light on the possibility that Professor Hill might have had an attachment or a feeling which would have led her to think about these things?

Senator Hatch yesterday put into the record some speculation, and that is what we are doing here, pure and simple. But you women know her well enough, so that I think you might have some insight into it, in terms of the case, which had the reference to "Silver" and reference to some other facts which came from another case. And without impugning any impropriety or wrongdoing, what do you think, Ms. Holt? I think you know her the best of anybody on the panel. Do you think it is conceivable that Professor Hill might really think this happened, when it didn't?

MS. HOLT: I think that's the only conceivable answer, Senator, because I do not believe it happened.

SEN. SPECTER: Well, you don't believe it happened and you can't find any motivation for her.

MS. HOLT: I can't find any motivation for her saying that it did happen.

SEN. SPECTER: Do you think she is the kind of a person who would come here under oath and say that it happened, if she didn't think it did happen?

MS. HOLT: I don't know. She didn't appear to be that type of person when I knew her.

SEN. SPECTER: You knew her second best, Ms. Fitch. Do you think it is possible that she really believes in her mind today that it never really happened?[*sic*].

MS. FITCH: I think it's possible. I may be on shaky ground here. I have read a little bit in psychiatry, but there is something called transference. I'm not talking now about Professor Hill, but just in general terms. My understanding of what transference means is that you may have strong feelings about someone and you're able to focus on someone who is either a therapist or someone who has been kind to you, and things get kind of muddled and they carry the burden of whatever someone else may or may not have done or what is something that you think actually happened.

So, there are any number of explanations, I would suspect, that would say that she is not a liar, but that this did not happen, but that, yes, she could probably pass a polygraph test, because she does sincerely believe that this happened with this person. And I say again that I do not believe in the allegations.

SEN. SPECTER: Well, have you seen anything in her personality or had any experience with her, because you knew her very well, which would give you some factual basis or some feeling that she might think that it happened, when, in fact, it didn't?

MS. FITCH: Senator, that's why I said I am not talking about Professor Hill, but just in general terms about this idea of transference. No, I can't say that I have.

SEN. SPECTER: Ms. Alvarez, what do you think about that possibility?

MS. ALVAREZ: I didn't know her well enough personally to be able to say that she was—that this would be something she would do. I didn't see her professionally as somebody who would do that. I do recall her being very ambitious, and—

SEN. SPECTER: Is this going to help her ambition?

MS. ALVAREZ: Well, she is—

SEN. SPECTER: Her life is not going to be any easier now.

MS. ALVAREZ: Well, I think she has now become, as I think somebody on this committee put it, the Rosa Parks of sexual harassment. You know, the speaking engagements will come, the book, the movie. I mean I don't know.

SEN. SPECTER: Do you think that's her motivation?

MS. ALVAREZ: I don't—I'm speculating. I have had to try and sort out what I think, why I think she might have done it. I think that it might have started off as a political, she was a political pawn, and the situation got out of control and she took it—

SEN. SPECTER: So, you think she is deliberately not telling the truth, as opposed to saying something that she thinks might have happened, when, in fact, it didn't?

MS. ALVAREZ: Yes, because I did not know her personally well enough to make a judgment on her personality and whether she was capable of that fantasy. My only way of looking at it is that it is a professional, I mean it is a personal move on her part, to advance her.

SEN. SPECTER: Ms. Berry, you have the final comment. You had started off with a quotation of the *New York Times*, which I asked Professor Hill about, saying that you thought there might have been a romantic interest that was denied. Do you think that—well, you've already said you don't think she's the kind of person that makes something up, but you disbelieve what she said. Do you think that, based on your knowledge of her, that there could be a situation where she thinks it happened, but, in fact, it did not?

MS. BERRY: A point I would like to make, I was listening some to Mr. Carr's testimony this morning or today, and he had indicated that Anita said to him that "I was harassed by my supervisor." Clarence Thomas was not the only supervisor that Anita had, and Mr. Carr seemed to make this gigantic leap, because he knew that she was on Clarence Thomas's personal staff, that the supervisor that she must have been referring to was Clarence Thomas.

SEN. SPECTER: Who were others who could be classified as a supervisor?

MS. BERRY: Mr. Roggerson was her supervisor in Congressional Affairs, and when I succeeded him to Congressional Affairs, he became the Executive Assistant, and so he was also her supervisor. How can I say this? Mr. Roggerson doesn't have such an impeccable reputation.

SEN. SPECTER: So, you think, in the case of one of the witnesses this morning, Professor Paul [*sic*] might just have the wrong man?

MS. BERRY: I am saying that's possible. He seemed to make that—he didn't identify. He said, "Anita Hill said to me that she was being harassed by her supervisor," and he said, "I dominated the conversation and, because she worked for Clarence Thomas, it must have been Clarence Thomas."

THE CHAIRMAN: Senator, it is time to switch.

SEN. SPECTER: If I may make just one more comment, Mr. Chairman. I had not heard what Senator Kennedy said this morning, and I waited until I got a transcript of the record, because I didn't want to make a comment, without being precise as to what Senator Kennedy had said.

When I got a transcript of the record about fifteen minutes ago, I told Senator Kennedy that I was going to raise this point, because I strongly disagree with what he said, but I wanted to be sure, before I took issue with it.

When Senator Kennedy had a turn earlier today, he said, "But I hope, Mr. Chairman, that after this panel, we are not going to hear any more comments unworthy, unsubstantiated comments, unjustified comments about Professor Hill and perjury, as we heard in this room yesterday."

I want to say that the comments I made yesterday were not unworthy, were not unsubstantiated or unjustified. On the contrary, they were well-based and well-founded in the record. It is a little late to debate it now, but I am prepared to do so, at your pleasure, Senator Kennedy.

SEN. KENNEDY: Well, Mr. Chairman, it is nonsense to suggest that Professor Hill committed perjury or anything remotely approaching it. It was very clear what she was saying to Senator Specter.

Initially, she said no one on the committee staff had suggested to her that Judge Thomas might withdraw quickly and quietly, simply because she made an allegation to the committee. Later, she said the possibility of withdrawal had come up, but in the context of a very different kind of conversation about the various things that might happen down the road as one of a broad range of possible outcomes, if Professor Hill reported what had happened. That's an obvious distinction between the two statements, and it is preposterous to call it perjury.

THE CHAIRMAN: Gentlemen, before you—

SEN. SPECTER: Just one reply, Mr. Chairman.

I regard that comment and characterization as preposterous. I did not start this argument, but I am not going to back away from it. To be in this committee room and to say that they are unsubstantiated is just patently wrong. I asked the question repeatedly, and there was no doubt about it. The witness was very evasive, and then the witness was really decisive in saying that no staffer had approached her with a suggestion that Judge Thomas might withdraw. Then, in the afternoon, in an unresponsive way and a way which really showed calculation, she slipped in a comment to the contrary. I think, having had some experience in the field, that what she said was just flatly untrue in the morning and she changed it in the afternoon. I think she did so knowing that it was a recantation and avoided a problem.

Thank you, Mr. Chairman.

SEN. KENNEDY: Well, if I could be recognized thirty seconds.

THE CHAIRMAN: Gentlemen, I will recognize the Senator from Massachusetts for thirty seconds, and then I respectfully suggest that this debate is likely to go on on the floor anyway, and I would ask that we end it. In the meantime, shortly after, I am going to ask the women on the panel whether they need a break. They have been sitting there a long time. I don't know how much people have to go.

I yield to my colleague from Massachusetts.

SEN. KENNEDY: Senator Specter has repeated effectively what he said in the transcript, when he said "I went through that in some detail, because it is my legal judgment, having some experience in perjury prosecution, the testimony of Professor Hill in the morning was flat-out perjury. She specifically changed it in the afternoon, when confronted with the possibility of being contradicted, and if you recant during the course of proceeding, it is not perjury, so I state very carefully as to what she had said in the morning."

But in the context of those continual denials, consulting the attorney, repeatedly asking the question, I believe this was at a time when I did interrupt. I know that the Senator from Pennsylvania didn't think it appropriate, but some of us thought he was attempting to put words into the mouth of Professor Hill. He went on and simply stated "was false and perjurious, in my legal opinion, and the change in the afternoon was a concession fatally to that effect."

Mr. Chairman, rather than going through the reference parts now and taking the time, I would like to ask that those parts of the record that refer to those exchanges be included now in the record, and the members can make up their own mind. The members can make up their own mind as to what conclusion they would draw.

SEN. SPECTER: That is satisfactory to me.

THE CHAIRMAN: Without objection, so ordered.

[The information referred to was entered in the record.]

THE CHAIRMAN: Now, let me canvas here for a minute, because you have been a long time sitting there.

Does anyone else have a question for this panel? Senator DeConcini, roughly how long do you wish?

SEN. DECONCINI: Five minutes or less.

THE CHAIRMAN: I will go down the line here.

SEN. SIMON: Five minutes.

THE CHAIRMAN: Five minutes.

SEN. HATCH: Five minutes.

THE CHAIRMAN: Five minutes, one minute.

We will give you a recess.

[Recess.]

THE CHAIRMAN: I think that the last questioner was Senator Specter. Senator Specter was the last one to question, correct?

SEN. THURMOND: So who is next?

THE CHAIRMAN: I think it is Senator DeConcini, and then Senator Hatch.

SEN. DECONCINI: Thank you, Mr. Chairman. I don't have too many questions.

Let me ask the panel, if I can, particularly Ms. Fitch and I guess Ms. Holt, it sounds like, from what you tell us today, that you were pretty good friends with Professor Hill. Is that a fair assumption?

MS. FITCH: We were good work friends. I was a good work friend with Anita Hill, yes.

MS. HOLT: We were professional friends.

SEN. DECONCINI: Professional friends.

MS. HOLT: And I use the word "professional" because we did not socialize on weekends or after work.

SEN. DECONCINI: In the course of that friendship, did she ever mention to you a friendship she had with Susan Hoerchner?

MS. HOLT: No, she did not.

SEN. DECONCINI: She did not? Or to Ellen Wells?

MS. HOLT: She had mentioned Ellen Wells.

SEN. DECONCINI: She had mentioned Ellen Wells? Can you recall?

How about you, Ms. Fitch? Did she ever mention either one?

MS. FITCH: I don't recall those names, Senator.

SEN. DECONCINI: Ms. Holt, what about Ellen Wells? Do you remember in what context that was mentioned?

MS. HOLT: I don't remember with any specificity, just that she knew Ellen Wells, and I recall having heard the name mentioned by Professor—

SEN. DECONCINI: Did she by any chance tell you, "This is one of my best, closest friends"?

MS. HOLT: No, she did not.

SEN. DECONCINI: Would you really have remembered that, you think, if she had said that?

MS. HOLT: Right.

SEN. DECONCINI: And John Carr, was that name ever—

MS. HOLT: I remembered her referring to a "John".

SEN. DECONCINI: To a "John," and not in any context close friend or some relationship?

MS. HOLT: I remember her referring to a "John" that she was dating.

SEN. DECONCINI: That she was dating.

Ms. Fitch, how about you?

MS. FITCH: Now, I don't recall that, Senator.

SEN. DECONCINI: Just not to leave anybody out, Ms. Berry, did—

MS. BERRY: I don't recall any such conversation.

SEN. DECONCINI: No such conversation.

Now I guess, Ms. Alvarez, this question is more to you. You know, listening to Judge Thomas here and his high regard and respect for then Ms. Hill, now-Professor Hill, you know, he doesn't have anything derogatory to say about her. He is just absolutely aghast and awash that this would happen, where your testimony is very critical of her. How do you equate that? Is that if he had a relationship with her in the professional field that was more compatible than the relationship that you had with Ms. Hill in the professional field?

MS. ALVAREZ: Why do you say I was critical of her? I don't think I was critical by saying—let me think how I described her—

SEN. DECONCINI: Let me just read it to you. It says, "She was opinionated, arrogant, and a relentless debater. She was the kind of woman who always made you feel like she was not going to be messed with, like she was not going to take anything from anyone. She was aloof. She always acted as if she was superior to everyone else, holier-than-thou." I think that is critical, but maybe—

MS. ALVAREZ: I don't know. Some people would call me arrogant, and some people would call me opinionated and a relentless debater.

SEN. DECONCINI: Nobody would call you arrogant. You are such a very nice lady.

MS. ALVAREZ: I don't think those are necessarily negative characteristics.

SEN. DECONCINI: You don't? Oh, okay.

MS. ALVAREZ: No. In some people's mind, they would think to say a woman was tough, a woman was arrogant, that would mean that—

SEN. DECONCINI: "Opinionated"—

MS. ALVAREZ: [continuing]—opinionated? No, I don't think that is necessarily—

SENATOR DECONCINI [continuing]—"arrogant, and a relentless debater," are not critical?

MS. ALVAREZ: If someone called me those things—

SEN. DECONCINI: Even two of those are not critical in your mind? Okay.

So my point is, did you hold her in high regard? Now I realize a lot has happened since then, and it is hard to look back on the nice side of somebody who—

MS. ALVAREZ: I did not have a problem with her professionally.

SEN. DECONCINI: You did not what?

MS. ALVAREZ: I did not have a problem with her professionally. I thought that I didn't like her superior attitude. I didn't like the way she kind of projected that onto the rest of the staff.

SEN. DECONCINI: Ms. Holt, you were asked a question about the Department of Education being suggested to be abolished by the Reagan Administration, and you said you were aware of that?

MS. HOLT: I had heard that, yes.

SEN. DECONCINI: You had heard that. You were also aware, or were you aware that there was ever a vote or even a debate on the Senate floor or House floor?

MS. HOLT: No, I wasn't aware of that.

SEN. DECONCINI: Yes. There wasn't.

MS. HOLT: There was a rumor.

SEN. DECONCINI: It was a rumor only, wasn't it, because there has never been a vote up here on Capitol Hill, on either the floor of the Senate or the House, to abolish, and there wasn't during those years. I just want the record to show that.

Now, Ms. Fitch, when you were answering Senator Grassley's question about the problem of speaking somebody's language, and that Clarence Thomas was going upstream or talked about the uppity blacks being different or something, do you have a feeling that there is some agenda here that is moving this or motivating this?

MS. FITCH: Senator, as a historian who has tried to look at the totality of the African-American experience in this country, my proclivity is to look at conspiracy theories, and I don't want to too closely associate that with this particular case. However, it would not surprise me that anyone, regardless of race, who hears a different drummer is at potential risk.

SEN. DECONCINI: Yes, potential risk.

MS. FITCH: And I am more comfortable thinking of it in those terms.

SEN. DECONCINI: So if you were extremely conservative, perhaps the liberal side wouldn't want you there, and might be involved in such a thing?

MS. FITCH: Well, Senator, that is a possibility, and it is also possible that conservatives might want to make it look like the—

SEN. DECONCINI: Yes, on the other side, from the other side, and if you were very strong on some ideological issue—

MS. FITCH: It is possible, Senator.

SEN. DECONCINI: [continuing]—such as abortion or *Roe v. Wade*, there could be some effort by those who opposed it or who opposed the right-to-life position.

MS. FITCH: I should probably say, though, Senator, one of the reasons I liked then-Chairman Thomas was that I am not a conservative Republican. I am a New York Rockefeller Republican, so we did not always agree. I consider myself a moderate, and he knew that.

SEN. DECONCINI: Thank you, thank you.

My last question is, just do you believe, each one of you, would you just state here for me, do you believe that Professor Hill was telling the truth when she testified here for some six hours. Ms. Alvarez?

MS. ALVAREZ: No, sir.

SEN. DECONCINI: Ms. Fitch.

MS. FITCH: No, sir.

SEN. DECONCINI: Ms. Holt.

MS. HOLT: No, sir

SEN. DECONCINI: Ms. Berry.

MS. BERRY: No, sir, absolutely not.

SEN. DECONCINI: Absolutely not. Thank you very much. I have no further questions.

THE CHAIRMAN: Senator Thurmond.

SEN. THURMOND: Senator Hatch.

SEN. HATCH: Let me just ask a few more questions, just to finish off what I had in mind.

In *The Washington Post* of September 9, 1991, the day before our hearings began, Anita Hill was quoted as follows, referring to a ten year-old article in which Judge Thomas made comments relative to his sister. Now here is what Professor Hill said before she made— this statement was made before she made any public charges of harassment: "It takes a lot of detachment to publicize a person's experience in that way."

She was also quoted as observing that Judge Thomas exhibited "a certain kind of self-centeredness, not to recognize some of the programs that benefited you." And she also was quoted as saying, "I think he doesn't understand people. He doesn't relate to people who don't make it on their own."

Now I would like to ask all of you, and we could start from you, Ms. Alvarez, across, did Anita Hill ever mention to any of you, at the time that you knew her, that she believed Clarence Thomas to be "detached" and that she thought he was "self-centered," that she believed that he failed to recognize the programs that benefited minorities and, most importantly, that she thought he did not "relate to people" and "didn't understand people"? Did you ever hear any comments like these from her?

MS. ALVAREZ: No, sir, I never did. I heard nothing but positive things about him, and everything he did in terms of helping her was an example of just the same thing.

SEN. HATCH: Ms. Fitch.

MS. FITCH: No, Senator.

SEN. HATCH: Ms. Holt.

MS. HOLT: No, Senator, and in fact her statement to the effect that he was unfriendly and couldn't relate to people could not be further from the truth. Even the members of the domestic staff talked to Chairman Thomas about their problems.

SEN. HATCH: And he talked to them?

MS. HOLT: And he talked to them.

SEN. HATCH: And he treated them equally?

MS. HOLT: He treated them equally.

SEN. HATCH: Now let me just ask this last question. There has been some indication that part of the problem here was that she was ambitious and desired a promotion in the department, and if I have it correctly, Allyson Duncan was promoted above her. Am I correct? She got the job? Ms. Holt, go ahead.

MS. HOLT: It wasn't actually a promotion. It was more recognizing Allyson as the chief of staff, as having supervisory responsibility in terms of assignments.

SEN. HATCH: But is it true that Anita Hill wanted that position or that recognition, to use your term?

MS. HOLT: She never indicated directly to me that she wanted it, no.

SEN. HATCH: How about the rest of you? Ms. Alvarez.

MS. ALVAREZ: It was common knowledge. I can't recall exactly who said what, but there were several times that people made reference to that.

SEN. HATCH: Ms. Fitch.

MS. FITCH: Senator, again, my experience is different because I was away, so any office-type politics I might not be aware of, so I am unaware of—

SEN. HATCH: But you were aware of her ambition and that she desired—

MS. FITCH: Oh, yes, she was ambitious.

SEN. HATCH: Nothing wrong with that. I am not implying anything wrong.

MS. FITCH: But I don't know about this specific position. I can't speak to that at all.

SEN. HATCH: Sure. And Ms. Berry?

MS. BERRY: She didn't indicate to me specifically, but I heard from other members from the Commission, throughout the Commission, that, yes, she desired that position.

SEN. HATCH: That is all I have, Mr. Chairman.

THE CHAIRMAN: Can you tell us for the record, Ms. Myers, who you heard it from, what other members, by name, you heard it from?

MS. BERRY: I could, but I won't. They haven't volunteered to come forward.

THE CHAIRMAN: Senator Leahy.

SEN. LEAHY: Ms. Holt, I was just confused by one thing. You may have already said this, but when did you leave the EEOC?

MS. HOLT: I am still at the EEOC.

SEN. LEAHY: When did you leave the employ of Clarence Thomas? I'm sorry.

MS. HOLT: In September of 1987.

SEN. LEAHY: In September of 1987, and the last call from Anita Hill, according to your log, was August of 1987. Is that correct?

MS. HOLT: Correct.

SEN. LEAHY: And then after that, you were no longer there, keeping the log. About a month later, you were no longer keeping the log. Is that correct?

MS. HOLT: That is correct.

SEN. LEAHY: And by the number of calls we have in here, she called an average of about once every seven or eight months, so the fact that there wasn't another call a month later, there is nothing unusual in that, is there?

MS. HOLT: No, sir.

SEN. LEAHY: But there seemed to be some inference by some here that she made that call and then suddenly cut off because she had been told that Judge Thomas was on his honeymoon or something. The fact is, a month later you were gone, and she didn't call that often anyway. We have six or seven calls logged in here, a handful of calls over several years. It averages about one and a half or so a year. I just didn't want the wrong inference to be left here.

Ms. Alvarez, you opined that possibly Anita Hill could have been doing this so she could make a movie. Let me tell you, after spending thirty, forty hours, whatever it is we have been here, I can't imagine anybody would want to spend thirty or forty minutes in this movie, and I don't really see that as a motivation.

But you did say one thing, and you were very emphatic on this answer, and I want to make sure I understood you right. You said that Judge Thomas never talked about sex matters at work. You were very emphatic about that. Is that right?

MS. ALVAREZ: That is right.

SEN. LEAHY: Including pornography or anything else?

MS. ALVAREZ: Right.

SEN. LEAHY: What about outside of work?

MS. ALVAREZ: Clarence and I were friends. We had been friends for many, many years, personal friends. Our kids went to the same school together. I knew his wife. We were going through a divorce at the same time and everything else. We had the kind of confidences, personal conversations, that friends have, that close friends have, and any more than that really is not relevant. I mean, at the office we were colleagues and the friendship part of it never—

SEN. LEAHY: Did you talk about pornography outside the office?

MS. ALVAREZ: No, sir, we never did.

SEN. LEAHY: Well, I am not sure I understand your answer. I am not really trying to trick you or anything here, but you said you didn't talk about pornography, didn't talk about sex matters at work. I asked you about outside of work, and—

MS. ALVAREZ: And I am trying to explain to you that Clarence and I knew each other very well, and that we had a personal friendship.

SEN. LEAHY: You didn't date?

MS. ALVAREZ: No, sir.

SEN. LEAHY: Do you want to add to that? I am not sure I understand. Do you know of him talking to anybody outside of work?

MS. ALVAREZ: I am sorry. Say this again.

SEN. LEAHY: Other than yourself, do you know of Clarence Thomas talking to people outside of work about either sex or pornography? Outside of yourself?

MS. ALVAREZ: No, sir. I just know that with me we, we had a friendship and that was it. I mean, we shared conversations that close friends share when you are going through divorce, when you are going through raising kids, all those sorts of things. The typical things that close friends talk about.

SEN. LEAHY: Thank you. Okay. I just wanted to clear that up.

And, Ms. Holt, you have certainly cleared up a question that was left hanging out here and I appreciate that.

Thank you, Mr. Chairman.

SEN. KENNEDY: [presiding]. Senator Thurmond.

SEN. THURMOND: I have one question I would like to ask Dr. Fitch.

Dr. Fitch, I believe you said that you visited Professor Hill in the hospital.

MS. FITCH: Yes, I did.

SEN. THURMOND: Do you know roughly when that was and why Professor Hill was there?

MS. FITCH: Senator, I know, I believe it was in 1983. I believe it was in summer, sometime between spring and summer. I don't, I can't give you an exact date. I did go to see her. I think she was in the hospital for a week and I do not recall that the nature—I don't recall what she was suffering from. It rang a bell that it might have had something to do with a stomach ailment, but I don't remember what the diagnosis was. I don't know that I ever knew.

SEN. THURMOND: What hospital was she in?

MS. FITCH: I believe, Senator, it was Capitol Hill Hospital. It is a hospital on the Hill and I think that is the name of it.

SEN. THURMOND: Thank you. Senator Brown.

SEN. BROWN: Thank you, Mr. Chairman.

Ms. Holt, occasionally, at least in our office, when people call in they will sometimes be given a home phone number. Occasionally, when we call back to other people we will have on file their home phone number as well as their office number.

I recognize it has been some time, but do you have any recollection as to whether or not Professor Hill had Clarence Thomas's home phone number or whether or not he had her home phone number?

MS. HOLT: I have no way of knowing that. I can only say that I did not give Professor Hill Clarence Thomas's home phone number.

SEN. BROWN: And you never referred her to his—to call him at home?

MS. HOLT: I did not.

SEN. BROWN: And you never got a feel for whether they chatted outside of office hours?

MS. HOLT: No.

SEN. BROWN: Thank you. A question to all of you. It may not be anything that we can add here, but I suspect most members are like I[*sic*]. You find the current divergence, or dramatic divergence in their testimony somewhat hard to explain.

In thinking about Clarence Thomas, was he the kind of person who would be different in the way he treated people, react to people, talk to people in private than he would be, let's say, when other people were present? Is there a significant difference in the way he behaved or talked or acted when you would be in an office sitting along with him versus where others could see or hear?

MS. HOLT: He always treated me with respect. He was a professional, and I had no problems whether there were twenty people around or whether we were alone.

SEN. BROWN: No significant difference in the way—

MS. HOLT: No difference at all.

SEN. BROWN: What about the rest of you? Any observations in that area?

MS. FITCH: I agree with what Ms. Holt just said. There was no difference.

MS. BERRY: I agree.

MS. ALVAREZ: I agree to a point. Because Clarence and I were friends outside of the office. I probably saw, I mean I would call him Clarence, you know. We talked about the kids and personal things that friends talk about that he would not have shared with people at the office.

SEN. BROWN: I was trying to go through and outline some of the traits that we have come to learn about him. I think all of us have come to learn about him. We have really listened to him for seven days. I don't know how close a friendship it has engendered, but I think this committee has come to know him pretty well as well.

But at least as I go through it, I find things like he is a serious person, and here is someone who after they were separated from their wife, a bachelor, in effect, again, sells his only car to pay for his son's tuition to school, and that is an unusually serious—I don't know many bachelors who sell their only means of transportation for their son's tuition. A very unusually serious person.

From the depositions I have read, this is someone who didn't tell dirty stories either in public or private, or even on camping trips. That he appears formal, intense, extremely hardworking, strict, and demanding are a couple of terms I have heard applied both to others around him and himself. I don't suppose there is anybody on this committee that doesn't think that what they need to do is work out every noon instead of eat or at least—I should speak for myself. I feel that need. And yet not many do it, or at least I don't.

I mean this is an extremely disciplined, serious individual. Is that a proper impression? Are there other descriptions you could give me of Clarence Thomas?

MS. FITCH: That is my description of him and one of the things that impressed me the most about him. And I think that those combinations of terms is what I meant when I thought of the word "decent" to apply to him in all ways.

MS. BERRY: But he is also generous, and supportive, and willing to promote people who work for him, kind. He is a good human being. Intelligent.

SEN. BROWN: The remarks he is alleged to have made and the conduct he is supposed to have done; that is, to ask someone out repeatedly and to pressure them to go out with you is an aggressive, is an aggressive personal act when someone says no to pressure them again. And it is almost confrontational in a personal way. To say those kinds of remarks is a very confrontational, hostile thing to do.

Were those traits present in Clarence Thomas?

MS. FITCH: No, Senator.

MS. HOLT: No, Senator.

MS. ALVAREZ: Not at all.

MS. BERRY: In fact, the Clarence Thomas that I first met was really kind of—I know it is going to be hard for you all to believe this, but he was really kind of socially shy. It took me maybe six months to get the man out of his office and to circulate among the employees, and at the Commission, you know, to greet them in the hall and to have lunch in their cafeteria, those sorts of things, because he is a relatively disciplined, serious individual. And the kinds of public relations things that I felt he needed to do, such as give public speeches and to greet the employees, and all of those kinds of things, it was like pulling hen's teeth to get the man to do that.

And then after he started doing that and saw the public reception to the real Clarence Thomas, that he was funny and smart and an articulate speaker, then it was hard for me to get him back in the office. But—

SEN. BROWN: Help me with one last question, if you would. If someone said to you to be personally very aggressive, as someone would be if they pushed someone to go out with them that wouldn't take no for an answer and said very, very gross things to them, someone said that was totally out of character, would that be an accurate statement? Would it be a gray area? How would you compare the contact that is described to Clarence Thomas?

MS. HOLT: Uncharacteristic, in a word.

MS. BERRY: Not Clarence Thomas at all.

MS. ALVAREZ: There is no way he is the man she alleges.

SEN. BROWN: Well, thank you.

SEN. KENNEDY: Thank you very much. Just before yielding to Senator Simon, I just want to make a comment about the panel. They are very strong supporters of Clarence Thomas. Understandable. They owe Clarence their jobs and they have great respect for him, and they are certainly qualified to speak on that.

But what they are not qualified is to psychoanalyze Professor Hill. And we have heard many reasons during the course of these hearings about concocted stories, about being pressured by various groups, and tonight we are hearing about schizophrenia, we are hearing about delusions, we are hearing about mental disturbances, and one has to just ask oneself how far will the proponents for this nomination go in trying to attack Professor Hill?

Senator Simpson.

SEN. SIMPSON: Mr. Chairman, did I hear you say "How far will the opponents go"? Was that what I heard?

SEN. KENNEDY: Yes. That is right.

SEN. SIMPSON: I think I am about to faint.

SEN. KENNEDY: That is fine. You can do it on Paul Simon's time.

SEN. SIMPSON: It will take a bigger room. I think I am about to go down.

SEN. SIMON: Mr. Chairman, first I want to thank the witnesses, and particularly Ms. Alvarez, who has been here twice in a very short period of time. And good to welcome Dr. Fitch, who is a former faculty member at Sangamon State University.

MS. FITCH: It's nice to see you.

SEN. SIMON: Ms. Holt, in your deposition—and you probably heard me read this earlier, you perhaps did—you say, on page 32, "Do you recall any other times Anita Hill called and you did not note that on the telephone log?" And your answer, "I don't." You repeat that later in this same log.

MS. HOLT: And I will state—

SEN. SIMON: Here this evening, you have added—and I know that sometimes people can refresh your memory, as you go on—you have said there were five or six times additionally where she called.

MS. HOLT: I said maybe five or six times. Like I think I mentioned before, when I responded to that question, I meant that I could not relate dates, times or years of when those calls came in.

SEN. SIMON: Well, that's not the question. If I can go over to page 44, also, "Do you have a recollection of Ms. Anita Hill calling Clarence Thomas any more times?" It doesn't say when, it says "any more times than may have sporadically shown up on these three pages?" Did anyone consult with you or advise you?

MS. HOLT: Absolutely not.

SEN. SIMON: So, between the time of your deposition and right now, the additional five or six times, you didn't talk to anybody about that?

MS. HOLT: You continue to say five or six times. It could have been two times, it could have been three times. You can't hold me to the five or six times. I'm not sure of that. I know for a fact that she called on instances when she was put directly through to Clarence Thomas.

SEN. SIMON: But earlier this evening, Senator Specter said, when I read the deposition, said Ms. Holt will testify that she called an additional five or six times. Do you know where he got that information?

MS. HOLT: I have no idea.

SEN. SPECTER: Mr. Chairman, I did not say five or six times. I said I was told that she would testify that there were calls made which were not on the logs, because the calls were received, but I did not say five or six times.

SEN. SIMON: Well, my recollection is you did say that, but we will let the record show, we will print the record and we will find out. Senator Specter at least admits that he said that you were going to testify about—

SEN. SPECTER: No, I don't admit anything, Mr. Chairman. I state a fact. I don't make admissions here.

SEN. SIMON: Well, he said—

SEN. SPECTER: Thank you.

SEN. SIMON: [continuing]—that you were going to testify to additional calls beyond the deposition.

MS. HOLT: I did not tell him that.

SEN. SIMON: You don't know where Senator Specter got that information?

MS. HOLT: I have no idea.

SEN. SIMON: I have no further questions, Mr. Chairman.

THE CHAIRMAN: [presiding]. Senator Thurmond.

SEN. KENNEDY: I think our time is up on this.

SEN. THURMOND: I just have a question I would like to propound.

All of you ladies have a close relationship with Judge Thomas. Did you consider him to be a clean, decent, thoughtful, caring man, who treated his women and co-workers, as well as women in general, with courtesy and respect? I would like for each one of you to answer that.

MS. ALVAREZ: Yes, sir, absolutely.

SEN. THURMOND: Dr. Fitch.

MS. FITCH: Most definitely, Senator.

SEN. THURMOND: Ms. Holt.

MS. HOLT: Absolutely.

SEN. THURMOND: Ms. Myers.

MS. BERRY: Absolutely.

SEN. THURMOND: All of you answered yes, is that correct?

MS. ALVAREZ: Yes.

MS. FITCH: Yes.

MS. HOLT: Yes.

SEN. THURMOND: Thank you. Is there anybody else on this side who has any questions?

SEN. SIMPSON: Mr. Chairman, I just have—I understand what Senator Kennedy is saying, but the word "schizophrenic" did not appear from anyone on this side of the aisle. The word "delusion" did not appear from anyone on this side of the aisle. That was in the testimony or the statement of the U.S. attorney who said that was an impossible thing, to use a lie detector. Those names, those hot buttons, those phrases did not come from us, and it is curious to me how anyone could say that, when Judge Thomas was asked questions about what Professor Hill's motivation was, that all of that entered the record, and that is all we are doing here.

So, I think just for the purposes of the record—and when you get to thinking about it, and all of us, as lawyers, have you ever seen a hearing in your life like this, where the opponents of the nominee and, in particular, a single witness, almost on a par in status with the nominee, is all out of balance—and that's fine, I have no problem with that, but let us all realize what is happening here. This is about Clarence Thomas, nominee to the U.S. Supreme Court, not Anita Hill and it seems to have tilted off in that extraordinary way.

One of the things that is in the public domain—and we have a rule, we have to see it for two days—I want to enter into the record this letter from Andrew S. Fishel, Managing Director of the Federal Communications Commission, where he said that he had listened to Ms. Hill testify, and he said, "At no time were any of the employees of OCR at risk of losing their jobs during this period"— this is the Office of Civil Rights at the Department of Education. They had a separate budget earmarked which was more than sufficient to avoid any staff cutbacks. He was involved in the office, I understand.

"Additionally, no employees were made to feel that their jobs were in jeopardy"—I keep hearing this come up all the time. Quite the opposite was true, he said:

"After Mr. Thomas announced his departure from OCR to go to EEOC,

Mr. Thomas made a special point of walking the halls of OCR to introduce Mr. Harry Singleton, his successor, to OCR staff in order to facilitate the continuity of leadership. Any explanation of Ms. Hill's rationale for leaving OCR to go to EEOC that is founded on her allegation that she would have lost her job at OCR is without basis."

I include that in the record, and I thank you, Mr. Chairman.

[The letter referred to was entered in the record.]

SEN. METZENBAUM: Mr. Chairman.

THE CHAIRMAN: Senator Metzenbaum.

SEN. METZENBAUM: Ladies, it has been a long evening, but before you go out of here, there were some other witnesses and one of those witnesses pointed out a letter that at that point had been signed by fifty Yale graduates who had graduated with Anita Hill and the number is now up to sixty-six. And there is such an inconsistency between—and it is so difficult to reconcile what you are saying and what they said.

I would like to share with you their letter.

"Dear Mr. Chairman, Senator Biden. It has been our privilege to know Anita Hill professionally and personally since the late 1970's when we were in law school together. The Anita Hill we have known is a person of great integrity and decency. As colleagues we wish to affirm publicly our admiration and respect for her. She is embroiled now in a most serious and difficult controversy which we know is causing her great pain.

"We make no attempt to analyze the issues involved, or to prejudge the outcome. We do, however, wish to state emphatically our complete confidence in her sincerity and good faith and our absolute belief in her decency and integrity.

"In our eyes it is impossible to imagine any circumstances in which her character could be called into question. We are dismayed that it has been. We know that it could not be by anyone who knows her. Anita has imperiled her career and her peace of mind to do what she felt was right.

"We know we are powerless to shield her from those who will seek to hurt her out of ignorance, frustration, or expediency in the days ahead. But we will have failed ourselves if we do not at least raise our voices in her behalf. She has our unhesitating, non-wavering support."

Now, the amazing thing about this letter is not only the strength of the support for this lady but the fact that it came from all over the world. There were sixty-six names on it. One of the names is signed by somebody in Paris, France. One of them is signed by somebody in London, Ontario. One of the names is signed by somebody in Sao Paulo, Brazil. One of the names is signed by somebody in Perugia, Italy, and from New York, and California, and Arizona, and San Francisco, and all over the country.

How do you reconcile the fact that these sixty-six people, who also knew her as you knew her, although at an earlier point, but they say that "we have known her as a person of great integrity and decency and that we have known her professionally since the late 1970's when we were in law school together"? How do you reconcile the fact? How do you explain it to us, sitting on this committee, that here are sixty-six people, who are obviously people of good repute ostensibly—Yale Law School graduates—and here are four people who worked with her, also people of good repute and good standing saying one thing totally different than these sixty-six Yale graduates are saying?

MS. FITCH: Senator, my response to that is that I am sure there are as many people and more who would say that, say the same thing about Judge Thomas. That's the only response I can have to the question you are asking. I don't know what to say.

MS. HOLT: Additionally a question comes to my mind about how long it has been since those sixty-six people have seen Professor Hill or have had any kind of—

SEN. METZENBAUM: I am sorry, I didn't hear that.

MS. HOLT: How long it has been since those people have had any interaction with Professor Hill.

SEN. METZENBAUM: No, they say specifically and I am not sure about the facts, that "we are privileged to know her professionally and personally since the late 1970's when we were in law school together."

Now, how much of that time they have seen her, I don't know. I have to assume that some of them have seen her more than others. I think fifteen of the names are from people here in Washington.

MS. BERRY: Well, I am sure that we had at least sixty-six women that were ready to come before this committee to tell them that Judge Thomas is a man of great decency and integrity if we are going to play the numbers game.

MS. ALVAREZ: You will have six times sixty-six and you had a group of people out there who will tell you exactly the same thing. It is just that you limited the time. We only have until Tuesday. We could go on with people who could come here and testify on Clarence's behalf and people who have worked with him and people who have known him.

MS. BERRY: And we are not intimidated by sixty-six names there and there are just four of us here.

MS. ALVAREZ: Even if they went to Yale Law School.

MS. BERRY: Exactly. [Laughter.]

THE CHAIRMAN: If everyone in the nation, everyone who went to law school who is not intimidated by someone who went to Yale Law School were here we would not have enough room if we piled them on top of one another. I just want the record to show that Yale Law School is a fine law school. I don't think it is any finer law school than a lot of law schools I can think of.

But having said that, a mild note of levity, I think your time is up, Senator.

SEN. METZENBAUM: It is in the record?

THE CHAIRMAN: It is in the record. I believe it is already in the record.

Now, does anybody on—Senator Kohl?

SEN. KOHL: Thank you, Mr. Chairman.

Some of you suggested possible motives for Ms. Hill to have done what she did. And I can understand that. But what I cannot understand and perhaps you can explain it to me, is what the motives would be of those four people who came here today, each one who had heard from Professor Hill over the past ten years, about these sexual harassment charges. Reputable people, people who had not talked to her over the past two years, had not talked to her over the past several months, but clearly reputable people who didn't know each other, came here from all walks of life.

And they testified that in 1981, 1982, 1983, and 1987, Professor Hill told them about what was happening.

MS. BERRY: I have already challenged Mr. Carr's statement. He said that Anita Hill told him that she was harassed by her supervisor. And he made the great leap that the supervisor that she was referring to was Clarence Thomas. And that, right there, is suspect to me when I know, for a fact, that Anita Hill had more than one supervisor.

SEN. KOHL: Okay. So in your case, you are saying her comments might have been about somebody else at EEOC? Her comments might not have referred specifically to him. All right, I think that is possible.

Diane.

MS. HOLT: Senator, I think I would question the fact that none of those people who Professor Hill told that she had been sexually harassed did not provide any advice. These were professional people. They knew what the recourse was. Nobody told her to go forward with her story.

SEN. KOHL: But the assumption there is that all four of them are lying.

MS. HOLT: That's not my assumption.

SEN. KOHL: But that is what you are saying.

MS. HOLT: No, I said I questioned that fact.

SEN. KOHL: I know but let's just move on to real talk. If you question that fact, you question the veracity of what they are saying.

MS. HOLT: I do, yes.

SEN. KOHL: All right, that is another way of saying in your opinion—

MS. HOLT: I question it, but I am not calling them liars.

SEN. KOHL: Well, we are just trying to use nice words, but I want to understand. You can say that, there is nothing wrong with it, but your explanation is that they are not telling the truth?

MS. HOLT: That's right, I don't believe it.

SEN. KOHL: I appreciate that.

And Ms. Fitch.

MS. FITCH: Senator, in discussing motivation I have said that I only understand my own. I cannot, I cannot try to discuss their motivation. I am sure they had the best intentions and wanted to be helpful to the person that they believe in. I don't know what else to say about that question. It is a question that I can't answer.

SEN. KOHL: Ms. Alvarez?

MS. ALVAREZ: No, likewise, I couldn't begin to put motivation or words into somebody's mouth or in their heads. I think that there was possibly some, like Phyllis talked about, there may have been, it may not have been who they all assumed it was. I can't really, I can't offer any more explanation than that. There may have just been a misunderstanding of what she had to say.

SEN. KOHL: All right. Just one other quick question.

Clarence Thomas has spoken here of a conspiracy, a lynching on the part of some white people that has a lot to do with what is happening. In fact, in his opinion, that is the major reason why we are here today and you, yourself, Ms. Alvarez, said "That we are beating up on the judge, and that this is a trumped-up deal" and so on.

But isn't it a fact that what we are dealing with here is a charge of sexual harassment by an African American against an African American? Isn't that why we are here today? Isn't that the fact of what brings us here today, an African-American woman who is charging an African-American man with sexual harassment? Is there something else that brings us here today?

I mean aren't we all here and hasn't a Senate committee convened to hold this hearing, because of a charge leveled at an African-American man by an African-American woman?

MS. BERRY: That's an old tactic in this country, Senator, that we use and I am sickened by that. That's the thing, I guess, that embarrasses me most about this situation is that a black woman would allow herself to be a pawn to destroy a black man. Have we reached the point in our civilization or in this country where people can't legitimately have points of disagreement without trying to destroy the person because you don't agree with what that person stands for?

And the chairman said, you might kill him but you are not going to kill his ideas.

SEN. KOHL: No, we are not suggesting—

MS. BERRY: There are a lot of other people out there who believe what Clarence Thomas says and his ideas are beginning to take root in the black community.

SEN. KOHL: That may well be so but what we are discussing here is a charge against an African-American man by an African-American woman. How do we wind up saying this is a racist conspiracy?

MS. BERRY: I haven't heard him use those terms. I heard him say a lynching.

SEN. KOHL: Ms. Alvarez?

MS. ALVAREZ: You are not investigating a sexual harassment charge.

SEN. KOHL: Of course we are. That's what the hearing is about.

MS. ALVAREZ: The statute of limitations ran out.

SEN. KOHL: An allegation of sexual harassment, that's what the hearing is all about.

MS. ALVAREZ: Well, no, an allegation of improper conduct.

SEN. KOHL: Again, an allegation made by an African-American woman against an African-American man.

MS. BERRY: Lynching doesn't necessarily have to refer to race.

SEN. KOHL: Well—

MS. BERRY: I mean what is happening to Clarence Thomas is, in my estimation, a—

SEN. KOHL: Ms. Alvarez, then I will be finished.

MS. ALVAREZ: No, I guess I am not sure quite the point you are trying to make.

SEN. KOHL: Well, I am trying to understand why you—

MS. ALVAREZ: You are trying to say this isn't a lynching?

SEN. KOHL: [continuing]—I can't understand why you are saying and that Thomas is saying that this is a racist conspiracy against—

MS. ALVAREZ: I did not say that.

SEN. KOHL: Well, you are saying, we, meaning the committee, are beating up on the judge.

MS. ALVAREZ: Yes.

SEN. KOHL: He is calling it a lynching and you are saying we are beating up on a judge, but what we are doing here is trying to understand whether there is any truth in the allegation made by an African-American woman against an African-American man.

MS. ALVAREZ: I think there is a much better way that it could have been done, not in this kind of forum—

SEN. KOHL: Well, that's true.

MS. ALVAREZ: [continuing]—and not in broad daylight and not on television and—

SEN. KOHL: Well, that's true, but the allegation, itself, is an allegation made by an African-American woman against an African-American man. That is just a fact.

MS. ALVAREZ: But what does that have to do? I mean that means it is okay to beat him up? I am not sure what you are saying. I am saying when I made that statement I think there was a better way for this whole thing to have been investigated and to have been handled. I think we did both of them a disservice by handling it the way we did, because you just beat him up in broad daylight and you took his name, his reputation, and his character and you can't give it back to him. That was my point.

THE CHAIRMAN: Senator, do you have more? Is that it?

SEN. KOHL: Yes. Thank you.

THE CHAIRMAN: Thank you.

If there are not any more questions I do have two very, very short questions. And Ms. Fitch, if I ever need an advocate you are the one I want to hire. You are all very good, but let me ask you this. I think that one of the points has confused me in this process not merely who is telling the truth because that perplexes me as much as it perplexes the American public apparently. I don't know what the American public thinks. I take that back. It perplexes me.

Now, you were asked a question by Senator Hatch a while ago, if I recall, that was an echo of an assertion that Judge Thomas made yesterday in a very articulate fashion and it was this:

That isn't this a stereotypical attack on a black man? Judge Thomas—and I am not criticizing his statement, I just want to understand it, and as a black historian maybe you can help me—he indicated that he believed this was—I won't use exactly his words, because they are not appropriate coming from my mouth—but something to the effect that if an uppity black person is being put down by other people, that's what this is about, putting down any black person who goes against the grain.

Now, I can understand that. What I can't understand though is how can one say that and not say the counter charges against Professor Hill are not equally, if not more stereotypical, of not taking seriously a black woman? How can one charge about stereotypical behavior apply to the judge and not equally apply to Professor Hill? This is not who is telling the truth—I am talking about this notion of stereotypical behavior we keep hearing hurled back and forth, across in front of me and this way as well, not by you but by others.

Can you shed some light on that point for me?

MS. FITCH: I am not sure I really understand the question.

THE CHAIRMAN: Well, the statement was made that the attack on Judge Thomas, along the lines relating to harassment, were stereotypical attacks on black men, they stereotyped black men.

MS. FITCH: Okay.

THE CHAIRMAN: And what I am saying is if that is true, and I am not arguing whether it is or isn't, is it not equally true to immediately question the veracity of a black woman who comes forward to make an allegation against a black man as preposterous? Doesn't that just as neatly fit into a stereotypical treatment of black women who dare speak up? That's my question.

MS. FITCH: I think I see where you are going to with this and in terms of both black men and white men, of course, that is a problem historically.

Yes, it is a no-win-no-win.

THE CHAIRMAN: That doesn't go to the veracity of anything. I am just trying to understand because I heard for the first time the other day the phrase stereotypical treatment of black men who dare run against the stream.

MS. FITCH: Yes, but in terms of the stereotypical response to black women it comes first from their experience with white men in this country. And I—

THE CHAIRMAN: I agree with that—

MS. FITCH: Yes—

THE CHAIRMAN: [continuing]—I agree with that, with white men.

MS. FITCH: [continuing] —yes, and of course, it can be extended to any other men.

THE CHAIRMAN: I understand, okay, thank you for clarifying that. Now, the absolutely last question I have is this: There was reference made earlier that there was a need to be able to establish a pattern of behavior. I don't know which of you said it.

MS. FITCH: I think I might have talked about patterns and in trying to explain why I take the judge's position in this and I am saying there was not any behavior that was ever evidenced by me over seven years by myself, hearing from anyone else and that established a portfolio for him for me.

THE CHAIRMAN: Okay, for you?

MS. FITCH: Yes.

THE CHAIRMAN: But you were not speaking as an expert in the field?

MS. FITCH: Oh, heavens no. I think—

THE CHAIRMAN: Because experts tell me that it is equally plausible and it happens as often that you have a sexual harassment incident, as well as you have sexual harassment incidents coming from a single person. So there is not a need to be able to establish a pattern of behavior in order to establish that there is sexual harassment.

MS. FITCH: Senator, I was very careful in the beginning to talk about possibility and probability.

THE CHAIRMAN: I see.

MS. FITCH: And I was addressing myself to probability.

THE CHAIRMAN: You are a good lawyer and witness.

MS. FITCH: Oh, God, I am not a lawyer.

THE CHAIRMAN: On behalf of the Senate, it is presumptuous of me to say that but you are extremely clear and precise and it is impressive. You all are impressive and I thank you all for being here. It has been very, very late. You have spent a lot of time and Clarence Thomas is, indeed, fortunate to have four such loyal supporters who obviously believe every word they said and their experiences are as they have cited and I appreciate it.

SEN. THURMOND: On behalf of this side of the aisle I wish to express appreciation to all of you and your splendid testimony.

MS. ALVAREZ: Thank you.

MS. BERRY: Thank you.

MS. FITCH: Thank you.

MS. HOLT: Thank you.

THE CHAIRMAN: Thank you all very much. It has been a long evening for you. It has been a longer evening, I might add, for the next panel who has been waiting.

Now, ordinarily what we had agreed to do was the next panel of witnesses was going to be a panel of several people testifying on behalf of Professor Hill. Professor Hill has contacted us and indicated that in the interest of time she is fully prepared to forego having that panel testify. So we will move that as her decision, not the committee's decision.

We will now move to the panel to follow that one. They will be testifying on behalf of and in support of the position of Judge Thomas, and that is our first is Stanley Grayson, vice president with the firm of Goldman Sachs in New York; the second is Carlton Stewart with the Stewart firm in Atlanta, Georgia; the third witness is John M. Doggett III, a management consultant in Austin, Texas; and the fourth is Charles Kothe, former dean of Oral Roberts University Law Center.

If you will all please come forward and before you sit we will swear you in if you will be prepared to stand and be sworn.

Do you all swear that your testimony will be the truth, the whole truth, and nothing but the truth, so help you God?

MR. GRAYSON: I do.

MR. STEWART: I do.

MR. DOGGETT: I do.

MR. KOTHE: I do.

THE CHAIRMAN: Thank you, and welcome. Thank you for your patience in waiting so long. Now let me ask the panel, is there any particular way in which you would like to proceed? Have you talked among yourselves how you would like to proceed?

MR. GRAYSON: We have not talked, but Dean Kothe has asked if he could go first.

THE CHAIRMAN: All right.

Dean, welcome. I know you have waited a long time. Your name has been spoken of often here, always positively, and so please begin your testimony, if you would.

Now again, gentlemen, I am going to ask you to keep your testimony relatively short, if we can, because you notice you will get a lot of chances to speak, because this panel has no reluctance to ask you questions.

Dean, please proceed.

TESTIMONY OF A PANEL CONSISTING OF:

STANLEY GRAYSON, Vice President, Goldman Sachs Law Firm, New York, New York

CARLTON STEWART, Stewart Law Firm, Atlanta, Georgia

JOHN N. DOGGETT III, Mangement Consultant, Austin, Texas;

CHARLES KOTHE, Former Dean, Oral Roberts University Law School

TESTIMONY OF CHARLES KOTHE

MR. KOTHE: Mr. Chairman and Senators, my name is Charles A. Kothe. I am of counsel to the firm of Clay, Walker—

SEN. THURMOND: If you don't mind, I would get close to the microphone so we can hear you all over the room.

MR. KOTHE: I am presently of counsel to the firm of Clay, Walker, Jackman, Dempson and Moller in Tulsa, Oklahoma.

During March of 1983 I was acting as the founding dean of the O.W. Coburn School of Law at Oral Roberts University (ORU). Being interested in our public relations and in our identity with the American Bar Association Accrediting Committee, I decided to have a program on civil rights. I had conducted many of them over the years.

I contacted the Equal Employment Opportunity Commission and talked to Clarence Thomas. I did not know him before that. He said he would come out to a seminar, and asked if he could bring a member of his staff, and I said of course. And so in April of 1983 we had a seminar on civil rights on our campus, and that is where I first met Anita Hill. In fact, the first time I talked with her, I recall, was at a luncheon at which Mr. Thomas was to be the featured speaker.

I learned at that time that she was from Oklahoma, and just out of the blue I said, "How would you like to come home and teach?" And she said, "I would like it."

And after the press conference that followed the luncheon, I told Chairman Thomas about my conversation and asked what he thought of it. He said, "Well, if that is what she would like to do, I would be all for it." And I said, "Well, do you think she would make a good teacher?" And I believe he said, "I think she would make a great teacher."

Following that, I arranged for her to be put in the process of filing applications which would go through our assistant dean. I wouldn't be involved in the paperwork until all of the recommendations were in. And sometime late in May I received her application, I believe, and all of the recommendations, and one from Chairman Thomas that was one of the most impressive, strongest statements in support of a candidate for our faculty that we had ever received.

Based upon that and, I believe, a conversation also with Chairman Thomas, I recommended to our provost that we engage her as a member of our faculty. That doesn't just happen perfunctorily at ORU, to get on the faculty because the dean says so. No one gets on the faculty at that school unless Oral Roberts approves, and after Oral Roberts, the chairman of the Board of Regents. And that happened in her case, and sometime in June she was offered a position on our faculty to take effect in August of 1983.

In 1984 I resigned as dean, to become effective in June, and during that time as she and I became better acquainted and I learned of her working on special projects, I spoke to her about my interest in civil rights, which had started with the act of 1964, and indicated I would be interested in some special assignments. And through her I was put in touch with Chairman Thomas, and led ultimately to my appointment in April of 1984, or maybe it was April of 1985, to a special assistant to Clarence Thomas at the EEOC.

During that time I had a number of assignments, one among which was, I wrote the 33-page report on the success story of Clarence Thomas, which was basically the improvements that he made and the progress he had made at EEO, and she conferred with me about that.

THE CHAIRMAN: I'm sorry. I didn't hear you. You were assigned to do what?

MR. KOTHE: I was assigned to work with the various persons in the EEO on the progress that was made from previous administrations. Anita had been working on a history of the EEO, and I put together a 33-page report which I labeled "The Success Story of Clarence Thomas", outlining the progress that had been made over previous years.

In 1986 ORU law school was closed, and Anita went to OU. I didn't keep in as close a touch with her at that time.

In April of 1987 a speech was made by Clarence Thomas in Tulsa before a personnel group, that I believe was arranged by Anita. She and I and my wife sat at the table together, and Clarence Thomas was there at that dinner.

After he spoke, he stayed at my home, which he has on several other occasions. The next morning we had breakfast together, and she attended the breakfast, and it was one of joviality and just one of joy. After that, as I recall it, she volunteered to take him to the airport in her sports car, of which she was quite proud.

During that period we were in touch only by telephone, and in April or May of 1987 she sent me a white paper on a project that had been under discussion for a seminar which she described as developing an EEO program that really works. The featured subject of that was to be sexual harassment, and I was to, as she outlined in the program, to open the program on that subject.

We had talked about it, and all the time we ever talked about it, never once did she tell me or hint to me that she had had any personal experience of sexual harassment; never once in any of that time that that was under preparation, or in any other of the discussions we ever had when she was on our faculty, when she was in my home, whenever we were together at any time, that Clarence Thomas was anything less than a genuinely fine person. In fact, she was very complimentary about him in every time we have ever talked together.

The last time she and I were together was in late 1987 or 1988, when we were both on the program for some personnel group in Tulsa. In discussing the preparation for that with her, I took what was generally my role of outlining the success story of Clarence Thomas. She took the technical part, and I think it had to do at that time with a case that involved pensions and civil rights.

And at that time, I believe Clarence Thomas had been married by that time, but in our discussions about him she was always very complimentary and I felt that she was fascinated by him. She spoke of him almost as a hero. She talked of him as a devoted father. She talked to me about his untiring energy. She never, ever, in all of our discourse, in all of those situations, ever said anything negative about him; and when we discussed the possibility of preparation for a seminar on sexual harassment, never said a word about her personal experience, or even her insights to any great degree.

In my experience with Clarence Thomas as a special assistant, I didn't have an office assigned, and frequently I would make my work station at the large conference table that he had in his office. Sitting there, I was able to observe him as he had discussions with some of the staff. Some of the employees would come, and other guests.

I traveled with this man for hours on end in automobiles, when we went through the swamps of Georgia together where he showed me where he was reared, and I have traveled with him by plane. I have been with him in business meetings, at banquets, at dinners in my home at least four times. We talked on to the end of the night in discussions of things that were of interest to both of us.

Never, ever in all of that time did I ever hear that man utter a profane word, never engage in any coarse conduct or loose talk. Always it was sincere, many times religious. We were both reading together, you might say at the same time together, the books by Rabbi Kushner, the one, *Why Bad Things Happen to Good People* [sic], and I suppose that is almost prophetic, and the other, *Who Needs God?* In fact, as we last talked about the one, *Who Needs God?* he built a sermon on that that he later gave in the pulpit at the church where he was married.

The last time I was with Clarence Thomas, he was our speaker at the Oklahoma Bar Association prayer breakfast, and on that occasion he told the story of his life and his spiritual experience, at the close of which he gave a prayer that brought tears to my eyes and many others there. That day we heard a man of God talk.

I have been with this man. He is a man of strength. He is a man of character. He is a man of high moral standing, and I tell you that it is not possible that he could be linked with the kinds of things that have alleged against him here. If it were true, it is the greatest Jekyll and Hyde story in the history of mankind. This is a good man, a man I have known, and a man I respect, and a man I think is worthy of a position on the U.S. Supreme Court.

THE CHAIRMAN: Thank you very much.

Now, since you have waited so long, we are going to continue that but, Mr. Doggett, if you could make your statement a little briefer, and the rest of you, so we get a chance to ask questions, since we are getting into past eleven. Mr. Doggett?

MR. DOGGETT: I appreciate that, Senator. About 6:30 this morning in Austin, Texas, I got a telephone call saying, "We would like you to get to Washington as soon as possible." Any of you who know about Austin, Texas know that that is not all that easy to do.

THE CHAIRMAN: Well, I am glad we waited this long so you could make it.

MR. DOGGETT: Well, I have been here for quite a few hours. I got here about 2:30 actually.

THE CHAIRMAN: I know it has been a long day. I appreciate that.

TESTIMONY OF JOHN N. DOGGETT III

MR. DOGGETT: I appreciate what you are trying to do, because this is a very difficult process. The charges that Anita Hill has made against Clarence Thomas, if true, would justify all of you and all of us saying that he would not be fit to serve on any court, not just the Supreme Court. In fact, those charges, if true and if filed formally, would raise serious questions about legal liability on his part and possibly criminal liability on his part.

I am also saddened by the process of having some of the best and brightest people in our country coming before the world, throwing mud. Clarence Thomas and Anita Hill, as I knew them back then, were good, decent, bright, committed people, and it is hard for me to be here knowing that one of them has to be destroyed if our nation is to be saved.

I appreciate how difficult what you are doing is. I don't think you have had a choice. Once those serious charges were made, you had no choice but to do what you could to find out whether or not there is any truth to them.

I have been impressed at the amount of work you and your staff have been able to do in such a short period of time. As a former litigator, I know I never would have tried to do what you have done in two or three days.

A week ago—well, let me tell you a little about who I am. I will try to be as short as I can, but I think this is very important.

I was born in a housing project in San Francisco, because my father left the East coast to be a minister to black workers who were coming from the South to work in the Navy Yard in San Francisco as part of the war effort. My family has had a commitment from the beginning to civil rights. My father was an associate of Martin Luther King. My father was the president of the NAACP, St. Louis branch, for ten years. My mother was a teacher who served inner city students for all of her life.

At every step of my education in the public schools of Los Angeles, I was told by white teachers that I was not going to be able to excel because I was black. And my parents told me, "Whatever they say is irrelevant. You are going to do the best you can."

To give you an example, when I was in high school I asked for the catalogs for MIT and Cal Tech, and the college counselor gave me the catalogs for Illinois Institute of Technology. When I was in high school, a good friend of mine who is now a tenured professor at Pomona College asked for an SAT application and she said, "You have to have your parents come here to get a SAT application." That is the world I grew up in.

I went to Claremont Men's College in 1965, and if you remember 1965, there was something called the Watts riots. That is what happened between my senior year of high school and my first year as a freshman. At Claremont Men's College, I was one of eight black students. All but two of us were freshmen. And when we would walk the streets of Claremont, people would stop and look at us. That is how strange we were.

And I can go on and I can go on and I can go on. I was the founding chairman of the Black Student Union of Claremont College, at the same time receiving an award from the ROTC as the most outstanding cadet in ROTC, in the midst of the Vietnam war, a war I opposed.

It was difficult for me to make a decision to come here, but I felt I had no choice. When I graduated from Claremont Men's College, I went to Yale Law School, and in my third year at Yale Law School, Clarence Thomas came as a first year student. My class at Yale Law School was the largest number of black students ever to be admitted at Yale Law School, and half of those who came never graduated.

My first year at Yale Law School also was the time that there was the Black Panther trial, that the hippies and the yippies came to New Haven. It was a tumultuous time, and my experience at Yale Law School was a time where we said, as black students, "We are going to be the best possible people we can, and we are going to work on admission standards that guarantee that we get the best people we can possibly get." Clarence Thomas was one of those people.

In my senior year, in my third year at Yale Law School, one of the things we all did, we black law students, was to put together a seminar, a pre-entrance program, a week or so, in conjunction with the administration, to make sure that we could tell our colleagues about the ropes, so that they could maximize their performance. And I remember some of the students who had come before me saying, "It is impossible for black students to score the same on the law school admissions test as whites. It is impossible for black students to have the same GPAs."

And there were a handful of us who said that was—well, this is the Senate, and there are people who don't like obscenity—but there were a handful of people who had a very strong and negative reaction to that. And I remember with pride when the dean of Yale Law School was able to come up to some of those people and say, "I have in my hand a list of fifteen applicants who are black, who have qualifications that meet the standards of anybody who is going to come to this law school."

I want to say that because that is my background.

When I graduated from Yale Law School, I took a job as a Reginald Hebrew Smith Community Lawyer Fellow, which is a special program the Government set up to make sure that legal service programs would have access to the best and brightest law students in the United States.

In the summer after I graduated, I took the bar exam at Connecticut while I was working full time as an attorney for New Haven Legal Assistance in New Haven. I studied for the bar examination in California, took that bar in February and passed it. In nine months I took two different bar examinations and passed them, and worked as a legal services attorney and then eventually as the director of the Office of Legal Services of the State Bar of California.

There is a lot more I could say. I am not going to say it right now, but I just wanted to let you know that I have worked all my life to fight for a very simple idea: That is that we people who happen to be black are as capable as anybody else.

I now am a management consultant. I have refused, even though I have been asked by clients, to apply for the 8(a) program, and to this year I have not participated in any so-called set-aside, affirmative action programs. And the only one I ever participated in was this summer, where all you had to say was that you were 100 per cent owned by blacks or by some other so-called minority group, because I wanted to prove that the reason people hired me was because I was the best there was.

I eventually went to Harvard Business School, where amazingly enough one of my friends was John Carr, the same John Carr who was here testifying on behalf of Anita Hill. And in fact, of Anita Hill, Clarence Thomas, and John Carr, John Carr is the person I am closest to because he is the person I knew the best. We were classmates at Harvard Business School.

I worked for Salomon Brothers during the summer. They offered me a full-time job. I turned them down. I joined McKenzie and Company here.

I met Anita Hill at a party in 1982, as far as I can remember, and I say as far as I can remember because, gentlemen, I had not thought about Anita Hill for eight or nine years, until I heard—until I read in the *New York Times* last Monday that she had made these charges against Clarence Thomas.

I was introduced to Anita Hill by a man named Gil Hardy, a Yale Law School graduate who eventually was a partner in the law firm that Anita Hill worked for initially. It is unfortunate that Gil Hardy is not here, and the only reason he is not here is that he is dead. He died in a scuba-diving accident off the coast of Morocco.

Gil Hardy knew Clarence and knew Anita more than anybody I know, and if he was here, we probably would not be here now.

I talked to Clarence on a number of occasions, and one of the reasons I came forward is that I remember those conversations, and Clarence told me—and let me tell you, at this time I was a Democrat, at this time I really had some reservations about whether or not the Reagan revolution was good for this country, at this time I was being hammered by Reaganites, because of my attitudes, and when I found out that somebody who had been a classmate of mine who I had assisted at Yale Law School was now in the position of being one of the top-breaking blacks in the Reagan Administration, I wanted to go talk to this man and find out what was going on, because I knew he would tell me the truth.

One of the things that Clarence Thomas told me that really stuck in my mind, and one of the reasons I said I've got to get this information to this committee and let them decide whether or not it is valuable, is that he said, "John, they call me an Uncle Tom. They are at my back. They are looking for anything they can use to take me out." He was quite aware of the scrutiny that he was under and the fact that his positions were very unpopular.

I also remember him talking about Bradford Reynolds, who at that time was the Assistant Attorney General for Civil Rights, and many of us, including myself, complained that this man was not qualified to lead the civil rights effort of the Justice Department. He said, "John, the Reagan Administration went to every black Republican lawyer it knew, and they all turned the job down, and so nobody can complain about Brad Reynolds being there. But I will tell you, one of my jobs is to make sure that I can try to keep this guy honest."

John Carr and I went to business school together. He was in the joint program. I had practiced seven years after Yale Law School and had decided that the only way to help poor people and people who were opposed, was to learn more about how the economic system worked, to learn more about how businesses worked.

Since John was in the joint degree program, after I graduated from Harvard and came down to Washington, DC, he remained at Harvard for another year and then went to New York.

In all the years that I have known John Carr, he has never mentioned knowing Anita Hill, and yet she stated that she dated that man and he said here that he would not call it dating.

In all the years that I have known Clarence Thomas, except for knowing that Anita Hill worked for him, he never mentioned her name. We never had any conversations about her. He mentioned the names of a number of friends. At times, it was clear he was very interested in trying to get me to know more black Republican conservatives, hoping to be able to convert me to the cause. He was not successful. But he never mentioned her.

And all the times that I had conversations with Anita Hill on the telephone and in person, that I observed her at parties of black Yale Law School graduates, she never ever talked about Clarence Thomas or talked about any problems or anything about that man.

I did have an experience with Ms. Hill just before she left to go to Oral Roberts University. And but for that experience, I would not be here, because other than that, my experience and relationships with Anita Hill was what I would consider very normal, cordial, and I thought of her as a decent person.

As you know, I submitted an affidavit to you. Ever since this committee released that affidavit to the press, the press has come to me saying would you talk about that affidavit. I said no, I am an attorney, I do not feel that is appropriate for me to discuss anything that is going to be discussed by this committee, before the committee has an opportunity to discuss it with me.

Ted Koppel's office called and said would you be on *Nightline*? Tom Brokaw's office called. Garrick Utley's office called. I even got a call a couple of days ago, saying, well, if you won't talk to us before you testify, will you show up on a *Good Morning* or *Today Show* after you testify? I am not going to do that. I am sickened by the fact that the best people, some of the best black people in this country, some of the best people in this country are participating in such a destructive process. But I respect the fact, Senators, that, given the severity of the charges, you had no choice.

There are many things that I could say. There are many things that I will say. I stand behind the affidavit that I submitted to you, and I look forward to the time when this body and your colleagues vote on the nomination of Clarence Thomas, and I very much hope that you confirm Clarence Thomas.

But there is one other thing that I want to say, before I wait to respond to your questions. My wife and I—my wife is here behind me—were at a Thai restaurant last night with a friend of ours who had flown in from Africa to do some business with us, and this all blew up in all of our faces. Another one of our friends came up to us and said, "John, I just want to look at somebody who is stupid enough to stand up to the world and say here I am, throw stones at me, throw knives at me, throw rocks at me."

Since you released my affidavit that I submitted to you, the press—I received a number of telephone calls, forty in two hours, immediately after. Most of them have been positive, but some of them have been negative and some of them have been threatening. One of them was a man who left a message that was very simple, "Boom, boom, boom, boom, boom," click, and he was not imitating the Eveready Rabbits.

I am from Texas, now, and those are supposed to be gunshots.

Last night, at that same Thai restaurant, a woman came out, as we were leaving, and said, "Shame, shame, shame, shame." I said, "Excuse me, do you know any of the people involved? Do you know Anita Hill? Do you know Clarence

Thomas? Do you know me?" She kept saying, "Shame, shame, shame, shame." I said, "Do you know any of the facts?" And she said, "You know nothing about PMS, and I can't stand any man who says a woman is unstable." I said, "But do you know anything about the facts?" And she said—and I'm sorry I have to say this—she said, "Put your penis back in your pants." [Laughter.]

This is somebody I had never seen before, somebody I do not know, somebody I hope I will never see again.

But I will tell you, Senators, I am not here for any other reason than to say I had information that I thought would be of use to you. You have decided this information is useful, and when this process is over, except possibly talking to people as I leave this building, I hope to never have to talk about this again.

SEN. DECONCINI: Mr. Stewart?

TESTIMONY OF CARLTON STEWART

MR. STEWART: Good evening, Senators, Senator Thurmond—I see that Senator Biden's seat is empty—and other distinguished members of the committee.

My name is Carlton Stewart. I am a graduate of Holy Cross College and the University of Georgia Law School. I was formerly house counsel to Shell Oil Company, in Houston, Texas, and Delta Airlines, in Atlanta, Georgia, respectively.

Additionally, I was a senior trial attorney with the Equal Employment Opportunity Commission, in Atlanta, Georgia, and later a special assistant to Judge Clarence Thomas, in Washington. Subsequently, I was a partner in the law firm of Arrington & Hallowell, in Atlanta, Georgia, and I am currently a principal in the Stewart firm in Atlanta, Georgia.

As aforestated, I was a special assistant to Judge Clarence Thomas at the Equal Employment Opportunity Commission during much of the time that Anita Hill was employed there. At no time did I hear any complaints from Ms. Hill concerning sexual harassment. At no time during my tenure at EEOC, did I observe or hear anything relative to sexual harassment by Judge Clarence Thomas.

In August of 1991, I ran into Ms. Anita Hill at the American Bar Association Convention, in Atlanta, Georgia, whereupon she stated, in the presence of Stanley Grayson, how great Clarence's nomination was and how much he deserved it. We went on to discuss Judge Clarence Thomas and our tenure at EEOC for an additional thirty or so minutes. There was no mention of sexual harassment nor anything negative about Judge Thomas stated during that time.

SEN. THURMOND: Would you pull the microphone closer to you, so that people in the back can hear you?

MR. STEWART: Okay. I will boom for you.

I have known Judge Clarence Thomas for more than thirty years, and I find the allegations by Ms. Hill not only ludicrous, but totally inconsistent and inapposite to his principles and his personality.

I will shorten this, so that we can get on with this. Thank you.

SEN. DECONCINI: Mr. Grayson?

TESTIMONY OF STANLEY GRAYSON

MR. GRAYSON: Thank you, Mr. Chairman, Senator Thurmond, members of this Judiciary Committee.

My name is Stanley E. Grayson. I reside in the city and state of New York. I am a vice president at the investment banking firm of Goldman Sachs & Company. Immediately prior to joining Goldman Sachs, approximately twenty months ago, I served as the deputy mayor for finance and economic development for the city of New York.

I am a graduate of the University of Michigan Law School and the College of the Holy Cross.

During the weekend of August 10, 1991, while at the hotel and conference headquarters for the American Bar Association's convention, in Atlanta, Georgia, I was introduced to Professor Anita Hill by Mr. Carlton Stewart.

At this meeting, Ms. Hill, Mr. Stewart and I sat and conversed for at least thirty minutes. During the course of our conversation, in the presence of Mr. Stewart, Ms. Hill expressed her pleasure with Judge Thomas's nomination, and stated that he deserved it.

During this time, Ms. Hill made no mention of any sexual harassment by Judge Thomas, nor did she in any way indicate anything that might call into question the character or fitness of Judge Thomas for the U.S. Supreme Court. To the contrary, she seemed to take great pride in the fact that she had been a member of Judge Thomas's staff at the Equal Employment Opportunity Commission.

SEN. DECONCINI: Thank you.

Dean Kothe, let me just ask you a question here. References are made here in different statements about a period of time when Judge Thomas was visiting you and apparently staying at your home. There was a dinner, where Professor Hill was invited and a breakfast the next morning where Professor Hill was invited, as was Judge Thomas, then Chairman Thomas, and that she drove Judge Thomas to the airport.

My recollection is that Professor Hill said that you asked her to do that. Do you recall those incidents, and did you ask her to do it? And if you did ask her to do it, did she leave any impressions, verbal or physical, that she didn't want to be with Judge Thomas or had any problem doing what you asked her to do, if you did ask her to take him to the airport? Do you remember the incident, first of all?

MR. KOTHE: Oh, yes, but you would have to describe the setting, to fully understand even the importance of your question.

You know, the part that offends me so much here is that Clarence Thomas has never been described. You say who is the real Clarence Thomas? Well, the real Clarence Thomas is a warm, wonderful human being.

SEN. DECONCINI: Yes, I understand that.

MR. KOTHE: Let me finish.

SEN. DECONCINI: Just address the area, if you will, please.

MR. KOTHE: Yes, I will. At that breakfast, if you ever heard him laugh, it would vibrate this room. Anita doesn't have just a modest little laugh, either, and the two of them were just laughing, and it was laughing at laughing, incidents they would bring up about things that they were privy to that I was not, but my wife and I would sit there and just watch these two people just enjoy one another, as you do when you are in his presence.

When it ended, time to go to the airport, whether I asked her to take him to the airport, I don't think it was that way. It was a question of his going to the airport and she just said, "Well, I'll take him," and that's the way I recall it. But it was in a setting of conviviality or joy.

SEN. DECONCINI: Of close friendship and respect in the—

MR. KOTHE: Oh, my, you would have had to have been there to understand it.

SEN. DECONCINI: Thank you, Dean, very much.

Mr. Doggett, your affidavit is of interest, of course, because if you want to draw something from it, you can, and if you don't want to, you don't have to. One thing you can draw from it is that perhaps Ms. Hill—when you knew her then, she was not Professor Hill, I don't believe—would somewhat fantasize as to a relationship that she thought she was going to have with you. Is that a fair observation or your interpretation?

MR. DOGGETT: That was the conclusion I came to, in response to what I felt was an absolutely bizarre statement she made to me at her going-away party.

SEN. DECONCINI: Thank you. I have no further questions.

THE CHAIRMAN: [presiding]. Senator Thurmond?

SEN. THURMOND: I have asked Senator Specter to propound to these witnesses.

SEN. SPECTER: Thank you, Mr. Chairman.

We have heard many impressive witnesses during the course of these proceedings, but I do not believe that we have heard any more impressive than this panel.

I want to divide the first portion of the fifteen minutes into two segments. Professor Kothe and Mr. Doggett have both submitted affidavits, which develop the statement of a fantasy on the part of Professor Hill, and I will examine both of them to see if there was any connection or any suggestion as to their use of the word "fantasy," and I can see Professor Kothe moving forward to suggest to the contrary, but I will come to that.

I first want to take up the testimony of Mr. Stewart and Mr. Grayson, because their testimony is much briefer, although by the time you finish your questioning tonight, you won't think so.

Going to a very important conversation which was held very recently, according to the statements of Mr. Stewart and Mr. Grayson, in August of this year, and a subject that I questioned Professor Hill about in detail, Mr. Stewart, you have already testified, and the critical part of your statement or your affidavit is, as follows:

"In August of 1991, I ran into Ms. Hill at the American Bar Association Convention, in Atlanta, Georgia, whereupon she stated to me in the presence of Stanley Grayson, how great Clarence's nomination was and how much he deserved it."

Mr. Stewart, are you sure that's the essence of what Professor Hill told you?

MR. STEWART: Absolutely.

SEN. SPECTER: Mr. Grayson's statement refers to the weekend of August 10, 1991, at the American Bar Association Convention, in Atlanta, Georgia, where he says he was introduced to Professor Hill by Mr. Stewart, and this is his statement: "During the course of our conversation, in the presence of Mr. Stewart, Ms. Hill expressed her pleasure with Judge Thomas's nomination and stated that 'he deserved it.' "

Mr. Grayson, are you certain that Professor Hill said that?

MR. GRAYSON: Yes, I am, Senator.

SEN. SPECTER: Later I'm going to come back to what Ms. Hill said by way of denial. But for the point of the first ten minutes, I want to move at this point to what Mr. Doggett and Mr. Kothe have had to say.

And, Professor, I want to start because of limitation of time, and you will be expanding in great detail on your statement, and I want to turn to the statement which you submitted on October 7th and ask you if you have a copy of that with you?

MR. KOTHE: I have the statement I submitted on October 10.

THE CHAIRMAN: Senator? Senator, I am not interrupting this. On an administrative matter.

SEN. SPECTER: Yes.

THE CHAIRMAN: In light of the hour, do you mind if I make an announcement about the remainder of the witnesses that people may be interested in knowing.

SEN. SPECTER: I would be glad to yield to you, Mr. Chairman.

THE CHAIRMAN: And I apologize, but this has just been decided.

We have now only one more panel of witnesses and it will be limited to an hour. Because I would like to read to the committee a letter that I sent after a number of conversations with my colleagues, Democrats and Republicans, to Ms. Wright, who was going to testify, or potentially going to testify, had been subpoenaed, and to Ms. Jourdain, who was going to corroborate the testimony of Ms. Wright.

This is the letter that I telefaxed to her lawyer in the office in downtown Washington a few minutes ago after extensive negotiations and discussions with Democrats and Republicans and Ms. Wright's lawyer.

"Dear Ms. Wright: It is my preference that you testify before the Judiciary Committee in connection with the nomination of Judge Clarence Thomas. But, in light of the time constraints under which the committee is operating and the willingness of all the members of the committee to have placed in the record of the hearing the transcripts of the interviews of you and your corroborating witness, Ms. Rose Jourdain, J-o-u-r-d-a-i-n, conducted by the majority and minority staff, I am prepared to accede to the mutual agreement of you and the members of the committee, both Republican and Democrat, that the subpoena be vitiated. Thus the transcribed interviews of you and Ms. Rose Jourdain will be placed in the record without rebuttal at the hearing.

I wish to make clear, however, that if you want to testify at the hearing in person I will honor that request.

Signed: Sincerely, Joseph R. Biden, Jr.

Postscript on the bottom I attached from Angela Wright: "I agree the admission of the transcript of my interview and that of Ms. Jourdain's in the record without rebuttal at the hearing represents my position and is completely satisfactory to me."

THE CHAIRMAN: Translated: Ms. Wright and Ms. Jourdain will not testify at the hearing. Their extensive interviews conducted by the majority and minority staffs will be placed in the official record available to all of our colleagues and to the press and the world, without rebuttal, in the record.

[The interviews referred to follow:]

TRANSCRIPT OF PROCEEDINGS

* * *

UNITED STATES SENATE

* * *

COMMITTEE ON THE JUDICIARY

* * *

In the Matter of the Nomination of
Judge Clarence Thomas to be an Associate
Justice of the U.S. Supreme Court

Thursday, October 10, 1991
Washington, DC

The telephonic interview of ANGELA DENISE WRIGHT, called for examination by counsel for the Senate Committee on the Judiciary in the above-entitled matter, pursuant to notice, in the offices of the Senate Committee on the Judiciary, Room SD-234, Dirksen Senate Office Building, Washington, DC, convened at 10:43 a.m., when were present on behalf of the parties:

CYNTHIA HOGAN, Staff of Senator Biden
HARRIET GRANT, Staff of Senator Biden
ANN HARKINS, Staff of Senator Leahy
WINSTON LETT, Staff of Senator Heflin
TERRY WOOTEN, Staff of Senator Thurmond
MELISSA RILEY, Staff of Senator Thurmond
MILLER BAKER, Staff of Senator Hatch
RICHARD HERTLING, Staff of Senator Specter

PROCEEDINGS

MS. HOGAN: Hi, Angela. This is Cynthia Hogan, from the Senate Judiciary Committee, in Washington.

I am sorry we are calling you a little bit later than we had anticipated, but it took us a little bit of time to get ourselves together this morning.

I wanted to let you know that, in addition to the people I told you would be here, there are several others. I told you last night that someone from Senator Thurmond's staff would be here and that I would be here. Of course, I work for Senator Biden.

There are actually two people here from Senator Biden's office, myself and Harriet Grant, and two people here from Senator Thurmond's office. As well, there are four other lawyers here who work for different Senators. I wanted to let you know that, before I put you on the speaker phone, so that you were aware that we were here. We also do have a court reporter, as I told you.

I am with Senator Biden. Now, if I put you on the speaker phone, I want each of them to identify themselves and to tell you who they work for. I want to reassure you that it still remains that only two people are going to ask you questions, and that is me and Terry Wooten, who works for Senator Thurmond.

I just wanted you to be aware that these other people are here, since I did not tell you that last night, and to make sure it was okay with you, before I put you on the speaker phone. If it is okay, I will ask each person to identify themselves for you, so that you are clear about who is here.

Is that all right? All right. Hang on.

MS. HOGAN: Ms. Wright?

MS. WRIGHT: Yes.

MS. HOGAN: All right. Why don't we just go around the room here. I want everyone to identify themselves for you, and I want to make sure we are on the record, so that you are aware of who is here.

MS. GRANT: Hi, Ms. Wright. I am Harriet Grant. I am with Senator Biden.

MS. WRIGHT: Okay.

MR. LETT: Ms. Wright, my name is Winston Lett, and I am with Senator Heflin.

MS. WRIGHT: Winston, what was his last name?

MR. LETT: Lett, L-e-t-t.

MS. WRIGHT: And with Heflin?

MR. LETT: Yes, ma'am.

MS. WRIGHT: Okay.

MS. HARKINS: Ms. Wright, my name is Ann Harkins, and I am with Senator Leahy.

MS. WRIGHT: Leahy?

MS. HARKINS: Leahy, L-e-a-h-y.

MS. WRIGHT: Okay.

MR. BAKER: Ms. Wright, my name is Miller Baker. I work for Senator Orrin Hatch.

MS. WRIGHT: Miller Baker, with Orrin Hatch?

MR. BAKER: Yes, ma'am.

MS. RILEY: Ms. Wright, I am Melissa Riley, and I am with Senator Thurmond's office.

MS. WRIGHT: Okay.

MR. WOOTEN: And I am Terry Wooten, with Senator Thurmond's office.

MS. WRIGHT: Okay.

MR. HERTLING: Ms. Wright, my name is Richard Hertling, H-e-r-t-l-i-n-g, and I am from Senator Specter's office.

MS. WRIGHT: Okay.

Whereupon,

ANGELA DENISE WRIGHT

was called for examination and testified, as follows:

By MS. HOGAN:

Q Ms. Wright, I am going to ask you again, mostly for the benefit of the court reporter who is here, just to state your name, your address, spell your name for us, so we make sure she gets that down.

A Okay. I will state my name and address and I will spell my name. I also would like to just preface whatever we are about to say. Okay?

Q Okay. That's fine.

A My name is Angela, A-n-g-e-l-a, Denise, D-e-n-i-s-e, Wright, W-r-i-g-h-t. What else did you want, my age or my address?

Q Both would be fine.

A Okay. I am thirty-seven years old. My address is—

Q I would also like to ask you to state where you are currently employed, but let me tell you that if you want to make your statement first, go ahead.

A Okay. Well, I will do both. I am currently employed as an assistant metro editor at *The Charlotte Observer*.

I want to preface what we are about to say by saying that I want to make it clear and I want it on the record that the information that I am about to give is not information that I approached anyone on Capitol Hill or on the Senate Judiciary staff with, but it is something that I have struggled with since I have seen Anita Hill on television on Monday night, and once I got a call from the Senate Judiciary Committee, that decision became quite obvious as to what I should do.

Now, I will take whatever questions you want.

Q Okay. I would like you just very briefly, if you could give us—and I mean very briefly—some background about yourself, say, your education and your job history, sort of, you know, one sentence.

A I have a degree in journalism from the University of North Carolina, at Chapel Hill. Prior to working at *The Charlotte Observer*, I worked as the managing editor of *The Winston-Salem Chronicle*. Prior to that, I worked for the National Business League in Washington. Prior to that, I was back in school in Chapel

Hill. Prior to that, I was at the EEOC. Prior to EEOC, I was at the United States Agency for International Development. Prior to that, I was at the Republican National Committee, and before that I was at the Republican Congressional Committee, and before that I was at the office of Senator—excuse me, Congressman Charlie Rose.

Q Ms. Wright, as I understand it, you know Clarence Thomas, is that correct?

A That is correct.

Q Can you tell us when you first met him?

A I first met Clarence Thomas in the late seventies, probably around 1978-79, when several black staff members of Republican congressional offices decided to form an organization called the Black Republican Congressional Staff Association. It was pretty much an informal organization that disbanded eventually on its own, but our purpose was to try and form some type of support group and some type of group that could convince other black political-type people that the Republican Party was a viable alternative to the Democratic Party.

Q I'm sorry, did you meet Clarence Thomas in the course of meetings of this association?

A Yes, that is correct.

Q And how often did you see him in this context? You know, give me a rough estimate.

A Probably only three or four times. The organization didn't last very long and I didn't go to every meeting that was held.

Q Okay. Did you consider yourself a friend of his at this time?

A No, an acquaintance.

Q Now, it is also my understanding that you worked with Clarence Thomas at the EEOC, is that correct?

A That is correct.

Q And can you tell us when you were hired at the EEOC and by whom?

A I was hired in March of 1984 by Clarence Thomas.

Q Can you tell me a little bit more about how you found out about a job, or did you approach him about a job? Can you give me a little bit of background about that?

A I was working as the Director of Media Relations for the United States Agency for International Development, when a friend of mine—well, I guess I should really say an acquaintance of mine—Phyllis Berry-Meyers, who was at the time Clarence Thomas's Director of Congressional Affairs, approached me at a reception on Capitol Hill and said that Clarence Thomas was in dire need of a Director of Public Affairs and would I be willing to talk to him about it, would I be willing to consider that position, and I said yes. She subsequently went to Clarence Thomas and told him that I would consider it, and sometime later I went over and talked to him about the position and he offered it to me and I left AID and went to EEOC.

Q And you joined EEOC, this was in March of 1984?

A Yes.

Q And your title was what?

A Director of Public Affairs.

Q And can you describe a little bit for me what your job responsibilities were?

A We had an office that had several public information specialists, a video department, and my job was to coordinate that staff—I think at the time there were twenty-seven maybe staff members there—and to produce in-house publications, to be the chairman's publicist, so to speak, his connection with the media, to answer media questions, to advise him on public appearances, his best contact with the media. He and actually other office directors, I was responsible for advising them on their contact with the media. We also produced seminars on the equal employment laws and things of that nature.

Q And did you report to Clarence Thomas?

A Yes, I did.

Q But you did at the same time work for others or handle publicity for other people, is that correct? I just want to make sure I understand—

A Publicity, if there was an office at EEOC that was involved in some issue and the media was interested in talking to that office director, generally the media came through me, asked me about setting up interviews with that particular person. It was not something that was required. There, of course, were some office directors who picked off directly from the media.

Q So, although you worked on publicity with other people, you reported directly to Clarence Thomas, is that correct?

A That is correct.

Q And can you give me a rough estimate of how much contact you had with him in the course of your employment?

A The contact with Clarence Thomas was pretty much a daily contact, in person or at least buzzing him on the phone from my phone to discuss questions from the media or some other course of business. You know, those were pretty turbulent times for the EEOC, and we had lots of questions from the press.

Q Sure. Did you consider your relationship with Clarence Thomas at this time to be strictly professional?

A I considered Clarence Thomas at the time to be—well, it was—I guess you could say it was strictly professional, in that there was no other contact between me and Clarence Thomas outside of professional activities.

Q Okay. Now, my understanding is that there are some statements or some comments that he made to you that you wanted to—I don't want to characterize them for you, but that you are willing to tell us about. Can you tell me were there comments that he made to you that maybe you considered inappropriate?

A Yes, I can tell you that during the course of the year that I worked for Clarence Thomas, there were several comments that he made. Clarence Thomas did consistently pressure me to date him. At one point, Clarence Thomas made comments about my anatomy. Clarence Thomas made comments about women's anatomy quite often. At one point, Clarence Thomas came by my apartment at night, unannounced and uninvited, and talked in general terms, but also conversation—he would try to move the conversation over to the prospect of my dating him.

Q I think if it is all right with you, we need to try and go through some of these comments very specifically. You have mentioned now that he came to your apartment one evening and I believe you said he came over uninvited, is that correct?

A Yes, that is correct.

MR. WOOTEN: Can we go back to maybe when it started, rather than—if that is the first contact, fine, but—

By MS. HOGAN:

Q I guess maybe I misunderstood. Was this the first time that you felt there was something inappropriate done by Judge Thomas?

A No, it was not.

Q Okay. Perhaps it would be easier if we could go back to the beginning. You became employed at the EEOC in March of 1984. Do you remember when the first comment or conduct that Clarence Thomas engaged in that you considered inappropriate?

A No, I do not.

Q Okay.

A Let me clarify one thing. The night he came by my apartment was the first and the only time he came to my apartment.

But, no, I cannot sit here and tell you I remember dates. What I can tell you is that this is a general course of action, this is an attitude and these are comments that Clarence Thomas has generally tended to make.

Q Okay. You mentioned just a moment ago that, generally, he pressured you to date him.

A Yes.

Q Was there anything that occurred along those lines prior to the time he came to your apartment, that you recall?

A Yes.

Q Okay. Could you tell us about that?

A Well, I will tell you about one—let me be specific here. We are talking about a thing that, you know, pretty much pops out of Clarence Thomas's mouth when he feels like saying this. We are not talking about, you know, traumatic single events here.

Q Right.

A We are talking about a general mode of operating. I can remember specifically one evening when the comment of dating came up, it was when we were having—the EEOC was having a retirement party for my predecessor, Alf Sweeney, which I had organized for Mr. Sweeney at Mr. Thomas's request, and we were sitting at the banquet table while the speakers and things were going through their speeches, and Clarence Thomas was sitting right next to me and he at one point turned around and said this is really a great job, blah-blah-blah, and he said and you look good and you are going to be dating me, too. That was not like the only time he said something of that nature.

Q Okay. Do you recall at all approximately when this banquet occurred?

A Approximately, it was early summer or late spring 1984. It was held at some type of officers club in Virginia. I can't remember what the officers club was, but at the time one of my staff members, John Hawkins, was a member of that club, and so he was able to procure it for us to have, you know, we would actually have, you know, a very elaborate retirement party for Mr. Sweeney.

Q Was it like a dinner banquet?

A It was a dinner banquet.

Q Okay. And you said that you were sitting at the banquet table with Clarence Thomas?

A Yes.

Q And when he made this remark to you about you would be dating him, was anyone else sitting there with you?

A Well, there were several people there at the banquet table, yes.

Q Do you know whether any of them heard this comment that Clarence Thomas made to you?

A I seriously doubt that any of them heard it.—He was sitting right next to me and this wasn't something he was shouting. He was talking, practically whispering, because there was actually a program going on.

Q Okay. Was this a well-attended event? Can you give me an idea of how many people may have been there?

A Yes, there were lots of people there, lots of influential people there, including congressmen, former Congressman and Mayor Carl Stokes, Congressman Lewis Stokes.

Q So, this was not simply EEOC employees?

A It was not simply EEOC employees. What we had done was to actually surprise Mr. Sweeney with a lot of old friends. In fact, his entire family was there. He did not know this banquet was happening, he did not know that these people would be there, and a lot of them were old journalists, like—I cannot remember the lady's name, a black journalist well-known in EEOC, and she just died last year—anyway, there were also lots of people from the EEOC there. It was actually crowded.

Q Now, after Clarence Thomas made this statement to you about you dating him—

A Excuse me, I just remembered, Ethel Payne is the name of this journalist I tried to remember.

Q I'm sorry, what was the last name?

A Ethel Payne, P-a-y-n-e.

Q After Clarence Thomas made this one comment to you, was there any further discussion of what he said?

A No.

Q Did you respond in any way to his comment?

A No, I never did.

Q And he did not follow up his comment with any additional discussion at that time?

A No, he did not.

Q Okay. Do you remember any other occasions on which he pressured you to date him?

A No, I do not. I can't give you dates and times and tell you that it was a general course of conversation.

MR. WOOTEN: Was the banquet the first time that Thomas had said something to you?

MS. HOGAN: This is Terry Wooten speaking, for your information.

MS. WRIGHT: Okay. No, Terry, it was not.

MR. WOOTEN: If we need to talk more about the banquet, go ahead.

By MS. HOGAN:

Q Was there anything else that occurred at the banquet that you recall, along these lines?

A No.

Q Do you remember specifically—now, I understand that you told us that there was this general environment of this, but do you remember any specific comments that Clarence Thomas made to you along these lines prior to this banquet?

A Prior to this banquet?

Q Correct.

A No, I cannot, any specific comments.

Q And what about after this banquet, do you remember any specific comments where he talked to you about dating him?

A No, I can only remember them in general.

Q Okay. Why don't you tell us what you remember, in general.

A In general, given the opportunity, Clarence Thomas is the type of person —well, let me back up a minute. In general, given the opportunity, Clarence Thomas would say to me, you know, "You need to be dating me, I think I'm going to date you, you're one of the finest women I have on my staff," you know, "we're going to be going out eventually."

Q And what do you mean by "given the opportunity"?

A Given the opportunity, you know, if there was no one else around or we were close enough that he could turn around and whisper something of that nature.

Q Do you ever recall him saying anything of this nature to you when other people overheard it?

A No.

Q If it is all right with you, you mentioned that this occurred once at your apartment.

A Yes.

Q Can you tell me a little bit more about that?

A He came to my apartment, I opened the door, I offered him a beer, we talked, he sat at what was actually a counter separating the kitchen from the living room area, we sat on bar stools and talked in general about general things and, you know, the conversation would turn to his desire to date me, and I would adeptly turn it to some other topic.

Q And this was the first and only time he was at your apartment?

A Yes, that is correct.

Q And he arrived uninvited?

A Yes, that is correct.

Q Did he say why he had come to your apartment?

A Not that I can recall. My recollection is that he was in the neighborhood or something, but I can't actually recall what he said when he came to the door or actually any specific things about the conversation, except for the nature of it.

Q So, you don't remember specific things he stated?

A No, I don't. You know, I wish I could apologize to you for that, but it is not the kind of thing I was taking notes about or I wasn't keeping a journal.

Q No, I certainly understand that it is a number of years ago, and we just appreciate your sharing with us what you remember. The only reason I am trying to ask, you know, for specific recollections is in case you have them, I want to make sure that we give you an opportunity to tell us.

A I specifically recall being at a seminar, I can't even tell you which seminar, because we had many of them, when Clarence Thomas commented on the dress I was wearing and asked me what size my boobs were.

Q This was an EEOC conference?

A This was an EEOC seminar.

Q A seminar. I'm sorry, you said it was out of town?

A Yes.

MR. WOOTEN: Can we go back to the time frame when you say Judge Thomas came to your apartment? I don't know that we got the time frame. Can you give us an approximate date?

MS. WRIGHT: Well, it was not in the summer, it was like it was cold, it was the end of fall or early winter.

By MS. HOGAN:

Q And do you know how he knew where your apartment was?

A Well, I lived in that same apartment for about five years on Capitol Hill, three blocks from the White House—excuse me, from the office building. Most of the people who knew me knew where I lived.

MS. HOGAN: I think it would be easier for her, if I continue.

MR. WOOTEN: If we could—

MS. WRIGHT: It doesn't matter to me how you want to—

MR. WOOTEN: I don't want to create confusion, but this is done in the time when you say Judge Thomas came to your apartment when you worked at the EEOC, is that correct or not? I don't want to put words in your mouth, but—

MS. WRIGHT: That is correct.

MR. WOOTEN: I am just trying to get a general time frame.

By MS. HOGAN:

Q This was during the year that you worked with Judge Thomas at the EEOC?

A That is correct.

Q In the fall or possibly the winter?

A Yes.

Q The next thing you mentioned was this EEOC seminar, do you have any recollection of when this occurred, approximately?

A No. We went to several seminars. In fact, my only recollection of it is that we were walking towards a meeting room and I was briefing him, giving him information on what this particular seminar was about; you know, the general run-of-the-mill things that public relations folks do and there were other people walking just ahead of us, people in his legal staff. But I can't remember which seminar that was, or which hotel that was. We held seminars in Denver, in Miami, I think, in Texas.

Q Do you remember what the subject of the seminar was?

A Well, the subjects of the seminar generally were about the laws under which EEOC operated and the laws that EEOC was charged with enforcing. We held community seminars to simply go to the communities and tell people, you know, this is what is qualified as age discrimination, this is what qualifies as sexual harassment, this is what qualifies as race discrimination and this is what the law says, and we had other, you know, experts from around the agency—lawyers and those type of people—to pretty much sit on panels and discuss all aspects of discrimination law.

Q So these were seminars that the EEOC gave on some type of regular basis?

A That's true, yes.

Q And they were given across the country?

A Yes.

Q And they were given to who? Was the public invited to these conferences?

A Yes, they were.

Q Okay, and can you give me an average of how many of these conferences you would attend with Clarence Thomas a year or in the year that you worked for him?

A I think during that year we had four or five. I can't say for sure, it is like four or five. But I want to make it clear that I did not attend them with him. I generally advanced him. My staff and I went out, prior to Clarence Thomas, or any of the legal people getting there.

Q Did he attend all EEOC seminars of this type that were given across the country?

A As far as I can remember, yes.

Q And you would do the advance work for all of these?

A Yes.

Q Okay, do you know whether anyone overheard the comment to him, the comment that he made to you in this hotel?

A No, I don't. If they did, they did not react to it.

Q Okay, did you tell anyone about it?

A No, I did not.

Not, let me put it, not, I did not walk away from that situation and go say, you know, "Guess what Clarence Thomas just said."

Q Okay.

A But in the course of other conversations that I had with other people, particularly women, about Clarence Thomas, yes, I have made—relayed that situation along with all others.

Q Do you recall any particular women that you spoke to about this?

A Yes.

Q Okay, could you tell me who they were?

A Well, I would be willing to name one of them.

Q Okay.

A Because it is interesting to me that that person is—this is sort of in a denial—but Phyllis Berry-Meyers was one of them.

Q And this is the same woman who initially contacted you about working for Clarence Thomas?

A Yes.

Q And what was her position? She worked at the EEOC, correct?

A She did, as Director of Congressional Affairs.

Q And you told her or discussed with her—

A She and I discussed Clarence Thomas on many occasions and the conversations were, of course, always varied depending on what the topic of the day was, but the conversations also generally ended up talking about Clarence and his approach to women, too.

Q Do you know whether you mentioned to her or to anyone else the comments, the comment that was made to you at Mr. Sweeney's retirement party?

A I can't sit down and remember specifically having that conversation with anyone, no.

Q Okay, and what about the fact that Judge Thomas came to your apartment. Do you remember if you ever mentioned that to anyone?

A Yes, I did.

Q And who did you mention that to?

A I would rather not say because I don't know if she would like to get involved.

Q Okay. Do you remember any other conversations with anyone else—men, women, anyone—where you discussed the comments made to you by Judge Thomas?

A No, I can't say—no, I don't remember any other specific conversations about Judge Thomas where I made references to those specific comments.

Q Okay, did you have any other conversations with people generally about Judge Thomas's conduct toward women in the office?

A Yes.

Q And can you tell us anything about those conversations? Who they were with or what the conversations consisted of?

A No, I can't. I mean when you work for somebody you generally talk about work and those people. I talked with Clarence Thomas about others, I talked with other people at EEOC about Clarence Thomas when I worked there, when I felt that perhaps some things he did were not, some positions he took were not the best ones to take, or some things he did were not the best things to do.

Q So these were—you just generally, you had conversations on various occasions with other employees at the EEOC that may have included some of these comments, or other comments about Judge Thomas's conduct towards women?

A Yes.

Q Okay.

A Well, let me say this, too. There were select people at EEOC that I would have had those conversations with. I would not talk in general to people at EEOC about that because Clarence Thomas and I were both political people and I was very conscious of what to say to non-political type people.

Q Okay, you mentioned that you did discuss generally with Phyllis Berry-Meyers?

A That's correct.

Q Do you recall what her reaction was when you discussed this with her?

A Yes, I do.

Q And what was her reaction?

A Well, I, I can almost quote her as a matter of fact, "Well, he's a man, you know, he's always hitting on everybody."

Q I'm sorry, I didn't catch the last.

A "He's always hitting on everybody."

Q Okay, do you remember any other specific comments that you might have made?

A No, I can remember one conversation with her went on for a while, but I can't tell you what else was said, you know, it was in general, the same kinds of comments.

Q Did you work closely with her in your capacity at the EEOC?

A Yes, pretty much, but, you know, her office, her responsibilities were very different. She worked as a liaison to Capitol Hill and I was a liaison to the media.

Q Okay, are there any other occasions on which you remember specific comments that Clarence Thomas made to you that you considered inappropriate?

A None that I can give you dates for, no.

Q Okay. Can you tell me how long you worked at the EEOC?

A For one year.

Q And can you tell me what the circumstances were of your leaving the EEOC?

A Yes. Clarence Thomas fired me.

Q And can you just describe for me the circumstances surrounding that?

A Sure. I came into my office one day and there was a letter in my chair and I opened that letter and it said, your services here are no longer needed as of—whatever two weeks from the date was—you know, you will no longer be employed by the EEOC.

And I read the letter. It was quite a surprise to me. I took the letter and I went upstairs to Clarence Thomas's office, whose secretary, Diane Holt, motioned me in without even, without any question. When I walked into his office, he was in the bathroom inside his office, and I sat down in the chair beside his desk and waited for him to come out. And when he walked out, I handed, I held the letter up and I said, 'What is this? What does it mean? Why are you firing me? And he says, "Well, well,—

[Pause.]

Q Ms. Wright, can you hear me?

A Yes, I can hear you.

Q Terrific, you were telling us about—

A I walked into his office.

Q Okay.

A Well, I said to him, you know, "What is this? Why are you firing me?" And he says, "Well, Angela, I've never been satisfied with your work."

I said, "Why have you not been satisfied with my work, and why have you not told me this up to this point?" He said, "Well, I told you to fire those folks down there, and you haven't fired a soul down there." And I said, "Well, Clarence, these people are career employees, not like I can just go in there and say you are fired. It takes almost an act of Congress to get them removed."

He said, "Well, I just in general am not satisfied with your work."

The day prior to that I had held a press conference on some issue that was real hot at the time, I don't remember what that issue was, but it was a very successful press conference. All the major media were there, *The Wall Street Journal*, *The Washington Post*, there were thirteen representatives there in all. And that morning, that I was sitting there talking to him, he had a press kit in front of him with almost an inch of press clippings. So I picked that up and I said to him, I said, "How can you say that especially today of all days, you sitting right here, with a press packet from a press conference that I just held for you yesterday that was very successful, when you guys were on the hot seat?"

And he said to me, you know, "I never needed you to get me any publicity. I could always call my buddy Juan Williams over at *The Washington Post* if I needed publicity."

And I said, "Okay, fine. Well, look if you—we are both political so that is your prerogative. You could tell me to go because you don't like the color of my shoes or something like that," I said, "But the point here is, Clarence, we are political and I don't believe this stuff you are telling me about why you're firing me, but I do have this question. Why did you decide to do this? If you wanted me to leave this position, all you had to do was say, go to your friends at the White House and call and see if you can get another appointment," I said, "but your intent was to make me unemployed. And why is that? I have been, I tried to be a loyal employee. I have tried to be your friend."

And he said, "Well, I never cared anything about loyalty and I don't care a whole lot about friendship." And I said, "Well—" I just pushed the chair away from the table, and I said, "Well, then, I hope you will be a very happy, successful man, but I doubt it."

And I walked out of his office and I went down to my office and I left EEOC. And that is the last conversation I ever had with Clarence Thomas.

Q If I could just go back a little bit. You said that the first notice that you received of this was in a letter that was left in your office?

A It was a letter, it was a letter that was left in my chair in my office.

Q And who was the letter signed by?

A By Clarence Thomas.

Q Okay, and at that time, you went up to his office?

A I did.

Q And do you remember anything else that was said between the two of you in the meeting in his office?

A I—I—I think I just said it just about verbatim.

Q Okay. Do you recall when this was?

A It was, as far as I can recollect, in April.

Q And that is April of 1985?

A Yes.

Q Was anyone else present during this conversation?

A No.

Q Do you think that your failure to respond to any of Judge Thomas's comments to you had anything to do with him firing you?

A You are not the first person who has asked me that question. Several people at EEOC asked me that question.

Q Do you remember who at EEOC asked you that question?

A Well, actually the man who was my predecessor who you can't confirm, because he is now dead, Al Sweeney, that was the first question that came out of his mouth. And there were other people there but I, I really hesitate to drag other people's names into this conversation who are not now at all affiliated with this issue. I don't mind discussing people who are, you know, who have already made a public comment on this, but I don't want to volunteer anybody else's participation.

Q Okay. Are there any other specific comments that Judge Thomas told you at any time that you want to tell us about?

A About the only thing I can tell you is that he did tell me at one point during that conversation when I asked him about why he was firing me that he was real bothered by the fact that I did not wait for him outside his office after work. It was a statement that I dismissed as one of his statements.

Q So you didn't follow up on that or respond to that?

A Well, I don't remember responding. You know, I wasn't a very happy person at that point. I was really trying to get to the truth of what was really going on and nothing he had said to me at that point sounded like the real deal.

Q Well, did that comment make you think that perhaps the firing had to do with your failure to respond to his comments?

A It did not make me think that at that moment. What I was thinking at that moment was he was grasping for all kinds of reasons. In retrospect I guess that is a possibility but that is not the first thought that came to my mind when he said it.

Q Okay. After you left the EEOC, what did you do next for employment?

A I did not—when I left the EEOC I went back to the University of North Carolina because I had not completed the work on my degree. I went back to finish school.

Q Okay, and you finished school when?

A In December of 1985.

Q And this was your bachelor's degree in journalism?

A Yes.

Q And following your graduation from the University of North Carolina, what did you do?

A I moved to Charlotte, North Carolina and I worked for a while as a substitute school teacher, actually I worked three jobs—as a substitute school teacher, as a radio news announcer, and as a freelance public relations.

I stayed in Charlotte for about, I guess that would have been, gosh, I would have come to Charlotte maybe in May of '86, and stayed in Charlotte until maybe September. And I went and just a month in Atlanta with some friends of mine there, just looking for work in Atlanta. And then went back to Washington, after someone that I knew called me up and asked me to take a position at the National Business League.

Q Okay, and following the National Business League, was when you went to *The Winston-Salem*—

A *Chronicle*, yes.

Q —*Chronicle*, okay. And following that, you went back to Charlotte and took your present job, is that correct?

A That's correct.

Q Now, on any of these occasions when you took employment after the EEOC, did you ask anyone at the EEOC for a recommendation?

A No, I did not.

Q Okay, did you give anyone's name at the EEOC as a reference to a potential employer?

A No, I did not, but on my resume the EEOC, of course, is listed as a former place of employment.

Q Okay, did you have any, have you had any contact with Judge Thomas since you left the EEOC?

A No, I have not.

Q Have you ever called his office or spoken to him by telephone?

A I have called his office on one occasion but I never got to speak to him.

Q And can you tell us about that one occasion?

A Yes. I had a friend who owns a telecommunications firm. He installed telephone systems in businesses. He had done lots of work on Federal military bases. And he had contacted me about trying to talk to anyone I knew who worked in the Government to perhaps see if they would be willing to talk to him about using his phone system.

And I placed a call to Clarence Thomas on his behalf. My call was never returned and I never tried again.

Q Who did you speak with? Did you call Judge Thomas at his office?

A Yes, I called and I talked with Diane, his secretary.

Q Okay, do you recall approximately when this call might have occurred?

A In the summer of 1987.

Q And you left a message with Clarence Thomas's secretary Diane?

A Yes.

Q And he never returned the call?

A That's correct.

Q Okay. Did you have any other occasions where you called him or his office?

A No, I did not.

Q Have you had any contacts since you left the EEOC with other employees of the EEOC who were there while you were employed there?

A Yes, I have.

Q And can you tell us whether in any of those conversations you discussed Clarence Thomas and any of the facts we have discussed today?

A Generally, when I talk with people who work at the EEOC, the conversation turns to Clarence Thomas, but no, not specifically about the things we are talking about right now.

Q Okay. Just one point of clarification on your degree from the University of North Carolina. You said you graduated in December of '85 or in May of '86?

A I completed the requirements in December of '85.

Q Okay.

A They mailed the degree to me, because I stay in Chapel Hill.

Q Okay. Ms. Wright, do you know Anita Hill?

A Do I know Anita Hill? I have never met Anita Hill, and I have never heard of Anita Hill before this week.

Q You are, I take it, aware of Professor Hill's allegations about Clarence Thomas?

A Yes, I am.

Q Do you feel that these allegations are in or out of character for Clarence Thomas, as you know him?

A I feel that the Clarence Thomas that I know is quite capable of doing just what Anita Hill alleges.

Q Do you have anything else you want to tell us today?

A No, I've told you all that I know.

MS. HOGAN: If you can bear with us just for one minute.

MR. WOOTEN: If you all have something, go ahead.

MS. HOGAN: If you will bear with us just for one minute, please.

MS. WRIGHT: Sure.

BY MS. HOGAN:

Q To go back briefly and follow up, you told us that in the conversation you had with Clarence Thomas when he fired you—

A Yes.

Q —he made a comment about you didn't wait outside his door for him at the end of the day. Is that accurate? I don't want to—

A That is correct.

Q Okay. Did you have any sense of what he meant by that comment?

A Not at the time, no, and I don't remember if I pursued it with him or not.

Q Okay. And did that lead you to—when he said that to you, was that in the context of explaining to you why he was firing you?

A Yes, it was. It was—excuse me just a minute, please.

Q Sure.

A [Pause.] He was—you know, I can't remember that specific part of the conversation. In general, he was talking about the kinds of things he felt that I should do, how I should report to him.

Q Okay.

A You know, I can't go back and say what exact words or which of his words preceded that or came out from that particular statement, but that statement was made.

Q Okay. In the conversations you had with other women at the EEOC about Clarence Thomas's conduct towards them, did any other women tell you that he had made specific references that they considered inappropriate?

A There were women who told me about specific references that he had made, but I don't remember them specifically saying that they considered it inappropriate. It was not—

Q Did they tell you that—did anyone else tell you that he had made comments to them about their anatomy?

A No, I don't remember that.

Q Did any of them tell you that he had made comments about wanting them to date him?

A Yes.

Q And do you remember any specifics with regard to what these women told you?

A Yes, but one woman that I can think of right now, particularly, was a married woman and I certainly would not like to discuss that.

Q Okay. Are you still there, Ms. Wright?

A I'm still there. We can finish. I am not trying to—

Q Okay. Sorry.

A Can I get you to hold on just a minute, so that I can get another call in?

Q Certainly.

A [Pause.]

Q When you say that he made comments to you and to other women about their anatomy, the only thing I believe you have mentioned to us specifically is that he made a comment about your boobs.

A Yes.

Q Were there any other specific comments about women's anatomy that you know of?

A Yes, Clarence Thomas talked about women's anatomy when he talked about the kind of women on his staff, he often said "I've got some fine women on my staff," and he would say things about individual people's anatomy.

Q And can you be any more specific than that, in terms of the type of comments he would make?

A I remember specifically him saying that one woman had a big ass.

Q And this was a comment that he made to you about another woman?

A I was not the only person in that room, come to think of it, but I can't remember exactly who was there.

Q But this was a comment that he made in your presence?

A Yes.

Q And do you remember any other specific comments?

A No, I don't.

MS. HOGAN: Okay. I think those are all the questions I have for you right now. Terry Wooten, who works for Senator Thurmond, is going to ask you some questions.

Terry, are you ready to go, or do you want to take a few minutes' break?

MR. WOOTEN: Do you want to talk to me for a minute on the side, or are you ready to go? I've got some things that I can ask and then you can come back.

MS. HOGAN: Ms. Wright, do you want to take a break for a few minutes, or are you content to go forward now?

MS. WRIGHT: I'm fine. Go ahead.

By MS. HOGAN:

Q I do have just one other question that I want to get on the record. Do you have anyone representing you, for instance, a lawyer?

A I have talked with friends who are lawyers, but I have not obtained legal counsel, no.

MS. HOGAN: Okay. Thank you.

By MR. WOOTEN:

Q Is anybody there with you now, or are you alone?

A I am alone, me and my dog.

Q Are you at work or are you home?

A I am at home.

Q You said that the first time that Judge Thomas made a comment to you was at a retirement party.

A No, I did not say that was the first time. That was one time, the time I remember.

Q Right. Could you go back and maybe tell us roughly when the first time it was that Judge Thomas had made some comment to you?

A No, I can't.

Q Is there any reason—you can't give us the context of maybe what he said the first time?

A No, I can't remember the first time, because it was one of a general pattern with Clarence Thomas to pop these things out of his mouth whenever he felt like it.

Q When can you say, roughly, when was the first time he made a comment to you—and I don't know if you can or not, but it is obviously a very serious allegation that he made other kinds of comments, and you are somewhat vague about what those comments were or when they took place.

A Okay.

Q I would just like to see if you can't think back and maybe tell us when was the first time or how long had it been when you were employed at the EEOC before he made the first comment.

A Oh, there is no doubt in my mind, it hadn't been very long, but I can't go back and tell you just what day or how many weeks. You know, Clarence Thomas I think felt very comfortable around me, and I want you to understand that I am not sitting here saying to you that I was sexually harassed by Clarence Thomas. I am a very strong-willed person and at no point did I feel intimidated by him. Some other woman might have, but these were not situations that I ran home and ruminated on and wrote down in my diary.

Q When he made these comments, how did you feel about it?

A I felt that he was annoying and obnoxious pretty much, but, you know—

Q Did you take them as a joke, or did you take them as something that maybe, you know, you had been harassed? You said you had not been harassed. I mean did you take them as a—

A Not sexually harassment, no.

Q I mean did—

A Harassment to me dictates some—I mean indicates some feeling that there is some threat. No, I never did feel threatened or intimidated.

By MS. HOGAN:

Q When you use the word "harassment"—this is Cynthia Hogan again—do you mean sexually harassed in a legal sense?

A I think that, yes, under the legal definition of sexual harassment, what Clarence Thomas did fit the legal definition, yes. I am not a lawyer, but as I understand it, that —

Q I'm sorry, it did fit the definition, as you understand it?

A As I understand it, yes.

By MR. WOOTEN:

Let me go back. You had said before you just made this statement that you didn't feel like you were sexually harassed, that you felt like you were more annoyed by it.

A Yes, I certainly did make that statement. But what I am saying to you is I am aware that, under the legal definition of sexual harassment, his actions fit the criteria. But was I intimidated to the point where I felt like filing a sexual harassment suit? No, I didn't consider filing then and I wouldn't file one now.

Q All right. The first specific time you remember that Judge Thomas said something to you was at the retirement party, that was the first time that you can say specifically this is what he said to me?

A Well, I think the use of the word "first" is what is bothering me. That is the one time when I can specifically remember the comment in the context of other circumstances.

Q Now, after that happened, were you annoyed or did you feel like you had been harassed, sexually harassed?

A Well, I think annoyed was a better term. I simply turned to Lewis Stokes, who was on my right-hand side and carried on a conversation with him.

Q All right. Did you ever tell anybody about that incident at all, the fact that Judge Thomas had made a comment to you at the retirement party?

A Well, I can't sit here and tell you that I had one conversation about that particular incident, no, but I can say that in the course of other general conversations, it is likely that I did, but I can't say that someone, that that was the focus of any other conversation I had, no.

Q Can you give us the name of any individual or individuals that you may have mentioned this to, the fact that something had been said to you at the retirement party?

A I could, but I am not willing to do that unless I would first check with them to see if they felt comfortable with me using their name in these proceedings.

Q Would you be willing to do that?

A I would be willing to check with them, yes.

Q Now, the second incident that you talked about to us is when Judge Thomas came to your apartment. Can you give us any indication as to how Judge Thomas knew where you lived?

A I had lived in the same apartment for five years on Capitol Hill, three blocks from the Capitol, on C Street. Duddington's Restaurant was literally by [my] back door. Anyone who knew me on Capitol Hill knew where I lived.

Q Well, let me ask you again: Was there any way —do you know how or have any indication as to how Judge Thomas would have known where you lived?

A No, I didn't ask him.

Q All right. Did you ever give him your address? Did you ever tell him where you lived?

A I think I probably wrote that down on the employment application.

Q All right. Other than putting that on the employment application, did you ever tell Judge Thomas where you lived?

A Not that I can recall. I mean that may have been part of our conversation at some point, but nothing significant enough for me to remember.

Q Well, if it was part of a conversation, I guess the question would be why would that come up in a conversation that you would have with Judge Thomas?

A I can't answer that, because I can't recall a conversation I had with him where that did come up. I am simply allowing for the possibility.

Q So, as best you can remember, you never told Judge Thomas where you lived or —

A No, I am not going to say I never told Judge Thomas where I lived. That is probably unlikely. I tell most people who you have any type of relationship with, when you talk with them at some point you get to the topic of where you live.

Q But you don't have any memory that he asked you about where you lived?

A No, I don't have any memory of that.

Q Now, you said that he came over in the winter —

A What I remember is that it was not hot, it was cold or cool.

Q Well, could you go back and recount maybe what you were doing at the time, did you have a doorbell, did he knock at the door? When you realized that Judge Thomas was there, can you just pick up from there and tell us what you thought first, and then what you did?

A Well, I went to the door and he was standing at the door, I opened the door and I said probably hello, how are you, come in. My guess is the conversation probably had something to do with what are you doing in this part of this neighborhood. I offered him a beer. We talked. He actually stayed for some time and talked.

Q Can you tell us approximately what time it was that he came over?

A No. I can remember about what time it was when he left, because it was after midnight and I was getting quite tired of the company.

Q Well, did you tell him that he needed to leave? You said he stayed there for some long period of time.

A I did not tell him he needed to leave. I probably made quite a few outward suggestions, like yawning and becoming distracted.

Q Were you drinking, as well, at the time?

A Yes.

Q Now, I am sure that if the person who was your boss came over, I assume there would be some conversation. Can you give us maybe a little more general information about what you discussed while he was there? Was this the first time he had ever been to your apartment?

A It was.

Q So, is it accurate to say that you were probably surprised when he came there?

A Yes, it is.

Q Well, can you just give us some indication of what maybe you generally talked about?

A I think, in general, we talked about the EEOC or changes he wanted to make there, most of them personnel changes. He talked often about wanting to clean out the public affairs department and fire all those folks down there, because they were just a bunch of incompetents. I am sure that was the thrust of it. We discussed that generally whenever we talked, but then he would also, of course, discuss his desire to date me, and I am very adept at turning the conversation towards some other topic.

Q All right. Can you be just—you said, I believe—my notes show that you said that you can't remember specific things. Let me ask you, if I could, Ms. Wright, to try to remember specific things. What did he say to you specifically about wanting to date you? Can you just be more specific about it? Because it is a very serious matter, in my judgment, to say that he came to your house. I mean if he came over to talk about work, that is one thing. If he came over to talk about other things, you know, that is another thing. We just need some informa tion from you about what he talked about, if you could be a little more specific.

A I understand that this is a very serious matter.

Q I am not trying to —

A But I want you to understand that I am telling you, as best as I can, what I know and what I have experienced with the man named Clarence Thomas whom you are about to name to the Court, and in this situation, if it were not for the situation at hand, you probably would not be talking to me. I know that you understand that I did not keep a journal, I did not write down his comments. I can only tell you in very general terms what my experience with Clarence Thomas has been.

Q Well, at the time that he came to your house, were you ever afraid of him?

A I was never afraid of Clarence Thomas.

Q Now, let's go back to this seminar that you said took place. I was just trying to get a rough time as to when you were at this seminar where you say Judge Thomas made some comment about your anatomy. Can you give us a rough time as to when that was?

A We had several seminars that year. The most I could tell you is that I can remember being at one of those seminars when Clarence Thomas made that comment. How can I tell you which seminar it was? Unfortunately, I know it would be most helpful for you, but I cannot tell you. I cannot remember that. Perhaps senility has set in at a young age here, but I can't remember that. We are talking of six or seven years ago.

Q Now, the term "boobs" came up. Is that a term that he used when he spoke to you?

A No, actually that is a term that I am using. Actually, what he said was what size are your breasts.

Q And at the time that statement was made, what was your reaction to it?

A I said something like I think you best concentrate on remembering the names of people you are going to be sharing the panel with.

Q All right. Let me ask you, on either one of these two specific occasions when Judge Thomas came to your house or to your apartment or that he made the comments about your anatomy, did you tell anybody at all about that, anybody that you could remember who could corroborate that you, in fact, told them about it?

A You know, I really don't mind cooperating with you, but at this point I truly feel like I have answered these questions that you are asking me already. Now, if you have something new you want to ask me, I don't mind answering them, but I am not going to go over this over and over and over again.

Q My question to you is: If Clarence Thomas would come to your apartment, just as though Senator Thurmond would come to my apartment, I think that would be a pretty big deal and I would probably tell somebody. My question to you is: Did you ever tell anybody that Judge Thomas came to your apartment?

A At one point today I already said yes, I did specifically discuss the fact that Judge Thomas came to my apartment with someone else whose name I don't care to use, participation of somebody who at this point is not a part of this proceeding.

Q Let me ask you, would you be willing to do that?

A I would be willing to call this person; Lyons is her name, if you—I guess that this person would mind because this person is still in a fairly political position.

Q Now, let's go to the time when you say that Judge Thomas had fired you.

You mentioned something about a press conference that you had held the day before.

A That's correct.

Q Was Judge Thomas agitated about that particular press conference?

A He did express some agitation at that press conference over the fact that Commissioner Gallegos was not there.

Q I see, and you said that he had said generally that he was never satisfied with your performance?

A Yes, he did say that.

Q Do you, did Judge Thomas ever get more specific than that, that you can remember?

A No, the only thing he said was that I didn't fire the people in my office that he wanted me to fire.

Q And can you, did you have the authority to fire people in your office?

A Political appointee, yes. I'm sure you understand about the authority to fire career employees, don't you?

Q Frankly, I don't, but I presume it is not easy to fire them.

A Career employees, let me just say career employees, you don't just walk in and fire a career Federal employee.

Q I would assume it would be difficult. But I guess my question is, and you may have answered it, is whether or not Judge Thomas was more specific with you about why you were being fired?

A No, he was not. But I think on that issue it might be, it might be important to point out, that you know, Judge Thomas gave me a wonderful recommendation when I took my current job. It's my understanding that he said to the person who called my references that firing me was the biggest mistake he'd ever made in his life. You can call that person, however, and ask her specifically what her words are. You can call my office and perhaps it is written in my files what he said, but I think that that, in itself, indicates, you know, or should be some indication of what I'm trying to tell you about that particular day. He was not specific. I never did believe whatever reasons they were that he gave me. My guess was that it was simply political, that there was someone more powerful than I who wanted a position as Director of Public Affairs.

Q Right. Obviously you don't think you should have been fired?

A No, I do not. I don't think I should have been fired, but I'm really happy that he did.

Q Okay.

A And let me point out, obviously he didn't think so either.

Q But because you say that he made, that was the biggest mistake that he'd ever made? Or a mistake that he had made to fire you?

A Yes. You know, I'm quoting someone on my staff, Mary Newsome, I mean someone at the newspaper who did the actual calls on my references so I don't want to put words in his mouth, that weren't there. I'm sure she wrote those comments down for the file, but you know, he said that I was a great employee and would be an asset to everybody's staff, etc.

MR. WOOTEN: If you will excuse me for just a minute.

[Pause.]

By MR. WOOTEN:

Q But you, since you were fired, you never—and this is a little bit unclear and somebody has asked me to clarify this—did you ever give Judge Thomas's name as a reference?

A I never gave his name as a reference.

MR. WOOTEN: Will you excuse us just a second.

[Pause.]

MS. HOGAN: Ms. Wright, would you like to take a break for a few minutes?

MS. WRIGHT: Yes, I would like to get a glass of water.

MS. HOGAN: Okay, that's fine.

[Pause.]

By MR. WOOTEN:

Q Ms. Wright, if we could just continue?

A Okay.

Q It is my understanding—and this is a question that someone else has asked me to ask—that Judge Thomas gave you a recommendation at some point, some kind of glowing recommendation. Is it from your current employer?

A Yes.

Q And the question would be, how did your current employer, if you know, how did your current employer have the opportunity or the ability to contact Judge Thomas if you had never used his name as a reference?

A When I apply for work, I generally, for my resume, [list] every place that I have ever worked before. People that were interested in hiring me at *The Charlotte Observer* did a thorough check and they called every place that I had ever worked before.

I mean you asked me if I have ever used Clarence Thomas as a reference. I take that to mean, do I list him as a personal reference of someone that I want to be called? The answer is, no, but I mean, you know, when I, my resume has every place that I have ever worked at in it, and I have no problem with people checking every place I have ever worked before.

Q Okay. Were you aware, obviously you were aware that Judge Thomas was nominated to the Supreme Court?

A Yes.

Q I presume that, in the process. I think he was nominated or the President announced his intent to nominate, it may have been July the first.

A I am aware of that.

Q Can you tell us just what your feelings were at the time that you heard he had been nominated to the Supreme Court?

A I never wavered in my feelings about that. I don't think, I don't think that Clarence Thomas is a good man and I did not think that he should be on the Supreme Court.

Q And that's based on what?

A It's based on several conversations that I've had with him and, my opinion of him that he's really a kind of, you know, not such a good person.

Q Well, is it based on the comments that annoyed you or is it based on something else?

A Well, I mean, I can, I can give you several comments that I've heard Clarence Thomas make that I think, you know, are unbecoming of any individual, period, but certainly unbecoming of someone who is going to spend the rest of his life on the Supreme Court.

Q Well, can you just—you said that you didn't think that he should be on the Supreme Court, could you just tell us why? So you say it's because of comments. Is it the comments that we've discussed this morning, or something else?

A No, they are comments other than what we discussed this morning. Let me name, I would say three. My predecessor, Al Sweeney, who was an older man and quite sickly. I, you know, Clarence Thomas in my opinion pretty much wanted to force him to retire. Obviously I benefited from that; once the position was open I was named Director of Public Affairs.

But I remember Clarence Thomas saying to me, "Al Sweeney is old, he's no good. He has one foot in the grave, and the other one on a banana peel."

A second situation here. I remember sitting in a staff meeting with Clarence Thomas and the majority white staff there, and Clarence and several of the legal staffers had gone to Mississippi for some type of meeting there. And one of the staff members were saying they felt pretty intimidated in Mississippi because they were with an interracial group, and I remember Clarence sitting there and rearing back in his chair with a cigar in his mouth and saying, "I have no problem with Mississippi. You know why I like Mississippi, because they still sell those little pickaninnies dolls down there. And I bought me a few of them too."

Okay? There was another occasion that I remember when Clarence was talking to Jeff—his last name was Funder or something, Funderburk or something like that and he was general counsel at the time. And Jeff was complaining about not being able to get money for something. I don't remember what that something was, mortgage or whatever. And I remember Clarence saying to Jeff, "Well, you know why you can't get any money, because you're not black enough. Now, if you wore a dashiki, and if you grew an Afro and put on a dashiki, you would get all the Government money you want."

I remember Clarence telling me that one of the people that Clarence wanted me to fire he wanted me to fire him because he said this man was "a sycophant". He wanted me to fire this other person because he said, "This man was a dufus."

You know, I am of the opinion that Clarence is, you know, not a very nice person. I was of that opinion before I left EEOC and even, I can assure you that even if I had left there under better circumstances, if he had thrown me the biggest party in the world, I would still be of the opinion that Clarence Thomas should not sit on the Supreme Court.

Q So what about his political philosophy? Does that weigh into your decision that you don't think he should be on the Court?

A Because of his political philosophies?

Q Right.

A No, his political philosophies are his own. He has a right to whatever opinions he wants, I mean, he holds on various issues. I am talking about character, pure and simple.

Q Well, let me ask you—I assume you are aware that the committee had a lot of hearings. We heard from a lot of witnesses.

A Yes.

Q I think we went for about eight days and most of them were covered on TV. Can you tell us why you chose to wait until now to come forward?

A Well, I think a more appropriate explanation of what is going on here is I'm answering questions that are just now being asked. But I must say that I was perfectly willing to keep my opinions to myself, except, of course, when asked about the Clarence nomination. I did not feel that it was a good thing, until I saw Anita Hill on television Monday night and my conscience started bothering me because I knew I felt from my experience with Clarence Thomas that he was quite capable of doing what she said. And it became a very moral struggle with me at that point.

I was struggling with trying to determine, trying to decide whether to say something, when I got a call from the Senate Judiciary Committee and that question became no longer a question.

Q All right, now you say that you got a call from the committee, when you decided you were going to come forward.

A Somebody first called me.

Q Can you tell us who that was?

A It was Dugas Mark Schwartz.

Q Do you have any idea as to how he got your name?

A He said that he had gotten information that I worked for Clarence Thomas. He knew of a column that I had written that was not going to be published detailing my opinion of this, of Hill's allegations.

Q I am sorry, your opinion of what?

A Of Hill's allegations.

Q I see, could you make that available to us?

A No.

Q Can you give us some general description of what you said?

A No, I'd rather not.

Because the column was not written with the intent of publishing it. It was written in the context of a discussion that I was having with my, with my supervising editor about becoming a columnist.

Q Okay, so the first contact you had was when somebody from the committee called you as opposed to you calling the committee?

A That's correct.

Q Has anybody from the committee—and I am not talking about just from Senator Biden's staff—but has any staff member, from any member in Washington, have they called you about this?

A No, they have not.

Q Can you just give us some indication as to how many conversations, how many times you have talked to congressional staff? And I presume you have just talked to Mr. Schwartz, you said?

A Two or three times.

Q Okay.

MS. HOGAN: I might state, for the record, that after—Ms Wright, correct me if I misstate anything—after you spoke to Mark Schwartz, I and Mark Schwartz called you back to set up today's telephone call. So I did speak with you last night about the procedures for today.

MS. WRIGHT: The answer may be yes, there was another woman involved and I am sorry to get into that issue but I remember only Mark Schwartz's name.

MS. HOGAN: I can state that it was me, but I just wanted to be clear that another conversation occurred at which I was a part.

MS. WRIGHT: Okay, thank you, yes.

By MR. WOOTEN:

Q Okay, when did you have the first contact with the committee, with Mr. Schwartz?

A Yesterday.

Q Okay.

A At probably about maybe five o'clock or something like that, I guess, I'm not really sure.

Q Okay, has anybody else—and obviously it wouldn't be any staff people—has anybody else called and urged you to come forward, or is this something you did of your own volition?

A People who know me who know that I know Clarence Thomas have suggested and urged me to make a statement since the day that Clarence Thomas was nominated, or at least since the day the nomination became public.

MR. WOOTEN: Give me just one second, I think we are pretty close to wrapping up here.

[Pause.]

By MR. WOOTEN:

Q When you decided to come forward and people had talked to you about coming forward, did you choose to come forward because of the statements that Judge Thomas made to you about dates, and the fact that he came to your house, or did you come forward because of his character, that you just didn't think he was somebody who should be on the Court?

MS. HOGAN: Excuse me, I just want to clarify that I am not misunderstanding something. My understanding, Ms. Wright, is that you did not come forward, that you were contacted by Mark Schwartz of the committee?

MS. WRIGHT: Actually I was just about to correct that, myself. I am sorry, Terry, but I cannot answer, I cannot answer the questions if you are going to insist that I decided to come forward. Obviously I did not come forward with anything. I am just answering questions that are just being asked of me.

By MR. WOOTEN:

Q Let me see [if] maybe I can rephrase. You said that other people had suggested that you come forward. I guess my question is, is the thrust of your concerns about Judge Thomas, is it the comments that he made to you, or is it just your general belief that he should not be on the Court?

A The thrust of my concerns at this point was to not watch a woman, who I believed in my gut to be telling the truth about a man who I believe to be totally capable of doing what she said he did, the thrust of my concern was not to watch her become victimized, when I knew of similar situations that I had had with Mr. Thomas.

Q I think we are very close, just maybe one or two questions, but we are very close to being finished.

A Let me just go on and clarify one other point I think you are getting to here, as far as whether I at any point felt the need to rush out and try and stop Clarence Thomas's nomination to the Supreme Court. The obvious answer to that is no.

Q All right.

Others have given me some questions, and I want to give everybody their chance to have their say through me, I suppose.

Let me ask you, do you need a break?

A No, I am fine, go ahead.

Q Let me ask you one other question, did you and Judge Thomas, I presume you all never had dated, or never did date, or never go to dinner or anything like that?

A That is correct.

Q Okay. Now, can you tell us maybe who was your closest friend at the EEOC during the year or so that you were there?

A I could but I would rather not mention that person's name without checking with that person to see how they felt about their name being mentioned.

Q Well, let me ask you this, would you consider one particular person your closest friend there?

A Yes.

Q And did you ever discuss the concerns you had, the annoyances you had with Judge Thomas with that friend?

A Yes.

Q You did? All right. Well, if you would, I think it may be helpful if you would check with that friend to see if he or she is willing to come forward.

A Okay, I will be glad to do that.

Q Okay.

A But you keep using the term, come forward. I can pretty much assure you that this person is not going to come forward or want to be very involved in this at all.

Q I understand that. Well, I think—and this is not to encourage you to do one thing or another, you are certainly free to do anything you want—but that is something that, of course, we are asking, because it would substantiate and support what you have said, you see?

A I understand. I really do, and I understand your responsibility to substantiate what I have said. And all I can do is tell you what I know and what my experience has been and you have to make your own judgments as to the veracity of those statements. You know, I have no problem talking to other people who could corroborate what I am saying but, surely you understand that this is not at all a pleasant situation to be in, and it is not something that even I take lightly, even though I think I have got the guts of a bull. But I don't necessarily relish the kind of fallout that comes from speaking up in this type of a situation.

And I'm not going to encourage anybody to do what I have done.

Q It is just a question of if they would mind committee staff contacting them to discuss what they may or may not know, but let me ask you just a couple of other questions.

Did you ever have evaluations at the EEOC prior to that time that you were fired by Judge Thomas?

A You say up to the time?

Q Or prior to the time.

A Yes, yes, I did.

Q And who evaluated you at that time?

A Clarence Thomas did.

Q And can you just tell us the gist of those evaluations, if you feel comfortable with that?

A I only—I remember only one evaluation and it was sort of a middle-line kind of evaluation. I wasn't satisfied with it. Obviously, I thought I was doing a pretty good job and I deserved a better evaluation, but it was one of those, you know—I don't even remember what the evaluation form was like. I just remember it was sort of, you know—if it was a scale of, you know, maybe a scale of A to F, it was a C.

Q All right, and you only have one evaluation that you can recall at this time? That's not a trick question; I'm just asking you, recalling the year that you were there.

A That's the only one that I remember, yes.

Q Okay.

A There could have been one that was great, but I don't remember that one.

Q All right, if you just give us one or two minutes, maybe we're closing to wrapping up. I don't know, but other people are—I want to be sure that everybody has a chance.

MS. HOGAN: I have just three or four questions to follow up with. Terry, do you want me to go ahead?

MR. WOOTEN: Yes, why don't you go ahead.

By MS. HOGAN:

Q Very quickly, Ms. Wright, because I know we've kept you a long time, and I appreciate your speaking with us, you were discussing before, the fact that Clarence Thomas had asked you to fire some of the career Federal employees on your staff.

It's my understanding that you, even with, you know, authority over your staff, would have needed cause to fire a career employee. Is that your understanding?

A Oh, yes, that's definitely my understanding.

Q And that's not the case with a political appointee, is that correct?

A No, that is not the case at all. I mean, surely, you guys know that that body is exempt from fair labor standards.

Q And you were a political appointee at the EEOC, is that correct?

A That is correct.

Q Okay, just a couple of more questions. You've stated that the type of comments that Clarence Thomas made to you that we've been discussing today were made on numerous occasions. Can you give us any sense of what the rate of these type of comments were? Did they occur once a month, did they occur once a week? You know, can you give us any general sense of that?

A Well, let's see, if I had to put it in a context of how many times I would see him and he may make a comment, I'd say probably it would be one out of four or one of out five encounters with him, you know, he may make some statement.

Q Okay, and these were statements specifically about you?

A Well, specifically about me and, like, you know, when are you going to date me, that kind of a thing.

Q Exactly, okay. Did he also make, then, statements about other women to you with any kind of regularity?

A No, not of that nature, if that's what you're asking. I mean, we may have discussed other women in the context of the way they were performing their jobs or something.

Q Well, I guess what I'm asking is, earlier you had told us that he did, on occasion, make statements about other women's anatomy in front of you, and I guess I'm asking was that an isolated incident that you described for us or did that also occur with some frequency.

A Oh, that's not something that I would say was frequent. Those are just what I remember as a couple of situations when that happened.

Q Okay, thanks. Also, just briefly, we discussed the comment that Judge Thomas made to you when you were at the EEOC seminar out of town when he asked about your breast size and complimented your dress, and I'm just wondering if you recall at all even generally what you were wearing at the time.

A No, I do not.

MS. HOGAN: Okay. That's all I have.

By MR. WOOTEN:

Q Did Judge Thomas—this is Terry again—did Judge Thomas ever say that he could[n't] ask you out of the EEOC because of the professional relationship he intended to have with his employees there?

A Did ever say that he couldn't ask me out?

Q Yes.

A No, he never said anything like that.

Q Let me ask you, do you know a Kate Simperande?

A Kate Simperande?

Q Simperade, Simperande?

A Yes, I do.

Q And have you ever charged her with any kind of racism before or—

A Yes, I did. When I left the AID, I wrote her a letter of recommendation saying that I felt she—I'm paraphrasing it, but I felt that she was quite unfair and racist and insecure and lots of other things.

Q Can you tell us what led to you writing that letter?

A I really don't think that's relevant. I mean, can you tell me why you want me to discuss my relationship with Kate Simerade?

Q Well, we would be interested if you had made allegations against other people.

MS. HOGAN: Is this—excuse me for a minute. Why don't we go off the record for a minute, if you can just hold on, Ms. Wright.

MS. WRIGHT: Okay.

[Discussion off the record.]

By MR. WOOTEN:

Q Let me ask you one more question. Again, I said earlier I thought we were close to the end, I think we are this time.

A Okay.

Q There's been a request to ask you a question, and obviously this may be something that you don't want to answer, but it's up to you. It's a question of who you voted for in the '80, '84 and '88 —

MS. HOGAN: No, no, no.

By MR. WOOTEN:

Q Well, let me ask you, do you consider yourself a Republican? You don't have to say who you voted for.

MS. HOGAN: You don't have to answer that question either.

MS. WRIGHT: I am a registered Republican.

MS. HOGAN: I'm not your counsel, but —

MR. WOOTEN: Okay, all right.

MS. HOGAN: I'm sorry to do this to you, Ms. Wright. Can you hang on for one more minute?

MS. WRIGHT: Sure.

[Discussion off the record.]

MS. HOGAN: Ms. Wright, this is Cynthia Hogan again. Let me put you on the speaker phone. I believe we have no further questions, but I just want to make sure that that's the case by putting you on the record.

Ms. Wright?

MS. WRIGHT: Yes?

MS. HOGAN: Terry, I'm aware you have no further questions?

MR. WOOTEN: We have no further questions, and thanks.

MS. WRIGHT: Okay, thank you.

MS. HOGAN: Ms. Wright, we appreciate it very much. We're sorry for taking up so much of your time.

MS. WRIGHT: All right.

MS. HOGAN: We appreciate your willingness to talk with us today. Thank you.

MS. WRIGHT: Bye-bye.

MS. HOGAN: Bye-bye.

[Whereupon, at 12:35 p.m., the interview was concluded.]

TRANSCRIPT OF PROCEEDINGS

* * *

UNITED STATES SENATE

* * *

COMMITTEE ON THE JUDICIARY

* * *

In the Matter of the Nomination of
Judge Clarence Thomas to be an Associate
Justice of the U.S. Supreme Court

Thursday, October 13, 1991
Washington, DC

The telephonic interview of ROSE JOURDAIN, called for examination by counsel for the Senate Committee on the Judiciary in the above-entitled matter, pursuant to notice, in the offices of the Senate Committee on the Judiciary, Room SD-234, Dirksen Senate Office Building, Washington, DC, convened at 2:15 p.m., when were present on behalf of the parties:

MARY DeOREO, Investigator, Staff of Senator Biden
MARK SCHWARZ, Staff of Senator Biden
TRIS COFFIN, Staff of Senator Leahy
MATT PAPPAS, Staff of Senator Heflin
BARRY CALDWELL, Staff of Senator Specter
MELISSA RILEY, Staff of Senator Thurmond

PROCEEDINGS

MS. JOURDAIN: Hello?

MS. DEOREO: Hi, Rose. This is Mary DeOreo, from the Senate Judiciary Committee.

MS. JOURDAIN: Yes.

MS. DEOREO: Rose, I want to tell you, before we go on the record, that there are sitting in the room with me representententatives from the majority side, Senator Biden's staff, Senator Heflin's staff, and Senator Leahy's staff, and there are also representatives from the minority side.

I will have them each introduce themselves to you, but first I want to introduce Mark Schwartz, who wants to make a few things clear with you, so you understand how it is we are proceeding. Mark is an attorney on Senator Biden's Judiciary Committee.

MR. SCHWARTZ: Rose, hi.

MS. JOURDAIN: Hi.

MR. SCHWARTZ: I just wanted to make sure you understood one point, which was that if this is going to be sworn testimony, which is the preference, that we have sworn testimony, you have the absolute right to have an attorney present, and we could not conduct such sworn testimony without either your having an attorney present or your saying it's okay for us to take your sworn testimony without an attorney present.

Now, before you answer that, the alternative for you is to say you do not want to have this be a sworn statement, in which case we will just take your statement on the record and not be sworn. That is your choice. I don't know if you have an attorney present with you.

MS. JOURDAIN: No, I don't. Hold on one minute.

[Pause.]

MR. SCHWARTZ: Are we on the record currently?

MS. DEOREO: Right now we are.

MR. SCHWARTZ: Okay. We are now on the record, so we will start the interview when the court reporter, at the appropriate time, can swear you in.

Whereupon,

ROSE L. JOURDAIN

was called for examination and was examined and testified, as follows:

By MS. DEOREO:

Q Ms. Jordan, this is Mary DeOreo.

A Ms. Jourdain.

Q Thank you. In fact, the first question is, would you please give us the proper pronunciation and spelling of your full name?

A Rose L. Jourdain, J-o-u-r-d-a-i-n.

MS. DEOREO: Thank you. Ms. Jourdain, we are going to go off the record for a moment. I am going to put you on hold.

[Discussion off the record.]

MS. DEOREO: Back on the record.

By MS. DEOREO:

Q Ms. Jourdain?

A Yes.

Q It's Mary again. I just want to clarify one point. Do you understand that you are sworn in?

A Yes.

Q And are you comfortable giving us your testimony, having been sworn in?

A I am quite comfortable. The only thing I want to ask you is that my address and phone number will not be made public, will they?

Q None of this will be made public, Ms. Jourdain.

A Okay.

Q Thank you. All right. Because I understand that this interview is taking place while you are at the Washington Hospital Center—

A Yes.

Q —so I am wondering—we are going to try to stay to the point and not take too long. I understand that you are not physically all that comfortable.

A That's true.

Q Thank you. Could you please give me some general background information about yourself, just education and some of the jobs that you have had, bringing us up to EEOC?

A All right. I am a graduate of Lake Forest College, I did graduate work at Northwestern University, I have taught school, I have had many, many different jobs, largely writing jobs. I have written a novel, I have written a television play, you know, produced a novel, produced a television play, I have written a textbook, and that's about it in a capsule.

Q And let me ask you, during all of this experience, can you give me some of your more recent employers that you had prior to coming to the EEOC?

A I was teaching school and then I came to Washington and—

Q Was that a public—

A —I worked for the Agency for International Development, but I went to the EEOC and then I went to the NEA—

Q Thank you. I would like now to ask you—

A —the National Education Association, not the National Endowment for the Arts.

Q Thank you, and I appreciate the clarification. Also, I can hear that you are speaking to someone in the room. Who is in the room with you?

A My daughter.

Q And what is her name, please?

A Jackie.

Q And her last name?

A Hayes.

Q Thank you. When were you employed at the EEOC?

A Now, I think, I believe it was 1980—I believe it was from November '83 to March '85, although—I think those are the correct dates.

Q That's fine, and I understand, with the interview coming at short notice, you haven't had a lot of time to go back and think about it.

A I have not.

Q What was your position at the EEOC?

A I was hired as a speech writer for the chairman Clarence Thomas.

Q And at that time, did you know Anita Hill?

A No, I never met her.

Q Did you know Judge Thomas professionally?

A I had never met the man until I walked into his office for the job interview.

Q During the course of your working as a speech writer for Judge Thomas, did you meet with him personally?

A Yes.

Q On a daily basis?

A Sometimes on a daily basis, sometimes on—it was an as-need-to-meet basis, really.

Q But you did have contact with him personally?

A Yes, and frequently.

Q Did you experience any sort of harassment from Judge Thomas?

A I personally, none.

Q Did you observe this behavior, alleged behavior from Judge Thomas towards anyone else?

A Well, he and I were generally in meetings discussing speeches or in full staff meetings, so there would have been little opportunity for that.

Q Thank you. Do you know Angela Wright?

A Yes, I do.

Q In what capacity?

A Angela Wright was head of the public relations department at the EEOC. I met her first at AID, and then she was also at EEOC. We became friends as a result of our working together.

Q As you were working together at both places?

A Yes.

Q Were you friends at AID?

A I did not know her until I became, you know, we became co-workers.

Q At AID?

A Yes.

Q All right. So, did you leave AID at about the same time and go over to EEOC?

A I went first.

Q Okay. Just for our own background information, were you fired from your job at AID?

A No, I left.

Q On your own volition?

A Yes.

Q Did Ms. Wright ever discuss with you any concerns or problems she was having in her encounters with Judge Thomas?

A Yes, she did.

Q Can you give me some specific details as to what Ms. Wright told you?

A When Ms. Wright first came in, she was very enthusiastic about her job. She was very happy to be there. As time went on, she became increasingly—she confided to me increasingly that she was a little uneasy and she grew more uneasy with the chairman, because of comments she told me that he was making concerning her figure, her body, her breasts, her legs, how she looked in certain suits and dresses.

Q Did she recount any specific experience?

A Well, for example, she told me he had come to her home one night unannounced, and she told everyone—for example, one time she came into my office in tears, said she had bought a new suit that I thought was quite attractive, it was just a regular suit for a person to wear to work, a woman to wear to work, and he had had evidently quite a bit of comment to make about it and how sexy she looked in it and that kind of thing, and it unnerved her a great deal.

She became increasingly nervous about being in his presence alone. As time went on, he asked her to have a meeting with him that was going to be a one-on-one meeting, which would not be unusual, you know, with the head of the public relations department, and these were scheduled in the evening, at the end of the workday, and she was increasingly uneasy about being there, and would say, why don't you wait for me and, you know, I really don't want to be there that long or alone with him, you know, not inviting me into the meeting, but just asking me to remain in the building until it was time for her—until she would be able to leave.

Q Were these conversations, Ms. Jourdain, between you and Ms. Wright, were there only the two of you, or were there occasions when someone else would be part of this specific type of conversation?

A I think most of the time that she spoke to me, I know most of the time she spoke to me alone. I really don't know that there weren't times that there were other people in the room, but there was probably only one, because she was not going to—she was not trying to bad-mouth the chairman.

Q Who would that other person—if there was someone else —

A Hold on a minute.

[Pause.]

My daughter said she was in the room once when we were discussing it.

Q And your daughter, again, for the record, is Jacqueline Hayes—

A Right.

Q —and she knows Ms. Wright?

A Yes, she does.

Q But not because she is an employee of EEOC?

A But not because she is an employee, because she is my daughter.

Q Thank you. Who did you talk to about Angela Wright's concerns concerning the chairman's behavior?

A I don't remember speaking to anyone about it. I may have spoken—I probably did speak to my daughter. I may have spoken to—I don't know that I spoke to anybody—I don't know that I ever spoke to anybody specifically about his behavior concerning her.

Q It would be pretty good gossip, there would be no one else in the—

A It would be gossip, but I have never been a person who was much into gossip.

Q All right. So, there was no occasion when someone was talking about the chairman, that you can recall saying, "Oh, by the way"—

A I wasn't very—I mean I was not interested in denigrating the chairman.

Q All right.

A I was not out to say, oh, he's a dog or this kind of thing. I was not interested in denigrating him at all.

MS. DeOREO: I am going to go off the record and put you on hold for a moment.
[Discussion off the record.]

MS. DeOREO: Back on the record.

Ms. Jourdain?

MS. JOURDAIN: Yes?

MS. DeOREO: Mark Schwartz, who is on Senator Biden's staff, has got some questions he would like to ask you.

MS. JOURDAIN: Yes.

By MR. SCHWARTZ:

Q Ms. Jourdain, do you know the dates that Angela Wright worked or was employed by the EEOC?

A I would not—I would believe it was shortly before December or end of November of—if I went there in November, I believe she came there in December. If I went there in October, she came there in December. I went very shortly before she did.

Q Could you give us an approximation as far as the year?

A [No response.]

Q Let me go back to my notes and repeat—

A I have a feeling it was '83 to '85. I am pretty sure of that. I'm pretty sure it was—

Q Just so that you understand, I don't want to be confusing, I understand you have already said that you were there approximately from November of 1983 to March of 1985. I just wanted to know what part of your tenure at the EEOC that Angela Wright was there, also.

A I'm not absolutely certain of these dates, but I think I'm correct, but I must say that I am not positive I'm correct on this issue. She would have been there from the November following my coming until the time I left.

Q So, approximately the later part of 1984 through March of '85?

A No, '83, I said '83.

Q Did you stay at the EEOC after Angela Wright left?

A I did not. We left at the same time.

Q Okay. Are you aware of the circumstances under which Angela Wright left the EEOC?

A No, I'm not, actually. She told me she got a letter from the chairman saying that her services were no longer required. I don't know that he gave her any reason. I believe that she told me—and here again, I have not committed it to memory, but it was a very curt, you know, a two-paragraph or a three-paragraph letter. I don't remember it. I had no reason to want to remember it.

Q You stated a little bit earlier that you were also fired from the EEOC.

A I was dismissed the same day as Angela, and Angela was like—

Q Ms. Jourdain—

A —when he wrote a letter of recommendation, withdrawing that letter of recommendation for me for another job, I had no problems with that, because I knew I had done a decent job for him, but I did ask him and he wrote a very strong letter, in fact, that the reasons for letting me go was that he had chosen to write his own speeches and, to the best of my knowledge, he never replaced me and did from then on write his own speeches, probably—I don't know this for sure—using somebody in part-time work, but I don't believe he ever [hired] another full-time—

MR. SCHWARTZ: I just want to put you on hold for one second.

Off the record.

[Discussion off the record]

MR. SCHWARTZ: Back on the record.

By MR. SCHWARTZ:

Q Ms. Jourdain?

A Yes.

Q We are back on the record. I just wanted to clarify one thing and Mary DeOreo is going to help me clarify it. I asked you a question, my last question, where I used the word, fired, and I just wanted to back-track for a second because you had earlier stated that the circumstances under which you left the AID were what?

A That I quit.

Q Okay, that you had quit. And the circumstances under which you left the EEOC were?

A I was dismissed.

Q Okay. I just wanted to be clear that my question went to the circumstances under which you left the EEOC?

A Mm-hmm.

Q Okay, fine, just so there is no confusion on the record.

A Now, the point that I am trying to make in my statement is that as time went on Angela Wright became increasingly upset and increasingly unnerved by what appeared to be more aggressive behavior on the chairman's part. She came to me—I am older than she—and she came to me oftentimes to ask advice what should she do? I mean we are talking about a time when sexual harassment was not a thing that women were talking about, and how to handle this. You know, what do you say? You know, I know that she had made it quite clear to him that she was not interested in developing a relationship with him outside of the workplace.

By MR. PAPPAS:

Q Ms. Jourdain, I am Matt Pappas and I work with Senator Heflin. I was just wondering about Angela Wright being dismissed from the EEOC. Did she ever give you any indication that she was bitter toward the agency or toward Clarence Thomas?

A No. I think that, I know that I was, I am certain that both of us were dismissed for a very similar reason and that was that we were increasingly ideologically opposed to the chairman's position. I know I was and I believe that that had a great deal to do with Angela's dismissal.

Q But she never indicated to you that she was —

A No. She never said anything about being bitter. In fact, I think she rather welcomed it because she was thinking about going back to school and doing some other things with her life anyway.

Q Okay.

A She was saving her money very carefully for a return to school so I don't think it was a major interruption of a career plan.

Q And she never said anything to you that would insinuate that she might have been let go because she would not enter into a relationship with Clarence Thomas?

A No. She never said that that was the reason. I know that she was upset and more and more upset, as I said by what she told me on—you know, she kept me pretty much informed on this because it was making her very nervous, on a more aggressive—not, you know, I am not speaking of a week-to-week more aggressive—but a seemingly more aggressive posture that—I mean his comments on her body and things. I am not saying that each week it got worse, but they were coming more frequently because she was telling me this more frequently.

And her thing was, gee, I want to go back to school. I want to get out of this, you know, I want to do something else with my life.

Q So at the time she was dismissed from EEOC, would you say that that was when it was at its worst? And what I mean by that, the advances that she alleged that Clarence Thomas made toward her?

A I can't say that for a—I can say that you are talking about a cumulative effect, you know. I am not saying that it was worse that week than it had been two months before, but the cumulative effect, I think was there.

MR. PAPPAS: All right, thank you.

By MR. COFFIN:

Q Hello, Rose, this Tris Coffin from Senator Leahy's office.

A Yes?

Q I was wondering if you could tell me a little bit more about the circumstances of Angela Wright's dismissal from EEOC. You said it had something to do with an increasingly—

A No. I am saying I don't know that that was it. I am saying I know that these were circumstances that were also happening at the same time. I don't know that these were the circumstances of the dismissal.

Q Did you ever hear a comment that Ms. Wright made that might have had something to do with her dismissal?

A Comment?

Q A particular comment?

A No. No, I don't know that.

Q Did you ever [hear that] Ms. Wright said of another EEOC employee or called another EEOC employee a faggot?

A No, I did not hear that. I heard a lot, but I didn't hear that one.

Q Okay.

A But nor do I want to give you the impression, under any circumstances, that I felt that, as I said before, that we have two situations here. We have a woman who is being increasingly, made increasingly, who is being increasingly unnerved, but I am not saying that her lack of responsiveness is the reason for her dismissal. I don't want that to be read into the record. I think there are two separate things going on there.

Q I understand you.

Can you give us a little more detail about these conversations between you and Ms. Wright where you discussed, where she would tell you about the increasingly aggressive behavior?

A Well, you know, for example, I was in my office, and she would come in and she would close the door. And you know, once she was, you know, once she was crying, and you know—

Q Okay, slow down.

A She is a very strong woman. She is not the kind of female that cries, you know what I mean.

Q Yes. I see, if you could just recall the first time she came into your office or the first time she told you these things. Tell us about that conversation.

A I don't remember the first—you know, we are talking about events that happened a long time ago. I can give you snapshot impressions but I can't tell you which snapshot came first.

Q Okay. So do you have a conversation in your mind, you are sitting in one chair and she is sitting in the other?

A I am sitting in the office, she walks in, slams the door and says, "Do you know what he said to me, do you know what he said to me?" And I said, "No, what did he say to you?" you know, because it has gone on before. And I think at this point it had something to do with her legs, you know.

Q And what would he say?

A I think it had something to do with, ooh, you have very sexy legs, or something like you have hair on your legs and it turns me on, or something like that. I thought, it was nutty, you know what I mean? It was that, but it was very unnerving to a young woman who is sitting there hearing this, you know.

Then there was a conversation about her bra size, and there was a conversation about a dress that she wore, I don't know why that was a dress that was to be commented on. It wasn't a skin-tight knit-type dress. There was another—you know, it was the constant kind of "Do you know what he did?"

Sometimes she laughed about it, you know. Sometimes it got on her last nerve. You know, sometimes it had happened so much that it was like you won't believe what this, what he said now, you know?

Q Yes, did you travel with Angela to—

A No, I never did.

Q You never did.

A Yes, I did once.

Q Where?

A We went to, we went to New York, the chairman, Angela and I went to New York to set up something. I don't even remember what it was. It was the only time we all went anywhere.

Q Okay. You mentioned earlier on that Ms. Wright said something to you about the chairman coming by her house. Could you tell me about that, please.

A Well, she called me up and she told me that he had had the nerve to show up in her house and come in and—

Q Was this—

A —sat down and made himself at home, and you know, what do you do about this kind of thing, you know?

Q Was this the next day?

A No, when that she told me?

Q Yes.

A I don't know whether she told me the next day or she called me up that evening, that same evening, and said, you won't believe what just happened.

Q Can you tell me step-by-step?

A No, I cannot tell you step-by-step on anything that happened six years ago.

I mean I cannot swear to any step-by-step, anything.

MR. COFFIN: Thanks.

By MS. DEOREO:

Q I want to ask before [we] go further, Ms. Jourdain, all of us are sensitive to the fact that these are uncomfortable days for you, physically uncomfortable days. How are you doing?

A It's, it's hard sitting here talking.

Q Can I ask, can you give us a few more moments? I very much would like representatives on the minority staff to have an opportunity to ask you some questions.

A All right.

Q Would you like us to take a little break and call you back?

A I would rather get through it.

Q Thank you. They are going to introduce themselves to you.

A All right.

MS. RILEY: Ms. Jourdain, I am Melissa Riley and I am with Senator Strom Thurmond's office and—

MR. CALDWELL: Ms. Jourdain, my name is Barry Caldwell and I am counsel to Senator Specter.

MS. JOURDAIN: All right.

By MS. RILEY:

Q Can you go back to when you worked with Ms. Wright, at AID?

A Mm-hmm.

Q Can you tell us, do you know the reason why Ms. Wright left AID?

A Yes. She was offered a much better position. I know that she was not happy there and she was offered a better position and she left. I believe that is the reason.

She was not happy and she had an opportunity to advance herself. She thought she did.

Q Okay. Could you tell us when was the last time you spoke with Ms. Wright?

A You mean, today?

Q Yes, Ma'am the last time you had a conversation.

A I think it's been about—I can't really. I mean it's been—gee, I haven't spoken with her in several days, I can tell you that. She knew that I was ill. And so she called me, she has called me since I have been in the hospital to see how I was doing.

Q Okay—Could you give me your best guess?

A Un-unh. In the hospital days start to run together.

Q I am sorry, I did not—

A I think it has been a week. Maybe, maybe ten, eleven days, something.

Q Okay. Going back to the episode that you mentioned that Clarence Thomas came to Angela Wright's house, can you give us at all any kind of time frame during the period that you specified that you worked at EEOC with her, during the year, do you remember any season?

A I have a feeling that my recollection of her telling me this, is that it was very cold out, and that, you know, it was not the type or time of year when people are out for a walk, you know, and just drop by somebody's house. So I think it was cold, it was kind of in winter. It might have been late fall.

Q Okay, and back to the last time that you spoke to her in a week or maybe ten or eleven days ago, did you talk about these episodes with Ms. Wright?

A About which episodes?

Q The episode of the house—

A No, I was talking about my illness.

Q Okay. So you never spoke to Ms. Wright about the episode with Clarence Thomas dropping by her house unannounced?

A I haven't spoken to her about that in a long time. In fact, that is why it is not really clear to me.

Q Okay.

A I mean the details of it are not clear.

Q But the episode, you didn't speak to her about the episode?

A I spoke many, a long time ago, but not, not not, we were talking about my, my being in the hospital.

Q That's fine.

Did you know Ms. Wright before you worked at AID?

A No.

Q Okay. How close a friend were you with Ms. Wright, would you socialize with her outside of work?

A Yes, we did. As time went on we became close friends. Not at first we weren't close friends, but we became closer because we worked together and we had projects that overlapped and we became friends. In other words, the public affairs office and the speech writer's office, you know, has things that they had to discuss. I mean, you know, those two offices or those two people needed to confer and we found that we had a lot of things we enjoyed in common, our opinions in common and became friends.

Q And your friendship continued after Ms. Wright went to EEOC and you joined her there or did—

A No, I was there first.

Q Okay, I am sorry.

A And she came over.

Q And your friendship continued at EEOC?

A Yes, it did.

Q Okay.

A In fact, it grew mainly because since that is when that relationship was there, because that was when she headed the public affairs office, and I was the chairman's speech writer.

Q And since you have, since you left EEOC and Ms. Wright left the EEOC, how much contact have you had with her over these years? Could you just take a guess?

A We have kept in contact with each other. You know, we were, you know, it's like anybody else that you know and you like and you hope to remain friends through life or at least keep up with them and see how they are doing and coming along. We have certainly kept up with each other. I think she is a friend of mine, yes.

Q Would you, say, call her on holidays or her birthday or would you just—

A I don't call anybody except my family on holidays and my birthday.

Q Okay. So what would you say, would it be infrequent contact since you left the EEOC?

A I think we talked, there were times that I called her about things that I was doing that I thought she might be interested in knowing about or give me some clues about how I might, you know, make some improvements and she did the same with me. She might be working on a story and call me up and say, I'm working on this, do you think, you know, where else do you think I might find some additional research material? I was working on several projects and I said hey, take a look at this and what do you think of it? And she responded.

Q Has Ms. Wright—

A These are episodic things, do you know what I am saying?

Q Yes, Ma'am. Has Ms. Wright called you recently working on a story about Clarence Thomas?

A No, un-unh. I didn't know she was.

Q I was just curious when you mentioned that.

A No, un-unh.

Q And you mentioned earlier that your daughter acknowledged that she had some knowledge of the conversations that you had with Ms. Wright about Clarence Thomas's inappropriate comments to Ms. Wright, can you give us a time frame about when your daughter would have known about these comments?

A No, she heard about them about the same time they were being made.

Q And how did she hear about them?

A She may have heard, she probably heard about them, she did hear about them when Angela was at my house and she may have been discussing it or was discussing it, you know, trying to figure out what should I do about this, you know? And it made a big impression on my daughter because she was young.

Q After Ms. Wright became upset about Clarence Thomas's advances towards her or his comments, I should say, did you try to, what advice did you give her?

A As I remember the situation, I said to her, you know, why don't you sit down and just discuss it with—I know that she had said to him, she had made it clear to him that she did not welcome these advances, and I said, just stay firm with it, you know, just don't let him think you are giving into it. You know, that you are becoming more, you are, that there isn't any kind of possibility of any kind of relationship here.

Q Did you, after Ms. Wright conveyed these comments to you, attempt to confirm his actions or did you try to investigate these comments or go to any other women and say, has he made these type of comments to you?

A I did not do that. I did not feel that I should discuss her business or his business with other staff members. I would never have said to anybody else on the staff that the chairman was saying these things, you know.

Q Did you consider them inappropriate?

A I—yes, I did consider them inappropriate and I did not feel that that would help him at all in the delegation of his duties to have women knowing that he was saying these kinds of things, but I didn't say anything.

MR. SCHWARTZ: Melissa, may we go off the record?

MS. RILEY: We are going to put you on hold for just a moment. Thank you.

[Discussion off the record.]

By MS. RILEY:

Q Ms. Jourdain?

A Yes.

Q Sorry about that. We have a couple more questions.

I was just curious, have you ever contacted Clarence Thomas for job references?

A Yes, I have.

Q And did he respond favorably?

A Extremely so.

Q And do you know if Ms. Wright ever contacted him?

A Yes, and he—and I know that she was delighted with the recommendation he gave her.

Q So she did attempt to contact him for a recommendation?

A Yes, and he gave both of us very good recommendations. In fact, you know, that being our—we needed them, you know.

Q A couple more questions, and then I believe one more person, a couple more people, have more.

Did you happen to attend a retirement party for Al Sweeney?

A Do you know, it seems to me that I did, but didn't he die?

Q I am not sure and I would hate to say anything about that. I just was curious if you attended the retirement party.

A I can't remember whether I attended his retirement party or his funeral. That sounds weird, but I think I did attend a retirement party for him, yes.

Q It may have been at perhaps some club in Virginia?

A No, I have never been to a club in Virginia.

Q Or a hotel, maybe, in Virginia?

A I don't recall.

Q That's fine.

Did Ms. Wright ever talk to you about comments that Clarence Thomas made to you at a retirement party?

A Made to me.

Q No, no, no, no. I'm sorry. Let me clarify that.

Did Ms. Wright ever speak to you about comments which Clarence Thomas made to her at a retirement party?

A No, I don't remember her ever saying anything like that—

Q Thank you.

A —any kind of comment about a retirement party.

Q No, let me clarify: Comments that Clarence Thomas made, inappropriate comments that Clarence Thomas made to Ms. Wright while attending a retirement party.

A No, I don't differentiate them as anything special.

You know what I mean?

MS. RILEY: Thank you, and I believe Mr. Caldwell has a couple of questions for you.

By MR. CALDWELL:

Q Hi, Ms. Jourdain. Just a couple of more questions and perhaps a couple of follow-up.

You said you went to the EEOC just before Ms. Wright.

A Yes.

Q Do you have a sense of how she found out about the EEOC job?

A I think she told me about the job. I think she knew the chairman. I mean, I think that—you know, they were both Republicans and they had met at some Republican functions. I think it was that kind of thing. You know, there are not many black Republicans, and so they all knew each other.

Q Right. You don't know if someone in particular introduced her to the chairman?

A I have no idea. It was not important, you know what I mean? It was just something that she told me about. I don't think that—he was somebody, it was a contact that she had. It was not anybody, you know.

Q I'm sorry. I missed that last part.

A He was a contact that she had. You know, in this city, who are your contacts?

Q Right. Okay. I guess, lastly, do you have a sense of why—and I hope I don't misstate this—why Ms. Wright is coming forward? Motive is the question. Do you have a sense of why she is coming forward now?

A Yes. Based on what I know about her, I would tend to believe—no, I don't tend to believe, I absolutely believe that she heard this young black woman on the television being raked over the coals, as though this experience that she was having was completely impossible, and you know, that a person in Clarence Thomas's position, black or white, would not have done this, and this woman was somehow coming from left field with some malicious agenda.

And having had a similar experience, I believe that Angela would have felt it her bounden duty to go on record saying that, and she is a very religious, very morally strong person. You know, she is a person who believes very much in right and wrong.

Q You said that you guys talked about these instances of the chairman's behavior while at the EEOC, and that you remained in contact as friends. Did she discuss her—

A Wait a minute. I don't understand your question.

Q Well, here is my question: Did Ms. Wright discuss with you her coming forward?

A No. When she called me, the last time I talked to Angela Wright, she called me to see how I was doing. She knew that I was sick. And if she mentioned it, it was in passing and it was not something that I was particularly involved in at that moment. Do you know what I mean? I was in a lot of pain, and my concentration unfortunately was on myself.

Q Okay. One last question. I understand that you are friends, but if you had to step back and look at Ms. Wright objectively, could you say there are any negative qualities about her that stick out in your mind? For instance, is she vindictive? Is she vengeful? Is she something along those lines?

A No, I cannot say that, nothing like that. No, no. No, no, no.

Q What about flirtatious?

A No, I don't think she is flirtatious. She is a very life-affirming human being. She believes in—she is serious. She can have a lot of fun, but she believes that life is a serious venture, that we are charged with certain responsibilities, those of us who have had advantages, to help other people.

Now if you are talking—the only thing I can think of that really, and that is not a negative, she tends to spend an awful lot of time with her dog and treat it more as a human being. That is the only thing that I can think of. I have said to her, you know, like this dog gets as much care as a lot of human beings, but that is the only thing I could ever think of that I would say was negative.

MR. CALDWELL: Okay. Thank you. I think Ms. Riley just has one or two other questions for you. Thank you very much.

By MS. RILEY:

Q Ms. Jourdain, I just wanted to go back and once again ask you a couple of questions regarding the time that Ms. Wright told you that Clarence Thomas came to her house unannounced. Could you tell me, did she happen to say how long he stayed at her house?

A No, I don't remember, but I think it was—she was—no, she did not. I don't remember if she did tell me that. I don't know that she told me that. I don't know that she told me that, but I do know that he arrived, he made himself at home, and all of this was rather presumptuous.

Q So you don't have a time frame as far as, did she happen to say how long he stayed at her house.

A No, I don't believe she ever said that. I don't believe she put it within a time frame. I think she was appalled at the presumptuousness of it.

Q And did she ever tell you what time of the evening he left, or the day or the morning or—

A It was not morning, and it certainly was not late at night. I mean, it wasn't that he stayed there until really late. I just don't remember. I don't know. I don't know, but given my feeling of the affair or the incident, it was probably something that he arrived around 8:30 or 9:00 and left around 10:30 or 11:00. I don't know.

MS. RILEY: Okay. I think that is all that I have.

By MS. DEOREO:

Q Ms. Jourdain, this is Mary DeOreo again.

A Yes.

Q On the same point Melissa was asking about, that same evening visit, did you have any understanding of how Chairman Thomas got to Angela Wright's house? Did they live within walking distance?

A I have no—to the best of my knowledge, I know she lived on Capitol Hill.

Q Fine.

A And to the best of my knowledge, he lived in Southwest.

Q I am not asking you to guess. I am asking do you —

A I don't know.

MS. DEOREO: Okay. That's fine.

I believe that the interview now is over, and Mr. Schwartz has some things he wants to talk to you about, on the record.

MR. SCHWARTZ: Ms. Jourdain, we are still on the record. I wanted to go back to the original point we had made at the beginning of the interview. Everyone here in the room when we went off the record before has come to an understanding, at least on our end, and just want to make sure it squares with yours: that since you have given a sworn statement, though none of us in the room would give a legal opinion as to the effect of that sworn statement, you should realize that the possibility would occur that if there were later found to be a contradiction in some sort of legal form, that could have legal consequences against you similar to perjury, in some sort of untoward consequences.

I am not saying that would happen, but because of that I wanted you to understand the implications of having sworn yourself in, and if you now feel uncomfortable with that and would like to take back your sworn part of it, we will just treat the testimony as we have all other interviews we have conducted during this proceeding, which is, it is out there for the informational purposes of the members of the committee. Now you should discuss that with your daughter.

MS. JOURDAIN: Hold on. Can you explain this to her, because I have to move.

MR. SCHWARTZ: Okay.

Hi. I'm sorry, what was your name again?

MS. HAYES: Jacqueline Hayes.

MR. SCHWARTZ: Jacqueline, I'm sorry. My name is Mark Schwartz, and we have in the room, I don't know if your mother has told you, we have attorneys representing both Senator Leahy, Senator Heflin, Senator Biden's staff, and Senator Thurmond and Senator Specter's staff, along with another member of Senator Biden's staff.

I just wanted your mother to understand that since she has agreed to give sworn testimony, that if at some point later there was found to be—and I am not saying there would be—some contradiction, that the ramifications of that, I could not swear to her that it might not be a potential problem with perjury. And I just wanted her to understand that, since she did not have an attorney present with her.

And if she feels uncomfortable about that, we have all agreed to treat this as we have all other statements, as unsworn and just for informational purposes. Do you understand?

MS. HAYES: Yes. Let me just explain that to her.

[Pause.]

MS. JOURDAIN: Hi. She explained this to me. You said that many of the people you interviewed did not make it a sworn statement?

MR. SCHWARTZ: To the best of my understanding—and you can correct me if I am wrong, Melissa or Barry—no one else has given a sworn statement to us.

MS. JOURDAIN: If no one else has given it, then I won't give one either. This is a statement but not a sworn statement.

MR. SCHWARTZ: Okay. The reason why we had requested that it be sworn is because of your current status in the hospital room and the unlikelihood that you would be able to testify before the committee. I just wanted you to understand that.

MS. JOURDAIN: Yes.

MR. SCHWARTZ: Okay. Is there anybody on the record who would like to make any more comments about this subject?

[No response.]

MR. SCHWARTZ: Okay.

MS. JOURDAIN: So now we are clear, this is no longer a sworn statement?

MR. SCHWARTZ: None of the parties involved in this on the majority or the minority staff or the Senate will treat this as a sworn statement taken under oath, so you can feel comfortable with that. It will be stricken from the record. Okay?

MS. JOURDAIN: Yes.

MR. SCHWARTZ: Okay, and before we go off the record, anybody else? Any comments? Any questions?

MS. DEOREO: I want to thank you very much. We are off the record now.

[Discussion off the record.]

MS. DEOREO: Back on the record.

Ms. Riley has one more question.

By MS. RILEY:

Q Ms. Jourdain, I apologize. I have one more.

A Okay.

Q Could you tell us if the incident when Clarence Thomas went to Angela Wright's house occurred while she worked at AID with you, or —

A No, at EEOC. I believe it was—oh, God. I'm sure it was EEOC.

MS. RILEY: Okay. Thank you.

MR. SCHWARTZ: Okay. That's fine.

Since we are still on the record, I will just state what your daughter said to us off the record, which was that if it could be arranged at a future time, that you would be prepared to give a sworn statement.

MS. JOURDAIN: Yes. In other words, since nobody else is giving a sworn statement, I would just as soon let it go as what I have done. If it becomes extremely, excruciatingly necessary and I can get it together, then I will do it.

MR. SCHWARTZ: Okay. Thank you very much, and we wish you a speedy recovery.

MS. JOURDAIN: Okay. Thank you.

MS. RILEY: We will be back in touch. Bye-bye.

MS. DEOREO: Bye-bye.

[Whereupon, at 3:08 p.m., the interview concluded.]

THE CHAIRMAN: And that will, at least as far as this committee's investigation at this moment of those two witnesses, end the matter. Now—and not in the matter in terms of judgment, in the matter in terms of witnesses.

So we are taking extensive testimony placed in the record by both majority and minority at the request of Republicans and Democrats as well as the potential witness. That is why I vitiated the subpoena, in spite of the fact I would have preferred her to be here. But, in light of the time constraints, I did not insist that that be done.

Now that means for the remainder of the night, I hope this doesn't encourage people to go longer than they otherwise would. For the remainder of the night, the only witnesses remaining are the four distinguished gentlemen before us and a panel of nine witnesses that are being produced by Judge Thomas, all women who worked in some capacity with him at, I believe EEOC. Don't hold me to that. It could be at Education as well.

Each will be by previous unanimous consent agreement limited precisely to three minutes. No more time will be allowed. And there will be sixteen minutes a side to cross-examine if anybody wishes to do that. I say that to the press and others who have been here so long trying to determine what the remainder of the witness list is.

SEN. METZENBAUM: Mr. Chairman?

THE CHAIRMAN: I yield to my friend from Ohio.

SEN. METZENBAUM: Mr. Chairman, I certainly think we should conclude the hearing with respect to these witnesses. But I wonder whether, in view of the fact that it is now 11:30 at night, and the next nine witnesses, of those nine I think seven of them are employed by the Administration either at the EEOC or at the Labor Department or the Department of Education, and two of them, one is a former secretary to Senator Danforth and one is a former chief of staff to Clarence Thomas—I wonder, Mr. Chairman, if we couldn't stipulate that all of that testimony will be very supportive of Clarence Thomas? I don't think there is any argument about that. I don't know why there is any reason to have to hear it. And frankly, I think in fairness to this committee and in fairness to the candidate that it would serve just the same purpose. We know what the testimony will be.

THE CHAIRMAN: I appreciate the Senator's request. And, as I hear from one of my friends from the far West and my right, not far right, a deal is a deal. They will be heard unless they choose to decide as two panels have on behalf of the witness, Ms. Hill, unless they so choose, they will be heard because we have a unanimous consent agreement to do just that.

Now, with that, I apologize to my friend from Pennsylvania. I hope someone has kept some notion as to how much time—how much time does the Senator have left? He has nine minutes left. Six minutes had expired when I interrupted. And you will have time to come back, if you wish.

SEN. SPECTER: Thank you. Thank you, Mr. Chairman.

THE CHAIRMAN: I apologize to the gentleman for the interruption.

SEN. SPECTER: Mr. Stewart, after Professor Hill said to you "how great Clarence's nomination was and how much he deserved it," did you continue to have a discussion with Professor Hill?

MR. STEWART: Correct.

SEN. SPECTER: Was there any mention at all of any sexual harassment by Judge Thomas of Professor Hill?

MR. STEWART: No mention at all, Senator.

SEN. SPECTER: Or any other unfavorable conduct of Judge Thomas?

MR. STEWART: No, none at all, Senator.

SEN. SPECTER: And, Mr. Grayson, after, as you have testified, Professor Hill said about Judge Thomas that he deserved it, referring to the Supreme Court nomination, was there any discussion by Ms. Hill of anything derogatory about

Judge Thomas?

MR. GRAYSON: No, Senator.

SEN. SPECTER: Is it Professor Kothe?

MR. KOTHE: Well, you use the Pennsylvania Dutch pronunciation. Actually it is "Kothe."

SEN. SPECTER: Professor Kothe?

MR. KOTHE: Kothe.

SEN. SPECTER: Professor Kothe—

MR. KOTHE: Right.

SEN. SPECTER: I would like you just to start, because time is limited and I can assure you there will be many questions on the body of your statement later, but because I want to move to Mr. Doggett in just a moment, I would like you to just read the final paragraph of your statement of October 7, if you would, please?

MR. KOTHE: I read it.

SEN. SPECTER: Would you read it, please?

MR. KOTHE: "I find the references to the alleged sexual harassment not only unbelievable but preposterous. I'm convinced that such is a product of fantasy."

SEN. SPECTER: Professor Kothe, did anybody suggest to you that you use the word "fantasy" in describing Professor Hill's conduct?

MR. KOTHE: No. In the second statement that I made on October 10 I left that off. That wasn't intended as words of art or scientific expression. It was just the instant reaction I had to this awful event. When I heard what the allegations were, my instant reaction was that it is just unbelievable, preposterous, and then I said that it must be a product of fantasy. Because if you just knew these people and knew Clarence Thomas, you would know that that couldn't possibly have been true.

SEN. SPECTER: Well, Professor Kothe, was there anything that you could point to in Professor Hill's conduct which would lead you in either an evidentiary or a feeling way to that conclusion of fantasy?

MR. KOTHE: No. I think perhaps my selection of words there was probably unfortunate. I have never seen Anita Hill in a situation where she wasn't a decent person, a dignified person, a jovial person. I have never seen her in a situation where actually you would say she is fantasizing in that sense. I almost regret that I used that in my first testimony.

SEN. SPECTER: Well, then how would you explain Professor Hill's charges against Judge Thomas in the context of your very forceful testimony in support of Judge Thomas?

MR. KOTHE: There is just no way of explaining it. How she ever was inclined to make such an observation is something that is totally beyond my comprehension. If you knew these two people as we all have known them, and evaluate that or equate that in the context of what has been alleged here, it just, it just couldn't be the same person, you wouldn't think.

SEN. SPECTER: Mr. Doggett, turning to your affidavit, and I am going to ask you for the conclusions first before you comment on the substance of your statement.

And permit me to comment I found your testimony of your professional background extremely, enormously impressive. And let me now move to the last line in the third full paragraph where you—well, why don't you read the last sentence in the third full paragraph on page 2, if you would, please?

MR. DOGGETT: "I came away from her going-away party feeling that she was somewhat unstable and that in my case she had fantasized about my being interested in her romantically."

SEN. SPECTER: And if you would now, Mr. Doggett, read the paragraph on page 3?

MR. DOGGETT: "It was my opinion at that time, and is my opinion now, that Ms. Hill's fantasies about my sexual interest in her were an indication of the fact that she was having a problem with being rejected by men she was attracted to. Her statements and actions in my presence during the time when she alleges that Clarence Thomas harassed her were totally inconsistent with her current descriptions and are, in my opinion, yet another example of her ability to fabricate the idea that someone was interested in her when in fact no such interest existed."

SEN. SPECTER: Now, Mr. Doggett, while your testimony has already, in effect, answered this question, I want to ask you explicitly did anyone suggest to you that you use the word "fantasy" in describing your conclusion about Professor Hill?

MR. DOGGETT: I talked to no one about my affidavit and the contents of my affidavit. I was quite frankly amazed when I heard the professor had used the same term. In fact, just to make it very clear, I have not talked to the judge, have not talked to any of these witnesses, I have not talked to the women that preceded us.

SEN. SPECTER: Now, Mr. Doggett, what happened between you and Professor Hill which led you to conclude that she was fantasizing?

MR. DOGGETT: At a going-away party for Anita Hill before she went to Oral Roberts University Law School, soon after I arrived and relatively early in that going-away party she asked me if we could talk in private, and I agreed, having no reason to see that that was inappropriate.

And she talked to me like you would talk to a friend who you are going to give some advice to help them "clean up their act." She said, "Something I want to tell you"—and this is what I have quoted in my affidavit, and it is the only part of my affidavit that talks about her statements that is in quotes because it was emblazoned in my brain because it was such a bizarre statement for me.

She said, "I'm very disappointed in you. You really shouldn't lead women on, or lead on women, and then let them down."

I came to a woman's going-away party who I really didn't know very well. She says, "Hey, let's talk in the corner," and she said, 'You led me on. You've disappointed me." And it is like, What? Where is this coming from?

I don't know about you, gentlemen. Washington, DC is a very rough town if you are single and you are professional, for men and for women. Most people come here to be a part of the political process. They have legitimate, real ambitions. And it is a lonely town, a difficult town to get to know people because people are constantly coming in and coming out.

I came to Washington, DC to be part of the business process. I was not interested in politics. I wanted to be an international management consultant. And the first time I met Anita Hill I sensed that she was interested in getting to know me better and I was not interested in getting to know Anita Hill. And, based on my experience as a black male in this town, I did everything I could to try not to give her any indication that I was interested in her, and my affidavit talks about that in some detail.

Even when I was jogging by her house and she said, "Hi, John," and we had a conversation, and she raised the issue of, well, since we are neighbors why don't we have dinner, I tried to make it very clear that although I respected her as a person and as a fellow alumnus of Yale Law School, and as somebody I thought was very decent, the only relationship I was interested in was a professional relationship.

And, as I stated in my affidavit, she said, "Well, what would be a good time?" and I was in my jogging clothes and so obviously I don't have a calendar with me. I said, "Well, I will check my calendar and I will get back to you." And I checked my calendar and I said, "Looks like Tuesday will work. You get back to me if that will work and let's talk about a place."

Later on with that dinner agreement, arrangements fell through, she gave me a call and said, "What happened?" I said, "What do you mean what happened? I never heard from you." She said, "Well, I never heard from you." And apparently, we both had expected the other person to call to confirm.

At the end of that "I never heard from you, I never heard from you," if I was interested in her the logical response would have been, "Well, since we didn't get together this time, let's do it again." There was no response, and there was a very awkward, pregnant pause and the conversation ended.

And I never saw Anita Hill again until that going-away party where she dropped that bombshell on me.

THE CHAIRMAN: Senator, your time is up.

SEN. SPECTER: Thank you very much, Mr. Chairman. I will come back the next round.

THE CHAIRMAN: Mr. Doggett, I don't doubt what you said, but I kind of find it equally bizarre that you would be so shocked. Maybe it has never happened to you.

I know a lot of men who call a woman and ask her out or ask to meet. Let me finish my comments here. Ask to have—decide to have dinner. Say let's get together for dinner, but afraid to say fully let's go out together for dinner. Let's get together. We live in the neighborhood, let's go to dinner. And then that person calls back or you call again and speak to her again and the date is set. And then for whatever reason she doesn't show up.

You are still interested. You call back. You say, "How come you weren't there?" You say, "Well, I thought that you were going to call." And you thought I was going to call, et cetera. And that goes back and forth. Then there is a pregnant pause and you hang up.

Maybe I am just accustomed to being turned down more than you were, when I was younger. But some men sit and say, "Geez. I wonder whether she's just bashful, that was the reason for the pregnant pause, or I wonder if she really wants me to call her back. She didn't say don't call me again. She didn't say I don't want to hear from you again. Maybe."

And then you see her a little while later at a party and she is leaving town. And you walk up to her and you say, you know, "Can I talk to you?" And she says, "Yes." And you walk over to the corner of the party and say, "You know, you really shouldn't let guys down like that. You led me to believe that you wanted to go out with me. You shouldn't do that to women—or to men."

And, if she turned around and said, "You're fantasizing. How could you ever think that? You must be demented? You must be crazy."

I don't think that is how normal people function. I mean, I don't doubt a word you said. But you go on and say you said, "I'll check my calendar and get back to you." You checked calendars, you got back to each other, the date fell—the date? We don't use dates these days, I know. The dinner fell through. You talk again and say, "What happened?" and she is silent. And she says, "What happened?" and you are silent.

You did not say to her, did you, don't call me again? Don't pay attention to me? I may be a virile person but don't pay any attention, just stay away from me? You didn't say anything like that did you?

MR. DOGGETT: I sure wish I had, Senator.

THE CHAIRMAN: Well, I wish you had too because maybe there wouldn't be this confusion. She may not be telling the truth, but how one can draw the conclusion from that kind of exchange that this is a woman who is fantasizing, this is a woman who must have a problem because she has turned—are you a psychiatrist?

MR. DOGGETT: Senator, I am trying to follow your question, but I may have to ask you to restate it.

THE CHAIRMAN: My question is are you a psychiatrist?

MR. DOGGETT: Absolutely not.

THE CHAIRMAN: Are you a psychologist?

MR. DOGGETT: Absolutely not.

THE CHAIRMAN: Well, how from that kind of an exchange can you draw the conclusion that she obviously has a serious problem? Where is the section? I want to find it here in your statement. You were stunned by her statement. You told her her comments were totally uncalled for and completely unfounded. Balderdash!

"I reiterated I had never expressed a romantic interest in her, had done nothing to give her any indication [I] might romantically be interested in the future. And I also stated the fact that I lived three blocks away from her, but never came over should have led her to believe something."

MR. DOGGETT: Pardon? I didn't hear what you just said, sir.

THE CHAIRMAN: The implication is that should have led her to understand that you weren't interested in her. Did she come up to you [and] say in mildly hysterical terms, why have you not called me or did she just make the statement straight, monotone, you shouldn't lead somebody on like that, or whatever the precise statement was? Can you characterize the way she said it? Did she sound very disappointed in you, you really shouldn't lead women on like that and then let them down? Or did she say, why did you do this? I am very disappointed in you? I mean can you characterize what it was like?

MR. DOGGETT: She was very, very intense, Senator. This was not—

THE CHAIRMAN: Describe for me how intense she was? Was her voice at a higher octave than normal?

MR. DOGGETT: She seemed very upset to me.

THE CHAIRMAN: Was her voice at a higher octave than normal, do you recall?

MR. DOGGETT: She seemed very upset, Senator.

Senator, my statement, my conclusion is based on a year and a half of experience, not just one afternoon jog on a Saturday in 1983.

THE CHAIRMAN: Well, tell me what else she ever said to you?

MR. DOGGETT: Okay. Examples, that is a very fair question, Senator.

THE CHAIRMAN: Thank you.

MR. DOGGETT: The first time I went over to Clarence Thomas's office, okay, the question is what else did she say to me?

THE CHAIRMAN: What did she ever say to you, yes.

MR. DOGGETT: A, she called me after the dinner fell through. I didn't call her. B, there were a number of months that—

THE CHAIRMAN: Let's stop there a minute. Wouldn't that lead you to believe that maybe she thought you might be interested or she wouldn't put her ego on the line to call a man?

MR. DOGGETT: Absolutely, Senator.

THE CHAIRMAN: All right.

MR. DOGGETT: What I have tried to say and what I am trying to say right now is that I did everything in my power with Professor Hill over the time I knew her to make it absolutely, positively clear that I was not interested in that woman.

THE CHAIRMAN: Did you say that to her? Did you say, Professor Hill, look, I mean, Anita, I just want to be clear before we get things out of hand here. I want to make it clear to you, I think you are a wonderful person, but I have absolutely no interest in you in anything other than professional terms. Did you ever say that to her?

MR. DOGGETT: There was never a need to do that because we never got to the level where I had given her enough encouragement where she felt that it was appropriate to—

THE CHAIRMAN: Well, give me more instances where she said things to you, that this just wasn't the one instance where she said, you know, you led me on or you led women on.

Tell me another instance.

MR. DOGGETT: Well, I think a perfect example of the conclusion that I came to when I was sitting at my computer in Austin, Texas was the statement that she gave under oath, before you two days ago, that she had dated John Carr. And the statement that John Carr gave under oath today that he would not characterize their relationship as a dating relationship.

THE CHAIRMAN: Now, wait a minute. John Carr said he went out with her.

MR. DOGGETT: That's right, and I believe, as I understand it—

THE CHAIRMAN: He said dating.

SEN. THURMOND: Let him get through.

MR. DOGGETT: Pardon?

THE CHAIRMAN: I am worried about your instances. What did she ever say to you, that led you to believe that she, in fact, had a clear understanding that you had no interest? You said that there were other instances, other than this occasion, where she said to you, I am very disappointed in you, you really shouldn't lead on women and then let them down.

MR. DOGGETT: Right.

THE CHAIRMAN: What else did she ever do or say?

MR. DOGGETT: Nothing else, Senator.

THE CHAIRMAN: That's it?

MR. DOGGETT: Absolutely, Senator, and if she hadn't said it and hadn't been upset to some degree with—

THE CHAIRMAN: Well, how was she upset again?

SEN. THURMOND: Well, let him get through, let him get through, let him answer.

THE CHAIRMAN: Okay.

MR. DOGGETT: It was her, she was intense. I do not believe she raised her voice, but this was not just, hey, guy, you know, be careful as you characterized it, this clearly bothered her. And I hear what you are saying, Senator, and I respect your opinion and I am not trying to argue with you but for me, in that time, in that room, that shocked me and maybe it would have not shocked you, it shocked me.

THE CHAIRMAN: I appreciate that. I do appreciate that. I sincerely do. Let me tell you what I thought when I first was told about this.

MR. DOGGETT: Okay.

THE CHAIRMAN: I thought it was the case of a woman walking up to someone she never had spoken to other than in passing business, watched him jog, said hello to them and then all of a sudden at a going away party walked up and called him aside and said, I don't know why you led me on like this.

That to me, if a woman did that to me, I may either think she is nuts or be flattered but I would wonder, at a minimum. I would walk away going "where did that come from?" Whether she called me or I called her, if I had agreed on one occasion to go to dinner with her, and if I had known that she had, if I felt that she had an interest in me, if the dinner date was broken, if she called me to ask me why.

If I said nothing and remained silent, and did not say, look, I just don't want to go out to dinner with you, I was just polite and said nothing. And then she came up to me and said that one sentence, I don't know how, quite frankly, a reasonable man could conclude from that to be stunned and shocked that this woman is fantasizing because she has a male complex—what was your phrase about complex? Come on, earn your salary. There is some place in there where you say, this must mean that she is used to be, this is a complex from being rejected by men.

MR. DOGGETT: It is on page 3.

THE CHAIRMAN: The fact, you believe "Ms. Hill's fantasies about my sexual interest in her were an indication of the fact she was having a problem with being rejected by men she was attracted to." It seems to me that is a true leap in faith or ego, one of the two. [Laughter.]

SEN. SIMPSON: Are we playing to the audience now?

THE CHAIRMAN: No, I am not.

SEN. SIMPSON: Well, then let's stop the crowd from responding. You have done that before and they have responded about six times now.

THE CHAIRMAN: If anyone else responds they are out and the reason I probably didn't is I am so intensely involved in this, I did not do that. Please, if anyone else responds I ask the police officers to move them out, I mean that sincerely.

MR. DOGGETT: Would you like for me to respond to your question?

THE CHAIRMAN: I would like you to say anything you want. I mean I truly would because I am having trouble understanding this one and I won't say anything more.

SEN. THURMOND: Now, take your time and say what you please.

THE CHAIRMAN: As long as you want.

MR. DOGGETT: I appreciate your concern.

THE CHAIRMAN: My confusion, not concern.

MR. DOGGETT: I assumed you were concerned also.

THE CHAIRMAN: No, I am not concerned.

MR. DOGGETT: I appreciate your confusion and I will do what I can to try to clarify it. A, I clearly reacted to this event differently than you would and I respect our differences of opinion.

B, there were a number of occasions when Gil Hardy and others who were black Yale Law School graduates made an attempt to bring together those of us who were in town, including people like me who were not practicing law and who were not involved in the political process, so that we could have social fellowship. We had parties, and other get-togethers.

I observed from a distance—and I am not a psychiatrist, I am not an expert, just a man—Anita Hill attempting to be friendly with men, engage them in conversation, initiate conversation, elongate conversations, and people talking with her and eventually going away.

THE CHAIRMAN: Can you name any of those men for us, for the record?

MR. DOGGETT: Sir, eight, almost nine years have gone by. If she had filed a sexual harassment charge—

THE CHAIRMAN: That's not the issue—

MR. DOGGETT: [continuing]—I would be able to do that because we would be in 1983 or 1984 given the statute of limitations. Which is why you have created a statute of limitations. It is too long, I cannot, sir.

I also remember, sir, the first time I went to Clarence Thomas's office, I was going to talk to somebody who was a classmate of mine about why he had become a black Republican Reaganite, because I had some real concerns. And as I went into his outer office, Anita Hill happened to walk by and she tried to stop me and engage me in conversation and acted as though she thought that since we were all black Yale Law School graduates, I should say, well, let's go in and talk with Clarence, which I did not.

Clearly, people can disagree as to whether or not my observations and conclusions are ones that they would make. But I assure you that based on my experiences and my observations of Anita Hill, both in terms of how she related to me and let's talk about the jogging incident, Senator. When I was running by I was timing myself with my watch and my interest was to run in place for maybe thirty seconds, be polite and keep going. The reason we continued to talk was because she wanted me to continue to talk. That is action on her part, sir.

THE CHAIRMAN: Can I ask you a question, why didn't you keep running?

MR. DOGGETT: Because the group of black Yale Law School graduates is a very small, a very close, and a very special group and it is like a family. Gil Hardy, the man who introduced Anita to Clarence Thomas, was one of the leaders of that group. We did what we could to be as supportive as possible.

Senator, I graduated in 1972. She graduated in 1980. She was significantly younger than me, she seemed to be lonely in this town. I was not going to try to make this woman feel that I was not going to be straightforward with her as a professional. There have been other women who have made it very clear to me that they have been interested in me and I have said, I am not interested. Anita Hill did nothing to deserve me to slam the door in her face. She was one of the Yale Law School black fraternity and there are very few of them, Senator.

Now, I agree that others may interpret my conclusions differently but that's how I saw it and that's why I said what I said.

THE CHAIRMAN: I appreciate that and I thank you very much.

Dean, did you work for Clarence—this is the first time I knew this, I should have read the record more closely—did you work for Clarence Thomas when you spent most time with Anita Hill, Professor Hill?

MR. KOTHE: I would have to say it this way. I worked for Clarence Thomas after I worked with Anita Hill. She was a professor on our faculty. When I retired as dean, I became special assistant to Clarence Thomas. I think in large part through what she did in initiating our arrangement.

THE CHAIRMAN: Thank you.

Now, from your testimony I got the impression though that the time that you spent the most time with Anita Hill was in setting up that conference you referred to on harassment.

Well, let me not say most time. You said there was a conference that you were setting up on harassment and Anita Hill was participating in that. And you were surprised that if she had been harassed she would have said something to you at that time. Were you working for the man that she alleges harassed her when you were surprised that she did not say something about harassment?

MR. KOTHE: Yes, sir, it was in 1987 and I had already been working with Thomas then—

SEN. THURMOND: Talk into the machine so that everybody can hear you.

MR. KOTHE: Yes, I had been working with Chairman Thomas at that time for probably two years.

THE CHAIRMAN: So I want to just make sure I understand. You made a statement which I thought was fairly powerful and obviously accurate. You said that one of the things you pointed to as evidence of the fact that Anita Hill's assertions are probably not true is with regard to a conference on harassment she worked with you in setting up. And you said, and I am paraphrasing, that if she had been harassed why would she not say to me that she had been harassed when the purpose we were getting together for was to discuss harassment?

And I ask you, in light of the fact that you worked for the man who allegedly harassed her, would it surprise you that she would not confide in you? Sir, I mean that sincerely?

MR. KOTHE: Well, precisely and that is what I said in my opening statement

THE CHAIRMAN: That's what I did not understand. Thank you.

MR. KOTHE: How could it possibly be that a person was talking to me about being a featured speaker on the subject of sexual harassment and never, ever have said I have been harassed. I have been exposed to this. I know it from personal experience, never ever?

THE CHAIRMAN: Now, what I am saying, Dean, as a trained lawyer does it surprise you that a person who says they were harassed now, would not say to you she was harassed when she would then have to tell you that the man who harassed her was your boss?

MR. KOTHE: It not only surprises me, it completely confounds me. How could it possibly be that a person as intelligent, as decent, as dignified as this young woman was could talk to me about having a program of sexual harassment and never say, I personally have experienced it?

THE CHAIRMAN: Thank you, very much. My time is up and I yield to Senator Thurmond.

SEN. THURMOND: Senator Specter.

SEN. SPECTER: Thank you, Mr. Chairman.

Mr. Doggett, we have been searching in the past week, and you are right when you talk as an experienced litigator, the speed with which this matter has been put together. I have never seen anything like it. I doubt that there has ever been as complex a matter as this put together in this kind of a hearing sequence, calling of witnesses and examination as we have proceeded with overnight transcripts in trying to move through in an orderly process.

And we are doing it at the mandate of the Senate and those of us who are doing it, at least this Senator has some concern about doing it at this speed. We are doing it the best we can. And we have been trying to figure this matter out.

And we have been going on the proposition most of the time, and it hasn't been very long, that either he is lying or she is lying. I have been trying to figure it out myself on the credibility issue or the perjury issue. And as the matter has evolved I have started to explore a third alternative. And that alternative was suggested to me when I read on the same day, which was last Thursday, the affidavits of Professor Kothe and the affidavit of Mr. Doggett.

And I had not seen, I still have not seen Professor Kothe's affidavit of the 10th. I have your affidavit of the 7th, where you had the word fantasy in, but as you say, you have changed it.

But I am fascinated, Mr. Doggett, by your pinpointing the John Carr issue. And I think that could bear some additional clarification because, as you testify about it, as I understand your testimony—

SEN. THURMOND: Senator, you had better wait a few minutes, somebody is talking to your witness. And let him get through.

SEN. SPECTER: Will somebody stop the clock.

THE CHAIRMAN: I apologize. I asked that they speak up. I just wanted to give the dean an opportunity, if he wanted to, to take a break at this moment if you want to and come back. I want the witnesses to know if they have to get up and leave and come back they can.

MR. KOTHE: Mr. Chairman, I have a requirement at this time. I would have to have something, protein or something.

THE CHAIRMAN: Yes, that's why I asked the staff to talk to you and, Dean, you are free to come and go. Or go. You don't have to come back. I sincerely mean it. The hour is late and you have a medical requirement and I understand that.

MR. KOTHE: I don't want to miss this.

THE CHAIRMAN: Senator Specter, understandably, says he needs the dean here to ask him questions.

SEN. SPECTER: I need the dean here, because I am going to talk about the dean's statement—

THE CHAIRMAN: Fair enough. Why don't we yield to some on the other side who can question, who does not have questions for the dean, but wishes to ask someone else questions, and then come back to you.

SEN. SPECTER: What do I have left, fourteen minutes?

THE CHAIRMAN: No, you can have as much time as you want.

SEN. SPECTER: Okay. Thank you.

THE CHAIRMAN: I yield to the Senator from Ohio.

SEN. METZENBAUM: Mr. Doggett, I haven't had a chance to read the full transcript of your testimony that was given in the telephone interview with several staff members representing Senator Biden, Senator Heflin, Senator Thurmond, Senator Leahy and Senator Specter.

But let me read you some portions of it, because I think we are talking about Anita Hill, and I think we need to also talk a little bit about Mr. Doggett, and this is a question to you:

> Now, since we have received your affidavit and since your statement has gone public, the majority staff has received word from an individual who said she worked with you at McKenzie. Answer: Yes.
>
> And she has made some allegations concerning yourself. Answer: All right. And did she give you a name? Answer: She did. And we will move to that. I wanted to let you know where this line of questioning was going, to turn at this time. Answer: All right. I am not surprised. This morning, we spoke with a woman named Amy Graham, who said she worked with you—

SEN. SPECTER: Excuse me, Senator Metzenbaum. Would you tell us where you are reading from?

SEN. METZENBAUM: Yes, page 64.

SEN. SPECTER: Thank you.

SEN. METZENBAUM: [reading:].

> Who said she worked with you at McKenzie & Company, and I believe you started down there in August of 1981. Answer: That is correct. Let me tell you generally what her allegations were, and then I will ask you some questions, and then I will turn back to Ms. DeOreo, to follow up with some questions. Answer: All right.
>
> Question: Ms. Graham indicated that, on her first day of work, when she met you, along with other people in that office; first of all very succinctly, do you remember Ms. Amy Graham? Answer: I do not. Question: You do not? Answer: I do not. She claims that, on her first day at work, at some point in the day, I believe she said—I don't have the transcript available yet, but at some point during the day you confronted her in the hall, in front of an elevator, and kissed her on the mouth and told her that she would enjoy working with you very well. She also—Answer: You know, I also got—I deny that. I didn't remember the woman, and that is outrageous. I also got a message on my answering machine after you guys went public with my affidavit, saying "This is your Texas whore from five years ago." Somebody, I don't know, never met, who decided that she was going to claim to be my whore. Question: Mr. Doggett, let me just tell you generally her allegation, and then I will give you adequate opportunity to respond. I think that, in all fairness, that you need to know what she said, and then you can respond overall. She also claimed that, during the time that she worked there—she was nineteen years old when she began work, she is twenty-nine years old now—she also claimed that at times, in front of the copying machine—and again, I am just going from my recollection, I

> don't have the transcript—that you would rub her shoulders at the copying machine. At the time, you suggested to her, "Oh, you are making copies, that is sort of like reproduction, isn't it?" She also said that some of your conversation dealt with sexual innuendo, there was sexual overtone in your talk. But what struck me, though, is she also said that you weren't in the office very much. So, first, if you could respond to Ms. Graham's allegations, and then I have some questions I want to discuss with you

I am still reading:

> Answer: I do not remember Amy Graham. If she was there, she was not there as an associate or as a researcher or as a consultant but was there as a part of the secretarial staff. I never made any comments or statements to anybody like that. I never did anything like that, so I categorically deny it. I am, quite frankly, not surprised that somebody has come out of the woodwork to make a claim like this. That's the nature of this business.

That is on page 76.

We now turn over to page 77, again the question—I was not present at this and I am only reading from the transcript:

> Question: Okay. Fine. So, I understand that you didn't have much conversation with Mr. Chisholm. Let me ask you, do you recall the name Joane Checci? Answer: Joane Checci, yes, I do remember that name. She designed business cards for me and stationery for me, when I was getting ready to leave the firm and become an independent consultant. Question: Do you recall ever touching Joane Checci? Answer: I never recall doing anything other than standing next to her. I may have brushed her when I was standing next to her, as she was designing business stationery, but I never remember. Question: Do you remember giving any neck massages? Answer: I don't remember, but if she had asked for one, I would have.

Then we go over to page 84:

> Question: Mr. Doggett, so I don't leave one more thing hanging out there that has been alleged against you, I want you to have an opportunity to clear your name. I recall one other thing Ms. Graham said. She said that, subsequent to your leaving McKenzie, she bumped into you on the street one afternoon or one day, and that she was still at McKenzie. She told you she had since that time received a promotion and that you responded, "Well, whom did you sleep with to get the promotion? Answer: All right. Question: Did that occur? Answer: I absolutely categorically completely deny that.

Mr. Doggett, you have an interesting series of questions and answers in this transcript. I wonder if you would care to tell us what are the facts with respect to these several ladies who have raised questions concerning your own conduct?

MR. DOGGETT: Senator, your comments about this document are one of the reasons that our process of government is falling apart.

First of all, Senator, I have a copy of the statement that this person met—it is called a transcript of proceedings. But, Senator, if you read this, it is a telephone conversation that she has with some staff members pro and against Mr. Thomas, and she is not under oath. I did not do any of the things that she alleged. In fact, the first time any of these issues were raised was the day before I was supposed to come here, eight and one-half years later.

I knew when I put my information into the ring, that I was saying I am open season. For anybody to believe that, on the first day of work, for a woman working in the xerox room, who is nineteen years old, a thirty-three-year-old black man would walk up to a nineteen-year-old white girl and kiss her on the mouth as the first thing that they did, whoever believes that really needs psychiatric care.

But let me talk about the facts, since you brought up this statement, which was not made under oath, which was not made consistent with any of the rules that you Senators are supposed to be responsible for, since this is the Judiciary Committee, let me talk about that, since you asked the question and went on and on and on.

During that time that she—I have read this statement. If she had made it under oath, Senator, I would go to court, but—

SEN. METZENBAUM: This isn't her statement. I am reading from your statement, Mr. Doggett.

MR. DOGGETT: The statement that you read from was a discussion with me, and consistently your staff people said, "I don't have the transcript, I don't remember the exact facts." Well, I have the transcript and the exact facts show this woman to be a profound liar who does not even remember the facts accurately.

She said—Senator, I would suggest we all turn to "Transcript of Proceedings of Ms. Amy Graham," the woman who has accused me, the liar, page 6: "I met John Doggett the first day I started there, which I remember correctly was probably Monday, March 20, 1982."

SEN. SPECTER: Mr. Doggett, what page are you on, please?

SEN. METZENBAUM: I don't have that.

MR. DOGGETT: Page 6 of the unsworn telephone conversation that Ms. Graham had with some staffers.

THE CHAIRMAN: Excuse me, let me interrupt for a minute.

MR. DOGGETT: I'm pissed off, sir.

THE CHAIRMAN: It is totally out of line with what the committee had agreed to—

MR. DOGGETT: I'm sorry.

THE CHAIRMAN: [continuing]—for there to be entered into this record any unsworn statement by any witness who cannot be called before this committee, and I rule any such statement out of order.

Now, I apologize for being out of the room. Was there any—

SEN. METZENBAUM: I was only reading from Mr. Doggett's own statement.

MR. DOGGETT: My statement was not under oath, sir. That was a telephone conversation and they said we staffers would like to talk with you, we have a court reporter there. I'm a lawyer, sir, it was no deposition, it was not under oath, as Ms. Graham's comments were not under oath. And since you have brought this up, I demand the right to clear my name, sir.

SEN. METZENBAUM: I was only reading from his statement, not from—

MR. DOGGETT: I demand the right to clear my name, sir. I have been trashed for no reason by somebody who does not even have the basic facts right. This is what is going on with Clarence Thomas, and now I, another person coming up, has had a "witness" fabricated at the last moment to try to keep me from testifying.

SEN. METZENBAUM: Well, Mr. Doggett —

MR. DOGGETT: I am here, I don't care, she is wrong, and I would like to be able to clear my name, sir.

SEN. METZENBAUM: Please do.

THE CHAIRMAN: Sir, you will be permitted to say whatever you would like to with regard to, as you say, clearing your name. If there was no introduction of the transcript of Amy Louise Graham in the record, then that is a different story. I was under the impression that had been read from. That has not been read from.

SEN. METZENBAUM: I did not read from that at all.

THE CHAIRMAN: It has not been read from, and I don't know what else took place, but—

SEN. METZENBAUM: I read from Mr. Doggett's questions asked of him—

THE CHAIRMAN: Mr. Doggett, please, as much time as you want to make—

SEN. METZENBAUM: [continuing]—by the staff of Senator Biden, Senators Heflin, Thurmond, Leahy and Specter. My staff was not even present. I am just asking you if you would please go ahead and respond in any manner that you want to clear your name.

MR. DOGGETT: Yes, sir.

SEN. SPECTER: Mr. Chairman, you were not here, but what happened is that Senator Metzenbaum was reading to Mr. Doggett from Mr. Doggett's unsworn statement of the telephone interview—

SEN. METZENBAUM: That's correct.

SEN. SPECTER: [continuing]—and that statement involved questions from Ms. Graham, who was questioned similarly in an unsworn statement over the telephone, and for Mr. Doggett to reply to what Senator Metzenbaum had asked him, since Senator Metzenbaum was basing his questions on what Ms. Graham had said, it is indispensable that Mr. Doggett be able to refer to what Ms. Graham said—

THE CHAIRMAN: It is appropriate for Mr. Doggett to refer to whatever he wishes to refer to at this point, in light of where we are at the moment.

MR. DOGGETT: Thank you, Mr. Chairman.

THE CHAIRMAN: So, Mr. Doggett, proceed.

MR. DOGGETT: I will tell you, Senators, before I talk about the specifics, I debated, myself and with my wife, whether or not to start the process that resulted in me being here, because this is vicious, and I knew, since anything I said was going to raise the question about the credibility of Professor Anita Hill, as a lawyer, that meant my character was open season.

I have never been involved as a candidate, although I have always said you can't complain about the process, if you're not willing to put your ass on the line —pardon me, I am sorry. I am sorry about that.

SEN. METZENBAUM: Mr. Chairman—

MR. DOGGETT: But I have said if you don't like the way the political process is, then you have to get into it and you have to get into the fray.

So, I said, okay, if I submit this information to this committee then I am open season and people are going to shoot at me, and I do not care. I have information I think the committee needs to hear. If they feel it is relevant enough for me to be here, I will be here and I will take whatever occurs.

But I will tell you, sir, I have had lawyers and professional people in Texas and around the country say that I was insane to subject myself to the opportunity to have something like this crawl out from under a rock. They have said I should have just stood on the sidelines and let it go by.

I am an attorney, sir—

SEN. METZENBAUM: Mr. Doggett—

MR. DOGGETT: [continuing]—I am a businessman and I cannot allow this process of innuendo, unsworn statements and attacks on characters to continue, without saying it is unacceptable.

Now, specifically, page 6 of her unsworn telephone conversation with Senate staff, dated the 12th of October, two days ago, says, "I met John Doggett the first day I started there, which, if I remember correctly, was probably Monday, March 20, 1972. At that—"

THE CHAIRMAN: I will let you continue, but you ought to seek your own counsel for a minute here. No one has read anything into the record, as I understand—

MR. DOGGETT: Now—

THE CHAIRMAN: No, wait, let me finish.

MR. DOGGETT: Yes, sir.

THE CHAIRMAN: [continuing]—that you may be about to read into the record. Let me say that anyone who asks you—that I think it is unfair—that you were in a telephonic interview, whether it is sworn or unsworn, are asked about an uncorroborated accusation that is not sworn to, and then in open session you are asked from your statement about that same statement, that's no different than as if it was introduced without—if the original statement were introduced, which is inappropriate. Now, all I am saying to you is this: I believe you are entitled to say whatever you wish to say here, and I believe we are beyond the bounds here.

MR. DOGGETT: I understand.

THE CHAIRMAN: The question I want you to think about is whether you want to further give credence to an unsubstantiated, unsworn-to statement of someone that may be completely lying. It is up to you to make that judgment. That is your call, but I would think about it.

MR. DOGGETT: I appreciate your comments and I apologize for getting angry.

THE CHAIRMAN: No, you have no reason to apologize.

MR. DOGGETT: No, I am going to apologize, sir. This is a difficult process. I have only been up here for a short period of time and you have been here, as I understand it, for a very long period of time.

Let me say, without reading the statement or putting in that "evidence," since I am under oath, comments made by this person, that they are wrong, that at the time the allegations, the unsworn allegations were made, I was in the midst of a major project with McKenzie & Company regarding the Comptroller of the Currency, where we had just found, from a computer analysis, that bank deregulation would result in bank failures and savings and loan failures that exceeded the historical limits of bank failures over the past ten years.

We were in the midst of that analysis, we were frightened by the information that we had found, and we were doing everything we could do to prove ourselves wrong, and it is in the context of that time that this person, whom I do not remember, claims that I would walk up to her and do that.

At the same time, Senator, I had just started a relationship with an attorney, a very intense relationship. The facts are wrong.

Second, that person, as read by Senator Metzenbaum, alleges that I was getting ready to leave the firm at that time. Senator, after I finished that Comptroller of the Currency study, in approximately April of 1982, in May of 1982, McKenzie & Co. sent me to Copenhagen, Denmark, to spend the summer working for our Danish office. That is not exactly an exit strategy, sir. That was one of the most prized assignments that the firm had.

The facts in this uncorroborated, unsworn-to statement are not even consistent with the facts of my life. So, without trying to put this thing into the record, all I can say is that I expected somebody to do something like this, because that is what this process has become, and one of the reasons I am here is to work with you gentlemen to try to take the public process back into the pale of propriety.

Now, second, when I was the director of the State Bar of California's Office of Legal Services, I had the opportunity to hire two deputies. Both of those people were women. In fact, when I knew that I was going to leave the state bar to go to Harvard Business School, the person I hired to replace me was a woman.

I have a very clear long record of commitment, sensitivity and support for women having the greatest role possible, but I am afraid that the outlandish allegations of Anita Hill are going to result in us feeling that it is inappropriate for us to be human beings with people if they happen to be women. Nobody would ever question me if I put my hand around this man, who I have never met.

THE CHAIRMAN: He might.

MR. DOGGETT: Well, maybe he would. [Laughter.]

But I hope we don't get to the point where if anybody by any way, accidentally or purposely, innocently touches somebody of the opposite sex, that becomes sexual harassment.

THE CHAIRMAN: I would really like this to end. Let the record show, and I am stating it, there is absolutely no evidence, none, no evidence in this record, no evidence before this committee, that you did anything wrong with regard to anything, none. I say that as the chairman of this committee. I think your judgment about women is not so hot, whether or not people fantasize or don't. You and I disagree in that.

MR. DOGGETT: Yes, sir.

THE CHAIRMAN: But you did nothing. There is no evidence, the record should show, the press should show, there is absolutely no evidence that you did anything improper, period.

MR. DOGGETT: Thank you, Senator.

SEN. THURMOND: Mr. Chairman, would it be proper to expunge from the record, then, that information that came out?

THE CHAIRMAN: Well, fine, but Senator, I would hope you would read from his statement of questions asked of him. It is a little bit like if someone asked me over the telephone, "Are you still beating your wife?" and I answer yes or no, it doesn't matter. I am still in trouble. And then someone says, "I am reading only from your statement, Mr. Biden. You are the one that mentioned your wife." I never did. And I know that is not what the Senator intended, but that is the effect. It is no different than just putting this unsubstantiated material in, and I want the record to show I don't think anything that is unsworn and I don't think anything in an FBI record is anything—up until the time it is sworn or the person is here to be cross-examined—is anything but garbage.

MR. DOGGETT: Thank you, sir.

THE CHAIRMAN: Senator, I apologize for the interruption—

SEN. THURMOND: Mr. Chairman?

THE CHAIRMAN: Yes?

SEN. THURMOND: Would it be proper for you to explain for the record those parts that you feel were improper?

THE CHAIRMAN: Yes, and I will.

SEN. THURMOND: Thank you.

THE CHAIRMAN: Now, Senator, please continue, not along the lines of what someone said he said, and he had to respond to what they said.

SEN. METZENBAUM: I am not saying what somebody said he said. I am asking him what he said. He said that he did not remember Ms. Amy Graham, that he did not know Amy Graham.

You also indicated that she was white and nineteen. How did you know that?

MR. DOGGETT: Senator, when your staff or the staff of the committee—

SEN. METZENBAUM: My staff has not been in touch—

MR. DOGGETT: Excuse me. When the staff of the committee—I corrected myself—made these allegations to me, one of the things I said, and if you read my complete statement, you will realize it is there, is that although I do not remember this person, that does not mean this person was not there; that it is possible that she did work at McKenzie and Company. I just do not remember her. I said that. Okay?

The second thing I did after the staffers of committee hung up was to call an associate of mine who started at McKenzie in the company with me, at the same time, a man named Carroll Warfield, and I asked him if he remembered this woman because I did not remember her name at all. I did not remember her face. Nothing about her came into my mind, but I knew it was possible she could have been there. Senator, it has been eight or nine years and I, even I can forget people.

He said, "Oh, yes, I remember her," and he was the one who indicated to me that she was white. That, as far as the age nineteen, I believe you read that when you read statements that I responded to from the Senate Judiciary Committee staff, and that is how we got the age nineteen, sir.

SEN. METZENBAUM: No, I think it was your statement, but we will just drop it, Mr. Chairman.

THE CHAIRMAN: All right. Thank you. Now let me make one other thing clear. The exception to unsworn statements being placed in the record is when the witnesses stipulate that they are admissible, when the parties mentioned in the statements stipulate they are admissible, and when the committee stipulates they are admissible, which is the case of the Angela Wright stipulation. That is different, so no one is confused later, that there is a fundamental distinction.

Now, Senator, who had the—

SEN. THURMOND: The distinguished Senator from Pennsylvania.

SEN. SPECTER: Well, thank you, Mr. Chairman. I was in the midst of questioning Mr. Doggett and Professor Kothe when we had to take a brief recess for Professor Kothe, so I shall resume at this point.

I think it is worth noting, Mr. Chairman, to amplify what Mr. Doggett has said —if I could have the attention of the chairman for just a moment—

THE CHAIRMAN: Yes. I'm sorry.

SEN. SPECTER: Late yesterday evening when we caucused and the chairman stated his intention to try to finish the hearings today—

THE CHAIRMAN: Yes.

SEN. SPECTER: [continuing]—I then reviewed what had to be done, and at about 6:45 this morning called Duke Short and said we ought to have Mr. Doggett here, and that is why he was called this morning at about 7 o'clock, he said—

MR. DOGGETT: 6:30, sir.

SEN. SPECTER: [continuing]—6:30 central time, so he has been on that track to accommodate our schedule so we could finish today.

MR. DOGGETT: I don't mind staying here as long as you need, sir.

SEN. SPECTER: Well, that is probably going to happen. [Laughter.]

MR. DOGGETT: I sense that.

SEN. SPECTER: I want to explore with you what conceivably—I don't want to overstate it—could be the key to the extremely difficult matter we are looking into. And I had said, shortly before my line of questioning was interrupted, that we have been working on the proposition that either Anita Hill is lying or Judge Thomas is lying.

And we have explored earlier today, with a panel of four women who favor Judge Thomas but who knew Professor Hill very well, the possibility that there could be in her mind that these things happened when they really didn't. And I developed that question after talking to a number of my colleagues, because we have been discussing this matter all day, and it originated with the two affidavits or statements, your affidavit, Mr. Doggett, and Professor Kothe's statement that was not sworn to, where the word "fantasy" was used.

And it may be that we are not limited to the two alternatives, one, that he is lying, two, that she is lying. Perhaps they both think they are telling the truth, but in Professor Hill's case she thinks it is true but in fact it is not. And you testified to a very interesting approach when you referred to the testimony of Mr. John Carr, whom you said you went to graduate school at Harvard with, where you made a key distinction between the way Professor Hill viewed the relationship and the way John Carr viewed the relationship. And I think it would be worthwhile if you would amplify that, as you had started to articulate it earlier.

MR. DOGGETT: Senators, at every step—in fact I remember when I was at Yale Law School seeing Senator Kennedy give a speech to people at Yale back in the early seventies—at every step of my education, at Claremont Men's College, at Yale Law School, at Harvard Business School, one of the things I tried to do was to provide assistance to make sure that black law students and Hispanic law students would have the best possible opportunity to do as well as possible, because I had something to prove, Senators. I had had people tell me that I could not be good because I was black, and I was out to prove them wrong.

Because of that, I was asked by my colleagues at Harvard Business School, in part because I was an older student and in part because of my commitment to excellence, to be the Education Committee chairperson for the African-American Student Union, and to organize tutorial study groups and other support activities to make sure that every one of our people had the best possible chance to do as well as possible, to excel. That is how I met John Carr.

I know John Carr, and I think I knew him well. I definitely know him better than I know the judge and I know the professor. I saw John Carr this May at Harvard Business School for our tenth Harvard Business School Alumni reception, reunion, and we talked.

In those ten, twelve years, John Carr has never mentioned Anita Hill to me. We have talked about women John Carr has had relationships with. I have called him up at times and said, "Hey, man, haven't you gotten married yet?" because we were that close, and he would say, "Well, you know, there really hasn't been anybody special." We have talked about the issue of John Carr's personal life, and her name never came up in the way that she described herself.

I, as the Senator asked me, am not a psychiatrist, I am not a psychologist, and so maybe I am not qualified to use the term "fantasy" from a professional standpoint. But as a lay person and an individual, that is what I felt. And given what

John Carr has said and has not said, given what the professor has said, given that she has described a series of activities where Clarence Thomas was obsessed with her—every time she said no, he would try to get her to relent and go out with him, over a period of years, obsessed with her—I have to deal with the realities that if he was so obsessed with her, why did he never talk to me about her or anybody else about her?

One of the things, Senator, that stunned—I won't use that word again—that amazed me about the testimony of the women who worked with Anita Hill and Clarence Thomas, is that they came up with conclusions very similar to what I put in my affidavit, and these are women I have never met. These are women who knew both of the people involved in this hearing at this stage far better than I did.

I was going to a gut sense, on male intuition. They were saying the same thing, without any communication between the four of them and myself, based on years of observation. I find that amazing.

SEN. SPECTER: Mr. Doggett, you heard the testimony of the panel with Ms. Berry on it? You were in the hearing room at that time today?

MR. DOGGETT: Hearing room at the end, and I was at the hotel looking at it on TV, sir.

SEN. SPECTER: So you saw the panel with Ms. Alvarez, Ms. Fitch, Ms. Holt—

MR. DOGGETT: I saw most of what they said, although I missed part of it as I was coming here to appear before you gentlemen.

SEN. SPECTER: Did you hear the part where Ms. Berry testified to amplify an interview which she had given to the *New York Times*, that Professor Hill was rebuffed by Judge Thomas?

MR. DOGGETT: I do not remember the exact facts, but I heard most of her response to the *New York Times*—

SEN. SPECTER: Well, I think it would be worthwhile for you to refer to whatever you heard of their testimony, in terms of their statements as to the relationship between Judge Thomas and Professor Hill, because their testimony was extensive as it relates to the approach you are articulating.

MR. DOGGETT: Right. My experience with Clarence Thomas and Anita Hill was inconsistent, as I said, with what she was alleging, and based on my experiences over a period of a year and a half with Anita Hill and over a period of seven or eight years with Clarence Thomas, I came to some conclusions as a lay person, as an individual, as an untrained non-professional, where I used the words "fantasies" and I talked about her possibly reacting to being rejected. I did that sitting in Austin, Texas, Thursday afternoon, on my computer with my word processing software.

Today, gentlemen, as you know, four women I have never met and have never talked with came to the same conclusion based on extensive experience and observations with Anita, with Professor Hill and Judge Thomas. Mine was just intuition, gentlemen. Theirs was based on experience, and we both came, all five of us came to essentially the same conclusion. That surprised me, but now I am not surprised.

SEN. SPECTER: Mr. Doggett, what similarities, if any, do you see between the description you have made of your own relationship with Professor Hill, where you categorized in your affidavit her response to being rejected, and the relationship which Professor Hill had with John Carr, where she had exaggerated the relationship as you have testified from your personal knowledge of the two of them, and the relationship with Judge Thomas, where she has represented the kind of a relationship which Judge Thomas has flatly denied and others who know the two of them think totally implausible?

MR. DOGGETT: In my case, Senator, which I obviously can talk about the clearest, she came up to me before we left—before she left for Oral Roberts University, and basically chastised me for leading her on, and gave me in effect advice that I should not in the future lead women on. I felt at the time, and the good chairman of this committee notwithstanding, I still feel at this point and I will always feel that that was totally inappropriate, given everything I tried to do to be a supportive older upperclassman, part of the Yale Law School group.

Regarding Mr. Carr, John Carr, Attorney Carr, my friend, I have had a series of conversations with this man over the past decade. He has never, ever said that he was dating Anita Hill. When he was here under oath he said, to paraphrase him, "I would not define our relationship as a dating relationship."

Regarding Judge Clarence Thomas I have the least information. because he never, ever at any time mentioned this woman to me. And at the time, the one time that I have concrete observation about her perception of how she thought she should be treated by me vis-a-vis Judge Thomas, she wanted to go into Judge Thomas's inner office at EEOC because she felt that was appropriate, and for me it didn't make any sense at all.

So in those three instances—my own personal experience, a statement by a business school colleague and friend of mine, and my one observation about Anita Hill and Clarence Thomas back, I believe, in 1982, there is a consistency in a perception of something that did not exist.

SEN. SPECTER: Mr. Doggett, do you think it a possibility that Professor Hill imagined or fantasized Judge Thomas saying the things she has charged him with?

MR. DOGGETT: You know, part of what makes this so unpleasant for all of us is that her charges are so clear, explicit, and extreme. I know how difficult it has been for me to even remember what happened back in 1982, so one of the things I did was take some time off from work to look at Anita Hill when she was testifying before this committee, and I will tell you gentlemen, she looked believable to me, even though the words she was saying made absolutely no sense.

I believe that Anita Hill believes what she has said. I believe, and I am saying this under oath, that there is absolutely no truth to what she has said. But I believe that she believes it.

I was impressed with her confidence, her calm, even though the things she was saying in my mind were absolutely, totally beyond the pale of reality.

Clarence Thomas told me in his office that "These people are going to shoot at me. I have a target on my back. It is one of my jobs to make sure that I am not going to be the black in the Reagan Administration that gets tarred and feathered."

Doing what she alleges that he did with her was a prescription for instant death. Clarence is not a fool. And quite frankly, Anita Hill is not worth that type of risk.

SEN. SPECTER: Thank you very much, Mr. Doggett. Very powerful.

Professor Kothe, just a question or two, and this is following up on what Senator Biden had asked you, and it relates to the testimony which you had given that Professor Hill was very complimentary about Judge Thomas. There has been considerable testimony given by people who have tried to explain Professor Hill's activities in the sense that she was controlled by Judge Thomas when she worked for him, and that even after she left him she needed him for a variety of assistance.

But my question to you is did there come a point where she had sufficient independence from Judge Thomas so that a continuation of laudatory, complimentary comments which you have testified about would tend to undercut her credibility that he had said these dastardly things to her early on?

MR. KOTHE: I am not so sure that I grasped the essence of your question. I don't know that she was ever dependent upon him for adulation. She had a continuing relationship, I think of a professional nature, with the EEOC. She was doing some studies and getting materials from them, and the things that we were working on together, we both derived information from the EEO office.

Just how extensive was her continued interaction with Chairman Thomas, I really don't know.

SEN. SPECTER: Well, let me break it down for you, Professor Kothe, to this extent. You have testified that you thought her charges were inconceivable, as I think you have earlier said. Is that correct?

MR. KOTHE: Yes. Absolutely.

SEN. SPECTER: And you have based that on your testimony that when you would talk to her about Judge Thomas she would consistently compliment Judge Thomas. Correct?

MR. KOTHE: Correct.

SEN. SPECTER: So, is it your conclusion that if she consistently said complimentary things about him that it could not be true that he had done these dastardly deeds?

MR. KOTHE: Yes, that would be my conclusion. It is just so utterly incongruent and inconsistent that a person that would speak of him almost reverently as a hero, as a person—a remarkable person, she would say, as a person of untiring energy, she spoke of him, as I said earlier, as a devoted father.

I have never heard her speak of him but in pretty much relatively glowing terms. Never have I heard her say anything critical about him, even when we were discussing the subject of sexual harassment.

So, in that situation with a person that I respected and a person that I admired, I just cannot in my mentations equate how utterly impossible, grotesque statements could be made about this person that she spoke of to me with such high admiration.

SEN. SPECTER: The follow-up question to that is some have sought to explain her continuing association with Judge Thomas on the basis that she needed him, that he was her benefactor. And my question to you is would it be necessary for her to go as far as she did in the kind of complimentary statements she made to you on a personal basis to maintain that kind of an association where she could go back to him, for example, for letters of recommendation?

MR. KOTHE: Well, certainly she needed no further letters of recommendation after she established herself as a teacher. She was a good teacher.

This is not a young woman that is obsequious and fawning and retiring. She was a very positive person. In our faculty meetings she was forthright. She was always a strong person. She didn't need Clarence Thomas to continue in her career of teaching, which she has done and become tenured at the University of Oklahoma.

SEN. SPECTER: So your conclusion was when she complimented Judge Thomas she meant it?

MR. KOTHE: I had no reason to believe she didn't.

SEN. SPECTER: And, if she complimented Judge Thomas, it would be totally inconsistent with his having said these terrible things to her?

MR. KOTHE: Utterly inconsistent.

SEN. SPECTER: And the final point is the one where Senator Biden asked you would she have been reluctant to talk to you in truthful derogatory terms considering the fact that you were in a sense an employee of Chairman Thomas?

MR. KOTHE: I wouldn't think there was any basis for her having a reluctance to disclose to me anything that was of that nature if, indeed, it were a fact. I think that our relationship was such that she could have confidence in me.

I didn't need the position with Clarence Thomas. She didn't need Clarence Thomas to keep the position she had. We were both ad hoc in that sense, working on something that was avocational with us, from the point of view of our then situation.

SEN. SPECTER: Thank you very much. Thank you, Mr. Chairman.

THE CHAIRMAN: Thank you, Senator. The Senator from Massachusetts indicates he would like to question.

SEN. KENNEDY: Just for a moment, Mr. Doggett. When you were at Harvard, did you say you headed the Afro students' organization for student assistance?

MR. DOGGETT: Senator, what I said was that in the second year I was asked by my co-students to be the chairman of the Education Committee, of what at that time was called the Afro-American Student Union.

SEN. KENNEDY: And that was a tutorial program for kids in Cambridge, or what was that?

MR. DOGGETT: No. Harvard Business School has a program to weed out people that it does not feel deserve an Harvard MBA. It is called hitting the screen. It is one of the most intense academic experiences that they have. The Afro-American Student Union is a membership organization of black American students at Harvard

Business School, and those of us who are second-years organized programs to do what we can, not only to prevent first-years from hitting the screen, but to do everything possible to make it possible for them to excel.

My fellow students asked me to be the chairperson of this committee and to organize programs for Harvard Business School MBA students in their first year.

SEN. KENNEDY: Well, that is fine. I was just interested in whether you were working through the Phyllis Brooks House or community programs. Because the Business School, I believe, has a program. I just wanted to see whether you were associated with it.

MR. DOGGETT: No, sir.

SEN. KENNEDY: Thank you very much.

THE CHAIRMAN: Senator Brown?

SEN. THURMOND: Senator Brown?

SEN. BROWN: Thank you, Mr. Chairman.

THE CHAIRMAN: I am sorry. I am sorry.

SEN. LEAHY: Mr. Chairman, we go twenty some odd minutes on that side, thirty-eight—I am sorry, forty-eight seconds on this side. Just a couple of questions.

SEN. THURMOND: Are we next over here?

THE CHAIRMAN: Well, apparently Senator Kennedy yielded the remainder of his five minutes.

SEN. THURMOND: Hold off for just a minute then.

SEN. BROWN: Okay.

SEN. LEAHY: Mr. Doggett, you said that in the years that you have known John Carr, he never mentioned knowing Anita Hill. You are not suggesting that John Carr didn't know Anita Hill, are you?

MR. DOGGETT: Absolutely not, Senator.

SEN. LEAHY: Okay.

MR. DOGGETT: It is clear that he did.

SEN. LEAHY: The fact that he didn't mention her to you is one thing.

MR. DOGGETT: Senator, I asked John Carr specifically about who he was going out with and whether or not he was getting married.

SEN. LEAHY: I understand. I think, though, that we should perhaps go by Mr. Carr's sworn statement here this afternoon. It might be the best testimony, rather than whether he thought it necessary to discuss it with you whether he knew her or not.

Now, in your statement you talked about how much you have known Professor Hill. You met her at a social function in 1982. You had two or three phone conversations in which you were primarily interested in having her get you in touch with Harry Singleton. You met outside, I think, Clarence Thomas's office. You bumped into each other jogging, and you explained how you jog in place, so you couldn't talk to her there. Somehow, other plans to go out fell through. Then you saw each other at a party and, according to you, Professor Hill said, "I'm very disappointed in you. You really shouldn't lead on women and let them down."

Now, you have described these contacts with her as minimal. Professor Hill, incidentally, testified she has little or no recollection of you. When I pressed her—and I asked her specifically—she said she thinks she recalls that you were tall.

Now, based on such minimal contacts with Professor Hill, how could you conclude that she had fantasies about your sexual interest in her, or do you just feel that you have some kind of a natural irresistibility?

MR. DOGGETT: My wife says I do.

SEN. LEAHY: Well, Anita Hill apparently doesn't say you do, Mr. Doggett.

MR. DOGGETT: Sir—

SEN. LEAHY: She doesn't even remember you.

MR. DOGGETT: No, she didn't say that, sir.

SEN. LEAHY: She said she barely remembers you. When I asked her to describe you she had some difficulty and thought that you were tall.

MR. DOGGETT: I looked at Anita Hill's face when you folks mentioned my name. She remembers me, Senator, I assure you of that.

Now, to answer your question, the reason I thought her statements were so bizarre was because our contact was so limited. If we had had much more contact with each other, and as the good Senator Chairman had said, she had come up to me at the end and said, "John, you know we've been seeing, running into each other time and time again," then her comment would have been much more understandable. Since we had had so little contact, I found it to be a bizarre comment.

SEN. LEAHY: You have remarkable insight into her: You are able to watch her face and know when we mentioned your name."By golly! John Doggett's name gets mentioned, this woman is, Wow!"

It really triggered a bell: is that what you are saying? I don't understand. Mr. Doggett, I know this has been an interesting experience for you. You have talked about how Tom Brokaw's office is looking forward—

MR. DOGGETT: Sir, it has not been interesting. It has been very painful, been very difficult. It has interfered with my life. It has resulted in me getting threats and obscene phone calls on my telephone, people approaching me and accosting me in public. This is not fun, sir.

SEN. LEAHY: But, Mr. Doggett, what I am saying is you had these very minimal contacts. Yet you have been able to analyze Anita Hill from just jogging in place and talking to her, and from talking to her on the phone a couple of times when you asked her to set up a meeting with somebody else, you are able to figure out that she has a problem with being rejected by men, and that she has fantasies about sexual interest in her.

Are you able to make such thorough judgments about everybody you meet for such a short period of time? And I mean that seriously.

MR. DOGGETT: I understand, Senator. I appreciate your question and I think it is a very fair question. Let me do what I can to try to assist you in understanding how I could say what I said.

The jogging incidence, I wanted to jog in place for a few seconds and then move on. She made it very clear that she would like the conversation to be more involved by her body language, by her questions: Well, where do you live? Why are you jogging in this neighborhood? I stopped jogging and we had a conversation that lasted between five or ten minutes. I don't remember exactly how long it was. It was a long time ago.

As I remember it, she was the one who initiated the suggestion that we have dinner. I also observed her from time to time at the Black Yale parties that we had. As she had conversations with me, my sense, unprofessional, limited as it was, was that she was trying to engage people in conversations and to prolong conversations. Based on my experience, it suggested an interest. I never saw any of those conversations result in people continuing to talk with her.

Now that is totally unscientific and it is just a point of view.

SEN. LEAHY: You don't have an aversion to long conversations, do you, Mr. Doggett?

MR. DOGGETT: When somebody is trying to, to use the terminology "hit on somebody," and the result is people walk away, and you see that happen more than one time, it leads you to believe, Senator, that maybe something is not working.

SEN. LEAHY: You said in your sworn affidavit that Anita Hill was frustrated not being a part of Clarence Thomas's inner circle.

MR. DOGGETT: That is correct, Senator.

SEN. LEAHY: From these minimal contacts, you were able to deduce that?

MR. DOGGETT: The look on Anita's face when we were in the outer office of Clarence Thomas's office at EEOC when I did not say, "I'm getting ready to talk with Clarence, why don't you come on in with me," the look on her face is the basis for that decision.

Now, you and anybody else may feel that I did not have sufficient information to justify making that opinion, but that is what I said and that is what I felt.

SEN. LEAHY: Let me make sure I understand this. By her body language, you knew that she was concerned about not being part of Thomas's inner circle? From the look on her face outside of Thomas's office when you spoke to her, you are able to discern what was in her mind? And then watching her on television, by the look on her face when I mentioned your name, you are able to draw other conclusions about her remembrance of you?

MR. DOGGETT: That is my sense, sir.

SEN. LEAHY: That is all right. I just want to make sure I understand your ability of perception.

And, Dean, you have testified that the Clarence Thomas you knew could not possibly have made the statements Anita Hill claims he made, and I understand that. You stated that very forcefully, sir.

Do you believe that the Clarence Thomas you knew could enjoy talking about pornographic movies? I mean, that is one of the things that was alleged. Anita Hill alleged that he talked to her about pornographic movies. Are you saying that the Clarence Thomas you knew wouldn't even enjoy talking about pornographic movies?

MR. KOTHE: I can't believe it. I can't just believe that this man would even think in terms of pornographic movies. All of my relationship with him was at such a high level, talking about books of religion and philosophy and the things that he was reading. I can't imagine this man would have any diversion in the area that you describe. I just can't.

SEN. LEAHY: I understand. I understand, Dean.

You are aware, however, that a supporter, a Ms. Coleman, has been quoted in the *New York Times* as saying that at law school he didn't talk about religion or philosophy, that he talked about pornographic movies?

MR. KOTHE: I didn't get that. Will you please say it again?

SEN. LEAHY: I said you said that the man you know would talk probably about books and religion, but you could not conceive of him talking about pornographic movies. You knew that one of his supporters, strong supporters—she has written a letter to me, in fact, in support of him—a Ms. Coleman, has been quoted in the *New York Times* as saying that Judge Thomas used to talk about pornographic films at law school? Does that surprise you at all?

MR. KOTHE: It does.

SEN. LEAHY: Thank you. And you have—just very quickly, you have no way of knowing from your own personal knowledge whether Anita Hill is telling the truth about what Clarence Thomas said to her?

MR. KOTHE: No.

SEN. LEAHY: And, Mr. Doggett, would your answer be the same? You know of nothing from your personal knowledge whether she is telling the truth or not? I know your opinion which you have expressed here. But of your personal knowledge, do you know?

MR. DOGGETT: I have absolutely no information.

SEN. LEAHY: And, Mr. Stewart, of your own personal knowledge?

MR. STEWART: My personal knowledge of Clarence Thomas would lead me to conclude that she was, in fact, lying.

SEN. LEAHY: But, of your own personal knowledge, you don't know whether Clarence Thomas sexually harassed Anita Hill?

MR. STEWART: No. I don't know that we, the term sexual harass or said the things she said[*sic*]. I think we are confused about all of that.

I will restate my statement and say that my personal knowledge of Clarence Thomas would make it incredible for me to believe the things she has alleged.

SEN. LEAHY: Do you know that Judge Thomas said that if somebody did the things that Anita Hill claims that he did, if somebody did that, Judge Thomas freely admits that that would be sexual harassment. But you don't know of your own personal knowledge whether that happened or not, is that correct?

MR. STEWART: I don't know that it happened. I conclude that Clarence Thomas did not do it.

SEN. LEAHY: Thank you.

Now, Mr. Grayson, of your personal knowledge, you don't know whether Clarence Thomas sexually harassed Anita Hill?

MR. GRAYSON: I have no personal knowledge.

SEN. LEAHY: Thank you.

SEN. HEFLIN: I will just ask one minute and that will do it. Dean, Clarence Thomas wrote a letter of recommendation for Anita Hill to you and she became a member of the law school at the Oral Roberts University. And is it correct that you wrote a letter of recommendation to the Dean of the University of Oklahoma Law School when she went there to teach at the University of Oklahoma?

MR. KOTHE: I think I talked to Dean Swank, I don't remember writing the letter.

SEN. HEFLIN: Well, he wrote, Clarence Thomas wrote you?

MR. KOTHE: Yes.

SEN. HEFLIN: Did you, in talking to the Dean of the University of Oklahoma Law School, did you give her a good recommendation?

MR. KOTHE: Oh, yes.

SEN. HEFLIN: A great recommendation?

MR. KOTHE: Yes.

SEN. HEFLIN: All right, thank you.

SEN. SIMON: Mr. Chairman, just one thirty-second comment to Mr. Doggett. When your counselor suggested the Illinois Institute of Technology rather than MIT or Cal Tech, let me tell you that counselor was recommending an excellent, superb school in Illinois. It was not a put-down.

MR. DOGGETT: All right.

SEN. LEAHY: The only trouble with that, Senator Simon, is that there is probably no one up at this hour of the night to see you say that plug, but we will make sure that you have a certified copy of the record in the morning.

SEN. THURMOND: Professor Kothe, I have two very brief questions. Knowing Clarence Thomas as you do, and knowing Anita Hill as you do, do you give any credibility to her charges against Clarence Thomas?

MR. KOTHE: The last part?

Would I what?

SEN. THURMOND: Do you give any credibility to her charges against Clarence Thomas?

MR. KOTHE: No, the answer is I do not.

I can't believe that she would even say that. I can't believe that she would put that kind of words in her mouth and I can't believe that she would ever say that about Clarence Thomas.

SEN. THURMOND: Well, do you give credibility to the charges or not?

MR. KOTHE: I do not.

SEN. THURMOND: What?

MR. KOTHE: I do not.

SEN. THURMOND: You do not.

The next question. You have had a close relationship with Clarence Thomas and Anita Hill. Do you believe the serious charges made against Judge Thomas by Professor Hill are true?

MR. KOTHE: I do not believe they are true.

SEN. THURMOND: You do not, that's all. I will yield to the Senator Simpson.

SEN. SIMPSON: It's been a long night and thank you so much Professor, and

Mr. Doggett, and Mr. Stewart and Mr. Grayson. I bet you two gentlemen wish you hadn't gone to the ABA convention in Atlanta if it was going to cost you this kind of a night, did you?

MR. STEWART: It's well worth it, Your Honor, to clear the name of Clarence Thomas.

SEN. SIMPSON: Let me tell you, it is true, you have to break it with levity because it does get so, it is so stunning. But I do ask you both, you two are really quite critical. And you have been asked very little but the questions you have been asked have been very important.

But you two are probably the two who have seen her most recently, and got an idea of her state of mind about Clarence Thomas in the midst of his travail. In other words, he has been in the tank now for 106 days. And you saw her in August and you spent thirty minutes with her, right?

MR. STEWART: If not longer.

SEN. SIMPSON: If not longer, and you talked about Clarence and lots of other things as we do, we lawyers at bar conventions.

MR. STEWART: Mostly Clarence, because that is what we had in common.

SEN. SIMPSON: And that was in an informal way, you are having a drink or just sitting, talking or just that was it?

MR. STEWART: The former.

SEN. SIMPSON: And she was very pleased about Clarence Thomas?

MR. STEWART: Yes.

SEN. SIMPSON: Or indicated that?

MR. STEWART: Yes, Senator.

SEN. SIMPSON: Proud of him, was she proud of him?

MR. STEWART: There seems to be—there was such euphoria, I would assume she was proud of him.

SEN. SIMPSON: You recall that and her voice and her demeanor?

MR. STEWART: Laughing, smiling, warm.

SEN. SIMPSON: And saying, isn't it great about Clarence?

MR. STEWART: And how much he deserved it and that, essentially in other tones that his hard work was paying off.

MR. GRAYSON: Senator, if I could comment. That particular afternoon was the first and only time I have met Anita Hill, and Mr. Stewart and Ms. Hill really spent a few moments sort of reminiscing, they both worked together. So, sort of as an observer, I clearly walked away from that meeting with the clear sense that Ms. Hill shared the excitement about Judge Thomas's nomination, and was, indeed, very supportive of it.

SEN. SIMPSON: Well, and I am sure you found her testimony here incredible.

MR. GRAYSON: Well, I think the reason we are here is incredible. It doesn't surprise me that she would say that after making all of these other allegations.

I would have to say on my end, I was a bit surprised by it. I am not a student of people but I think to the extent of watching the interaction and the discussion, I was indeed surprised that the reaction was that she [saw] Carlton's enthusiasm for the judge and didn't want to—I don't remember her exact words—but basically didn't want to ruin the mood of the little meeting that took place. If that is, in fact, the case, my response would be that she is very good because that was not clear in my perception of the conversation that took place.

SEN. SIMPSON: Well. I thank you, very much for coming. And I realize the serious reason that you are both here. And Mr. Doggett, you have been dealing with the issue of what you saw of her and what she said to you. I accept your summary of your affidavit and your testimony as something you feel very strongly about. And apparently if someone else does not that is truly a difference of opinion.

But to you, from your background and the way you describe it, I understand your reaction and I believe it sounds like a natural reaction to you. And you, Professor, thank you. You have been very kind and very patient, and I would like to, if I were in law school, I would have loved to be under your tutelage. I had some rugged rascals that nearly drive me insane. I needed kindness, I needed kindness and sweetness that you could have given to me.

SEN. LEAHY: They succeeded, Alan.

SEN. SIMPSON: And as for Leahy—

SEN. LEAHY: Alan, I think you succeeded in that insanity drive.

SEN. SIMPSON: You see what happened to Leahy and I, we were in a hearing here one day and a courier came in and he said, I am looking for a bald-headed guy with gray hair and glasses and homely as hell and they said there are two of them, meaning myself and Leahy.

So I want to tell you if we all started to trot out what we did in law school that ought to be a riot for the American public. I don't know what Clarence Thomas did in law school, but I got a hunch about it. And I believe *Playboy* came out while I was in law school and I remember reading it for its articles and its editorial content. So maybe we can just drop all reflections of what we did in law school, what we watched. It is like doctors going to medical school and calling their cadaver certain names, you know, and lawyers doing all the black humor and the white humor and the ghastly humor and the grotesque and the drinking. Well, some of you may have missed law school.

Anyway I thank you for coming and—

MR. STEWART: Senator, may I make one comment?

SEN. SIMPSON: Yes, sir.

SEN. THURMOND: I believe we have six minutes left on this round.

SEN. SIMPSON: Mr. Stewart had a comment.

SEN. LEAHY: One thing I do want to say in fairness to the professor when I quoted from the *New York Times* Ms. Coleman's discussion of the X-rated films, the professor obviously had not seen that article. I am not going to go back to it—but out of fairness to him, could somebody from the staff just give that to the professor, please?

SEN. SIMPSON: Mr. Stewart had a question.

MR. STEWART: I would just like to make one comment. I understand the need for levity at this late hour but we are here for a very, very serious matter. I think we need not lose sight of the fact that separate and apart from Supreme Court confirmation, Clarence Thomas is a sitting Federal judge. This process has treated him, in the last several days, like he is a foreman in a manufacturing plant. We are dealing with claims that are—that's a nullity at law.

Allegations come in ten years, eight years, whatever, way beyond the statute of limitation and I think we need to keep these things in focus and in vogue when we are trying to make a decision about who is telling what. We have two witnesses today for Ms. Hill who were told two different things. Two were told that she was being sexually harassed by her supervisor and two were told by her boss.

We still don't know who they are. There were giant leaps in logic to conclude that it was Clarence Thomas, but that is clearly not the case. Many were asked the question of why we are here? We are here because of a leak, not because of allegations, but because of a leak. This is publicized because of a leak by the committee, somebody on the committee.

Clarence should not be the person who receives the brunt of this. The very same rights that they accuse him of being against, they took from him by leaking this information.

That's all I have.

SEN. THURMOND: I have propounded the question to Professor Kothe and I want to ask a second one and I just put one question to you three gentlemen.

Even though Anita Hill may believe what she said was true, in your opinion, is there any merit in the charges made by her against Clarence Thomas?

MR. GRAYSON: In my judgment, Senator, absolutely not.

SEN. THURMOND: Mr. Stewart?

MR. STEWART: In my judgment, Senator, absolutely not. Whether they are lies or a product of fantasy, they should be dismissed.

SEN. THURMOND: Mr. Doggett?

MR. DOGGETT: Absolutely not. Clarence has been trying to do some things that are extremely important for this country and for any of the things that Anita said to have been true would have totally made it impossible for him to be successful.

SEN. THURMOND: I believe, Dean Kothe, you have already answered that question.

MR. KOTHE: Yes, I share with those views.

THE CHAIRMAN: Are we prepared to dismiss this panel?

I am sorry. Senator Brown?

SEN. BROWN: Mr. Chairman. I have a few brief questions and I will try to make them brief.

Dean Kothe, your statement indicates that you saw Professor Hill and Judge Thomas together on a number of occasions. Do you remember how many occasions?

MR. KOTHE: I don't think I said a number of occasions. I said I saw them in Washington, in my home, at the seminar, that was about it.

SEN. BROWN: Could you characterize for us the nature of the conversations between them, the way they acted toward each other?

MR. KOTHE: Oh, it was most friendly. And, in fact, it was a matter of joviality and a lot of laughter. You know, when you are around Clarence Thomas in a relaxed mode, it is a time of joy. And they would reminisce about certain situations that I was not privy to in their experience in Washington and people that they would talk about and they would talk and laugh. But it was always one of pleasure.

SEN. BROWN: Did you detect any latent hostility in the relationship?

MR. KOTHE: Oh, no, you couldn't possibly have.

SEN. BROWN: Did you have any occasion in the time you knew Clarence Thomas to see him off-guard, see him in relaxed situations?

MR. KOTHE: I tried to convey that. I have ridden with him in a car for three hours down in Georgia, right in the swamps where he said he was reared. I have been in offices with him. I have been on several college campuses with him. I have been with faculty. I have been with students. I have been in my home when we just stripped down and getting ready for bed and in my library and just talking for a couple of three hours.

SEN. BROWN: In those relaxed situations, did his vocabulary include any of the words we have talked about in these hearings?

MR. KOTHE: I said this over and over again, I never ever heard this man use a profane word. And like I am experienced with other lawyers and other men and in a long discourse inevitably there is a story somebody wants to tell. I never heard him tell a dirty story, so to speak, or make an off-color remark.

It just has to be that this man in the situations I have seen him in would have to be the greatest actor in history to have disguised this part of his nature that has been described here, this totally unreal.

SEN. BROWN: Thank you.

Mr. Doggett, I liked your reaction to something. In reading through the transcript or reading through your testimony, your statement, it has been some time since I have been in a situation as an unmarried person, so I am not sure I am an expert on this at this point, but the conversation that took place seemed to me could be nothing more than someone flirting with you.

Specific[ally], the language, the conversation that you had with Professor Hill at the time, Anita Hill at the time, that the words could have been simply a way of flirting, not terribly serious in their content other than engaging. Would you comment on that?

MR. DOGGETT: I never perceived Anita to be flirting with me. I perceived her to, as a man, be indicating that if I was interested in getting to know her better that she would be interested.

SEN. BROWN: You thought the words were quite serious, not—

MR. DOGGETT: Sir, the comments that she made at the going away party to me, seemed to be very, very serious and that is how I took them.

SEN. BROWN: Mr. Stewart, one thing, Professor Hill here indicated that it was you who made the comment about Judge Thomas being, at least my recollection is that Judge Thomas being so well suited for the Court and wasn't it wonderful, and so on. And that rather than her instigating those remarks, that she merely maintained a politeness during that period without formally objecting but without her uttering those words.

Are you quite certain that those words came from Professor Hill?

MR. STEWART: I am absolutely certain that not only did they come from Ms. Hill but that they were surrounded by euphoria and a continuation of kudos for Judge Thomas that lasted more than a few minutes, that lasted almost over thirty minutes.

The one thing Anita Hill and I had in common was Judge Thomas. That was the subject of conversation. There were no negatives, there were all positives and Mr. Grayson was there and he had not met Ms. Hill before that very instant.

SEN. BROWN: Thank you.

Mr. Chairman, I want to yield back but if I could just make a note about the legal research that Senator Simpson did in law school.

We had a student in Colorado's law school, who did legal research because he took certain pictures out of the magazine and appended them to his answer in torts and in two or three places he received the highest grade in the class.

I will yield back.

THE CHAIRMAN: It is time to end this panel. Thank you, very much.

SEN. SIMPSON: Mr. Chairman, I just have something to enter into the record because my friend from Vermont talked about Lavita Coleman in a rather negative way and I wish that he had finished the sentence.

She also said that neither she nor the other students were offended by his amusing comments about pornographic material and then she said, Ms. Coleman, now a lawyer in Washington continued: "Indeed we would have been hypocrites to have been offended since very few of us failed to attend one or more similar films that were shown on the Yale university campus while we were in school." We did not even do that in Laramie. So that shows you how far behind the curve we were, but then she went on to say and I end with this sentence, she called, this is the same woman about this pornographic stuff, she called him, calling Clarence Thomas—"Particularly sensitive and caring regarding the professional and personal concerns of the women he knows and with whom he has worked and she seriously doubted that he harassed Professor Hill."

That is what is wrong with this process, right there.

SEN. LEAHY: Well, Mr. Chairman, as the Senator from Wyoming knows, I prefaced that by saying that Ms. Coleman is a very strong supporter of Clarence Thomas.

And the only reason I brought it up and sent the whole newspaper is that it would be in context for Professor Kothe because he had said that he just could not imagine under any circumstances Judge Thomas going to an X-rated movie. That was the sole point of it. But as I have also stated, Ms. Coleman is a strong supporter and has written to me strongly in support of Judge Thomas.

THE CHAIRMAN: Thank you, gentlemen. I truly appreciate your willingness to be here as long as you have. There is only one consolation you all have; there is a panel of nine people to follow you. Just be thankful you're not among them.

Thank you very much.

SEN. THURMOND: We thank you very much for your appearance.

THE CHAIRMAN: Our next and last panel—it is almost inappropriate to say welcome at this hour of the night, but I thank you all very much for your willingness to be here, and particularly for your willingness to be here at this late hour.

As I indicated to you a moment ago, we are going to insist on the three-minute rule that was announced beforehand, notwithstanding the fact, I am told, there are two witnesses who were going to be here, and for understandable and appropriate reasons, in light of the hour, are not here.

But let me ask the timekeeper, when the clock goes on, will the yellow light go on, with one minute to go? So, when the amber light goes on, you will have a minute. One of you asked me how will you know when we are getting near three minutes, and Ms. Johnson indicated to me that she was pregnant and due at any moment, and so I strongly urge my colleagues not to have it that they be responsible for her being here any longer than is necessary. If I can't convince you, on my behalf, to stop questioning, I hope that you will have some consideration for Ms. Johnson, who has not asked for any. I am using you as a ploy, Ms. Johnson, to try and see if we can move this thing along.

Now, our panel is made up of Patricia Johnson, Director of Labor Relations at the EEOC; Pamela Talkin, former chief of staff for Clarence Thomas at the EEOC; Janet Brown, former press secretary for Senator John Danforth; Linda Jackson, research associate, Department of Education; Nancy Altman, formerly of the Department of Education; Anna Jenkins, a former secretary at the EEOC; Lori Saxon, former assistant for congressional relations of the Department of Education; and Connie Newman, Director, Office of Personnel Management.

Thank you all very much.

Now, I was asked by the panel, they apparently have decided how they would like to proceed, and I would just yield to the panel to proceed in three-minute intervals seriatim, and we will finish.

I beg your pardon, I am required to swear you all in. I am sorry. Do you swear that the testimony you are about to give will be the truth, the whole truth, and nothing but the truth, so help you, God?

MS. JOHNSON: I do.

MS. TALKIN: I do.

MS. BROWN: I do.

MS. NEWMAN: I do.

MS. JACKSON: I do.

MS. ALTMAN: I do.

MS. JENKINS: I do.

MS. SAXON: I do.

THE CHAIRMAN: Thank you very much.

TESTIMONY OF A PANEL OF:
NANCY ALTMAN, formerly of the Department of Education
PATRICIA JOHNSON, Director Labor Relations, Equal Employment Opportunity Commision
LINDA M. JACKSON, Social Science Research Analyst, EEOC
JANET H. BROWN, Former Press Secretary to SEN. JOHN DANFORTH
LORI SAXON, Former Assistant For Congressional Relations Department of Education
PAMELA TALKIN, Former Chief of Staff, EEOC
ANNA JENKINS, Former Secretary, EEOC
CONSTANCE NEWMAN, Director, Office of Personnel Management.

TESTIMONY OF PATRICIA CORNWELL JOHNSON

MS. JOHNSON: Good morning, Chairman Biden, Senator Thurmond and other members of this committee.

I am Patricia Cornwell Johnson, and I currently work as the Director of Labor Relations of the Equal Employment Opportunity Commission. I received my Bachelor's Degree from the American University here in Washington, and my law degree from the Georgetown University Law Center. I am a member of the bar of the District of Columbia, the U.S. Supreme Court, the U.S. Court of Appeals for the District of Columbia Circuit, as well as the majority of other U.S. Courts of Appeals.

I received my labor relations training at the National Labor Relations Boards. I moved from there to corporate America, then to a major transit authority, before going to the EEOC. I work in an area that is dominated by men and I have never met a man who treated me with more dignity and respect, who was more cordial and professional than was Judge Clarence Thomas.

Shortly after joining the Commission—and I must apologize to my mother for making this statement on worldwide TV, and I am grateful that she is asleep—then-Chairman Thomas became aware that I used profanity in some exuberant exchanges with union officials. Chairman Thomas made it clear to me that that was unacceptable conduct which would not be tolerated. I was shocked because up until that time, such language had indeed been acceptable, almost expected—it made me "one of the boys." Chairman Thomas insisted that his managers conduct themselves in a manner that was above reproach and he held himself to that same high standard.

I had occasion to meet with Chairman Thomas alone to discuss labor relations and strategies. He was always professional. As a labor attorney with approximately fifteen years of experience, I have drafted policy statements concerning sexual harassment, I have trained managers concerning what constitutes harassment, how to deal with such allegations.

Furthermore, with a previous employer, I was a victim of sexual harassment. It was the most degrading and humiliating experience of my professional career. I confided in friends and family concerning the best manner to confront it. I did confront it and I eventually left that position. But I must tell you that, during the time I had to continue to work with the perpetrator I avoided contact, especially one-on-one contact with him, and since leaving that position I have never had any further contact with that man.

I do not believe these allegations that have been leveled against Judge Thomas. Moreover based on my professional experience, as well as my personal experience, I do not believe that a woman who has been victimized by the outrageously lewd, vile and vulgar behavior that has been described here would want to have, let alone maintain, any kind of relationship with a man that victimized her.

THE CHAIRMAN: Thank you very much, and thank you for staying within the time. Whoever is next please move forward.

TESTIMONY OF LINDA M. JACKSON

MS. JACKSON: Chairman Biden, Senator Thurmond and members of the committee: I would like to correct the record. I am employed as a social science research analyst at the EEOC.

When I first met Clarence Thomas in 1981, he was Assistant Secretary for Civil Rights in the Department of Education. My work required him to contact his office to secure certain data and information. After finding out the type of information I needed, Clarence Thomas indicated that any follow-up contact I had with his office should be through his aide, Anita Hill. He described her as someone who would help me navigate and put me in touch with the right people at OCR. He spoke in terms any mentor would use, explaining she was very bright and knowledgeable about the workings of OCR.

During that time, Anita and I began to have lunch and discuss both work and personal things. She referred to Clarence Thomas with admiration, and never once mentioned anything was going wrong at work. She seemed excited to be a special assistant to a very visible public official. I never saw any strained relations between them, whenever I saw them together in the workplace or at a meeting. She would generally look at him with a smile on her face and have the kind of positive demeanor that would suggest she respected and liked him as a person.

We often discussed the social scene in Washington. In the context of such discussions, it seems that she would have mentioned something, if she were having a problem at the office, even if she did not name a specific person. Subsequent discussions I had with Anita also yielded no mention of anything improper on the part of Clarence Thomas.

It is difficult for me to believe that Anita would follow her supervisor to another agency, if he was subjecting her to the things she has alleged. I remember Anita Hill as an intelligent woman and one who would have found some way to retain her job at the department or find another in either the public or private sector, if she were unhappy.

After meeting Clarence Thomas through my job, I ran into him in the hallway of my apartment building and found we lived in the same place. We began to have numerous conversations about work, politics and personal issues. We became very good friends in the process.

I believe I know the basic nature of this man better than most people in this room. I believe, unequivocally, Clarence Thomas's denial of these allegations. This is a very honorable man who has the highest respect for women. He always treated me with utmost respect and was more sensitive to women than most men I know. He never engaged me in discussions of any kind that could be considered demeaning to women.

He was often troubled by those women he knew, both professionally and women who were having difficulties with personal problems, particularly treatment by male friends, coworkers or spouses. He and I had numerous conversations about abuse of women, physically, emotionally and verbally. You see, Senators, he helped me pick up the pieces of my own crushed spirit, after I left an abusive marriage.

His sensitivity and honor, his respect for women, his helping attitude toward all people in need, makes these allegations even more ludicrous.

THE CHAIRMAN: Thank you very much.

Who is next?

TESTIMONY OF JANET H. BROWN

MS. BROWN: My name is Janet Brown, Mr. Chairman.

SEN. HATCH: Would you pull your microphone over, Ms. Brown?

MS. BROWN: Yes, I will.

SEN. HATCH: I would love to hear you.

MS. BROWN: This will be very brief.

I have known Clarence Thomas very well for twelve years. We worked for two years very closely here in the Senate on Senator Danforth's staff. He is a man of the highest principle, honesty, integrity and honor in all of his personal and professional actions.

A number of years ago, I was sexually harassed in the workplace. It was a demeaning, humiliating, sad and revolting experience. There was an intensive and lengthy internal investigation of this case, which is the route that I chose to pursue. Let me assure you that the last thing I would ever have done is follow the man who did this to a new job, call him on the phone or voluntarily share the same air space ever again.

Other than my immediate family, the one person who was the most outraged, compassionate, caring and sensitive to me was Clarence Thomas. He helped me work through the pain and talk through the options. No one who has been through it can talk about sexual harassment dispassionately. No one who takes it seriously would do it.

I don't subscribe to the belief that men, because they are men, don't understand sexual harassment. My husband, my father and my brother understand it. Clarence

Thomas understands it. And because he understands it, he wouldn't do it.

SEN. KENNEDY: [presiding]. Ms. Saxon?

TESTIMONY OF LORI SAXON

MS. SAXON: I worked at the Department of Education in the Office for Civil Rights from September 1981 until September 1982. I was twenty-four years old at the time. I was the confidential assistant to Clarence Thomas. In that capacity, I handled congressional relations and public affairs. My office was just down the hall from Anita Hill's during her tenure at the Department of Education.

I never saw any harassment go on in the office. The office was run very professionally. Clarence Thomas and Anita Hill were always very cordial and friendly in their relations. There was never any evidence of any harassment toward any of the female employees. I dealt with Anita Hill on a daily basis in performing my duties. She was happy in her position and she liked working for Clarence Thomas.

Anita Hill never indicated to me that he was harassing her. Clarence Thomas generally left the door of his office open, so if he had any meeting with Hill or any other employees, they were in view. He operated with an open-door policy with every member of the staff, regardless of gender. I never saw him meet in private with a female employee, without someone else present. Unless it was a group meeting and there were many staffers present, the door would be open and his secretary would be right outside the door.

Anita Hill was the only special assistant who accompanied Clarence Thomas to the Equal Employment Opportunity Commission, upon his appointment in August of 1982. Anita told me that she was very excited about the opportunity to work for the chairman of the EEOC. She related to me that she was pleased that Clarence was taking her with him.

I believe Anita Hill's statements that she felt pressures to accompany Clarence Thomas to EEOC, because of fears of losing her job, are simply untrue. I and the rest of the senior staff of the Office for Civil Rights found other positions within a few months. That is how the process of being a political appointee worked.

I was Clarence Thomas's confidential assistant for a year. My job required that I meet with him at least once a day. He never made an inappropriate advance, uttered any off-color remarks, or used coarse language in my presence. I was younger and more politically active than Anita Hill. I introduced him to my friends in Washington, the political community and very social settings. I was the first person to bring and introduce him to a luncheon with Thomas Sowell and others at the Capitol Hill Club. During this entire period, he never made any inappropriate actions toward me or any other female with whom I saw him.

I understand what women in this country go through in the area of sexual harassment. There is no place for sexual harassment in the workplace. I experienced perhaps a different kind of harassment, by being a victim of a violent crime. I know what it is to have one's face violated. I know what it feels like to feel helpless and humiliated.

Let me assure you in no uncertain terms that no harassment took place in the workplace at the Office for Civil Rights.

SEN. KENNEDY: Thank you very much.

Ms. Altman.

TESTIMONY OF NANCY ALTMAN

MS. ALTMAN: My name is Nancy Altman. I consider myself a feminist. I am pro-choice. I care deeply about women's issues. In addition to working with Clarence Thomas at the Department of Education, I shared an office with him for two years in this building. Our desks were a few feet apart. Because we worked in such close quarters, I could hear virtually every conversation for two years that Clarence Thomas had. Not once in those two years did I ever hear Clarence Thomas make a sexist or offensive comment, not once.

I have myself been the victim of an improper, unwanted sexual advance by a supervisor. Gentlemen, when sexual harassment occurs, other women in the workplace know about it. The members of the committee seem to believe that when offensive behavior occurs in a private room, there can be no witnesses. This is wrong.

Sexual harassment occurs in an office in the middle of the workday. The victim is in a public place. The first person she sees immediately after the incident is usually the harasser's secretary. Co-workers, especially women, will notice an upset expression, a jittery manner, a teary or a distracted air, especially if the abusive behavior is occurring over and over and over again.

Further, the women I know who have been victimized always shared the experience with a female co-worker they could trust. They do this to validate their own experience, to obtain advice about options that they may pursue, to find out if others have been similarly abused, and to receive comfort. Friends outside the workplace make good comforters, but cannot meet the other needs.

It is not credible that Clarence Thomas could have engaged in the kinds of behavior that Anita Hill alleges, without any of the women who he worked closest with—dozens of us, we could spend days having women come up, his secretaries, his chief of staff, his other assistants, his colleagues—without any of us having sensed, seen or heard something.

SEN. KENNEDY: Thank you very much.

Ms. Jenkins.

TESTIMONY OF ANNA JENKINS

MS. JENKINS: Chairman Biden, Senator Thurmond and other members of the committee, my name is Anna Jenkins, and I reside in Silver Spring, Maryland. I am a staff assistant in the Office of Policy Development at the White House. I was not asked by the White House to give a statement. I went to them and asked if it was okay for me to give a statement.

I have been a Federal employee since December 1965 and worked for the Equal

Employment Opportunity Commission from May 1970 to September 1989, with intermittent details to the White House under the Carter and Reagan Administrations.

I was employed as a secretary in the EEOC's Office of the Chairman in the Executive Secretariat as a staff specialist. During my tenure with the Office of the Chairman, I served under five chairpersons, William Brown, John Powell, Lowell Perry, Eleanor Holmes Norton, and Clarence Thomas. In September 1989, I left the EEOC to join the Bush Administration, Office of Policy Development.

When President Reagan appointed Clarence Thomas as chairman of the EEOC, I was the only employee left in the chairman's office from the previous administration. Upon Judge Thomas's arrival at the agency, I worked directly for him as his secretary until his confidential assistant Diane Holt and legal assistant Anita Hill came onboard. He brought them from the Department of Education.

Prior to Anita Hill joining the staff, she appeared quite anxious to work for the EEOC. In fact, she called Judge Thomas several times to inquire about the status of her appointment.

I recall the first day Ms. Hill reported to work at EEOC. She was very pleased and excited about being able to select an office with a big picture window overlooking the Watergate Hotel and the Potomac River.

I had daily contact with Anita Hill and Judge Thomas. We shared a suite of offices consisting of a reception area, conference room, kitchen, and five offices. Judge Thomas's conduct around me, Anita Hill, and other staffers was always proper and professional. I have never witnessed Judge Thomas say anything or do anything that could be construed as sexual harassment. I never witnessed him making sexual advances toward any female, nor have I witnessed him engaging in sexually oriented conversations with women.

I have witnessed Judge Thomas and Anita Hill interact in the office. At no time did the relationship appear strained nor Anita appear uncomfortable with the relationship.

I understand that at Anita's press conference she denied knowing Phylis Berry. I was confused by her denial, since Phylis Berry often visited the office while Anita worked there. I have seen them exchange greetings.

In closing, I wish to emphasize that I have the highest regard and respect for Judge Thomas. In light of my experience with him and the way I have seen him conduct himself around other females, I find this harassment allegation unbelievable.

SEN. KENNEDY: All right.

Ms. Newman.

TESTIMONY OF CONSTANCE NEWMAN

MS. NEWMAN: Constance Newman. I appreciate the opportunity to appear before you.

I am both saddened and optimistic as a result of these proceedings. I am saddened because of the way in which the raw nerves of America have been touched, the raw nerves of racism and sexism, leading to too much mistrust between too many of us. Many of these feelings are just below the surface of this great nation, and we are all the victims of it. We are all hurt in some way by the side of America that allows bigotry and unfairness to exist. We must come to terms with what is unfair in this basically fair nation.

I am saddened for my friend Judge Clarence Thomas, and his family. All who are in public life must sympathize with their plight.

I am saddened for Professor Anita Hill. Her life will never be the same. I don't know her, but I must believe that she must be a talented and conscientious woman, or she would not have completed the tough educational requirements of Yale Law School or be a tenured professor at a major law school. She must be a concerned black woman, or she would not have chosen to work in civil rights.

What was her motivation? Frankly, I do not know. I do not even want to speculate.

The waters are muddy around sexual harassment now, but I am optimistic. I am optimistic because I believe that as a result of these proceedings, you will know what I know about Judge Thomas. He is competent, he has integrity, he has true grit, and I do believe that these proceedings will make him even stronger and even more sensitive.

I have known him for ten years. That does not mean that we have not disagreed. We have. We have argued. Through the years he has changed his mind some; I have changed mine a little. But I have not changed my view about the basic decency and integrity of this man. I know him and have worked with him. I have worked in the halls of EEOC. Not once did I hear a hint of improper conduct. I would have heard. I heard of disagreements, but not improper conduct.

Finally, I am optimistic that positive change will take place as a result of these proceedings. America has seen and understood some of the delicate issues that we must face and will appreciate the governmental process, painful though it may be.

THE CHAIRMAN: You are a great optimist, Ms. Newman, but I am so delighted to hear somebody say that.

Ms. Talkin.

TESTIMONY OF PAMELA TALKIN

MS. TALKIN: As chief of staff of the EEOC for three years, I reported directly to then-Chairman Thomas. We worked very closely. We traveled together frequently, and we spent innumerable hours alone together and as many hours in the company of other women.

Judge Thomas was adamant that the women in the agency be treated with dignity and respect, and his own behavior towards women was scrupulous. There was never a hint of impropriety, and I mean a hint; never a gesture, never a look, never a word, never body language, none of the things that we women have a sixth sense about and that very few men have any sense about. [Laughter.]

THE CHAIRMAN: Thank you. [Laughter.]

MS. TALKIN: Needless to say, there was nothing explicit or coarse in his language. Judge Thomas viewed such conduct, and I quote, as "repugnant," "reprehensible," "deplorable," and "despicable." He would not tolerate it.

I have been in the work force for over thirty years. During that time I have endured varying degrees of sexual harassment, sometimes serious, sometimes subtle. I view myself as very alert to this; some of my men friends say, overly sensitive. It is in that context that I tell you that I have never met a man as sensitive. He has a feminist's understanding of sexual politics. He is a man who loathes locker room talk.

This is a man who, when I had momentary lapses of language, looked discomfited and never responded in kind.

This is a man who looked at his shoes when other men were craning their necks to look at a woman.

This is a man who spent countless hours talking to me about his efforts to raise his adolescent son to be a decent, dignified, reverent man of women, and urging his son to treat his teenage female companions with dignity and respect despite his raging hormones.

This is a man who understood the inherent imbalance of power in the workplace between men and women, and frowned upon even consensual romantic relationships because he did not want one woman in the agency to even mistakenly believe that her dignity had been compromised.

I have spent over eighteen years enforcing laws against employment discrimination, and I can tell you that I have never worked in a work environment where any individual, man or woman, was more committed to establishing a workplace free from discrimination and harassment. It is the saddest of ironies to me that the behavior that Judge Thomas found most abhorrent is the behavior that he is now being accused of.

THE CHAIRMAN: A very powerful statement, Ms. Talkin.

I apologize for being out of the room while some of you were testifying. I don't believe there are any questions from the panel. Your statements speak for themselves.

Before I dismiss this panel, though, I have an announcement to make, and that is that having spoken with Senator Danforth, and Senator Danforth representing, and that is enough for all of us, that he has spoken with Clarence Thomas—no, has not?

SEN. DANFORTH: Mr. Chairman, I have not. If you would like me to call him on this matter, I will—

THE CHAIRMAN: I think before I—

SEN. DANFORTH: [continuing]—but I can absolutely guarantee what the answer will be.

THE CHAIRMAN: Well, I think it may be useful to call.

SEN. DANFORTH: All right.

THE CHAIRMAN: And I think that out of an excess of caution, because this is of such consequence, not that I doubt your judgment on this, but it is—I will withhold. I will excuse the panel, but we will just recess in place for a minute here, and I ask everyone to wait just a minute because I will have an announcement, depending on the phone call, about tomorrow's proceedings that will— today's proceedings. Yes, I am sorry, it is two o'clock.

SEN. HATCH: You may want to wait, as well. You may just want to wait.

THE CHAIRMAN: Well, this two o'clock is better than two o'clock two nights ago. Then I was sitting in a dentist's chair, so it is getting better. At least we are in good company.

Let me suggest once again that Judge Thomas is indeed fortunate to have such friends and supporters as all of you women that are here, and again I thank you, truly thank you, for being here, and particularly at the hour. This is an unusual time to be summoned to the committee—now you weren't summoned—to come to the committee, to testify anywhere in the world, let alone here in this old magnificent room. So thank you all, and you all are dismissed.

SEN. THURMOND: If I may say a word?

THE CHAIRMAN: I'm sorry. I beg your pardon. Senator Thurmond would like to say a word.

SEN. THURMOND: Mr. Chairman.

On behalf of the Republican Senators I wish to commend you for your appearance and for the excellent statements you have made. And because you have made such outstanding statements, we have no questions on this side of the aisle.

THE CHAIRMAN: I won't characterize why anybody has no questions, but nonetheless, seriously, thank you all very, very much for being here.

Excuse me. Yes?

SEN. METZENBAUM: Mr. Chairman, I just said the chairman made a valiant effort to justify to the American people why we got a salary increase. We have been here until two o'clock.

THE CHAIRMAN: No, I learned a long time ago not to attempt to ever justify anything like that, and I am certainly not going to

SEN. SIMPSON: Mr. Chairman, if I may just, not a question, but it is very helpful to hear from women like we have heard over these days, who have been victims of sexual harassment, which is a very important thing for us. We hear it, we know it, we have hearings, but to hear it from you and especially to hear your reaction to it, and what you do and what your network is, and what it is in the workplace, and how that really works in real life, is very, very helpful and very, very informative for me. And I have a very enlightened woman that I have been living with for thirty-seven years, but she has enlightened me a great deal more these last days. So thank you again. Powerful statements.

SEN. KENNEDY: I believe you are excused. Thank you. [Laughter.]

THE CHAIRMAN: Gentlemen and ladies and everyone here, and members of the press who have been also equally as patient, both Judge Thomas and Professor Hill have decided that they do not wish to appear tomorrow.

Now there is one caveat. Senator Danforth has represented and indicated, with good reason, that having talked with Judge Thomas earlier, that if Ms. Hill didn't come back, he would not come back, and vice versa. But we formally haven't spoken to him this evening, so that if there were any change it would be six o'clock in the morning. There is no way to physically reach him. There is a recording on.

So, at any rate, I see no reasonable probability that anyone will change their mind. Based on that, this entire proceeding is ended.

[Whereupon, at 2:03 a.m., October 14, 1991, the committee was adjourned.]

APPENDIX A

LETTER AND AFFIDAVIT FROM SUKARI HARDNETT, FORMER SPECIAL ASSISTANT, EEOC, WASHINGTON, DC

Members of the Senate Judiciary Committee
U.S. Senate
Washington, D.C. 20510

October 13, 1991

Dear Senators,

I worked as a Special Assistant to Clarence Thomas at the EEOC from 1985 to 1986. I am writing because I am amazed and outraged at the "fatherly ambience" that he is getting away with projecting as an image of his office. Let me make it clear: I am not claiming that I was the victim of sexual harassment.

Clarence Thomas pretends that his only behavior toward those who worked as his special assistants was as a father to children, and a mentor to proteges. That simply isn't true. If you were young, black, female and reasonably attractive, you knew full well you were being inspected and auditioned as a female. You knew when you were in favor because you were always at his beck and call, being summoned constantly, tracked down wherever you were in the agency and given special deference by others because of his interest. And you knew when you had ceased to be an object of sexual interest — because you were barred from entering his office and treated as an outcast, or worse, a leper with whom contact was taboo. For my own part, I found his attention unpleasant, sought a transfer, was told one "just doesn't do that," insisted nonetheless and paid the price as an outcast for the remainder of my employment at EEOC.

I can understand why some of his special assistants are coming forward to his defense: he is the most powerful black man they know and possibly, the most influential they will ever know. They want to retain contact because they will need it to survive and to advance in a very tough world. But the atmosphere of absolute sterile propriety permeated by loving, nurturing but asexual concern is simply a lie. Women know when there are sexual dimensions to the attention they are receiving. And there was never any doubt about that dimension in Clarence Thomas' office. I have told all of this to Senate staff including the Chairman's staff in the weeks following the nomination. But in light of the importance which both ambience (in his office) and credibility have now assumed in these hearings, I felt obliged to communicate this in writing in order to put this on the record publicly.

Sincerely,
Sukari Hardnett
Address Deleted

APPENDIX A, CON'T

AFFIDAVIT

(District of Columbia)
Sukari Hardnett, having been duly sworn, make the following statement:
1 I worked as a Special Assistant to Clarence Thomas at the EEOC from 1985 to 1986.
2 I am amazed and outraged at the "fatherly ambience" that he is getting away with projecting as an image of his office.
3 I am not claiming that I was the victim of sexual harassment
4 Clarence Thomas and those who have tested on his behalf would have us believe that his only behavior toward those who worked as his special assistants was as a father to children, and a mentor to proteges. That simply isn't true.
5 If you were young, black, female, reasonably attractive and worked directly for Clarence Thomas, you knew full well you were being inspected and auditioned as a female.
6 You knew when you were in favor because you were always at his beck and call, being summoned constantly, tracked down wherever you were in the agency and given special deference by others because of his interest.
7 You knew when you had ceased to be an object of sexual interest — because you were barred from entering his office and treated as an outcast, or worse, a leper with whom contact was taboo.
8 For my own part, I found his attention unpleasant, sought a transfer, was told one "just doesn't do that," insisted nonetheless and paid the price as an outcast for the remainder of my employment at EEOC. That is why I resigned and left the EEOC.
9 Statements made under oath by Clarence Thomas' staff were simply untrue. They asserted I had been dismissed because of failure to pass the bar. Untrue. They characterized my position as a kind of law student internship. Untrue. I held the position of Special Assistant and my desk was located in the Chairman's suite.
10 I believe I understand why some of his special assistants are coming forward to his defense. He is the most powerful black man they know and possibly, the most influential they will ever know. They want to retain contact because they will need it to survive and to advance in a very tough world.
11 But as respects the atmosphere of absolute propriety, they were either totally unaware of the reality or they engaged in active misrepresentation. It is certainly possible that some were in fact accorded the genuine respect they described.
12 To maintain that Clarence Thomas' office was untainted by any sexuality and permeated by loving, nurturing but asexual concern is simply a lie.
13 Women know when there are sexual dimensions to the attention they are receiving. And there was never any doubt about that dimension in Clarence Thomas' office. I know it. Clarence Thomas knows it. And I know he knows it because he discussed some of the females in his office with me.
14 I have told all of this to Senate staff including the Chairman's staff in the weeks following the nomination. In light of the importance which both ambience (in his office) and credibility have assumed, I felt obliged to communicate this in writing in order to put this on the record publicly.

Sukari Hardnett
Address Deleted

Subscribed and sworn to before me
this 14th day of October, 1991.
Kathleen Jordan
Notary Public
My Commission Expires October 31, 1994

Appendix B
Submitted Material Not Included in the Text

FBI Affidavit, Oct. 11, 1991 (Submitted by Sen. Simpson.)
Green, Donald H., Att'y, Pepper, Hamilton &Scheitz, Washington, D.C. Letter in defense of Anita Hill's work performance at Wald, Harkrader & Ross.
Herold, J. Radley, Judge, Westchester County Court, NY. Prepared statement, observations on senatorial hearings for Supreme Court nominees.
Smith, J. Clay, Prof. of Law, Howard Univ., Washington, D.C. Letter and reports on EEOC prior to Clarence Thomas's chairmanship.
Thomas, Clarence. Answers to written questions by Senators Biden, Byrd and Levin.

Material in Opposition to Confirmation of the Nominee

Abrams, Rbt., Att'y Gen'l., State of NY. Letter.
Age Discrimination Victims Reparations Registry, NY, NY. Prepared statement.
Asian-American Legal Defense and Education Fund. Prepared testimony.
Blumrosen, Alfred W., Prof. of Law, Rutgers Univ., Newark, NJ. Prepared testimony.
California Women Lawyers, Anne D. McGowan, Pres. Letter.
Catholics for a Free Choice, Washington, DC. Report,"Natural Law and the Nominee: What Natural Law Does Clarence Thomas Defend?" by Anthony Battaglia, PhD.
Franklin, John Hope, Prof. Legal History, Duke Univ. Law School. Letter.
Grey, Tomas C., Prof., Stanford Univ. Law School, Stanford, CA. Revised testimony.
Holtzman, Elizabeth, Comptroller, City of NY. Letter.
Instituto Puertorriqueño de Derechos Civiles of Puerto Rico, Ralph Rivera, Gen'l Coordinator. Article, "Opposition to the Nomination of Judge Clarence Thomas to the Supreme Court of the United States".
Lawyers for a Democratic Alternative, Andrew A. Rainer, Chair. Letter.
Lawyers for the Judiciary, Chicago, IL. Prepared statement.
Letter signed by 134 Constitutional Law Profs. and Law School Deans.
Mink, Patsy T., U.S. Rep. Testimony.
Nat'l Committee for Constitutional Integrity, John B. Minnick, Co-Chmn. Letter.
Nat'l Committee on Pay Equity, Claudia E. Wayne, Ex. Dir. Prepared statement.
Nat'l Council of Jewish Women, NY, NY. Prepared testimony.

Appendix B, con't

Nat'l Education Ass'n. Prepared statement.
Nat'l Federation of Business and Professional Women's Clubs, Inc., of USA, Pat Taylor, Nat'l Pres. Prepared statement.
Nationalist Movement, The, Richard Barnett, Learned, MS. Prepared statement.
Organization of Chinese Americans. Prepared Testimony.
Samar, Vincent. Article, "The Problem with Supreme Court Nominee Clarence Thomas's Natural Law Views".
United Electrical Radio & Machine Workers of America, Rbt. Kingsley, Political Action Dir. Prepared statement.

Material in Support of Confirmation of the Nominee

American Indian Alliance. Letters.
Coalitions for America, Paul M. Weyrich, Nat'l Chmn. Partial list of state legislators supporting Clarence Thomas. Articles, "A Unique Contribution to America", "A Response to Judge Thomas's Critics" by Thomas L. Jipping.
Coleman, C. D., Sr. Bishop, Christian Methodist Episcopal Church, Dallas TX. Letter.
Dawkins, Rev. Maurice A., Port of Spain, Trinidad and Tobago. Letter.
District of Columbia, Black Republican Scholarship Fund, Connie Mack Higgins, Chmn. Testimony.
Evans, Samuel L., Philadelphia, PA. Prepared statement.
Int'l Narcotic Enforcement Officers Ass'n, John J. Bellizzi, Exec. Dir. Testimony.
Iwo Jima Black Veterans, Frederick D. Gray, Chmn. Letter.
O'Bannon, Michael J., Pres., Federal Focus Inst. Prepared statement.
Stafford, Bobby B., law firm of Raby & Stafford, Alexandria, VA. Statement.
US Justice Foundation, Gary G. Kreep, Exec. Dir. Prepared statement.
Williams, Juan. Article, "Open Season on Clarence Thomas", *Washington Post*, Oct. 10, 1991 (Submitted by Sen. Hatch).
Tollett, Kenneth J., Prof. of Higher Educ., Howard Univ., Washington, DC. Letter.

APPENDIX C

RESULTS OF THE SENATE VOTE TO CONFIRM CLARENCE THOMAS, NOVEMBER 15, 1991

For Confirmation (52)

Democrats:
Boren (OK)
Breaux (LA)
DeConcini (AZ)
Dixon (IL)
Exon (NE)
Fowler (GA)
Hollings (SC)
Johnston (LA)
Nunn (GA)
Robb (VA)
Shelby (AL)

Republicans:
Bond (MO)
Brown (CO)
Burns (MT)
Chafee (RI)
Coats (IN)
Cochran (MS)
Cohen (ME)
Craig (ID)
D'Amato (NY)
Danforth (MO)
Dole (KS)
Domenici (NM)
Durenburger (MN)
Garn (UT)
Gorton (WA)
Gramm (TX)
Grassley (IA)
Hatch (UT)
Hatfield (OR)
Helms (NC)
Kassenbaum (KS)
Kasten (WI)
Loff (MS)
Lugar (IN)
Mack (FL)
McCain (AZ)
McConnell (KY)
Murkowski (AK)
Nickles (OK)
Pressler (SD)
Roth (DE)
Rudman (NH)
Seymour (CA)
Simpson (WY)
Smith (NH)
Specter (PA)
Stevens (AK)
Symms (ID)
Thurmond (SC)
Wallop (WY)
Warner (VA)

Against Confirmation (48)

Democrats:
Adams (WA)
Akaka (HI)
Baucus (MT)
Bentsen (TX)
Biden (DE)
Bingaman (NM)
Bradley (NJ)
Bryan (NV)
Bumpers (AR)
Burdick (ND)
Byrd (WV)
Conrad (ND)
Cranston (CA)
Daschle (SD)
Dodd (CT)
Ford (KY)
Glenn (OH)
Gore (TN)
Graham (FL)
Harkin (IA)
Heflin (AL)
Inouye (HI)
Kennedy (MA)
Kerry (MA)
Kerrey (NE)
Kohl (WI)
Lautenberg (NJ)
Leahy (VT)
Levin (MI)
Lieberman (CT)
Metzenbaum (OH)
Mitchell (ME)
Mikulski (MD)
Moynihan (NY)
Pell (RI)
Pryor (AR)
Ried (NV)
Riegle (MI)
Sanford (NC)
Sarbanes (MD)
Sasser (TN)
Simon (IL)
Wellstone (MN)
Wirth (CO)
Wofford (PA)

Republicans:
Jeffords (VT)
Packwood (OR)

INDEX A
ALPHABETICAL LIST OF WITNESSES

INDEX B
COLLOQUY

Index B con't

INDEX C
REFERENCES IN THE TEXT

INDEX C CON'T